Census Users' Handbook

Edited by

Stan Openshaw

GeoInformation International
A Division of Pearson Professional Limited
307 Cambridge Science Park
Milton Road
Cambridge CB4 4ZD
United Kingdom
and Associated Companies throughout the world

Copublished in the United States with
John Wiley and Sons, Inc, 605 Third Avenue, New York, NY 10158

First published 1995

British Library Cataloguing-in-Publication data
A catalogue entry for this title is available from the British Library.

ISBN 1 899761 06 3

Library of Congress Cataloguing-in-Publication data
A catalogue entry for this title is available from the Library of Congress.

ISBN 0-470-23481-4 (USA only)

Printed in the United Kingdom
by Bell and Bain, Glasgow

This book is dedicated to all who are interested in the collection, use, research and future of census data.

Contents

List of plates

List of contributors

Editor
Stan Openshaw, School of Geography, University of Leeds

Authors
Mark Birkin, School of Geography, University of Leeds and GMAP Ltd
Chris Brunsdon, Department of Town and Country Planning, University of Newcastle upon Tyne
Steve Carver, School of Geography, University of Leeds
Tony Champion, Department of Geography, University of Newcastle upon Tyne
Martin Charlton, Department of Geography, University of Newcastle upon Tyne
Graham Clarke, School of Geography, University of Leeds
Mike Coombes, NERRL Research Co-ordinator, CURDS, University of Newcastle upon Tyne
Hywel Davies, London Research Centre
Daniel Dorling, Department of Geography, University of Newcastle upon Tyne
Elizabeth Middleton, Census Microdata Unit, Faculty of Economics and Social Studies, University of Manchester
Liang Rao, GIS/Trans, Boston, USA
Phil Rees, School of Geography, University of Leeds
Ian Turton, School of Geography, University of Leeds (Appendix 11A)
Colin Wymer, Department of Town and Country Planning, University of Newcastle upon Tyne

Preface

Welcome to the 'third' census users' guide and handbook that has been produced to commemorate the appearance of the 1991 Census. First out was the Market Research Society's *An Introductory Guide to the 1991 Census* (NTC Publications, Henley) – a very basic, highly descriptive, introductory guide for marketeers. The other two books, *The 1991 Census User's Guide* (HMSO, London) and this *Census Users' Handbook* (Longman, London), are much more substantial and highly complementary efforts.

Such a flurry of book writing is a result of three factors: first, the importance of the census as a data source; second, a tribute to the original foresight of David Rhind who over a decade ago spotted an important need; and third, an unfortunate lack of co-ordination between sociologists interested in a social survey and social science perspective and geographers mainly interested in a spatial one. Ideally, there should have been only one 1991 Census users' guide/handbook coming from the academic sector, not two. However, there are two books and they are highly complementary. There is very little overlap, and they could easily have been volumes 1 and 2 of a boxed set. In terms of content, the Dale and Marsh guide is almost entirely census descriptive with little concern for analysis or application, whereas this handbook continues the format and structure of the first *Census User's Handbook* edited by David Rhind and focuses more firmly on the analysis and spatial aspects of census data.

The Rhind original, published in 1981, provided practical guidance in the use and analysis of what was then and still is today the single most important dataset available to geographers, planners, social scientists, market researchers, government officials, spies etc. In many ways, how the data were collected, validated and stored is of nothing more than passing interest to most census users. If you want a single comprehensive reference source of this information then read the Dale and Marsh *1991 Census User's Guide*. In many ways, it is more important to know not what the census is, but what can be done with it, what analysis tool might be most usefully applied to it and, because the census is predominantly a spatial database, how the various geographical aspects and problems this causes can best be handled. It is these questions that this *Census Users' Handbook* seeks to answer.

A new handbook is required because in the last 10 years the need for advice and information about census-related analysis technologies has undoubtedly intensified. Not only has the number of potential and real census users increased by about two orders of magnitude but the computing hardware and software environments have almost completely changed beyond all recognition, first by the introduction of the personal computer (PC) and subsequently by the tremendous increase in available computational power. It is now easily forgotten that in the early 1980s census processing was a large-mainframe-based mainly research activity, with relatively few experts or users. Mapping census data involved a major effort of time and patience. In the 1990s there is probably little that cannot now be done on a cheap PC or workstation offering equivalent or better computing capabilities for much less than a thousandth of the price in less than a day. In addition, the geographical information system (GIS) revolution of the mid-1980s has greatly eased the task of manipulating and mapping census data, as well as providing an ever increasing amount of census-relevant digital map data. Furthermore, the 1990s are a time when census analysis has filtered down to schools and is no longer the domain of the expert. So, in many ways the world of the 1991 Census is vastly different in terms of computing aspects and the size of the user community than that of the 1981 Census. Indeed the entity that has changed least is the census itself and to a lesser extent also the available census analysis technologies.

I remember well that one of David Rhind's original objectives in assembling his 1981 handbook was a desire to make census analysis tools available for users. I think his original intention was to focus on a set of techniques and associated software. With respect to the latter, we have both failed, although no doubt keenly interested readers could contact the contributors of interest. However, both handbooks have succeeded in presenting an array of useful census analysis technologies.

However, census technology is only one, albeit important, dimension to a census user's handbook. Not only should there be advice for users but there should be an attempt to address some of the census-related wider organizational issues. The census is an extremely important data source in a period of historically unprecedented change. Census user's handbooks and guides can make an important contribution to the forthcoming 'future of the census' debate only if there is a critical commentary. This handbook is independent of the UK Census Agencies. The views it contains are those of authors and what they believe; there was no need to apply 'anti-boat rocking' filters. This is important because many criticisms of past censuses have never been made public and, in consequence, perhaps because of this fear of OPCS or GRO(S) disapproval, the census is not as good a product as perhaps it might have been. This is not to say that this handbook is overtly critical, but only that where criticism is warranted or made it remains on public record and has not been sanitized or removed during editing.

To summarize, the justification for this particular *Census Users' Handbook* is the need to update the original 1981 Rhind-edited handbook to meet similar user needs for an advanced source of information about analysis relevant to the 1991 Census. A census handbook is not an introductory guide to census data nor a description of what the census is and how it was collected, but a collection or manual of census-relevant technologies that might be helpful to census users wishing to make the most of the 1991 Census. This is important because good census usage requires knowledge not just of what the census is but also of the problems of analysis and advice about what methods and techniques to use to get the most from it. The Dale and Marsh guide does little to meet this need. It is important to appreciate that increasingly the census data are not results that are of value in themselves, but are inputs into increasingly complex analysis procedures. This 1991 *Census Users' Handbook* continues the tradition started by the Rhind original. Hopefully, with the passage of time, it will be perceived to be just as useful as was the original.

Stan Openshaw
August 1993

Acknowledgements

We are indebted to the following for permission to reproduce copyright material:

Office of Population Censuses & Surveys for Figures 2.3, 2.4, 2.6 and 10.1; *The Cartographic Journal* of the British Cartographic Society for Plates II and III, *Transactions of the Institute of British Geographers* for Figure 4.1.

While every effort has been made to trace the owners of copyright material, in a few cases this has proved impossible and we take the opportunity to offer our apologies to any copyright holders whose rights we may have unwittingly infringed.

1

A quick introduction to most of what you need to know about the 1991 Census

S Openshaw

Editor's note

Some people might think that census analysis is hard. Well, it's not really, not anymore. Once upon a time you could get a PhD for applying statistical analysis to census data. Some even wrote books about their experiences. However, census analysis is no longer hard or difficult or in many instances at the leading edge of methodological research. It is, however, extremely useful. This chapter attempts to demystify the whole business, provide a quick introduction of the basics, and then via a question and answer session try and communicate some of the experiences of a quarter century of playing with researching, analysing and enjoying census data.

1 Getting started

This book is written for users and prospective users of computer databases or files containing data from the 1991 Census with an interest in analysis for research and applied purposes. An obvious question that many such newcomers to census data ask is 'How do I get started?' Such users will not initially want to read either the complete set of OPCS/GRO(Scotland) Census Newsletters or the 49 or more 1991 Census User Guides, nor will many have the time or inclination to attend one-, two- or five-day courses on the 1991 Census. Nor will they necessarily wish to read about the history of the census or to read *The 1991 Census User's Guide* (Dale and Marsh 1993) to find out what is there and how it got there. This chapter starts then by trying to describe, as simply as possible, what census data exist and how they were created, and then offers a guided meta-path into the census itself with a focus on application.

It all happened on and about Sunday 21 April 1991 when everyone in the UK was supposedly asked to complete the census questionnaire. The responsibility for designing the census questionnaire, for collecting the data and for processing it rests with the Office of Population Census and Surveys (OPCS) in England and Wales and with the General Register Office (GRO) in Scotland and Northern Ireland. Census enumerators knocked on doors and delivered the questionnaire during the previous week and collected the completed forms the following week.

The census is really only a large household survey that is organized, processed and applied in a manner familiar to those interested in household surveys. However, it differs from the usual sort in four ways: (i) its length and complexity (you would not normally dare to ask so many questions that are complicated to fill in, although the questions themselves are fairly innocuous); (ii) a projected 100% coverage of households, creating large data volumes; (iii) a unique high response rate mechanism (it is illegal not to complete the questionnaire) and (iv) by the care with which the data are coded, checked, processed and safe guarded. No wonder the total cost is estimated to be £140.5 million or about £7 per household.

Perhaps surprisingly, the census questionnaire in England only contains 24 questions, 5 relating to the household and 19 to the individuals living within it. It may seem strange that 24 questions can generate a census dataset that is

Table 1.1 Principal 1991 Census questions

Household questions
- type of accommodation
- number of rooms
- tenure
- amenities
- car and van ownership

Individual person questions
- name
- sex
- date of birth
- marital status
- relationship in household
- whereabouts on census night
- usual address
- term-time address
- usual address one year ago
- country of birth
- ethnic group
- long-term illness
- whether working, retired, looking after house etc.
- hours worked per week
- occupation
- name and address of employer
- address of place of work
- daily journey to work
- degree, professional and vocational qualification

seemingly so complex to understand, handle and analyse. However, the complexity is not due to the numbers of questions; indeed, as Table 1.1 shows, the content and coverage of the census questions are in fact unremarkable and very straightforward. If the 1991 Census results could have been distributed to users in the form of coded responses to the census questionnaire then much of the added complexity might have been avoided, although the users would now have to recode the data themselves and this is not as simple as it appears because of its hierarchical structure. The natural hierarchical structure of census data reflects the fact that the household information part of the questionnaire is common to the individuals living within it, household sizes vary and thus the number of individual records also vary, and relationships between household members can be quite complex. Nevertheless, in some European Union countries (i.e. Italy) census data are distributed in a raw coded form, without names and addresses, and to some extent the UK Sample of Anonymized Records (see Chapter 12) is of this format. However, the need to preserve the confidentiality of UK census data has precluded the distribution of the coded individual census records. In Britain access to the individual data has only ever been possible by very special off-line arrangements, e.g. the OPCS Longitudinal Study (see Dale and Marsh 1993; Chapter 12), or by requesting special tabulations from the OPCS. The situation in Northern Ireland was different in that coded census data at the individual level appear to have been available from both the 1971 and 1981 Censuses, but seemingly they now follow the OPCS and GRO(S) model. It is interesting to note that there has perhaps been too much concern about census confidentiality based on political exaggeration and pseudo-science; and that even now the 'real' confidentiality risk in the reporting of the census is a largely unknown quantity. The standard response has been to 'play safe' even if this damages the data and many subsequent applications that are based upon it.

Since user access to the coded individual census data is not considered possible in the UK, the census results are presented as cross-tabulations of the census questions reported at different levels of geography, designed in a way that will not allow a single person to be identified. The complex nature of the 1991 Census results almost entirely from the production of nearly 100 tables based on many

Table 1.2 Census tables and cell counts

Census		Total tables	Maximum cell count
1971	SAS	35	462
1981	SAS	53	5 517
1991	SAS	83, 84, 86	9 069
	LBS	95, 96, 99	20 219

Notes: Not all tables are available for all of the UK: the SAS contains 83 tables for England, 84 in Wales and 86 in Scotland. Likewise, the LBS table numbers are country specific. SAS are available down to census enumeration districts, whereas the LBS are only available down to wards.

different permutations of the original 24 questions. Since users have no access to the individual census data records, the OPCS and GRO(S) have had to design and create a large number of standard output tabulations in order to meet a wide diversity of information needs. Indeed designing these output tables and consulting with users about their layout and content is traditionally a major part of the census planning task. Moreover, as the number of census users has increased, so too has the magnitude of the task. The resulting explosions in tables and the numbers of identifiable individual counts or cells contained within them is shown in Table 1.2. The provision of some of the data only for certain countries (e.g. Welsh speakers in Wales) means that not all the census data are available across the entire UK, but most are.

Another slight complication with the 1991 Census is the distinction between Small Area Statistics (SAS) which are available down to the smallest census output area (census enumeration district, ED) and the so-called Local Base Statistics (LBS) which are only available down to census wards (see OPCS User Guides 24, 25 and 38). However, with very few exceptions the LBS tables contain all the SAS tables plus much more as well, although whether or not all these data are needed at such a coarse level of geography is an unanswered question.

Users need to know about these tables and the cells within them because the census data are accessed by specifying which cell counts you need or which table you would like printed. For example, if you wish to create a variable such as 'percentage owner occupied' using the SAS data then you will need the census data items

table S19 cell 6 number of owner-occupied houses
table S19 cell 1 number of households

and a means of performing rudimentary arithmetic operations on the numbers. Software such as SASPAC will then help do the rest for you (see Chapter 2). Alternatively, there may well be other pathways you could follow to obtain the data, e.g. in paper form via a County Monitor or via some other, perhaps CD-ROM based, software system (see Chapter 3). Defining your data for extraction from the census database is by far the most time consuming, boring and error-prone part of census analysis. SASPAC trivializes the computing aspects but still leaves the user with the now much harder task of defining and then selecting the variables of interest. This can be either very easy when there are few well-defined variables or highly complicated when there are alternative definitions to consider and many variables.

As a data user you will also need to identify which, of several, different levels of census geography you are interested in. In England and Wales the basic spatial unit for which census tables are available is the census enumeration district (ED). This is essentially the area covered by a single census enumerator and typically contains about 200 households or 450 people. However, EDs vary greatly in size and no SAS data are reported for EDs with less than 50 residents and 16 resident households. The 1991 EDs are unfortunately different from those used in 1981. In Scotland they do things differently. They use output areas (OAs) to report the

Table 1.3 Standard census output areas

Output areas: England and Wales
enumeration district (EDs)
ward
district
county
postcode sector
Output areas: Scotland
output areas (OAs)
postcode sector
regions

census tables which are larger than the areas used for enumeration (a useful development). The OAs are also comparable with 1981 OAs and postcode related. Table 1.3 summarizes the available choice (see also OPCS User Guide 27).

It is possible to change the geography by aggregation to about 30 different sets of areal units (see Chapters 4 and 5). SASPAC has a special command to create user-defined zones. In the geographic information system (GIS) age this aggregation need no longer be exact, nor restricted only to traditional zonal objects; e.g. you may wish to estimate populations for retail catchment areas or living within 2 km of a rail-route or located on a certain rock type within 15 km of a particular point.

2 A few complications you need to bear in mind

A few other census-data-related complications are important and you need to know a little about them.

(a) Some of the 'hard to code' census questions (i.e. occupation, relationship, qualification, journey to work) are only coded for 10% of the data, which can introduce substantial uncertainty at the small area scale. For example, a census ED which has 100 households in it will have 10% coded data based on 10 of them. This causes two problems: first, the results contain sampling error with a level of uncertainty that reflects the size of the ED; second, a more widespread problem, it is easier to obtain much more extreme results in census areas with small population owing to small number effects. Unfortunately, EDs, OAs and wards vary in size and the variations are not random but tend to reflect urban–rural population densities which can create a geographically structured pattern of systematic spatial variations in data precision. These problems need to be handled explicitly by census analysis procedures, rather than ignored.

(b) Various confidentiality-preserving data-blurring methods are applied to the SAS and LBS data. This can result in percentages that exceed 100%!

However, the effects should be neutral on any analysis, or so it is usually claimed.

(c) SAS data are not released for areas with less than 50 usually resident persons and 16 resident households (double the minimum sizes used for the 1981 Census), whilst the LBS data are only reported for wards with 1000 or more residents and 320 or more resident households. These restrictions are simultaneously quite reasonable and absurd. There is no real scientific basis for them. Maybe they work well, maybe they have no effect; the problem is that no-one really knows! However, what they do is damage the data. It seems perverse that errors are deliberately introduced into data that were most painstakingly collected and supposedly error free. Is it sensible and safe to make policy decisions on expensive census data that are known to be wrong? Chapter 13 considers further some of these issues.

(d) The census variable definitions and also the census EDs (in England and Wales) change from one census to the next, making comparisons between 1971–81–91 difficult (at the small area scale see also Chapters 3, 6 and 10). Again there are good reasons for these problems. Historically, this was more readily acceptable than today. It causes many problems, devalues the usefulness of this and previous censuses, and hides the processes of change about which there is no other source of information.

(e) There is imputation of missing data in an attempt to reduce bias in the census by inventing census data for 'missing' households. If people wish to hide from official surveys, perhaps because of now historic poll-tax fears, then it is very difficult by definition to identify who they are, where they live and how many they are. Whether the 1991 Census missed large numbers or small numbers is a matter for extensive debate (see also Chapter 13). However, imputation is also a most serious source of additional error and uncertainty. If, as seems likely, the 'missing million' were concentrated in certain types of area and location, then their non-enumeration may well have generated a major source of non-random error of the worst kind.

(f) The spatial nature of census data makes the use of standard statistical methods problematic; in particular, tests of significance can be both misleading and wrong. Also the volume of the data increases the importance of data reduction and data descriptive visualizations in one, two and three dimensions. Chapters 6, 7, 8 and 9 cover these and related issues.

(g) Whilst mapping census data and census atlas making is now a fairly trivial task, there is the major problem that the census itself contains no digital boundary information. The 1991 Census (like those of 1981 and 1971) provides only an approximate, error-prone, 100-m grid reference for each ED. This is really inadequate in the 1990s, particularly as it is left to the census user to buy or capture the relevant census boundaries in a digital form. The 1990s are a time when GIS are accepted technology and the problems of separating the arcs from the attributes should have been avoided (see Chapters 4, 5 and 13). The census does come with an ED to unit postcode directory, but sadly it is not the definitive gold standard it should have been. Yet it is useful and does provide a basis for linking census and non-census data. In these and related matters, you really need to be an expert or invest a considerable amount of time and effort if you are a beginner. As always, if you can find a local expert then you will save much time and effort.

(h) In addition to EDs and OAs there are special EDs (SEDs, called special output areas (SOAs) in Scotland) which contain 100 or more persons in communal establishments on census night (i.e. prisons, hospitals, aged persons' homes). Military bases are not reported in the census. Ships are covered by special shipping EDs or OAs. Areas which are too small are termed restricted and only basic counts are reported. The census data would always have been better without such complications that undoubtedly cause some users to analyse 'ships' by mistake.

3 Steering a path through the census document maze by questions and answers

Another way of helping users cope with the heap of available 1991 Census information, the various documents, computer systems, guides and handbooks is to ask a series of meta-questions. It is noted in passing that question and answer sessions of this sort rarely appear in print. Maybe there are good reasons for this, but they can also provide a useful introduction to census material.

In the following text these abbreviations are used:

CUH1 the 1981 Rhind-edited *Census User's Handbook* (Rhind 1983)
CUH2 this 1991 handbook
CUG1 the Market Research Society guide (Leventhal *et al.* 1993)
CUG2 the ESRC/OPCS guide (Dale and Marsh 1993)

Chapters (if relevant) are designated by a hyphen and number, so this chapter is designated CUH2-1.

To help readers, the questions are grouped into three broad categories: basic general questions, more specific questions, and advanced.

3.1 Some basic general questions

Q. I want to use the 1991 Census.

A. Fine, but you have to be much more specific than that. In particular, what aspects are you interested in? What applications, what data, at what level etc.?

Q. I don't know, I'm just a beginner; what can I read that might help me?

A. Mm! If you want to read about censuses in general then start with CUH1 and then this chapter. If you want to know lots of details about the 1991 Census then read CUG2 from cover to cover. If you want a quick and brief overview then try CUG1.

Q. I want some summary statistics for districts and counties.

A. Look for the relevant County Monitors, you may not need to do any computing, or use SASPAC to print some tables. Maybe the numbers you want are already in published tables which can be obtained from either a library or an HMSO bookshop. If not, then investigate whether the tables you desire are available in either the Small Area Statistics or the Local Base Statistics and thus could be generated by SASPAC.

Q. I am baffled about the whole census business. Can you recommend something really simple to get me started?

A. Read CUG1, it's nice and easy going, or else seek help from a locally available expert; or consider a course.

Q. I am not computer skilled but want some 1991 Census data. What do you recommend so that I can have some results by tea-time?

A. Be careful – maybe growing roses or watching football might be a safer and more appropriate activity. Playing around with census data is not for the totally uninitiated. Alternatively, be prepared to spend a few weeks becoming an expert, but it might well take longer than you expect.

Q. I want some maps of census data. How do I go about it?

A. Refer to an expert. Basically you will need (i) census data, (ii) boundaries to go with the data, (iii) a mapping package that can cope and (iv) an ability to apply item (iii) to items (ii) and (i). Then you need to decide how best to present the data (see CUH2-6), and what 'story' you want it to tell.

Oh! You thought that mapping data was a purely objective exercise, did you? Well, it can be, but be aware that choice of colours, the choice of class intervals, the choice of census geography and the choice of study region can all influence the visual impression gained by viewers of the map (Monmonier 1991). You need to have a story that you want the map to support. Alternatively, if mapping is designed to help you explore the data, then there are often more powerful methods that you should also consider using, e.g. the various statistical procedures in CUH2-7,8,9. Monmonier's ideas of how to make nonsense of the census are well worth reading.

Q. I want some census data. Where do I get it from and how much will it cost?

A. How long is a piece of string? The cost depends on who you are, what you want and what you intend to do with it. Either read CUG2 or ring the OPCS or GRO(S) for advice. Academics and local government consortia members have, or may have, a special deal; see CUH2-3.

Q. I want to use the census to identify certain individuals.

A. Well, don't: because (i) it's probably illegal, (ii) more importantly it simply cannot be done and (iii) if you claim to have done it you will be guilty of being both mischievous and wilfully wrong. Moreover, it may result in your organization being banned from access to the census. All census users have to sign an agreement which prohibits them from trying to identify individuals and from claiming to have done so.

Q. Are there any better data sources than the census for Britain?

A. It depends on what you want. The census is supremely good in terms of the variables it contains for April 1991. Other commercial sector databases will in general not be as good in terms of coverage. *BUT* (note the capitals) the non-census data may (i) be more recent, (ii) contain different variables that might be more useful; (iii) approach the accuracy of census data whenever sample sizes are sufficiently large or there is complete coverage (e.g. share registers); and (iv) may be more useful when attention is focused on identifiable individuals rather than aggregate statistics for small areas. Also, the bias contained in many non-census data sources may not matter. For example, in a marketing context you may not be bothered about not having data for people who are not mail order responsive or who might be thought to be unlikely prospects (i.e. the very poor, the very old and the rich). Indeed, the census being a more or less complete count of everyone is less useful, because not everyone is equally mail order responsive. So bias and whether it matters is application context dependent.

Q. Do I need SASPAC before I can do anything with the 1991 Census?

A. No, but it certainly can make accessing the data much simpler. If you are a non-programmer and a non-expert in statistical packages, then SASPAC makes it easy for you to select, manipulate, tabulate and extract census data IF you have access to SASPAC (see CUH2-2,3). However, and this is an important point, please don't think that the 1991 Census is hard either to analyse or use. It's not! In fact it has never been easier to perform census analysis. You may be able to meet most, maybe all, of your analysis needs using a spreadsheet. Historically, many users have done useful analysis with a calculator whilst others will today find word-processors, statistical packages and GISs provide more than adequate platforms.

Q. Are you saying that I do not need SASPAC to do useful things with the 1991 Census data?

A. Yes. Much depends on what you mean by 'useful things'. Purpose is important. A GIS expert will naturally find a GIS far more useful. A database user will want to use a favourite database. The *raison d'être* for SASPAC has now gone. If you have access to census data via it, then use it. If you don't, then don't worry – you're probably not missing much.

Q. I am very concerned that the census is not completely correct.

A. No large complex computer database will ever be 100% accurate. Even if the 1991 Census was 99.9% right, this would still imply that 20,000 household records would be incorrect. CUG2-6 provides a good discussion of the validation of census data, so read it.

Whilst it is impossible to be precise, it might be guessed that the census is about 90% to 95% accurate, although the 10% coded data need to be handled more carefully. In both cases, levels of accuracy depend on the size and the nature of the areas of interest. When attention is focused on the smallest census areas, then the error (more precisely described as uncertainty) may now exceed 50%. Also, there are different types of census 'error' which might affect different areas differently. These include sampling error in the 10% coded variables, data blurring for confidentiality reasons, imputation of missing data, non-response which may be more characteristic in certain types of area although there is no way of knowing for certain, coding errors, people lying either deliberately or accidentally, computer error, and data ageing.

Indeed data ageing rapidly becomes the dominant source of uncertainty about census data. They become out of date at different speeds and with different consequences in different places. In many ways, the census is least useful in those parts of Britain which are changing!

Q. I am a member of the public and want some census data for my parish church/bingo hall/boys club/OAP workshop. How do I get some?

A. Ah well! As a member of 'Joe Public' who helped pay for the census via your taxes etc., you may be mortified to discover that you are not allowed 'free' access to it unless what you want appears in a census publication which is in your local public library. Not only are you not allowed free access, but the databases, software for accessing the data etc. are all 'owned' by commercially minded organizations who will expect you to pay for it! In short the 1991 Census was not conceived of as a public data resource but one that was designed for the use and needs of a relatively exclusive group of 'experts'. Maybe, therefore, it does not matter that it is hard to access and that there is no public access to the computer databases. Alternatively, maybe it should be a public information source, since the public created it and paid for it. It is about us so why cannot there be public access to it? No doubt there will be, one day.

Q. The variables I am interested in are either not in the census or have not been coded in the way I need.

A. This may be your fault. Each census is preceded by a lengthy user participation phase in which potential users are consulted about what the census includes, the prospect for new variables (there are five new questions in 1991 on such exciting topics as long-term illness, central heating, term-time student addresses, ethnic origins, and numbers of hours worked) and table output. However, there has always been a reluctance to ask certain types of questions (e.g. on income) and actually getting new questions added is by no means easy. All too often new ideas are withered away owing to lack of support (external and internal), lack of obvious firm promises of payment for the additional variables, and in 'census speak' because the added burden of including the question would outweigh the benefits of collecting such data or they are perceived as likely to attract adverse political commentary. The census planning process has traditionally been very conservative and performed in expectation of the prospect of political censure at almost any moment. It is also a somewhat obscure process in that there is no public record of how significant decisions of user importance are made.

If the data coding is a problem, then with the 1991 Census there is a chance that you might be able to obtain your own tabulations based on the Samples of Anonymized Records (SAR) (see CUG2-11 and CUH2-11). Also, it is sometimes possible using microsimulation and iterative proportional fitting to manufacture your own pseudo-data that are consistent with known information. In this manner, you can create your own census data estimates for variables not included in the census, e.g. income. See CUH2-12 for details.

Q. Why do we have a census?

A. Partly tradition since 1801 and partly because there was no alternative source, until recently. It seems that no-one has really been brave enough to disrupt the census tradition (see CUH1-1). Whether it is sensible to continue it many more times is perhaps increasingly debatable (see CUH2-13).

Q. Why are England and Wales census data organized differently from those for Scotland (and Northern Ireland)?

A. Not such a silly question. One explanation is ethnic bloodymindness. Another is organizational differences. Another is the more advanced nature of the census in Scotland with a greater willingness to innovate and try new ideas. Another is that Scotland is a much smaller country and is therefore easier for the census to cover. Yet another would attribute the differences to stupidity at a time when it is quite reasonable to expect that the same information be available for the same areas uniformly throughout the UK (and Europe).

3.2 More specific questions and answers

Q. The census documentation, guides etc. have not been written or designed for the complete beginner. What can be done about it?

A. Yes, this is true. Maybe you will have to wait for the 'Ladybird' book of the census to be produced. On the other hand, census data are being used in school projects so there is, in principle, no great intrinsic difficulty. Complete beginners have to start somewhere so why not begin with the simplest of the census guides (CUG1) and work your way up; or else jump in at the deep end and learn about the census via the SASPAC manuals (see CUH2-3).

Q. Where can I get some more advice about the census?

A. If you are an academic then for a while at least you can write to the Census Support Officer, Census Dissemination Unit, Manchester Computing Centre, Manchester University, Oxford Road, Manchester M13 9PL. In the longer term (i.e. post-1996) you should try the ESRC Data Archive, University of Essex, Wivenhoe Park, Colchester, Essex CO4 3SQ. If you are a non-academic then write to either Census Customer Services, OPCS, Segensworth Road, Titchfield, Fareham, Hampshire PO15 5RR; or Census Customer Services, Census Branch, General Register Office for Scotland, Ladywell House, Ladywell Road, Edinburgh EH12 7TF; or Census Customer Services, Census Office, Department of Health and Social Services, Castle Buildings, Stormont, Belfast BT4 8RA. If you are a member of the public then try your local town hall, probably the Planning Department; or even the relevant County Council or Regional Authority. If you are a member of local government or a local service provider then try also the town hall or County Council. See also CUH2-3.

Q. What is the hardest part of coping with the 1991 Census?

A. Just getting going. You need to start somewhere and it is not always obvious where. Maybe a good starting point is to acquire SASPAC user manuals and just try and get some data/results out. Then delve into the various documents, guides and handbook. You can buy *SASPAC User Manual: Parts 1 and 2* from the London Research Centre, Parliament House, 81 Black Prince Road, London SE1 7SZ. See also CUH2-2,3 and CUG2-7, 8.

Q. What is the hardest part of SASPAC?

A. Trying to cope with the mainframe (or PC) on which it is located.

Q. I have just returned from an introduction to the 1991 Census course and it all seemed rather mystifying and complex. What can you advise?

A. Well you could try a DIY approach and read CUH2 or CUG1 in conjunction with SASPAC manuals. The course was probably too academically focused; it may have assumed too much knowledge of idiosyncratic computer systems, and typically attempted to obscurate rather than clarify (a widespread academic disease). After all, courses have to appear difficult to justify their cost and/or existence. Maybe also first-time users need to know more about what the census can provide prior to attending.

A final piece of advice. Experience suggests that many courses are useful because they provide handouts or workbooks with examples in them. All you have to do is substitute your variables for theirs, replace their data definition command by yours etc.; and provided you have spelt the words right it will work. Encouraged by this success, you then go and extemporize on the theme, read manuals and generally gain confidence from your initial success. Alternatively, if it fails, ask for help; and you at least have the basis for getting going. Remember the census is *easy* and never before in human history has census data been so easy to get at and use. So, off you go!

Q. Which packages are most useful in analysing census data files?

A. It depends on who you are and what you want to do. Spreadsheets, databases, mapping packages, statistical packages and GIS can all be used. Sadly none really copes with the special nature of census data; e.g. the statistical packages assume that the census data are equivalent to survey data collected by simple random sampling (this is only applicable to the SAR, see CUH2-11). The mapping and GIS packages offer none of the visualization procedures that might be most appropriate for use with the census; in particular the map patterns can be dominated by variations in size of census area. There are ways of fixing this problem (see CUH2-5,6 and CUG2-9). There are no zonal ranking procedures that handle the spatial representational aspects of census data, and no generally available multivariate classification packages that handle small number problems properly. So, why worry? Use whatever software you have available, and then ponder a little about the unresolved complexities and whether they may matter.

Q. The 1991 Census is extremely complex with up to 20,000 variables available. How on earth does anyone make any sense of it?

A. Yes, there are up to 20,000 variables but they were generated from only 24 questions! Quite simply the 24 variables can be recoded and cross-tabulated in many billions of different ways. For example, age can be recoded in various ways; occupation likewise. What the 1991 Census makes available is a carefully selected and designed subset of these possible cross-tabulations. The hardest part might well be deciding and then finding which variables are of greatest relevance to your needs.

A very useful aid is the METAC91 meta-database about the 1991 Census tables (Williamson 1993). It runs on a PC and allows you to search for census variables of interest. This is helpful because it can save time and assist the discovery of hitherto unknown census statistics hidden away in the 100 census tables, probably embedded in one of the numerous subtables within the tables.

Q. Census geography is confusing because the words have no natural meaning. How can I cope? I am not a geographer.

A. Not being a geographer is irrelevant. Census geography certainly was not designed by a geographer – it just sort of emerged, by default. It's a mess! The easiest way of coping is to imagine a set of areas ranging from small to large. In England and Wales, the smallest zone is the census ED (consisting of about 20 to 200 houses), the ward (with a population of a few thousands), the district (i.e. your local authority) and county. In Scotland, the smallest areas are termed output areas (collections of postcodes) and these aggregate into postcode sectors, districts and regions. What has geography got to do with it? The key is to remember that, although the census data relate to individuals and to households, they are aggregated to geographic areas – hence the term census geography. This preserves your privacy and confidentiality, since data about yourself and your family are merged with the data of many other persons who live nearby and there is no way of distinguishing your data anymore. This loss of information causes many problems even if it is an effective means of preserving confidentiality.

Q. I have heard rumours about the missing million. What exactly does this tell us about the reliability of the 1991 Census?

A. There are two possible responses. One is that it really does not matter much because the census data have been adjusted to take it into account. Another view is that it does matter because there might well be many more than a million missing, since it is only an estimate, and because the missing people may be concentrated in particular types of area. On the other hand, how large is this source of error compared with the changes that have already taken place since the census was taken? Indeed, the lack of census update mechanisms and its rapid data obsolescence will soon become far more serious matters than a missing million here or there.

Q. Could the census not be made easier?

A. Yes. A more flexible, user-controlled, data access and customized table design system would have removed the need for up to 20,000 values for large numbers of census areas. Chapter 13 discusses this aspect further. There is no real reason why a more flexible and less rigid system could not have been used with the 1991 Census, and even fewer reasons why it cannot be used in any future census; otherwise the census dinosaur will collapse under the weight of its own obsolete and rigid output complexity.

Q. What would have been the impact of not having a 1991 Census?

A. It is difficult to know whether it would have made that much difference to those areas of planning and public administration in which the census really matters. Remember, until 1993 the 1981 Census was still being used, which suggests that at the very least many census-significant planning processes are robust or insensitive to large-scale data inaccuracy. This is not an ideal state by any means. Population forecasts and resource allocation mechanisms might have been poorer than they already are. Maybe the principal effects would have been psychological; but maybe also it would have stimulated the availability of new data sources that would eventually help mitigate the short-term effects. The census can increasingly be viewed as an outdated concept even if there is still a need for census-like data for small areas based on extremely large samples or full enumeration. In the 1990s information technology era, it must be possible to create more up-to-date databases of census-like data that are of relevance to many of the applications which at present use census data. The problem is that this would probably require a complete overhaul of HM Government's statistical and data infrastructure. This might well happen, but the pace of change seems to be exceedingly slow.

Q. Was the census worth its cost as a small sample survey could have provided equivalent information?

A. This fallacy needs to be squashed. The statement is at best applicable only for statistics reported for large geographic areas. The principal value of the census is that it is still the only source of reliable and comparable data for small areas with complete coverage of Britain's population. It is not designed to be a sample but to be comprehensive. It provides a 'gold standard' against which all other household surveys and databases can be compared. It becomes particularly useful at the small, sub-local authority, geographical scales, often used for policy, planning and research purposes; and it is here where sample surveys cannot compete at present because even the largest sample sizes are still too small.

If you wish to follow up this point then the SAR (see CUG2-11; CUH2-11) is a 1% and 2% sample of households and persons. You can investigate at what spatial level the cross-tabulations become unreliable, although for confidentiality reasons the data are not available for small geographical areas where, of course, the limitations of such small sample sizes would be most visible. If you really want to do without a census then the best route is to seek to provide census-like data from government's existing databases perhaps in conjunction with commercial sector data. Sample surveys are not substitutes or adequate replacements despite a certain amount of spurious appeal.

Q. Can the census be analysed in a non-spatial and non-geographical way?

A. Yes. The geographical nature of the census with the fascinating picture it provides of small area variations in a number of interesting variables often detracts from the nature of the census as a large household survey. If the geographical details are ignored, then the census can appear as a simple British household survey type of data source. You can look at up to 20,000 cross-tabulated counts and no doubt some of these will show fascinating details about the socioeconomic and demographic condition of Britain's population in 1991. The SAR is worth looking at, because you can create your own variables (see CUH2-11) or link the census with non-census data to fabricate new variables of interest (see CUH2-12). Indeed there is a veritable goldmine of untapped social-science-relevant information just awaiting research attention. Maybe the SAR is the natural route for many social scientists to start to appreciate the importance of the census as a survey data source.

3.3 More advanced questions and answers

Q. What is the relevance of asking how many bathrooms you have?

A. Clearly, this is relevant to plumbers! It is also supposedly a measure of inverse deprivation. Herein indeed lies one of the major structural weaknesses of the census, in that many of the variables are surrogates or proxies rather than direct measurements of underlying social conditions. Does it matter if you do not have central heating? Surely, it is more important to know whether you have adequate heating and the financial resources to switch it on in winter. Likewise, what is the point of asking about long-term illness when there should be better sources of the information?

Q. What is the best way of handling or reducing aggregation effects in census data?

A. One solution is always to use data for the smallest possible areas, as this will naturally tend to minimize the impact of aggregation damage. However, this does not adequately deal with the associated spatial representation problems. Geographers have been very slow to appreciate the consequences of studying data for zonal or areal entities. No two zonal objects (or zonal cases) are identical. They may vary in physical size and geometric shape, in terms of internal data heterogeneity, and by their ability to capture or represent underlying spatial patterns. For example, a zone big enough to capture an entire village or town will provide a very different spatial data 'picture' than one which only represents part of a village or town. Villages and towns vary greatly in size and shape; as a result the ability of the same level of census geography to represent whole or parts of settlements varies tremendously. In some cases, the zoning system may be quite good, in other places disastrously bad. Now imagine the problem at a microscale. The result is that any zoning system contains a spatially varying level of internal heterogeneity and thus varies in terms of its representational accuracy. Essentially, this source of spatial data error is out of control. All the census analyst can attempt to do is to reduce the impact.

CUH2-5 suggests that one way of controlling the impact of zones on the results is to design new levels of spatial aggregation that have some geographical property in common. For example, zones of approximately equal population size will at least contain census data at a similar level of precision (and sampling error in the 10% of data). Small number effects will have been standardized. Ideally, the census output areas themselves should have been designed by the census agencies to be similar in size and social homogeneity (as might be measured by tenure type). This was once impossible because of the computational complexity it could cause, but it is now much less of a problem although it would have to be done by the OPCS or GRO(S). However, all that users can do with the 1991 Census is to re-aggregate the census EDs, wards and postcode sectors into larger and more size homogeneous and perhaps internally homogeneous areal units.

Q. I am interested in ranking wards by a *Z* score statistic. What advice would you offer?

A. *Don't*! First, wards, despite the availability of 20,000 LBS, are a relatively poor level of census geography. They vary too much in size and internal heterogeneity to be a useful set of areas for any serious analytical purpose (a fundamental criticism still not understood by many applied users, especially in a certain government department). Second, a *Z* score statistic computed for areas is biased by spatial autocorrelation in the data (this tends to reduce the standard deviation and inflate the *Z* score). Third, ranking wards ignores the fact that the wards are not themselves comparable objects – some are, some are not. It is a bit like comparing chalk with cheese – they are not the same. Ranking assumes that all wards are comparable objects. Fourth, it tends to emphasize small number problems (wards with small populations can more readily assume more extreme values) and to de-emphasize wards with highest levels of internal heterogeneity. Finally, there is the difficult problem of designing a sensible and sensitive univariate index for the ranking. We live in a highly multivariate world. The census is an extremely multivariate dataset. How on earth can you develop a univariate index by which to rank areas? It would be much better to use a multivariate classification despite the greater complexity it entails (see CUH2-5,8).

Q. I am interested in creating a set of 50 or so general census-related indicator variables. Where might I find a set of good 1991 definitions?

A. That's not so easy. The variables you use need to reflect purpose. Then you need to try and reduce redundancy in topic coverage by either scrutinizing correlation matrices or using factor analysis. A good introduction is in CUH1-4, 5, 7. If you are feeling energetic then you could easily start with 400 or so derived variables with a view to reducing them to 40 or 50 sets of not too highly correlated 'important variables'. The literature on geodemographic systems will give you some pointers, as will the social geography and factorial ecology literature.

In reality, at the end of the day you just have to sit down and derive variables to cover whatever topics are relevant. Be careful to avoid (i) mixtures of 10% and 100% coded data in the same variable; (ii) sets of variables that add to 100% (closed number set problems); (iii) variables which are multimodal or highly skewed (they will muck-up your standard statistical methods); (iv) variables with different definitions or interpretations in different parts of the UK (e.g. in Scotland houses tend to be smaller); (v) variables dominated by missing data; (vi) variables known to be suspect (i.e. migration is usually problematic); and (vii) data for very small areas in which extreme values due to small number effects dominate.

Then, having derived some variables, do check them very carefully; remember the old dictum 'garbage in, garbage out'. Wrong data do not produce good results! So look at both minimum and maximum values – are they what you expect? If OK, then have a look at some one-dimensional histograms. If OK, then maybe the data might be worth doing something with (see CUH2-6,7).

Q. I think I may have found something of major significance/importance/value from analysis of 1991 Census data. Should I buy some champagne to celebrate?

A. Maybe yes, maybe no. Quite often wrong data can produce the most spectacularly interesting results. So first check for data errors; then check again! If still OK, then try and replicate your results somewhere else; or feed in some randomized version of the data (i.e. randomly swop individual variables from randomly selected different cases; do this enough and you will end up with a randomized census data file) and re-run. There are major problems somewhere if you still get interesting results. If still OK, then maybe you should celebrate.

Q. I have just found that my results are significant at $p = 0.000,001$ (or even $p = 0.000,000$). What does this really mean?

A. Significance levels often have no real meaning when applied to census data, as they relate to sampling error. For example, suppose your correlation coefficient is significantly different from zero at $p = 0.000,000,01$. So what! If you have a large enough number of zones, a correlation value of 0.01 may well be regarded as significantly different from zero but you should not get too excited about it. However, census data are also often not strictly speaking a random sample; there is often no sampling error to worry about. In which case a correlation of 0.000,01 is different from 0.000,00 and no statistical testing is needed! So be careful and don't overdo the significance testing.

Another complication to worry about is that the spatially autocorrelated nature of census data tends to invalidate the standard statistical tests. The standard error estimates are often too small, and whole books have been written on statistical analysis of spatial data without much practically useful outcome. If you really want to test hypotheses on census data then consider the use of Monte Carlo significance tests (see also CUH2-7,9).

The best way to regard tests of significance is as a hurdle. If your statistic fails the hurdle, then maybe you should not be too excited about it. If it passes, then try and find some other reason for believing it. If you really want benchmarks to compare your results with, then you will have to use Monte Carlo methods to be on the safe side.

Q. What census data checking would you recommend?

A. Look at the minimum and maximum values of your variables. Then apply some simple exploratory data analysis methods, such as those described in CUH1-4 and CUH2-7. You can also try bootstrapping. This works as follows: take a random sample (with replication) of the observations and redo your analysis, and then repeat 1000 times or so (Good 1994). This will build up a distribution of results which gives you some indication of how stable your results are. Another method is to add random noise to the data (to reflect data uncertainty) and then repeat your analysis 1000 times or so. Again the spread of results will contain useful information.

Q. What data transformation would you advise?

A. None, probably; unless it is considered to be really critical. Transforming data greatly complicates interpretation. For example, the statement that there is a high correlation between unemployment and poor housing means something. The statement that there is a high correlation between the arcsin of log unemployment and the unfurnished rented housing raised to the power of 0.335 is completely meaningless. If you wish to use linear statistics then their beauty is their simplicity. If you wish to wander into the nonlinear world then don't expect simplicity.

Q. The census relates to a night-time situation. How can I estimate populations for 12 noon?

A. You cannot. Indeed, the day-time distribution of census variables is spatially completely different. We have only the most tenuous information about these day-time distributions, e.g. as contained in the journey-to-work data. So this is a major and unavoidable defect in census data. It has some important implications; e.g. in emergency planning, daytime population distributions matter but only night-time distributions are available. This defect applies to all non-census data as well. Maybe there should have been a special census question asking where the residents were at mid-day on the previous Friday.

Q. Some people consider that continuous, surface, representations of census data are more useful than discrete values for zones. For example, they reduce modifiable areal unit effects and provide a more natural and better description of the spatial patterning of census variables. Can this be recommended as a substitute for traditional small area statistics?

A. It all depends on (i) your purpose and (ii) the quality of the surface generalization. It has to be recognized that the data incorporated in the census are discrete and spatially discontinuous. It is a simplification and a generalization to represent such data for both zones and surfaces. In a zonal representation there is a loss of information due to aggregation and patterns can change abruptly at zonal boundaries. Some new patterns are created and others disappear. It is also an unintelligent process in that neighbourhood information and local data gradients are not taken into account. The continuous surface representation does deal with the latter but in an arbitrary fashion. In both cases the data are smoothed and, in the latter case, the values are the figment of some mathematical function's imagination. So neither are ideal, although the discrete zonal representation is closer to the raw data.

If the objective is to visualize census data, then certainly three-dimensional representations can look spectacular. Also, variables such as population density are most naturally viewed as surfaces. However, whether or not a three-dimensional representation of two-car households makes much, or any, sense depends on the quality (and locally adaptive nature) of the surface modelling process and whatever else is draped on top of it to provide location finding information, or even interesting covariates. However, one of the advantages of the surface representation is the ability to perform cross-area aggregation, e.g. to merge census with remotely sensed data or to estimate census data for areas that do not match any of the available census geographies. The errors in this type of data manipulation need to be carefully considered.

On the other hand, scientific visualization can turn flat and boring traditional census mapping into colourful three-dimensional displays. Why worry too much about the accuracy of the representations if the objective is to communicate broad patterns (rather than micro details). Obviously care is needed but that apart there are a myriad of alternative presentations that might be useful, so experiment!

Q. Is it possible that geodemographic classifications of Britain's residential areas can now be produced without using 1991 Census data?

A. Yes. Database companies such as ICD and NDL/CMT hold large individual-level databases containing census-like data about millions of people. The NDL database in 1993 is estimated to contain information about 14 million people and the CMT equivalent has 7 million. Many of these people are mail order responsives. When such data are aggregated to census EDs, then it is likely that the results will be better than the 10% census data but worse than the 100% at such small area levels (see CUH2-11 and CUG1-7). Resampling or reweighting might well prove useful as a means of removing bias and improving the quality of the data. The principal methodological difficulty is the need to incorporate in 'census' analysis procedures for handling large-scale variations in data precision. On the other hand, in a marketing context, many of the census variables are used as proxies for missing data, e.g. income. With the NDL/CMT data, income information is available, greatly simplifying the analysis process and making the results more relevant to marketeers. It might be argued, therefore, that geodemographic systems based on non-census data might be more useful, as well as being updatable products. Time alone will tell when the empirical comparisons are performed (see also CUH2- 8).

Q. I am a commercial user interested in exploiting the census as a value adding product. What advice can you give me about the choice between different geodemographic systems?

A. First, it is useful to note that, of all the broad classes of census users, the commercial user is probably the least well catered for. The Census Offices have seemingly been overly concerned to avoid 'getting the census a bad name' and thus have failed either to provide top-class standard geodemographics (using internally available data at the postcode level or even non-blurred data at census ED level) or to make the census agencies a particularly attractive commercial proposition. It is almost as if commercial users have been an embarrassment. Presumably this reflects the view that the census has no role in a consumer-led revival out of the early 1990s economic recession. This assumption might well be wrong.

As for the choice between geodemographic systems, maybe the superficial differences do not matter much. The errors in the geodemographic targeting process seem to result mainly from other aspects of the process, namely over-simplified consumer behaviour modelling. Ideally, the 1990s are a time of customized client-specific geodemographics, incorporating a wide range of non-census data, and the era of the general purpose system has in fact ended (see CUG1-7 and CUH2-8).

Q. Is a 10-year gap between censuses tolerable in the 1990s during a period of unparalleled socioeconomic change?

A. No, but this has become the fashion. With the sole exception of 1966, there has never been a mid-decennial census, mainly owing to lack of government support. Typically, it is assumed to be too expensive. Also the length of time it has traditionally taken for the data to be made available (i.e. the last of the 1991 Census data were available in 1994) makes the prospect of the five-year census somewhat embarrassing, although there is no reason why this should continue to be so bad. There is also an important emerging need to be able to update the census on an annual basis, with estimates good enough to be used at the small area scale. The fact that these data do not already exist is a grave deficiency in information provision.

Q. How easy is it to use census data in decision making and how directly relevant is it?

A. In planning the location of an aged persons' home, the census will help identify a 'good' location in April 1991. The question is whether this will remain a good location for the next 30 years. Indeed this illustrates another fundamental weakness of the census. It is a snapshot, but many spatial-decision- making processes require a forecast of change. The census database is only a starting point for decision making, and it only provides a small part of the information support that is needed. The failure to retain geographical comparability between the censuses in England and Wales compounds these problems. It follows then that the census needs to be accompanied by modelling and prediction of change to be of maximum use in spatial decision support. It is interesting that the census agencies are, in fact, well placed to do this, if the needs were clearly articulated and identified as important. Without this dynamic element, the census is clearly of less value in many decision-making contexts than it could be.

Q. Does government make best use of census (and other) data resources?

A. Probably not. The uncertainty reflects the relative and context-dependent nature of what might be regarded as 'best use'. Ideally, data should be accurate, contain relevant information and be up to date. None of this applies to 1991 Census data as they are used in many applications. For example, if you wish to target small areas for special action then you need *accurate* measurements of *relevant* variables for all the small areas in the UK. The census only goes part of the way; for instance, the best measures of deprivation are not entirely census based but are income and social security related but these data are not in the census and never will be. As information technologies improve, so the limitations of the census as a relevant data resource are more and more exposed. Once upon a time there was nothing else; this is not true anymore.

Q. I would like some code to compute spatial variograms on census data. Where might I get it from?

A. You should write to any relevant authors in this book. Alternatively, if you know what the words mean, then maybe you could write your own software to do it.

Q. What is secondary copyright?

A. The census agencies claim that Crown Copyright applies to both the raw census data and any results obtained from it. They could probably seek to charge copyright payments if the secondary results are then used in some commercial exercise. This is somewhat pernicious in that ownership of the data has been extended beyond the data to which it applies, e.g. to the parameters in a regression model built on census data but then applied to non-census data. It is clearly a 'grey' area and users need to tread carefully.

Q. Is it not unfair to be overly critical of the 1991 Census and is there not a danger that an important data resource will not be properly used or appreciated?

A. By tradition, censuses attract criticism. It is nearly always possible to do better and as a result the census concept has evolved. The criticisms that matter concern whether or not the 1991 Census could have been significantly better for about the same cost. Maybe, the answer might just have been 'yes' on this occasion. However, having stated the criticisms it is not clear (and never is) who is to blame. Is it individuals or is it the system, or is it a mix of both? Are the internal impediments real or illusionary, or are they psychological perceptions of possible constraints? Who really knows? What we do know is that 'they' (whoever 'they' are) do the best they can in difficult circumstances. But is this good enough? Maybe someone should find out.

Q. Does the need for a 2001 Census mainly reflect the failure of government to organize its corporate data resources properly?

A. Yes. There is little doubt that there will be a 2001 Census although in theory many of the data, and much more besides, already reside in various government-owned computer systems. It is ironic that once there was no alternative to the census; but now there is, it is still easier to continue the census concept not just here in Britain but throughout the world. Those who write census handbooks are quite glad about this.

4 A guide to the 1991 Census user's guides and handbooks

With two census user's guides already published plus this *Census Users' Handbook*, the census user might well be excused for being confused. Which one should he or she read first? Which is the best value for money? Which is most suitable for a given application or theme? It is useful to review the contents and coverage of all three census user's guides and then provide a path through them all.

Table 1.4 *A Census User's Handbook* (1983) edited by D. Rhind (Methuen, London)

Chapter	Title
1	Censuses past and present
2	The 1981 Census and its results
3	User needs: an overview
4	Univariate analysis: presenting and summarising single variables
5	Creating new variables and new areas from the census
6	Mapping census data
7	Bivariate and multivariate analysis: relationships between census variables
8	Multivariate analysis of census data: the classification of areas
9	Analysing change through time
10	Linking census and other data
11	Microdata and the British Census

4.1 The original Rhind edited (1983) *Census User's Handbook*

This handbook was written at a time when the census was just starting to become a major focus of research and applied attention. The 1981 Census was the first census that was 'easy' to access via standard software (SASPAC or even SPSS) in computing environments that were more than powerful enough (just, in some cases) to cope with the 1981 SAS. There were the beginnings of an expanding user community (in academia, in government and in commerce) and a desperate need for some advice over and above the traditional but often terse descriptive documents provided by the OPCS and GRO(S). It is interesting that this need continues to this day.

Table 1.4 presents the contents of the 1983 *Census User's Handbook*. As can be seen, this Rhind original had to attempt to cover all aspects of the census, its history and content, as well as provide methodological and technical advice that census users might have found useful. It is noted that the perspective was that of the quantitative geographer interested in applied census analysis. Also, raising awareness of the census and related issues was another important underlying theme.

The strong focus on the analysis of census data is quite apparent with about half the book devoted to relevant techniques. It is also interesting that the content of the remainder of the book is shared between describing what the census is and offering thoughts about its future.

Table 1.5 *An Introductory Guide to the 1991 Census* (1993) edited by B. Leventhal, C. Moy, J. Griffin (NTC Publications, Henley-on-Thames)

Chapter	Title
1	Introduction
2	Census methodology
3	Census outputs
4	Differences within the UK
5	Analysis of census data
6	Samples of Anonymized Records
7	Special classifications
8	Further data sources
9	Lifestyle data
10	Projecting the census forward

4.2 The Leventhal *et al.* edited (1993) *Introductory Guide to the 1991 Census*

This was produced by the Market Research Society Census Interest Group and was only published after a tremendous struggle. The objective is narrowly focused and the book is primarily aimed at those involved with market research, both practitioners and the clients who employ them. The editors write: 'It is our aim to provide straightforward and accessible help, so that readers can discover how the census works; what can be produced from it; the limitations of the various reports and outputs; and what other sources work well with the census' (Preface). Table 1.5 summarizes the contents.

Clearly this is a useful, highly descriptive, often fairly brief, and low-level introduction to the census for marketeers. There is very little methodological and advanced analysis content and this reflects the characteristics of the target audience. Most of the book provides a description of census data.

4.3 The Dale and Marsh edited (1993) *1991 Census User's Guide*

This book was partly funded by the ESRC and is published by the HMSO. It can therefore be regarded as the 'official' OPCS-approved census user's guide to the 1991 Census. It clearly benefits but also suffers in various ways from its OPCS sponsorship. This guide seems to have set itself the limited but useful task of providing a comprehensive information source about the 1991 Census. It is almost 100% description, often in immense detail, of the 1991 Census. Of the 398 pages only 21 are concerned with mapping and spatial analysis; see Table 1.6 for a summary of its contents.

It is clearly useful for users to have a definitive published single reference source of census information but it will not help them do much or any analysis. Compared with the 1983 Rhind handbook, this Dale and Marsh book is massively unbalanced. Census users could discover everything they need to know about the 1991 Census from other OPCS and GRO(S) publications; indeed,

Table 1.6 *The 1991 Census User's Guide* (1993) edited by A. Dale and C. Marsh (HMSO, London)

Chapter	Title
1	An overview
2	The content of the 1991 Census: change and continuity
3	Census geography: I An overview II A review
4	Fieldwork and data processing
5	Privacy, confidentiality, and anonymity in the 1991 Census
6	The validation of census data I Post enumeration survey approaches II General issues
7	Output from the 1991 Census: an introduction
8	The 1991 Local Base and Small Area Statistics
9	Mapping and spatial analysis
10	Migration, transport and workplace statistics from the 1991 Census
11	The Sample of Anonymized Records
12	The OPCS Longitudinal Study
13	Population censuses in Northern Ireland: 1926–1991
14	Wither the Census?

presumably they have had to do this already because the availability of the census data pre-dated the book by at least six months. However, it will no doubt fill a niche as a reference source.

4.4 The Openshaw edited (1995) *Census Users' Handbook*

This book retains a reasonably close affinity with the 1981 Handbook, particularly with respect to its focus on methodological and applied analysis aspects. Table 1.7 summarizes the chapter headings; it will be noted that about three-quarters are concerned with the methodological and analysis aspects of using census data. It is therefore a real census users' handbook. In some respects it may be regarded as being 'advanced'. Yet no apology is offered. It is not sufficient merely to describe what the census offers by way of data, leaving analysis to the discretion of the user. The census is a far too valuable and important data resource for such a *laissez-faire* approach, especially as the applied use of census data presents a plethora of hard methodological problems. To quote Rhind (1983): 'We confidently anticipate no less than 10,000 people in Britain making direct use of the 1981 Census statistics and decisions arising from some of these uses will ultimately touch the lives of millions' (p. xviii). Rhind clearly got a zero in the wrong place, but the real point he is making is that there is a large and growing base of census users who use census data in all sorts of decision making

Table 1.7 *Census Users' Handbook* (1994) assembled by S. Openshaw

Chapter	Title
1	A quick introduction to most of what you need to know about the 1991 Census
2	Putting the census on the researcher's desk
3	Accessing the data via SASPAC91
4	Dealing with census geography: principles, practices and possibilities
5	GIS and the census
6	Visualizing the 1991 Census
7	Analysis of univariate census data
8	Classifying and regionalizing census data
9	Further analysis of multivariate census data
10	Analysis of change through time
11	Samples of Anonymized Records
12	Using microsimulation to synthesize census data
13	The future of the census

that affects us all. It is extremely important that there is a source of expert advice in census analysis, an area where conventional statistical packages are not so helpful. This census users' handbook attempts to meet some of these needs.

The census is also a most important data source. This has always been true, but it is becoming clear that the traditional UK census concept is now seemingly in some need of revision. Unlike the other two census books, this book is independent of the OPCS. It has not been given their blessing (nor denied it), nor has it been subject to their scrutiny. It is simply an independent effort and it is no less likely to be 'right' or 'wrong' because of this fact. However, being independent does provide an opportunity for perhaps a more objective and occasionally, where appropriate, a more user-oriented critical view of the census, the OPCS and GRO(S) than that which is likely to be found elsewhere. Where relevant, also a constructive proactive stance is offered.

This book is a handbook of facts, ideas, methods and advice for the 1991 Census user who wants, or needs, to get the most out of census analysis. In many ways also, it should be recognized that the 1991 Census is a census in transition. Whatever happens in 2001, it is certain to be different in various ways. In particular: (i) the integration of census data, digital map data and GIS will be complete; (ii) the census database should be annually updatable; (iii) census data storage will be in computer memory; (iv) artificial-intelligence-based (rather than conventional statistical) analysis methods will revolutionize what can be done with census data, and (v) the output areas and fixed tables concepts should have been replaced by more dynamic and flexible procedures. These and related developments are events that we can only look forward to; meanwhile let us enjoy the 1991 Census data we already have and focus our minds on making the best of what we have.

To aid the reader, a short editor's introduction prefaces each of the chapters.

5 Using the Handbook

There are a number of different ways of viewing the contents. These are illustrated as follows by a series of meta-walks designed for different interest groups.

Walk 1:	the beginner	Chapters 1 – 4, 6, 7, 10 should appeal
Walk 2:	the advanced	Chapters 6 – 9, 12 and 13
Walk 3:	the statistician	Chapters 7 – 9, 12
Walk 4:	the planner	Chapters 1 – 6, 10, 11, 13
Walk 5:	the geographer	Chapters 1 – 11, 13
Walk 6:	the marketeer	Chapters 6, 8, 10 – 13
Walk 7:	the government statistician	Chapters 1, 4, 6, 12, 13
Walk 8:	the UK Census Offices	Chapters 1–13
Walk 9:	critics of the Census	Chapters 1, 4, 10, 13
Walk 10:	social survey	Chapters 11, 12

References

Dale, A and C Marsh 1993 *The 1991 Census User's Guide*. London: HMSO.
Good, P 1994 Permutation Tests. Berlin: Springer Verlag.
Leventhal, B, C Moy and J Griffin 1993 *An Introductory Guide to the 1991 Census*. Henley: NTC.
Monmonier, M 1991 *How to Lie with Maps*. ASPRS Special Publications.
Rhind, D 1983 *A Census User's Handbook*. London: Methuen.
SASPAC 1992 *SASPAC User Manual: Parts 1 and 2*, CST 450, 1st edn. London: London Research Centre, April.
Williamson, P 1993 METAC91: a database about published 1991 census table contents. Working Paper 93/18, School of Geography, University of Leeds, Leeds.

2

Putting the census on the researcher's desk

P Rees

Editor's note

The very brief census overall view contained in Chapter 1 is supplemented by this in-depth account of what information is provided by the 1991 Census. It is not an account of the census process but a view of what the census actually provides. Whilst the focus is on the academic uses of the census, the chapter is also of much wider interest, providing a handy digest of the available information and offering some examples of census analysis likely to be of applied value. Finally, it serves as a timely reminder that in virtually every university in the UK there are groups of geographers and others working on the analysis of the 1991 Census. Users with queries or problems relating to census analysis should try and establish contact. There is a tradition of isolationism in UK census research that helps no-one and can so easily be cured by a letter or telephone call.

1 Introduction

The 1991 Census of Population was carried out in all parts of the UK on 21 April 1991. Since that day the Census Offices of the UK have been engaged in preparing extensive sets of data for submission to Parliament and for sale to users. To provide the higher education community with access to the computer-held versions of the census outputs, the Economic and Social Research Council (ESRC) and the Joint Information Systems Committee (JISC) of the Higher Education Funding Councils of England, Wales and Scotland have been collaborating, with help from the Department of Education, Northern Ireland (DENI), in making arrangements for the purchase and dissemination of census data.

Section 2 outlines the system of collective purchase and dissemination of the data that is in place. Sections 3–5 describe the various census datasets, roughly in order of their delivery to the academic community. Many more details on each of these datasets can be found in other chapters in this volume. In Section 6 a guide is provided for users on how to overcome the problems of building census datasets that are comparable between 1981 and 1991, a problem peculiar to England and Wales. Section 7 offers advice on how to construct small area population estimates for intercensal years forward from the 1991 Census base. Section 8 describes the different ways in which researchers can access and hold data from the 1991 Census as input to their research projects. The penultimate section, Section 9, provides a short illustrative application – an analysis of a new census variable, limiting long-term illness – while the last section, Section 10, reviews the achievements of the Census Programme.

2 The system of dataset provision and use

2.1 The Census Programme

Students and researchers in the academic community (higher education) are privileged that a system of purchasing, supporting and disseminating the machine readable outputs of the 1991 Censuses of Population in the UK has been set up by the ESRC and JISC in collaboration with DENI. Some £3.12 million (ESRC £1.5 million, JISC £1.5 million and DENI £0.12 million) are being spent on the central purchase and support of the principal datasets and their dissemination to users throughout the academic community. This activity is currently known as 'The ESRC/JISC 1991 Census of Population Programme'. It will be referred to as the Census Programme in the rest of the chapter.

2.2 Use of the census data

Use of the statistics is free at the point of use, as long as users have registered with the relevant dissemination unit and have assented to the conditions of use agreed by ESRC on behalf of ESRC/JISC with the Census Offices and other data suppliers. It must be stressed that census data can only be used for academic research and teaching, and that if higher education institutions wish to incorporate census data in commercial products or projects they must negotiate the appropriate licences and fees with the Census Offices or other suppliers.

2.3 The Census Offices of the UK

The Census of Population is administered by three Census Offices. The Office of Population Censuses and Surveys (OPCS) has responsibility for England and Wales; the General Register Office, Scotland (GRO(S)) administers the Scottish census; the Census Office, Northern Ireland (CONI) carries out the census in that part of the UK. The three Census Offices collaborate closely and two, OPCS and

GRO(S), produce closely aligned census outputs. The Northern Ireland census outputs have always been somewhat different, although in collaboration with the ESRC/JISC Census Programme CONI will produce Small Area Statistics (SAS) on a basis comparable with that adopted in Great Britain.

The addresses of the Census Offices and the names of key personnel for contact are provided in Appendix 2A.

2.4 Organization of the Census Programme

The components of the Census Programme are set out in Table 2.1 and the names and addresses of principal investigators are listed in Appendix 2A. Fuller details

Table 2.1 Arrangements for the maintenance and dissemination of census data to the UK academic community under the ESRC/JISC 1991 Census of Population Programme

The Components	Location	Access/Content
1 Census datasets	MCC, Manchester	Registered users via JANET
	Data Archive	CD-ROM datasets from DA
	Other sites	Registered users via LAN
2 Locational datasets	MCC, Manchester	Registered users via JANET
	EUDL, Edinburgh	Registered users via JANET
	Other sites	Registered users via LAN
3 Units	CDU, Manchester	Via JANET
	CMU, Manchester	Via JANET
	DA, Essex	Via JANET
	LSSP, City	Via JANET
4 Training Programme	City/Manchester	User's Guide to the 1991 Census
	Southampton	Tutorial and user guides
	Leicester/MRRL	Sample datasets
	Leicester/MRRL	Trainer resource base
	Cardiff	Training workshops
	Manchester/City	Training programme
5 Development Programme	Southampton	Spatial models of census data
	Southampton	Aggregation issues
	Warwick	Occupation definitions
	Manchester	US Census lessons
	Leeds	Population synthesis, migration analysis
	Leeds	SARs project
		Aggregation issues
		Classification project
6 Seminar Programme	Meetings	e.g. Census Analysis Group Conference Sept 1993, Newcastle
7 Research Programme	For 1994–5	14 projects
8 Co-ordinator	Leeds	To any census user in the academic community

of the programme are provided by Rees (1992a). Here some of the key characteristics are highlighted.

The datasets are held and supported centrally by a series of ESRC- and JISC-funded units. Users access the data via the national academic computer network called JANET. A set of projects aimed at providing training in the use of census data is distributed around the country: users can obtain advice from their nearest project personnel. Particular methodological problems are being addressed by a series of development projects at a variety of universities. A seminar programme provides a forum for reporting on the results of this work and forms a collaborative network. One of the tasks taken on by the Census Analysis Group members at Leeds and Newcastle was the creation of a machine-readable version of the County Monitor/Scottish Region Monitor data, which provided researchers with a simple national dataset in December 1992 (see Section 3).

2.5 Model of the data agreements

The Census Programme plays the very important role of negotiating conditions under which the data may be used. Figure 2.1 sets out the general structure of the data agreements that have been or are being entered into. Five organizational levels are recognized.

Level 1 consists of the data suppliers such as OPCS. *Level 2* is the academic community, which is represented by ESRC on behalf of ESRC, JISC and DENI, the funding organizations. Link 12 represents the contracts or agreements entered into by ESRC and the supplying organization. Some agreements are relatively simple (e.g. the SAS/LBS agreement between ESRC and OPCS/GRO(S)), while others are extremely complex (e.g. the Samples of Anonymized Records contract between ESRC, the University of Manchester and OPCS/GRO(S)).

Level 3 contains the data distribution organizations, which have been licensed by ESRC to hold and distribute census datasets and to provide users with the

LEVEL 1: the data provider (e.g. OPCS, EDLINE)

LINK 12 (Contract or agreement)

LEVEL 2: the academic community (e.g. ESRC/JISC)

LINK 23 (Distributor Agreement)

LEVEL 3: the data distributor (e.g. University of Manchester)

LINK 34 (End User Licence)

LEVEL 4: the academic community organization (e.g. University)

LINK 45 (Individual Licence)

LEVEL 5: the user (e.g. individual researcher or student)

Fig 2.1 The general model of data agreements.

means of access. Each of the data distributors holds an End User Licence (Link 23) from ESRC and is provided with funding to supply data services.

At *Level 4* are the higher education institutions or other academic organizations which take responsibility for the behaviour of their individual users. At a minimum, this may mean just administering the relevant user registration system for the data distributor; at a maximum it may involve holding the complete copy of a national dataset and running their own user registration system (e.g. as at the University of Newcastle).

Level 5 involves the individual user within an academic organization, a researcher or a student, who registers to use a particular dataset. Users are issued with individual licences or their equivalent.

Both higher education institutions and individuals may find themselves filling in many registration forms and may complain about the time consumed and the obligations incurred. However, these are a very small price to pay for access to extremely valuable data.

2.6 An overview of the census datasets

Table 2.2 summarizes the main outputs from the 1991 Census of Population. The top part of the table lists the principal sets of printed documents which have been produced. These are available in the libraries of higher education institutions.

The bottom part of the table lists the principal computer-held datasets, which are described in more detail below and in other chapters. By the time this volume is published, all of the datasets except special tabulations (which are not the concern of the Census Programme) will have been produced and made available.

3 County and district datasets: monitor data

This section describes a dataset built up from the County and Region Monitors for Great Britain, which provides an extensive set of variables for all 67 county/region units in Great Britain and all 459 districts. There are 67 county/region units because Inner and Outer London are separately distinguished. These data provide a means of quickly testing out ideas and hypotheses on a national scale before launching into the more time-consuming tasks of data extraction and analysis on finer spatial scales. Section 7 outlines an application in which they are used.

3.1 The 1991 Census County/Scottish Region Monitor data files

A set of files has been created at the University of Leeds containing the data published by OPCS, GRO(S) and CONI in the County Monitors (England and

Table 2.2 The principal outputs from the 1991 Censuses of Population: months when first available to the academic community

Outputs	England and Wales	Scotland	Northern Ireland
Printed documents, available in libraries			
National Preliminary Reports	07/91	07/91	11/92
National Summary Reports, Part 1	03/93	03/93	11/92
National Summary Reports, Part 2	08/93	08/93	na
National Summary Monitors	12/92	12/92	
Topic Statistics Reports	01/93–09/94		01/93–12/93
County Reports, Part 1	07/92–02/93		na
Scottish Region Reports, Part 1		07/92–02/93	
County Reports, Part2	01/93–06/93		na
Scottish Region Reports, Part 2		01/93–06/93	
County Monitors	07/92–10/92		na
Scottish Region Monitors		07/92–10/92	
Machine-readable statistics			
County Monitors	12/92		
Scottish Region Monitors		12/92	
Northern Ireland Pseudo-Monitor			12/92
Local Base Statistics and Small Area Statistics, 100%	07/92–01/93		11/94
Local Base Statistics and Small Area Statistics, 10%	02/93–05/93		na
ED-to-PC Directory	01/93		
Area Master File	06/93		
Higher Areas Index		08/93	
Special Workplace Statistics	07/94	07/94	na
Special Migration Statistics	05/94	05/94	na
Samples of Anonymized Records (2% individual; 1% household)	07/93	07/93	08/94
Longitudinal Study 1991 Update	01/94	na	na
Special Tabulations	1994	1994	1994

Source: OPCS and GRO(S) (1992d, p.20; 1992a) and personal communication.
Notes: na, not available. All dates after September 1994 are estimated.

Wales), Region Monitors (Scotland) and the Summary Report (Northern Ireland). The files were input under DOS as ASCII files and ported to UNIX for testing and checking. They were then transferred to Manchester for general access.

Full details about the files available to the academic community at Manchester and at Leeds are given in Table 2.3. To use the files, the census users can port them from Manchester to their own systems and then use the Statistical Package for the Social Sciences (SPSS) for analysis. The users will need to port both the data files and the SPSS data description files, and create SPSS system files on the local system. The SPSS system files held on the Leeds library disk can be used

Table 2.3 The principal Great Britain files assembled from County/Scottish Region Monitor data

County/Scottish region data for Great Britain: Tables A to L
cogbal.dat = data arranged in fixed format, described in
cogbal.sps = SPSS command file with data description

District data for Great Britain: Tables B to L
digbbl.dat = data arranged in fixed format, described in
digbbl.sps = SPSS command file with data description

The following files were prepared at Newcastle and contain all the data for Great Britain districts for each table separately:
Tableb, Tablec, Tabled, Tablee, Tablef, Tableg,
Tableh, Tablei, Tablej, Tablek, Tablel

These files can be found by using the gopher menus at midas (cs6400.mcc):
1 datasets information
3 UK Census of Population Statistics
I 1991 Local Base and Small Area Statistics
II Helpful files
II tables for counties/districts from members

directly or ported by Leeds users or by other users of SUN OS version UNIX systems.

Alternatively, users can port from Manchester a set of files suitable for use in a spreadsheet package (e.g. MS-EXCEL). These files contain the district data for Great Britain: each file contains all the data from one table in the County/Scottish Region Monitors. The district data refer exclusively to 1991, while the County/Scottish region dataset also contains data from the 1981 Census and 1991 variables computed from a population base similar to that used in 1981 (slightly smaller than the 1991 population base).

3.2 Warnings about the data

The data were input from the published monitors at the University of Leeds by Census Programme project personnel. They were then distributed to selected Census Analysis Group members preparing papers for presentation at the Royal Geographical Society on 2 December 1992 (e.g. Rees 1992c, 1993a).

The data have been independently checked by Census Analysis Group members at Leeds and Newcastle in completely different formats. The checks were of three kinds: (i) checking of each data item against the monitor item by an individual different from the inputter; (ii) checking of the internal consistency of table figures (within narrow bounds); (iii) checking of district numbers against county numbers; and (iv) checking of every element in the Newcastle version of the files against the corresponding element in the Leeds files. However, no guarantee can be given that all items are correctly represented, and users should report any errors to Keith Cole at Manchester or Phil Rees at Leeds (see Appendix 2A for addresses).

Users will undoubtedly wish to use the County/Scottish Region Monitor data to infer absolute numbers from the percentages in the tables. They should be aware that any absolute figures in the files derived from the rounded percentage figures in the monitors will usually differ somewhat from those published in the County/Region Reports because of the calculation process involved.

It is now possible to replace the percentage data contained in these files by the absolute counts given in the relevant district or county LBS or SAS file. However, you may still find these files of use (i) in getting a quick overview of a topic area for the whole country prior to extracting the data from the dozens of files containing the LBS/SAS data and (ii) in training researchers or students in the use and interpretation of census data.

4 Small Area Statistics: SAS and LBS datasets

The generic term Small Area Statistics (SAS) has been used in the past to refer to machine-readable/computer-held census data produced for areas smaller than local government districts. However, the terminology is more complicated in the 1991 Census. The term Small Area Statistics refers to a set of tables/counts that are supplied for the smallest areas recognized: enumeration districts in England and Wales, output areas in Scotland and enumeration districts in Northern Ireland.

A second, fuller set of tables/counts is available from the 1991 Census for larger subdistrict units: wards in England and Wales, and postal sectors in Scotland. These are called Local Base Statistics (LBS). The SAS contains about 9000 counts while the LBS contains about 20,000 counts.

Both the SAS and the LBS are divided into two sets: the first and larger set contains tables/counts which report on variables which were 100% coded; the second and smaller set reports on variables which were coded only for 10% of forms, because of the labour involved in assigning codes to the answers to open-ended questions.

4.1 The SAS and LBS data for Great Britain

Virtually the whole of the 100% SAS and LBS for Great Britain for the standard geographic units were delivered to the Census Dissemination Unit at Manchester by the end of March 1993 and have been available to all registered users since then. Tables 2.4, 2.5 and 2.6 list the full range of datasets and contain information on the supplementary geographies for which SAS and LBS tables were delivered

Table 2.4 ESRC/JISC 1991 Census of Population Programme purchase of SAS, LBS and related materials for England and Wales

Areas		**£**
Small Area Statistics		
Enumeration districts		226 808.00
Wards		19 860.00
Districts		806.00
Counties		110.00
Standard statistical regions		18.00
National (England and Wales)		4.00
Parliamentary constituencies		1 486.00
Regional Health Authorities		39.75
District Health Authorities		532.65
Postcode sectors		17 488.00
Civil parishes/communities in Wales		22 518.00
European constituencies		185.50
Subtotal		289 855.90
Local Base Statistics		
Wards		37 237.50
Districts		1 511.25
Counties		206.25
Standard statistical regions		33.75
National (England and Wales)		7.50
Parliamentary constituencies		2 103.75
European constituencies		262.50
Regional Health Authorities		56.25
District Health Authorities		753.75
Subtotal		42 172.50
ED-to-PC Directories:	County files	11 120.00
	National file	3 200.00
Maps of EDs on microfilm:	First set	7 200.00
	9 sets at £1800.00	16 200.00
Total, England and Wales		369 748.40

Note: Prices exclude media, handling and VAT.

later in 1993. In 1994 further data were added for secondary areas such as wards, localities and regional electoral divisions in Scotland, while data for urban and rural areas are to be produced for England and Wales.

4.1.1 Areas for datasets purchased by the ESRC Census Programme

The Census Programme is purchasing from the Census Offices sets of SAS and LBS for as many of the alternative geographies as are on offer. The full purchase lists for England and Wales, for Scotland and for Northern Ireland are given in Tables 2.4, 2.5 and 2.6 respectively.

Table 2.5 ESRC/JISC 1991 Census of Population Programme purchase of SAS, LBS and related materials for Scotland

Areas		**£**
Small Area Statistics		
Output areas		70 964.00
Postcode sectors		2 336.00
Districts		106.00
Region		24.00
Scotland		2.00
Parliamentary constituencies		142.00
European constituencies		16.00
Health Board Areas		30.00
Civil parishes		183.40
Subtotal		73 803.40
Local Base Statistics		
Postcode sectors		4 380.00
Districts		198.75
Region		45.00
Scotland		3.75
Parliamentary constituencies		266.25
European constituencies		30.00
Health Board Areas		56.25
Subtotal		4 980.00
Postcode-to-output areas index:	All regions	2 636.00
	National	7 096.40
Total, Scotland		88 515.80

Note: Prices exclude media, handling and VAT.

Table 2.6 ESRC/JISC 1991 Census of Population Programme purchase of SAS and related materials for Northern Ireland

Areas	**£**
Small Area Statistics	
Enumeration districts ($N = 3729$)	7 458.00
Wards ($N = 566$)	1 132.00
Districts ($N = 26$)	52.00
Belfast Urban Area ($N = 1$)	2.00
Northern Ireland ($N = 1$)	2.00
Parliamentary constituencies ($N = 17$)	34.00
Health Board Areas ($N = 4$)	8.00
Education Board Areas ($N = 5$)	10.00
Postcode sectors ($N = 23$)	800.00
Subtotal ($N = 4749$)	9 498.00

Notes:
Prices exclude media, handling and VAT. The costs are set against ESRC investment in a collaborative project with CONI.

You may ask why machine-readable tables of statistics for higher level geographies are being purchased when they could be produced by aggregation from the smaller enumeration district/output area or ward/postcode sector information. There are three reasons for so doing.

1. The SAS and LBS tables are subject to a process of adjustment, in which 0, +1 or −1 is randomly added to a cell count to blur data and preserve confidentiality. Aggregated versions of small area tables will include sums of these adjustments. The higher geography tables (e.g. district or county) are not adjusted and therefore provide good check totals for the small area populations.
2. Only one set of organizations, the Census Offices, carries out the tabulations, avoiding disagreements between users employing different procedures to effect aggregation.
3. The marginal cost of higher geography tables is very low.

4.1.2 The SAS and LBS files at Manchester Computing Centre

The Census Dissemination Unit at Manchester Computing Centre (MCC) has aggregated county files to give SAS and LBS files for standard regions in England and national tables for England, Wales and Scotland. To check what files are available, registered users able to log-on to the MIDAS system at MCC can issue the command gopher to obtain the latest information.

4.1.3 SASPAC91: the extraction package

To use the SAS and LBS datasets, the user will need to consult the relevant manuals (SASPAC 1992) to put together the necessary information for data extraction. Three types of information are needed: (i) the SASPAC91 commands that will find, extract, manipulate and output the data required; (ii) the table and variable codes that identify the sets of counts required by users; and (iii) the geographic codes for the areas for which counts are needed. OPCS and GRO(S) (1992a, b) provide the table layouts, table codes and code numbers for counts within tables together with a simple index of topics. SASPAC (1992) also provides the same information in its Part 2, which must be used to yield the correct table code in non-standard cases. A guide to the SASPAC91 package for accessing the SAS and LBS data is provided in SASPAC (1992), Part 1. Williamson (1993) provides a database tool, called MetaC91, for finding out about table contents, variable locations and variable classifications in the SAS/LBS and in the Samples of Anonymized Records.

Details of how to construct the names of input system files and instructions for running the SASPAC91 package at MCC are given in MCC (1994). A guide for accessing SASPAC91 across the JANET network from another site is provided by Census Analysis Unit (1993). A full set of class notes and exercises is provided in Rees (1993b).

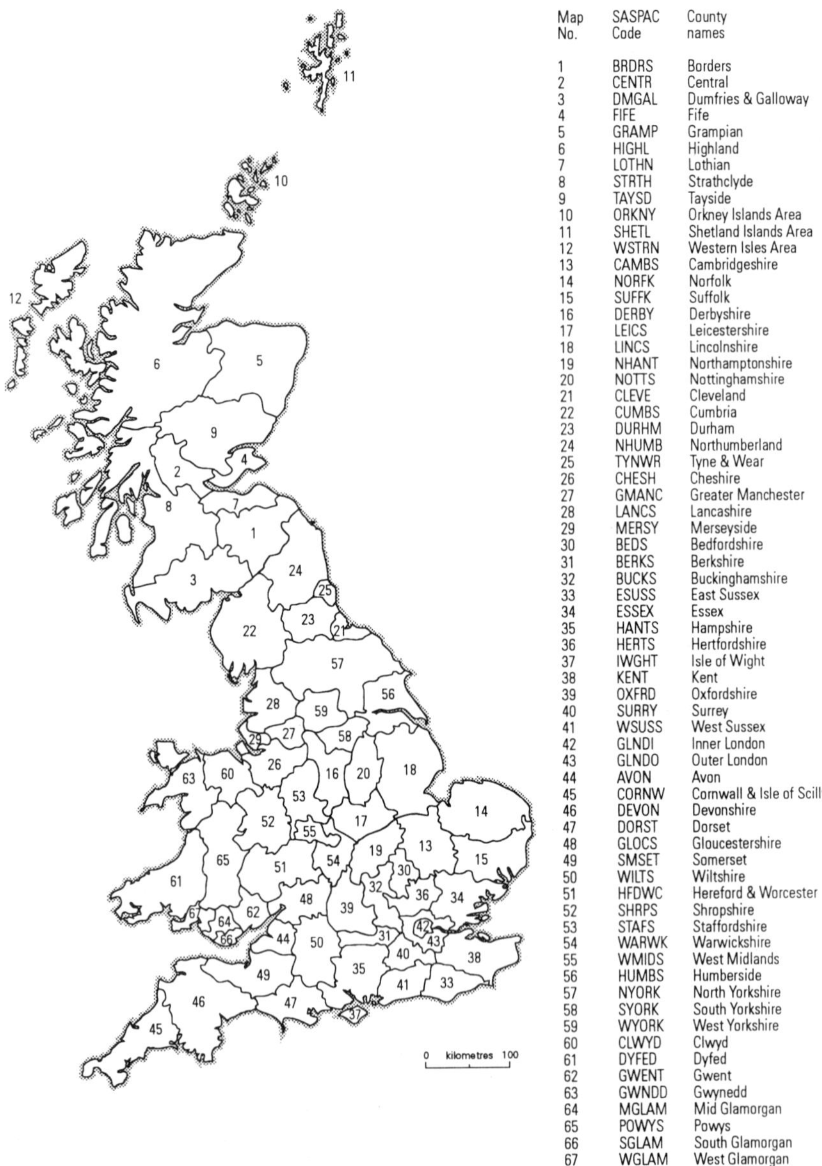

Map No.	SASPAC Code	County names
1	BRDRS	Borders
2	CENTR	Central
3	DMGAL	Dumfries & Galloway
4	FIFE	Fife
5	GRAMP	Grampian
6	HIGHL	Highland
7	LOTHN	Lothian
8	STRTH	Strathclyde
9	TAYSD	Tayside
10	ORKNY	Orkney Islands Area
11	SHETL	Shetland Islands Area
12	WSTRN	Western Isles Area
13	CAMBS	Cambridgeshire
14	NORFK	Norfolk
15	SUFFK	Suffolk
16	DERBY	Derbyshire
17	LEICS	Leicestershire
18	LINCS	Lincolnshire
19	NHANT	Northamptonshire
20	NOTTS	Nottinghamshire
21	CLEVE	Cleveland
22	CUMBS	Cumbria
23	DURHM	Durham
24	NHUMB	Northumberland
25	TYNWR	Tyne & Wear
26	CHESH	Cheshire
27	GMANC	Greater Manchester
28	LANCS	Lancashire
29	MERSY	Merseyside
30	BEDS	Bedfordshire
31	BERKS	Berkshire
32	BUCKS	Buckinghamshire
33	ESUSS	East Sussex
34	ESSEX	Essex
35	HANTS	Hampshire
36	HERTS	Hertfordshire
37	IWGHT	Isle of Wight
38	KENT	Kent
39	OXFRD	Oxfordshire
40	SURRY	Surrey
41	WSUSS	West Sussex
42	GLNDI	Inner London
43	GLNDO	Outer London
44	AVON	Avon
45	CORNW	Cornwall & Isle of Scilly
46	DEVON	Devonshire
47	DORST	Dorset
48	GLOCS	Gloucestershire
49	SMSET	Somerset
50	WILTS	Wiltshire
51	HFDWC	Hereford & Worcester
52	SHRPS	Shropshire
53	STAFS	Staffordshire
54	WARWK	Warwickshire
55	WMIDS	West Midlands
56	HUMBS	Humberside
57	NYORK	North Yorkshire
58	SYORK	South Yorkshire
59	WYORK	West Yorkshire
60	CLWYD	Clwyd
61	DYFED	Dyfed
62	GWENT	Gwent
63	GWNDD	Gwynedd
64	MGLAM	Mid Glamorgan
65	POWYS	Powys
66	SGLAM	South Glamorgan
67	WGLAM	West Glamorgan

Fig 2.2 The counties of England and Wales and the regions of Scotland and their SASPAC91 file names at Manchester Computing Centre.

Figure 2.2 provides a list of the counties for which SAS and LBS files are available together with the names which have been assigned to the files by the Census Dissemination Unit at MCC.

4.1.4 A meta-database for finding variables

One of the problems faced by users of the 1991 Census SAS and LBS data is the sheer volume and complexity. Time and care must be taken in reviewing table contents to discover whether a particular cross-tabulation is present. One of the Census Programme projects at Leeds has developed, in collaboration with OPCS, Titchfield, a meta-database of variable definitions and cross-tabulations with reference information on where these are to be found in the SAS, LBS and County Reports. This meta-database is available as an executable IDEALIST file for use on a PC. Williamson (1993) provides a user manual and a floppy disk with the meta-database.

4.1.5 Grid reference errors in the SAS

The enumeration district (ED) grid references should be checked when used as a small number of errors have been detected. A file of corrections available at MCC should be consulted when using either the SAS ED centroids or the ED-to-postcode directory.

4.2 The SAS data for Northern Ireland

4.2.1 The ESRC and CONI agreement

The ESRC and CONI have reached agreement about the production of SAS for Northern Ireland from the 1991 Census. The Census Programme has funded a project, undertaken by staff from Queen's University Belfast, to produce software to generate SAS tables using the database package SIR. The software has been used by CONI to produce the SAS datasets. The tables are designed to match those for Great Britain as closely as possible and follow the same confidentiality rules (including blurring through the random addition of 0, +1 or -1 to table cells for the two smallest sets of areas) with the same thresholds as in Great Britain. The SAS tables have been produced for the areas shown in Table 2.6.

4.2.2 Comparability of Great Britain and Northern Ireland SAS

The Great Britain SAS/LBS and Northern Ireland SAS are not precisely comparable because there were differences in the questions asked. No ethnic question was asked in Northern Ireland. Instead a question on religion was asked. A classification by religion is used in those tables where an ethnic classification appears in the Great Britain SAS. There are differences in the way the education variable is tabulated: the Northern Ireland Census asked about secondary qualifications, not higher qualifications.

All of the Northern Ireland tables are based on the full set of returns (100% data); no sampling was undertaken. In addition, no imputation (for wholly absent households) was carried out after the Northern Ireland census.

The Northern Ireland SAS were released in 1994. It is therefore possible to carry out accurate analyses of the population of the UK at small area scale for the first time!

4.3 The enumeration district to postcode directories for England and Wales

These have been installed at MCC and can be searched using UNIX editors or special software. These files can be used to convert census statistics for census areas into census statistics for postal areas.

4.4 The Area Master File for England and Wales

The Area Master File (AMF) defines areas in terms of the smallest areal unit needed to give a full specification and provides the OPCS codes to identify each territorial unit. The AMF is available to users at MCC. To the AMF will be added codes for user-defined areas of general interest. For example, researchers at the University of Newcastle have added the link between 1991 wards and postcode sectors and their functional region classification.

4.5 Provision of the 1991 Census on CD-ROM

One means of storing and delivering the large data volumes of the census is to place them on CD-ROM. The ESRC Data Archive are placing the SAS and LBS data for the country on a set of CD-ROMs for distribution to the academic community. Users should contact the Data Archive for details of registration and supply. The CD-ROMs are intended for use by individual researchers or research teams (all of whom need to register as users).

5 Other census datasets

The other datasets which are being produced from the 1991 Census include two databases containing individual records (the Samples of Anonymized Records and the Longitudinal Study) and two involving interaction data (the Special Migration Statistics and the Special Workplace Statistics). We also describe the digitized boundary datasets which will contain the Ordnance Survey (OS) co-ordinate descriptions of census area boundaries suitable for input by users to mapping and geographical information system software. The datasets are described in order of their delivery to the academic community.

5.1 The Samples of Anonymized Records

The Census Offices have produced, for the first time, public use samples of individual and household records from the 1991 Census. The Census Programme is the sole purchaser (and funder) of this new dataset. A description of the main features will be found in Marsh and Teague (1992), together with a full bibliography of the papers which argued the case for the dataset.

There are two Samples of Anonymized Records (SAR):

1. a 1% sample of households;
2. a 2% sample of individuals.

The SAR have been produced for Great Britain, and separately for Northern Ireland. These two sets of SAR will be merged for a subset of common variables to form the UK SAR.

The 1% household sample is coded geographically to standard regions within Great Britain. This coarse level of spatial disaggregation is designed to protect the anonymity of the sample.

The 2% individual sample is coded geographically at a much finer scale to local authority areas that have combined populations of 120,000 people or more. The areas are shown in Figure 2.3 and the areas are listed in the key to the figure.

The SAR are made available to the academic community by the Census Microdata Unit (CMU) at the University of Manchester for online and batch tabulation by users or for porting to their own institutions. The datasets can be accessed via one of the following database packages: SPSS, SAS and QUANVERT (see Appendix 2B for definitions). The CMU also offers a tabulation and advice service to academic users and a commercial service to outside users. A Census Programme project at the University of Leeds supervised by Stan Openshaw has prepared a UNIX-based tabulation system for accessing the SAR in a flexible way that exploits the power of modern workstations. The system offers users advice on the statistical significance of their cross-tabulation and a variety of tabulation indexes and tests. It can be ported to UNIX systems with sufficient data storage capacity.

It is therefore possible for users to produce their own cross-tabulations of census data from the SAR in a way that meets the needs of their research more precisely than do the published and preset tabulation datasets. However, in doing so they should always be aware that the tables produced are sample estimates and proper statistical inference procedures should be used to determine what are significant differences and relationships.

5.2 Digitized boundary data and other locational reference data

It is important to know where census areas are located. To answer the question 'where?', several different types of locational reference data are being purchased by the Census Programme: census codes and associated grid references, indexes, digitized boundary data and maps.

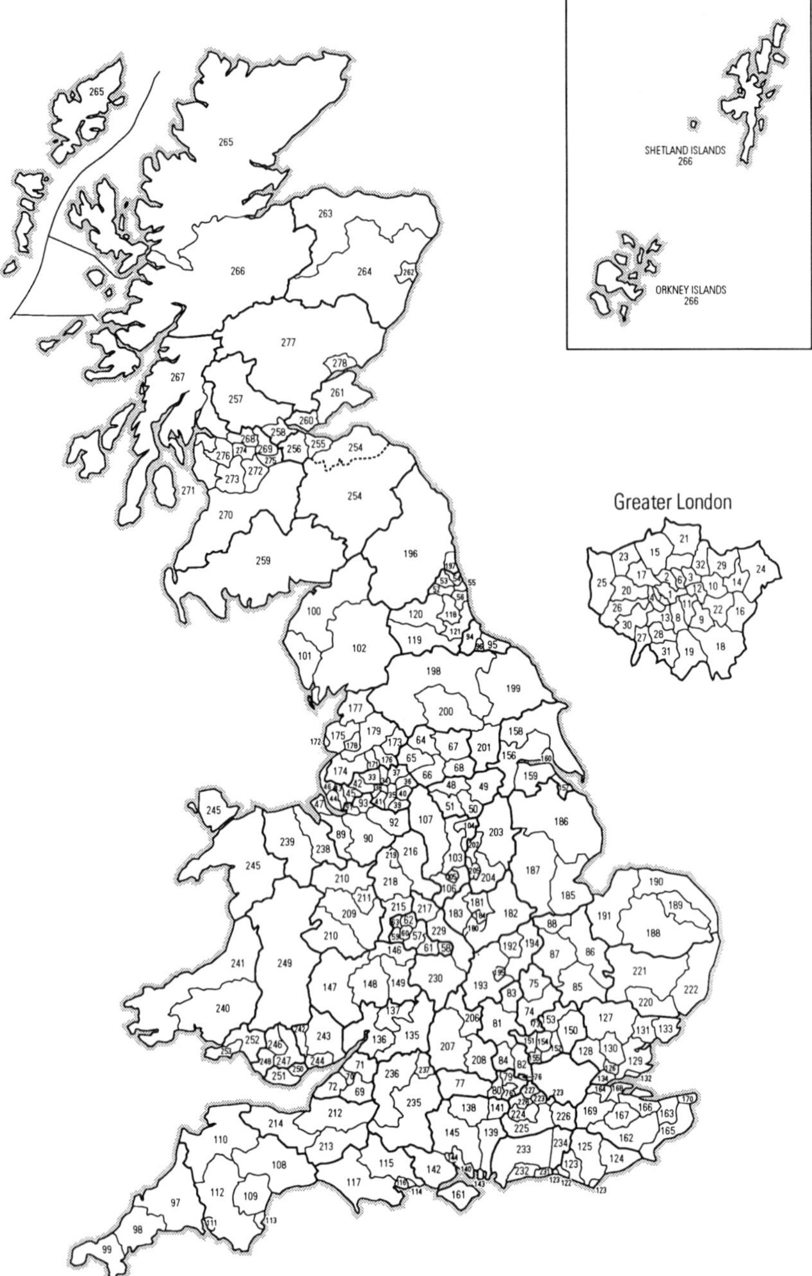

Fig. 2.3 The areas for which Samples of Anonymized Records (2% individual sample) are available in Britain. Source: Marsh and Teague 1992; 1991 Census, Crown Copyright. ESRC/JISC purchase.

Key to Fig.2.3

001 City of London; Westminster, City of
002 Camden
003 Hackney
004 Hammersmith and Fulham
005 Haringey
006 Islington
007 Kensington and Chelsea
008 Lambeth
009 Lewisham
010 Newham
011 Southwark
012 Tower Hamlets
013 Wandsworth
014 Barking and Dagenham
015 Barnet
016 Bexley
017 Brent
018 Bromley
019 Croydon
020 Ealing
021 Enfield
022 Greenwich
023 Harrow
024 Havering
025 Hillingdon
026 Hounslow
027 Kingston upon Thames
028 Merton
029 Redbridge
030 Richmond upon Thames
031 Sutton
032 Waltham Forest
033 Bolton
034 Bury
035 Manchester
036 Oldham
037 Rochdale
038 Salford
039 Stockport
040 Tameside
041 Trafford
042 Wigan
043 Knowsley
044 Liverpool
045 St Helens
046 Sefton
047 Wirral
048 Barnsley
049 Doncaster
050 Rotherham
051 Sheffield
052 Gateshead
053 Newcastle upon Tyne
054 North Tyneside
055 South Tyneside
056 Sunderland
057 Birmingham
058 Coventry
059 Dudley
060 Sandwell
061 Solihull
062 Walsall
063 Wolverhampton
064 Bradford
065 Calderdale
066 Kirklees
067 Leeds
068 Wakefield
069 Bath; Kingswood; Wansdyke
070 Bristol
071 Northavon
072 Woodspring
073 Luton
074 Mid Bedfordshire; South Bedfordshire
075 North Bedfordshire
076 Bracknell Forest; Slough
077 Newbury
078 Reading
079 Windsor and Maidenhead
080 Wokingham
081 Aylesbury Vale
082 Chiltern; South Buckinghamshire
083 Milton Keynes
084 Wycombe
085 Cambridge; South Cambridgeshire
086 East Cambridge; Fenland
087 Huntingdonshire
088 Peterborough
089 Chester; Ellesmere Port and Neston
090 Congleton; Crewe and Nantwich; Vale Royal
091 Halton
092 Macclesfield
093 Warrington
094 Hartlepool; Stockton-on-Tees
095 Langbaurgh-on-Tees
096 Middlesbrough
097 Caradon; North Cornwall
098 Carrick; Restormel
099 Kerrier; Penwith; Isles of Scilly
100 Allerdale; Carlisle
101 Barrow-in-Furness; Copeland
102 Eden; South Lakeland
103 Amber Valley; North East Derbyshire
104 Bolsover; Chesterfield
105 Derby
106 Erewash; South Derbyshire
107 Derbyshire Dales; High Peak
108 East Devon; Mid Devon
109 Exeter; Teignbridge
110 North Devon; Torridge
111 Plymouth
112 South Hams; West Devon
113 Torbay
114 Bournemouth
115 Christchurch; East Dorset; North Dorset
116 Poole
117 Purbeck; West Dorset; Weymouth and Portland
118 Chester-le-Street; Durham
119 Darlington; Teesdale
120 Derwentside; Wear Valley
121 Easington; Sedgefield
122 Brighton
123 Eastbourne; Hove; Lewes
124 Hastings; Rother
125 Wealden
126 Basildon
127 Braintree; Uttlesford
128 Brentwood; Epping Forest; Harlow
129 Castle Point; Maldon; Rochford
130 Chelmsford
131 Colchester
132 Southend-on-Sea
133 Tendring
134 Thurrock
135 Cheltenham; Cotswold
136 Forest of Dean; Stroud
137 Gloucester; Tewkesbury
138 Basingstoke & Deane
139 East Hampshire; Havant
140 Eastleigh; Fareham; Gosport
141 Hart; Rushmoor
142 New Forest
143 Portsmouth
144 Southampton
145 Test Valley; Winchester
146 Bromsgrove; Wyre Forest
147 Hereford; Leominster; South Herefordshire
148 Malvern Hills; Worcester
149 Redditch; Wychavon
150 Broxbourne; East Hertfordshire
151 Dacorum
152 Hertsmere; Welwyn Hatfield
153 North Hertfordshire; Stevenage
154 St Albans
155 Three Rivers; Watford
156 Boothferry; East Yorkshire Borough of Beverley
157 Cleethorpes; Great Grimsby
158 East Yorkshire; Holderness
159 Glanford; Scunthorpe
160 Kingston-upon-Hull
161 Medina; South Wight
162 Ashford; Tunbridge Wells
163 Canterbury
164 Dartford; Gravesham
165 Dover; Shepway
166 Gillingham; Swale
167 Maidstone
168 Rochester upon Medway
169 Sevenoaks; Tonbridge & Malling
170 Thanet
171 Blackburn
172 Blackpool
173 Burnley; Pendle
174 Chorley; West Lancashire
175 Fylde; Wyre
176 Hyndburn; Rossendale
177 Lancaster
178 Preston
179 Ribble Valley; South Ribble
180 Blaby; Oadby & Wigston
181 Charnwood
182 Harborough; Melton; Rutland
183 Hinkley & Bosworth; North West Leicestershire
184 Leicester
185 Boston; South Holland
186 East Lindsey; Lincoln; West Lindsey
187 North Kesteven; South Kesteven
188 Breckland; South Norfolk
189 Broadland; Norwich
190 Great Yarmouth; North Norfolk
191 Kings Lynn and West Norfolk
192 Corby; Kettering
193 Daventry; South Northamptonshire
194 East Northamptonshire; Wellingborough
195 Northampton
196 Alnwick; Berwick-upon-Tweed; Castle Morpeth; Tynedale
197 Blyth Valley; Wansbeck
198 Craven; Hambleton; Richmondshire
199 Ryedale; Scarborough
200 Harrogate
201 Selby; York
202 Ashfield; Mansfield
203 Bassetlaw; Newark & Sherwood
204 Broxtowe; Gedling; Rushcliffe
205 Nottingham
206 Cherwell
207 Oxford; Vale of White Horse; West Oxfordshire
208 South Oxfordshire
209 Bridgnorth; Shrewsbury & Atcham
210 North Shropshire; Oswestry; South Shropshire
211 The Wrekin
212 Mendip; Sedgemoor
213 South Somerset
214 Taunton Deane; West Somerset
215 Cannock Chase; South Staffordshire
216 Staffordshire Moorlands; East Staffordshire
217 Lichfield; Tamworth
218 Newcastle-under-Lyme; Stafford
219 Stoke-on-Trent
220 Babergh; Ipswich
221 Forest Heath; Mid Suffolk; St Edmundsbury
222 Suffolk Coastal; Waveney
223 Elmbridge; Epsom & Ewell
224 Guildford
225 Mole Valley; Waverley
226 Reigate & Banstead; Tandridge
227 Runnymede; Spelthorne
228 Surrey Heath; Woking
229 North Warwickshire; Nuneaton & Bedworth; Rugby
230 Stratford-on-Avon; Warwick
231 Adur; Worthing
232 Arun
233 Chichester; Horsham
234 Crawley; Mid Sussex
235 Kennet; Salisbury
236 North Wiltshire; West Wiltshire
237 Thamesdown
238 Alyn and Deeside; Delyn; Wrexham Maelor
239 Colwyn; Glyndwr; Rhuddlan
240 Carmarthen Dinefwr; Llanelli
241 Ceredigion; Preseli; Pembrokeshire; South Pembrokeshire
242 Blaenau Gwent; Islwyn
243 Monmouth; Torfaen
244 Newport
245 Aberconwy; Arfon; Dwyfor; Meirionnydd; Ynys Mon-Isle of Anglesey
246 Cynon Valley; Rhondda
247 Merthyr Tydfil; Rhymney Valley; Taff-Ely
248 Ogwr
249 Brecknock; Montgomeryshire; Radnorshire
250 Cardiff
251 Vale of Glamorgan
252 Lliw Valley; Neath; Port Talbot
253 Swansea
254 Berwickshire; Ettrick & Lauderdale; Roxburgh; Tweeddale; East Lothian; Midlothian
255 Edinburgh City
256 West Lothian
257 Clackmannan; Stirling
258 Falkirk
259 Annandale & Eskdale; Nithsdale; Stewartry; Wigtown
260 Dunfermline
261 Kirkcaldy; North East Fife
262 Aberdeen City
263 Banff and Buchan; Moray
264 Gordon; Kincardine & Deeside
265 Caithness; Ross & Cromarty; Skye and Lochalsh; Sutherland; Western Isles
266 Badenoch & Strathspey; Inverness; Lochaber; Nairn; Orkney Islands; Shetland Islands
267 Argyll and Bute; Dumbarton; Inverclyde
268 Bearsden and Milngavie; Clydebank; Strathkelvin
269 Cumbernauld & Kilsyth; Monklands
270 Clydesdale; Cumnock & Doon Valley; Kyle & Carrick
271 Cunninghame
272 East Kilbride; Hamilton
273 Eastwood; Kilmarnock & Loudoun
274 Glasgow City
275 Motherwell
276 Renfrew
277 Angus; Perth & Kinross
278 Dundee City

Table 2.7 Locational reference datasets

Census codes and grid references

1 The census codes for small areas which locate them within larger areas, e.g. 08DAFN15 = enumeration district 15 within Headingley ward (FN) in Leeds district (DA) in the county of West Yorkshire (08) in England
2 The grid references for centroids within each small area (contained within the SAS)

The Small Area to Postcode Indexes

1 The enumeration district to postcode directory for England and Wales (part of the SAS purchase)
2 The postcode to output areas index for Scotland (from GRO(S))

Digitized Boundary Data

1 The digitized boundaries for EDs in England and Wales (from the EDLINE consortium)
2 The digitized boundaries for unit postcodes in Scotland (from GRO(S)).
3 The digitized boundaries for enumeration districts in Northern Ireland (under negotiation)

The Area Indexes

1 The Area Master File for England and Wales, which lists for each ED the other areas it belongs to, not just the standard census areas of wards, districts and counties, but also the urban/rural classification of the Census Offices, parliamentary and European constituencies, special programme areas and so on
2 The OA–Higher Area index file for Scotland
3 An Area Master File for Northern Ireland similar to that for England and Wales
4 To the Area Master Files for Great Britain have been added codes for the Functional Regions developed by the Centre for Urban and Regional Development Studies at the University of Newcastle upon Tyne, under a small project funded by the Census Programme

5.2.1 The machine-readable datasets

There are four types of locational data (Table 2.7): (i) the grid references for centroids within each small area found in the lowest level SAS; (ii) the small area to postcode indexes for England and Wales and for Scotland; (iii) the digitized boundaries of the smallest areal units in each census country; and (iv) the area indexes which list the other areas to which the smallest units belong. Together these data provide a very powerful base for the geographic analysis of the census data.

5.2.2 Access to the datasets

The locational reference information is brought together for users at two sites: the Census Dissemination Unit at Manchester and the Data Library, Computing

Service, University of Edinburgh. At Edinburgh, the Census Programme has funded a project, called UKBORDERS, to provide a general interface to users for extracting the locational reference data in the form needed for analysis. This might, for example, involve requesting digitized boundary data for a region for wards, with the reduced number of co-ordinates needed for thematic mapping, or it might involve defining all the small areas within a certain distance of a central point. These facilities will be accessible over the JANET network.

5.2.3 *The maps*

The Census Initiative has purchased 10 copies of ED planning maps on a 1:10,000 OS grid background for England and Wales on microfilm. These microfilm sets have been distributed to higher education sites involved in the Census Programme, including Manchester, Edinburgh, Newcastle, Leeds, Leicester, Southampton, Warwick, Cardiff, Birkbeck and King's College London. Individual higher education institutions may wish to purchase paper subsets of these ED maps for local users to consult. For example, the University of Leeds has purchased a set of ED planning maps covering West Yorkshire.

For Scotland, GRO(S) are providing the digitized boundary co-ordinates for all output areas suitable for the production of transparent overlays which can be placed over published OS map sheets. Edinburgh Data Library provides such a service to Scottish users at cost. This may also be an effective solution for higher education institutions in England and Wales but only if they already hold the OS coverage.

5.3 The Special Migration Statistics

Two sets of Special Migration Statistics (SMS) have been produced by the Census Offices for Great Britain. Set 1 provides two tables of simple counts for all inter-ward/postcode sector flows of migrants recorded in the 1991 Census. Set 2 provides up to 10 tables of cross-classified counts (11 in Scotland and Wales) for inter-district flows of migrants in Great Britain. Full details are provided in OPCS and GRO(S) (1993). The SMS data are held at the Census Dissemination Unit at the University of Manchester.

Software to access the SMS and the Special Workplace Statistics (SWS) has been written by the Census Programme for use at MCC (Rees and Duke-Williams 1994).

5.4 The Special Workplace Statistics

The SWS Set C will contain journey-to-work statistics from the 1991 Census on a census ward/postcode sectors geography. The datasets are held for general academic use at MCC and can be accessed using the software described above.

5.5 The Longitudinal Study

The OPCS Longitudinal Study (LS) is a set of records of various events held by OPCS relating to just over 1% (4/365ths) of the population of England and Wales (about 560,000 people). These can be linked in a variety of ways for analysis. Initially, all people born on each of four dates each year were selected from information given in the 1971 Census. From 1971, as new births occur on these four dates each year and as immigrants with these birth dates register with the National Health Service, these people join the LS. The records of the members of the LS found in the 1981 Census were added to the database and by the end of 1994 the records of LS members traced in the 1991 Census had been added.

The LS datasets are mounted on OPCS's own mainframe computer and accessed by academic researchers through the LS Support Programme within the Social Science Research Unit (SSRU) of City University (see Appendix 2A for contact addresses). Academic researchers must apply via the SSRU to the OPCS for permission to access particular LS subsets. The LS unit at SSRU can then assist the approved applicant by constructing requested tables or by helping the user with the necessary data processing on the OPCS mainframe. The LS unit runs courses for current and potential users and provides extensive documentation and a newsletter.

5.6 Special tabulations

It is possible for users to order their own tabulations from the Census Offices if none of the datasets being purchased by the Census Programme meets their requirements. However, a charge is made for these tabulations by the Census Offices and there is likely to be a queue of user requests.

We now turn from an account of the datasets provided by the Census Offices and purchased by the Census Programme to a consideration of one of the commonest problems faced in analysis: that of comparison of results from the 1991 Census with those from 1981.

6 Constructing a geography of change for small areas

We describe the issues that must be considered when using SAS from the last two censuses in 1981 and 1991 to construct a picture of demographic change over the intercensal period.

The issues are discussed in the context of the demographic characteristics (sex and age) available in the census statistics, but most of the points made have application to the other population attributes recorded in the censuses. Why should we be interested in age–sex detail for the population? The answer is that the demand for many of the goods and services provided for the population varies significantly by age and sex. Both local authorities and private companies therefore require estimates and projections with age–sex detail. The starting points for such estimates and projections are the census counts.

Ideally, we would like to construct for the intercensal decade tables of exactly comparable age–sex disaggregated populations for exactly comparable areas in 1981 and 1991, together with the demographic components that show how the earlier set of populations has evolved into the later. This will involve identifying the role of cohort replacement, mortality and migration in particular. For ages under 10, fertility data are also required.

6.1 Small areas defined

It is useful, initially, to define the range of meanings applied to the term 'small area' in the census. By small areas is usually meant areas that are subdistrict in geographical scale. Districts are the smallest governmental unit with elected councils and taxation and spending powers in the UK. There are 485 of these: London boroughs, metropolitan districts, county districts (England and Wales), districts within Scottish regions or local government districts (Northern Ireland).

Small areas range in size from the English and Welsh ED which can contain only a few hundred persons to an electoral ward in a large metropolitan district which can house 20,000 people. It is important to understand the nature of the alternative types of small areas before embarking on analysis of population change. The user of SAS will be very lucky indeed to find all the relevant data in 1981 and 1991 and for years in between reported for consistently comparable areas.

6.2 Types of small area

There are four general types of subdistrict small area: (i) areas used in administering the census; (ii) areas used in administration or reporting between censuses; (iii) postal areas; and (iv) areas used for specific planning or marketing purposes by public or private organizations.

Demographic statistics are produced for the first two sets of areas. These may be converted into statistics for the third and fourth types of areas through perfect or imperfect aggregation. By perfect aggregation we mean that the small areas add up exactly to the relevant postal or planning areas; imperfect aggregation implies that the fit of small areas into postal or planning areas is not exact.

6.3 Small areas used in the censuses of 1971, 1981 and 1991

Censuses in the UK have always involved the employment of enumerators, who distribute, collect and check household census forms. Their workloads are defined as covering all addresses in an area known as an enumeration district. EDs are defined by the Census Offices in collaboration with local authorities to equalize enumerators' workloads, subject to nesting constraints that they fit into certain larger administrative areas such as electoral wards in the year of the census and local government districts. EDs are redefined at each census to reflect any changes in the boundaries of the administrative areas and to respond to major changes in population distribution due to house building or demolition.

EDs are used to report census results in *England and Wales* in 1981 and 1991, but only a subset of these will be comparable. There was no continuation of the grid square output produced for the 1971 Census and the option of using postal geography to achieve real compatibility was rejected on grounds of cost. In 1981 OPCS defined census tracts which were aggregations of 1971 and 1981 EDs that fell within the same boundaries. About 60% of EDs were the same while the other 40% had to be put together into larger areas. No census tract outputs have been produced for 1991 and the responsibility for producing comparable areas has been left to users.

Figure 2.4 shows the ward and ED boundaries at the 1981 and 1991 Censuses for a large English city (the metropolitan district of Leeds). The ward boundaries do not change whereas those for the EDs have altered.

EDs were used in *Scotland* to report census results in 1981, but they were planned as aggregations of the smallest area of postal geography, the unit postcodes. GRO(S) recognized the importance and difficulty of maintaining areal comparability between censuses and took steps to ensure this. It separated the census 'input' area (the ED) from the census 'output' area. All census returns were given detailed unit postcodes. What this meant was that data gathered using one set of unit postcode aggregations could be output for an entirely different set. Scottish output areas from the 1991 Census have therefore been designed to coincide with the EDs of the 1981 Census.

In *Northern Ireland* the grid square approach defined in 1971 has been maintained by the Census Office in order to provide comparability between 1971, 1981 and 1991 for kilometre grid squares in rural areas and 100-metre grid squares in urban areas. However, the range of counts provided for grid squares is low (809 in 1991) for confidentiality reasons. Therefore, ESRC funded a team at Queen's University Belfast to produce SAS for 1981 EDs used by CONI. These are available to the academic community via the Data Archive, University of Essex, or the Census Dissemination Unit. The Census Programme of ESRC/JISC/DENI funded a comparable project in 1993–4 in collaboration with CONI to produce SAS from the 1991 Census for EDs (see Appendix 2A for contact names and addresses).

From this account it is therefore apparent that comparison of the results of the 1981 and 1991 Censuses in Scotland will be comparatively straightforward.

Fig. 2.4 The geography of the census in an English city: (a) Leeds Metropolitan Districts electoral wards, 1981 and 1991 Censuses; (b) Headingley ward enumeration districts, 1981 Census; (c) Headingley ward enumeration districts, 1991 Census. Source: 1981, 1991 Censuses. Crown Copyright: OPCS ED maps.

In Northern Ireland a small set of statistics for comparable areas can be employed, but otherwise the problems of comparison will the same as in England and Wales. It is in England and Wales that the researcher is faced with the greatest problems. The rest of Section 6 therefore concentrates on the situation in this census country.

6.4 Areas used for reporting between censuses

Between censuses the electoral ward is used for reporting the counts of electors from the annual electoral registers in all census countries. Vital statistics counts (births and deaths) are reported for wards in England and Wales and for postal sectors in Scotland. Because of these important roles, census statistics are also reported for wards in 1981 and 1991.

Two considerations need to be borne in mind if the decision is taken to use wards as the small areas for studying population change.

1. Ward boundaries are subject to systematic review and adjustment by the Boundary Commissions of England, Wales, Scotland and Northern Ireland. Revisions may occur to the boundaries of wards or to the number of council seats allocated to a ward in order to make the number of electors per seat more equal and to preserve the equivalence of the votes of people living in different areas. On the basis of a sample of districts studied by the author it appears that about half of the districts in England and Wales experienced radical boundary changes between 1981 and 1991. Minor changes to ward and district boundaries may occur also as a result of road or housing estate construction.
2. Care should be taken in merging statistics from different sources. It should always be assumed that the different sources provide independently ordered statistics until proved otherwise. For example, the ward order in the vital statistics files provided by OPCS for intercensal years often differs from both the 1981 and 1991 Census order.

Currently, the mid-year population estimates produced by OPCS and GRO(S) are not disaggregated by ward, but consideration is being given to development of such estimates.

6.5 Postal areas

The geography of the postal system for the UK has recently been described in detail by Rhind *et al.* (1992). Increasing use is being made of this geographical system because a great deal of administrative and marketing data have the postal address with full postcode recorded.

It is possible to obtain precise census data for any postal area in Scotland either by amalgamating output area statistics or by requesting special tabulations. In

England and Wales and in Northern Ireland SAS tables are provided for postcode sectors.

To make it possible to obtain approximate census data for smaller postal areas, the ESRC Census Programme has purchased the ED-to-postcode directories for England and Wales. These will contain for every ED a list of the whole postcode units (PUs) or part-postcode units (PPUs) that intersect with the ED and the number of households in each PU or PPU. It should be relatively easy then to use these counts as appropriate weighting factors in an aggregation of ED statistics to the desired postal geography. Researchers may wish to write their own software to do this or use aggregation procedures within existing software (e.g. SASPAC which contains such a facility).

6.6 Building a comparable set of ward statistics

6.6.1 Aggregation of enumeration district statistics

Let us assume that you have selected the ward as the most convenient unit for measuring and projecting intercensal change, but that ward boundaries have changed between censuses. It is relatively straightforward to use ED SAS data to convert the 1981 Census figures to the new geographic base. For each ED it is necessary to identify the new wards that the ED falls into and the proportions of the ED that fall in each new ward. These proportions can be obtained through inspection of ED boundaries and new ward boundaries on equivalent base maps and by making estimates of area proportions using eyeball or graphical methods. Account may be taken of the underlying distribution of population revealed on the OS base map at this stage. If digitized boundary data for both EDs and new wards are available, then use can be made of overlap analysis functions provided in most geographic information system (GIS) packages (e.g. ARC-INFO, ATLAS-GIS, IDRISI). The assumption behind using such overlap analysis is that the population is evenly distributed within the ED.

Overlap analysis used in this way has been criticized as not providing accurate estimates, but this has been in the situation where the new areal net is comparable in scale to the ED. Wards will be some 10 to 100 times the size in area and population of EDs, so that the assumption of uniformity in population distribution need be applied only to the relatively few EDs falling in more than one ward.

6.6.2 Conversion of old ward statistics to new ward statistics

A second problem that will present itself if the ward boundaries have changed is the need to convert intercensal statistics (e.g. vital statistics) to the new geographic base. This can be done by using the 1981 Census ED to new ward population analysis described above to construct a matrix showing the proportions of 1981 ward populations falling in the new wards.

Let $\boldsymbol{T}$ be such a transformation matrix. Each element T_{ij} in the matrix is defined as

$$T_{ij} = P_{ij}/P_i \tag{2.1}$$

where P_{ij} is the population located in old ward i and new ward j and is given by

$$P_{ij} = \sum_{e \in i} P_e w_{ej} \tag{2.2}$$

where P_e is the population of ED e and w_{ej} is the proportion of the population of ED e assumed to fall into new ward j. The new ward statistics are then given as

$$X_j = \sum_i T_{ij} X_i \tag{2.3}$$

More precision may be gained by using ED populations for particular ages that are closely associated with the component variable to be transformed. For example, to transform death counts for wards, you might wish to use the population aged 70+ rather than the total population.

Although such procedures are relatively crude, they can be regarded as very cost effective compared with purchasing special tabulations of the relevant data from national agencies. Local agencies, however, may have set up the databases of statistical records in such a way that such retabulations are relatively easy to accomplish.

6.6.3 A general methodology for flexible zones

In the course of analysing population change between censuses or projected change beyond the last census, comparisons may be needed for any arbitrary set of zones. Figure 2.5 sets out such a flexible zone routine which has been developed by GMAP Ltd, University of Leeds, for five metropolitan districts as part of the West Yorkshire Population Model and Information System (WYPMIS).

The top part of the diagram details the datasets that need to be assembled, the methods of preparation and sources. The input datasets consist of the relevant ED data from the 1991 Census, the digitized boundaries of EDs and the digitized boundaries of the new zones. From the second and third inputs are developed, through overlap analysis, ED to new zone assignment lists with weights attached to each new zone in an ED list. The standard data from the WYPMIS for 1991 wards are then disaggregated to ED level by applying ED to ward proportions based on census count variables and re-aggregated to new zones employing the ED to new zone lists. An alternative route through the

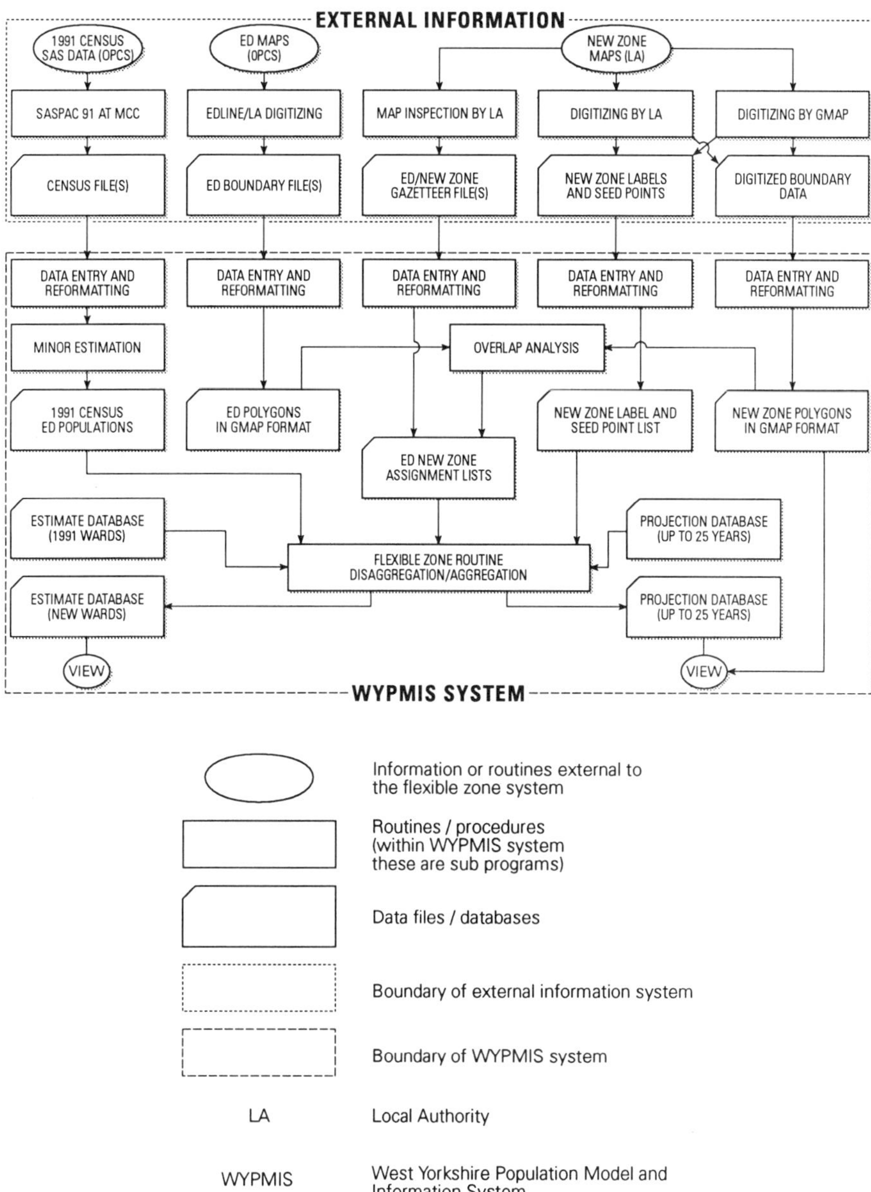

Fig. 2.5 The structure of a system for producing geographically flexible outputs.

system involves the direct input of an ED–new zone gazetteer file, bypassing the overlap analysis.

Of course, the estimates produced for the new zones are likely to be less reliable than those for the 1991 wards for which many more direct counts are available, but considerable value is added to the system by combining census data from two area levels (ED and ward).

6.7 Population bases and under-enumeration

There are a number of issues that need to be addressed concerning the exact definition of the population included in the 1981 and 1991 Censuses, and the degree to which each census suffers from under-enumeration.

6.7.1 The 1981 and 1991 population bases

Both 1981 and 1991 Censuses report populations on a resident basis. In other words, records of persons or households actually present at an address other than their normal residence are transferred back and counted in the area of usual residence. However, the two Censuses treat wholly absent households differently. In 1991 these households were invited to submit forms on their return to their residence, and in addition procedures were used to impute the sizes and characteristics of absent households which enumerators ascertained were in residence but which did not return census forms. There was also under-enumeration detected in both censuses by post-census checks (the Post Enumeration Survey (PES) in 1981 and the Census Validation Survey (CVS) in 1991) in the form of households missed by enumerators, dwellings misclassified as vacant and under-enumeration of residents in households. In addition, there was evidence of other under-enumeration not accounted for by the CVS in 1991.

Table 2.8, taken from the National Monitor for Great Britain (OPCS and GRO(S) 1992d), shows the consequences of adopting different population definitions on any comparison. Use of the 'Resident population on a 1981 base' (row 1a) suggests that the population in Great Britain decreased by 0.04% over the decade. Use of the resident counts in 1981 and 1991 suggests that it increased by 2.5% over the decade. Allowing for coverage adjustments in both censuses (row 2) suggests that the population grew by only 2.1%. To convert the census populations into mid-year estimates it is necessary to add students at their term time addresses and subtract them from their residences reported at the census and also to allow for changes between census data in April and mid-year. When this is done (row 4) the results suggest that the population grew by 2.3% over the 10 years.

The Census Offices provide advice to users on which data to use when making comparisons (OPCS and GRO(S) 1992d, p. 25):

> where the user requires population numbers by age, by sex, or by administrative area, rather than any relationship with other census topics ... the

Table 2.8 Comparison of census with mid-year population estimate: Great Britain, 1981 and 1991

Population element	1981	1991
1 Residents counted in census	53 557	54 889
1a Resident population 1981 base	53 557	53 340
1b In wholly absent households – enumerated	na	680
1c In wholly absent households – imputed	na	869
2 Coverage adjustments	1 246	1 053
2a In wholly absent households	1 005	na
2b Net under-enumeration accounted for by CVS	215	299
2c Under-enumeration not accounted for by CVS	26	754
3 Other adjustments	12	113
3a Definition of residents, e.g. students	8	69
3b Timing change – census day to 30 June	9	44
3c Other changes	–5	0
4 Registrar-General's mid-year estimates of residents	54 814	56 055
Under-coverage in main census tables	2.3%	1.9%

Source: OPCS and GRO(S) (1992d, Annex A, p.25).

mid-year population estimates should be used in preference to the Census resident counts.

This has considerable implications for anyone studying intercensal change for small area populations. The figures in Table 2.8 suggest that the census counts from 1981 and 1991 that get closest to the mid-year estimate of change are the 1981 and 1991 resident population bases (2.5% increase compared with 2.2%). Alternatively, the researcher should first adjust both 1981 and 1991 census counts to their mid-year equivalents. This will involve adjusting small area populations by the ratio of the estimated population in an age–sex group to that for the local government district in the census.

Table 2.9 shows the boost factors applicable to the England and Wales population census counts that convert them to mid-year estimate numbers. The most severely affected age–sex groups are young males, as might be expected. Table 2.10 provides sample comparisons for the County of North Yorkshire. The census count changes are inferred from the 1981 base populations and percentage distributions for 1981 and 1991 given in the County Monitor for North Yorkshire. Overall these counts show North Yorkshire's population growing by 4.8% over the intercensal decade. The second set of figures is computed for the same County Monitor age groups from the 1981 and 1991 provisional population estimates. The overall change using these statistics is estimated as 6.5%. The biggest differences are for the smallest age groups, 16–17 and 85+, and are substantial. However, all differences are in the same direction

Table 2.9 Boost factors to convert census counts into estimate counts, allowing for under-enumeration

Age	Persons	Males	Females
All ages	1.02	1.03	1.01
0–4	1.03	1.04	1.03
5–9	1.03	1.03	1.02
10–14	1.02	1.02	1.01
15–19	1.02	1.03	1.01
20–24	1.06	1.09	1.02
25–29	1.06	1.08	1.03
30–34	1.02	1.03	1.01
35–39	1.01	1.02	1.00
40–44	1.01	1.01	1.01
45–84	1.00	1.00	1.00
85+	1.05	1.10	1.04

Source: OPCS and GRO(S) (1992d), p.10).

and of the same magnitude, so that it is probable that the pattern and direction of change, if not its magnitude, would be reasonably estimated using census counts.

What effect do these observations have on non-demographic characteristics? Clearly, if those characteristics are closely associated with age and sex, then application of correction factors based on the total population only will not be sufficient. Where the SAS or LBS datasets provide cross-tabulations of the characteristic by age (e.g. headship status, ethnicity), it should be fairly straight-

Table 2.10 Population change, 1981–91, using census monitor and population estimate data, North Yorkshire

Age groups (from County Monitor Table E)	Percentage change 1981–91 using Table E, 1981 base population	Percentage change 1981–91 using 1981 mid-year and 1991 provisional mid-year estimates	Difference
0–4	16.5	17.7	1.2
5–15	−14.5	−11.6	2.9
16–17	−19.8	−27.5	7.7
18–29	9.4	10.9	1.5
30–44	12.3	15.1	2.8
45–pen	7.0	9.8	2.8
pen–74	−1.6	−0.2	1.4
75–84	18.2	19.6	1.4
85+	66.0	59.8	6.2
Total	4.8	6.5	1.7

Source: OPCS Census Monitor CM32 and OPCS mid-year population estimates. All data are Crown Copyright.

forward to adjust the census counts to reflect differential under-enumeration. However, there are far fewer such cross-tabulations in the 1981 SAS than in the 1991 SAS, and we may have to make do with a single correction factor.

6.7.2 Student populations

One of the adjustments reported in Table 2.8 to the census counts is the transfer of student populations to their term-time addresses. Table L10 in the LBS provides information for each ward that enables this transfer to be effected in a systematic way for 1991 census counts.

6.7.3 Age group definitions

To carry out proper comparisons between the age structure of small area populations in 1981 and 1991, it is necessary to give careful thought to the selection of age groups. Preliminary analysis of age group change using the Census Monitor dataset (Rees 1993a) is fraught with difficulty because of the irregular nature of those ages: 0–4, 5–15, 16–17, 18–29, 30–44, 45 to pensionable age, pensionable age to 74, 75–84 and 85+. It is not possible to trace members of one of these age groups in 1981 into the 1991 population. The 0–4 year olds become 10–14 years old ten years later but are joined by persons born in 1981–6 who become aged 5–9 and by persons aged 15 who ten years earlier were aged 5. Regular age groups are needed with one-, five- or ten-year age intervals depending on the detail required. A person aged 0 in 1981 is aged 10 in the next census, assuming survival. Persons aged 0–4 survive to be 10–14. Persons aged 0–9 survive to be aged 10–19 at the next census. Using these regular age groups it is then possible to distinguish the effects of cohort replacement from those of mortality and migration. Which interval should be chosen for the analysis? This depends very much upon the resources available for handling the data and the use to which the data will be put. In a study of small area populations in Swansea, Rees (1991) estimated ward populations between 1981 and 1989 using five-year age groups, and these were used as benchmark populations for entry into a model for projecting ward populations for five-year intervals (e.g. 1981–6, 1986–91, 1991–6, 1996–2001). In a study of small area populations in Bradford (part of the WYPMIS project (Rees 1992d)), single year of age populations were employed and estimated for each mid-year from 1981 to 1991. The associated projection model uses a one-year time interval (1991–2, 1992–3 and so on).

There are no problems about deriving quinquennial (and therefore decennial) age group counts to age 85+ from the 1981 SAS and 1991 SAS and LBS. However, single year of age counts are provided in the 1981 SAS only for private household populations to age 24. It is therefore necessary to assume the same distribution of population within a five-year age group in the whole resident population to obtain an estimated count by single years of age. No single year of age information is provided beyond age 24, and disaggregation factors need to be derived from national census or estimate tables. In the 1991 LBS single year of age populations are provided in Table L38 for wards for residents in households and these can be used to disaggregate the five-year age distribution of the whole resident population further.

7 Building small area population estimates from census data

Censuses provide detailed population counts every 10 years. It is clearly important to be able to update this information after each census and to be able to adjust those intercensal estimates after the publication of a new census. Here we comment briefly on ways in which census population counts can be employed in small area estimation.

7.1 The forward component method

The usual method of population estimation involves estimating the components of demographic change year by year and adding/subtracting these from the census population.

The population in a small area is estimated as follows:

$$P(t+1) = P(t) + B - D + N \qquad (2.4)$$

where P stands for population, B for births, D for deaths and N for net migrations, all for a time interval t to $t+1$ (one year later). The first interval in the estimation is from census day in April to mid-year (70 days in 1991, 66 days in 1981). Births and deaths are published by OPCS and GRO(S) for wards/postcode sectors on an annual basis, so that it is necessary to combine data from two calendar years:

$$B = 0.5B(t) + 0.5B(t+1) \qquad (2.5)$$

$$D = 0.5D(t) + 0.5D(t+1) \qquad (2.6)$$

In the case of the interval between census day and mid-year, some 70/365ths (1991) or 66/365ths (1981) of the vital statistics counts are used.

The final component that needs to be added is net migration. This is not measured directly but must be obtained indirectly, using other ward counts such as the electoral register.

$$N = E(t+1) - E(t) \qquad (2.7)$$

where $E(t)$ is the estimated count of electors in ward i at mid-year t. Electors are counted on 10 October in each year, so that the estimated mid-year count is an interpolation between successive registers. Because registers are actually published in mid-February after the October registration, great care must be taken not to enter incorrect statistics into these procedures. This net migration estimation fails to take account of any losses through mortality or any gains through the registration of new electors who attain electoral age. These are all subsumed in the estimate. An additional problem is that the reliability of the electoral register declined significantly with the introduction of the poll tax from 1989 onwards.

A more reliable method is therefore needed to estimate the extent of net migration into or out of small area populations. Now that the 1991 Census SAS and LBS have been published we can use census populations to estimate net migration over the decade:

$$N(1981\text{–}91) = P(1991) - P(1981) - [B(1981\text{–}91) - D(1981\text{–}91)] \qquad (2.8)$$

So far the estimation method has been defined for all age populations. It is possible to decompose all the components by age and sex using a variety of estimation techniques which are discussed in more detail by Rees (1990).

7.2 The iterative proportional fitting method

An alternative method for estimating age-disaggregated small area populations involves the technique of iterative proportional fitting. The essence is that the matrix of populations by ward and age available from the SAS of the census is rolled forward (i.e. aged year by year) and adjusted to constraints consisting of the district population estimates by age (five year) and sex and estimates of ward populations at each year based on interpolated electoral counts and some census data. The ward by age and sex matrix is iteratively adjusted to fit the district totals by age and sex and the ward population totals. In this way it is possible to produce estimates of single year of age populations for wards for each year between censuses.

7.3 Adjustment of small area population estimates

Both of the techniques described above produce post-censal estimates. Once the next census is published it is possible to check on the validity of the estimates and to make adjustments so that the time series starts with the 1981 Census counts and finishes with the 1991 Census counts. Note, however, the advantage of the iterative proportional fitting method: the adjustment of census counts to mid-year district estimates recommended earlier is automatically made.

Attention is now given to the methods by which census users may access the computer-held datasets purchased by the ESRC/JISC Census Programme.

8 Access to the datasets

There are a variety of ways to access the census and related datasets. The exact method will depend on both the particular dataset involved and the arrangements made at each higher education institution. The different models of access are first described and then a detailed example is provided.

8.1 Models of access

The following models of access currently exist. By dataset in this context is meant fairly complete copies of major subsets of census and related data rather than extracted data that the researcher will use immediately.

1. Access via JANET indirectly to datasets via a gateway (e.g. to LS via LSSP).
2. Access over JANET directly to datasets held at a data distributor (e.g. CDU at MCC or UKBORDERS at EUDL).
3. Access via a campus LAN directly to datasets ported to a campus mainframe or distributed system (e.g. a SAS/LBS subset on a PC file server).
4. Access to datasets ported to the computing system of an individual user (e.g. SAS/LBS on CD-ROM).

8.2 An example of access

To access the census data you will need to learn how to accomplish a sequence of tasks. These may appear complex but are really quite simple once you have been shown them by an expert user. The following example describes how University of Leeds census users currently access SAS and LBS census datasets using model 2.

8.2.1 Registration

The user fills in the registration form obtained from the Helpdesk Office in the Computing Service, which sends the form to the CDU at MCC. It takes about a week for registration requests to be processed but registration lasts for as long as the researcher or student remains at the higher education institution.

8.2.2 Homework

The user consults the key manuals and decides which variables or tables to extract.

8.2.3 Starting at a networked personal computer (PC)

The user accesses the local preferred PC server from a PC on the campus network. The method varies from department to department, from PC cluster to cluster. For example, on my own PC I issue a single command given the name 'novell' which activates a communication program and produces the prompt

```
F:LOGIN>
```

8.2.4 Logging on to the general purpose server

The user then logs on to the campus general purpose server (gps) (a large SUN) using

```
telnet gps
```

and is then prompted for a user id and password.

8.2.5 Logging on to the remote database server (cms.mcc)

Once logged on to the gps, the user issues a tailored telnet command

```
telnet midas
```

and logs on to the MCC Cray Superserver 6400.

8.2.6 Running the extraction software (SASPAC91)

The user prepares a command file for SASPAC91 using an editor (e.g. GNU emacs) and then runs the commands using

```
saspac userjob
```

where userjob.cmd is the name of the file with the SASPAC commands. If successful, files of results are generated.

8.2.7 Using file transfer protocol (FTP) to move data home

To move the results back to Leeds, the user logs off the Manchester system. This places the user back on the gps. Then the command

```
ftp
```

is issued and the user logs on to cms.mcc again. A command such as

```
get userjob.prn
```

will transfer the file of printed table results back to the Leeds gps in a few seconds.

8.2.8 Using file transfer protocol to move data to the PC

The file can be moved, if necessary, to the user's PC by using ftp from the PC. Again details vary across campus. On my PC I issue a tailored ftp command

```
ftp gps
```

and issue the command

```
get userjob.prn
```

The file is moved from the gps to the PC as userjob.prn for further use.

The details of how this direct access is achieved will differ from campus to campus, but the computing services of most higher education institutions should be able to set up such a system (or something simpler).

You will find that it is becoming progressively easier to do work across JANET and that there are good training materials being developed by the Census Programme to help you in this respect (e.g. Census Analysis Unit 1993; Rees 1993b). Several university departments now run classes for undergraduate students across JANET, with no major difficulty.

9 An illustrative application: limiting long-term illness

Most of the material provided in this chapter so far consists of information about information. We should not conclude without at least a peek at some of the fascinating results beginning to emerge from an analysis of the 1991 Census. Here we report a preliminary investigation of one of the new census variables, that recording limiting long-term illness.

9.1 The map of limiting long-term illness

Figure 2.6 plots the percentage of the population reporting limiting long-term illness (LLTI) for counties and Scottish regions (using the Monitor dataset). The map shows simultaneously (i) a gradient from the south and east (lower reported illness) towards the north and west (higher reported illness), (ii) more reported illness and higher mortality in denser urban counties than in less densely populated areas, (iii) particularly high levels of LLTI in coalfield counties (Durham,

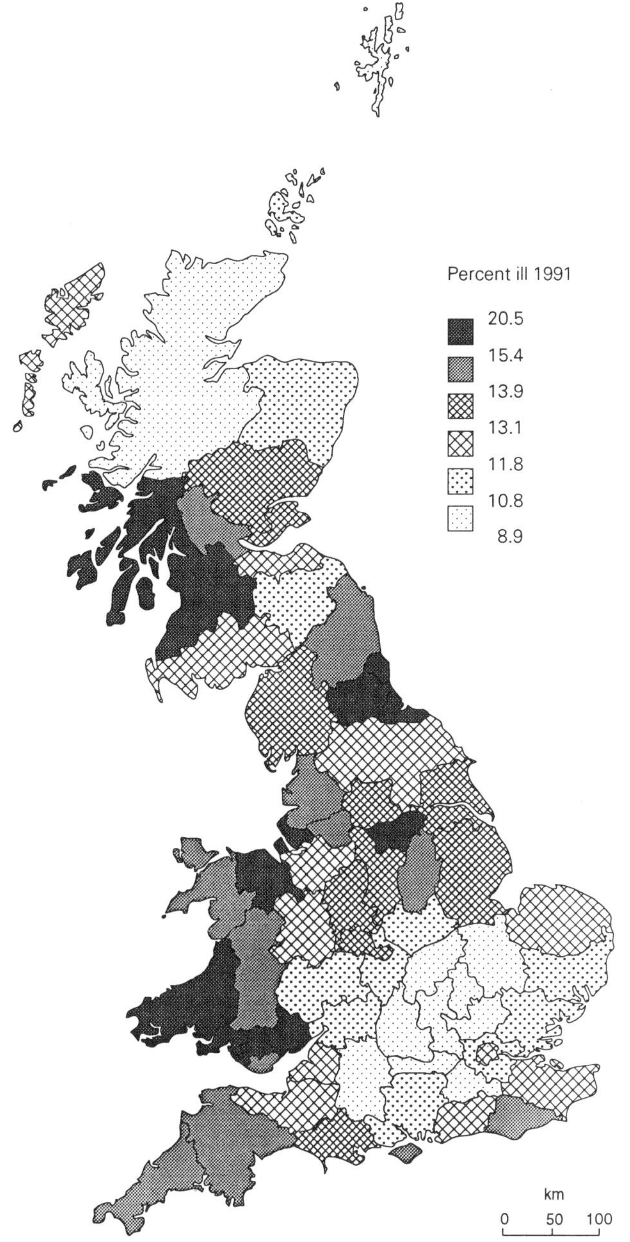

Fig. 2.6 The distribution of limiting long-term illness. Source: 1991 Census, Crown Copyright. ESRC/JISC purchase.

South Yorkshire, Gwent, Mid Glamorgan and West Glamorgan), (iv) lower levels of reported illness in Highland and Island Scotland and higher levels of reported illness in North and West Wales than mortality statistics would suggest and (v) higher values of illness in some south and east coast counties.

The influence of a history of coalmining and placement of a population in Scotland, Wales or England is confirmed when we compute the average illness percentages in a cross-tabulation of coalfield status and culture class (Table 2.11). Counties/Scottish regions were assigned to one of three coalmining statuses through inspection of a map of counties overlaid on a map of coalmining activity in the late 1950s: 0 equals no coalfield in the county; 1 means a minor amount of coalmining has taken place over the past half century; 2 means that coalmining was a major activity in the area.

The table shows that as we move from no coalfield status to major coalfield status the percentage reporting LLTI consistently increases with one minor exception (the one minor coalfield region in Scotland). Welsh counties score higher and Scottish regions score lower on LLTI than their English equivalents. The two variables seem to play an independent role.

These casual observations need rigorous testing, however, before we can accept them as possible causal candidates.

9.2 Hypotheses about the distribution of limiting long-term illness

The map patterns can be used to suggest six hypotheses about the distribution of LLTI:

1. LLTI is positively associated with degree of deprivation in the population.

Table 2.11 Limiting long-term illness by coalfield and culture status

	Cultural class (nation)			**Total**
	Scottish	**English**	**Welsh**	
Coalfield status	**[0][a]**	**[1]**	**[2]**	
No coalfield [0]	11.5[b]	12.0	14.8	12.0
	(8)[c]	(32)	(2)	(42)
Minor coalfield [1]	14.0	13.1	15.5	13.9
	(1)	(6)	(3)	(10)
Major coalfield [2]	13.8	15.0	19.1	15.5
	(3)	(9)	(3)	(15)
Total	12.3	12.7	16.7	13.1
	(12)	(47)	(8)	(67)

Notes:
[a]Dummy value assigned to class.
[b]Percentage of the population (1991 population base) reporting limiting long-term illness.
[c]Number of counties/Scottish regions.
Source: 1991 Census, County/Scottish Region Monitors, Crown Copyright. Contained in file cogbal.dat (Leeds) (see Table 2.3).

2. LLTI is negatively associated with degree of affluence of the population.
3. LLTI is positively associated with extreme old age.
4. LLTI is positively associated with density of population.
5. LLTI is positively associated with a history of coalmining in the county/ Scottish region.
6. LLTI is higher in Wales and lower in Scotland, other things being equal.

These hypotheses have been framed substantively rather than statistically. Using statistical inference we attempt to reject null hypotheses of no relationship between LLTI and a possible explanatory variable.

9.3 The association of limiting long-term illness with explanatory indicators

Table 2.12 sets out Pearson's correlation coefficients between LLTI and the selected 15 explanatory indicators. Only 7 of these variables produced coefficients

Table 2.12 The correlations between limiting long-term illness and selected socioeconomic indicators

Variable		Correlation	Min	Max
Dependent variable				
E13	% limiting long-term illness	1.00	8.9	20.5
Potential determinants of LLTI				
F03	% males economically active, 16–64, full-time	–0.70**		46.0
F07	% males economically active, 16–64, unemployed	0.67**		4.8
G11	% households with 2 or more cars	–0.63**	11.3	38.8
COAL	Coalfield status	0.61**	0	2
G10	% households with no car	0.56**	17.8	53.9
CULT	Cultural status (country)	0.44**	0	2
H02	unshared detached housing unit	–0.34**	1.0	68.1
E09	% aged 75–84	0.22	4.3	9.0
G04	% households renting from local authority	0.19		3.6
G07	% households lacking or sharing WC, with no central heating	0.18	0.1	3.3
G08	% households exclusive use of WC, with central heating all rooms	–0.15	63.0	93.6
G02	% households owner-occupier	–0.08	47.1	77.4
D02	Persons per hectare	–0.07	0.1	78.1
E10	% aged 85+	0.06	1.2	2.5
H07	% housing unit shared	0.04	0.0	0.9
Potential consequence of LLTI				
SMR	Standardized Mortality Ratio (UK = 100), persons, all ages, 1980–6	0.49**	84.3	121.2

Note: **, Significant a the 0.01 level (99% confidence).

significantly different from zero at the 0.01 level. The rest were not significant at the 0.05 level.

The first step is to pick out from the battery of variables that can be computed from the census counts a set of indicators that we hope will measure the explanatory factors suggested in the hypotheses. Initially this was done by inspecting the definitions. Five deprivation indicator candidates were selected, five affluence candidates, two old-age indicators and a density variable together with dummy variables for the coalfield and cultural statuses captured in Table 2.11. These are listed in Tables 2.12 and 2.13. It turns out that several choices were poor: e.g. the variable 'dwellings shared (H07)' is now such a rare phenomenon with a maximum of 0.9% suffering this deprivation that it could not possibly account for LLTI which affects 13.1% of persons and more than 20% of households.

The significant list includes deprivation indicators (percentage unemployed and percentage of households with no car), affluence indicators (percentage of males aged 16–64, economically active and working full-time – a measure of participation in the primary labour market; percentage of households with two or more cars available; percentage of households living in an unshared, detached house), coalmining history and cultural status.

The tenure indicators of deprivation and affluence (percentage of households renting from a local authority or equivalent; percentage owner occupied) proved insignificant. These sectors of the housing market are now so diverse that tenure is no longer a good socioeconomic discriminator. The amenity indicators (percentage of households lacking or sharing a WC, without central heating; percentage of households with exclusive use of WC, with central heating in all rooms) also proved insignificant. The correlation coefficients for the old-age indicators also proved to be low, particularly that for the percentage of the population aged 85 and over. The density variable exhibits a correlation opposite in sign to that implied by the hypothesis put forward above. The correlation analysis provides no support for the third or fourth hypotheses.

The influence of coalmining history and national cultural status, identified in Table 2.11, was confirmed by positive and significant correlations in Table 2.12.

9.4 Testing the hypotheses: regression models of limiting long-term illness

Each of the hypotheses listed earlier can be subjected to testing using regression analysis. The results are reported in Table 2.13. Each block of the table reports the beta (standardized) regression coefficients associated with the independent variables included in the particular hypothesis test. The standardized regression coefficients measure the change in the dependent variable produced by a relative change in the independent variable. For example, a 1% change in the level of unemployment across counties/Scottish regions would produce, holding the other hypothesis 1 variables constant, a 0.62% change in LLTI.

Hypothesis 1 does achieve an *F* value significantly different from zero but the overall variation in LLTI associated with deprivation indicators is only 54%. The

Table 2.13 Regression results testing hypotheses about the distribution of limiting long-term illness

Hypothesis 1: deprivation			$F = 14.8^{**}$ $R^2 = 0.54$
F07	% males unemployed	0.62**	
G04	% rented from LA	–0.33*	
G07	% lacking/sharing WC	0.20*	
G10	% households with no car	0.28	
H07	% households sharing WC	–0.32**	
Hypothesis 2: affluence			$F = 43.0^{**}$ $R^2 = 0.78$
F03	% full-time	–0.53**	
G02	% owner-occupier	0.37**	
G08	% central heating	0.24**	
G11	% 2+ cars	–0.65**	
H02	% detached	–0.20**	
Hypothesis 3: extreme old age			$F = 16.1^{**}$ $R^2 = 0.33$
E09	% aged 75–84	2.05**	
E10	% aged 85+	–1.90**	
Hypothesis 4: density			$F = 0.3$ $R^2 = 0.01$
D02	Pop per ha	0.07	
Hypothesis 5: coalfield status			$F = 39.1^{**}$ $R^2 = 0.38$
COAL	Coalfield status	0.62**	
Hypothesis 6: cultural status			$F = 15.6^{**}$ $R^2 = 0.19$
CULT	Cultural status (country)	0.44**	
Combined model: stepwise			$F = 82.5^{**}$ $R^2 = 0.91$
COAL	Coalfield status	0.21**	
D02	Pop per ha	–0.25**	
F07	% males unemployed	0.33**	
CULT	Cultural status (country)	0.44**	
G11	% 2+ cars	–0.42**	
E09	% aged 75–84	0.70**	
E10	% aged 85+	–0.53*	

Notes:
The coefficients reported are standardized beta coefficients.
*, significant at the 0.05 level (95% confidence); **, significant at the 0.01 level (99% confidence).
For hypotheses 1 to 6 the SPSS Enter procedure was used. For the combined model the SPSS stepwise inclusion procedure was used.

percentages in local authority housing and in shared housing have negative partial regression coefficients, signs contradicting the hypothesis. This means we should probably reject them as reliable deprivation indicators. However, there is ample evidence of the effect of unemployment on LLTI. This variable is retained in the combined regression model shown in Table 2.13.

Hypothesis 2 can also be accepted and the affluence variables show strong associations collectively with LLTI. Both the owner-occupied and central heating variables show signs opposite in direction to the hypothesis and must therefore be dropped as affluence indicators.

The regression equation for hypothesis 3 achieves a significant F value but the overall fit is poor. The percentage of the population aged 75–84 shows a positive regression coefficient in line with the hypothesis, but that for the percentage aged 85 and over shows an opposite sign. It may well be that a selection effect is operating here: survival to very old age is enhanced by lower than average LLTI. Note that the age variables do get included in the combined model.

Although by itself the density variable records an insignificant regression coefficient, it figures in the combined model when its association with other variables is taken into account. However, the sign of the partial regression coefficient is negative, opposite in direction to hypothesis 4.

Both coalmining history and national cultural class are significant and are included in the combined model.

The stepwise regression of the combined model reported in the last block of Table 2.13 picks out the most influential indicators. Indicators representing the explanations put forward in hypotheses 1, 2, 3, 5 and 6 achieve significance at the 1% level, while density and percentage aged 85+ play roles opposite to the ones originally hypothesized.

9.5 Summary and critique of findings

To sum up, the evidence suggests that counties/Scottish regions with higher levels of unemployment and with a history of coalmining experience higher levels of LLTI and that these effects are enhanced in Wales compared with England or Scotland. Counties/Scottish regions with high levels of participation of men in full-time employment and with high percentages of households having two cars or more available have lower levels of LLTI. Allowing for the influence of these indicators and their correlation with density there is evidence that more densely populated areas have lower LLTI levels. The variation between areas in the share of the population that is reasonably old does appear to increase the percentage of LLTI, while the areas with highest percentages of the very old show lower percentages, other factors being held constant. This has been interpreted as a survival and selection effect.

These analyses have been based on area average values from the Monitor dataset and are thus liable to what is known as the 'ecological fallacy' (spurious associations). However, such is the detail of tables provided in the LBS that many of the hypotheses can be explored directly for all areas. For example, it is possible to compute the probability of LLTI given broad age group for all LBS areas and thus to explore the conundrum posed by the old-age associations reported here. It is also possible to measure the strength of the unemployment and affluence factors more directly. This could lead to a shift in the dependent variable to be explained from a simple percentage to an age standardized value, or the variation across geographical units in the probabilities of LLTI given age, unemployment, full-time employment could become the subject of investigation.

It will also be possible to explore the combined effect of all these hypotheses at an individual scale using tabulations from the 2% SAR, and to relate these to contextual effects. The rich information provided by the 1991 Census opens up very many new avenues for social science research.

10 Concluding remarks

The 1991 Census is the latest in a long line stretching back to 1801 of comprehensive counts of the British population. The content of the census questionnaire has not changed radically in recent decades. What has changed dramatically is the volume of published output from the Census Offices and the potential for analysis by researchers. For example, the SAS and LBS datasets of the 1991 Census provide two to four times as much information as was available from the 1981 Census SAS. The great potential for new analysis is revealed in the discussion of the new LLTI variable.

This chapter has also outlined the set of issues that must be addressed when small area population change is being investigated. Census data can be seen to be essential to such investigations, but the limitations of the 1981 and 1991 Census counts must be appreciated and the information must be combined with best estimates of other demographic components in order that the sources of change be properly identified.

To deliver Census datasets to researchers' desks has required an extensive programme of collaborative activity, which has been described in this chapter. That such an enterprise can be carried out on a communal basis is testimony both to the skills of all participants and to the commitment of large numbers of people in both government service and higher education to seeking the objective truth about the state of the nation's population. By the start of 1995 British academics could have on their desks (if they have a networked PC or one with a CD-ROM) unrivalled access to statistics about the 57 million people that live on our offshore islands.

Acknowledgements

The author wishes to thank ESRC/JISC for their support through grant A507345001 for Coordination of the Census Programme, his colleagues in the academic community for their efforts in providing the building blocks of the Programme, and the ESRC Secretariat for their hard work in ensuring that the Programme runs smoothly. All users owe a debt of gratitude to Professor Catherine Marsh, who sadly died in January 1993, for her leadership in persuading the Census Offices to produce and make available to the academic community the new Samples of Anonymized Records. The author is also extremely grateful to all his colleagues in the different Census Offices for all their efforts in carrying out the complex task of a decennial census and in converting the returns into an extremely rich set of databases, which will be extremely valuable inputs to academic research.

The following people provided considerable help in preparing the Census Monitor datasets described in the chapter. At Leeds Yu-Xian Jin keyed in the county data; Paul Williamson keyed in the district data and carried out the consistency checking and error correction; Oliver Duke-Williams carried out a check on the district data. At Newcastle Tony Champion organized a thorough round of checking; Daniel Dorling reformatted and aggregated the data and subjected it to consistency checks; Mike Coombes, Colin Wymer and Marilyn Champion checked individual parts of the data.

Appendix 2A Useful contacts

2A.1 ESRC

Mr Jeremy Neathey
ESRC
Polaris House
North Star Avenue
Swindon SN2 1UJ

Tel 0179 341 3000 (switchboard)
Fax 0179 341 3001

2A.2 Census Offices

Mr Ian White
Census Division
Office of Population Censuses and Surveys
St Catherines House
10 Kingsway
London WC2B 6JP

Tel 0171 242 0262

Mrs Lin Graft
Mrs Celia Curtis
Census Customer Services
Office of Population Censuses and Surveys
Segensworth Road
Titchfield
Fareham
Hampshire PO15 5RR

Tel 0132 981 3800
Fax 0132 981 3532

Mr Frank Thomas
Census Customer Services
General Register Office (Scotland)
Ladywell House
Edinburgh EH12 7TF

Tel 0131 334 0380 ext 217
Fax 0131 314 4344

Mr Trevor Evans
Census Office for Northern Ireland
Department of Finance and Personnel
Parliament Buildings
Stormont
Belfast BT4 3SW
Tel 0123 252 1440
Fax 0123 252 1073

2A.3 Census Programme units and projects

2A.3.1 Units

(1) The ESRC Data Archive

Professor Denise Lievesley
ESRC Data Archive
University of Essex
Wivenhoe Park
Colchester
Essex CO4 3SQ

Tel 0120 687 2001
Fax 0120 687 2003
Email archive@essex.ac.uk

(2) The LS Support Programme

Dr Heather Joshi
LS Support Programme
Social Statistics Research Unit
City University
Northampton Square
London EC1V 0HB

Tel 0171 477 8485
Fax 0171 477 8583

(3) The Census Microdata Unit

Professor Angela Dale
Ms Elizabeth Middleton
Department of Econometrics and Social Statistics
University of Manchester

Oxford Road
Manchester M13 9PL

Tel 0161 275 2000 ext 4876
Email cmu@manchester.ac.uk

(4) The Census Dissemination Unit

Mr Keith Cole
Dr Virginia Knight
Census Dissemination Unit
Manchester Computing Centre
University of Manchester
Oxford Road
Manchester M13 9PL

Tel 0161 275 6066
Fax 0161 275 6040
Email k.j.cole@mcc.ac.uk
v.knight@mcc.ac.uk

(5) The UKBORDERS project

Mr Peter Burnhill
Dr Donald Morse
Edinburgh Data Library
Computing Services
University of Edinburgh
George Square
Edinburgh EH8 9LJ

Tel 0131 650 3301
Fax 0131 662 4809
Email p.burnhill@edinburgh.ac.uk
donald.morse@edinburgh.ac.uk

(6) The Northern Ireland project

Dr Ian Shuttleworth
Department of Geography
School of Geosciences
Queen's University
Belfast BT7 1NN

Tel 0123 224 5133 ext 3359
Fax 0123 232 1280

2A.3.2 Training programme

(1) The 1991 Census User's Guide

Professor Angela Dale
Census Microdata Unit
Faculty of Economics & Social Studies
University of Manchester
Manchester
M13 9PL

Tel 0161 275 4721
Fax 0161 275 4722
Email a.dale@manchester.ac.uk

(2) Tutorial and user guides for the 1991 Census of Population

Dr Mike Clarke
Deputy Director
GeoData Institute
University of Southampton
Highfield
Southampton SO9 5NH

Tel 0710 358 3565
Fax 0710 359 2849

Dr David Martin
Professor Neil Wrigley
Department of Geography
University of Southampton
Highfield
Southampton SO9 5NH

Tel 0170 359 5000/3762
Fax 0170 359 3729
Email ggi08@ibm.soton.ac.uk

(3) Sample datasets to illustrate different applications, different media

Dr Allan Strachan
Dr H M Hearnshaw
Midlands Regional Research
Laboratory
Bennett Building
University of Leicester
University Road
Leicester LE1 7RH

Tel 0116 252 3849
Fax 0116 252 2200
Email rrl@leicester.ac.uk

Mr David Walker
Senior Lecturer
Department of Geography
Loughborough University of
Technology
Loughborough LE11 3TU

Tel 0150 922 2741
Fax 0150 926 2192
Email d.r.f.walker@lut.ac.uk

(4) Using the 1991 Census: a trainer's resource base

Dr Mitchell Langford
Dr Allan Strachan
Midland Regional Research Laboratory
Bennett Building
University of Leicester
University Road
Leicester LE1 7RH

Tel 0116 252 3849
Fax 0116 252 2200
Email rrl@leicester.ac.uk

(5) A series of training workshops for users of the Census of Population and related data

Mrs Teresa Rees
Social Research Unit
University of Wales College of Cardiff
PO Box 906
Cardiff CF1 3YN

Tel 0122 287 4463
Fax 0122 287 8845

Dr Stephen Littler
School of Institutional Management
University of Wales College of Cardiff
PO Box 906
Cardiff CF1 3YN

Tel 0122 287 4175
Fax 0122 287 4446
Email littler@cf.ac.uk

(6) Training programme on the Census of Population and related government surveys

Professor Angela Dale
Faculty of Economics & Social Studies
University of Manchester
Manchester
M13 9PL

Tel 0161 275 4721
Fax 0161 275 4722
Email a.dale@manchester.ac.uk

2A.3.3 Development programme

(1) Interpretative analysis of social change using spatial models of census data

Dr David Martin
Department of Geography
University of Southampton
Highfield
Southampton SO9 5NH

Tel 0170 359 5000
Fax 0170 359 3729
Email ggi08@ibm.soton.ac.uk

(2) A new approach to the 'aggregation' issue in Census data analysis

Professor Tim Holt
Department of Social Statistics
University of Southampton
Highfield
Southampton SO9 5NH

Tel 0170 359 2518
Fax 0170 359 3846
Email socstats@ibm.soton.ac.uk

Professor Neil Wrigley
Department of Geography
University of Southampton
Highfield
Southampton SO9 5NH

Tel 0170 359 5000
Fax 0170 359 3729

(3) Occupational definitions and coding conventions: the 1981 and 1991 Censuses of Population

Dr Peter Elias
Institute for Employment Research
University of Warwick
Coventry CV4 7AL

Tel 0120 352 3286
Fax 0120 354 2241

(4) American census data handling techniques and the British census

Mr Robert Barr
Department of Geography
University of Manchester
Oxford Road
Manchester M13 9PL

Tel 0161 275 3648
Fax 0161 273 4407
Email r.barr@manchester.ac.uk

(5) Using the 1991 Census for population synthesis and analysis of migration

Professor Philip Rees
School of Geography
University of Leeds
Leeds LS2 9JT

Tel 0113 233 3341
Fax 0113 233 3308
Email p.h.rees@leeds.ac.uk

Dr Mark Birkin
School of Geography
University of Leeds
Leeds LS2 9JT

Tel 0113 244 6164

Dr John Stillwell
School of Geography
University of Leeds
Leeds LS2 9JT

Tel 0113 233 3315
Email john@geog.leeds.ac.uk

Dr Debbie Phillips
School of Geography
University of Leeds
Leeds LS2 9JT

Tel 0113 233 3318
Email debbie@geog.leeds.ac.uk

(6) ESRC Census Research Unit – work on aggregation

Professor Stan Openshaw
School of Geography
University of Leeds
Leeds LS2 9JT

Tel 0113 233 3321
Fax 0113 233 3308
Email stan@geog.leeds.ac.uk

2A.3.4 Census Analysis Group: Steering Committee

Dr Tony Champion
Department of Geography
Daysh Building
The University
Newcastle upon Tyne NE1 7RU

Tel 0191 222 6000 ext 6437
Fax 0191 262 1182
Email tony.champion@newcastle.ac.uk

Dr John Stillwell
School of Geography
University of Leeds
Leeds LS2 9JT

Tel 0113 233 3315
Fax 0113 233 3308
Email john@geog.leeds.ac.uk

Professor Philip Rees
School of Geography
University of Leeds
Leeds LS2 9JT

Tel 0113 233 3341
Fax 0113 233 3308
Email p.h.rees@leeds.ac.uk

2A.3.5 Census Co-ordinator

Professor Philip Rees
School of Geography
University of Leeds
Leeds LS2 9JT

Tel 0113 233 3341
Fax 0113 233 3308
Email p.h.rees@leeds.ac.uk

Appendix 2B Glossary of acronyms

ARC-INFO	geographical information system software
ATLAS-GIS	geographical information system software
CD-ROM	compact disk – read-only memory
CDU	Census Dissemination Unit
CMU	Census Microdata Unit
CONI	Census Office Northern Ireland
C91	Census 1991 PC data access program
DA	ESRC Data Archive

DBD	digitized boundary data
DENI	Department of Education Northern Ireland
ED	enumeration district
EUDL	Edinburgh University Data Library
EDLINE	digitized ED LINE boundaries in England and Wales
ESRC	Economic and Social Research Council
EXCEL	spreadsheet software package
GIS	geographical information system
GRO(S)	General Register Office Scotland
HMSO	Her Majesty's Stationery Office
IDRISI	geographical information software for the PC
JANET	Joint Academic Network
JISC	Joint Information Systems Committee
LAN	local area network
LBS	Local Base Statistics
LS	Longitudinal Study
LSSP	Longitudinal Study Support Programme
LLTI	limiting long-term illness
MCC	Manchester Computing Service
MRRL	Midlands Regional Research Laboratory
NHS	National Health Service
OA	output area
OPCS	Office of Population Censuses and Surveys
QUANVERT	fast database package by QUANTIME Limited
QUB	Queen's University Belfast
SARS	Samples of Anonymized Records
SAS	Small Area Statistics *also* Statistical Analysis System
SASPAC	SAS Package for the 1981 Census
SASPAC91	SAS and LBS Package for the 1991 Census
SIR	Survey Information Retrieval package
SMS	Special Migration Statistics
SPSS	Statistical Package for the Social Sciences
SSRU	Social Statistics Research Unit (City University)
SWS	Special Workplace Statistics
UKBORDERS	package for accessing DBD for UK
UNIX	a computer operating system

Appendix 2C User Registration Form for the SAS/LBS

This page may be copied by users wishing to register to use the Census

MANCHESTER COMPUTING CENTRE
Census Dissemination Unit (CDU)

SAS/LBS DATASETS USER REGISTRATION FORM

Application to use the machine-readable datasets for
Small Area Statistics and Local Base Statistics and Related Material
from the 1991 Census of Population

I apply for authority to use the 1991 Census of Population Small Area and Local Base Statistics and related material. I agree to accept and abide by the Conditions of Use.

FULL NAME: ______________________________

DEPARTMENT: ______________________________

INSTITUTION: ______________________________

FULL ADDRESS: ______________________________

____

TELEPHONE NO: ____________________ EMAIL: ____________

STATUS: Staff Member ☐

Postgraduate (Research) ☐

Postgraduate (Taught) ☐

Undergraduate ☐

Other, please specify ______________________

MCC (VM/CMS) USER NAME: ______________________

Keyword description of intended use of data and related material:

continued

Research Council or organization funding the work in which the data and related material may be used:

ESRC ☐ Other Research Council ☐ Other Research Body ☐

UFC ☐ PCFC ☐ HEFC(EW) ☐ HEFC(S) ☐ HEFC(NI) ☐

LEA ☐ Other ☐

Length of time that registration requested for:

1 year ☐ 2 years ☐ 3 years ☐ 4 years ☐ 5 years ☐

6 years ☐ 7 years ☐ 8 years ☐ 9 years ☐ 10 years ☐

Students should register for the remaining length of their course. Contract researchers should register for the remaining length of their projects.

Is the work likely to require permission from the Census Offices under the Conditions of Use?

Yes ☐ No ☐

If yes, the user should contact the relevant Census Office and obtain the necessary permission or licence.

SIGNATURES

Person applying: ______________________ Date: __________

Supervisor (for students): ______________________ Date: __________

MCC representative: ______________________ Date: __________

Comments by applicant:

Please return this form to: User Services, MCC, Oxford Road, Manchester M13 9PL. A copy will be returned when authority has been granted.

For MCC use: Reference no.: ______________________ User name: ______

Access granted (date): ______________________ Signature: ________

References

Census Analysis Unit 1993 *Accessing the Census: a Suite of Exercises to Access the 1991 and 1981 Census at MCC.* Midlands Regional Research Laboratory, University of Leicester.

Dale, A and C Marsh (eds) 1993 *The 1991 Census User's Guide.* London: HMSO.

Marsh, C and A Teague 1992 Samples of anonymised records from the 1991 Census. *Population Trends* 69 (Autumn), 17–26.

Manchester Computing Centre (MCC) 1994 *Guide to accessing the Census* 1991 (SAS/LBS) *and* 1981 *(SAS) data using SASPAC.* CSS 604, Manchester Computing Centre, University of Manchester.

OPCS and GRO(S) 1992a *1991 Census. Definitions*, Cen 91 DEF. London: HMSO.

OPCS and GRO(S) 1992b *User Guide 24: Local Base Statistics.* Titchfield, Hants: OPCS.

OPCS and GRO(S) 1992c *User Guide 25: Small Area Statistics.* Titchfield, Hants: OPCS.

OPCS and GRO(S) 1992d *Great Britain. National Monitor.* London: OPCS.

OPCS and GRO(S) 1993 *User Guide 34: Special Migration Statistics.* Titchfield, Hants: OPCS.

Rees, P 1990 *A Manual for Subnational projections.* Unpublished manuscript, School of Geography, University of Leeds.

Rees, P 1991 The projection of small area populations: a case study in Swansea, Wales. In P Hooimeijer, G A Vander Knaap, J Van Weesep, R I Woods (eds) 1994 *Population Dynamics in Europe: Current Issues in Population Geography.* Netherlands Geographical Studies 1.73 Royal Netherlands Geographical Society, Department of Geography, University of Utrecht, Utrecht, 141-58.

Rees, P 1992a The ESRC/UFC-ISC 1991 Census of Population Initiative: delivering the data of the decade. *ESRC Data Archive Bulletin* 51, 12–22.

Rees, P (ed) 1992b Census analysis: planning the way ahead. A report on the launch seminar of the Census Analysis Group, April 6–7th 1992. Working Paper 92/13, School of Geography, University of Leeds.

Rees, P 1992c The demographic structure of Britain's population: first results from the 1991 Census. Working Paper 92/23, School of Geography, University of Leeds.

Rees, P 1992d Projecting the population of urban communities. Paper presented at the US/UK Seminar on Migration in Post-Industrial Societies, University of Southern California, August 1992. Forthcoming in *Environment and Planning A.*

Rees, P 1993a Demographic structure and change, 1981–91: results from the 1991 Census. *Town and Country Planning* 62 (March), 46–9.

Rees, P 1993b *Census Data, Block III of GP2H 1992/93: Class Documents and Exercises.* School of Geography, University of Leeds.

Rees, P and O Duke-Williams 1994 The special migration statistics: a vital resource for research into British migration. Working paper 94/19, School of Geography, University of Leeds.

Rhind, D, J Raper and J Shepherd 1992 *Postcodes: The New Geography.* Harlow: Longman.

SASPAC 1992 *SASPAC User Manual: Parts 1 and 2*, CST 450, 1st edn. London: London Research Centre, April.

UMRCC 1990 *The 1981 SASPAC Manual, Parts 1 and 2.* Manchester Computing Centre.

Williamson, P 1993 A meta-database for the SAS and LBS datasets of the 1991 Census of Population. Working Paper 93/18, School of Geography, University of Leeds.

3

Accessing the data via SASPAC91

H Davies

Editor's note

Historically, accessing census data for small areas distributed on computer media has been a major problem. The 1966 Census data (on punch cards) required the user to write special software. The 1971 Census data available on magnetic tapes also required special software both to read the seven-track ICL tapes (if you are not an ICL site the horrors of this still linger on) and to extract the cells of interest (never an easy task because of the cross-tabulated nature of the Small Area Statistics). All over the UK people re-invented programs merely to read the data which meant that end-users could only get access to the data via a systems programmer. The development of SASPAC for the 1981 Census and the availability of the data in a character form capable of being read by non-ICL systems changed all this. However, the installation of a portable SASPAC created another burden, which often required what seemed like heroic efforts. However, SASPAC did work and it revolutionized the way users accessed the 1981 Census. This chapter continues the SASPAC story.

However, it is important to realize that SASPAC is not the only way of accessing census data. Even in the early 1980s some people preferred to use SPSS to access the data; and it could do this extremely well. I myself never used SASPAC, preferring instead to write my own programs in FORTRAN. The situation today is much more fluid. There are many different routes to accessing small area census statistics; SASPAC91 is just one of them. However, for many local authorities and census users in universities it is likely to remain the predominant path to the Small Area and Local Base Statistics data. Fortunately, it is simple to use and some useful manuals have been written.

OK, I know, census data file extraction and data creation is the really boring part of census analysis. However, it is also a most essential part of the analysis process and if it is done badly or is wrong everything else that follows will also be wrong, so grit your teeth and get it right! So if you feel SASPAC91 is boring then you can always consider the even more boring alternative of writing your own code to extract those bits of the 1991 Census you need. Why not see SASPAC as a front-end to other systems, if it doesn't do what you want. Maybe, you don't even need to use it; indeed, it should not be overlooked that many census user needs will be met from the published census results.

1 Introduction

The 1991 Census of Population in Great Britain, which was held on the night of 21–22 April 1991, will generate a vast mass of statistics over the next few years that will provide a uniquely rich source of geographically based information.

These statistics will be an invaluable source of information to demographers, town planners, social researchers and a whole host of others requiring a 'snapshot' of the demographic characteristics of areas or of changes in such characteristics over time. They will be used by public sector organizations such as local and health authorities in planning the allocation of scarce resources, and by private companies to target their most profitable local markets, throughout the 1990s and into the twenty-first century.

The primary source of statistics are the Local Base Statistics (LBS) and the Small Area Statistics (SAS) – a set of standard variables and tables produced by the Census Offices. The SAS, which consist of some 9000 counts or variables, are made available for each of over 140,000 small areas in Great Britain, while the LBS are released for each of some 8300 administrative areas and contain more than 20,000 counts. The contents of the SAS and LBS are described in Census Offices' User Guides 24 and 25.

The quantity of information contained within these datasets is such that a system based on machine-readable storage and retrieval of the statistics becomes almost essential. The SAS for an 'average' local authority district, consisting of 350 enumeration districts (EDs), would occupy some 21,000 pages of computer output and would require nearly 6 yards of shelf space to store.

The Census Offices make these datasets available only in machine-readable format compatible with mainframes, and their customer supply files contain only data. That is, they do not contain any descriptive text such as the text associated with the row and column headings of the tables.

The supply by the Census Offices of the SAS and LBS to customers only on mainframe-compatible media caused difficulties to many users who wished to install their data on microcomputers. On behalf of the SASPAC user community, the London Research Centre negotiated with Manchester Computing Centre (MCC) for the data files to be made available on PC-compatible media to sites requiring the service. In addition, recent technological developments have meant that bulk storage media such as CD-ROMs have become more readily available. This has been reflected in the SASPAC consortium's production of the full national database on a set of CD-ROMs for use with SASPAC.

Once the census statistics have been installed on their machines, users will be looking for software that will not only allow the huge quantity of statistics to be stored and retrieved efficiently, but which will allow them to interrogate the statistics in a meaningful manner without a great amount of preparation in creating database dictionaries and file specifications.

SASPAC (Small Area Statistics PACkage) is software that has been designed with primarily this objective in mind. It is tailor-made for the storage, interrogation and analysis of the 1991 Census of Population statistics and has been designed to meet user requirements on mainframes, minicomputers and microcomputers. It is user-friendly with efficient and easy links to other proprietary software.

Through SASPAC, the statistics are available for retrieval and interrogation as and when required by users. Amongst facilities available to users are the following:

- selection of areas for further analysis, on the basis of their demographic characteristics or their distance from a fixed location;
- creation of derived variables from existing ones, through use of arithmetic operators, for immediate or later use;
- creation of new areas of specific interest through aggregation of existing areas;
- ranking of areas according to user-selected characteristics of their population;
- merging of other datasets, including 1981 SAS, with the 1991 Census statistics;
- production of interface files for transfer of data to other software for further analyses or presentation.

For some users of SASPAC, the results of the 1991 Census will be their first introduction to the world of census data analysis. The software has been designed to accommodate this lack of experience. However, no amount of user-friendliness in the software can overcome a lack of knowledge of the SAS and the LBS. It is therefore very important that users of SASPAC acquaint themselves with the details and background of the relevant statistics through reading the Census Offices' guides. In this respect, probably the most important are User Guides 3, 24, 25 and 38 (available from the Census Offices), together with the Definitions volume which is published by HMSO.

2 Basics of SASPAC

SASPAC has been developed primarily to facilitate user access to, and interrogation of, the SAS and LBS produced from the 1991 Census of Population. However, its use is not confined to these datasets, since it can cope with any dataset which is geographically referenced and in which the same items of information are available for all areas on the file.

When a dataset is first introduced to SASPAC, other information must also be supplied so that the files created for future use with the software – known as

SASPAC system files – contain intelligence which allows easy retrieval of required items of information.

When a census dataset is introduced to the software, the additional information is supplied through the medium of a data definition language (DDL) file. A DDL file is a file that contains information about the data contained within a dataset to be read by SASPAC. Its primary function is to detail the number of tables represented within the dataset and the number of cells within each table. An exception to this requirement for a DDL file is a 1981 SAS file which was created as a SASPAC81 System file on the same machine operating system. Such files are referred to as SASPAC4 files.

Non-census datasets can also be read by SASPAC, but in these cases the additional information is supplied by the user in the form of formatting statements relevant to the input dataset.

Having read a dataset, SASPAC then converts the data from the standard character format into its own internal format for more efficient and economic storage. These files – the SASPAC system files – are unique to SASPAC and cannot be read by other software. The creation of these files, a process termed loading, is a once-and-for-all operation, and means that once data are loaded into SASPAC the original raw data are no longer required for direct access and may either be disposed of or stored for archival purposes.

This flexibility in the introduction of datasets to the software allows access to the following datasets, amongst others:

1981 Census SAS
1981 Census Special Workplace Statistics (Sections A and B)
1991 Census Special Workplace Statistics (Sections A and B)
JUVOS Statistics
user-generated datasets that are SAS-type in structure

The system files, because of the way in which they are constructed, are very much smaller than their parent raw data files, and this has beneficial consequences for users, especially those using microcomputers, in terms of the storage requirements for the census statistics.

The system files, once created, will be available for later access and interrogation by the user. The data can be manipulated within SASPAC, and data for new areas may be created, for immediate or later access. SASPAC will enable the user to produce a variety of reports on any of the statistics stored on a system file or created during a run. It also makes it easy to export census data for further analysis and presentation using other spreadsheet, database, graphical or mapping software.

The only difference in the functionality of SASPAC on the largest mainframe and a microcomputer of a given base configuration is that, on the latter, users may create WKS and DBF output files directly. The absence of this ability on mainframes is related to the fact that the internal representation of binary files – which is what WKS and DBF files are – is different on mainframes from that on microcomputers. WKS and DBF files created on a mainframe would therefore not be interpretable on a microcomputer system.

SASPAC is a batch-oriented item of software in which the requirements of users are indicated to the software through a series of commands, and these commands taken together in the appropriate order create a command file. It is this command file that is at the heart of every SASPAC operation.

Users of the software in an MS-DOS or UNIX environment have an advantage over users in a batch environment on a mainframe or minicomputer, in that the former have access to a full interactive menu-driven front-end which generates the command files necessary to operate SASPAC. The availability of this user-friendly interface means that users of the software on microcomputers do not need to know the command language and syntax in detail.

3 History of SASPAC

SASPAC was originally developed for the interrogation and analysis of the 1981 Census of Population and was used by nearly 200 organizations on a large variety of mainframes and minicomputers. It was probably amongst the most portable software packages ever written. In the introduction to the 1981 version of this handbook, David Rhind wrote that 'the project had transformed the way in which census statistics are used in Britain'.

The 1981 software was so successful that it was nominated as the joint winner of the 1983 British Computer Society Social Benefit Award. Its use in polytechnics and universities was so widespread that it became the *de facto* standard census analysis package, and was taught on a variety of courses.

In 1987, the portability of the software was exploited by Northern Software Technology in conjunction with Greater Manchester Research, who successfully installed the 1981 version of SASPAC on an 80386 MS-DOS system and made it available as SASPAC4/386.

Following the success of the 1981 venture, LAMSAC (the co-ordinators of that development) initiated discussions on the provision of similar software for 1991. A demand among local authorities and other public organizations was immediately perceived, and following consultations with potential users of the software, user requirements were drawn up and a contract for the development of the software was awarded to MVA Systematica, in partnership with Northern Software Technology.

On the closure of LAMSAC in October 1989, the ownership of the development was transferred to the Local Government Training Board (now the Local Government Management Board (LGMB)) and the management of the project to the London Research Centre, which has continued to undertake this task on behalf of the LGMB.

Following the 1981 Census of Population, SASPAC provided easy access to the data, and it is a measure of its success that as users of census statistics started to plan for the 1991 Census of Population a common demand was that SASPAC91 be developed to continue the 'tradition'. In less than 10 years SASPAC has become the industry standard for census data storage and interrogation. Thus it can be said that in the last ten years little has changed in the software used to interrogate SAS. What has changed, and dramatically, is the means of accessing the software and the people undertaking the accessing.

In 1983 (in *BURISA Newsletter 61*), I described the system which had recently been brought into operation at the Greater London Council (GLC) which allowed users virtual on-line access to the whole of the London database at ED and ward level. Under this system, users were relieved of the task of depositing a deck of punched cards with the central computer resource for submission at an indeterminate time, and instead were able to submit jobs from remote terminals, initially of the teletype form and later of VDU form, and know that the job would be submitted almost immediately. It has to be said that the GLC experience was not shared by other users of SASPAC, among whom it was common to find people who were restricted to overnight turnaround on their jobs.

It is the latter users who will notice the greatest change brought about by the technological advances made during the last 10 years, and more specifically, the last five years.

The 1981 version of SASPAC was designed as a batch-run, mainframe program, although one authority asked for it to be mounted on a DEC PDP-11 mini. This proved to be impossible, but such was the pace of change and the improvement in memory management that it proved possible, by 1988, to mount exactly that software on a Compaq 386 microcomputer.

Despite its inherent user-friendliness, SASPAC suffered from the need for users to be aware of the operating system requirements and job control language (JCL) of their particular mainframe in order for them to assign appropriate channels and make the correct connections between the software and the hardware. Here again, at the GLC we were a privileged group in that, through good relationships with the computer department, catalogued procedures were set up which hid most of the JCL from users. They were then left with the relatively simple task of identifying a few basic parameters such as file names in order to submit jobs.

Now, with the increasing availability of microcomputers, this restriction on use is diminishing, and users of SASPAC will not only have no need to know the command structure of the software but will also only need a very limited knowledge of the operating system (MS-DOS).

With the increasing use of networks, there are further options open to all users of census data. It could be envisaged that the data for the area of an organization's interest could be held on a central server, with a network of users in different departments, or within the same department, holding the software and data of particular interest on their own machines. Data could be down-loaded as and when required from the central server, which could be a mainframe, a mini or even another micro.

In this way, the users of census statistics become much more diffuse, with less reliance being placed on a central information resource to provide information for the separate departments. It could well be argued that there are dangers in this approach, in that inexperienced users of census statistics not having adequate knowledge of any limitations in the data may draw invalid statistical conclusions and produce spurious results.

Additionally, with such easy access to the software and data, there is a great danger of a proliferation and duplication of files on the system. An abundance of 'sleeping files' or 'sleepers' – files created and used once for a particular job, and left dormant on the system without documentation – is a particular problem with such a system.

These dangers were present under the GLC system, and it required the introduction of standards in file saving and good practice in documentation of files created to alleviate the problem. Even so, duplication and 'sleepers' to some extent were inevitable, and it requires very good practice to eliminate them from any system.

Correct use of the statistics will always be a problem, and could even occur where data were supplied by experienced users to inexperienced end-users. It is how the end-user presents the results that really matters. It is therefore important that the experienced users within an organization inform colleagues in other departments of the pitfalls and limitations of the census data, either through continuing dialogue or through information notes.

4 Structure of SASPAC

The language of SASPAC consists of a set of commands which nest together in predefined ways to create a command file. A command file is a series of commands which tell SASPAC what files to read; what areas on the file to consider; what manipulation of the data is to be done; what areas and/or variables are to be output; and what format the output is to appear in.

A typical SASPAC command file would contain the following basic elements:

INPUT
SELECT
MANIPULATE
SELECT FOR OUTPUT
OUTPUT

Not all of these elements have to be present in every command file, but every command file must input a file and produce some output.

SASPAC commands generally consist of three elements:

Mandatory keywords
Optional keywords
User-supplied names or identifiers, which may or may not be mandatory

Probably the most commonly used command will be:

INPUT <FILETYPE> FILE [NAME] [=] <filename>

which is the command used to instruct SASPAC which file is to be read during the current task. In this example certain conventions are used. These are that items enclosed in square brackets are optional, while those enclosed in angular brackets are user defined. Also elements in upper case are keywords recognized by SASPAC whereas those in lower case are user supplied. Thus in the above example the user has the option to include the keyword NAME, while the filename is supplied by the user and is mandatory.

In general, each of the keywords must be delimited by at least one blank. This means that the command

INPUTSYSTEM FILE TESTFILE

would generate an error condition, since SASPAC would not recognize the keyword INPUTSYSTEM.

In understanding the way in which SASPAC operates, it is important to bear in mind the different types of file which the software accesses at different times. Reference has already been made to command files, system files, SASPAC4 and DDL files. In addition to these, there are a further nine distinct file types.

Before considering the file types referenced by SASPAC, a brief description of the task-based structure of the software will be of value. SASPAC undertakes the following tasks:

LOAD
CONVERT
TRANSFER OUT
TRANSFER IN
FORMAT
RE-ZONE
REPORT

Each of these tasks has a specific function, as defined below, and requires the use of specific commands. Some commands are common to many tasks; others are used for one task only. The purpose of each of the tasks is as follows.

Load:

Used to introduce a data file to SASPAC. The LOAD task reads the raw data and creates a system file in SASPAC's own internal format.

Convert:

Used to introduce a SASPAC4 file to SASPAC. The Convert task reads the system file created by the 1981 version of the software and creates a new system file in SASPAC's own internal format.

Transfer Out:

Used to replicate a 1991 system file in order to move it to a different computer operating system, e.g. mainframe to micro.

Transfer In:

Used to introduce to SASPAC a file which the software itself had created during a Transfer Out task, as output from a system file, at another installation or on a different machine.

Format:

Used to introduce to SASPAC a file which contains card image representations of the standard SAS and LBS pages and tables, and all the necessary information for the correct positioning and representation of variables on these pages and tables. The Format task reads these files and creates files containing the same information in a compressed form internal to the software.

Re-zone:

Used to create new areas from thc cxisting areas held on system files. The Re-zone task reads system files and aggregates user-specified areas on these files to create new areas. These areas are then available for later retrieval on the newly created system files.

Report:

This is the major task undertaken by SASPAC. The Report task reads system files and allows users to undertake manipulations of the data prior to outputting reports in a variety of formats.

To undertake each of these tasks SASPAC, as already stated, requires access to a variety of file types. Specifically, these are as follows:

Command files
Configuration file
Report files
Log files
Interface files
Transfer files
Framework data files
OPCS data files
Framework files
System files
SASPAC4 files
DDL files
Gazetteer files

The contents of each of these file types is as follows.

Command files:

These files contain a list of instructions which SASPAC will interpret and in response will undertake the tasks required by the user. A typical command file would be

```
INPUT SYSTEM FILE NAME = TESTFILE
INCLUDE 02BDFA01 02BDFA09
PRINT VARIABLES S010001 TO S010002
OUTPUT PRINT FILE = TESTPRIN
END
FINISH
```

Instructions which are too long or too complex to fit onto a single 80 character line may be continued onto succeeding lines by the use of a '/' character.

Configuration file:

This file is supplied with the software but may be modified for local requirements. It is a card image file which contains a number of the default values and system parameters which are used by the software. Sample lines from a typical configuration file on a PC system would be

```
COMMAND FILE DIRECTORY NAME = \SASPAC\COMMAND
SYSTEM1 FILE DIRECTORY NAME = D:\SASBACK\SYSFILES
PRINT COMMAND OF SYSTEM = SASPRINT.BAT
PAGE LENGTH = 55
PAGE WIDTH = 80
MAXIMUM PAGES = 200
```

Report files:

These are files to which SASPAC will write all report output, whether the request is for listing of variables or printing of pages, tables or profiles.

Log files:

These are files to which SASPAC will echo all commands in the input command file and to which all generated system messages will be sent. The log files will contain all information required to ascertain whether a job ran correctly, and if not, why not. A log file will automatically be generated every time a SASPAC command file is processed.

Interface files:

These are files to which SASPAC will write when there is a requirement to export data to other software. There are six different types of interface files available to the user, and the choice will be dependent on the software to which the data are to be exported. These interface files are

Formatted files
Delimited files
DIF files
DBF files
WKS files
Matrix files

Transfer files:

These are files which SASPAC will write to when there is a requirement to export the complete dataset for input to SASPAC on a different operating system, or will read from when importing a dataset from a different operating system.

Framework data files:

These are files which contain card image representations of the standard SAS and LBS tables together with all the necessary information required for the correct positioning and representation of variables on these tables. They may also be created by users to define tables for non-SAS/LBS datasets which may be input to SASPAC, or for producing user-designed tables of the SAS or LBS.

OPCS data files:

These are files which contain card image representations of SAS and LBS, or any other SAS-type datasets to be read by SASPAC. They may be files created as standard output by the 1981 version of the software or, despite the name, they may be files containing the user's own data. The use of the name OPCS is generic and is intended to include GRO(S).

Framework files:

These are files which contain internal representations of the pages and tables associated with any dataset to be read by SASPAC, and all the necessary information for the correct positioning and representation of variables on these pages and tables. They will have been created during a Format task from the appropriate framework data files.

System files:

These are files which contain internal representations of the data within any dataset to be read by SASPAC. They will have been created during a Load task from the appropriate OPCS data files, during a Convert task from the appropriate SASPAC4 files, or during a Transfer task.

SASPAC4 files:

These are files which contain internal (to the 1981 version of the software) representations of the data within any dataset to be read by SASPAC. They will have been created during a Load task in either version 3 or version 4 of the 1981 software.

SASPAC4 files will only be available to SASPAC if they were created on the same operating system as that to be used for the current implementation. Thus, system files created on SASPAC4/386 in an MS-DOS environment will be usable with the microcomputer version of SASPAC but, for example, 1981 files created on an ICL/VME machine will not be directly usable with SASPAC on an IBM/MVS implementation.

DDL files:

These are card-image files which contain information on the content of datasets to be introduced to SASPAC during the loading of raw census data. They tell SASPAC the number of tables represented by a dataset, and the number of cells or counts within each table.

Gazetteer files:

These are files which are used to facilitate the creation of new zones. In the 1981 version of the software, users had to specify each old area which was to be aggregated into a new one, either individually or as ranges of codes. The gazetteer file concept allows users to use existing or specially created files of area allocation to facilitate new area creation.

For example, users may already have a file which defines their specific areas of interest in terms of EDs (whole or part). Such a file would be introduced to SASPAC as a gazetteer file, and the creation of the data for the specific areas would then be mechanical, without the need for further user input. A typical gazetteer file would have the following layout:

```
01ACAA01  01
01ACAA02  01  0.50
01ACAA02  02  0.50
01ACAA03  03
01ACAA04  01  0.75
01ACAA04  03  0.25
```

This file would be accompanied by the following commands in the Command file:

```
INPUT GAZETTEER FILE NAME=GAZ1 /
EXISTING ZONE   COLS 1 TO 8 /
SCALE FACTOR    COLS 15 TO 22 /
NEW ZONE COLS 9 TO 14
```

There is also a facility for new zone labels to be provided within the gazetteer files.

Users of SASPAC on microcomputers will find that the software has its own internal convention for naming the files which it uses and creates. Within the MS-DOS environment all files, whether related to SASPAC or not, have a name of the form

Root.Extension

where 'Root' consists of up to eight characters and 'Extension' up to three characters. The characters may be either alphabetic or numeric, and in some cases other special characters may be used. However, for safety, it is often better to restrict file names to alphabetic or numeric characters.

Table 3.1 File name extensions looked for by SASPAC on a PC under MS-DOS

File type	Extension
Command file	CMD
Configuration file	CFG
Report file	PRN
Log file	LOG
Interface file	
Formatted file	FMT
Delimited file	DEL
DIF file	DIF
DBF file	DBF
WKS file	WKS
Matrix file	MAT
Transfer file	TRF
Framework data file	FWD
OPCS data file	TXT
Framework file	FWK
System file	SYS
SASPAC4 file	S81
DDL file	DDL
Gazetteer file	GAZ

Some software will recognize certain extensions as being specific to that software. For example, MS-DOS will recognize any file with an extension of EXE, COM or BAT as a file containing a command or commands which it can execute or act upon. Similarly, the spreadsheet package LOTUS 1-2-3 will assume that any file with an extension of WKS is a file containing data in its own internal format.

SASPAC is consistent with this naming convention by allowing users to allocate their own root, but the extension is automatically allocated by the software depending on the circumstances in which the file is created.

The root allocated by the user may be descriptive of the task undertaken or may follow some other naming convention decided by the user.

The file name extensions automatically created and looked for by SASPAC on a PC under MS-DOS are given in Table 3.1. In addition to knowing what type of file to look for when undertaking particular tasks, SASPAC also knows where to look for these files.

When the software is delivered, an integral part of it is the configuration file which tells SASPAC where the different files types that it uses are to be located and found. This configuration file may be amended to suit the requirements of individual installations. On microcomputers it may be changed, either temporarily or permanently, through use of the interactive menu system.

Throughout the period of its operation, SASPAC will automatically allocate the different file types to their correct locations, so that housekeeping becomes a comparatively simple affair.

On microcomputers, the executable software will be resident on a single

Table 3.2 Default subdirectories for each file type

File type	Subdirectory
Command file	\SASPAC\COMMAND
Configuration file	\SASPAC
Report file	\SASPAC\REPORT
Log file	\SASPAC\LOG
Interface file	\SASPAC\INTERFAC
Transfer file	\SASPAC\INTERFAC
Framework data file	\SASPAC\FRWDATA
OPCS data file	\SASPAC\OPCS
Framework file	\SASPAC\FRWORK
System file (1)	\SASPAC\SYSFILES
System file (2)	\SASPAC\SYSFILES
System file (3)	\SASPAC\SYSFILES
SASPAC4 file	\SASPAC\SASPAC4
DDL file	\SASPAC\COMMAND
Gazetteer file	\SASPAC\COMMAND

directory, with the different files being stored in separate subdirectories of this directory. The default directory is named SASPAC.

All files of a given type, with the exception of system files, will be allocated to a single directory. System files are allowed to be allocated to up to three subdirectories for 1991 system files and an additional one for SASPAC4 system files, to allow different users on the same system to create their own data files for their own use, if necessary.

At installation, a set of default subdirectories (defined by the configuration file) is created by the installation program supplied with the software. On a microcomputer, the default subdirectories for each file type are as given in Table 3.2. A similar naming convention is used, as available, on other hardware configurations.

Reference has already been made to the construction of a simple command file as consisting of the following elements:

INPUT
SELECT
MANIPULATE
SELECT FOR OUTPUT
OUTPUT

These command files may be stacked so that the step from the bottom of one to the top of another is identified by the keyword command END, while the bottom of the whole pile is identified by the keyword command FINISH.

On meeting the command FINISH, SASPAC will immediately terminate execution and will ignore any commands which may follow it. This command must be preceded by an END command, which in turn must be preceded by some form of output command, otherwise SASPAC will report an abnormal termination of execution.

As SASPAC allows for sequential tasking, a command file could have the following structure:

```
INPUT
SELECT
MANIPULATE
SELECT FOR OUTPUT
OUTPUT
END
INPUT
SELECT
MANIPULATE
SELECT FOR OUTPUT
OUTPUT
END
FINISH
```

The two SASPAC commands (END and FINISH) that have been introduced here must be present in all command files. The FINISH command must only be present once – otherwise abnormal termination will occur – while the END command may be present more than once, depending on the number of tasks to be undertaken during the operation of the command file.

Now that we have seen the basic structure of a command file and have considered what SASPAC expects to be told before it can undertake a program run, let us look in greater detail at how a command file is structured. In particular, we shall consider various basic examples of tasks which users might wish to undertake.

5 Benefits of using SASPAC

5.1 Intelligent interpretation of Census Offices' data files without user preparation

The datasets produced by the Census Offices are in the form of very large numbers of 80 byte card-image records. These records contain the data classified by table, together with certain 'header' information related to the area for which the data are produced. The tables are as defined in Census Offices' User Guides 24 and 25. Although the datasets are defined in terms of these tables, the accompanying text is not contained within the datasets. Table 3.3 shows the typical layout for the first few records of an ED level fixed format file.

Information on the codes used in these files and the format of the records is given in the Census Offices' User Guide 21, but users of the data will require

Table 3.3 Layout of part of a typical 1991 OPCS dataset

11OPCS 0142215/10/921991 SAS E290618P									
210429		127232	124577		512390039491	1			
22									
3104Isle Of Wight									
3203									
3302									
41001	00700071211								
53001	118939	114801	54340	60461	4138	2036	2102	2323	2323
53002	1336	987				1595	1595	746	849
53003				1720	1720	823	897		
53004		8293	2981	1448	1533	5312	2331	2981	7828
53005	2647	1272	1375	5181	2274	2907	465	334	176
53006	158	131	57	74	127232	117782	55788	61994	9450
53007	4367	5083	121262	117124	55676	61448	4138	2036	2102
53008	124577	120439	57245	63194	4138	2036	2102		

forms of access to the data whereby they will have no need to understand the complexities of structure of the datasets.

Through SASPAC, interrogation of the statistics is made available to users, whereby a loading process introduces intelligence into the dataset such that the content of each location within the dataset is allocated a variable name by which users will address such variables. These loaded datasets are referred to as SASPAC system files and would be created by a command file similar to the following:

```
INPUT SYSTEM FILE NAME = IOWDISTH
INPUT DDL FILE NAME = SAS91
OUTPUT SYSTEM FILE NAME = IOWDISTH
END
FINISH
```

Note that the apparent conflict in name between the input and output files is easily resolved by the configuration file within SASPAC, so that, in the PC environment, the former would have the extension .TXT, while the latter would have the extension .SYS, and each would reside in its relevant subdirectory.

Once loaded, the parent TXT file may be consigned to the archives, with the SYS file being held on-line, or on a medium available for easy retrieval.

5.2 Storage of data files in an economical and efficient manner

The size of the datasets will be dependent upon the area level, and whether they are SAS or LBS. Table 3.4 shows the size of the Census Offices' datasets in general terms, while Table 3.5 indicates the sizes of the datasets for a 'typical' English county.

It is estimated that the SAS dataset for the whole of Great Britain would be

Table 3.4 Sizes of Census Offices' datasets

Level	kbytes per area on file SAS	LBS
ED / OA	39	–
Ward / Postcode sector	44	98
Local authority / County / Scottish Region	75	167

of the order of 7 gigabytes when delivered by the Census Offices. The size of the SAS dataset at ED level for Hampshire (the English shire county with the greatest number of EDs) is about 130 megabytes.

One of the primary benefits of SASPAC is that the first task it undertakes is the compression of the datasets supplied by the Census Offices. On the fixed format files there is a very large amount of wasted space (as can be seen from Table 3.3), due to the counts not occupying the full width of the allocated field and also because, in many cases, the data are sparse, i.e. a large number of the counts are zero.

One way that SASPAC can reduce the file size is by stripping away these zero counts and unnecessary blanks. It is calculated that the system files will be approximately 16% of the size of the corresponding fixed format files for EDs and output areas. At the ward or postal sector and district level the scope for compression of files is reduced by the comparative lack of zero counts, and so at these levels the system files may be closer to 25% or 30% of the size of the original files (Table 3.6).

5.3 Allowance for easy access to the data files by persons who are not 'computer-literate'

The datasets for interrogation by users could be made available as copies of the data files supplied by the Census Offices. This would require the user to

(a) have knowledge of the content and construction of the data files;
(b) have detailed knowledge of the operating system relevant to the hardware platform on which the data files reside;
(c) have fairly detailed knowledge of a programming language to interrogate the data files.

Table 3.5 Sizes of Census Offices' datasets for a 'typical' English county

Level	Number of areas on file	File size in Mbytes SAS	LBS
ED	2000	78	–
Ward	200	9	20
Local authority and county	11	1	2

Table 3.6 Approximate sizes of SASPAC system files

Level	kbytes per area on file SAS	LBS
ED / OA	6	–
Ward / Postcode sector	10	16
Local authority / County / Scottish Region	23	39

Alternatively, they may be supplied as data files specific to SASPAC, where the software and data files together contain 'intelligence' relating to the content of the data files. This would require the user to

(a) have some knowledge of the content of the data files;
(b) have a basic knowledge of the operating system relevant to the hardware platform on which the data files reside;
(c) have basic knowledge of the method of operation of SASPAC.

5.4 Ability to produce individual or tabulated items of information as printed reports

When the Census Offices' datasets are loaded into SASPAC – a process which creates the system files – the software adds intelligence to the files such that each item of the dataset becomes uniquely referenced, thereby facilitating future interrogation of the datasets.This is done by allocating an identity consisting of the table number and location within a table to each variable found within the dataset. Such an operation makes use of the information contained within the Census Offices' User Guides 24 and 25, where count identifiers are allocated within tables.

Under this system, any variable within the SAS or LBS is identified by a code of seven or eight characters. In England, all variables are allocated seven character codes, but an eighth character is used to identify national (Scottish and Welsh) variations in some tables.

The variable identifier code is built up as follows: first character (alpha), dataset identifier (L / S); second and third characters (numeric), table identifier; fourth to seventh characters (numeric), location within table. To identify the national variations, a second alpha character (S or W) is used between the dataset identifier and the table identifier. Thus a code of S150001 would be used to identify a count in Table 15 in England, while in Scotland the similar count would be identified by SS150001. It should be noted that only where there is a national variant is the additional alpha character used.

Since the table identifier is built into the variable identifier, individual tables may be selected by reference to the appropriate part of the code.

However, as has been seen earlier, the datasets as provided by the Census Offices consist only of the counts or variables, and the textual information required to produce tabular output is not made available with the data. To enable users of the statistics to produce appropriate tables, SASPAC contains files (known as framework files) which contain the appropriate text for all tables, along with information as to which variables are to be output within the body of the table.

To produce tabular output, a user of SASPAC would require a command file of the form

```
INPUT SYSTEM FILE = S91AYEDH
INPUT FRAMEWORK FILE = NTSAS132
PRINT TABLES S01 TO S04
OUTPUT PRINT FILE = TABPRINT
END
FINISH
```

while to produce output consisting of individual variables the command file required would take the following form:

```
INPUT SYSTEM FILE = S91AYEDH
PRINT VARIABLES S010001 TO S010007
OUTPUT PRINT FILE = TABPRINT
END
FINISH
```

5.5 Ability to select areas for interrogation or output by area identifier

The naming convention adopted by the Census Offices for all areas in England and Wales is as it was in 1981. Each ED has a unique eight-character identifier which is constructed from the codes of its encompassing areas as follows:

02AYFC01	8-character enumeration district identifier
02AYFC	6-character electoral ward identifier
02AY	4-character local authority district identifier
02	2-character county identifier

The county identifiers are allocated within the range 1–56 across the whole of England and Wales such that each county has a unique two-character identifier. Similarly the local authority district identifiers are allocated within the range AA–TT such that each district has a unique identifier.

However, the ward identifiers always start at FA within a district, and the enumeration codes always start at 01 within a ward. It follows that to identify a local authority uniquely its two-character code is sufficient, while to identify a ward the local authority code must be attached to the appropriate ward code. Similarly, an ED must have its encompassing ward and local authority codes attached to be uniquely referenced.

The area referencing system in Scotland is similar, but it additionally recognizes the fact that the output areas used in Scotland are based on postcoded boundaries and that they are subdivisions of thc 1981 EDs. There is therefore the possibility of a ninth character being used where 1981 areas have been split. The other levels of the code are as in England and Wales, with output areas replacing EDs, and postcode sectors replacing wards. The higher level in Scotland is referred to as the Scottish Region.

The county or Scottish Region code is to some extent superfluous owing to the uniqueness of the local authority codes, and so it is perfectly in order to refer to six-character ED codes and to four-character ward codes.

SASPAC recognizes both the short and long codes for all areas, so that users may select particular areas of interest for further analysis or output. If there was a requirement to restrict the printed output to be produced from a file to selected areas, the command file required would contain an additional command as follows:

```
INPUT SYSTEM FILE = S91AYEDH
INCLUDE AYFC06 AYFC09 AYFG11
PRINT VARIABLES S010001 TO S010007
OUTPUT PRINT FILE = TABPRINT
END
FINISH
```

5.6 Ability to select areas for interrogation or output by value of a count or counts

Many interrogations undertaken by users of the census statistics will involve the analysis of areas where certain demographic characteristics may be more highly concentrated. For example, an education department may wish to identify areas with a high proportion of 0–4 year olds. To do this they will wish to isolate those areas where that proportion is greater than, say, 6%. The command file required for such a task would require first the calculation of the appropriate percentage and then selection of areas satisfying a criterion. This would be achieved by the following command file:

```
INPUT SYSTEM FILE = S91AYEDH
YOUNG=(S020008/S020001)*100
DESCRIBE VARIABLE YOUNG DP=2 DPSD=2 LABEL=% AGED 0 TO 4
SELECT IF YOUNG GT 6
PRINT VARIABLES WITH STATISTICS YOUNG
OUTPUT PRINT FILE = PRINTVAR
END
FINISH
```

Note that in this example a new variable (YOUNG) has been created from two existing census counts. S020008 represents the total number of 0–4 year olds, while S020001 represents the total usual resident population. Normal arithmetic conventions may be used to create any new variables from existing ones.

5.7 Ability to select areas for interrogation or output by distance from a fixed point

Each ED in England and Wales, and each output area in Scotland, has an associated Ordnance Survey grid reference (OSGR) which locates its centroid. In England and Wales this centroid has been allocated 'by eye' so that the centroid is population weighted, but in Scotland it is allocated by appropriate software following the digitization of boundaries.

The OSGR is of the form AB23456789, and SASPAC contains a conversion utility which translates this into a pair of co-ordinates (easting and northing) which represent distances in a horizontal and vertical direction from a fixed point of origin a little to the southwest of the Scilly Isles.

The availability of this OSGR, and the derived easting and northing, means that distances between zones, and distances of zones from a fixed point, may be calculated. This is done through use of Pythagoras's theorem such that the distance D in kilometres of a zone with easting E and northing N from a fixed point with easting e and northing n is calclulated as

D = (SQRT((E–e)**2 + (N–n)**2))/100

where the ** symbol is used to denote exponentiation and SQRT represents square root. The resolution in the OSGR provided by the Census Offices is to 10 m, and so division by 100 is necessary to translate the result into kilometres.

Combination of this distance calculation with printing with statistics and use of the IF–THEN–ELSE option within SASPAC allows users to create totals for areas lying within circles centred on a given point and with set radii. The following command file will calculate the distance of each ED on the input file from a fixed point (53300, 19650) and will create new variables which, depending on the distance of the ED from the point, will contain either zero or the total usual resident population of the ED.

```
INPUT SYSTEM FILE = '\SASPAC\SYSFILES\S91AYEDH.SYS'
DISTANCE=(SQRT((EASTING-53300)**2+(NORTHING-19650)**2))/100
DESCRIBE VARIABLE DISTANCE DP = 2 DPSD = 2 /
   LABEL=DISTANCE/ FROM ENFIELD TOWN
IF DISTANCE LE 1 THEN D=1
IF DISTANCE LE 1 THEN POP1=S010064 ELSE POP1=0
IF DISTANCE LE 2 AND DISTANCE GT 1 THEN D=2
IF DISTANCE LE 2 AND DISTANCE GT 1 THEN POP2=S010064 /
   ELSE POP2=0
IF DISTANCE LE 3 AND DISTANCE GT 2 THEN D=3
```

```
IF DISTANCE LE 3 AND DISTANCE GT 2 THEN POP3=S010064 /
   ELSE POP3=0
SELECT IF D LE 3
PRINT VARIABLES WITH STATISTICS DISTANCE S010064 D POP1/
   POP2 POP3
OUTPUT PRINT FILE = '\SASPAC\REPORT\CU4.PRN'
END
FINISH
```

In this example the value of S010064 – the total usually resident population – is only allocated to the appropriate new variable if the distance falls within the appropriate range.

It should be noted that the / character is used with two different meanings in this example. First, it is used in the creation of the variable representing distance to enable division, and second it is used on the next line in the description of the variable to indicate a continuation line. There is no conflict between the two, since SASPAC can infer from the context the appropriate meaning to allocate to the symbol.

5.8 Ability to aggregate areas to create new areas

The EDs defined by the Census Offices are primarily areas created for the collection of census statistics. They have no other administrative basis, and in themselves they are of little interest. However, their boundaries were drawn so that they took into consideration, as far as possible, the requirements of authorities for special areas. This means that more appropriate areas for the statistics, such as housing estates, development areas etc., may be created from the base statistics.

SASPAC assists users in the creation of new areas in one of two ways: through input of constituent areas as a string, or through use of a gazetteer file.

In the first of these options, users must define individually each of the existing areas which constitute a new zone. This constitution may be achieved by adding together areas of the same or different levels, or by subtracting areas from a higher level. The areas are identified by their area codes as discussed earlier. In the following example, a new zone is to be created by taking all EDs bar three within a ward and adding these to other enumeration districts. To undertake this task requires the use of two levels of input system files, and this is achieved through two INPUT SYSTEM FILE commands.

```
INPUT SYSTEM FILE = S91AYWDH
INPUT SYSTEM FILE = S91AYEDH
READ IN SERIES
NEW ZONE ID=AREA01 NAME = New zone 1
USING AREAS AYFC-AYFC02-AYFC08-AYFC09+AYFD12 /
   +AYFE14+AYFE17
```

```
OUTPUT SYSTEM FILE NAME = NEWFILE
END
FINISH
```

The user is not limited to the creation of a single new zone, and the pair of commands NEW ZONE and USING AREAS could be used as many times as were necessary to create the required number of new areas.

The other option for creation of new areas involves the use of a file which provides a full listing of the linkages between new and existing zones. The format of the gazetteer file is user defined so that as long as the file contains the relevant information relating to the existing and new zones, along with any necessary scaling factors, it does not matter what order they appear in, nor where on the record they lie.

The gazetteer file facility allows Scottish users of the software to easily recreate their 1981 ED information from the output area information. This is achieved by creating a file with the output area code in columns 1–9. By definition columns 1–8 of this file will contain the 1981 ED code. A command file such as the following will therefore automatically create a new system file containing new zones which are the 1981 EDs.

```
INPUT SYSTEM FILE = OAFILE
INPUT GAZETTEER FILE = SCOTGAZ /
   EXISTING ZONE COLS 1 TO 9 /
   NEW ZONE COLS 1 TO 8
OUTPUT SYSTEM FILE = EDFILE
END
FINISH
```

5.9 Ability to create new counts

Reference has already been made to the requirement to create new counts from the census variables, primarily to facilitate the creation of percentages or proportions. SASPAC allows users to calculate new variables through use of the normal arithmetic operators of addition, subtraction, multiplication and division. In addition, exponentiation and square root functions are available, and brackets may be used to force the priority of processing as defined by normal arithmetic logic.

Since many areas, especially at the ED level, will suffer from thresholding due to confidentiality restrictions, division by zero is a very real possibility. To avoid this occurrence, SASPAC includes an IF–THEN–ELSE facility which will allow users to specify division only if the divisor is greater than zero.

In the following example, a new variable representing the percentage of households renting from a local authority or new town is to be calculated only if the total number of households (S220001) is greater than zero.

```
INPUT SYSTEM FILE = S91AYEDH
IF S220001 GT 0 THEN LARENT=(S220325/S220001)*100 ELSE/
   LARENT = 0
DESCRIBE VARIABLE LARENT DP=2 DPSD=2 LABEL=% /
   Renting from LA
SELECT IF LARENT GT 60
PRINT VARIABLES LARENT S220325 S220001
OUTPUT PRINT FILE = LAPRINT
END
FINISH
```

In this example, an added refinement has been imposed on the output in that only areas where the percentage renting from a local authority or new town is greater than 60% will be passed to the output print file.

5.10 Ability to merge with other census or non-census data files

SASPAC has been primarily designed for the interrogation of the 1991 Census of SAS and LBS. However, it is not restricted to those datasets. It will in fact allow access to any dataset that is similar in construction to them, i.e. any dataset which consists of a geographically referenced set of counts which may or may not be arranged on a tabular basis but which has the same information available for all the geographic areas on the file.

This means that the 1981 statistics for small areas are accessible through SASPAC as are locally collected information from surveys or customer / client records. SASPAC allows users to define their datasets in such a way that they may be interpreted by SASPAC so that system files may be created from them. Once the system files are created, they may be used in exactly the same way as the system files created from the base census datasets.

5.11 Ability to rank areas on the basis of their demographic characteristics

When output is produced from SASPAC, the default order is for areas to be arranged in exactly the same order as they were on the input files. Normally this is in ascending alphabetic / numeric order of the area identifier. In certain instances, there will be a need for the output to be reordered so that the order will depend upon the value of some variable or variables.

For example, the following command file would produce output in which the areas would appear with the area with the highest percentage of households renting from a local authority or new town at the start and that with the lowest percentage at the end:

```
INPUT SYSTEM FILE = S91AYEDH
IF S220001 GT 0 THEN LARENT=(S220325/S220001)*100 ELSE/
```

```
   LARENT = 0
DESCRIBE VARIABLE LARENT DP=2 DPSD=2 LABEL=% /
   Renting from LA
SORT LARENT DESCENDING
PRINT VARIABLES LARENT S220325 S220001
OUTPUT PRINT FILE = LAPRINT
END
FINISH
```

5.12 Ability to export data to statistical, mapping or graphics packages, in a format which may be specific to the importing software or of a generalized format

SASPAC as an item of software was never intended to be a full statistical analysis tool which would allow users to undertake all their required interrogations and analyses within it. It was recognized at its conception that there were already in existence, and use, items of software which were more ideally suited to the statistical, graphical and mapping analysis of the census statistics.

What these software tools did not do was allow easy storage of and access to the mass of statistics produced by the Census Offices. In a way, SASPAC was seen as the interface between the user and the datasets – an interface which allowed easy retrieval, following basic manipulation, of required subsets of the statistics and then porting of these subsets into a more appropriate tool for further analyses and presentation.

The hooks by which SASPAC hangs data onto these other software tools are the interface file outputs which are available to users of the software. The particular hook to be used in any particular circumstance depends upon the needs of the receiving software, but there are sufficient hooks within SASPAC to satisfy the needs of virtually any other item of software.

The interface file output formats which are available within the PC environment are:

FORMATTED
DELIMITED
WKS
DBF
DIF

The first two of these are simple ASCII files, and could be used to import statistics to almost any other item of software. However, one of the other three may be more efficient in certain cases. For example, if the receiving software was EXCEL, then a WKS file would be used, and this would be achieved through use of a command file similar to the following. In this command file, the percentage of households renting from a local authority or new town, as already considered, is to be further analysed in EXCEL.

```
INPUT SYSTEM FILE = S91AYEDH
IF S220001 GT 0 THEN LARENT=(S220325/S220001)*100 ELSE/
   LARENT = 0
DESCRIBE VARIABLE LARENT DP=2 DPSD=2 LABEL=% /
   Renting from LA
SAVE VARIABLES ZONEID LARENT S220325 S220001
OUTPUT WKS FILE = LARENT
END
FINISH
```

In this example, the variable ZONEID is specifically named as a variable to be written to the WKS file, whereas in previous examples no mention was made of it. This is because the area identifier (ZONEID) is automatically written to a print file, while for interface files there are no default output variables.

6 The future

SASPAC is now in use at more than 300 organizations, and the number of users is very much greater than this since the method of licensing for most organizations refers to site licensing.

This means that within a local authority, for example, not only will the software be in use within the main census user department – probably the Planning Department – but it will also be in use in other departments such as Housing, Social Services etc. Additionally, the software may well be in use on a range of platforms, so that it is possible for a single organization to be using SASPAC on a mainframe, a UNIX platform and a PC running under MS-DOS.

This wide range of usage means that a significant pool of expertise is being developed which in turn means that ongoing support for the software is guaranteed, and this support will become apparent in the enhancements and variations of the software which will appear.

Already the software has been enhanced to allow users to access the Census Offices' ED-to-postcode directory and to use it in the analysis of their own local postcoded information or to create postcode-based areas of census statistics. Other enhancements will take account of changes in technology since the beginning of the development of SASPAC. One of these addresses the growth of graphical user interfaces (GUI) in recent years.

At its inception in 1987, SASPAC was seen as an item of software which adhered to the 1981 standard for accessing the statistics from the Census of Population. This meant that it was to be designed as batch-oriented software primarily designed to operate in a mainframe environment. At that time, only a few users saw any potential in developing a microcomputer version of the software, despite promptings from the project management. It was feared that anything developed to run on a microcomputer would be a severely downgraded version of the software.

It was only when Northern Software Technology, in conjunction with Greater Manchester Research, successfully ported the 1981 code to operate on a microcomputer without any loss of facilities compared with the mainframe version that it became clear that SASPAC would have to be developed for use in the microcomputer environment.

By that time, though, the foundations of the development had been laid, and the microcomputer and mainframe versions of the software were seen as the same development. The only concession to the fact that in a microcomputer environment the processor was solely devoted to the user was that a front-end menu-driven interface was developed which made it easier for novice users to produce command files.

The menu-driven interface (SASMEN) was developed to be operational purely in a DOS environment, although the needs of UNIX environments were considered during its production. The result is that it has now been ported to UNIX environments.

While the user was accessing SASMEN, no other software could be utilized, and therefore there was no way in which the user could swap between software. For example, users could not have a print file open at the same time as a word processing package with a view to copying and pasting from one to the other.

With the advent of GUI environments such as WINDOWS, users of microcomputers came to enjoy the advantages of having greater control and power over their ability to 'mix and match' with different software. Additionally they were able to access many items of software without being required to have any great knowledge of the operating system. This last feature was, to a great extent, replicated by SASMEN.

An early re-release of SASPAC provided a version which would operate perfectly well as a DOS application under WINDOWS. By this method, the SASMEN screen became a window instead of occupying the whole screen, and users were able to utilize some of the facilities available under WINDOWS. However, in allowing users to enjoy all the benefits of WINDOWS, a full WINDOWS application would need to be developed.

The positive responses from within the SASPAC user community to the availability of software which was totally compatible with WINDOWS gave a clear indication that further development work on producing a WINDOWS application would be especially welcomed. It was in response to such demands that the development of a GUI version of SASPAC is under investigation.

Since the development and future management of SASPAC remains firmly in the hands of the users, the project itself is responsive to changing user needs, and this will continue through the life of the product.

Further information regarding SASPAC and its availability may be obtained from

The SASPAC Help Desk
London Research Centre
81 Black Prince Road — Tel 0171 627 9693 / 9696
London SE1 7SZ — Fax 0171 627 9606

4

Dealing with census geography: principles, practices and possibilities

M Coombes

Editor's note

The census is a spatial dataset, unavoidably so. Census geography is therefore of critical importance and it is one of the principal areas in which major deficiencies still exist in the census. This chapter provides a detailed discussion of the principles and possibilities. It is designed to help users cope with the 1991 Census, to develop a better understanding of the problems and to inform debate about future possibilities. The reader might wish to link this chapter with the geography section of Chapter 2, the GIS examples in Chapter 5 and the analysis of census change in Chapter 10.

Census geography is critical to the value of the data from any census. For example, the 37 recommendations of a multidisciplinary team (Marsh *et al.* 1988) as to social scientists' needs from the 1991 Census included nine which were exclusively or partially on census geography. Yet the issues involved are rarely about geography for its own sake, such as a call for census data on environmental features like the number of trees per house or (as in the Newcastle City survey of 1986) data on where the household does most of its shopping. On the contrary, many issues of census geography are concerned with 'taking the geography out' of the data, in the sense that the users' freedom to access and manipulate the census should not be constrained by the areas for which the data are made available. This chapter is therefore *not* centred on geographical issues for their own sake nor primarily on the value of census data for various geographical analyses. The aim here is to help all census users to understand the importance of census geography and its implications for the usability of the data. The first section of the chapter briefly explains the role of geography in most modern censuses; this is followed by a short explanation of the principles currently underlying census geography in Britain. The third section then describes how these principles have been applied in 1991, first in England and Wales, and then in Scotland and Northern Ireland. Next, the implications for users are indicated, and the ways in which users can deal with these issues are outlined. The final section briefly considers some possible future developments in census geography.

1 What's so geographical about the census?

Population census information is collected about people – about individuals and their households and housing. The two principal organizing principles are time and space, as shown by the fact that this book refers to the *1991* Census of *Britain*. Many of the key debates over census strategy revolve around these two dimensions. For example, there is pressure from Eurostat for the census data from all European Union countries to be more comparable. To make our census data less distinctively British would be to emphasize space – comparison with other countries – at the expense of time, because the data would probably become less comparable with data from earlier British censuses as a result.

The dilemma of comparability through time versus comparability across space will crop up again in several different contexts in this chapter. Another aspect of the link between time and space is the way constraints are imposed on the current geography of census-taking as a result of the need for data on *change* imposing a limit on the extent to which 1991 practice can differ from that of 1981 (or earlier). This constraint applies most obviously to the questions which are asked and the variables they generate, but it applies equally to the areas used for reporting data, so comparability through time looms large among the principles of census geography. Of course, these comments may not apply so strongly to less historically minded countries such as the USA where innovative approaches may be more readily adopted (Bureau of the Census 1989), but this chapter is exclusively concerned with the current practice – and practical opportunities – within the UK.

It may not be immediately obvious just how critical a role geography plays in shaping census outputs. The list of volumes published, for example, is dominated by the multi-topic volumes which refer to a specific area such as a county. Perhaps geography has become such an ingrained part of the census that no alternative organizing principle is even considered. Yet it *would* be possible for the long list of area-based census volume to be replaced by outputs which are organized on a very detailed occupation or class breakdown, for example. On this scenario the national single-topic volume on social structure would be replaced by a whole series of volumes which each cover just one specific socio-occupational group: each would have page after page of cross-tabulations of other variables for that group of the nation (rather than for one area of the country, as it is in the current system). The time dimension could then contribute data not on *geographical* migration (from a question about address one year previously) but instead on *social* mobility (having asked about status a year ago). Whereas the emphasis upon space leads to complex questions over where to allocate people who were not at their usual address on census night, an emphasis on social position would have to devote considerable energy to dealing with the ambiguous allocation of people of very different status in the same household – let alone those who are retired, unemployed or being retrained. The point being made here is simply that there is nothing inevitable about organizing data by its spatial dimension, and the exact methods used in any census for this spatial coding are all the more open to debate.

For the purpose of this chapter, then, issues of census geography are primarily rooted in the ways in which the British census is currently organized. Geography is so central to the organization of the census that the chapter needs to start by tracing the principles of British practice back to the key census policy issue of confidentiality. Only when these principles are recognized is it possible to understand the British approach to the geography of census taking and reporting – and what it means for the user.

2 Principles underlying census geography

Privacy may be something of a British obsession in general, but confidentiality is a concern of census-takers in most countries. For example, the widespread public disbelief in the confidentiality of computerized census files in West Germany led to their equivalent of the British 1981 census being abandoned. The first 'line of defence' in the British census is that names and addresses are not even entered onto the computer files (HM Government 1988). However, full postcodes *are* now entered onto the files, but these codes are not accessible to users because some households could be uniquely identifiable from tabulations by individual full postcodes. The simple fact is that location is the only census variable which has such detailed coding: there are nearly 1.5 million different postcodes. By way of contrast, the occupation coding identifies the next most detailed variable in the census, with less than 500 categories. Even if many more could be recognized, only the most exceptional categories would identify distinct individuals. For example, an occupation coding would have to be extraordinarily detailed to identify 'head of state' separately – but Buckingham Palace is sufficiently isolated *spatially* for it not only to have a distinct postcode but also for its census enumeration district (ED) to stand apart from others in central London (as shown in Fig. 6.6 of Chapter 6). Thus the geography of the census is potentially the way in which 'the genie can get out of the bottle' so far as releasing confidential data. The user, of course, is concerned with the other side of the coin: the ways in which EDs – and census geography generally – thus become the framework for controlling the ways in which the data can be assessed.

It is impossible to exaggerate the importance of the confidentiality issue in shaping census geography. The size of area for which any dataset is released is entirely determined by the possibility of identifying individuals. The minimum size of area has to be increased when there is to be an increase in the number of variables which are to be made available (because of the increased potential risk of identifying individuals). The trade-off between numbers of areas and numbers of variables for 1991 Census datasets is illustrated in Table 4.1 (fuller information on the areas used for different census outputs is provided in OPCS and GRO(S)

Table 4.1 1991 Census reporting units in England

Building block areas	**Approximate number of areas**	**Approximate number of counts**	**Output for which this is the minimum area**
Postcode units	1 250 000	1	Household count
Enumeration districts (EDs)	110 000	10 000	Small Area Statistics (SAS)
Groups of EDs/postcodes	Not fixed	600[a]	Special Workplace Statistics (SWS)
Wards	8 000	90[a]	Special Migration Statistics (SMS)
'Super EDs'	See text	20 000	Local Base Statistics
Districts	350	Not known	Topic statistics (some)
Groups of districts	250	50[b]	Sample of Anonymized Records (individual records)
Counties	50	Not known	Topic Statistics (more variables)
Regions	10	40[b]	Sample of Anonymized Records (household records)
Country	1	Not known	Topic statistics (remaining tables)

Notes: [a]There are also the statistics relating to the flow – which is zero in the vast majority of cases – to or from any other zone in this set of areas; thus the 250 statistics on each flow in the SWS could be seen as producing a dataset of 2,000,000 variables (250 × 8000 other wards, as origins/destinations) for *each* ward in a full set of ward-to-ward SWS flow matrices!
[b]These are the variables reported for each record; arguably this number should be multiplied by the number of records in the area to provide a number of 'data items' which is comparable with the number of counts in the other lines in the table.

(1992), while Denham (1993) sets out, particularly in his Fig. 3.1, the relationship between these sets of areas). For example, twice as many counts are included in the Local Base Statistics (LBS) as in the Small Area Statistics (SAS). EDs are the basic unit for SAS, but almost all EDs will be too small for them to be used for publishing LBS. These cross-tabulations will include many cells with just one person or household possessing a distinctive combination of characteristics. The new Samples of Anonymized Records (SAR), on the other hand, are made up entirely of individual observations, so the minimum size of population (for areas used to locate the home location of individual records) was set at 120,000.

Geographical aggregation is so inseparable from the issue of confidentiality that there is a particular term – 'differencing' – for the possible problem arising from publishing data for slightly different small areas (OPCS and GRO(S) 1988). The concern is that calculating the difference between the statistics for two areas would effectively reveal the data for the small area which represents the difference between the two boundaries. An example will illustrate the issue. In the planning stage for the 1991 Census, there was a commitment to report SAS for 'Pseudo EDs' (OPCS and GRO(S) 1988). These areas were defined as the nearest equivalent to EDs which could be created by grouping whole postcode units. In many cases the boundary between an ED and its equivalent Pseudo ED is just one or two houses. Differencing the data for the two areas would allow full SAS to be generated for these very small areas, clearly contravening the basic principles of the trade-off between area detail and data detail. In retrospect, it is scarcely credible that OPCS could ever have considered so clear a contravention of their long-standing vigilance over differencing.

The standard response to the danger of differencing is to ensure that each level of unit for which data are published fits within a hierarchy. The point of the hierarchy is that a unit at any level is a grouping of the smaller areas at the lower levels. The result is that any area which lies between officially recognized boundaries, whether these boundaries are at the same or different levels, must be made up of whole units at the lowest level. It is because of this constraint which is imposed on the availability of data at higher levels that it is essential to be concerned about the definition of the lowest level units – the building block areas – for which any dataset is made available. A consequence of the hierarchical principle is that there will be pressure to publish data for the smallest possible units to meet the current confidentiality constraints. This constraint ensures that, when aggregated, these building blocks can fit as closely as possible to the boundary of other areas. The disadvantage of this approach for the user is that the outcome of the attempt to identify the smallest feasible building block areas, for any dataset, is likely to be a unique set of boundaries. This is the reason why the smallest areas for reporting SAS do not match to the areas for reporting other census datasets, or the areas for reporting parallel data from other sources (e.g. unemployment statistics), or indeed those EDs used for reporting the SAS from earlier censuses.

To sum up, census geography exemplifies key principles of the Government Statistics Service (GSS). The overriding concern with confidentiality determines the minimum size of building block areas. The GSS anxiety over differencing imposes the hierarchical rule on the options for higher order units. This in turn puts pressure on the definition of building blocks so that they are as small as is allowed by the confidentiality constraints at that time. The consequence is that each set of building blocks tends to be unique to that particular census, with severe disadvantages for the study of change (which requires compatibility with earlier censuses) or of complex issues such as deprivation (which require the merging of census and other datasets). It is now time to turn to the 1991 Census in more detail to identify how these GSS principles have been put into practice.

3 1991 Census geography

The main features of 1991 Census geography are outlined in this section. The first part identifies the basic geographical data which are built into the 1991 Census. The second part sets out the principal implications for census outputs, and the section ends by distinguishing the different approaches to the geography of census outputs which have been taken in England and Wales, Scotland and Northern Ireland. Anyone who is unfamiliar with the areas used for 1991 Census output across Britain may be helped by studying Fig. 3.1 in Denham (1993).

3.1 The geographical coding of census data

The full postcode is the finest detail location coding of each census record on the 1991 Census computer files. In addition, the ED code is added to the record. One important point to note at the outset is that this information was recorded by the census enumerator, or was later captured by the Census Offices' coders, rather than being left to the respondent. As a result, the location coding should generate substantially more accurate data than much of the other detailed census data, which relies upon the self-completion sections of the form. The 1981 post-enumeration validation survey, for example, showed that most of the self-completed data included substantial levels of error at a very detailed level of breakdown (Britton and Birch 1985). This can be contrasted with the lower error levels which were considered unsatisfactory in the far more detailed spatial coding of the 1981 data (Neffendorf and Hamilton 1987). Indeed, the locational data are considered quite unsatisfactory if their error levels exceed 1% (e.g. the initial release of 1991 ED grid references had to be exhaustively corrected when just 1 in 50 was found to be inaccurate).

The other point to stress at the outset is that few people in the 1991 Census are associated *only* with the location where they completed the census form. All people who on census night were not at their usual address also had their usual residence's location captured, so that they could be assigned to either area's data (depending upon which census 'base' the analysis uses). Similarly, students and schoolchildren who live away from home during term time had this address captured too so that an area's population could be counted using either base. Anyone who had moved in the 12 months preceding census night (about 1 in 10 of the population) also had their address a year before captured. These data form the basis for the migration data which also use current address to create a matrix showing where people have moved to and from. The final type of location which is coded affects well over a third of all people, because it is the workplace of those who are in employment. Only 10% of these records are coded, but this is sufficient to provide another matrix of movement which uses two location codings – the journey-to-work dataset.

For all these 'remote' addresses, the location is coded by postcode. The place of enumeration is also postcoded, but it is also identified by the ED of which it is part. The size of EDs varies according to the expected difficulty of travelling between addresses and of obtaining responses, because each ED is designed to present a similar effective workload for the enumerator. A typical urban ED covers a few hundred people, but a typical rural ED might include less than a hundred. Large institutions like hospitals or prisons are created as special EDs (SEDs), with other distinctive EDs created to cover people who were at sea on census night. More details of the way in which EDs are defined, with maps of some examples (including the contrasting system in Scotland), can be found in Clark and Thomas (1990).

The census-taking procedures only provide guidelines on roughly how many EDs a district will be divided into: experienced census administrators will also recognize how the area might be efficiently divided to minimize enumerators' travel times. Around these broad guidelines, however, there are very many options as to the precise alignment of ED boundaries. Consequently, it is not too difficult to ensure that every statutory boundary for which SAS must be available is recognized by an ED boundary. However, those parishes whose populations are too small for SAS to be published for them individually are grouped together in the EDs used for census output.

Even given the constraints of matching statutory boundaries, there is still considerable flexibility in the detailed drawing up of ED boundaries. As a result, the Census Offices allow each local authority (LA) to participate in the process so that they can obtain SAS accurately for any of their own internal boundaries (e.g. of housing estates). For the 1991 Census, a small number of English LAs chose to align EDs with postcode boundaries. The crucial points which arise for the census user from these factors are that in England and Wales

- the ED boundaries in any LA may have been defined to meet any of several different criteria, so may or may not allow SAS to be compiled from them by accurately grouping to match any other set of boundaries (e.g. postcode sectors);
- most 1991 ED boundaries, in any given area, are different to a greater or lesser extent from those in 1981 and 1971; and
- the administrative criteria for ED planning were applied differently in different LAs, so it is not possible to create consistently comparable definitions of finely detailed areas across the whole country.

These implications can be seen as arising from the lack of a 'standard' set of small areas for statistical purposes. In the final section of this chapter we consider whether there is any realistic alternative.

3.2 The geography of census output

The administrative details of census-taking would be irrelevant to the census user if the data reporting took the postcode as the universal building block area. This is the case in Scotland, as will be discussed more fully later. Data for England and Wales, however, continue to use the ED as the building block for SAS – thus areas for data output are restricted by the boundaries designed for data input, and of course by the principles of census geography which were outlined earlier.

Table 4.1 provides the basic information on which areas are the building blocks for the various datasets from the 1991 Census. Apart from EDs, most of these sets of areas are familiar units such as LAs. The key exception is the building blocks for the LBS. The minimum size requirement is too large for almost all EDs, and also for wards in many rural areas. The implication is that a set of 'super EDs' is needed, grouping wards in sparsely populated areas and splitting those urban wards with very large populations. A 'feel' for this problem can be obtained from the ward and ED maps given in OPCS and GRO(S) (1991): a tremendous loss of detail would result if moving from the ED scale meant having to make do with ward level data (and this loss of detail is far greater in metropolitan areas where wards have far larger populations). Surprisingly, the OPCS have not identified these 'super EDs' in the same way as they defined EDs. Instead they have allowed anyone interested to define these building blocks in any LA, as long as no-one else has done so previously. It is to avoid possible differencing that the first set of 'super EDs' identified in any LA must become that LA's definitive LBS building block areas. This policy has clearly led to an extreme version of the three points made above in relation to EDs – *inconsistency* in definition between LAs, *instability* from one census to another, and *implausibility* as a basis for identifying other areas for which census data will be needed. These are three crucial issues for many data users when considering the definition of building blocks.

This is not the place to detail the precise set of building blocks for which each census dataset is to be published. Readers requiring more detail than that which is given in Table 4.1 are referred to the relevant User Guides or to the Definitions volume (OPCS and GRO(S) 1992). The principles of the GSS approach to confidentiality have been re-emphasized in the discussions leading to the newest dataset, the SAR. Marsh *et al.* (1991) had to demonstrate the level of risk to confidentiality which is associated with different possible minimum sizes of area for location coding the individual data. The other census dataset which includes individual records is the Longitudinal Study (LS), and this is not published at all because confidentiality is ensured by detailed checks on every table produced from the raw data. The scale of this task must, in principle, rise inexorably with each new set of output, in order to ensure that no new table is sufficiently similar to the ever increasing number of previous tables (so compromising confidentiality through the possibility of differencing).

This problem was the fundamental objection to the proposed innovative software which might allow users to access raw census data directly (Rhind and Higgins 1988). Although the individual output could be readily checked against confidentiality constraints, the system would also have to check the danger of differencing by imposing the same constraints on the hypothetical outputs which could be generated by combining the new output with (combinations of) every other output which the system had ever produced previously. In short, the flexibility offered by the proposed new access system directly contradicted those principles of census geography which led to fixed building blocks, and to the hierarchical aggregation of these to prevent differencing. Of course, 'Barnardization' could be seen as some protection in all these questions of confidentiality, but this would require it to be applied separately to each accessed dataset – which would often lead to the embarrassing result of larger areas having lower values than small areas which they encompass.

3.3 Contrasts within the United Kingdom

Do these principles inevitably lead to the use of EDs as the basic census building block areas? The experience in Scotland shows that this is not the case. For the 1991 Census there, input and output areas have been entirely disentangled. Output areas (OAs) have been defined to be, in effect, the smallest possible areas for reporting SAS. The constraint of matching statutory areas remains, but ED boundaries are ignored because they are defined purely for census-taking and are not relevant to users' needs. Consequently, the OAs were defined to maximize their utility for users in general, and the solution was to align them with postcode geography. Two great advantages of this policy are that census data can be readily merged with data from all the non-census sources which are increasingly based on postcode geography (Raper *et al.* 1992), and also that change data are more readily calculated. The latter advantage follows from the Scottish experiment in 1981 with the use of a postcode base for census output. Postcodes remain relatively stable compared with other areas smaller than LAs, such as wards. 1991 SAS can now be aggregated readily to the postcode-based areas for which 1981 SAS are already available. All this has only been made possible by investing more in census processing for Scotland than for England and Wales. In fact, the initial investment for the 1981 Census extended so far as recoding the 1971 SAS so that these data too became available for postcode-based areas. Scotland's policy of non-minimal investment has been maintained for 1991 by using geographic information system (GIS) techniques to ensure that OAs offer the maximum number of areas which pass the SAS size threshold. It has also ensured that all OAs *do* pass the threshold, so Scotland has no equivalent of the special EDs in England and Wales (i.e. small areas whose populations are too small for their SAS data to be published at the ED level).

Comparability of 1971–81–91 data has also been provided for by the census in Northern Ireland. The basic area unit used there is the grid square – the stable small area unit which was a forerunner of postcode geography as the candidate 'standard' area (CRU *et al.* 1980). Unfortunately, the population size of some 1-km squares is small, so the dataset available for these units has barely a tenth of the counts of the SAS. Grid squares also suffer from the disadvantage of not being used in many other datasets, thus inhibiting the merging of census with other datasets, and of being excessively arbitrary. Clearly, grid squares are inherently arbitrary in their 'boundaries' and so are unsatisfactory as building blocks to identify the divisions between areas such as housing estates. The tragic 'green line' which divides the communities of Belfast is an obvious example of a border which needs to be recognized with far more precision than is possible using grid squares (even the 100-m squares available in urban areas).

The 1991 Census data for Scotland and Northern Ireland, then, provide intriguing contrasts to the position in England and Wales. All three countries adhere to the GSS policy of protecting confidentiality by only releasing data for hierarchical aggregates of carefully chosen building block areas (apart from the lack of 'fit' of grid squares into LAs in Northern Ireland). It is the practice of OPCS which is distinctive, because no single policy of ED definitions is applied across the whole of England and Wales. In contrast, census users north of the border can be confident that OAs have a consistent basis to their definition throughout the whole of Scotland, although of course these areas are not readily comparable with EDs south of the border or with Northern Ireland's grid squares. The census user in England and Wales is also the least well served in terms of consistency of small area definitions through time, so that compiling a database on change at the small area level is a major task. However, the Northern Ireland census user is offered by far the lowest volume of small area data (although an academic research project is creating a set of areas similar to EDs).

Perhaps the most intriguing feature to have arisen from this discussion has been how little convergence there has been in census policies in the three countries. After the aborted proposals for OPCS to extend to England and Wales in 1991 the Scottish postcoding of its 1981 Census (OPCS and GRO(S) 1985), the theme became to 'use similar procedures' as in 1981 (OPCS 1987). In practice, this has largely meant fossilizing the distinctive approaches to census geography in each country. This incompatibility – compounded by the inconsistency of ED and 'super ED' definitions within England and Wales – is ironic in an era when the censuses of all European Union countries are to move towards greater comparability.

4 Implications and opportunities

In this main section of the chapter, concerns over the usability of census data are first codified as seven 'tests' by which to evaluate any approach to census geography. Second, the different approaches to be found in the 1991 Census are evaluated. Next, the user is alerted to problems and opportunities for comparing 1991 Census data with earlier censuses, and then with non-census data. The final discussion focuses on the geography of 'real world' areas, such as settlements and neighbourhoods.

4.1 What are the users' needs?

Users' assessments of 1991 Census geography will clearly depend entirely on the particular uses to which they wish to put the data. Even so a number of questions are likely to occur to many different users, and some of these questions have already been indicated in the preceding discussion.

1. Are the building blocks the smallest that the confidentiality restrictions deem to be possible (to allow maximum flexibility of aggregation)?
2. Is each of the areas in a set of building blocks, or other set of areas, defined on a consistent basis across the country?
3. Does this set of areas represent (parts of) 'real world' entities, such as settlements, which can thus be recognized using these boundaries?
4. Does the set of areas allow comparison with previous census(es) at this level, or for some minimal grouping of areas to create consistent boundaries?

The increasing use of GIS techniques for handling census data has prompted other questions which, though not irrelevant to other users, are particularly important to GIS users.

5. Does the set of areas cover the whole of the country without leaving any locations whose data are too sparse to allow them to be published?
6. Are the boundaries of these areas available in digital form?
7. Can these areas be readily and accurately linked by their location coding to the areas used in many non-census datasets?

These seven tests represent a user's benchmark against which to evaluate any approach to the geography of census output.

4.2 The three approaches compared

Scottish 1991 Census data users can be assured that their census geography passes all these seven tests. Most of the points have been made in the previous section. The OAs are consistently defined (test 2) to maximize the number of areas allowable (test 1) while covering the whole of Scotland (test 5). OAs are based on the widely used postcode units (test 7) which were also the basis for 1981 SAS and 1971 RSAS (test 4). Their definition was undertaken with a GIS using digital boundaries (test 6) which are then analysed to define which OAs cover each of Scotland's built-up areas (test 3). The GIS can also help to deal with boundary changes by cross-referencing an area as being part of one LA at one time and another at a later date. Higher level areas are groupings of OAs, so that problems only tend to arise where two such groupings do not 'nest' into each other hierarchically. For example, the built-up areas may have to have two definitions, one being the original OA-based definition (for SAS analyses) and the other being based on the OA groupings which are the smallest areas for LBS (the Scottish equivalents of 'super EDs'). However, this is an inconvenience which is inevitable in this context and so is no fault in the Scottish approach to census geography.

What about the Northern Ireland approach based on grid squares? The advantages of grid squares certainly include digital boundaries (test 6), and they have been used for previous censuses (test 4). However, the earlier discussion made clear that grid squares are unsatisfactory in most other respects: they are not the smallest units which are possible in urban areas (test 1), nor are they large enough to avoid data suppression in rural areas (test 5) – and although they are certainly consistently defined (test 2), geometric consistency is scarcely a benefit for the analysis of census topics (although it can ease some of the technical obstacles in the way of data visualization (Tufte 1990) which can be a vital first step towards analysis). In fact, this consistency can be over-stated since coastal and border squares are less than full size (and the effect of the grid on the curved surface of the earth produces areas in northern Scotland which are not square anyway). It is even more obvious that grid squares do not match up to physical realities such as settlements (test 3) and that very few other data are available for grid squares (test 7).

More users will be accessing data on England and Wales than on either of the other countries. Once again, the earlier discussion has covered the main features of census geography based, in this case, on (super) EDs. This approach can fare no better than the Scottish one in matching a two-tier system into fixed boundaries such as those of settlements (test 3). Unfortunately, it is less successful in meeting all the other six tests – although the lack of digital ED boundaries (test 6) in previous censuses has been resolved, apart from uncertainties over the location of some SEDs.

Are the problems users face with the England and Wales data as intractable as those posed by the Northern Ireland dataset? Users can do little about the lost opportunities for more detailed LBS areas (test 1), or the unavailable SAS for suppressed EDs (test 5). The remaining issues, however, might in principle be addressed by further grouping of the published data:

- to match the areas used for earlier censuses (test 4);
- to match areas used for other data altogether (test 7); or
- to make the areas more consistent across the country (test 2).

These three points will now be considered in more detail. Some of the more fundamental issues raised cover problems which are faced by even the relatively advantaged census users in Scotland.

4.3 Census geography and the analysis of change

Table 4.1 shows that for some 1991 Census outputs the district is the smallest area of publication. This may seem to be an unproblematic starting point for the matching of the 1991 Census with data from earlier censuses. Although local government reorganization is once again getting under way, this has not yet affected the 1991 Census. Superficially, then, the 1991 districts provide a consistent 'geography' back to 1981 – and indeed the 1971 data were re-released for this set of areas (which were brought in by the mid-1970s local government reorganizations). However, piecemeal adjustment to district boundaries through the 1980s 'moved' over 1% of Britain's population. County reports always include detailed specification of LA boundary changes: it is essential to check these and, where there has been a change, to seek to reallocate the LA's building block areas in *one* of the censuses so that it more closely matches the other census's definition of the area. Clearly, not to do so can generate entirely spurious radical changes in an LA's population size (e.g. a surprising 'fall' in South Oxfordshire's population, which is purely due to the transfer to Oxford City of an area housing over 10,000 people). It may be less obvious that an area's profile (e.g. unemployment rate) may be affected almost as much. This is because the areas transferred tend to have been distinct from the other parts of their former LA; consequently the profile of the 'donor' LA in particular may be substantially different without the transferred area.

The principal means of dealing with change in the definition of areas at one level, then, is to regroup the areas at a lower level to make the boundaries match. How is this to be done? In the case of LAs, the number of boundary changes are relatively few and are well documented. Consequently it is fairly straightforward to implement a manual adjustment to 'look up' files which indicate the grouping of lower level areas to LAs. The position is less encouraging for smaller areas (although OPCS can supply lists of ward and parish changes between censuses in England and Wales). Inspection of maps is one method to try matching the boundaries from different censuses, but this is scarcely a feasible solution except for small study areas – especially since the maps are far from easy to access or, indeed, read.

The increasing availability of GISs can automate this process in a number of ways (Martin 1991), the most familiar of which is probably Point in Polygon (PIP). One census's boundaries (polygons) are used as 'targets' into which the centroids (points) of the other census's areas are allocated. An alternative solution, which does not need a GIS, uses centroids rather than boundaries for the 'target' areas and simply finds each area's nearest 'target' area from the other census. It is crucial to remember that any process of this kind only aims to be a 'best fit' and so introduces more error into any analysis of change. The crucial safeguard is to ensure that the analysis takes place at a higher level than that of the areas which were used as input to the 'best fit' procedure. For example, 1981 ED centroids could be matched as nearly as possible to 1991 ED centroids, but the merged dataset should then only be analysed for groups of EDs (such as 'super EDs', wards or postcode sectors) so that the majority of the error is cancelled out by the aggregation process. The same outcome could be achieved by taking the polygons of the higher level 1991 areas and allocating the 1981 EDs to them by a PIP using a GIS.

4.4 Linkage to non-census data

The increasing availability of GIS is leading to a more flexible approach to the problems of linking census geography to other datasets' areas. For example, the academic community is purchasing 1991 ED polygons and centroids to support a strategy in which each researcher can devise the most appropriate linkage between sets of areas on a project-by-project basis. This strategy presumes that GIS competence is sufficiently widely available for each researcher to be able to

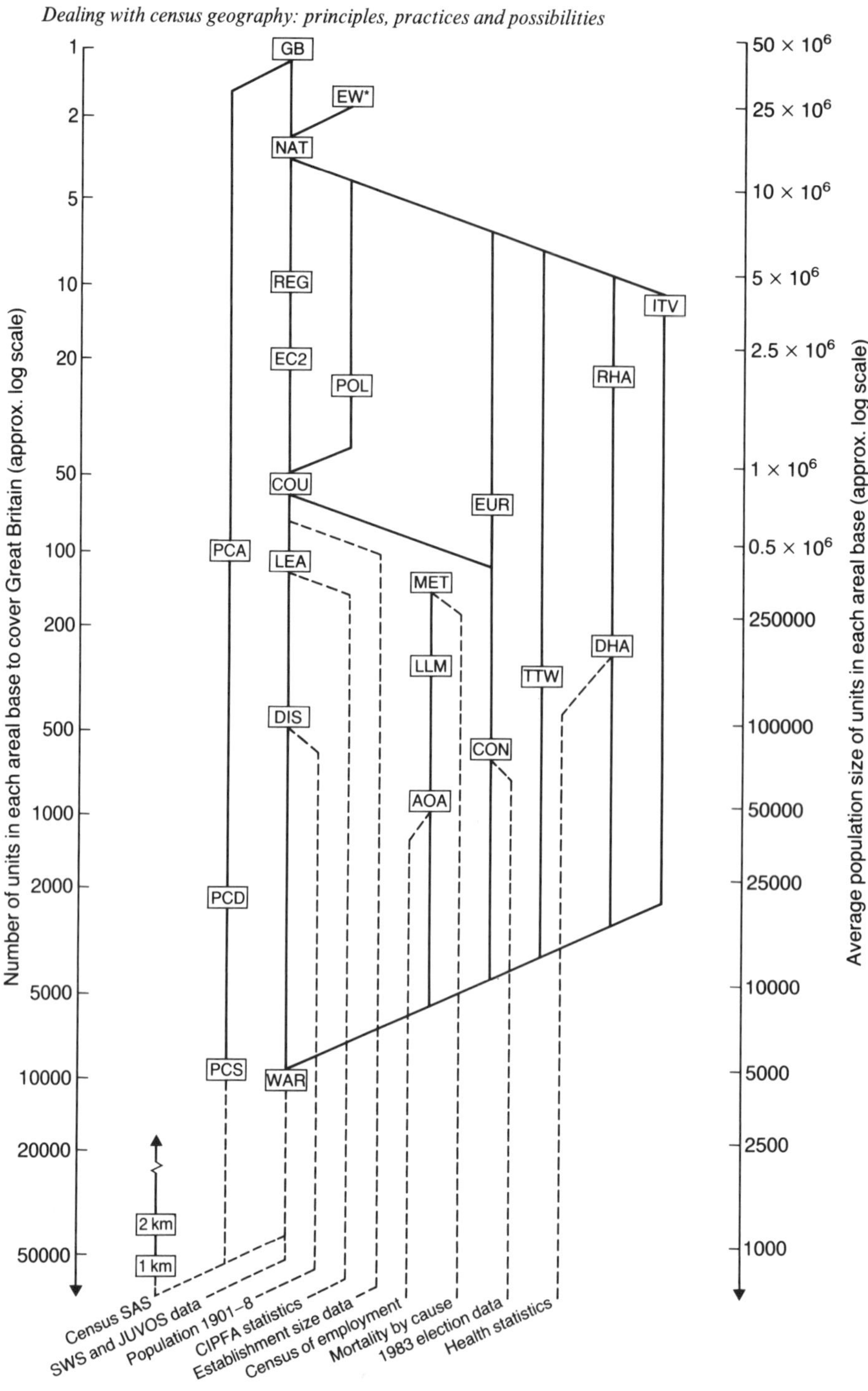

Fig 4.1 Areal bases, aggregations and datasets: a sample (see facing page for key). After Owen *et al.* 1986. Reproduced with the permission of the Transactions of the Institute of British Geographers.

manipulate the data in the way which best suits each project. The previous philosophy was based on the scarcity of expertise and techniques for manipulating small area data: the strategy was then to create a few 'centres of excellence' which would address the most frequently faced problems and make the solutions available to others at a centralized location. Some 'look up' files were thus deposited in the ESRC Archive at Essex University, e.g. the Super Profile neighbourhood classification of 1981 EDs (Charlton *et al.* 1985). More generally, the NOMIS geographic database retrieval facility at Durham University (Townsend *et al.* 1986) has provided many academics with a wide range of 1981 Census output areas (and now provides 1991 data for wards and larger areas). NOMIS also offers access to many labour market databases, although a basic spreadsheet is the only form of analysis provided for statistics from different datasets. Analysis functions are even more limited within the BBC Domesday Videodisc (Owen *et al.* 1986), which is another means of access to 1981 Census data for a variety of different areas (also presented alongside other datasets).

Figure 4.1 shows the set of links – each of which involved a 'look up' file – which determined the types of areas for which each dataset was made available on Domesday (Owen *et al.* 1986). The important point about Fig. 4.1 is that the linkages which were implemented had been checked against minimum standards of boundary matching – any user could then access data for a range of different types of area, with confidence that they would not be depending on a 'best fit' which was not sufficiently accurate. The current strategy, on the other hand,

Key to Fig. 4.1

AOA	Employment Office Areas (amalgamated to create a stable set for time series 1971–81)
CON	Parliamentary constituencies (as presently defined)
COU	Counties/Scottish Regions
DHA	District Health Authorities (and equivalent areas in Wales and Scotland that replaced Area Health Authorities)
DIS	Districts/Boroughs/Island Authorities
EC2	European Level II Regions (Metropolitan Counties and regional remainders)
EUR	European Assembly constituencies
EW*	England and Wales (*does not cover the whole of Britain; this is the only areal unit of this type in the figure)
GB	Great Britain (totals)
ITV	ITV Regions (there is one definition that approximates the regions without overlap; each is also available in full)
LEA	Local Education Authorities
LLM	Local labour market areas (as defined by CURDS; see text references to Functional Regionalization)
MET	Upper Tier of CURDS Functional Regionalization (Metropolitan Regions and Freestanding Regions; London FR also separate)
NAT	Nations (England, Scotland and Wales)
PCA	Postcode areas (as defined by the initial letter(s) of each postcode, e.g. 'SR' or 'G')
PCD	Postcode districts (as defined by the full first part of the postcode, e.g. 'WC1A' or 'S3')
PCS	Postcode sectors (as defined by the full postcode except the last two letters)
POL	Police Authorities (approximated in the case of the boundary of the Metropolitan force)
REG	Regions (the so-called Standard regions such as East Anglia and Wales)
RHA	Regional Health Authorities
TTW	Travel-to-work areas (defined in 1984 by CURDS for the Department of Employment)
WAR	Wards (England & Wales)/Postcode Sectors (Scotland) as used in the 1981 Census of Population
1 km, 2 km	Enumeration districts as rasterized into grid squares of size varying from 1 to 10 km

leaves the users to undertake the 'best fit' and to judge its quality themselves. Inevitably, some users will fall into a trap provided by the flexibility of GISs – carrying out analyses which are distorted in places where the 'best fit' was inadequate. This disadvantage is counterbalanced by the many new possibilities which the previous rigid approach denied. For example, Fig. 4.1 provides no link from the District Health Authorities (DHAs) into Local Education Authorities (LEAs), because in a few parts of the country DHAs are larger than LEAs. In most areas, however, the opposite is true and the current flexible approach should encourage users to assess the needs of their own research and, for example, to undertake analyses of the link between education outcomes and DHA-specific census data (e.g. on children in households including people with long-term illness) for a large sample of areas.

In principle, the linking of 1991 Census data with non-census information poses the same problem as linking with data from previous censuses. The problem arises because the areas used for the 1991 Census are subject to subsequent change (e.g. LAs) or are completely *ad hoc* (e.g. EDs). Linkage can take place in either direction, in the sense that census data can be grouped into areas not used for census output, or non-census data can be grouped into census areas. For the latter approach, the Central Postcode Directory (CPD) has provided a 'look up' between postcodes and wards since the 1981 Census. A major improvement in 1991 is the decision by OPCS to make available a listing of the postcodes covered by each ED. Where postcodes are split by EDs, the count of households which is to be produced for all postcodes will also be available for these part postcodes. Thus the increasing number of postcoded non-census datasets can be related to census geography – by users with the necessary computing facilities. More complex programs will be needed to use this 'look up' file in the other direction (i.e. to group census data to approximate areas based on groupings of postcodes which are not part of the census hierarchy of areas).

In practice, it is more often the case that census data are being used to provide general or contextual information in a multi-source dataset focused on the issues addressed more directly by the non-census data (Audit Commission 1991). For example, an analysis of crime patterns will need census data to understand the social background to the variation between areas, but the main focus is on the crime information. This leads to using the non-census areas for the analysis because specialist data sources, such as crime statistics, are often produced for a specialist set of areas (such as the area covered by a police station) and their boundaries are likely to be available only on paper maps. Moreover, the specialist areas may have a 'real world' significance for that issue – the definition of the police station's area may represent many years' experience of 'the patch' and be the most appropriate way to divide it up so as to identify a local community with its distinctive features in relation to crime.

In these circumstances the most effective approach is to group census units to match the areas used by the non-census dataset, rather than vice versa. This is also the most efficient approach because locational data are needed for each of the many areas to be grouped, but for relatively few 'target' areas. The CPD and the new 'look up' file of postcodes to EDs now provide a *basic* method of achieving the widespread need for a 'best fit' of census areas into non-standard areas (especially as there is now more ready access to census areas' boundaries and centroids). Some databases from which census data are obtained may provide a grouping option automatically, in the way in which NOMIS does. If the study area overall is small then the grouping 'look up' list can be obtained manually by inspecting maps. If the grouping will involve many census areas, usually because there are many 'target' areas, then the most efficient approach will often be to digitize the latter areas and to PIP the census areas' centroids into them to create the 'look up' file. Thus census data may usually be linked to the areas used for the statistics on the main issue of an analysis – of crime, employment, housing or whatever – and this is more often the appropriate direction for linkage to take place because these non-census boundaries frequently have some significance for that issue. The discussion here has thus moved to the last question which was raised at the beginning of this section: how readily can census areas be grouped into 'real world' boundaries?

4.5 The 1991 Census and the geography of Britain

The preceding discussion has dealt with the single-purpose 'real world' boundaries for which single-issue non-census datasets are often released. The remaining problem relates to those boundaries which are relevant to a wider range of issues – neighbourhoods, settlements and localities or communities.

An earlier section of the chapter mentioned the 'urban areas' which OPCS (in collaboration with the Ordnance Survey) identify as built-up areas in terms of census areas. These boundaries are accurately defined to be groupings of EDs in England and Wales, and OAs in Scotland. Equivalent areas were identified in 1981 – called 'localities' rather than 'urban areas' in Scotland – but users interested in change analysis will have to create their own 'look up' file of one census's building blocks into the other year's definition of urban areas (although this will be easier in Scotland because of the stability of building block areas as a result of the postcode base). The more fundamental issue to be faced is whether to analyse the change experienced in the urban areas as they were at the start of the period *or* the changes which led up to the situation which is reflected in the current settlement definitions. This is a question faced by any change analysis which is focused on a form of change which will affect the units of observation themselves. The same is true, incidentally, for an analysis of people's changing social status – the analysis could be in terms of the experience of people classified either by their original status (e.g. what proportion of labourers became managers?) or by their present situation (e.g. has the unemployment rate increased among people who currently have professional qualifications?).

The final challenge is perhaps the most intractable – the definition of socio-geographic boundaries. Consistent definitions of neighbourhoods or localities were traditionally either *formal* (e.g. a grouping of 'areas whose workers are mostly employed in mining') or *functional* ('areas whose workers are mostly employed in the Rhondda Valley'). Both types of definition have been applied to

1971 and to 1981 data, so the user has a range of existing boundaries for analyses based on areas prior to 1991. In the period after the release of 1991 Census data there has been the predictable surge of new 1991-based definitions.

Formal groupings of areas have become most familiar as the neighbourhood classifications which are usually implemented at the ED level (e.g. Charlton *et al.* 1985). The aim is to present a categorization of *types* of area: they then tend to make this search for area types all the more difficult by seeking a classification which will be relevant for a multitude of different purposes (Openshaw 1989). Because they do not take account of the location of EDs, either explicitly (by considering their centroids) or implicitly (by considering movement data which tend to link together adjacent areas), these classifications produce groupings which are usually made up of areas which are very scattered around the country. In fact if two adjacent EDs *are* grouped within the same neighbourhood type – along with many other EDs in many other locations – this only indicates that they have similar characteristics: there may be very little binding the two EDs' populations together in the community sense which would be implied by stating that they are the *same* neighbourhood. For example, they may be very similar suburbs of the same city but separated by a motorway or some other barrier which prevents them forming parts of an integrated neighbourhood. In fact, this notion of integration is one which is more properly addressed by a functional classification. A final word of warning on neighbourhood classifications concerns their labelling, particularly of those versions used in marketing applications. Many describe the neighbourhood types using labels such as 'rural/suburban/inner city' or 'newer/mature' and so forth. The problem is that the relevant data (e.g. distance from main urban centre, age of buildings etc.) are not part of the census data which were analysed. Consequently, users should be very careful to check and rely on the statistical characteristics of the neighbourhood typologies, derived from a genuine analysis of census data, rather than interpret their analyses on the basis of the area type names.

The most familiar functional area definitions in Britain are perhaps the set of Travel to Work Areas (TTWAs) which are the government's official form of local labour market areas (LLMAs). These will be redefined once the necessary 1991 Census commuting data are available. The commuting data (SWS) is one of the last census outputs to be published, so many LLMA researchers have to wait before they can benefit fully from any of the 1991 SAS and LBS. This is because they often need to base their analyses on the new TTWAs, and these areas will not be available until after an analysis taking six or nine months following the release of the SWS. However, the functional patterns of links between town and country do not change very rapidly, so that even the LLMAs of the 1971-based 'Functional Regions' (Coombes *et al.* 1982) are still found to be useful for many research purposes. This relative robustness is largely due to the fact that functional definitions focus on links which have a strong distance deterrence (i.e. people are reluctant to travel unnecessarily long distances to work). Distance is one feature of the country which is unchanging, and the inertia it imposes is only marginally affected by gradual increases in personal mobility and localized changes to transport networks.

There are several other features of functional area definitions which make them valuable to many different census users, and particularly those studying variation across the country in the change from one census to another. These features provide a useful summary of some points which have been rehearsed several times in this section. First, the scale of most LLMAs is itself helpful, with most including a population of 50,000 or more. The benefit of scale is that, although considerable effort will be involved in compiling 'look up' files manually or with a PIP, errors of mismatch between the groupings of different building block areas (e.g. 1981 and 1991 wards) will be unlikely to distort the results significantly. This is because the average number of building block areas per LLMA should be high enough for most error at the building block level to cancel out. Obtaining a high value on this ratio, between 'input' and 'output' areas, is the main guideline by which to assess the likely robustness of a 'best fit' between sets of areas (although it is crucial to check whether the ratio varies strongly between parts of the country, since it may be high on average but still dangerously low in a substantial minority of places).

The second benefit of LLMAs results from their aim to be meaningfully comparable areas, i.e. to all be functionally separable labour markets. Each LLMA of any significant size will include at least one urban area, given the geography of Britain. The result is that to a substantial degree there is an equalizing of urban–rural contrasts between LLMAs. For example, the 1991 Census is known to suffer from an unprecedentedly high level of under-enumeration and this problem is thought to be concentrated in urban areas. A comparison of the 1981–91 population change of LAs thus contains an important bias which will be accentuated by the way many district boundaries include solely urban or rural areas. The LLMAs' mix of urban and rural areas, on the other hand, tends to disperse the problem. Of course, some LLMAs *are* more urbanized than others, but this is a genuine geographical aspect of urban–rural variation, which LLMAs are well suited to portray accurately, rather than an artefact of arbitrary boundaries. This question of under-enumeration, incidentally, is one which was fairly unfamiliar in Britain – although not in Northern Ireland – until 1991: it has important implications for many users of small area data, which include some units where the problem is likely to have been very high, and at the small area level the problem remains undiluted by grouping the affected units with any less problematic neighbourhoods.

5 Prospects

It is only possible to discuss options for the role of geography in the 2001 Census procedure by first distinguishing the three uses of the census geography term 'base' – which may be applied to the finest detail coding of census returns *or* to the smallest areas for census output *or* to the smallest unit in census administration. In the 1981 Census of England and Wales these three types of building block coincided as EDs, but by 1991 the postcode unit was the finest detail coding whereas the largest census dataset (the LBS) is not being published for areas as small as EDs. Thus EDs are no longer the building blocks for coding or for much of the census output. The question for the 2001 Census, then, is what should be

- the finest detail coding area,
- the smallest OA and
- the individual enumerator's area – the ED.

The experience of the 1991 Census throughout Britain has been dominated by the reduced level of enumeration. It is unlikely that the 'changing social environment' (Clark 1992) will make a fuller enumeration easier in future censuses, with two consequences for census geography. The first consequence is a reduction in the strength of those arguments which are based on censuses' universal coverage and their exact count of the population. In particular, the argument that the geography must exactly fit with certain pre-existing boundaries, such as those of parishes, is reduced if the resulting population counts are already far from exact measures because of their dependence upon imputation and the unmeasurable local variation in levels of under-enumeration (Mills and Teague 1991). In any case, areas such as wards often change between censuses, so there seems little point in taking these 'moving targets' as inviolable.

The second consequence is that it is more difficult to predict in advance which areas are likely to meet the population thresholds for OAs. For the 1991 Census, the fuller detail provided by LBS in comparison with SAS results in the need for larger OAs to protect confidentiality. Creating dataset-specific OAs increases the problems arising from the difficulty of predicting the numbers of people included in any area. This is because each set of OAs has its own population minimum, and users do not want to have to wait until each OA's population level has been checked against the minimum requirement. These delays are made worse by the need to build up each set of OAs as a grouping of the smallest set in order to avoid possible differencing problems. From this perspective, the Scottish approach to 1991 Census geography has clear advantages because its use of GIS gives flexibility to allow OAs to be quickly adjusted until the population minima are met. The other important advantage to the user of the Scottish approach is that the whole country is then covered by OAs for which data can be published: there are no areas for which data are suppressed because the population minima remain unmet.

A particular example of the problems which can arise in the absence of a GIS-based approach is shown by the OAs for 1991 LBS in England and Wales. The policy has been to allow one user in each district to define the OAs for LBS in that area, on a 'first come, first served' basis. To avoid any subsequent 'differencing' problems, no other OAs will then be allowed for LBS in that district. This approach is clearly unsatisfactory for many other users because these OAs

- may be much larger than they might have been (so that internal heterogeneity remains high);
- will have been defined purely to meet that user's needs, which may result in a bizarre set of boundaries; and

- cannot be considered to be part of a national set of OAs which have been defined on similar criteria, thereby making up a broadly consistent set of areas for comparative local studies (e.g. of deprivation).

From the discussions here, then, a number of guidelines can be proposed.

1. It is important to separate the decision on each dataset's OAs from the definition of EDs (i.e. the area used for administering the data collection).
2. The finest area of coding needs to be the building block of a GIS, so that the areas can be optimally grouped into the hierarchy of OAs (for different datasets).
3. Each set of OAs should be defined as consistently as possible across the whole country (not left to individual users on a 'first come, first served' basis).
4. Every set of OAs should provide a complete coverage of the country, without any area's data being suppressed.
5. There is now less validity for arguing that OAs must nest exactly into pre-existing administrative areas.

It is clear that the GSS's long standing concern with confidentiality – and hence differencing – is likely to persist to 2001 and beyond (OPCS *et al.* 1993). Taking this concern together with the five guidelines above, the Scottish approach to census geography becomes all the more attractive. As described earlier in relation to the 1991 data, this approach is not only sympathetic to the guidelines developed here, it also provides the increasingly important benefit of ready linkage with non-census data through the use of whole postcode units as the finest coding area. This conclusion recalls the view of the Chorley Report (1987) that users need a postcode basis for data coding in the census, and so leads to the call for a postcode-based set of OAs for 2001 Census geography throughout the UK.

Acknowledgements

The author is grateful for the comments on a draft version of this chapter which were made by Alex Clark (OPCS) and Tony Champion and Dan Dorling (fellow authors here in Newcastle).

References

Audit Commission 1991 Numbers that count : making good use of the 1991 Census. *Information Paper 7*. London: Audit Commission.

Britton, M and F Birch 1985 *The 1981 Post Enumeration Survey*. London: HMSO.

Bureau of the Census 1989 Computer mapping and more! First Census TIGER file available. *Diffusion* 6, 16–17.

Charlton, M E, S Openshaw and C Wymer 1985 Some new classifications of census enumeration districts in Britain: a poor man's ACORN. *Journal of Economic and Social Measurement* 13, 69–96.

Chorley Report 1987 *Handling Geographic Information* (report to the Department of the Environment's Committee of Enquiry, Chairman Lord Chorley). London: HMSO.

Clark, A M 1992 1991 Census: data collection. *Population Trends* 70, 22–7.

Clark, A M and F G Thomas 1990 The geography of the 1991 Census. *Population Trends* 60, 9–15.

Coombes, M G, J S Dixon, J B Goddard, S Openshaw and P J Taylor 1982 Functional regions for the Population Census of Great Britain. In D T Herbert and R J Johnston (eds) *Geography and the Urban Environment 5*. London: Wiley.

CRU, OPCS and GRO(S) 1980 *People in Britain: a Census Atlas*. London: HMSO.

Denham, C 1993 Census geography: an overview. In A Dale and C Marsh (eds) *The 1991 Census User's Guide*. London: HMSO.

HM Government 1988 *1991 Census of Population*, White Paper (Cm 430). London: HMSO.

Marsh, C, S Arber, N Wrigley, D Rhind and M Bulmer 1988 The view of academic social scientists on the 1991 UK Census of Population: a report of the Economic and Social Research Council working group. *Environment and Planning A* 20, 851–89.

Marsh, C, C Skinner, S Arber, B Renhole, S Openshaw, J Hobcraft, D Lievesley and N Walford 1991 The case for samples of anonymised records from the 1991 Census. *Journal of the Royal Statistical Society A* 154, 305–40.

Martin, D 1991 Geographic Information Systems and their Socio-economic Applications. London: Routledge.

Mills, I and Teague, A 1991 Editing and inputing data for the 1991 Census. *Population Trends* 64, 30–7.

Neffendorf, H and D Hamilton 1987 Locational referencing applications – the Central Postcode Directory review. In *Applications of Postcodes in Locational Referencing*. London: LAMSAC.

OPCS 1987 *Census of Population, England and Wales: the Geographic Base*. London: OPCS.

OPCS and GRO(S) 1985 *Government Statistical Service Geographic Data Base* (Proposal CEN P3/26/1). London: OPCS.

OPCS and GRO(S) 1988 Geography and output areas for SAS. *Census Newsletter* 7, 8–10.

OPCS and GRO(S) 1991 Local and small area statistics: prospectus. *1991 Census User Guide* 3.

OPCS and GRO(S) 1992 *1991 Census: Definitions*. London: HMSO.

OPCS, GRO(S) and Census Office Northern Ireland 1993 Report on review of statistical information on population and housing. OPCS Occasional Paper 40. London: HMSO.

Openshaw, S 1989 Making geodemographics more sophisticated. *Journal of the Market Research Society* 31, 111–31.

Owen, D W, A E Green and M G Coombes 1986 Using the social and economic data on the BBC Domesday disc. *Transactions of the IBG* 11, 305–14.

Raper, J, D Rhind and J Shepherd 1992 *Postcodes: the New Geography*. London: Longman.

Rhind, D and M Higgins 1988 Customer-selected results from the 1991 Population Census using IKBS and highly secure technology. *ESRC Data Archive Bulletin* 39, 9–11.

Townsend, A, M Blakemore, R Nelson and P Dodds 1986 The National On-Line Manpower Information System (NOMIS). *Employment Gazette* 94, 60–4.

Tufte, E R 1990 *Envisioning Information*. Cheshire, CT: Graphics Press.

5

GIS and the census

M Charlton, L Rao and S Carver

Editor's note

The GIS revolution changes the entire context in which users see and use census data. Suddenly the census is seen in a much broader context, as only one part of the geographical mosaic. It is just one layer of geography at a not too fine resolution among perhaps 200 other layers. It is noted that all good GIS packages now contain the databases and mapping functions that 10 years ago would have required you to link SASPAC and GIMMS! They also trivialize many previous 'hard' census analysis and display tasks. Their present limitations are their focus on the visual rather than the statistical and the difficulty (really inconvenience) of linking the two aspects of analysis. However, in many ways the greatest strength of a GIS in a census analysis context is not the mapping or database functionality, or its ability to provide another way of accessing and mapping census data, but the tools it contains for manipulating census data together with other geographical information. For example, it can answer various spatial queries such as what the population is of 0–10 year olds living within 1 km of a particular road. This is useful. Much more useful is its ability to re-engineer census geographies in non-straightforward ways, e.g. create zoning systems that are composed of areal entities that are similar in size or shape or social heterogeneity. This is a basic prerequisite for sensible geographical analysis and is one of the greatest gifts that GIS can give the census user: a freedom from the tyranny of fixed arbitrary census geography.

1 Introduction

This chapter deals with some issues in using census data with geographical information system (GIS) software and hardware. We begin with a brief look at the developments in using spatially referenced census data over the past 20 years, and continue with those considerations relevant to using census data in the context of GIS.

The second part of this chapter presents a number of examples using the ARC/INFO system. This does not imply a preference for ARC/INFO as being the 'best' for the tasks. However, ARC/INFO is widely available among the academic community as a result of the activities of the Combined Higher Education Software Team, and the authors have used it extensively in their research and teaching. This chapter should not be read in isolation, but is related to both Brunsdon's chapters on statistical analysis and also to Dorling's chapter on visualization. GIS is not an end in itself, it merely provides some tools to assist in the analysis of the data. There will be occasions when it plays a major part in providing the results of analysis, and there will be many other occasions when it is entirely inappropriate. Note that none of what follows assumes that the analyst has access to ARC/Census, the ESRI census analysis package.

2 Developments in GIS

2.1 The last 20 years

Unlike the 1971 and 1981 Censuses of Population, the 1991 Census is characterized by a plethora of hardware and software with which it may be analysed. In 1971 there was no SASPAC, diffusion of statistical packages was very limited, there was an almost complete absence of mapping software, the microcomputer and the workstation had yet to be invented, and most computing was centred around mainframe computers in centralized locations accessed mainly through punched card readers. The problem of devising the algorithms to determine whether a point lay inside a plane region had yet to be addressed satisfactorily.

However, these shortcomings did not prevent analyses of census data; in their crudest form, an analysis of the patterns within the data would take the form of printing off all the tables for each enumeration district (ED) and filing them for later manual analysis. In the late 1960s, following the introduction of SYMAP in the USA, several mapping packages were developed in Britain. For example, the LINMAP (LINe printer MAPping) was developed by the Department of the Environment (DoE) for plotting 1966 Census indicators using character symbols on line printers. In the early 1970s a Geographic Information Manipulation and Management System (GIMMS) was developed at Edinburgh University. Afterwards, several statistical analysis packages, such as SPSS and SAS, added graphics and mapping functions for general usage. Although there were mapping programs these did not have a complete topological data structure to represent the real world; they were only able to plot maps on a line-printer, and later on a colour plotter, and only a few were able to display vector features on computer screen (i.e. Tektronix monitor). Nevertheless, these early often crude developments laid down the foundation of computer-aided design (CAD) and GIS.

Before the 1981 Census, the majority of users had to rely on the standard population statistics produced by the OPCS, which were limited in both the contents and the geographical units used. At that time only a programmer or a statistician could get more information out of the census by writing programs to process the raw data. After the cancellation of the 1976 mid-term census, the Local Authorities Management Services and Computer Committee (LAMSAC) set up a 1981 Census Working Party (University of Durham and University of Edinburgh) for the development of a small area statistics package (SASPAC). It provided a reasonably user-friendly front-end so that users could have much easier access to the raw data of the 1981 Census. By 1991, the SASPAC was developed for a wider range of computer platforms (i.e. VM/CMS by the University of Manchester and the PC by the London Research Centre). GIMMS was used by many as the mapping system for census data throughout the 1980s, although, for more specialist applications, coding one's own software was still a necessity. However, with the widespread diffusion of the microprocessor during the 1980s, the technological improvements in mass storage and software developments in the USA, the UK picture changed rapidly. The acquisition of the ARC/INFO system by Birkbeck College in 1985 may be taken as a turning point; the publication of the Chorley Report and the ESRC's Regional Research Laboratory Initiative have also been powerful driving forces.

The rapidly falling cost of computer power and the widespread introduction of distributed processing on UNIX workstations has helped to fuel the diffusion of GIS and the picture in 1993 from the point of view of the census analyst is very different from the position in 1971. Texts on GIS are widespread, ranging from the encyclopaedic (Maguire *et al.* 1991), the generalist textbook (Star and Estes 1990; Laurini and Thompson 1991), to the more social science oriented (Martin 1991). The *International Journal of GIS* provides an academic forum, and there are associated publications, e.g. *Mapping Awareness*, *GIS World* and *GIS Europe*, aimed at a more general readership. In the UK, the Association for Geographic Information publishes an annual yearbook, while many a practitioners' bookshelves bend under the weighty volumes of software manuals and papers from US and European GIS conferences. As well as paper information, those with access to Internet can find GIS issues being considered on the comp.infosystems.gis discussion group (available by listserver as GIS-L), and ESRI run a listserver for discussion of ARC/INFO specific issues. If that is not enough, users with time to spare can trawl the global information dustbin using the gopher facilities now available at many universities.

Current applications of GIS are wide ranging including not only natural sciences but also the social sciences, planning, AM/FM (Automated Mapping/Facilities Management) and even archaeology. The use of GIS for the analysis of socioeconomic data is now a typical end-use of new systems by academics, government, utilities and commercial users. Some systems vendors have already identified this as a major market area and now provide specialist facilities for census-based analyses in their systems, e.g. ESRI's Arc/Census. On a different level, there is an ever growing literature on GIS applications in socioeconomic data analysis and, more specifically, the UK Census of Population (Martin 1991).

Today, it is virtually impossible to consider handling census data without also considering GIS.

2.2 What is a GIS today?

GIS has been defined in various ways. It is usual in doing so to cite its range of functionality; e.g. GIS provides the user with a consistent framework for the input, storage, retrieval, analysis, manipulation, display and integration of spatially referenced data. More succinctly, GIS is an advanced and comprehensive computer tool box for the management and analysis of spatial data including census data.

The situation regarding GIS software has changed markedly from the mid-1980s. The penetration of GIS into the academic sector has initially been slow because of the high costs involved, with GIS software being, in general (or at least in terms of commercial prices), vastly more expensive than the machines which are used to run it. The use of GIS in academia has received a boost, however, in the form of a site licensing agreement between CHEST (Combined Higher Education Software Team) and ESRI (Environmental Sciences Research Institute), the originators of ARC/INFO. ARC/INFO is one of the most popular vector-based GISs on the market (it also supports raster and image processing) and despite being expensive to buy at commercial rates is now available to all UK academic institutions at a minimal cost. There are also a number of cheaper GISs on the market oriented towards teaching (e.g. IDRISI from Clarke University, USA) and some are even distributed free (e.g. GRASS from the US Army which can be down-loaded directly across the international computer network). The result is that GIS has now taken off in the UK academic sector with many systems installed in all universities. These are not just limited to geography departments and central computing facilities; many systems are being installed in a range of departments as diverse as zoology, surveying and archaeology. GIS has even been used in theology. It also seems that GIS software is increasingly available in local and central government.

The software itself has developed to such an extent that the supply of new features, speed and reliability keep pace with user demand. Yet many user applications of GIS in the field of census analysis are still limited to simply mapping the data at different spatial levels, i.e. UK wide, regional, county, district, ward and ED levels. Much of the advanced analysis capabilities of GIS, such as map overlay, are only just starting to be used.

The hardware accompanying GIS systems has also come a long way since the 1981 Census. Powerful GIS can be run on humble desktop PCs with enough speed and memory for most users, especially with the advent of the 80486 and Pentium chip and cheap IBM clones with high capacity disks. Workstations are now replacing older mainframe computer set-ups in most universities and other major organizations providing direct user access to large amounts of computer power and disk storage. This is an important consideration for users using GIS with very large datasets such as the census and ED boundary files. The quality of output devices, including visual display units (VDUs) and hardcopy, have all increased dramatically since 1981. The 1980s have seen many advances in the resolution of VDUs with the introduction of CGA, EGA, VGA and now super VGA graphics for PC users. Hardcopy devices cover a range of monochrome and colour devices to suit a range of applications and budgets. These include dot matrix printers, inkjet plotters, bubble-jet plotters, thermal wax plotters, pen plotters, electrostatic colour plotters and laser printers. In fact, there is quite a bewildering array of hardcopy devices on the market with which GIS can communicate via standard interface languages (e.g. PostScript, HPGL, PCI etc.). Many new GIS users of the 1991s have simply no appreciation of how sophisticated and easy to use the technology has become compared with 10 years ago, or even five years ago.

In addition to communicating between devices GIS usage of census information will often entail transfer of digital information between systems at remote sites many kilometres apart. Transfer of census tables is easy enough as ASCII files via file transfer protocol (ftp), but transfer of boundary information is different. Boundary files will usually be transferred in a particular format depending on their source and a variety of transfer formats exist. These include the Ordnance Survey Transfer Format (OSTF), the National Transfer Format (NTF) and Digital Line Graph (DLG) format. These will have to be converted into a format readable by the GIS being used. Most GIS provide the user with routines for doing this.

These are a number of common uses of a GIS. In terms of the analysis of census-based information, six primary functions are defined.

2.2.1 Geo-referencing

A GIS allows the computation of relationships between spatial entities, e.g. assigning the census data to the relevant spatial units or geographic features on a digital map. Aggregation and cross-area referencing of census data become straightforward in a GIS. For some spatial analysis such as autocorrelation and zoning, the contiguity of spatial entities is needed; only a GIS can present the geographic features in a realistic way.

2.2.2 Spatial measurement

A GIS provides various geometric functions which allow the measurement of distance, area and density, e.g. it calculates the area of wards and finds the centroids of EDs. The NEAR command in ARC/INFO can also calculate the shortest distance between a point and a line. These functions can be used to obtain the basic measurements, such as the size of built-up areas and travel-to-work distances, which may be required by further spatial and statistical analysis.

2.2.3 *Spatial representation and visualization*

In a GIS, the distribution of population can be represented by symbol points (of different sizes) or by density shades (of different colours), so that the relationships between spatial objects can be visualized on a graphic terminal or a colour plotter. Since the objects and their attributes are interrelated, spatial queries can also be made by selecting the objects on the screen or by entering the attribute value.

2.2.4 *Spatial aggregation*

Because the spatial objects and their relationships are identifiable or separable in GIS, aggregation or disaggregation can be easily achieved. In ARC/INFO, the commands DISSOLVE and UNION can group any spatial objects which are adjacent and have one or more attribute value in common. In recent years, many statistical models have been incorporated into GIS. For example:

- Spatial ordering: one adapted ARC/INFO command uses a Peano curve – a self-similar space-filling curve – to calculate the position of each point (node, arc mid-point, polygon centroid) in order to obtain the compact shape of groups (Bartholdi and Platzman 1988).
- Fuzzy classification, e.g. fuzzy *c*-means clustering algorithm (Bezdek 1984): in general, the method is to assign each spatial feature (a polygon or point) with a membership value between 0 and 1 according to one classification criterion, and then to use other criteria to justify the value of the membership of each feature; at the end an overlay classification index can be obtained. In census analysis, different sizes of grid cells or circles can be used to aggregate the features in order to get the average values of their memberships (Burrough 1989; Fisher and Pathirana 1990).
- Kriging uses generalized linear regression techniques for minimizing an estimation variance defined from a prior model for a covariance. In ARC/INFO, the kriging function is used to calculate semivariance values for a set of randomly distributed points with z values. The semivariance can be modelled to create a lattice surface or graphed as a semivariogram.

In addition to covariance and semivariance, the correlation can also be used to measure the spatial variability when the spatial relationships (distances or contiguities) are put into consideration. The GRID module in ARC/INFO offers an interactive modelling environment using Map-algebra as the data-manipulation language for any cell-based spatial aggregation and classification in different resolutions.

2.2.5 *Spatial overlay*

GIS can create a relationship between the spatial features held in two separate map coverages (or layers). For example, in ARC/INFO the IDENTITY command can be used to identify the postcode label points that lie within wards; the INTERSECT command can produce a new coverage which keeps the topological attributes of two input coverages where the features are intersected or in common; and the UNION command simply combines the two input coverages into a new one. The overlay functions allow a GIS to store the multiple datasets at different spatial levels or for different spatial units.

2.2.6 Cell-based modelling and surface modelling

Unlike the cell-based primitive GIS in the 1970s, the new cell-based models can accurately portray continuous surfaces. The GRID module in ARC/INFO can process any discrete data and transfer them to other forms of spatial features, e.g. from raster to vector, and from grid cells to lattices or a triangular irregular network (TIN). If a zone does not have data, the GRID and TIN models can compute a value for this zone based on the continuous surface. For census analysis, a GIS can generate a three-dimensional surface to visualize the results and this can be a useful way of complementing more traditional map displays.

3 Census data in GIS

A GIS could not work on data without a geographical reference. Basically there are two choices we need to make regarding data models when choosing a GIS with which to analyse census data. We have to choose between raster- or vector-based systems and layer-based or object-oriented systems. In the case of the former, it is now largely a matter of personal choice and is no longer a critical technical issue. The level of detail obtainable using vector-based systems is undeniably greater for the same amount of disk storage used, but for the majority census-based applications of GIS the resolution offered by most raster systems is more than adequate. Where vector-based systems come into their own is in the analysis of network information such as traffic flows, travelling salesmen problems and shortest path definition.

A more serious decision regarding choice of system is that between layer-based and object-oriented approaches. In layer-based systems, data are stored and integrated as thematic map layers. In the case of the census, we may then have one layer containing ED boundaries and ED level data (which then enables us to create further layers such as ward and district level data by aggregation), one layer containing postcode boundaries and data, one containing the locations of customers and related data and another containing the road and rail network. These are then integrated by overlaying one on top of the other to define spatial and logical relationships. In an object-oriented database, on the other hand, all data including EDs, wards, postcodes, customer locations, roads and railways together with associated information are stored in a single layer as individual objects. This has obvious implications for the way we handle the relationships between objects and the way in which we integrate and analyse census data. The layer-based approach is probably the most intuitive and easy to use for handling census data and so the rest of this chapter is based on this premise. It is possible that the situation might well be reversed by the next census in 2001.

3.1 Census data coverage

In the case of the 1991 Census, digital boundary coverages are available from a number of suppliers. The alternative to using (and paying for) someone else's digital boundary data is to digitize them yourself. The trouble here, apart from it being a time-consuming process, is that you can run into copyright problems.

When using census data with digital boundary files it is necessary to form a link between the census data (attribute data) on the one hand and the boundary data on the other, be they EDs, wards, districts or counties. To do this we need to use the ED code, ward code, district code or county code respectively, which is attached to the attribute data in the census tables. In most cases this is a simple one-to-one relational link with each area code linking directly to one area in the boundary data. The main exception to this rule is in the case of islands which share the same area code as the area to which they belong on the mainland.

Other forms of linkage between census data and other data or boundary files may be performed. It is possible to assign postcodes to a particular ED although there are many more postcodes than there are EDs. Several postcodes may therefore fall within the same ED and it is necessary to use a postcode-to-ED lookup table to perform the link between the two. A problem arises here in that the postcode geography is not the same as the census geography (i.e. postcode boundaries do not follow and nest inside census boundaries, except in Scotland). This means that postcodes near the edge of an ED may overlap its boundary making it necessary either to make an assumption about which ED the postcode lies mainly within or to assign part of the postcode to one ED and part to another. OPCS tables linking part EDs to part postcodes are available for this purpose (OPCS 1993).

With the census boundaries, which are hierarchical, it is possible to aggregate smaller units such as EDs into larger units such as wards, districts, counties and regions. This is simply a matter of knowing which ward an ED belongs to, grouping all the ED boundaries and data into ward groups, totalling up the attribute data and removing internal ED boundaries. Similarly, wards can be aggregated into districts, districts into counties and counties into regions in the same fashion. The disaggregation of data from larger spatial units to smaller spatial units is not quite so easy. If we needed to do this, say for example to disaggregate ward data into ED level boundaries, the problem lies in how to divide up the census data between the EDs making up a particular ward. Typically we would be forced to assume that the variable of interest (e.g. population) is evenly distributed across the larger areal unit and thus can be divided into the smaller areal units on the basis of area. However, population, car ownership, number of dependants etc. are not evenly distributed over space and so there are obvious difficulties with this technique. Despite much research, this problem has not yet been adequately resolved; indeed it may never be, so a pragmatic solution might be all that can be used.

Linkages may be created between census data and geographic features such as transport networks and city blocks using geometrical relationships. This is possible using a GIS by calculating the nearest ED centroid to the point, line or area representing the feature of interest and using this ED as the assigned code. Overlaying geographical areas on census boundaries which do not match gives rise to cross-area aggregation problems similar to those encountered in overlaying postcode boundaries on the census boundary data. Users clearly need to take these errors into account although GIS typically provide no tools to help deal with error propagation issues (see Openshaw 1989).

All the boundaries for all the different areal units from countries (England, Wales, Scotland and Northern Ireland) to EDs are available in digital form for the 1991 Census, although they were never part of the census and have to be acquired separately. For the 1981 Census a full set of digital boundaries was not available from any source. The highest level of resolution was the ward with only the area centroids being available for the ED level, thus limiting the scope of GIS analysis at this most detailed level. This was mainly because the effort involved in digitizing 130,000 ED boundaries using early 1980s technology was too great. Several efforts were made to generate an artificial set of ED boundaries from their centroids using Thiessen polygons, and Martin (1989) discusses another technique for mapping census data from ED centroids using kernels.

Finally, it is noted that many of the problems and opportunities for using GIS with census data are new. The 1981 data pre-dated the GIS revolution and, for much of the UK, there was never any small area census boundaries available in digital form. Most census GIS users are therefore on the early slope of a learning curve. One indication is that the term GIS is only referenced eight times in Dale and Marsh (1993).

3.2 Choice of data model

Analysis of census data in a GIS can take on various forms and various levels of complexity, from simple data retrieval to complicated models. Data retrieval may be spatial or aspatial. Aspatial retrieval refers to the selection of features or data, e.g. EDs, on the basis of certain criteria specified by the user. These usually take the form of simple rule-based database queries, e.g. find all EDs with a population greater than 100 people or find all the EDs with a mean household size of five people. Simple logical operations may also be included in this kind of database query, e.g. find all the EDs with a population greater than 100 and over 50% council property. Data retrieved in this manner may then be displayed on the screen for scrutiny by the user.

Spatial data retrieval involves a certain level of locational information in the retrieval operation. At its most basic, spatial data retrieval may be the interaction between the user and the computer screen using the mouse or other pointing device to point at an object or feature and ask 'What is this?' Other spatial queries may be based on the topological or geometric relationships between objects or features. We may ask the GIS to retrieve all EDs adjacent to or within another type of spatial unit such as a national park or postcode sector, or we may ask the GIS to retrieve all EDs within 1 km of a motorway.

The following census-related examples might be viewed as an extension of ESRI (1993). Readers not interested in GIS technicalities could well decide to skip the next few sections. Hopefully, those interested in using ARC/INFO with the 1991 Census will find the examples and suggestions helpful. The following examples use ARC/INFO version 6.1.1 operating on a UNIX workstation, so that the command syntax is case sensitive. Because ARC/INFO uses INFO as its database management system, all commands in INFO, including the names of infofiles and data items, must be entered in upper case, but when calling a non-INFO file the file name must be kept the same as it is in the operating system. In most ARC modules, upper or lower case commands are treated the same.

In the ARC/INFO model, the digital map data and the associated attribute data are referred to as a coverage. The model is vector based, so coverages may contain either point, line or polygon information. There are facilities to deal with raster information and raster/vector conversion, but they have not historically formed the core of the system. A coverage is a single layer and will only contain one type of data – the coverage is given a name by which it is referred to in commands. The attribute data are stored in feature attribute tables: the point attribute table (PAT), the arc attribute table (AAT) and the polygon attribute table (PAT). These files can be accessed or processed through INFO or TABLES modules and thus are called infofiles. Those kept in their original format (e.g. ASCII) are called data files. If possible, try to use TABLES to manipulate the infofiles, instead of using the INFO module directly.

3.3 Data input

One of the fundamental issues is how census data are input to GIS software. This involves the creation of a spatial database which contains the geometric information relating to the position of the centroids and boundaries, and also the creation of a textual and numeric database containing the census area codes, associated names and (most probably) an extract from the SASPAC91 data files.

In ARC/INFO, the attributes of a polygon are related to the polygon through its label point (with an unique id). Therefore the simplest way to relate the census data to an ED coverage would be to create the centroids of ED polygons and then to join the census table to the PAT using the common spatial identifier, e.g. the OPCS code. Indeed, in the absence of extensive digital coverage of the 1981 ED boundaries, this was often a starting point for many analyses. The centroid coordinates are stored in the data file, and can be extracted via SASPAC91. There are several methods, but the goal is to create a point coverage which contains the ED code in its PAT. You will need access to a file editor – this may be a word processor on a PC, vi or emacs on a UNIX box, edit/edt on VMS systems or xedit on a CMS system. If you have access to a statistical package program, such as SPSS or SAS, or you can write simple BASIC, FORTRAN or C programs, this will also be helpful, but only to provide some shortcuts.

SASPAC91 can be persuaded to extract the ED code and the associated easting and northing with the following commands:

```
INPUT SYSTEM FILE NAME=eddata
SAVE VARIABLES EASTING NORTHING
OUTPUT DELIMITED FILE NAME=coords
END
INPUT SYSTEM FILE NAME=eddata
SET COUNTYCODE ON
SAVE VARIABLES ZONEID
OUTPUT DELIMITED FILE NAME=edinfo
END
FINISH
```

This will create two comma delimited files with the ED code and its associated easting and northing. The system file names will be specific to the installation being used, and the output file names should conform to local conventions. For example, at Manchester University the two output files would be named *EDDATA* and *EDINFO* (both with extension name *DELIMITD*).

Before input to ARC/INFO, the two files will need some small alterations. The *ZONEIDS* will be surrounded by single quotes – these should be removed (most edit programs have a global search and replace facility which should help here). The *EDCODES* will be prefixed by the county number – if this is not desired, then omit the SET COUNTYCODE ON instruction.

The GENERATE command requires that every point has a sequence number, the user id. These should be added to the coordinates by hand (if you do not program or have access to SPSS or SAS), or through a program, or by any other convenient means. GENERATE expects to find the keyword END as the last line in the file. The file should look something like

```
1,56231,66752
2,56243,66452
3,56226,66397
.
.
.
1265,52183,60818
END
```

Note that the user ids need not start at 1. We shall assume that the names of the files are *coords.txt* and *edinfo.txt*. The creation of the centroid database is as follows:

```
[ARC]:          GENERATE EDCENTROIDS
[GENERATE]:     INPUT coords.txt
                POINTS
                QUIT
[ARC]:          BUILD EDCENTROIDS POINTS
```

GENERATE creates a coverage, in this case named *EDCENTROIDS.* It has to be instructed where to find the coordinate file and the type of data that are in the file. The BUILD command creates a PAT which initially contains four items, area and perimeter (both zero), an internal sequence number (which would be *EDCENTROIDS#* in this case) and a user id (in this case *EDCENTROIDS-ID*). The PAT is accessed through TABLES. An infofile, *EDCODE.LIST*, is also used to store the ED code:

```
[ARC]:          TABLES
[TABLES]:       DEFINE EDCODE.LIST
                EDCODE,8,8,C
                <return>
                ADD FROM edinfo.txt
                QUIT STOP
```

The ED code is an eight-character entity. At the moment, however, the *EDCODE.LIST* infofile exists outside the coverage PAT. The two infofiles can be merged thus:

```
[ARC]:  JOINITEM EDCENTROIDS.PAT EDCODE.LIST ~
            EDCENTROIDS.PAT EDCENTROIDS#~
            EDCENTROIDS-ID LINK
```

The operation of JOINITEM, which takes two infofiles and merges them, can seem rather complex to the uninitiated. The *EDCENTROIDS#* item in the PAT contains the internal sequence number of each ED, and this is the same as the record number for the corresponding ED code in *EDCODE.LIST* – the link option instructs JOINITEM to carry out the merge using this information. When it has carried out the merge successfully the *EDCODE.LIST* will be stored in *EDCENTROIDS.PAT* immediately to the right of *EDCENTROIDS-ID.* (N.B. a title (~) is used as a line continuation symbol in ARC/INFO.)

Once the coverage has been created, it should be checked visually and a sample of EDs should be queried spatially to check that locations and *EDCODE* are correct. This is most easily accomplished in ARCPLOT.

```
[ARC]:          ARCPLOT
[ARCPLOT]:      & STATION 9999
                MAPEXTENT EDCENTROIDS
                POINTS EDCENTROIDS
```

```
IDENTIFY EDCENTROIDS POINT *

/* select a point with the mouse to view its attributes */
```

Unless the data refer to Cornwall or perhaps Devon, there will be a single point in the lower left corner of the screen and a cluster of points in the upper right corner. This is because SASPAC91 places the shipping EDs at a location with easting and northing both zero. These should be removed. There are a number of possible routes here: either they can be removed interactively using ARCEDIT and the coverage rebuilt; or the ADDXY command can be used to add the eastings and northings to the PAT and then the RESELECT command can be used to extract those with non-zero eastings and northings. Using the latter option, the commands would be

```
[ARC]:         ADDXY EDCENTROIDS
[ARC]:         RESELECT EDCENTROIDS FINALEDS POINT
[RESELECT]:    RESELECT X-COORD = 0 and Y-COORD = 0
               <return>
```

The procedure may seem initially rather complex; it is composed of a series of simple steps. It can be generalized to deal with most point datasets, e.g. the postcode-to-ED lookup files.

There are some points to note. SASPAC91 outputs the coordinates of the centroid to 10 m resolution. If it is intended to integrate the data with other coverages stored at different resolutions, then the coordinates of either coverage will have to undergo coordinate transformation (a procedure for this is described later in this chapter). Initial investigations into the locations of the coordinates carried out in early 1993 suggested that a small proportion are in error. One interesting exercise is to compare the location centroids of the EDs with ones calculated from the postcode-to-ED lookup tables; because the lookup table carries population counts, it is possible to calculate unweighted and population locations for the centroid. You should ensure that you are using the latest OPCS or GRO(S) updated coordinates.

3.4 Data import and conversion

If you have managed to obtain digitized ED boundaries, or ward boundaries, in ARC/INFO export format, you can create the coverage very quickly. The filename will end in .e00; perhaps eds.e00 (or a series of files with extension names e01, e02 etc., for example). The IMPORT command will accomplish the database creation

```
[ARC]: IMPORT COVER eds ED_BOUNDARIES
```

which will create a polygon coverage named *ED_BOUNDARIES*, assuming that *eds.e00* was exported from a polygon coverage. The DESCRIBE command will report on the coverage contents:

[ARC]: DESCRIBE *ED_BOUNDARIES*

It is sometimes the case that boundaries arrive in a form which cannot apparently easily be imported into an ARC/INFO coverage. The Geoplan postcode sector boundaries are one example – each sector is digitized as a closed polygon with an identifier and the number of vertices in the polygon boundary, the whole being stored as an ASCII file. The authors have found that one route into ARC/INFO for such data is to use its facility to read MOSS files (MOSS is a public domain GIS produced by the US Department of the Interior). If the boundaries can be reformatted into MOSS format (there is an example of this format in the ARC/INFO manual), then the MOSSARC command can be used to read the data in, and CLEAN can be used to create polygon topology. For example, if the coordinates are in a file named *boundaries.moss:*

[ARC]: MOSSARC *boundaries.moss EDS_MOSS* POLY
[ARC]: CLEAN *EDS_MOSS EDS91* # # POLY

It is possible that further processing with ARCEDIT to tidy up the boundaries may be required. The PAT will also require some attention; MOSSARC puts the identifier (which it refers to as the subject value) into an item named DATA which is 30 characters in length.

3.5 Map projection and scaling

Like a paper map, the digital map is also a mathematical representation of the real world. Because many coordinate systems have been used to register the features on earth's surface, the projection is required in GIS. In order to overlay features stored in different coverages, we must give these coverages the same projection, the same coordinate system and the same scale.

The coordinate system of a coverage is registered by at least three controlling points. In ARC/INFO four points, called tics, are used to define a coverage – the fourth tic is for checking the accuracy of the map digitizing. Therefore the project procedure is to change the four tics' easting and northing from a map coordinate system to the 'real world' coordinate system. Only a few map projections, however, are in common use: Lambert's conformal conic, Transverse Mercator and stereographic. In the UK most maps are in Ordnance Survey Grid Reference (OSGR) which is already flat, so no projection is needed.

Map scaling is the process of inferring the size of a feature on a map from the actual size of its entity in the real world. The scale is expressed as a ratio of map size to actual size. The digitized line is a sample of the line drawn on the map by a cartographer – it is one of an infinite number of possible samples. As such it contains uncertainty, arising partly from the choice of the sample points and the accuracy with which the sample point was digitized. If manual digitizing is being employed, there are no hard and fast rules which determine where the sample points should be chosen – generally a curve is sampled more densely than a straight line. Some digitizing tables support 'stream digitizing' in which points are sampled when the cursor has moved a given distance, perhaps 0.5 mm – this may lead to over-sampling for straight lines and under-sampling on quickly changing curves. The accuracy of the sampled point depends on the operator (digitizing is a tiring process) and the stability of the medium on which the source map is printed (paper is much less stable than Mylar film).

One vendor of digitized ED boundaries has captured them from the Ordnance Survey's archive of 1:10,000 scale maps, and claims an accuracy of ± 4 m on the ground. On a 1:10,000 map, a distance of 1 mm on the map represents a distance of 10 m on the ground. This implies that, for each point, the digitizing is to an accuracy of ± 0.4 mm. If you decide to use data captured from 1:250,000 scale maps, and overlay this with data captured from 1:10,000 scale maps, then problems may well arise with registration. The whole issue of error propagation is still receiving attention, and it is rare for a GIS to assume that lines are other than accurately digitized. Table 5.1 summarizes some useful map scale translations.

3.6 Extending the attribute tables with census data

The nature and extent of the census data and the sorts of analysis that it permits are developed elsewhere in the book. One may wish to use the GIS as a cartographic tool, mapping some derived census variable, or the results of some analysis (perhaps the residuals from a regression model), or the results of a classification exercise. The software permits such data to be used in other ways, some of which are outlined below. The results might be maps, further data to be returned to a statistical program, or a report.

The numeric and textual data are sorted in an infofile and may be either permanently merged with the boundary PAT or temporarily joined through the

Table 5.1 Map scale and 'real world' distance

Map scale	1 mm (map unit)	1 inch (map unit)
1:1 250	1.25 metres	104.17 feet
1:2 500	2.50 metres	208.33 feet
1:10 000	10 metres	833.33 feet
1:25 000	25 metres	2 083.33 feet
1:50 000	50 metres	4 166.67 feet
1:100 000	100 metres	8 333.33 feet
1:250 000	250 metres	20 833.33 feet
1:625 000	625 metres	52 083.33 feet

use of RELATE. There are good reasons for using relates – they keep down the size of the PAT and they are a flexible means of data handling (one set of boundaries will suffice for a number of different analyses).

It is desirable that the data to be linked to the boundary data contain the appropriate area code. In this way, the chance of linking the attribute data to the area data will be minimized. Assuming the attribute data to be stored as a comma separated file in *mydata.dat*, one procedure is as follows:

```
[ARC]:        TABLES
[TABLES]:     DEFINE DATA1.DAT
              WARD_CODE,6,6,C
              VAR1,4,7,B
              VARIABLE2,4,12,F,2
              VARIABLE3,4,7,B
              .
              .
              .
              <return>
              ADD FROM mydata.dat
              SORT WARD_CODE
              LIST
              QUIT STOP
```

It is important that the data be sorted on the area code, as this is used to optimize the speed of the relational join.

```
[ARC]:                RELATE ADD
[Relation Name]:      WARD1
[Table Identifier]:   DATA1.DAT
[Database Name]:      INFO
[INFO Item]:          WARD_CODE
[Relate Column]:      WARD_CODE
[Relate Type]:        ORDERED
[Relate Access]:      RO
```

This adds a relation to the current relate environment. The command prompts for further information: (a) the name of the relation *WARD1*; (b) the infofile which contains the information we wish to have related to another *DATA1.DAT*; (c) the name of the relational database management system we are using – INFO/TABLES; (d) the name of the item in the infofile from which the relate is done – *WARD_CODE*; (e) the name of the item in the related infofile which is to be related to the previous item; (e) the type of the relate (there are a number of options here – we use ordered because we have sorted the infofile on the Relate Column); (f) the nature of the access rights to the related file (again there are a series of options here – read-only will prevent any accidents). The relation can be saved in an infofile for later use. To refer to an item in related a infofile, it needs to be prefixed by the relation name followed by '//'. For example, in mapping some variables:

[ARCPLOT]: POLYGONSHADES *WARDS WARD1//~ DENSITY DENSITY.LUT*

4 Spatial analysis using ARC/INFO

Once input into a GIS as boundary point data and attribute data, census data may be used with a whole series of GIS operators, both spatial (i.e. concerning the geographical location of the data) and aspatial (i.e. concerning the data itself). GIS operations on census data include basic data display and mapping, spatial and aspatial data retrieval, query, integration and modelling.

The basic display of information in tabular or map form is probably the simplest of GIS operations relevant to census data, although this can be done using any database. Choropleth mapping of census variables is in turn probably the most frequently used method of data display. It is difficult to avoid a book or paper which uses census data without seeing one of these maps. In the early 1980s it was likely that such maps were drawn using a mapping package such as GIMMS. In the late 1980s and today, GIS packages are largely superseding basic mapping packages for the mapping of census data. To use GIS only for mapping is to ignore a major part of its functionality in being able to interrogate and integrate geographical datasets in a manner not previously possible via simple mapping packages.

4.1 Spatial aggregation analysis

It is often desirable to create a new set of areal units from an existing set of building blocks. For example, we might wish to define a zoning system for some modelling study where the zones are aggregates of complete EDs. Again, some policy areas might be required which are aggregates of EDs or wards. If we have ED boundaries, we may wish to create the ward and district boundaries which sit above them.

We shall assume that we have a coverage of ED boundaries in some area of interest. To create the new areas requires the production of a lookup table linking each ED with the ward (for example), or district, in which it lies. This is relatively easily accomplished. We start by assuming the existence of an infofile containing only the ED codes; the data item will be eight characters in width. The ward code is formed by removing characters 7 and 8, and the district code is formed by removing characters 5 to 8 inclusive. A sequence of operations would proceed along the following lines:

[ARC]: ADDITEM *EDLIST.DAT EDLIST.DAT WARD_~ CODE 6 6 C*

```
[ARC]:          ADDITEM EDLIST.DAT EDLIST.DAT~
                  DISTRICT_CODE 4 4 C
[ARC]:          TABLES
[TABLES]:       SELECT EDLIST.DAT
                MOVE ED_CODE TO WARD_CODE
                MOVE ED_CODE TO DISTRICT_CODE
                SORT
                LIST
                QUIT STOP
```

We add two extra items to the *EDLIST.DAT* infofile, namely *WARD_CODE* and *DISTRICT_CODE*, of six and four characters width respectively, to receive the new codes. Then in TABLES/INFO we copy the existing *ED_CODE* to the new items; INFO will truncate them at the right-hand end. We will require the infofile to be sorted on the *ED_CODE* item.

The business of aggregating the boundaries is accomplished by the DISSOLVE command, which requires the user to specify the name of the coverage containing the source zone definitions, a name of the new coverage which will contain the boundaries of the zones we wish to create, and a dissolve item (the names of the new zones). The lookup table we have just created will provide us with the dissolve item – how do we link it with the boundary data? We assume that our boundary data attribute table contains the *ED_CODE* item which we used in creating our lookup table.

We need to create a temporary link between the boundary data and the lookup table. This is accomplished thus:

```
[ARC]:               RELATE ADD
[Relation Name]:     CENSUS_LINK
[Table Identifier]:  EDLIST.DAT
[Database Name]:     INFO
[INFO Item]:         ED_CODE
[Relate Column]:     ED_CODE
[Relate Type]:       ORDERED
[Relate Access]:     RO
```

Thus to create the ward boundaries from the ED boundaries:

```
[ARC]:        DISSOLVE ED_COVERAGE WARD_COVERAGE~
                CENSUS_LINK//WARD_CODE POLY
```

The resulting coverage of ward boundaries will have an item *WARD_CODE* in its PAT containing the ward codes from the lookup table. Creating the district boundaries is as simple an operation.

The ability to relate infofiles is a very powerful process – as well as providing flexibility in the handling of the geometry data, it also prevents the attribute tables becoming unnecessarily large in size. Although disk space is a relatively inexpensive commodity, we can improve efficiency by keeping redundancy in the database to a minimum.

4.2 Spatial overlay analysis

One of the operations which GIS permits is the computation of statistics for one set of areas which have been derived from another set of areas. For example, suppose that ED boundaries, and the Small Area Statistics to go with them, have been loaded into ARC/INFO. It is possible to create census profiles for school catchment areas whose boundaries we already have in digital form. It is almost inevitable that the school catchments will cross some ED boundaries, so there will be some edge effects in the results.

There are a number of possible techniques, varying in acceptability. If it is assumed that the population is homogeneously located within an ED, then a simple pro-rata based on the areas of the EDs and the school catchments might be sufficient. We could carry out another weighted pro-rata based on the postcode-to-ED lookup tables. We could also carry out some statistical modelling along the lines suggested by Flowerdew and Openshaw (1987).

The simple pro-rata involves the geometric intersection of the ED and school catchment boundaries. If we wish to calculate the population then we proceed as follows:

```
[ARC]:     INTERSECT ED_COVERAGE SCHOOL_COVERAGE ~
               SCHOOL_ED_COVERAGE POLY # NOJOIN
```

The polygons which are created as a result of the intersection contain sequence numbers from the *ED_COVERAGE* and from the *SCHOOL_COVERAGE*. This allows us to set up relations in INFO to merge the ED data with the school data. It will be necessary to add an item to the polygon attribute table for the school coverage to contain the population totals:

```
[ARC]:     ADDITEM SCHOOL_COVERAGE.PAT~
               SCHOOL_COVERAGE.PAT TOTALPOP 4 8 B
```

Then, the relational database management system in ARC/INFO can be used to merge in the ED populations. Assume that these data are stored in an item named *USUAL_RESID* in the ED coverage, and proceed as follows:

```
[ARC]:     INFO
[INFO]:    ARC
           PROGRAM ADDUP
           SELECT SCHOOL_COVERAGE.PAT
           CALCULATE TOTALPOP = 0
           SELECT SCHOOL_ED_COVERAGE.PAT
```

```
RELATE 1 ED_COVERAGE.PAT BY ED_COVERAGE# ~
    WITH LINK
RELATE 2 SCHOOL_COVERAGE.PAT BY~
    SCHOOL_COVERAGE# WITH LINK
PROGRAM SECTION TWO
CALCULATE $2TOTALPOP = $2TOTALPOP +~
    $1USUAL_RESID  * ( AREA / $1AREA )
PROGRAM SECTION THREE
END
<return>
RUN ADDUP
QUIT STOP
```

Once this INFO program has been run, the *TOTALPOP* item in the *SCHOOL_COVERAGE.PAT* attribute table will contain the 'interpolated' values derived from the ED coverage. An alternative would be to write the weights required for each ED out to a file so that they could be used, say, to create new system files for SASPAC that relate to the catchment areas.

The overlay functions provide a way to use census information for evaluating the catchment of a particular service, such as bus passengers and customers of a supermarket. Whatever the service is, its catchment area can be defined by an overlay process. For example, the catchment area of a bus operator can be obtained by generating a buffer along the bus route or around each stop (Fig. 5.1). More accurately, the walking/driving time zones from a supermarket can be drawn with the ALLOCATION and CONTOUR commands in ARC/INFO. Thus, the catchment polygons can be superimposed onto the census data coverage so that the proportion of the catchment areas can be calculated and used to estimate the ratio of population.

Figure 5.1 shows a route evaluation system developed on ARC/INFO using census data in Merseyside. After the INTERSECTION of an ED coverage and a built-up area coverage, the density of population can be calculated by the residential areas. The catchment analysis can be performed at a smaller scale or lower level.

4.3 Analysing changes between censuses

Digital boundary data for the 1981 EDs are not available for most of the UK, the exception being Scotland and a few counties. Unless the analyst has access to a set, then mapping and analysis will have to take place at the ward level (for which boundaries are available) or some synthetic boundaries will have to be created for the 1981 ED centroids, perhaps using Thiessen polygons.

The process of taking data from the 1981 SASPAC and creating an ED point coverage is similar to that described above for the 1991 data. Unless the 1981 data have been loaded into the SASPAC91, the user will have to contend with SASPAC's matrix files. The grid references (to 100 m resolution) and ED codes

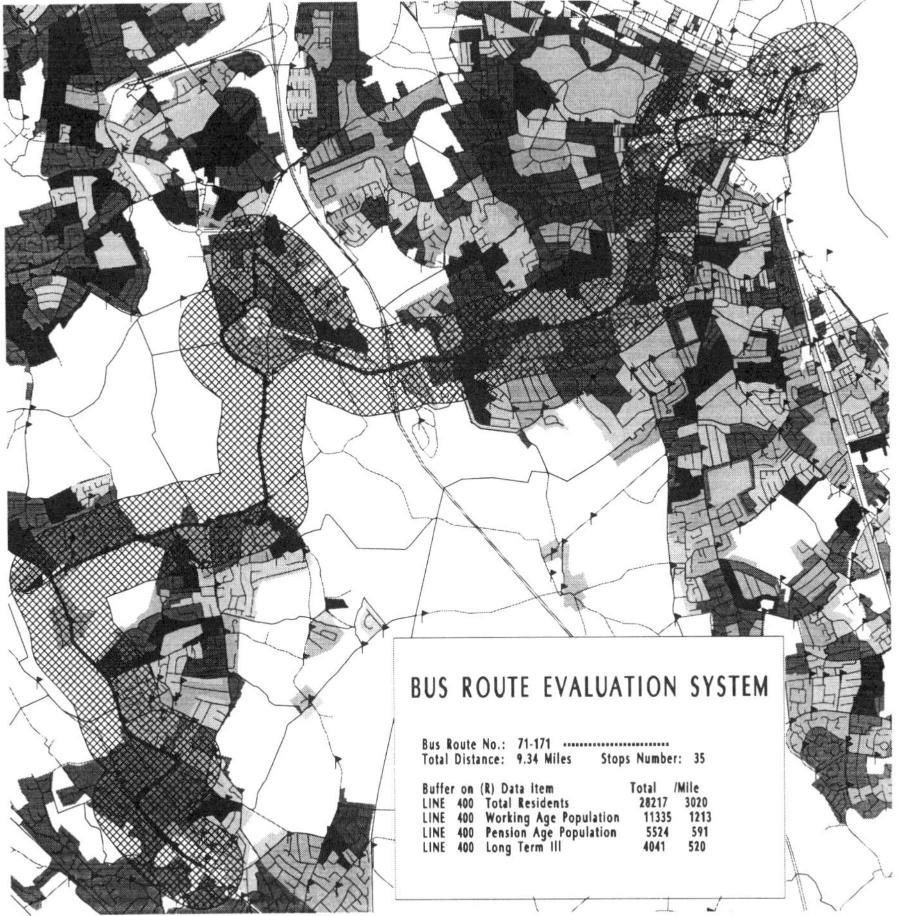

Fig. 5.1 The population catchment of a bus line (buffering distance: 400 m).

contain the header records for each ED. The relevant reformatting can be carried out using a simple program or some of the facilities in SPSS or SAS.

Boundaries may be synthesized using Thiessen polygons – these can be quickly created in ARC/INFO using the THIESSEN command. Note that the new coverage is no longer a point coverage but a polygon coverage (there are a number of GIS operations which convert from point or line data to polygon data). For example:

[ARC]: THIESSEN *ED81_CENTROIDS ED81_POLYGONS*

Displaying these polygons reveals that they are all convex, and at the edge of the study region the polygons can look rather unusual. There are a number of operations which are possible here to improve the look of the coverage, of which the simplest is to intersect a county boundary (or some other boundary, as appropriate) with the Thiessen polygons:

[ARC]: INTERSECT *ED81_POLYGONS COUNTY81 ~ ED81_COUNTY*

The PAT will require a little reorganization to remove unnecessary items – the DROPITEM command is useful here:

[ARC]: DROPITEM *ED81_COUNTY.PAT ED81_COUNTY.PAT ~ COUNTY81#*
[ARC]: DROPITEM *ED81_COUNTY.PAT ED81_COUNTY.PAT ~ COUNTY81-ID*

More sophisticated 'improvements' might involve intersecting the Thiessen polygons with ward boundaries; the process can be automated through the use of the ARC/INFO Macro Language.

More useful from the point of view of change analysis would be to take the 1991 ED boundaries and intersect them with the 1981 ward boundaries and recalculate the 1991 values on the 1981 spatial base. If 1991 ED boundaries are not available, then either Thiessen polygons may be created for them or the centroids can be assigned 1981 ward codes (as in the fire example below). A slightly more sophisticated analysis would take the postcode-to-ED lookup file and assign 1981 ward codes to the postcodes – this would then form the basis of a population-weighted assignment of the 1991 data to the 1981 areas. This is an occasion where GIS is only part of the process of analysing census data and intercensal change. However, the importance of not neglecting the errors in these GIS operations is emphasized. GIS cannot make good all the differences in spatial information, and attempts to overlay incompatible 1981 and 1991 Census ED boundaries is just one example. If such areas are created and the match-up is not perfect, then users of the data need somehow to carry forward some of the resulting uncertainty. Openshaw *et al.* (1991) describe one general method for doing this.

4.4 Transferring point information to census areas

Another area in which we can exploit the capabilities of GIS is the aggregation of non-census point-referenced information to an areal base for which we have census information. This has been used extensively, notably in epidemiological studies. For example in a study of cancer cases in northern England, childhood cancer cases were given postcodes, grid references for the postcodes were obtained from the Central Postcode Directory, and the resulting point locations were intersected with ward boundary data to allow the calculation of rates and Poisson probabilities for the different cancer types (see Openshaw *et al.* 1987).

In this example, we assume that information relating to, for example, fires in residential areas has been postcoded, and that a map of fire incidence is desired. We can obtain the counts of households from the census. Depending on which version of the Central Postcode Directory is available, the grid references will be to 100 m or 10 m resolution – we shall assume that they are to 100 m resolution and that the ward boundaries are to 1 m resolution. It is important to realize that resolution and accuracy are not the same and should not be confused .

If the grid references are captured in a file, with some suitable user ids, we can use the GENERATE command to create a point coverage. Suppose the file *house_fires.dat* contains lines of the form

```
1, 4532, 5613
2, 4723, 5529
.
.
.
2134, 4428, 5123
END
```

then we create a point coverage:

```
[ARC]:          GENERATE HOUSE_FIRES
[GENERATE]:     INPUT house_fires.dat
                POINTS
                QUIT
[ARC]:          BUILD HOUSE_FIRES POINT
```

As before, GENERATE needs to know the name of the coverage to create, the location of the input data and the type of input data. A point attribute table for each fire is created using the BUILD command.

However, at the moment, the fires data are stored to 100 m resolution and the ward data are assumed to be to 1 m resolution. How can we integrate the two? If we multiply the eastings and northings for the fire locations by 100 then we shall achieve the desired resolution, although note that we have not altered the accuracy of the data – we need to be aware that there might be some south-western bias in the locations. The transformation required is simply accomplished:

```
[ARC]:       CREATE FIRES1M HOUSE_FIRES
[ARC]:       TABLES
[TABLES]:    SELECT FIRES1M.TIC
             CALCULATE XTIC = XTIC * 100
             CALCULATE YTIC = YTIC * 100
             LIST
             QUIT STOP
[ARC]:       TRANSFORM HOUSE_FIRES FIRES1M
```

The information required for the transformation is contained in the TIC file for the untransformed coverage: we begin by creating an empty coverage containing only the tics from the untransformed coverage. In TABLES we select the tic file for the coverage to receive the transformed data, and we multiply the tic values (in the XTIC and YTIC items) by 100; it is helpful to list the infofile to check that the calculation has been specified correctly. Finally the TRANSFORM command is used to accomplish the transformation.

There are two commands which are appropriate to compute the geometric intersection of the fire and ward coverages. Both will create a new point coverage containing the data from the fire coverage and the information for the ward in which each fire is located. The IDENTITY command will create a new coverage which contains all the points from the fire coverage (including those which fall outside the physical extent of the wards); the INTERSECT command will exclude any fires which lie outside the location of the ward boundaries. The choice of command will be dependent on the context of the study. We shall use the IDENTITY command:

[ARC]: IDENTITY *FIRES1M WARDS1M FIREWARD* POINT #~
NOJOIN

The # specifies a default 'fuzzy tolerance' (the minimum distance between points in the output coverage). It is calculated as the minimum fuzzy tolerance in the two input coverages. The NOJOIN parameter instructs IDENTITY only to add the ward's internal number (the item name is *WARDS1M#*) to the PAT of the output coverage. This helps to keep coverage sizes to a minimum; the relate environment is used to merge information from the ward PAT and its associated files. The frequency counts can then be generated using the FREQUENCY command:

[ARC]: FREQUENCY *FIREWARD.PAT FIREWARD.DATA*
TABLE#
[FREQUENCY]: WARDS1M#
END
END

The FREQUENCY command prompts for one or more frequency items. As we only want to know the frequency in each ward, then we use the internal number which was added to the PAT by the IDENTITY command. The output infofile contains two items *FREQUENCY* and *WARDS1M#* – there are others but these need not concern us now.

We may find it helpful to add in some extra items to the *FIREWARD.DATA* infofile to receive the ward code, the calculated rates per household and area:

[ARC]: ADDITEM *FIREWARD.DATA FIREWARD.DATA~*
WARD_CODE 6 6 C

```
[ARC]:     ADDITEM FIREWARD.DATA FIREWARD.DATA~
               RATE_HH 4 12 F 2
[ARC]:     ADDITEM FIREWARD.DATA FIREWARD.DATA~
               RATE_HA 4 12 F 2
```

Finally we can calculate the rates: we need to relate a number of files together, first to get the ward codes from the *WARDS1M* PAT using the *WARDS1M#* item and also to compute the rate per hectare:

```
[ARC]:     INFO
[INFO]:    ARC
           SELECT FIREWARD.DATA
           RELATE 1 WARDS1KM.PAT BY WARDS1KM# WITH~
               LINK
           MOVE $1WARD_CODE TO WARD_CODE
           CALCULATE RATE_HA = ( FREQUENCY / $1AREA ) /~
               10000
```

Next we get the household counts. First we clear the existing relates and then we set up a new relate with a census infofile:

```
[INFO]:    /* continue */
           RELATE 1 WARD_COUNTS.DATA BY WARD_CODE
           CALCULATE RATE_HH = (FREQUENCY /~
               $1HOUSEHOLDS) *10000
```

In each case, the related file is given a number. We can then refer to items in the related file by prefixing the item name we require with $ and the relation number. Despite the apparent complexity, this is all really straightforward.

4.5 Three-dimensional representation of population distribution

The density or concentration of population can be represented by a three-dimensional surface if we agree that the social and economic characteristics of an area are influenced by its neighbouring areas. In other words, the spatial changes are continuous. First we need to find a way to measure the density of population – using a grid to aggregate the point-based data is one of the common methods (section 4.4). Then using TIN in ARC/INFO, Thiessen polygons can be generated about these points. Finally changing the *Z* factor, the surface can show the dramatic areal changes of the distribution of population. Figure 5.2 gives a three-dimensional representation of unemployment rate in the Greater Manchester area, 1991. The following commands provide a quick way to generate and to view such a surface model in ARC/INFO (version 6.1.1):

```
[ARC]:          ARCTIN EDCENTROIDS EDTIN POINT ~
                    UNEMPLOY # 1000 100
.
.
.
[ARCPLOT]:      MAPEXTENT UNEMPLOY
[ARCPLOT]:      SURFACE TIN EDTIN LINEAR 100
[ARCPLOT]:      SURFACEDEFAULTS
[ARCPLOT]:      SURFACEDRAPE MESH ALONGY 100 1
[ARCPLOT]:      SURFACEDRAPE ARCLINES ED_COVERAGE 3
...
```

5 Designing zonal boundaries optimized for use with census data

5.1 Handling census data for unnatural areas

A major problem with the 1991 Census, and indeed all previous censuses, concerns the nature of the geographical entities used to report the census statistics. As Morphet (1993) correctly points out, the census EDs are not 'natural' areal units. The same criticism applies even more to wards, postcode sector geography and districts. The criticism is that the availability of digital boundary information represents an invitation for users to map data using various census geographies whilst failing to realize that the areal entities being presented in cartographic form are neither comparable entities nor natural units for presenting data about the socioeconomic and demographic condition of people. The spatial variation reported by choropleth maps might easily have been created by the modifiable areal problem (Openshaw 1984). The need to chop continuous space into discrete lumps can cause all manner of problems. Some of the census boundaries will reflect real changes in the underlying urban mosaic; however, many others might be purely arbitrary. Morphet (1993) argues that 'the only significant ED boundaries are those to be found between different but homogeneous EDs' (p.1274) and that 'out of many thousand ED boundaries in the

Fig. 5.2 The three-dimensional surface of unemployment rate in Greater Manchester.

1981 Census map of Newcastle, only two, amounting to less than 200 m of boundary length, are significantly located at the boundary of areas of different social composition' (p.1276).

Martin and Bracken (1991) attempt to avoid some of the discrete space problems by representing census data as a surface. Martin (1989) argues that this avoids the limitations of choropleth mapping and it is certainly easily handled by GIS – there are many graphical functions for viewing surfaces in three dimensions. However, continuous space representations, no matter how cleverly done, cannot escape from the fact that the data being measured by the census are not continuous. People and households do not exist in the form of a surface! But, equally, EDs, wards and all other census geographies are not optimal ways of representing their characteristics either. We can but echo Harvey (1969) when he warned against the misuse of areal units designed for one purpose (census collection or safe data reporting) for another purpose. The question is what can be done about it.

5.2 Designing new areal units for specific purposes

One possible solution is to use the power of GIS technology to re-aggregate the small area census data into larger areal entities that are less arbitrary in terms of a specific purpose or application. Clearly this is not ideal – some very important patterns will have already been lost by the original aggregation to EDs and wards – but there are still some benefits in re-engineering the census geography so that in specific ways the aggregated data possess at least some global levels of comparability and some of the extreme anomalies of arbitrary aggregation have been removed. This argument was first developed by Openshaw (1978) but it is only now that the tools are available that will in principle allow census users to apply zone design methods easily to the 1991 Census.

A number of re-aggregation criteria can be identified:

1. areas that possess similar levels of heterogeneity in terms of census variables of interest;
2. areas that are of an approximately equal size and shape; and
3. areas that provide an efficient partitioning of space and are of an approximately similar nature.

The simplest of these is little more than a contiguity constrained classification of census data (see Chapter 8). However, much more elaborate zone design criteria involve the use of complex aggregation optimizing procedures, variants of Openshaw's Automated Zoning Procedure (AZP) (Openshaw 1979, 1984). The following sections report the results of an ARC/INFO-based Zone Design System (ZDES) (Openshaw and Rao 1995) designed for use with 1991 Census data.

For illustrative purposes a ward level census dataset for Greater Manchester County is used. It contains 214 zones in digital form and a small number of census

Table 5.2 Zoning results

From 214 wards to 10 zones	Object	Best of 10 random runs	Tabu search	Simulated annealing
Equal number of working age population	Total variation	6.741%	2.83%	2.832%
Location allocation of working age population	Function result	5884.1	5725.8	5720.4
Correlation between unemployment rate and distance to the centre	Positive (+1.000)	+0.999995644	+0.999996754	+0.999998677
	Negative (-1.000)	-0.996967132	-0.999237188	-0.999499776

variables. The complexity of the AZP type of optimization problem depends on the number of census zones (N) available for analysis and the desired number of output zones (M). As N becomes large in relation to M so the aggregation 'freedom' inherent in the data rapidly increases and the optimization task becomes fairly trivial. Here $N = 214$ and $M = 10$ presents a problem of a modest to low degree of difficulty and is presented for illustrative purposes.

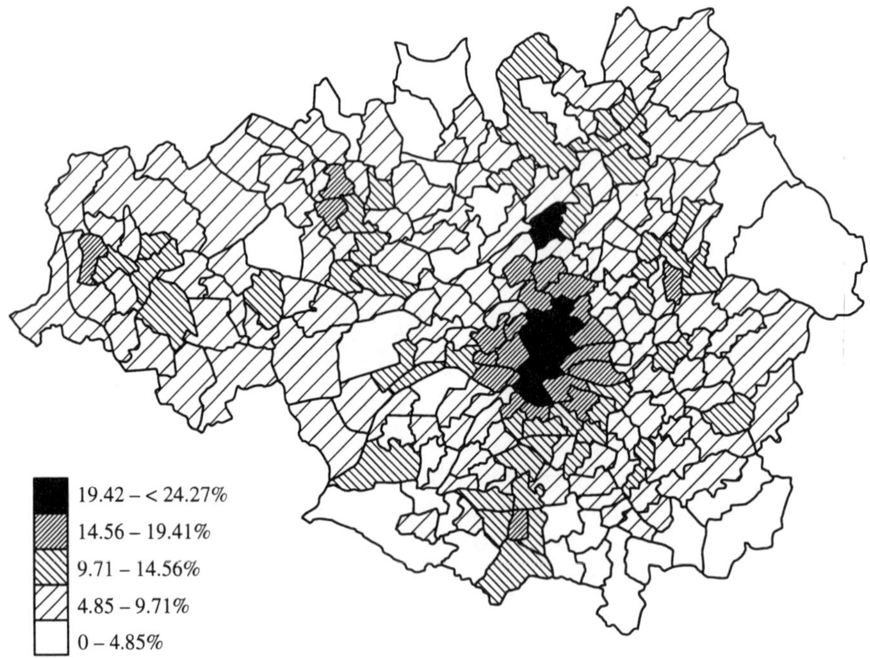

Fig. 5.3 The unemployment rate by wards.

5.3 Example 1: Designing census zones of approximately equal size in terms of a specific census variable

The oldest form of purposeful zoning system explicitly designed for a particular purpose is the electoral areas. In the UK, parliamentary constituencies are designed to be of approximately equal size to ensure fair democratic representation. Similar criteria are also relevant for ensuring a reasonable spatial representation of census data. The concept of cartograms (see Chapter 6) is one way of achieving this goal in a cartographic context. Deliberately searching for an aggregation of N areas into M new areas such that each of the M new areas contains an approximately similar number of a specific census variables is another way of solving the problem. There is no guarantee of course that there is a unique solution to this type of problem but, if this is important, then one can be enforced by imposing other constraints (i.e. approximate shape equality) on the optimization process.

Table 5.2 gives the results of seeking to aggregate the 214 wards into 10 regions in Great Manchester County. The fit is quite good. Of more interest here is the resulting map of percentage unemployment for zones which no longer vary in terms of the number of economically active. Figure 5.3 shows the original ward level map, whilst Fig. 5.4 presents the results for the engineered zoning system.

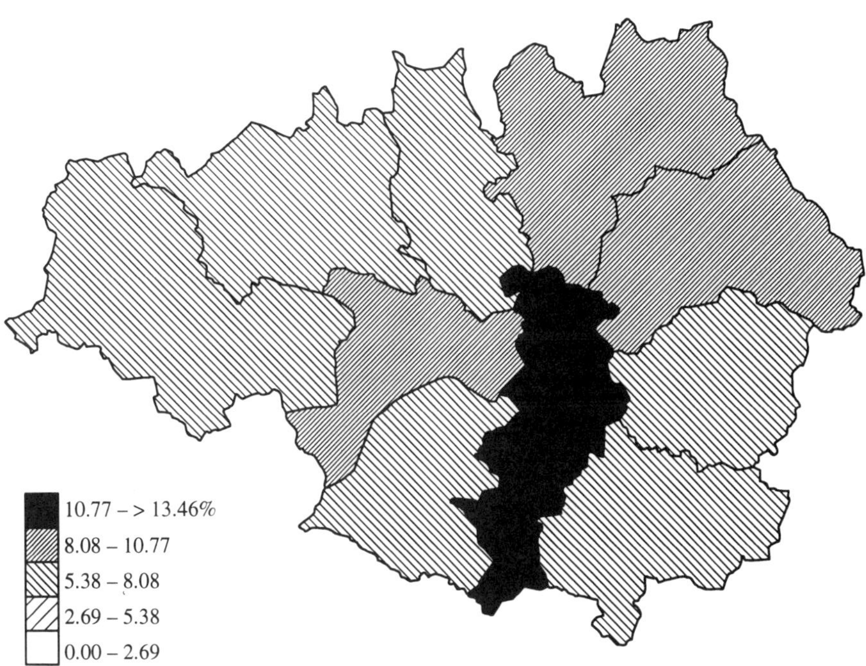

Fig. 5.4 The unemployment rate by districts.

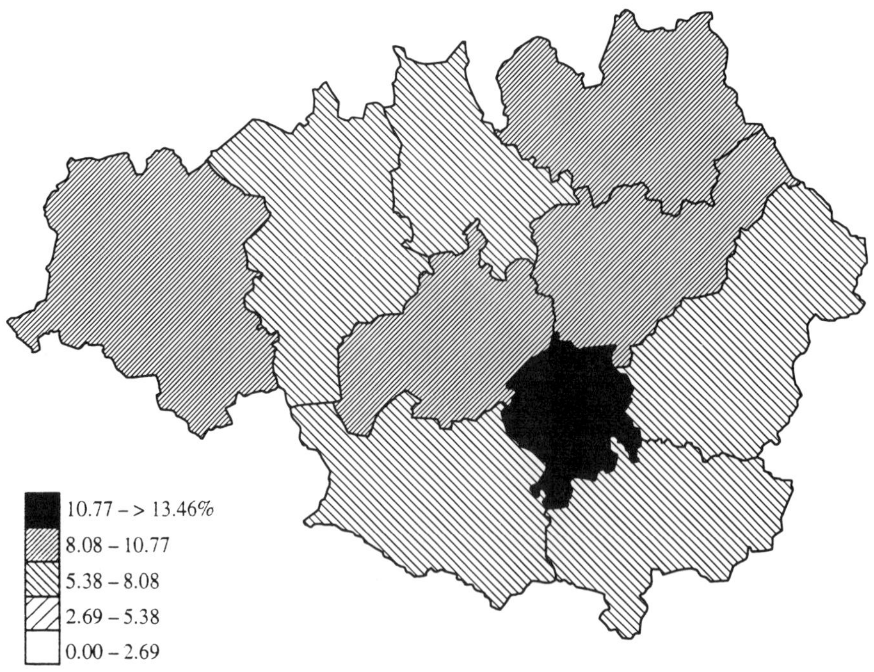

Fig. 5.5 The unemployment rate by new zones with location allocation on working age population.

5.4 Example 2: Designing zones to provide an efficient partitioning of space

Another generally useful zone design criterion is to seek an efficient partitioning of space such that a census variable distributed over the region of interest is well served. This is the classic location-allocation problem but it can also be an aggregation criterion (Goodchild 1979). The objective function is to find M points around which the wards are allocated to the nearest point such that the weighted sum of distances is minimized. Figure 5.5 presents the unemployment results for these zones.

5.5 Example 3: Designing zones to optimize correlation coefficients

The final example serves both as a warning of the danger of ignoring modifiable areal unit effects (see also Openshaw and Taylor 1981) and as a source of inspiration as to how a new set of spatial analysis tools might be devised. First, it is noted that quite often the aggregational freedom inherent in census data can be exploited by a zone design algorithm to produce virtually any result. Figure 5.6 shows the results of maximizing a negative relationship between unemployment and distance from the city centre. Figure 5.7 shows the results of maximizing

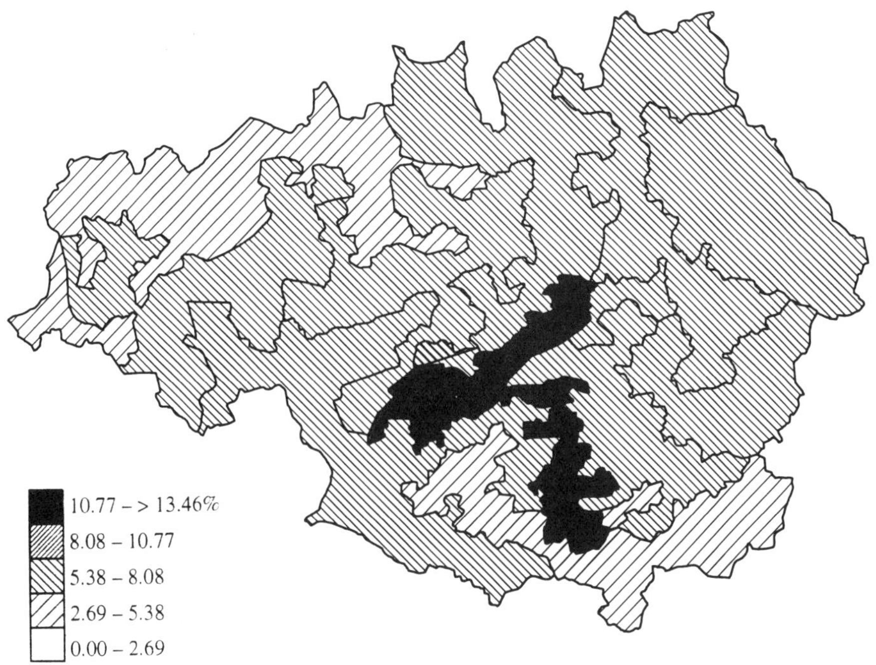

Fig. 5.6 The unemployment rate by new zones with negative correlation between unemployment rate and distance to the regional centre.

a positive correlation. Here the spatial data are made to fit the model by manipulating the zoning system. Distance is measured from the weighted zone centroid – hence the weird zones sometimes needed as the suburbs are relocated in the town centre! However, as Openshaw (1984) pointed out, the resulting zoning systems provide a visualization of the interaction between model and data at a given spatial scale and, far from being a problem, this aspect of the modifiable areal unit problem might actually be useful. It is left as an exercise for the interested census user to consider how to utilize this technology most effectively.

5.6 Suggestions for the future of census geography

Users need geographical flexibility in census data. However, this process is not just a matter of designing spatial building blocks that link to postcodes or match key administrative boundaries and which aggregate nicely over a fixed range of scales. It should also allow the users to define their own output areas, subject to confidentiality (i.e. minimum size) constraints. Users interested in ranking areas should be ranking areas that are simultaneously of a similar size (for data precision purposes) and of a similar nature (for geographical social comparability purposes). Users interested in studying socioeconomic variations within towns

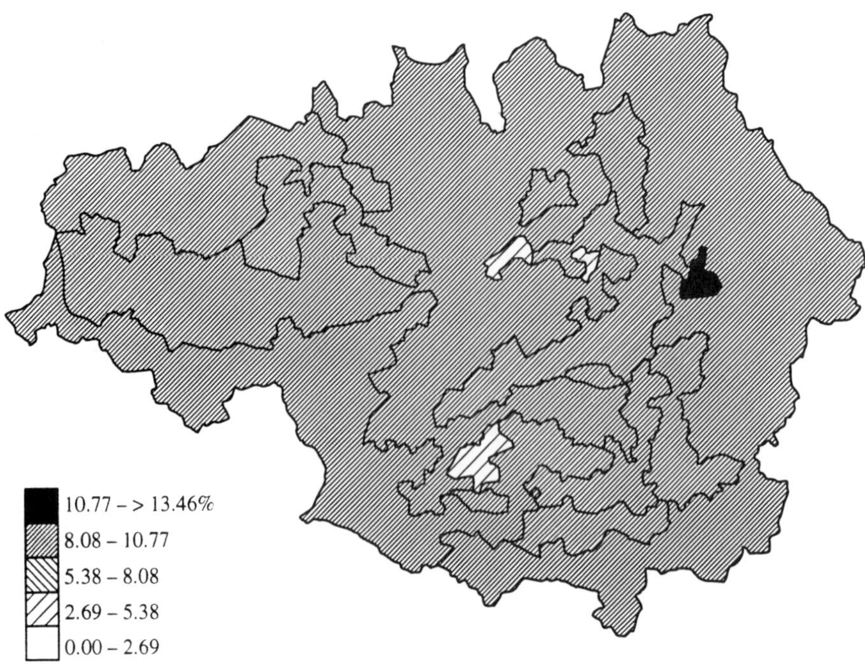

Fig. 5.7 The unemployment rate by new zones with positive correlation between unemployment rate and distance to the regional centre.

need to use areal entities that respect rather than disguise or remove significant differences. The definition of what is significant is, quite reasonably, application dependent. GIS tools such as SDS provide a means by which census users could in 2001 design whatever census geographies would be deemed best for their purposes, and for many users there may be more than one of these. Alternatively, the census agencies could themselves offer explicitly designed census zoning systems with respect to three or four principal zonal definition criteria.

6 Conclusions

GIS is not merely concerned with cartographic display of census data. Each census seems to be accompanied by a rash of census atlases. It has been observed that, as computers get more and more powerful and we are inundated with software which exploits that power, we can produce rubbish at a greater rate than at any time in the history of the world. The GIS vendors are only too willing to tread a path to our doors to sell us the ultimate solution to all our problems. The problems associated with the analysis of spatial data, and the integration of GIS and spatial data analysis, are currently receiving attention (Fotheringham and Rogerson 1994, Goodchild *et al.* 1992). Whilst the mathematical treatment by

Griffith (1993) may be difficult for many, a useful review of what is covered in spatial data analysis is given in Upton and Fingleton (1985). As yet few GIS systems provide adequate facilities for spatial data analysis (Openshaw 1991). GIS is not, and never will be, a panacea. However, it does significantly extend the available census analysis tool-kit. It increases the usefulness of 1991 Census data in a number of ways: (i) a wide range of spatial data manipulation options is available; (ii) it allows easy linkage with other spatial information available in a digital form; (iii) it puts the census database into a broader context – as a GIS data source the census is fairly low resolution information; (iv) it provides a comprehensive set of mapping tools; and (v) it offers a framework within which, one day, really useful spatial and geographical analysis might be performed. The 1991 Census user cannot ignore GIS in many spatially oriented applications and it is confidently expected that its importance will increase throughout the 1990s.

References

Bartholdi, J J and L K Platzman 1988 Heuristics based on spacefilling curves for combinatorial problems in Euclidean space. *Management Science* 34, 291–305.

Bezdek 1984 FCM: the fuzzy *c*-means clustering algorithm. *Computers and Geoscience* 10 (2–3), 191–203.

Burrough, P A 1989 Fuzzy mathematical methods for soil survey and land evaluation. *Journal of Soil Science* 40, 477–92.

Dale, A and C Marsh 1993 *The 1991 Census User's Guide.* London: HMSO.

ESRI 1993 *Understanding GIS: the ARC/INFO Method*, Environmental Systems Research Institute, Redlands, CA.

Fisher, P F and A S Pathirana 1990 The evaluation of fuzzy membership of land cover classes in the suburban zone. *Remote Sensing and Environment* 34, 121–32.

Flowerdew, R and S Openshaw 1987 A review of the problems of transferring data from one set of areal units to another incompatible set. Northern RRL, Research Report 4, Universities of Newcastle upon Tyne and Lancaster.

Fotheringham, A S and B Rogerson 1994 *Spatial analysis and GIS.* Basingstoke: Taylor & Francis.

Goodchild, M 1979 The aggregation problem in location-allocation. *Geographical Analysis* 11 (3), 241–55.

Goodchild, M, R Haining and S Wise 1992 Integrating GIS and spatial data analysis: problems and possibilities. *International Journal of Geographic Information Systems* 6 (5), 407–25.

Griffith, D A 1993 Advanced spatial statistics for analysing and visualizing georeferenced data. *International Journal of Geographic Information Systems* 7 (2), 107–24.

Harvey, D 1969 *Explanation in Geography*. London: Edward Arnold.

Laurini, R and D Thompson 1991 *Fundamentals of Spatial Information Systems.* London: Academic Press.

Maguire, D J, M F Goodchild and D W Rhind (eds) 1991 *Geographical Information Systems: Principles and Applications*. Harlow: Longman.

Martin, D 1989 Mapping population data from zone centroid location. *Transactions of the Institute of British Geographers* 14 (1), 90–7.

Martin, D 1991 *Geographic Information Systems and Their Socioeconomic Applications.* London: Routledge.

Martin, D and I Bracken 1991 Techniques for modelling population related raster databases. *Environment and Planning A* 23, 1069–75.

Morphet, C 1993 The mapping of small-area census data – a consideration of the role of enumeration district boundaries. *Environment and Planning A* 25, 267–78.
Openshaw, S 1978 An empirical study of some zone design criteria. *Environment and Planning A*, 10, 781–94.
Openshaw, S 1979 A geographical solution to scale and aggregation problems in region-building, partitioning, and spatial modelling. *Transactions of the Institute of British Geographers* 2, 459–72.
Openshaw, S 1984 *The Modifiable Areal Unit Problem*, Catmog 38. Norwich: Geo-Abstracts.
Openshaw, S 1989 Learning to live with errors in spatial databases. In M Goodchild and S Gopal (eds) *The Accuracy of Spatial Databases*. London: Taylor and Francis, 263–76.
Openshaw, S 1991 Developing appropriate spatial analysis methods for GIS. In D J Maquire, M F Goodchild and D W Rhind (eds) *Geographical Information Systems: Principles and Applications*. New York: Longman, 389–402.
Openshaw, S and Rao, L 1995 Algorithms for re-engineering 1991 census geography. *Environment and Planning A* (forthcoming).
Openshaw, S and P Taylor 1981 The modifiable areal unit problem. In N Wrigley and R J Bennett (eds) *Quantitative Geography*. London: Routledge, 60–70.
Openshaw, S, M Charlton, C Wymer and A W Craft 1987 A mark I geographical analysis machine for the autmatic analysis of point data sets. *International Journal of Geographic Information Systems*, 1, 335–58.
Openshaw, S, C Charlton and S Carver 1991 Error propagation: a Monte Carlo simulation. In I Masser and M Blackemore (eds) *Handling Geographic Information*. New York: Longman, 78–101.
Rao, I and S Openshaw 1994 A spatial design system for census data: a toolbox for Arc/Info. Working Paper, School of Geography, University of Leeds.
Star, J and Estes, J 1990 *Geographic Information Systems: An Introduction*. Englewood Cliffs, NJ: Prentice Hall.
Upton, G and B Fingleton 1985 *Spatial Data Analysis by Example*. New York, Wiley.

6

Visualizing the 1991 Census

D Dorling

Editor's note

Visualization is one of the latest rediscoveries in science. It is an area where considerable progress is likely during the 1990s and one which might be expected to revolutionize traditional census cartography. Maybe census maps can become alive by merging computer visualization with virtual reality concepts. Indeed, increasingly the world has to be viewed from and within databases, which in some senses constitute a new universe of information. As humans we are blinded by the multi-dimensional and multivariate complexity of the census databases we can now create – often we cannot see the patterns for the detail. We cannot even clearly see the branch on which the leaf we are studying is located, let alone the tree or the forest of which it is part. Visualization is a step towards reducing this data blindness.

This is not a standard handbook chapter. It does not describe 'best practice', take the reader through the options they have, or provide a succinct summary of the field. This is because there is, as yet, no accepted wisdom to the methodology of census visualization, no set of all-singing all-dancing computer packages, no weighty academic legacy of papers on the subject. Visualization – the study of information through graphical means freed from manual restriction by the advances in scientific computing – is still very new. What this chapter aims to give is a flavour of visual techniques which can be used to study census data and which will become generally accessible in the decade following the 1991 Census. First the arguments for visualization are made, and examples are then given using the hierarchy of census geography to structure the chapter. Speculation on some possibilities for entirely new visual representations are given towards the end. The aim of this chapter is to show how visualization of the census can engage our imaginations in new ways to address age-old questions about society.

1 Visualization

> We must create a new language, consider a transitory state of new illusions and layers of validity and accept the possibility that there may be no language to describe ultimate reality, beyond the language of visions.
>
> (Denes 1979, p. 3)

Visualization is the dream that we can turn statistics into pictures which portray the complexity of the reality which we, from our experiences, know to exist. The British census provides millions of numbers concerning the people of this country. These numbers can be reduced to a few totals, averages and deviations, but such simple statistical manipulation alone cannot convey to us the grand structure and near-infinite subtlety of society which we know them to have captured (McCormick *et al.* 1987). What if it were possible to reconstruct part of what it actually means to live in Britain today – from the way in which 20 million census forms were completed – through pictures? This dream is not new.

From some of the first computer-drawn maps of the Swedish 1980 Census came the idea that there could be new ways of bringing masses of statistics to life through pictures:

> From the diagrams which display households suddenly appeared a throng of people who with muted voices told of their lives, of their loneliness, of their joy in their children and of their hopes on their behalf.
>
> (Szegö 1984, p. 20)

It needs to be made clear that the subject of this chapter is not illustration (to illustrate means, in dictionary terms, to clarify, make clear, pure or transparent). Graphic illustration of the census merely involves taking a few numbers and turning them into a pretty picture which is more interesting for publication than a table (for an example, see Plate I). Simple graphs and charts, maps and diagrams are included in this category as they can contain only a few variables, even if they are of the most elaborate design. This is not visualization, which is defined in practical terms as the process of making visible what was hidden in huge tables of figures, often too large to be printed on paper (Tufte 1983). Visualization involves the creation of new solutions for a dilemma of our times – having too much information to comprehend when using conventional analytical techniques.

Social scientists in particular have a more serious and ironic problem in trying to understand census data using conventional statistics. They already *know* too much about the subjects they are studying for the simplistic findings from these studies to be enlightening. Statistics has been defined as 'the study of the unknown' (Tanur *et al.* 1985), being able to find structure in complex variable patterns – such as the influences of a variety of pesticides on crops or the discovery of clusters between alloys of many metals. But when it comes to the study of that with which we are most familiar – our social world – these techniques can often produce embarrassingly naive results, 'discovering' what was either already well known, or results which are artefacts of the technique. The application of visualization is thus appropriate in this area because it can simultaneously both show us what we expect to see and allow us slowly to reshape our perceptions of reality. Superficially the working of images is explicit (Marr 1982) – the literal opposite of *black box* techniques where the computer produces, say, a cluster analysis purporting to represent social inequality and you are implored by the weight of convention to accept its validity.

The pictures created through visualization may not show a pattern. This may be either because there is no pattern to find or because the information has not been looked at in the right way. Imagination in design is needed, but also a great deal of trial and error, in order to find an effective way of uncovering unknown patterns in census statistics (Tukey 1965). A scientific approach is needed to make sure that the pictures illustrate what was intended without unintended bias. An artistic approach is needed to ensure that the overall creation is acceptable to the mind and eye which are being asked to analyse them (Robinson 1989). Visualization requires the combination of disparate skills, and the existence of some structure to find, for it to be seen as successful.

The eye reads pictures, the mind analyses them: people respond and the public can react. To have presented, before our eyes, images detailing the nature of the society in which we live forces us to question more emotively the reasons for society's current evolution, by thinking about the quality of our lives and of the lives of others around us. The census is our decennial snapshot of British society (Rees 1992). The challenge is to show, as best we now can, how the picture looks this time round.

The census is amenable to visualization because of the strengths of the inherent structures to be found in society and the quality of the geographical referencing which census tables contain. What makes the census particularly valuable for social science is not the wealth or depth of the questions that it asks (for they are few and shallow), but rather the great spatial detail that is provided – showing how each neighbourhood, each block of streets, each hamlet, differs socially from its neighbours (for every place in the country simultaneously). The social structure of our society is manifest most directly through the spatial distribution of its people (Pred 1986) and so through mapping the census we can obtain a glimpse of the complex social landscape which we imagine to exist (Census Research Unit 1980).

In the first *Census User's Handbook* there is a chapter by the editor on 'mapping census data' (Rhind 1983). The advances reported in that chapter had altered census cartography significantly, and took many previously manual methods to their automated limits. Computer cartography had only recently become widespread, so for the first time maps of the census were not constrained by what it was possible to produce by hand (see Chapter 5). Cartographers began to experiment with new forms of mapping, but forms which could still largely be thought of in terms of traditional land maps – constrained by the tenets of a discipline rooted in mapping for military purposes, where the size and value of territory, rather than the lives of people, were all-important (Harley 1989). It is intriguing that census cartography combines two ancient tools of war: to put it simply, cartography maps land to be fought over (Sternberg 1993) and census statistics count men to fight! It is important not to forget the original reasons why all this information was collected and that the state paid for it to happen.

Now that we can shed some of the constraints of traditional mapping (both in theory and practice) and adopt some of the new possibilities of computer graphics, many researchers are moving into visualization (MacEachren 1992). It is worth reiterating that visualization, in a theoretical sense, means to make visible what is hidden – in this case, what is hidden in the reams of statistics now issued about Britain's people, households and dwellings. We want to be able to see what is happening to all the people of this country, to those living in tower blocks as much as those living in rural estates. We do not want to map the use and nature of British land, but to portray the employment and nature of the people in Britain. Here we are not concerned with 'census mapping':

> Census maps, and related data, are used for three purposes: to locate census areas in relation to other places; to display census data in an effective and parsimonious way; and, to carry out analytical operations such as calculating the population characteristics of the catchment population of a major store.
>
> (Barr 1993, pp. 250–1)

The Office of Population and Census Statistics has released over a billion statistics derived from the 1991 Census. We could whittle these down to a few numbers: 54,156,067 people, an unemployment rate of 9.5%, a few measures of statistical deviation; a table of 60 'key statistics', or the results of a hypothesis test. But that would not do justice to understanding the wealth of information that has been collected. The desire of visualization is to grasp as much complexity as possible, to see what all these figures have to show, not to simplify but to comprehend. As a result very different axioms from conventional mapping emerge:

> Detail cumulates into large coherent structures ... *to clarify, add detail.*
>
> (Tufte 1990, p. 37)

Social structure often has a fine texture to it in which the microcosm reflects the macrocosm, like the patterns of fractal mathematics now so easily revealed by the computer (Mandlebrot 1983). There is so much detail that it would be almost impossible to draw a single picture by hand which fairly reflected the spatial composition of our society. The best method for visualizing a set of data will depend on the patterns that exist in those data which, in turn, cannot often be found without visualization. So a recursive search for a successful image is often needed, and in this a multitude of different techniques can be used. This chapter demonstrates the use of a few of these for visualizing census data in the hope that this will inspire others to experiment further.

The human eye–brain system has evolved to search for, and analyse, spatial patterns (Marr 1982). At speed it can spot order, repetition, grouping and inconsistencies in a picture. These are the very things researchers are looking for in a society. If we can turn these numbers into pictures we may be able to use the census to understand society better than we have been able to before, to learn something which we did not know, rather than merely to confirm our expectations.

2 Census geography

> The practices through which social structure is both expressed and reproduced cannot be divorced from the structuring of space and the use of spatial structures.
>
> (Pred 1986, p. 198)

Visualization of census data does not have to be spatial. Nevertheless it is that aspect which is concentrated on in this chapter. The reason for this is that the greatest advantage of census information over other social surveys is that it provides us with, in effect, thousands of identical simple surveys which were taken at the same time in every locality. Most other surveys are restricted in only providing information for a single place, or for a sparse national sample, or for only a few regions or districts of the country – even though they might provide much more detailed data about their more limited subjects.

The finest spatial level of output of the 1991 Census in England and Wales is the enumeration district. Each enumeration district contained, on average, 400 people and consisted of just a few streets or a single block of flats in towns and cities, part of a village or a hamlet in the country. There were over 113,000 enumeration districts in 1991 in England and Wales (see Chapter 4 for how Scotland differs). We have been given information about very many small groups of people and all their neighbours. It is therefore the spatial aspect of these data which gives them their value.

For each enumeration district a national grid reference to an accuracy of 100 m is given in what are called the *Small Area Statistics*. This is supposed to identify the centre of population of the area. The points were chosen by hand and in the first release of the statistics many hundreds were found to have been misplaced! However, for the first time, digital boundaries of the enumeration districts have been produced, in theory delimiting precisely where 'on the ground' people were counted (these were released during 1993). Enumeration districts are likely to range in size from less than one-thousandth of a square kilometre (the base of a high rise block) to over a hundred square kilometres (encompassing empty moorland in the most remote areas). It would not be surprising to find the largest being more than a million times the area of the smallest – whilst still containing fewer people.

How might we go about visualizing the characteristics of people in so many areas, which vary so much in size? Figure 6.1 shows a grid drawn over a 'normal'

Fig. 6.1 1981 equal population grid squares from smoothed enumeration district cartogram, 30,000 people squares.

equal land area map of the British Isles. The grid is not uniform but is violently stretched and twisted. It is made up of almost 2000 squares which (on the mainland) each contain 30,000 people. There are many such squares in the large cities, but few in the more rural areas. The picture is more complex than this, however; in East Anglia, for example, the effect of Norwich can be seen, like a weight pulling the fabric of some giant net inwards. Each square contains the same number of people, yet some cover great swathes of land while others are barely visible. Perhaps it would be more sensible to pull all the lines straight to form a rectangular grid, ensuring that each square would be of equal size so that their populations are more fairly represented than on a traditional map. An *equal population cartogram* would have been created (Tobler 1973a), but more on that later.

In 1981 digital boundaries were available only for wards, of which there were over 9200 in England and Wales and into which enumeration districts were nested. The electoral wards varied in population from 498 (Lower Swaledale) to 41,502 (Birmingham, Weoley), and in land area from 19 hectares (Skipton Central) to 44,789 hectares (Upper North Tyne). Thus they exhibit a skewed distribution in which the majority are small in area where people huddle together on the land. On a conventional national grid projection only a small proportion of the wards are visible. Figure 6.2 shows these wards' boundaries for the whole country, with an inset focusing in on London. At almost every level of magnification there are some wards which cannot be seen and others (usually containing the fewest people) which dominate the image. Simply because the census provides geographical information using only one projection does not mean that that projection must be maintained (although almost all mapping does this). Similarly, we do not have to use the raw counts of the people it lists, but can transform these to use more meaningful scales.

What satellite imagery has shown us most vividly is that people do not appear on photographs of the earth's surface – they are not like fields, rivers or mountains. People are tiny, houses are tiny: something that may appear obvious, but which is all too quickly forgotten in conventional census cartography. More importantly, people are very unevenly distributed over most of the land surface of Britain, so that if a traditional equal area map projection is chosen for anything larger than a small part of a city, gross over- and under-representations of different social groups will be presented in the image. It should never be forgotten that:

> mapping can be extremely informative but it can also mislead.
>
> (Rhind 1983, p. 171)

The information in the census concerns people and households. In visualizing these, a primary aim should be that each person and each household is given equal representation in the image. Current computer versatility allows this, so a principal challenge of visualizing the 1991 Census is to achieve it. In Fig. 6.5 of the *User's Handbook* of the 1981 Census a handmade cartogram of 19 districts was presented. Figure 6.3 shows an equal population cartogram of the more than

Fig. 6.2 Census ward and Scottish part postcode sector boundaries.

Plate I The distribution of population by county in 1981.

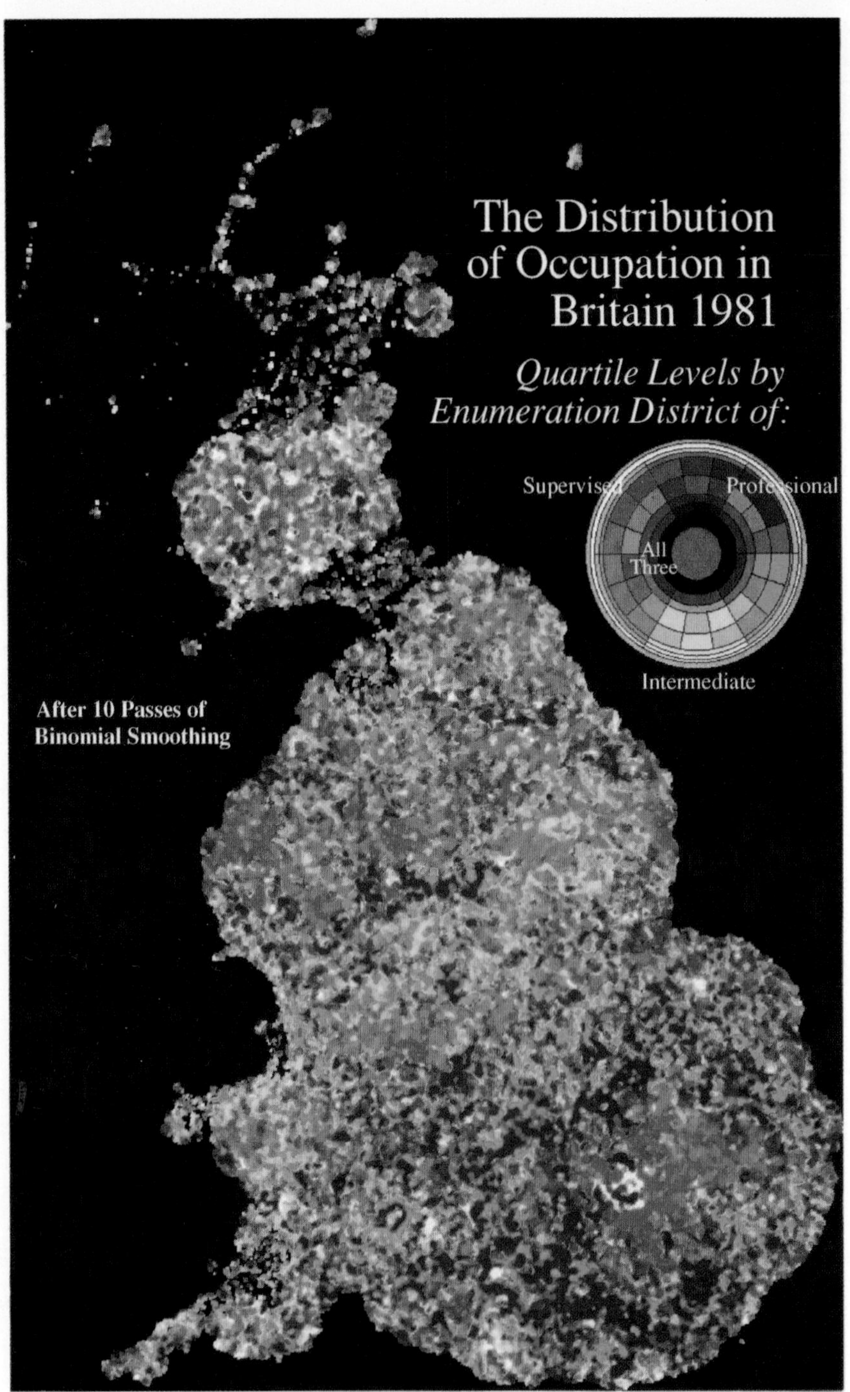

Plate II The distribution of occupation in Britain, 1981, after 10 passes of binomial smoothing. Reproduced with the permission of *The Cartographic Journal* of the British Cartographic Society.

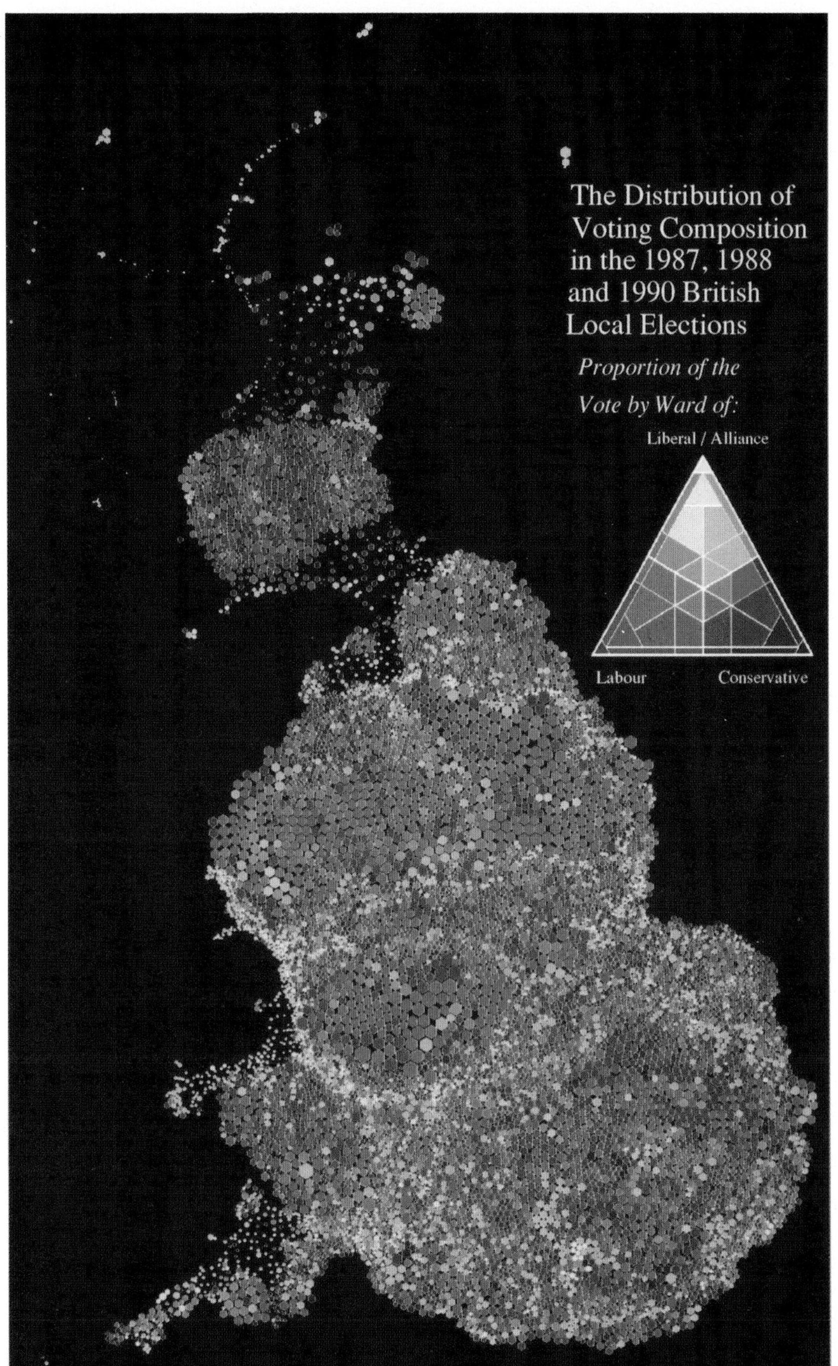

Plate III The distribution of voting composition in the 1987, 1988 and 1990 British local elections. Reproduced with the permission of *The Cartographic Journal* of the British Cartographic Society.

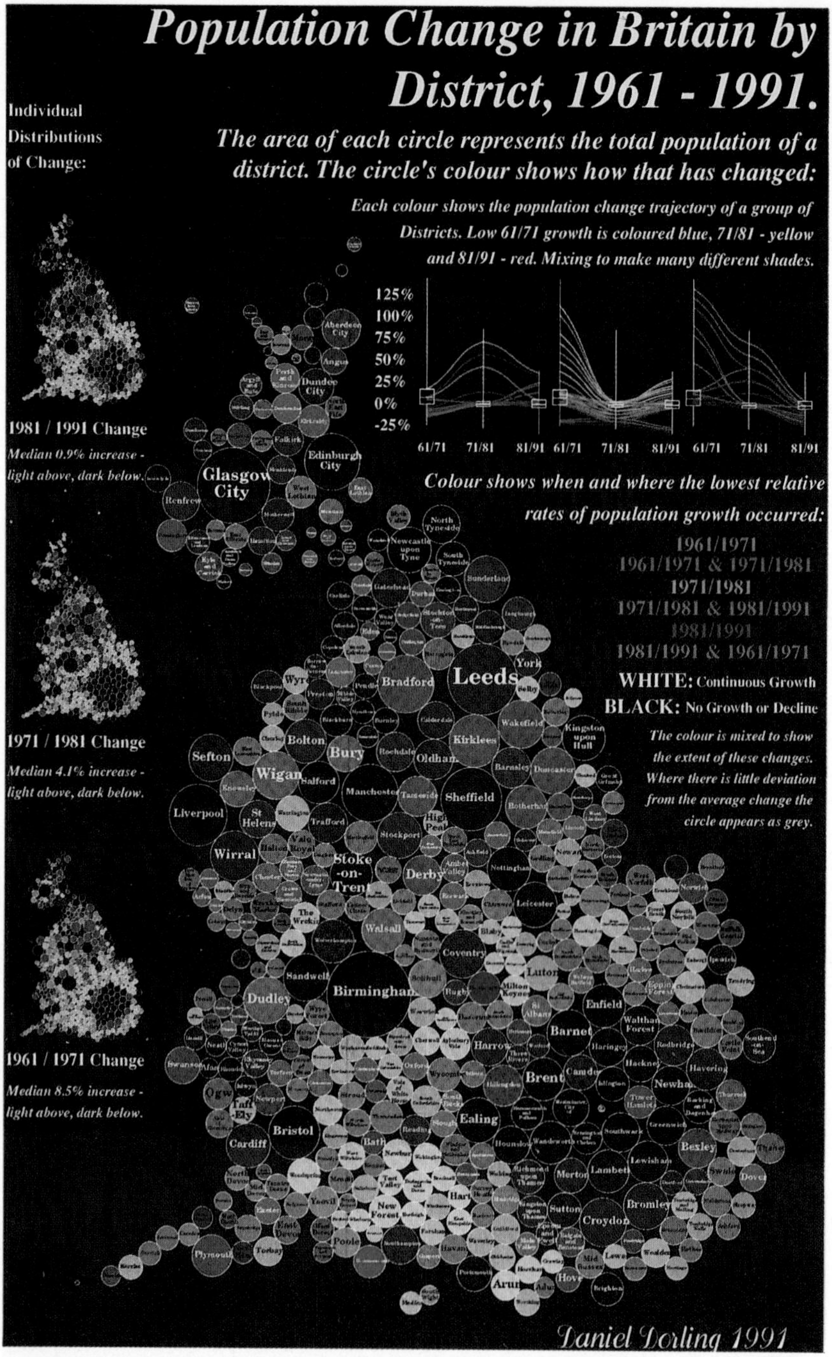

Population Change in Britain by District, 1961 - 1991.

Individual Distributions of Change:

The area of each circle represents the total population of a district. The circle's colour shows how that has changed:

Each colour shows the population change trajectory of a group of Districts. Low 61/71 growth is coloured blue, 71/81 - yellow and 81/91 - red. Mixing to make many different shades.

125%
100%
75%
50%
25%
0%
-25%

61/71 71/81 81/91 61/71 71/81 81/91 61/71 71/81 81/91

1981 / 1991 Change

Median 0.9% increase - light above, dark below.

Colour shows when and where the lowest relative rates of population growth occurred:

1961/1971
1961/1971 & 1971/1981
1971/1981
1971/1981 & 1981/1991
1981/1991
1981/1991 & 1961/1971
WHITE: Continuous Growth
BLACK: No Growth or Decline

The colour is mixed to show the extent of these changes. Where there is little deviation from the average change the circle appears as grey.

1971 / 1981 Change

Median 4.1% increase - light above, dark below.

1961 / 1971 Change

Median 8.5% increase - light above, dark below.

Daniel Dorling 1991

Plate IV Population change in Britain by district, 1961–91.

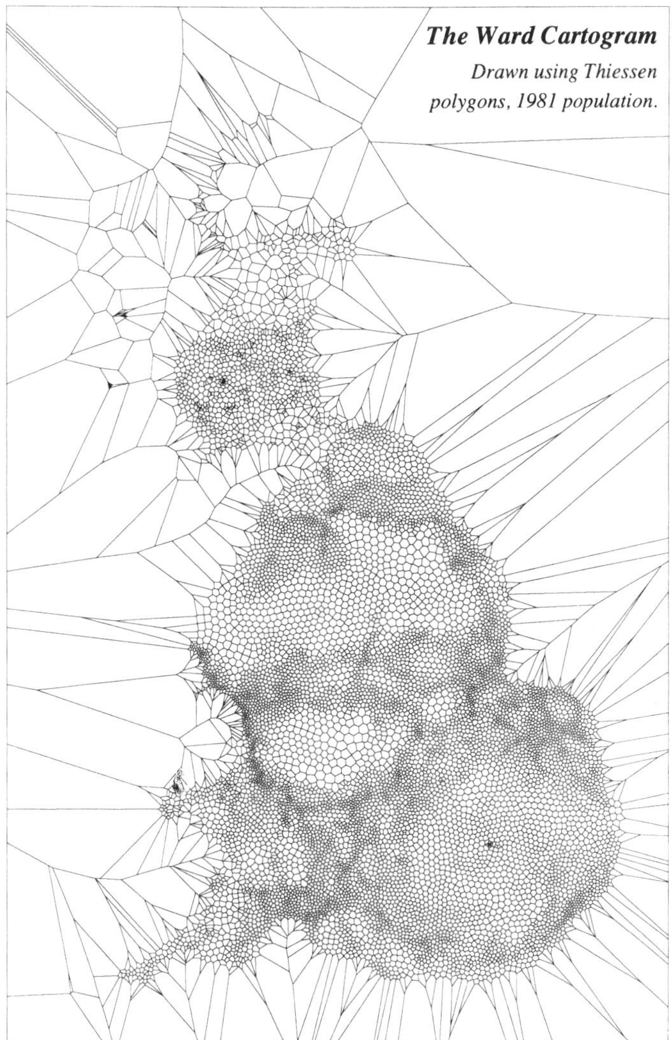

Fig. 6.3 The ward cartogram drawn using Thiessen polygons, 1981 population.

10,000 wards of Britain based on the 1981 Census. In effect, the lines in Fig. 6.1 have been straightened (for more details see Dorling 1995). Thiessen polygons have been used to make the projection appear continuous and to create the 'stained glass window' effect as the populated areas meet the sea. Clipping a coastal boundary would result in a neater if less interesting image (see Chapter 5 for an explanation of these terms). The cartogram represents one level of abstraction beyond the land (choropleth) map – one level closer to the maps of social landscape we are aiming to see.

On the type of cartogram from which Fig. 6.3 was derived, every ward is represented by a circle. Each circle's size is proportional to the population of that ward. Traditionally these cartograms have been used in mapping election results, and Plate III (described in Section 5) illustrates this. In this approach, most wards on the cartogram have been placed adjacent to wards that they share common boundaries with, although occasionally this has not proved possible (thus it is a 'noncontinuous area cartogram' in the terminology of Olson 1976). Even when reproduced to the page size of this book each ward is made visible in a single image. Here is a projection upon which it is possible to show the fortunes of every group of people at something akin to the neighbourhood level, nationally, without a particular bias against those groups who happen to live in the most densely populated areas.

At what spatial level, however, should we be looking at society? Now that the creation of high resolution area cartograms is practical we are not restricted to using the lowest administrative level (Hunt 1968) or the smallest artificial areal units (Census Research Unit 1980) that are visible. We can use whatever level we choose. There is a wealth of good advice to be followed in making the choice of scale, however:

> Even given these resources, it is essential, in general terms, to use the most detailed data available for mapping ...
>
> (Rhind 1983, p. 183)

We can even begin to go below the enumeration district level and redistribute census statistics in a dasymetric fashion using the locations of unit postcodes – if we so choose (see for example Fig. 6.5, which is explained later). (Dasymetric mapping means to shade the pieces of land upon which people live.)

Nevertheless, the choice of how many places to adopt and show on paper does affect the techniques we can use for the visualization of census data. It also affects the number of independent variables we can investigate simultaneously, and the degree of detail with which we can investigate each one. Basically, the more areas we wish to see at once, the less we can see about each – there is a finite (if large) amount of detail that a single image can contain and remain comprehensible. To decide how much *spatial* detail to see necessitates deciding how much *social* detail to omit. To do that, we must first know how much detail there is in the census variables.

3 Portraying variables

The 1991 Census asked just over only a dozen basic questions; however, each question has a number of possible answers (see Chapter 9). For example, 'where were you born?' is divided into over a hundred possible replies (nation-states). 'Where do you work?' is categorized into possible flows to over 10,000 wards, and is then cross-classified by 'what do you do?' To begin it is often simplest to narrow down to a single yes/no answer, which can be converted into a proportion when reported for the group of people living in an area. This proportion can be represented in an image using a shade of colour. Enhancement using different colours like the colours for different heights on a traditional physical geography map is possible but runs the risk of creating patterns that are artefacts of where the colour boundaries lie.

A multitude of statistical methods (see Chapter 7) can be used to match variable proportions to shades of colour. The areas can be ranked by their proportions and grouped by above or below average, quartiles or even percentiles. However there is a lot to be said for portraying detailed information in as direct and simple a form as possible (see Tobler 1973b). The images will often be difficult enough to interpret without having to bear in mind that the figures have been manipulated in a complex way before being converted to shades of colour. Continuous shading of areas is in the spirit of visualization because the aim is not to produce maps from which individual values can be accurately read (a table or database is better for this), but to produce images in which the overall distribution is accurately portrayed.

Even if we do not impose arbitrary categorical boundaries for shading (according to the variable depicted) we will still be using arbitrary spatial boundaries for calculating the value of the area in the first place. Figure 6.4 illustrates what is called the modifiable areal unit problem (Openshaw 1984a). In the figure, four conventional choropleth maps of the same unemployment measure from the census are shown shaded according to a single continuous scale. All that differs between the maps are the areal units – the boundaries used – to calculate and portray the variable. The figure shows which choice of boundaries has the greatest influence for this distribution, and where they make little impact on the impression gained. For instance, the high unemployment rate of the town of Corby is quite resilient to the different ways in which that place can be delimited. The problem is that, in general, this effect will be different for each distribution.

The modifiable areal unit problem can be handled in a number of ways. The simplest is merely to illustrate it by using multiple boundaries, and with interactive visualization it is possible to redraw images instantly using different boundaries to see the effects of these choices. A more sophisticated approach to this problem is to think more carefully about what areas are meaningful to visualize. A set could be specifically defined (e.g. housing market areas) or 'fuzzy boundaries' could be used – for instance by employing kernel mapping methods (see Brunsdon 1991 for an explanation).

Arbitrary boundaries, however, have their greatest influence on the impression gained in their use for portraying statistics, not in their use for calculating them. If the whole of a county is shaded dark grey because levels of unemployment are particularly high in one of its towns, is our image accurately reflecting reality? Just because proportions are calculated for one area does not mean they have to be shown using a scaled down replica of the boundary of that area (i.e. by choropleth mapping). David Martin (1991), for instance, makes a strong case for virtually never using traditional choropleth mapping.

Dasymetric mapping, where only the points where people actually live are shaded, has long been advocated to produce more realistic pictures. The most

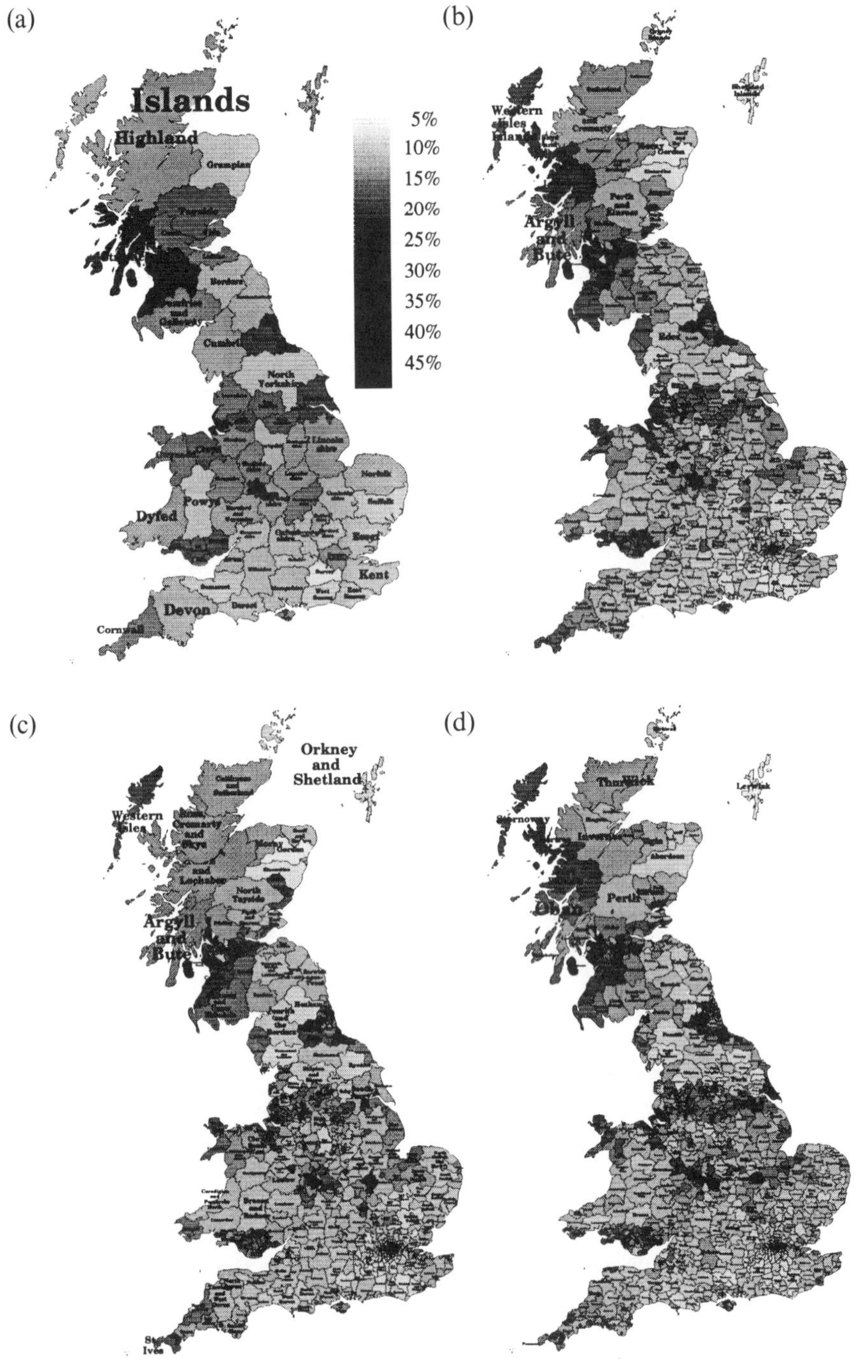

Fig. 6.4 Annotated choropleth maps, shaded by the 1981 unemployment rate: (a) counties and Scottish regions; (b) local government districts; (c) parliamentary constituencies; (d) amalgamated unemployment office areas.

detailed digital data source available to the academic community to achieve this 'automatically' is the central postcode directory which gives a reference for each of over 1.6 million postcodes in Britain. Each postcode has been linked to a 1991 enumeration district (from the addresses on the census form) so it is possible to map dasymetrically below the finest level of enumeration. This method could be enhanced further by introducing a degree of chance into the graphics by 'spraying' colour slightly at random around each postcode to reflect the fact that dwellings are spread out around these points, and that we cannot be sure of their reliability (Barr 1993, p. 251)!

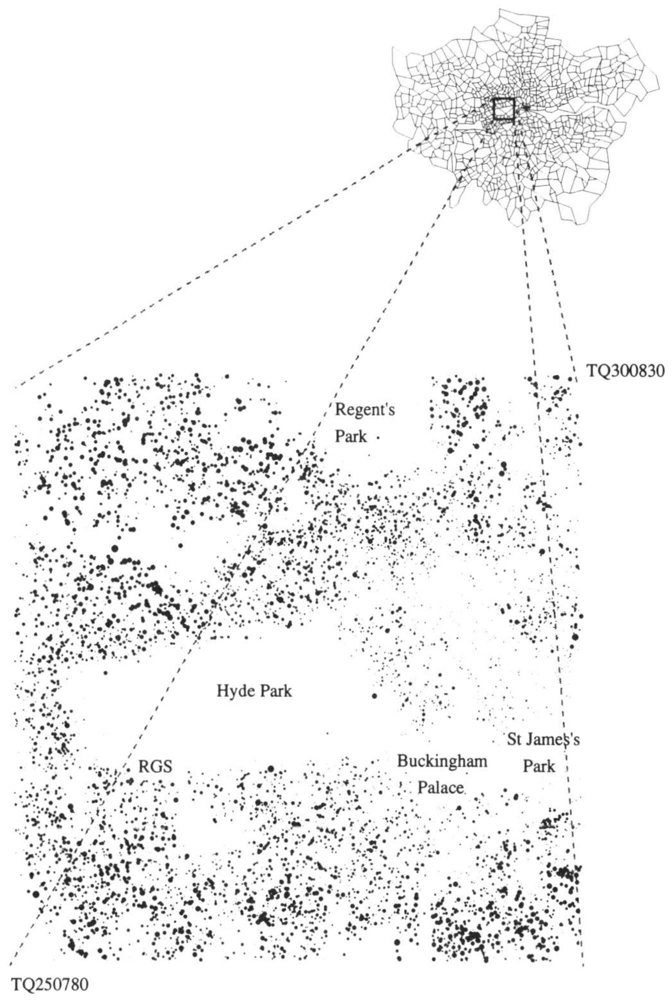

Fig. 6.5 The distribution of households by postcode in 1991. Inset shows 25 km^2 round the heart of London. The area of each circle is in proportion to the number of households at that location.

But what do we see when we visualize using these methods? Figure 6.5 takes Fig. 6.2 a stage further, zooming into central London by postcode. Unfortunately, as we more accurately portray physical reality we are left with less and less space in which to show social reality. Even in the most densely populated part of Britain, what dasymetric mapping shows best are those areas which it leaves colourless. The parks, rivers and roads of the capital stand out most clearly on a dasymetric map of any variable for a city like London, and then most prominent are the isolated places, which usually contain least people and for which averages and proportions are least meaningful.

The severity of the modifiable areal unit problem for conventional thematic mapping is due to the fact that greatest emphasis is given to those places containing fewest people – where the arbitrary movement of boundaries can have the most severe effect on the values calculated. If the same set of unemployment statistics as was used in Fig. 6.4 is mapped on population cartograms as in Fig. 6.6, the arbitrary boundaries can be seen to have much less influence on the impression gained. Our methods of visualization must be robust if one arbitrary choice or another is not to lead us to misinterpret what is important.

Already the number of things to be kept in mind has multiplied and we have so far only considered visualizing a single simple proportion over a few areas. Researchers soon tire of this simplicity and wish to look at several variables to see how they are related. It is obviously possible to produce several univariate pictures side by side for comparison, but it rapidly becomes apparent that only the simplest of cross-references can be made between them (e.g. 'are the same areas shaded lightest?'). What is required is the inclusion of several variables in the same image. Methods of doing this are discussed later; what is important here is to stress the basic decisions which need to be made about the variables before the drawing can begin. It must also be realized that as we increase the complexity of our design, so too we decrease its ability to be more generally understood. At one extreme we are producing pictures for our exclusive use and need not worry as to whether they are meaningful for others – at least not until the results have to be demonstrated.

Variables can be mutually exclusive; for instance it is not possible to have been born in two different places, or to be both in and out of work. Variables can also be called exhaustive when they cover all eventualities: for instance, 'born in Britain' or 'born outside Britain'. Visualizing two mutually exclusive and exhaustive variables only requires the portrayal of one independent variable (as the second can be derived from the first) and is thus a much simpler problem than simultaneously visualizing two independent variables such as the proportions of people born outside Britain and the proportions unemployed (in each of thousands of places).

The visualization of independent variables also raises the risk of invoking the 'ecological fallacy' (Openshaw 1984b). The fact that in a particular area there are significant proportions of two groups of people should not imply that there is any evidence that the two groups include the same people (at least not until the sum of their proportions rises above 100%). Often there are cross-tabulations in the census statistics which show apparent simple correlations to be false. A classic example is that areas that tend to have high proportions of people born outside

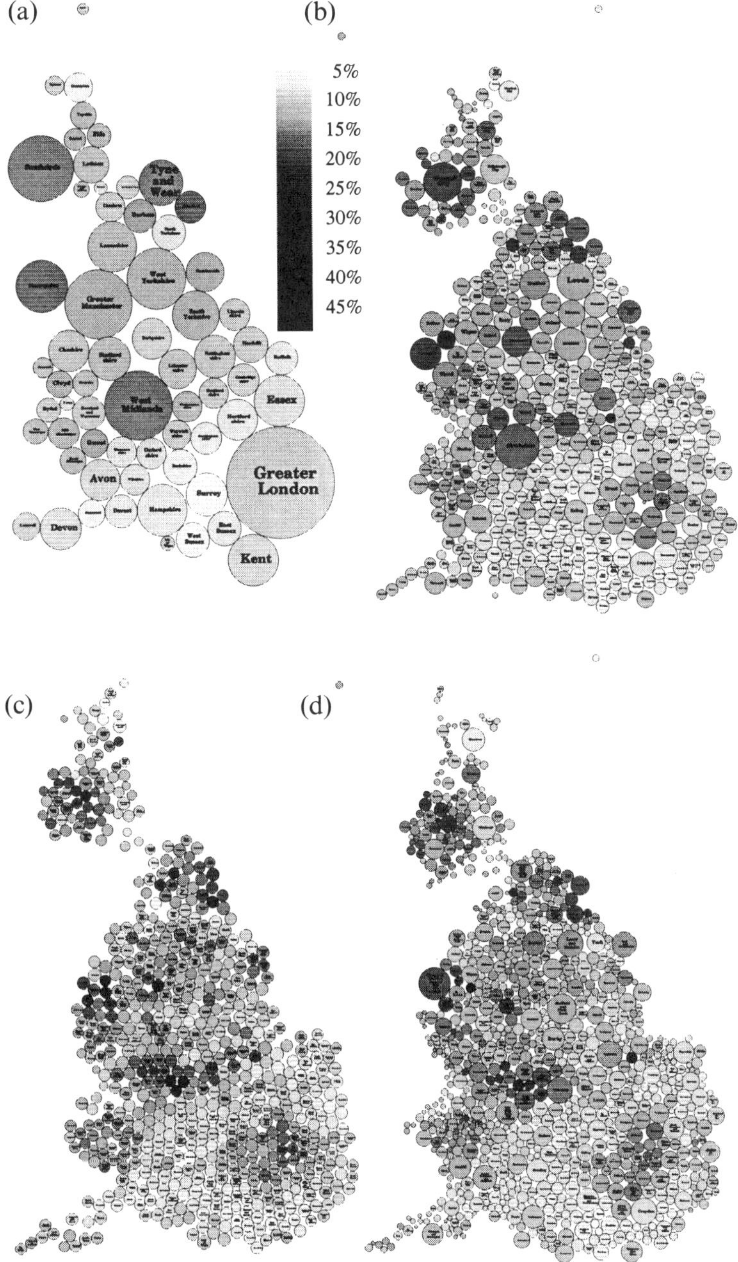

Fig. 6.6 Annotated equal population cartograms, shaded by the 1981 unemployment rate: (a) counties and Scottish regions; (b) local government districts; (c) parliamentary constituencies; (d) amalgamated unemployment office areas.

Britain often also tend to have the lowest average levels of qualifications; however, it is usually not the 'lifetime migrants' who have the lowest number of degrees or HNDs. But what is the best way to visualize the pertinent features of a table of statistics such as these, for and in each area?

When faced with such complex problems, the temptation is to reduce the variables to categorical values. For instance, when investigating the spatial relationship between unemployment and, say, 12 social groups, each social group could be assigned a colour, and the social group with the highest or lowest unemployment rate in each area would determine that area's colour. A dozen variables, each with a practically continuous range, will have been reduced to a single variable which can only take 12 values. It is important to be aware of how much information is being thrown away by such a process (which is also heavily dependent on the arbitrary boundaries drawn between social groups: 'who is a manual worker and why should we use that category or any other?').

Let us suppose, however, that a single image is required to display the relationships between social group and tenure, where we have a matrix of perhaps 12 variables by 7 for each area. One possibility would be to subtract the national matrix of proportions from each local matrix and choose to categorize that area by the greatest deviation shown, e.g. to show 'an unusually low number of professionals buying their homes'. Whether it is possible to do this depends on the structure in the data and the number of categories which emerge. Often we have to admit defeat and use several images (or amalgamate many of the district variables). We must also take account of the inherent variability of such statistics (particularly if taken from the 10% census), so as not to identify an insignificant change as important (Cole 1993).

Finally it must be pointed out that the census contains information not only about people in areas but also about people moving between areas. Flows of people migrating and commuting are some of the most interesting datasets which have been derived and the most challenging and rewarding to visualize: challenging, because instead of a single set of areas we now have a matrix of areas to represent, i.e. the flows between each area and all the other areas – squaring the number of 'objects' which might need to be rendered visible. To do so, however, would be rewarding because there is so much to see in flows, which are the most spatial of spatial data (unemployment can be studied without looking at its geography but migration, by definition, cannot).

Before we look at how matrices of variables and flows can be visualized, it is necessary, in an attempt to be systematic, to look first at the visualization of the most simple of variables – proportions – over the greatest number of places possible (without dasymetric mapping), i.e. all enumeration districts.

4 Visualizing enumeration districts

> ...within any town as in the region as a whole there is a pattern. The poor housing, schools and levels of unemployment will tend to be concentrated

> in certain districts – as they are concentrated in inner city areas of large conurbations of this country. At the level of the region, too, there is a pattern, increasingly clear and changing.
>
> (SEEDS 1987, p. 6)

Enumeration districts represent the finest level at which census data are released in England and Wales (in Scotland the situation is slightly different – see Chapter 4). As has been detailed in Section 2 above, there are over a hundred thousand enumeration districts in Great Britain, with many thousands of statistics being reported independently for each from the 1991 Small Area Statistics. How can that national pattern across this finest level of resolution be seen?

An A4 sheet of paper (or an average computer monitor) is roughly 50,000 square millimetres in area, excluding a little space for margins and borders. If each person were to be given equal area then the scale would be just over 1000 people per square millimetre (irrespective of the areal units used). Three average enumeration districts would then have to be squeezed into each square millimetre. At this size they can only be shown by a speck of colour (although still larger than the dot on the top of this letter 'i'). What would an image, which purported to show the characteristics of so many communities, look like?

At the simplest level each enumeration district dot is shaded either pure black or pure white. Figure 6.7 shows the distribution of Irish-born people living in Britain by enumeration district in 1981. An enumeration district was shaded black if it had more than the median average proportion of Irish-born residents. Thus half the country (on the cartogram) is black and the other half white. The major metropolitan centres appear as dark clusters, while a more speckled appearance is given to those areas where the concentrations are less clear cut. Although only black and white are used here, at this scale the dots can merge to create shades of grey at the fringes.

Many more elaborate shading schemes than this can be envisaged. For instance, only those enumeration districts which held the most highly concentrated half of the Irish-born population could be coloured. Alternatively, a series of grey-scales could be used; the darkest for the most highly concentrated 10% down to the lightest for the enumeration districts with the lowest proportions of Irish-born. Szegö (1984) has suggested that the border (in the case of Great Britain, the sea) be coloured a neutral grey rather than the usual white. It might even be more appropriate to use a colour not on the grey-scale. The fact that it can be claimed that such subtle changes can affect our impression of an image is not a weakness of visualization but a strength, as we learn that there are many ways of seeing the same pattern, each literally in a slightly different light.

The mixing of shades to create textures, too, can be seen as an advantage and can even be enhanced by smoothing the image to achieve some desired level of *generalization*. Plate II shows the result of using 10 passes of the most basic binomial filter (through which, in each dimension, each point is given a new value equal to half its old value and a quarter of its two closest neighbours – Tobler 1989). In the figure the very complex distribution of occupational groups has

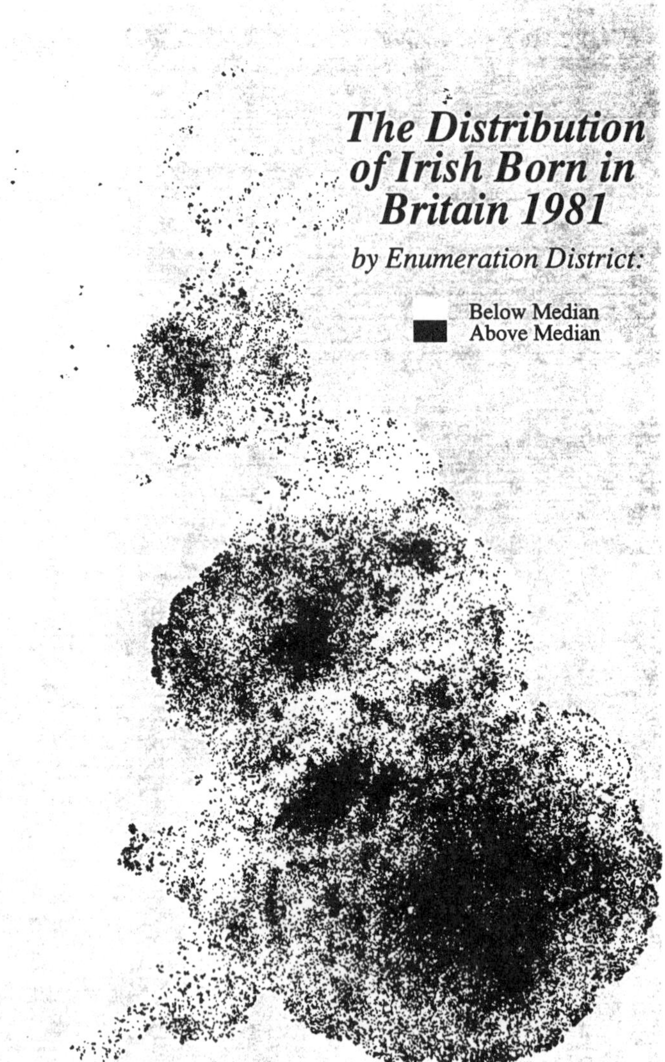

Fig. 6.7 The distribution of Irish born in Britain, 1981, by enumeration district.

been smoothed. Where three-colour mapping (see below) is being used to illustrate subtle trivariate interactions of people by class, generalization very much simplifies the image and is particularly useful when reductions in size are required, but as with all these decisions it changes the impression of the distribution. Watching the generalization take place as an animation can be very enlightening – but that subject too is reserved for later discussion.

While black, white and grey-scales are most appropriate when looking at a single distribution (as we can best distinguish shades without colour), if the wish is to study more than one variable at once we must consider the use of colour.

On almost any microcomputer screen colour is now taken for granted, but high resolution, high quality printing and publishing can cause difficulties (this chapter for instance is limited to four colour prints). Much can be seen with colour which could not be visualized in black and white.

Colour can be used to make grey-scale images appear less drab, although this does not make the best use of the opportunities which colour offers and may result in the picture being more poorly understood (as fewer levels of distinct hues can be distinguished than can shades of grey). For the presentation of categorical data, however, colour is almost a necessity, as distinctly different shades are what is required. The most challenging use of colour in visualization comes when an attempt is made to maximize both the advantages of the distinction between hues and the continuity of saturation (and/or lightness). This strategy is needed when we wish a single colour to represent the levels of three dependent – or two independent – variables through the mixing of colours.

Two-colour, or bivariate, mapping now has quite a strong tradition in cartography. It can be done in many different ways but here just one possibility is outlined. Suppose enumeration districts were coloured according to the proportion of people born in Ireland – using red when this statistic was in its highest quartile, white when in its lowest, and with two shades of pink in between. Overlay this distribution with that of people born in Asia, coloured similarly but with shades ranging from blue to white. Where there were high concentrations of both groups the enumeration district would be coloured purple, white for neither, red for mainly Irish and blue for mainly Asian and with various shades in between. The basic geographical distribution of these two groups across the whole of Britain could be made visible at the highest level of resolution on one (admittedly garish!) page. A pure red dot (representing an enumeration district with the proportion of people born in Ireland in the top quartile) by a pure blue dot (proportion of Asian-born in the top quartile) might look to the eye as purple, but would that be a disadvantage? After all, the dots were only so different because of the imposition of an arbitrary line drawn for the benefit of enumeration. If the line had been drawn another way both areas might have been coloured pure purple. Shading of this kind, at this resolution, can make up for some of the difficulties of the modifiable areal unit problem (see above) by producing images which are to an extent free from the arbitrary effects of the precise delimitation of enumeration districts, because of our eyes' natural ability to generalize the image (Arheim 1976).

The next obvious step after two-colour shading is three-colour, or trivariate, colouring. This is the most sophisticated possibility when there is only a pinprick to shade. Three primary hues of varying intensity will produce a unique colour for every possible combination (while more than three colours do not). When images use three-colour shading, the patterns formed are usually much more complex. It is often the case, however, that the more complex a picture is, the more there is that can be learnt from it. This is not necessarily easy, but can be very rewarding in terms of gaining new insights.

The example of generalization (Plate II) shows clusters of enumeration districts nationally where the occupation of 'heads of households' is predominantly 'professional' (blue), 'intermediate' (yellow) or 'supervised' (red). Where there is a concentration of professional workers, for instance around Greater London, the area will appear bright blue. Where there are high proportions of people in both intermediate and supervised occupations (but not in professional occupations), for instance around central Birmingham, areas of orange emerge. Superficially, there is not a great deal of difference between this kind of image and a CAT (computer-aided tomography) scan, with the latter showing a slice through the human brain and the former a slice through society. One important difference is that a great deal of training is needed to interpret a map of the brain, with which most of us are unfamiliar, whereas a map of human society can be much more quickly understood (as we constitute it) and so can show more complex structures.

Because the three distributions of occupations spatially 'repel' each other (people in different classes of job tend not to live in the same streets), the primary colours chosen, red, blue and yellow, dominate this image. If the variables chosen had been birthplace (subdivided by, say, Irish, Asian and Afro-Caribbean), then a great many places would be coloured either black (high proportions of all three) or white (very low proportions) because these groups tend to cluster together, although many more subtle mixes of colours would also be visible. In Plate II the sharpest divide is shown to be in Inner London, where a white buffer appears between the blue centre of the capital and its red core. This is where the spatial generalization procedure failed to merge the colours because social divides along this boundary are too great.

One final word of warning about colour. The apparent colour of an object is affected by the colours surrounding it. Isolated spots of unexpected colour stand out in otherwise uniform areas far more than they do where there is already great spatial variation. The colour of each object you see is, in fact, the result of a mixture of colours on the page that is unique to every distribution shown. This is not so grave a problem when visualizing geographic space as it is with other subjects. To live in the only (hypothetical) enumeration district in Northumberland which has more than a quarter of its population born in Asia is a very different experience from living in an enumeration district in London with a similar proportion of the population born in Asia (where this proportion is not at all unusual). We must just understand that our pictures can be as subjective as the conclusions we draw from them – and the decisions which led to their creation – despite the explicit consistency of their design. Each apparent weakness of a visualization technique may also be argued to be a strength, although the apparent strengths of such positivism can easily be turned about to list obvious weaknesses.

5 Visualizing census wards

> Human beings make a strange fauna and flora. From a distance they appear negligible; close up they are apt to appear ugly and malicious. More than

anything they need to be surrounded with sufficient space – space even more than time.

(Miller 1934, p. 318)

There are many ways in which enumeration districts could be amalgamated to form larger areas for study. We must always have a reason for discarding so much information in amalgamation. The reason for using wards is that they are the lowest level of official British administrative geography for which non-census information about our society is widely disseminated. They are also the smallest areas for which political officials are elected, and so have some purpose other than enumeration. There were over 9500 census wards in England and Wales in 1991. Again the situation is somewhat different in Scotland and so Chapter 4 should be consulted for those interested in the nomenclature more generally. Here, purely for convenience, Scottish Part Postcode Sectors are considered alongside English and Welsh wards for the purposes of visualizing the census.

The 1991 Census contains much more detailed information at the ward level in the *Local Base Statistics*, allowing far finer subdivisions of population characteristics to be made than are available in the Small Area Statistics. How, though, should we begin to investigate the distribution of people by, for example, nearly a hundred countries of birth, at the level of the 10,000 wards in the country? This can obviously not be adequately achieved with a single map: although if that were the goal (for instance to produce a map for a ward-based atlas of the whole census) how might that goal be approached? One option, which has been alluded to before, is to start using colours to represent categories rather than representing variables.

With areas larger than pinpricks (see Figs 6.2 and 6.3) we can be more sure of recognizing particular shades of colour. Thus, a more sophisticated statistic could be chosen than the usual averages or quartile ranges. Each ward could be categorized by the place of birth which most deviates from the usual proportion. So a ward with every single one of its residents born in England might be sufficiently unusual to be labelled 'English-born', whereas one with just 10 residents born in Trinidad and Tobago might qualify, according to whatever statistic was devised, as being unusually 'Trinidadian and Tobagan-born'. Each continent (of birth) could then be given a primary or secondary colour, shades of which would be used for many of the individual countries. Thus a choropleth cartogram, like a physical geographer's soil or vegetation map, would be created highlighting those towns of greatest diversity of birthplace and those of most homogeneity.

Some statistical sophistication may be needed to avoid just highlighting 'quirks' in the figures. Estimates of sampling error may have to be made if, for instance, data from the 10% sample of census forms is being used – particularly when measuring the numerical change over time of quite small groups. It might be found that their proportions of the whole population would have to alter substantially for a change to be significant enough to be worth showing. The reliability of even the '100%' results may at times also need to be questioned (see Chapter 2), for instance in mapping the change over time of the location of young men (the category which is known to be least well enumerated in the 1991 data) (Simpson and Dorling 1994). These problems are not, however, reasons for avoiding mapping at the ward level. The aggregation of data increases 'accuracy' only in the most trivial of senses.

Plate III shows a cartogram based on the night-time populations of all wards in Britain, used to visualize the results of the British local elections of 1987, 1988 and 1990 combined (all three years have to be included to get a complete coverage of the country). Each ward has been coloured according to 36 categories of election result, ranging from cyan for a Conservative marginal where Liberal came second and Labour third to blood red for a ward where only a Labour candidate stood. The standard electoral triangle (Upton 1991) is used as a key in which the colours of all the possible categories are displayed to indicate the proportions of the vote they represent. To explain adequately just this one diagram would take several pages of text. That is not the purpose here: what is of interest for this chapter is that this degree of detail is possible (Dorling 1993).

The lace-like patterns of local voting tally very closely with those of occupation which were shown in Plate II (as has been known for a long time, but can now be demonstrated visually). Features such as the concentration of Liberal seats on the edge of Inner London and Liberals' generally high propensity to appear where there is a greater degree of social mixing might have been missed in a conventional statistical analysis (where the 'answers' have to be known to some extent before the 'questions' can be posed). The fact that everywhere there are small clusters of bright blue ('safe' Conservative seats) surrounded by purples (Conservative/Labour marginals) encroaching on reds with almost infinite repetition might well also be missed without visual analysis – as too might the stark message of leftwing support from most of the electorate in recent local elections.

Returning to the visualization debate, more flexibility of depiction could be introduced by altering the ward's shape, e.g. to arrows or teardrops (such as is discussed in the next section). Such techniques can be effective when there are marked regional variations, but can be confusing when the pattern is more diffuse. The effectiveness of using changes in the shape, size, orientation and colour of each ward's depiction depends both on the actual pattern of the variable portrayed and on how easy it is for the mind to relate that particular variable to each mode of representation. Can we easily think of that variable as dark or light (e.g. unemployment 'black spots'), as one particular colour (e.g. party affiliations as red, yellow and blue), up, down, left or right (commuting), wide or thin (range of available tenures perhaps), large or small (economic status)? In the ward cartogram shown earlier (Fig. 6.3), size is used to represent total (night-time) population, but could be used to show the daytime population after the effects of commuting have been included. Thus in urban areas the circles would overlap whilst rural areas would appear empty. The circles could then be coloured by, say, predominant 'mode of transport to work', so showing how the transformation took place.

Much more elaborate graphics schemes than this could be devised, but with each ward having less than 5 mm^2 in which its population can be represented, even on a cartogram, it is best to restrict the options to (albeit more elaborate) shading and colour schemes. In the above example, the overlapping in city centres would be problematic; on the other hand, if all wards were scaled so that even the largest did not overlap, then very few would be visible. There is still more information to be shaded, however, because, as opposed to most enumeration districts (for which there are no comparable data over time), we can amalgamate the enumeration districts of previous censuses to fit approximately into the current ward boundaries and so calculate – and hence visually express – approximate changes over time (even when the ward boundaries have altered; further details are given in Dorling 1994a). It is then possible to ask whether the total population has gone up or down or how the characteristics of the population have changed. Almost inevitably, the image will have to depict the areas as they existed at one particular date. But how best to present this information?

If there were 200 people out of work in a ward of 2000 'economically active' adults in 1981, and 224 seeking work out of 2800 in 1991, then the number of unemployed has risen by 24 while the percentage has fallen by two percentage points (from 10% to 8%) or a fifth. Which change statistics we choose to show will often dramatically alter our final image, as will the way in which we choose to show them. The purpose for which we are visualizing the information has to be the prime motivation for which statistics we choose to portray. If the interest is in planning the provision of benefit offices then it may be the absolute change that is of most relevance. If it is in the state of the labour market, then the shift in proportions may be more useful; alternatively, if it is in the changing chance of individuals being unemployed, then the relative changes could be chosen.

If we are interested in the changes not just between two dates but between 1971, 1981 and 1991, we would probably draw separate pictures for changes between pairs of dates but could then go on to compare the 1981–91 change with the 1971–81 change. Is the change accelerating or decelerating, reversing or continuing? However, to understand a picture of 'change in change' requires simultaneous understanding (and preferably visual depiction) of the absolute change and of the original and current levels of the variable. Complex analysis must remain comprehensible. The rate of growth or decline of a newly immigrant population makes little sense without having an idea of the initial size of that population. With more than three time periods included, there may be no option but to use separate maps – because the temporal patterns will tend to break up the spatial ones. More elaborate methods of depicting change are discussed in the next section.

Even greater challenges are posed by the portrayal of what in many cases actually causes the changes – flows of people. Flow is much more than change; flows describe how things change, e.g. how the night-time population becomes the daytime population (through travel to work, travel to school and so on). A greater amount of information is contained by a matrix of flows than in a vector of change, and hence the difficulties (and benefits) of visualization are similarly magnified. The prevalence of, say, commuting flows to a single city centre could be depicted by shading other places so that the higher the proportion of its resident workforce commuting to that centre then the darker it is shaded. If we have over 10,000 places (as in the case of wards nationally) then 10,000 different maps could be drawn! The Special Workplace Statistics of the census do, in fact, give us this level of information, further broken down by many of the characteristics of those commuting. The challenge for visualization is to transform this huge matrix into a condensed visible form to see the structure and the disparities.

Luckily, there is inherent structure in travel-to-work flows which makes their spatial depiction, even at this level, not too problematic. Between the 10,000 wards in Britain there could, theoretically, be as many as a hundred million movement streams. Rather unsurprisingly, less than 1% of these actually occur in an average year. However, the flows are often heavily biased in one particular direction (towards towns in the morning when commuting), so much so that we do not need to show this. If we plot only those flows where more than 2% of the employed population of a ward work in another ward, our diagram will show the daily movements of just over half the workforce in space (at an almost individual level). Figure 6.8 shows how these look on an equal area projection, and illustrates how much more is now possible than was even thought plausible 10 years ago:

> In short it is unlikely that more than thirty flows can be shown successfully on one map and planning the design of a flow map is singularly difficult – 'try it and see' is an essential element of such map creation.
>
> (Rhind 1983, p. 176)

Whether any number of flows can be visualized successfully depends on the inherent structure of those flows. Twenty million individual flows converging within only a few hundred groups are not difficult to understand, whereas 10,000 flows going in all directions would look much like any other set of 10,000 randomly scattered lines. With migration there is less spatial conformity to the movements because the subjects are no longer constrained by travel-time. But even changing the way we determine what is a significant flow to plot can dramatically alter the image created. Figure 6.9 shows the effect of measuring the propensity of movement (by dividing the numbers of commuters by the workforce living in the wards of origin and destination). Drawn on a cartogram base for clarity, London dominates the image with its low central night-time population. Manchester creates a distinct cluster because it has a single 'Central Business District' ward, whilst there are almost no flows to be seen in Birmingham using this measure (because it has a much more dispersed pattern of employment). Without seeing this picture, how can you know what effect a particular choice of statistics might have?

Figure 6.9 also highlights some of the serious difficulties in depicting flows between a large number of areas. The modifiable areal unit problem is rife in flow mapping because the *size* of an area influences the rate of flow (as smaller areas will have fewer flows within them, and hence a higher proportion of flows out of them – one further reason for Birmingham's absence in Fig. 6.9). The *shape* of the area can also have a drastic effect. Long thin wards are more likely to have higher rates of in and out flow than more compact ones (because, even if people were moving at random in a long thin ward, they would be closer to a boundary and therefore more likely to cross it and thus be registered as a 'flow'). The

Fig. 6.8 Daily commuting flows between English and Welsh wards in 1981. Flows of more than 2% of the employed population at the area of residence are drawn as thin lines to their workplace. Fifty per cent of all commuters are included – 10,319,230 people.

problem does not diminish when large areas are used. Between standard regions, most of the migration or commuting is due to flows of people who live near the boundaries of these regions and commute or migrate just a few miles across the border. Flows between non-contiguous areas may have more significance, so charting those alone could partly overcome the problem of the influence of each area's size and shape.

Fig. 6.9 Daily commuting flows between English and Welsh wards in 1981. All flows which satisfy the following inequality are drawn as thin lines:

$$\frac{m_{ijst}}{p_{is}\,p_{js}} > \frac{1}{25{,}000}$$

where m_{ijst} is the number of people moving from place i to j between times s and t, p_{is} is the number of people at place i at time s, i is the place of residence, j is the place of work, s is night-time and t is daytime. Flows of over 1000 people are drawn as thick lines.

The 1991 Census data will allow us to draw new maps of both commuting and migration flows. Suppose we were interested in seeing how the flow maps (at this level of detail) had changed: how the static structure of change had itself changed – the spatial distribution of the differences between two matrices. To illustrate the difficulties of this problem it is best to use an example. Suppose 1000 people commuted in 1981 from town A to town B while some 800 moved in the opposite direction daily. Between 1981 and 1991 the working population of town A rose from 20,000 to 25,000, while that of town B fell from 50,000 to 40,000. In 1991 1100 workers commuted from A to B while only 700 moved from B to A. What, in a nutshell, had happened? Now imagine trying to describe the situation when A and B are represented by several thousand small places. The solution of this visualization problem is left as an exercise to the more ambitious reader!

6 Visualizing places

> Images are only images. But if they are numerous, repeated, identical, they cannot all be wrong. They show us that in a varied universe, forms and performances can be similar: there are towns, routes, states, patterns ... which in spite of everything resemble each other.
>
> (Braudel 1979, p. 133)

The sorts of problem described in the previous sections become progressively easier to handle when there are fewer places involved and hence more space to show the characteristics of (or interactions between) these places. A further advantage is that people at least have an idea where districts, towns and regions are, and so can transcribe what they see back to what they know as reality, better than they can from a map of over a hundred thousand areal units (within which they have to learn to navigate in a new kind of space). However, the disadvantages of only visualizing census information at the level of the district (constituency, labour market or whatever) is that much of the fascinating spatial detail on society which the census provides is jettisoned. Further, many of the tentative solutions that arise from using spatial detail to overcome difficulties such as the modifiable areal unit problem and the ecological fallacy, which become possible when the maximum detail of the information is retained, also have to be abandoned.

This section has been left towards the end because once the objectives are widened it becomes more difficult to provide useful prescriptions. Once you have the scope to vary the shape, size and other features of your visual representations of places, then the design constraints loosen. Instead of trying to define the limits of what is possible under these conditions, it is therefore more appropriate to give a few examples of what is plausible. There is one overriding maxim, however: if the design is to show the overall pattern as well as that within localities, the representations chosen must be able to *meld* into a single image, to be composed of patterns but also to be able to form an overall pattern. They must be able to create what is called a *gestalt* – an organization which is more than the sum of its parts, a picture which can reflect a whole facet of our society (for many more imaginative examples see Szegö 1987 or Tufte 1990).

Beginning with the most simple embellishments, the circles that have been used in so many of the examples in this chapter can be turned into 'pies' or concentric rings to show the relative sizes of subsections of the population (by, say, country of birth) or substrata of a phenomenon through time (immigration over time, for instance). Figure 6.10 illustrates rings being used to show the changing spatial distribution of county level unemployment differentials over time. Influential practitioners have rarely found either of these methods to be effective because

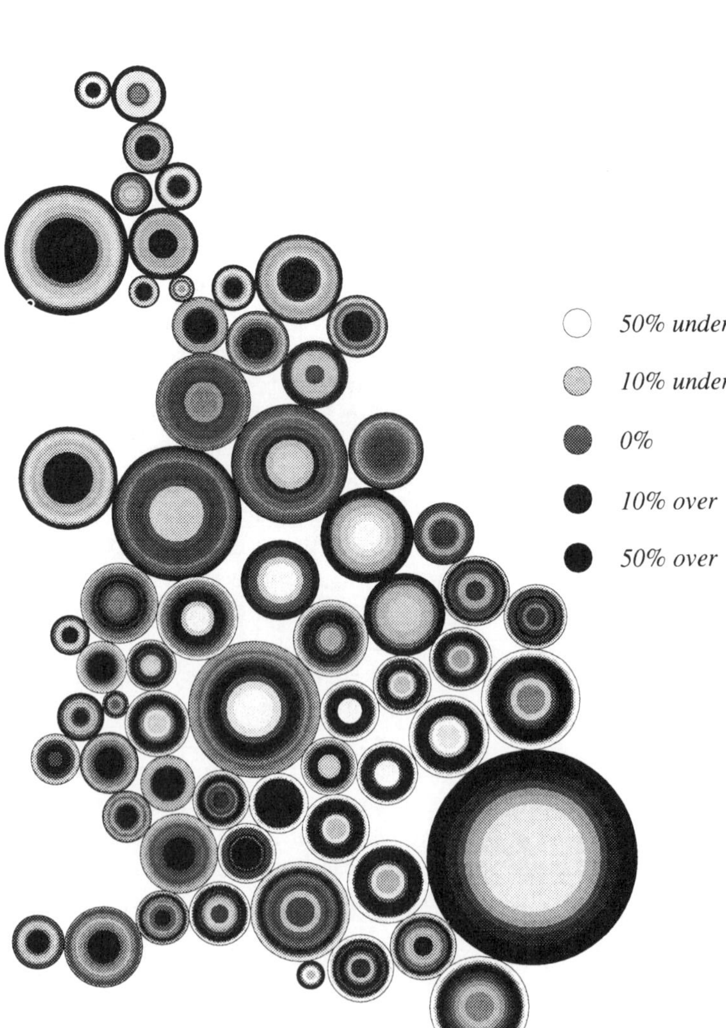

Fig. 6.10 The space–time trend of unemployment in Britain, 1978–90, on a 1981 county population cartogram, outer rings being most recent years and the scale indicating deviation from space–time independence.

the 'superimposition of several images destroys each of them' (Bertin 1981, p. 182). The use of numerous pie charts on a map is a pet hate of many cartographers, because they incorporate multiple sins of graphic design. People are unable to judge angles easily and certainly cannot compare them in different sized circles across (what often ends up being) a garishly coloured map. Pies and rings are simple graphics, and often suffer from not being well thought out in terms of how they might tessellate.

If we were interested in showing multivariate information about a single place we would probably not use pies but would draw charts. The simplest chart is made up of bars, one bar for the level of each variable. Thus we could show, for instance, the number of people employed in eight types of industry simultaneously. If we divided the bars we could also show the proportions of workers who are male or female. By having the bars horizontal and extending both right and left our chart begins to look like a 'population pyramid' – one side for either sex. By reflecting the pyramid again (this time in the horizontal) the population could be further subdivided, by say part-time and full-time workers – a 'population cross'. Draw one of these crosses in each of hundreds of places and the interactions of some 32 variables can be depicted across space.

Figure 6.11 shows how the visual realization of such a process might look, depicting the variance in employment by industry for parliamentary constituencies. The dominance of areas in the centre of London and other major cities is clear, creating mushroom-shaped pyramids where many more people work in administration, finance and services than in manufacturing. The widths of the bars of the pyramids have been scaled to reflect the national proportions of people working in each industry. The coalmines of the East Midlands and the dearth of jobs in many parts of Scotland (at that time) can both be identified. This is not an example of thematic mapping for two reasons. First, it is too complex to expect people to understand easily at a first glance (indeed interactive magnification on a computer screen is needed to appreciate fully the structure it shows). Second, it is less 'representing political features of the earth's surface' (from the *Concise Oxford Dictionary*) than a visualization of (making visible) what just happens to be related to the earth's physical surface. The details of this point are somewhat prosaic, but in essence the figure fails as an illustration because you already have to know what you are looking at to know what you are looking for.

One problem with bar charts is that the order in which variables are placed along the chart greatly influences the visual impression given, and that order is arbitrary. If the order of the industries, say, were made the same as their national rankings, then charts where a gradual rise was broken would show areas where the industrial mix was at odds with what would be naively expected if all places mirrored the national distribution. What is most important about these symbols (as with all *glyphs* – 'sculptured characters or symbols') is that they create a recognizable shape. It is the outline of the bars that is important, so colouring the whole symbol a single shade creates a single object – admittedly with 32 appendages – which is simple enough to be relatively easily compared across space.

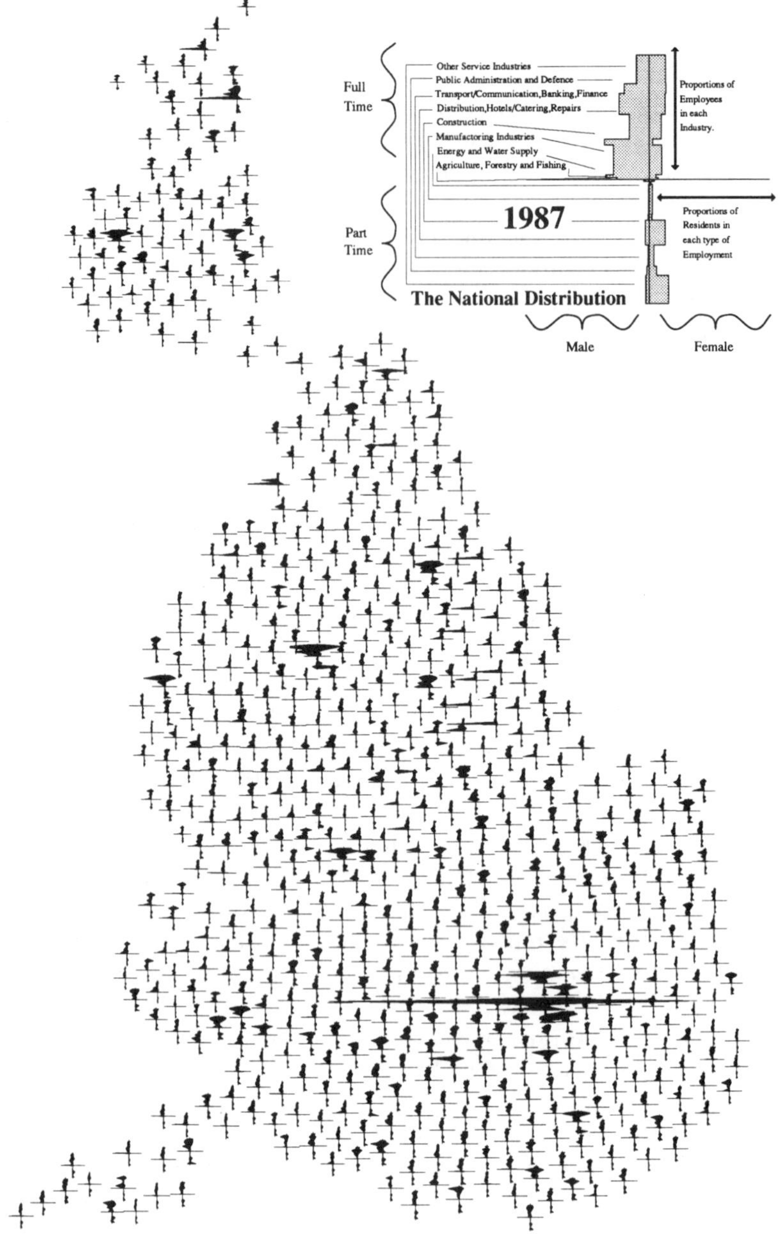

Fig. 6.11 The distribution of employment by industry, status and gender, 1987. The area of the blocks is in proportion to the number of jobs in each sector, in each constituency.

However, the fundamental difficulty remains. Bar charts, graphs and pyramids were originally designed to stand alone, and thus often contain enough complexity and detail as single entities, and too much when many are displayed simultaneously as map symbols. To be used in a spatial context, glyphs must generalize and simplify the information if the overall patterns are to be understood, particularly if more than a few dozen areas are to be compared. As the number of areas increases, so too do the differences between areas. The industrial structure becomes less predictable and the population structure more varied. Unfortunately as the symbols get smaller comparison becomes more difficult. We must design simple glyphs which do not require a great deal of space, and which the eye can quickly comprehend without excessive examination.

The most basic, traditional glyph which can satisfy the above criteria is the arrow. The use of lines to show flows between thousands of areas has already been discussed. Once we have the space to give the arrows width, size, shape and colour they can show much more detail of the flows they depict. The visual advantage of arrows is that their aggregate expresses a form of its own. Like a flock of birds in flight, groups of arrows pointing in a similar direction appear to be *going* that way; they form a single object. This is exactly the impression we wish to create.

One subject which is particularly amenable to the use of arrows is the depiction of change over time in three mutually exclusive variables. Although this technique has been used in Britain mostly to show three-party swings between general elections (e.g. Upton 1991) it could be used to depict change in any census variables – the change from 1981 to 1991 in the proportions of three groupings of socioeconomic groups falling into social classes could be a good example. The direction of the arrow can represent the direction of change as a vector with, for example, 'up' meaning an increase in the 'top' group, 'right' indicating an increase in the 'middle' group and an orientation towards the 'left' showing a rise in the 'lower' group (see the discussion below on Fig. 6.15 for further explanation). The length of the arrow would indicate the magnitude of the change. The size of the arrow would be in proportion to the size of the groups, while the position of the arrow is determined by the location of the place it represents. The colour of each arrow could illustrate the proportions of people in each class in 1991, to give more meaning to the changes in direction (see Dorling 1992 for examples).

In one sense, nine dimensions would be seen in this relatively simple picture – two for position, two for direction, three for colour and one for each of length and size; but that would be a gross exaggeration. The position of the place is shown by two *dimensions*, while the image is representing seven very closely knit *variables*. It is the strength of the relationships between the variables that allows so much to be depicted. The arrows would work well in this example because direction would be meaningful, and the three variables which made up direction would really be one – change in class composition. If the image worked well it would be because the spatial relationships between the classes chosen were strong enough for discernible patterns to emerge.

Glyphs more complex than arrows have been specifically designed to allow quick comparison of the overall pattern of multivariate information where less simple structures are expected and where the change in direction of more than three mutually exclusive variables may be of interest. In the literature the best known of these are *trees* and *castles*, where various aspects of a basic shape are altered to produce many variations of an underlying structure which are easily comparable. It is the maintenance of this basic structure which aids our visual assimilation of the objects into an image. What distinguishes these symbols from many of the objects described above is that they have been specifically designed to be used as glyphs – to be compared quickly with one another.

Castles have various parapets, which alter in height and aspect as the values of the variables change. In many ways they are simply an embellishment of the bar chart, altered so as to allow the mind to form an impression of the general 'shape' of the place more easily using a more familiar symbol. Bar charts can only go up or down, have a peak here or there, but they are still charts. Castles appear more as single objects, and so it is hoped that an overall impression from a whole 'country's worth' of these can be obtained. Kleiner and Hartigan (1981) used castles to represent the varying fortunes of 15 companies over 25 years, grouped recursively into clusters of similar companies forming separate 'towers' of a single castle. The census variables provide numerous complicated classifications which could benefit from similar forms of visual expression.

Kleiner and Hartigan (1981) also introduced the use of 'trees' in order to show changes in variables which can be recursively grouped (because a tree recursively branches). The image of a tree is visually familiar and thus relatively easy to interpret. Just as castles grew out of bar charts, trees have grown out of the simple graphic symbol of the weather vane (used to show average wind directions through the lengths of eight radial 'spokes'). Rather than order the spokes as a wheel, they have become the branches of a tree. This works because we are used to seeing tree-like objects which vary in shape but have a rough symmetry about them. The order in which the variables are assigned to the branches and twigs is crucial for the impression gained. It is usual to place the total population variables at the base, put the smaller subgroups to the sides and so on. Whether this works or not depends on the variance in the information being depicted. A relatively convincing 'wood' can be created; thickets, copses and spinneys of different species can be identified (i.e. overall tendencies for trees to have a certain combination of features in certain parts of the picture, and for other combinations never to occur). Figure 6.12 shows the use of trees to depict different aspects of the British housing market. The branches show different categories of housing, their widths being the number of sales in any one year and their lengths the average prices. Their areas, then, are in proportion to the value of the submarket and they sum to the total value of the housing market in each place. This is not census information but it could easily be combined with statistics such as the number of people buying their homes to enhance that information.

The most contentious glyphs created to date are based on human faces, drawn by Herman Chernoff. Faces, it is argued, are the visual image we are best equipped and experienced to decipher. We naturally combine their features to interpret moods such as happy or sad, sly or dull. What is more, we can easily compare faces to look for family resemblances or the mood of the crowd. Faces

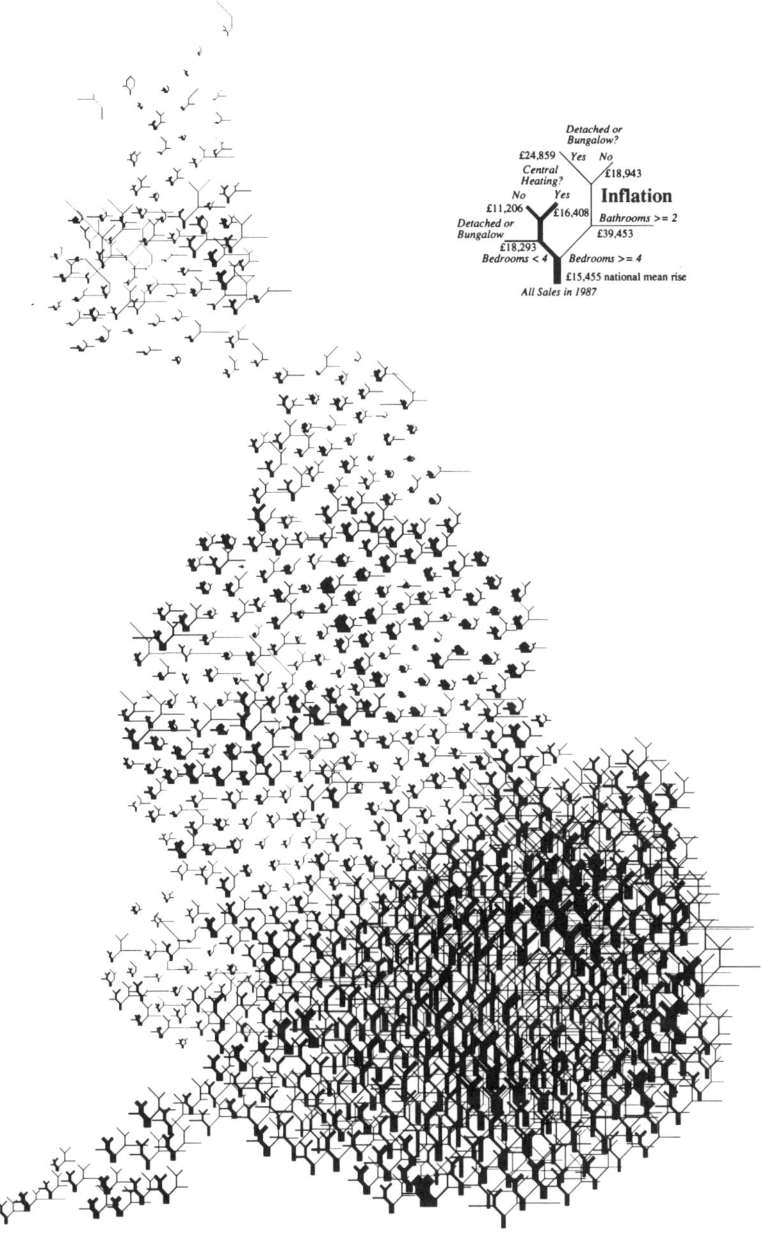

Fig. 6.12 The changing distribution of housing by price, attributes and sales, 1983–7. The area of the branches is in proportion to the total housing inflation by each set of attributes, in each constituency.

maintain a basic structure in which even a slight variation often holds meaning.

The original Chernoff faces aimed to show the values of as many as 18 variables simultaneously (Chernoff 1973). These have been criticized because certain different combinations of variables could result in the same visual expression and because the order in which so many variables were assigned to features had a drastic effect on the impression gained. The example shown (Fig. 6.13) portrays only five variables, using just 11 Bezier curves to construct the faces which reflect their values (further details are given in Dorling 1994b). The image combines variables from the last two figures and introduces some more, to show how these glyphs can be used to compare statistics which do not fall into simple groups or categories.

Figure 6.13 was developed as part of a study of social change between the 1983 and 1987 British general elections, with each parliamentary constituency being represented by a face. The size of the face is drawn in proportion to the electorate, the shape of the face by house price change (fat if rising more than average, thin if less), the shape of the mouth by employment (smile if rising), the width of the nose by electoral turnout (big if rising) and the eyes by industrial structure (large low eyes for more service employment, small and high on the face where other industries predominate). The 'disappointment' of parts of the north is clear in the signs of gloom in those constituencies' 'faces'! Scotland's 'faces' are thin (where house prices rose slowly), while many inner city noses are small as turnouts are low. Colouring the faces by the change in the vote would allow the spatial connections between these social changes, and electoral change, to be seen where and if they occurred. There is, of course, a great danger here of evoking the ecological fallacy in quite a spectacular way. These are the 'faces' of places, not people.

Strong local relations in space are perhaps the clearest message to be formed by the images shown here. Sharp divisions are also immediately apparent, as are more gradual changes. The faces can be seen to be reflecting places' *reactions* to a changing social situation. In this sense they are the ultimate form of spatial reification – giving a place lifelike characteristics and opinions which it cannot actually have. Chernoff faces are contentious for the very reason that they are seen as useful. Peoples' reactions to faces are much stronger than their reactions to more neutral objects, which are claimed to depict information more objectively. In perception, there is a continuum from personal likes and dislikes of certain colours in maps to individuals' strong reactions to cartoon faces. Visualization of social information, however, is all about engaging our imaginations and emotions. The emotional response to Chernoff faces can therefore be thought of as a strength as well as a weakness.

A more serious criticism of the use of glyphs is that they can overload the viewer with information: too much is being asked of the eyes and the mind. In this section it has been shown how badly designed symbols are impossible to decipher spatially, while better thought out images can help the viewer form higher level structures from the simple pictures of collections of places. It is a mistake, however, to think that these symbols can add another dimension to the two we have on paper. Glyphs show multivariate structure, not multidimensional

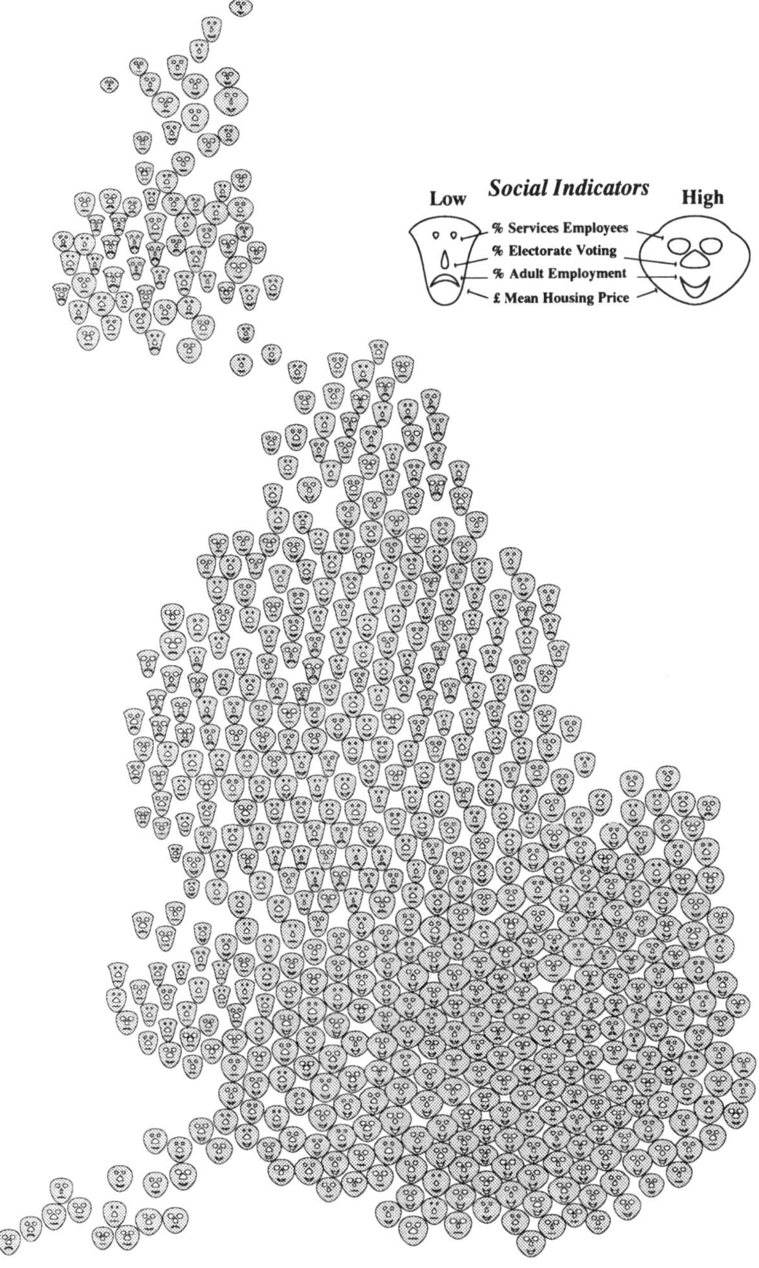

Fig 6.13 The distribution of voting, housing, employment and industrial compositions in constituencies in 1987. Facial features are in proportion to the relative values of the social and economic characteristics of the areas they represent.

form. We can look at a great many categorical aspects of many places simultaneously, but varying the features of an object is not a good substitute for varying its position because different combinations of colour and shape can only imply simple relationships, such as correlation over time.

Just because we have the space to use more sophisticated symbols does not predicate the use of more simple graphical techniques to tackle complex problems. Plate IV attempts to depict the changes in population over the three decades from 1961. Three-colour mixing on a cartogram is used. Places are black when their populations have declined faster than the national average during each of the three periods 1961–71, 1971–81 and 1981–91, and white when they have consistently risen more quickly. The rural belt of the home counties is white while most of Inner London is black. More subtle shades of colour characterize other changes. Much of the southwest (and Tower Hamlets) is green because the last decade has seen a reversal in its long-term population decline. The urban/rural fringe districts are orange as their populations grew fastest in the 1960s, after which stricter planning controls were applied and demographic factors came into play.

The wealth of information which can be gained from using sophisticated techniques such as these appears great. But there is a good deal we are not able to see in the structure (which in the last example is derived from less than 2000 statistics). This is because we cannot show change over time and space simultaneously in two dimensions (although the graphs in the figure try to give an idea of the kinds of temporal movements involved). Features such as the colour of an object have no geometry and so are limited to conveying only a few values. To attempt to see into a real third dimension we must begin to think in terms of volume, discussed in the final section of this chapter, a possibility which becomes feasible when we only wish to view a few regions simultaneously.

7 Visualizing regions

> The world is complex, dynamic, multidimensional; the paper is static, flat. How are we to represent the rich visual world of experience and measurement on mere flatland?
>
> (Tufte 1990, p. 9)

This penultimate section begins to explore the possibilities when the spatial distributions over just a few dozen areas are the interest. These are the numbers involved with, for instance, English counties, or with standard regions. While it is generally poor geographical practice to look for patterns in society at such an aggregated level, there are a few advantages in so doing. First, much non-census information is only available at these levels, including many of the results of annual official surveys. Second, people are even more likely to be familiar with the concept of regions than, say, districts and so have less to learn in order to begin to understand the image (not always a good thing). Most importantly, however, once we become interested in changes over time and other subjects which involve a more detailed geometry, the simplicity of regions compensates for the complexity of the subject.

There are some new forms of census information which are only available at these relatively crude levels of aggregation. The 2% Sample of Anonymized Records of individuals is available only for aggregations of districts where more than 120,000 people live. The 1% sample of individual households is geographically disaggregated by only 12 standard regions. The Longitudinal Study, which links the records of a 1% sample of individuals between censuses, traditionally provides information only down to the district level, with many analyses suppressed for areas smaller than regions. Thus there is a great deal of interesting census information for which very little spatial detail is available but which we still wish to visualize (partly because it is often of a very complex nature).

A second reason why we might wish to use such crude geography is to look at change over time in the years between censuses. A practical example is in the monitoring of migration flows, where the most spatially detailed information available between censuses is for the hundred or so Family Health Service Authorities of England and Wales. The National Health Service Central Register of patient movements provides a full migration matrix at this level of aggregation since 1975 on a quarterly basis. The advantage of having so few areal units is that more sophisticated graphic techniques can be employed.

Figure 6.14 shows the migration streams comprising various percentages of all the recorded moves between 1975 and 1976. A population cartogram is used to ensure some clarity; two concentric circles are placed at the centre of each area being represented, their size in proportion to the numbers of in- and out-migrants, with a black circle uppermost indicating an overall loss of people and the net flow being proportional to the gap between the circles (and vice versa for white). An arrow is drawn between each pair of areas with a significant flow, with its width in proportion to the number of people moving and the arrowhead pointing in the direction of net flow. If the reverse flow is also significant, it is placed on top of this (so as not to be obscured), with its arrowhead at the other end of the line. A white border is then placed around each arrow to distinguish it from the general tangle of lines. One graphical subtlety is the sorting of all these arrows so that the ones between contiguous areas are drawn uppermost, the ones between second-order contiguous areas below them, and so on. The most important decision to make, however, is always which flows to show and which to ignore, by determining what is a 'significant' movement.

By raising and lowering the level of significance you choose, the picture becomes more or less cluttered as lines appear and disappear. A sequence of images showing how the structure builds up can be quite revealing (Dorling 1991). The Pennines appear as a formidable barrier to movement, while the northwest cluster of areas is one of the last groups to connect to the national network of migration streams. Animation of the image, as the level of significance changes, highlights this quite well and helps understanding of a very complex diagram. The much higher general rates of migration in the southeast can be readily distinguished from the figure, with a Wash–Exe line dividing that dense mass of lines from the much lower levels in the north. Use of the population

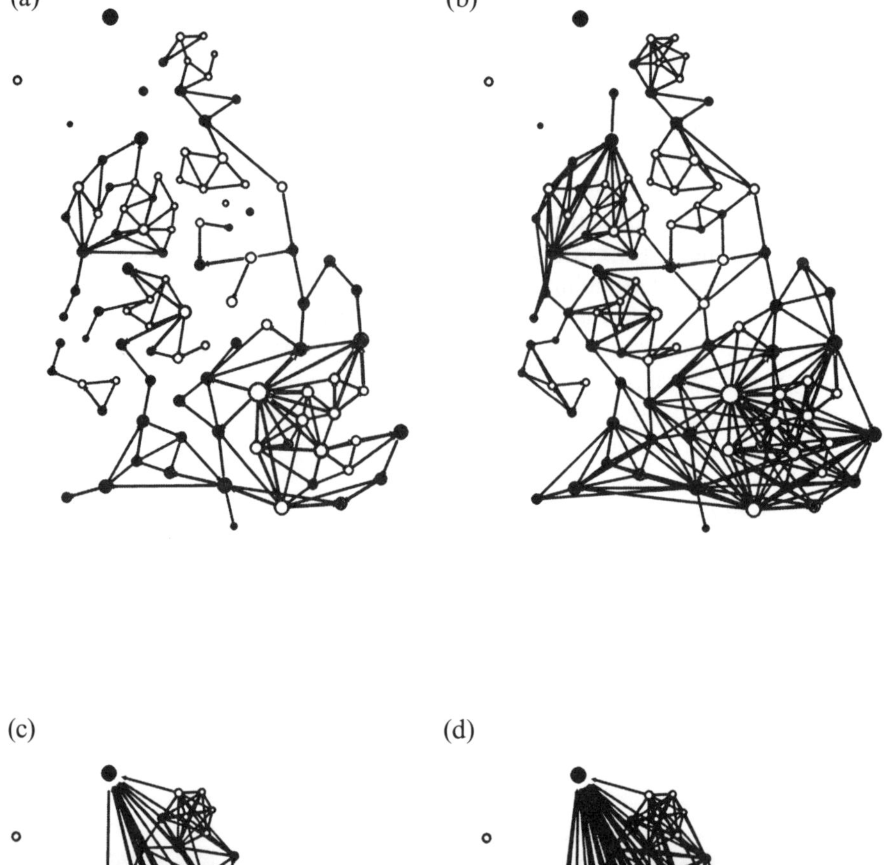

(c)

(d)

Fig. 6.14 Migration flows between family practitioner areas (1975–6). The percentage of all recorded moves is (a) 36%, (b) 48%, (c) 65% and (d) 75%.

cartogram as a base gives the density of lines (and the areas of the circles) some meaning. The tightness of flows between the areas of the northeast is clearly apparent, represented by the 'hexagon' of areas in the top right. The strong connections between the single northernmost area, representing Scotland, with parts of London is also very obvious: Scottish migrants flow right the way across the country, generally avoiding the places in between.

It is much more difficult, however, to explore graphically the spatial nature of changes to the flows over time. This can be demonstrated by taking a simpler problem than the migration example. Unemployment data are now available at very frequent intervals at a highly disaggregated level. In the past, this detail was not available and the further we go back in time the less detail there is. Suppose we wished to investigate how the levels of unemployment had changed annually at a fine level from the end of the 1970s to just before the latest census was taken. If, for each of over 800 (unemployment office) areas, we want to show 12 levels of unemployment, how could this be done?

Nationally, the level of unemployment varies dramatically over time. If we were just to plot the crude rates it would be very difficult to distinguish between different areas. What is of interest here is the time a particular level of unemployment is 'unusual' for a particular place and a particular time. To measure this, the conventional technique is to calculate an expected level (given the place and year) and subtract that from the actual level. How then can we show these 12 deviations? Using an area cartogram in which the places are represented by circles, the simplest option is to show each deviation by colouring (different greys) each one of the 12 rings in each circle. Figure 6.10 has already illustrated this technique. Using an analogy with the cross-section of a tree, the outer rings can represent the most recent years and the inner core the first year in the series. Each ring should have its area in proportion to the total workforce of that year. Where a place such as London is light in its centre and gets darker around its edge, that signifies that the level of unemployment there is rising from below the national trend to progressively further above it. Many places on Merseyside, Tyneside and Clydeside have a dark core and dark circumference and are paler in between, indicating that these places did 'relatively well' when unemployment levels were at their highest nationally, because they were then not so unusual in having their high levels (this also illustrates a problem of using such simple measures). Oxfordshire is the only county which clearly is improving consistently against the national trend, at least up to 1990.

If phenomena are found to be too complex for representation in this way, one form of escape is to look at even fewer cases or places. With just 12 regions it is possible to stop mapping the geography entirely and just use charts. Classically, a line chart is used with one line for each region, the horizontal axis being time and the vertical axis being the value of some variable. For visualization purposes we could begin to break the rules a little: only show lines when they were interesting, choose in which order they were to overlap, give them a thickness which altered along their length, hang other symbols off them, or even let them bifurcate (i.e. split) if it is appropriate to divide a region into two at some point. All we are doing is exploring and embellishing from a basic graphical model, but freed from the restrictions of having to represent the geography of the situation in some standard form. The graphical possibilities then very quickly become limitless. Because we are not trying to illustrate the numbers but to understand them better, we do not need to stick to accepted templates.

A good example of what becomes possible when you are no longer trying to show geographical patterns is provided by triangular graphs which use space to show the relationship between three dependent variables across many places when there is no wish to show the spatial relationships of places with each other. Figure 6.15 demonstrates this with local election results collected for the 'divisions' which county councillors represent (areas somewhat larger than wards). Over 3000 places are shown, again as circles, their areas in proportion to their electorates and their positions within the triangle determined by the share of the vote of each of the three major parties (where one party was not represented, a histogram is built up on the side of the triangle opposite the missing party's apex). The places form

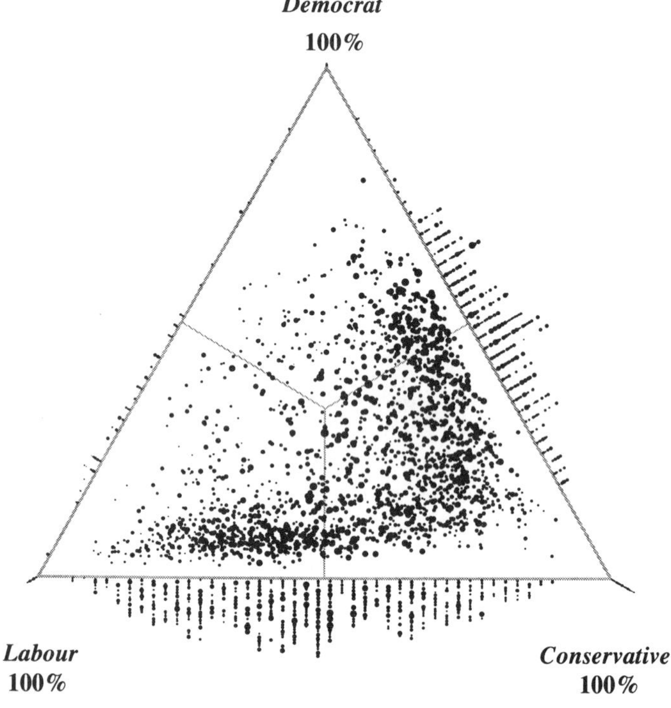

Fig. 6.15 1989 county council elections: English voting composition. Every electoral division won by one of the three major parties is shown by a circle on the diagram. The area of the circle is in proportion to the total vote. Independent candidates are counted as Conservative where no Conservative opposed Labour or Liberal nominees. The position of the circle indicates the composition of votes in that division. Distance from each apex measures the support for a party from total to none. Divisions falling on the sides of the triangle are projected as a histogram of two-party support.

a shape in the 'variable space' of the triangle. In this case they demonstrate one stage in the polarization which was taking place in 1989 as the cluster of divisions formed a V shape – seats either aligning on the Labour–Conservative apex or along the Democrat–Conservative line. Changes in the shapes formed on these triangles over time can produce very interesting patterns.

One method increasingly being advocated for studying change over time (and other changes) in visualization is animation. In studying elections it was with changes between triangular graphs that this writer found animation to be most useful, because drawing lines between points on the graphs quickly created a mess (Dorling 1992). The other major uses for animation are in panning and zooming over a very detailed image, or in illustrating very simple movements to a large audience – for instance the movement of the 'centre of population' of a county over time (Monmonier 1992). In general, flying over landscapes created by raising the ground by the level of some social variable may not be a particularly useful way of understanding its distribution – but others might disagree. Where animation and perspective viewing might be most useful, however, is in studying the geometry of the more complex abstract worlds we might create – a landscape where distance is drawn in proportion to travel-time for instance; but here we are quickly departing from what it is possible to visualize with census data.

When creating the illusion of a surface on a two-dimensional medium, depth cues have to be used – perspective and shading. But if that surface, created by the values of one variable over space, is to be coloured according to the distribution of another variable, the information is lost and confounded. It it lost because it cannot be seen (being behind part of the surface), and it is confounded because shading and shadow intermingle. To really appreciate three-dimensional geometry you must be able to fly around that surface, or at least be able to 'rock' the image from side to side. In doing this, however, you are never quite able to get a hold on what you are looking at (Kaufman *et al.* 1990, p. 162). A surface is not an alternative for a choropleth map, because on the one hand it contains more information and on the other hand it contains less. A surface expresses geometry – distances between objects on the surface are defined – so 'shortest' routes can be seen which are not always straight lines. This is an advantage when a geometry is being defined explicitly, but if you are not trying to measure distances in terms of, say, years of unemployment, then the advice which applied to the precursor of the perspective view still applies today:

> – it is extremely wise to avoid contour mapping of census data.
>
> (Rhind 1983, p. 190)

We do not think in a three-dimensional geometry – many tests have shown this (Parslow 1987). The geometry of visual thinking is essentially two dimensional. Many people cannot actually perceive depth (Young *et al.* 1988, p. 419). Another disadvantage to be remembered is that we have poor visual memory (there is just too much to remember). Of course, there are problems with even the most basic of visual techniques: the emotional overtones of colour are perceived differently by different people; the colour blind cannot see the full trivariate range; and, of course, some people cannot see at all. Visualization is not a panacea. With information as rich as that from the census you can quickly exhaust the possibilities before you are able to study the features which you are most interested in. You can, however, always then invent new possibilities.

8 Conclusion

Visualization of the census is not an easy subject to cover in just one chapter because there is so much more that could be said and drawn. I have not discussed the practicalities of visualization – the hardware and software – because these are changing so quickly. All the illustrations shown here were produced by simple programming and the in-built software of a standard 'Acorn' British school microcomputer. If you pay a significant amount of money for a 'visualization package' it should be able to do a great deal more than this. There is still an advantage to programming from scratch, however, because totally new ideas cannot be implemented using other people's applications. Programming languages are also becoming simpler to learn. Geographical information systems (GIS), on the other hand, have severe limitations in this field:

> In fact few of the graphical operations feasible in a GIS are going to be appropriate for census data.
>
> (Barr 1993, p. 267)

Traditional problems of visualizing the census can be superseded if a new methodology is adopted. Difficulties such as boundary change need not be a problem since, as people move, so do the collating boundaries move around them, eternally attempting to encompass them. An animation of changes in the population can also incorporate change in the boundaries. If cartograms are used, places 'disappear' and are 'born' as they shrink and grow in line with their populations and geographical definitions. Use of cartograms also avoids the age old problem of wasting most of the paper showing the characteristics of the fewest numbers of people at the expense of the majority – who often are those about whom we know the least, who tend to be poorer, less visible in our cities and on our maps.

On the subject of flow mapping, which this chapter has dealt with at several stages, it should be pointed out that not all flows are spatial – flows between tenure and social groups can be measured from the Longitudinal Study; flows on and off the unemployment register can be seen, as can flows of votes between parties measured by electoral surveys. All these aspatial forms of flow represent challenges for future new methods of visualization. Depicting how these matrices of flows have changed over time is an even more challenging problem waiting to be addressed, and after that, showing the spatial component of these changes!

Graphic depiction has come in and out of fashion in cycles over the last 200 years (Beniger and Robyn 1978). Its resurgence is usually caused by the invention of new printing technologies and the availability of more abundant information, so we should not be surprised to see a rise in visualization as, internationally, data from the multitude of 1990 and 1991 Censuses are released and high quality graphics workstations become widespread. When dasymetric mapping was first used in the British census of 1851, it was a time-consuming and laborious process. Now we can do this using the postcode-to-enumeration district lookup file in a matter of seconds. Our methods may be quicker, but how much of an innovation do they represent?

A new challenge to census visualization is to see how time and space can be transformed to represent more clearly the patterns within them, on paper or in animation (Rucker 1984). A landscape where distance is travel-time has been mentioned above and should be possible to create. Ultimately we ask: can we compare the evolution of one thing with the flows of another and the distribution of yet others without collapsing reality into dimensions which cannot contain its complexity? One dream of this writer is to make possible the interactive visualization of a single dynamic map of Britain which can be asked to show whatever variables you wish to see in a given form, from whichever census, for any areal units, using any projection that can be defined.

Pictures of spatial social structure should have the power to reflect the complex tapestry and delicate lace-work of the relations between people, through the places in which they live and the spaces they create. As we are inundated with the greatest volume of information about our society that we have ever had in digital form, new methods and methodologies will inevitably be created to study it. In all this technological excitement we should always remember to ask – why, for whom and for what are we looking?

Acknowledgements

Thanks are due to Tony Champion, Mike Coombes, James Cornford and David Dorling who all commented extensively on the first draft of this chapter. The research this chapter is based on was funded by the Strang Doctoral Studentship of the University of Newcastle upon Tyne between 1990 and 1991, a Joseph Rowntree Foundation Fellowship between 1991 and 1993 and a British Academy Fellowship since then.

References

Arheim, R 1976 The perception of maps. *American Cartographer* 3 (1), 5–10.

Barr, R 1993 Mapping and spatial analysis. In A Dale and C March (eds) *The 1991 Census User's Guide*. London: HMSO.

Beniger, J R and D L Robyn 1978 Quantitative graphics in statistics: a brief history. *American Statistician* 32 (1), 1–11.

Bertin, J 1981 Graphics and Graphic Information Processing. Berlin: Walter de Gruyter.

Braudel, F 1979 *The Wheels of Commerce*. London: Fontana.

Brunsdon, C 1991 Estimating probability surfaces in GIS: an adaptive technique. *EGIS '91 Proceedings*, Brussels, 155–64.

Census Research Unit 1980 *People in Britain – a Census Atlas*. London: HMSO.
Chernoff, H 1973 The use of faces to represent points in *k*-dimensional space graphically. *Journal of the American Statistical Association* 68 (342) 361–8.
Cole, K 1993 Sampling error and the 10% small area statistics. Manchester Computer Centre Newsletter 22, University of Manchester.
Denes, A 1979 Isometric systems in isotropic space: map projections: from the study of distortion series 1973–1979. New York: Visual Studies Workshop Press.
Dorling, D 1991 The visualization of spatial social structure. PhD thesis, University of Newcastle upon Tyne.
Dorling, D 1992 Stretching space and splicing time: from cartographic animation to interactive visualization. *Cartography and Geographical Information Systems* 19 (4), 215–27, 267–70.
Dorling, D 1993, Map design for census mapping. *The Cartographic Journal* 30, 167-83.
Dorling, D 1994a Visualizing the geography of the population with the 1991 Census. *Population Trends* 76, 29-39.
Dorling, D 1994b Cartograms for visualizing human geography. In H Hearnshaw and D Unwin (eds) *Visualization in GIS*. Chichester: Wiley, 85-102.
Dorling, D 1995 Visualizing changing social structure from a census. *Environment and Planning* A 27 (2).
Harley, J B 1989 Deconstructing the map. *Cartographica* 26 (2), 1–20.
Hunt, A J 1968 Problems of population mapping: an introduction. *Transactions of the Institute of British Geographers* 43 (April).
Kaufman, A, R Yagel, R Bakalash and I Spector 1990 Volume visualization in cell biology. *Visualization '90, Proceedings of the First IEEE Conference on visualization*, San Francisco, 160–7.
Kleiner, B and J A Hartigan 1981 Representing points in many dimensions by trees and castles. *Journal of the American Statistical Association* 76 (374), 260–76.
MacEachren, A M 1992 Visualization. In R Abler, M Marcus and J Olson (eds) *Geography's Inner World: Pervasive Themes in Contemporary American Geography*. New Brunswick, NJ: Rutgers University Press, ch. 6.
Mandlebrot, B B 1983 *The Fractal Geometry of Nature*. San Francisco: Freeman.
Marr, D 1982 *Vision*. New York: Freeman.
Martin, D 1991 *Geographic Information Systems and Their Socioeconomic Applications*. New York: Routledge.
McCormick, B H, T A Defanti and M D Brown (eds) 1987 Visualization in scientific computing – a synopsis. *IEEE Computer Graphics and Applications* 21 (6).
Miller, H 1934 *Tropic of Cancer*. London: Grafton (quote from the 9th edn, 1965).
Monmonier, M 1992 Directional profiles and rose diagrams to complement centrographic cartography. *Journal of the Pennsylvania Academy of Science* 66 (1), 29–34.
Olson, J M 1976 Noncontinuous area cartograms. *Professional Geographer* 28 (4), 371–80.
Openshaw, S 1984a *The Modifiable Areal Unit Problem*, Catmog 38. Norwich: Geo-Abstracts.
Openshaw, S 1984b Ecological fallacies and the analysis of areal census data. *Environment and Planning A* 16, 17–31.
Parslow, R 1987 A new direction for computer graphics. *Computer Bulletin* September, 22–5.
Pred, A 1986 *Place, Practise and Structure; Social and Spatial Transformation in Southern Sweden: 1750–1850*. Totowa, NJ: Barnes and Noble.
Rees, P 1992 The data of the decade. Paper presented to the Censuses Analysis Group Meeting, University of Leeds, 6–7 April.
Rhind, D 1983 Mapping census data. In D Rhind (ed) *A Census User's Handbook*. London: Methuen.
Robinson, A H 1989 Cartography as an art. In D Rhind and D R F Taylor (eds) *Cartography Past, Present and Future*, 91–102.

Rucker, R 1984 *The Fourth Dimension: Towards a Geometry of a Higher Reality.* Boston: Houghton Mifflin.

SEEDS 1987 *The South–South Divide.* Harlow: South East Economic Development Strategy Association.

Simpson, S and D Dorling 1994 Those missing millions: implications for social statistics of non-response to the 1991 Census. *Journal of Social Policy* 23 (4), 543-567.

Sternberg, B 1993 Military and civilian GIS work in tandem. *GIS Europe* 2 (3), 16–17.

Szegö, J 1984 *A Census Atlas of Sweden.* Stockholm: Statistics Sweden, Central Board of Real Estate Data, Swedish Council for Building Research, and the University of Lund.

Szegö, J 1987 *Human Cartography: Mapping the World of Man.* Stockholm: Swedish Council for Building Research.

Tanur, J M *et al.* (eds) 1985 *Statistics: a Guide to the Unknown.* Belmont, CA: Wadsworth and Brooks/Cole.

Tobler, W R 1973a A continuous transformation useful for districting. *Annals of the New York Academy of Sciences* 219, 215–20.

Tobler, W R 1973b Choropleth maps without class intervals? *Geographical Analysis* 3, 262–5.

Tobler, W R 1989 An update to numerical map generalization. In R B McMaster (ed) *Numerical Generalization in Cartography.* Toronto: Cartographica, University of Toronto Press.

Tufte, E R 1983 *The Visual Display of Quantitative Information.* Cheshire, CT: Graphics Press.

Tufte, E R 1990 *Envisioning Information.* Cheshire, CT: Graphics Press.

Tukey, J W 1965 The future processes of data analysis. *Proceedings of the Tenth Conference on the Design of Experiments in Army Research Development and Testing,* Report 65-3. Durham, NC: US Army Research Office, 691–725.

Upton, G J G 1991 Displaying election results. *Political Geography Quarterly* 10 (3), 200–20.

Young, F W, D P Kent and W F Kuhfeld 1988 Dynamic graphics for exploring multivariate data. In W S Cleveland and M E McGill (eds) *Dynamic Graphics for Statistics.* Belmont, CA: Wadsworth.

7

Analysis of univariate census data

C Brunsdon

Editor's note

It is taken for granted that many users will input census data into statistical packages. However, this is not always helpful because of the special nature of census data for geographic areas. This chapter provides some practical advice as to how users should proceed and outlines a number of appropriate techniques.

1 Introduction

1.1 Looking at a single variable

On first inspection of any set of data, there are a certain number of questions that are often of interest. How are the values of a variable of particular interest distributed? Are there any cases with exceptionally large or small values of some variable? What associations are shown between certain groups of variables? Data drawn from the 1991 census are no exception to this, and the aim of this chapter is to suggest to the census user a set of statistical techniques that may be helpful in answering questions of this sort. Broadly, the techniques may be divided into *univariate* and *multivariate* methods, i.e. those examining individual census variables in isolation and those exploring the associations that may occur between several variables. Only univariate techniques will be considered here, since multivariate methods will be covered in a later chapter. Another useful distinction between methods is that of *exploratory* approaches as opposed to *modelling* or *hypothesis* based approaches. The former require few assumptions about the input data and are used to describe or summarize the data, highlighting any interesting or unusual characteristics that may become apparent. The latter are more concerned with calibrating formulae suggesting quantitative relationships between variables, and formally testing hypotheses of association between variables. These may often require very rigorous assumptions about the data.

It is intended here to give an overview of univariate approaches, together with some recommendations – and warnings of pitfalls – that may be of use when presenting or analysing univariate datasets taken from the census. Many important patterns can be identified by the study of single census variables, and most of the methods presented here will require little effort and are easily interpreted. It is always important to carry out some univariate analysis on any variables used in a study. Indeed, it will be argued that some univariate analysis should be a prerequisite for many of the multivariate analysis techniques.

1.2 A geographical context

The geographical nature of census data is particularly relevant to all forms of analysis. The methods presented here will not be as explicitly spatial as those involving mapping demonstrated in the chapters concerned with geographical information systems (GIS) and visualization, but nonetheless consideration of the spatial nature of the underlying data is essential in their interpretation. This last statement has more consequences than one may initially imagine. For example, many of the commonly used statistical tests were derived on the assumption that each observation in the dataset is independent of the others. With geographical data this is rarely the case between nearby zones. This would suggest that many methods offered by the commercially available statistical packages are inappropriate. In fact the outlook is not as bleak as it may first appear – but it is important that the census user does not carry out analysis blind to these considerations.

1.3 Graphical and exploratory approaches

A final but important practical consideration is the use of computer packages to carry out analysis. Since the last census a decade ago, great advances have been made in microcomputing and graphics which can be put to good use for census data analysis. For the purposes of exploration and displaying of results, graphical presentation may sometimes prove to be a more effective and direct means of communication than tabulation. In addition to this, modern computer software also offers scope for interaction. Thus, users are encouraged to experiment with different display formats, and different models, obtaining almost instant responses to any changes requested. This allows a very different and perhaps more adventurous approach to that necessarily adopted in previous censuses, when computer time was costly and graphics display a highly coveted and tightly rationed resource.

2 Presenting and analysing individual variables

2.1 Overview

There are many occasions where the distribution of a single census variable is of interest. Even when dealing with groups of several variables, it is important not to overlook the characteristics of each variable in its own right, since these can often have consequences on the outcome of multivariate analysis techniques. Thus, a knowledge of reliable and helpful univariate techniques is essential for any census-based study. The techniques that are of most use are those that can generally be described as exploratory, in that they can be used to discover many interesting (and perhaps unexpected) patterns or features that may be contained in the data. For univariate studies, much of the emphasis should therefore be placed on presentation. At this early stage in the analysis, little is known about the data and many interesting questions can be raised. Are there any general trends in the data? Are there any exceptional values going against the trends? The aim of the first part of this section is to present a set of techniques that will help to answer general questions of this sort.

2.2 Displaying the raw data

For a given variable, census data usually come in the form of a table or computer file. They consist of some quantity, such as 'the percentage of people who are economically inactive' calculated for a set of regions, typically enumeration districts or census wards. These are treated as fundamental spatial divisions, in that only variation between these areal units may be observed – information about internal variation is excluded from the dataset. For each such region, the value of the variable is tabulated, usually alongside the name (or code) for the region.

A typical example is given in Table 7.1, for the proportion of households with heads in professional occupation by county from the 1991 Census. What is apparent from this table is that, while serving as a useful way of finding individual pieces of information (e.g. looking up the rate for Hertfordshire), it gives little indication of the overall pattern of employment in the country. It is hard to see whether there are a handful of well-off counties with others lagging far behind, or a smooth progression from good to bad with some representation of most levels between. A more helpful presentation format to highlight this type of information is the *stem and leaf display* (Tukey 1977). This combines the graphical information of a bar chart with the more precise quantitative information found in the table. First, the data items are sorted in numerical order. Then some of the most significant digits of each data item are used to label each bar. Finally, the bars themselves are composed of the next most significant digit. This is best shown by example, and the data from Table 7.1 are shown in this form in Fig. 7.1.

This gives a much clearer picture of the distribution. It can now be seen that a large number of counties distribute themselves around the 16% level, spreading

Table 7.1 Proportion of households with heads in professional occupations by county from the 1991 Census

County	Households SEGS 1,2,3,4,13	Total	Percentage of total
Avon	6 333	33 394	18.96
Bedfordshire	3 458	17 409	19.86
Berkshire	5 881	23 362	25.17
Borders	680	3 676	18.50
Buckinghamshire	5 317	19 305	27.54
Cambridgeshire	4 133	20 594	20.07
Central	1 418	9 381	15.12
Cheshire	6 674	32 483	20.55
Cleveland	2 349	19 616	11.97
Clwyd	2 199	13 971	15.74
Cornwall	2 718	15 484	17.55
Cumbria	2 703	17 205	15.71
Derbyshire	5 051	33 119	15.25
Devon	6 224	34 822	17.87
Dorset	4 513	22 473	20.08
Dumfries and Galloway	902	5 063	17.82
Durham	2 642	22 031	11.99
Dyfed	1 781	11 750	15.16
East Sussex	5 269	26 173	20.13
Essex	11 327	52 581	21.54
Fife	1 755	11 695	15.01
Gloucestershire	3 717	17 954	20.70
Grampian	2 903	16 546	17.55
Greater London	45 608	250 731	18.19
Greater Manchester	13 908	94 425	14.73
Gwent	2 045	15 505	13.19
Gwynedd	1 365	8 165	16.72
Hampshire	10 143	51 203	19.81
Hereford and Worcestershire	4 722	22 221	21.25
Hertfordshire	8 960	33 446	26.79
Highland	1 110	6 435	17.25
Humberside	4 552	30 469	14.94
Islands	326	2 395	13.61
Isle of Wight	799	4 384	18.23
Kent	10 280	52 403	19.62
Lancashire	7 913	50 114	15.79
Leicestershire	5 298	29 710	17.83
Lincolnshire	3 390	19 824	17.10
Lothian	4 591	26 623	17.24
Merseyside	7 192	52 889	13.60
Mid Glamorgan	2 147	18 781	11.43
Norfolk	4 562	25 730	17.73
North Yorkshire	4 992	24 181	20.64
Northamptonshire	3 277	18 861	17.37

Table 7.1 *cont.*

County	Households		
	SEGS 1,2,3,4,13	Total	Percentage of total
Northumberland	1 829	10 760	17.00
Nottinghamshire	5 361	35 718	15.01
Oxfordshire	3 925	17 838	22.00
Powys	670	3 878	17.28
Shropshire	2 359	13 079	18.04
Somerset	2 935	15 374	19.09
South Glamorgan	2 458	13 430	18.30
South Yorkshire	5 751	47 576	12.09
Staffordshire	5 899	35 814	16.47
Strathclyde	11 205	82 434	13.59
Suffolk	3 845	21 562	17.83
Surrey	11 108	35 360	31.41
Tayside	2 266	14 302	15.84
Tyne and Wear	5 103	42 360	12.05
Warwickshire	3 462	16 643	20.80
West Glamorgan	1 637	13 139	12.46
West Midlands	12 668	93 623	13.53
West Sussex	6 008	24 873	24.15
West Yorkshire	11 368	74 708	15.22
Wiltshire	3 297	18 200	18.12

% Household In SEGS 1-4 and 13		County Name
11	4	Mid Glamorgan
12	00015	
13	25666	
14	79	
15	001223778	
16	57	
17	0122345678889	
18	012235	
19	01689	
20	115678	
21	35	
22	0	
23		
24	2	West Sussex
25	2	Berkshire
26	8	Hertfordshire
27	5	Buckinghamshire
28		
29		
30		
31	4	Surrey

Fig. 7.1 A stem and leaf display for the data of Table 7.1.

about 5% either way, but also there is another more affluent and smaller cluster at around 25%. Finally, one county (Surrey) has a value of 31% and is ahead of even this cluster, with the nearest county to it falling 4% behind. Two important features of the stem and leaf plot are illustrated here. First, because it retains much of the exact numerical information in the dataset, it is possible to identify the original cases easily. For example, it can easily be seen that the percentage values in the upper cluster are 25.2%, 26.8% and so on. These can be checked back against the original data to see which counties comprise this affluent cluster. Second, it also highlights outstanding values in the data. This is best illustrated by the Surrey example given earlier. This illustrates an important principle. There may be general trends in the data (the two main clusters) but there are often one-off exceptions to these trends. To gain some insight into the processes giving rise to the data, one must consider both the trends and the counter-examples. It is often the case that graphical (or semi-graphical) exploratory methods on the raw data can both identify the general form of any patterns or trends in the data and highlight any exceptions to them.

The stem and leaf method provides a useful way of displaying relatively small datasets but is of less value when datasets become large. Since each data item requires one character (excluding the overheads of the label bars, title and so on), it becomes clear that displaying information for all 10,444 UK census wards, for example, is impractical on a single book page or sheet of paper, unless the size of the text is so small that it becomes illegible. In this case a *histogram* is a better alternative. This is a bar graph in which the area of each bar is proportional to the frequency count of data items in each of a set of value classes. A histogram of the previous variable, but based on census wards, is shown in Fig. 7.2. As with the stem and leaf diagram, information about the 'shape' of the distribution is conveyed, but there is no longer the exact quantitative information.

Again it is possible to see certain outlying values here. A small number of wards have 100% of their households with heads in professional occupations.

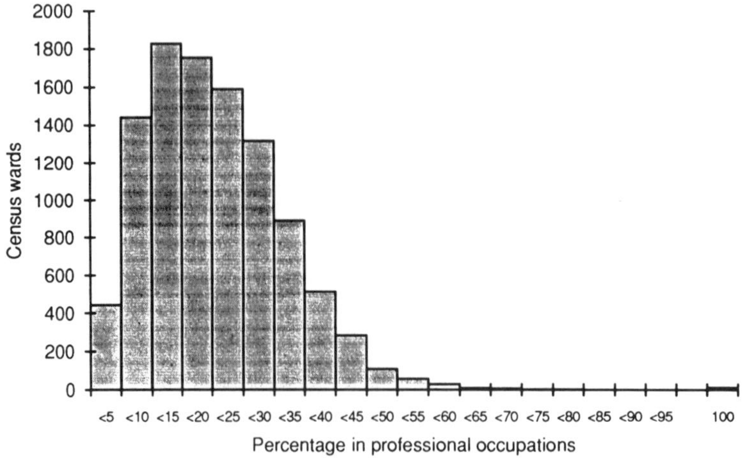

Fig. 7.2 Histogram of the percentage in professional occupations – class width 5%.

Fig. 7.3 Histogram of the percentage in professional occupations – class width 1%.

This is somewhat surprising, but many of these wards are in the centre of the City of London and have total populations of less than 20. As before this demonstrates that it is important to discover the exceptional cases as well as the general trends.

An important choice when drawing histograms is that of class width. In Fig. 7.2 each class had a width of 5%, but if a different width is chosen, this may affect the appearance of the histogram. In Fig. 7.3, the same variable is charted with class widths of 1%.

Although conveying a similar general pattern to the first histogram, this has a more 'ragged' appearance. It also reveals that a certain number of wards have no households with heads in professional employment at all, and that this is in opposition to the trend in the distribution (which generally falls off from 10% to 2% for the variable under scrutiny). It is also important to consider sample sizes when using a histogram of this type. In the 1991 Census there were 1252 wards having a base population of less than 50. With the computation of percentages, these can lead to a number of problems. For example, there is a peak at 66% on this histogram, but since this value represents precisely two-thirds of the denominator it is much more likely that one of the smaller wards will have this value than 65% or 67%. A similar argument could also explain the peak at 50% and possibly some others. It is sometimes important to identify 'quirks' in the data of this sort, particularly when it is intended to input these results into some more sophisticated analysis methods, as some of these methods may be sensitive to these artificial clusters.

The role that the histogram has played here is therefore twofold. It has identified the general trends in the data, but has also identified some unexpected facets and outlying values. The effectiveness of this was increased greatly when we created a histogram with relatively small class sizes, although clearly decreasing these over-enthusiastically could create problems due to sparsely represented classes. A rule of thumb that has been suggested in the previous handbook (Evans

1983) is that the number of classes should equal the square root of the number of values, rounded up. Beyond this, it is often practical to choose round numbers close to those suggested by this rule as cut-off points between classes. For example, for 10,444 wards, the square root rule suggests that 121 classes are used. This gives cut-off points that are multiples of 0.8264%, but it may be more sensible to work with 1% sized classes. Using an interval of 1% makes the values associated with each of the histogram bars clearly discernible. This has worked reasonably well in the above example, and in fact the previous suggested width would have been less effective at identifying the small numbers problem.

Summing up, then, it is important to carry out a graphical analysis before moving on to more complicated techniques. Not only does it identify general patterns in the data, it often provides a striking indication of unexpected patterns or outstanding cases. A stem and leaf plot is a useful way to achieve this if the number of data cases is small but is impractical for more than a few hundred values. A less detailed alternative could then be a histogram, which shows distribution shape but no longer identifies individual values. Histograms having large class widths tend to show general trends in the data but smooth out any irregularities. At times this may be desired, but in an exploratory analysis it is generally important to identify these irregularities rather than eliminate them. In this case relatively small class widths are recommended, such as those obtained using the guidelines above.

2.3 Simple descriptive statistics

In addition to the graphical summaries suggested in the last section, it may also be necessary to obtain some information about distributional characteristics of variables of interest in tabular form. This would be particularly helpful when comparing several variables, since it is simpler to list the information on a single page than to draw many histograms or stem and leaf plots. Several measures have been proposed to describe the distribution of some variable. The two most common approaches are those based on *moments* of the distribution of the variable and those using *quantiles,* sometimes called *order-based* methods. In both cases a set of numerical measures is provided to summarize the average level, degree of spreading and general shape of the distribution observed. As will be seen below, the order-based methods tend to be less sensitive to extreme or outlying cases, but they may require more computation as they involve sorting (or at least partial sorting) of the dataset. It may well be the case that neither option is universally 'best', the suitability of each method resting on the amount and the values of outliers in the data and the size of the dataset itself.

2.4 Moment-based statistics

Two of the most commonly used measures of distribution are the *mean* and *standard deviation.* The mean describes a central tendency in the data in such a way that all absolute deviations from this number sum to zero. It is therefore a form of average. However, having this information for a distribution is not particularly helpful in isolation. It gives no indication of how much spreading of value occurs on either side of this central quantity. The standard deviation is often used to supplement this, as it is a measure of how much the individual data items are dispersed from the mean. It is based on the squares of deviations of individual data items from the mean. The squaring of the quantities causes deviations of the same size above and below the mean to influence the calculation identically. The standard deviation is in fact the square root of the mean values of these squared deviations.

This approach of taking mean values of powers of deviations about the mean can be generalized to any integer power k. In general the kth moment of the data about the mean can be written as

$$\frac{\sum_{i=1}^{n} (x_i - \overline{x})^k}{n}$$

Thus the standard deviation is the square root of the second moment. When $k = 3$, this quantity is no longer always positive and reflects the degree of asymmetry that the data values show about the mean. If there is a distribution with a long tail (see Fig. 7.1), there will be a large number of observations a long way above the mean. These will have positive deviation values, which when cubed will give even larger positive amounts. Since there are few observations a long way below the main value, these positive values will not be countered by an equal number of large negative contributions. Thus the value of the third moment will be positive. If the converse were true and there were a number of observations falling below the mean but few above, then the third moment would be negative. Thus, the third moment measures an aspect of the shape of the distribution. Zero indicates a symmetrical distribution (such as the typical Gaussian), negative values suggest a long tail below the mean and positive a long tail above it.

Finally, it may be seen at this stage that such a measure will be scale dependent. For example, if rates running from 0 to 1 were used instead of percentage rates, the third moment would change by a factor of 10^6. To compensate for this, the crude figure is divided by the cube of the standard deviation. The resultant quantity, which is scale invariant, is called the *skewness*.

One final measure of shape sometimes used in conjunction with skewness is the *kurtosis*. This is based on the fourth moment in the same way as skewness is based on the third. It can usually be thought of as a measure of 'flatness' of the distribution. A typical bell-shaped distribution may have a value of around 3, but a uniform distribution in which all values are equally likely to occur may have a value that is close to zero. Like a standard deviation, kurtosis cannot be negative since it is based on an even powered moment, although some computer packages 'normalize' the figure by subtracting 3. An important feature of kurtosis is that it cannot be considered independently of skewness. Evans (1983) identifies the problem that kurtosis tends to increase with increasing magnitude of skewness, since many census variables are percentages and constrained to the range 0%–100% and any long tails tend to contribute to flat regions in the distribution. It is thus hard to consider the interpretation of a given kurtosis figure in its own right. Given these difficulties of interpretation, it is advised that at least for data exploration the census user pay considerably less attention to kurtosis than to skewness.

From this discussion, a recommended moment-based summary would be given using the mean, standard deviation and skewness of the distribution for each variable. These are readily computed in most statistical packages, and some spreadsheets. However, it would be unfair to leave moment-based summaries without pointing out one of their major drawbacks. Returning to the ward-based data illustrated in Figs 7.2 and 7.3, consider the effect of those outlying wards having rates of 100%. The summaries are given for datasets with these wards first included and then excluded in Table 7.2.

While the outliers have not greatly affected the mean and standard deviation in each case, the skewness of the first set is noticeably higher than the second. This is particularly alarming for this dataset, since the outliers (wards having a rate of 100%) only numbered 166 out of 10,444 total observations. Only 1.5% of the dataset has caused a change of about 20% in the skewness measure. This is a fundamental problem with moment-based methods. They can be extremely sensitive to outlying observations. Owing to the large number of observations in this case, the mean and standard deviation were less noticeably affected, but with smaller samples similar phenomena can occur with these statistics also.

2.5 Order-based statistics

The final part of the last section suggests that in some cases a set of descriptive statistics that are less sensitive to outliers would be of value. One step towards this would be to sort the data and base the summary statistics on points read off along the sorted list. For example, the value that ranks exactly in the middle of the sorted dataset, the *median,* gives a measure of centrality, in a similar way to the mean. However, this quantity is not affected by the precise value of the more outstanding cases. These cases will rank near the top or bottom of the dataset, but however extreme they are they cannot affect the position of the middle ranking values in any significant way.

Table 7.2 Summary of ward-based rates for head of household in professional employment

Dataset	With outliers	Without outliers
Mean	17.1%	17.0%
Standard deviation	11.6%	11.2%
Skewness	1.665	1.346

There is still one practical problem. If the dataset has an even number of values there is no single central value dividing the list exactly in half. In this case it is usual to take two central values and average them. Thus, with a 17 sample dataset (e.g. European regions in the UK) the median is the ninth ranking value, but with an 18 sample set it would be the average of ranks 9 and 10.

This notion can be extended to give measures of spread, as well as central tendency. Looking at the values that are one-quarter and three-quarters of the way along the sorted list gives a pair of values called *quartiles*. The distance that these are apart, the *inter-quartile range*, gives a measure of spread within the data. Again, these values will not be affected by the extremity of the maximum and minimum values since they are chosen solely on the basis of their rank. This measure combined with the median can then give an indication of the central point of the data distribution and the degree of spread about this centre. As before, there may be problems if there is not an exact three-quarter or quarter point, but similar averaging methods to those for medians are applied (see for example Tukey 1977).

To bring the approach in line with the moment-based approach, it is now necessary to provide a measure equivalent to the skewness of the data. One simple way to do this is to consider how quartiles behave when different types of skewness occur. If the data are positively skewed, having a long upper tail, then the upper quartile will be correspondingly high but the lower tail will be relatively close in value to the median. If the skewing is negative, the converse will be true. In the first case, the centre point between the upper and lower quartiles will lie above the median, but in the second it will lie below it. Thus the quantity

$$\text{median} - \frac{Q_u + Q_l}{2}$$

(where Q_u and Q_l are the upper and lower quartiles) gives an order-based measure of skewness. Information for this measure is based on data towards the centre of the distribution rather than on outliers. For the dataset considered in Table 7.2, the order-based summaries are given in Table 7.3. It can be seen here that there is only a relatively small effect on the summary statistics when the outlying cases are removed.

Further information about the shape of the distribution can be obtained by looking at other values on the sorted list of variables. Generally, statistics based on points at some proportion of the way along the sorted list are referred to as *quantiles*. For example, points that are exactly one-eighth of the way along the list are octiles. It is sometimes informative to look at some of these other values

Table 7.3 Order-based summaries for the dataset in Table 7.2

Dataset	**With outliers**	**Without outliers**
Median	18.56	18.51
Inter-quartile range	15.36	15.37
Asymmetry	0.544	0.574

as well as the quartiles, to gain a better impression of distributional shape. For example, looking at the first and last octile gives more information about the shape of the distribution further out from the central point. Further information about skewness can also be obtained from looking at the centre of these two octile points, as well as the mean and centre of the inter-quartile range. A more comprehensive discussion of this idea may be found in Velleman and Hoaglin (1981).

2.6 Box and whisker plots

It is important to bear in mind that while these forms of summary are useful they are not a substitute for the graphical techniques put forward earlier. The order-based statistics are resistant to outliers in a given sample, and so give a good description of the remainder of the data, but the values of outliers themselves are part of the story. Generally these are best discovered and examined with the earlier graphical methods. The main advantage of the statistical summaries is that they may be tabulated and compared for different regions, or different variables. However, one helpful compromise between the two approaches is the *box and whisker plot*. This takes up less space on the printed page than a histogram or stem and leaf plot, but still conveys graphical information about the data. Because of its smaller size, it is possible to compare several of these directly on a single page.

A diagram of such a plot is given in Fig. 7.4. The box contains the area between the quartiles (with the median marked off), and the tails of the distribution and the outliers are also indicated.

Outliers are nominated by testing each data value to see if it lies outside the range (median–3 × inter-quartile range, median + 3 × inter-quartile range). The outermost edges of the 'whiskers' in the plot correspond to the most extreme values in the dataset that are still within this range. Because the box and whisker

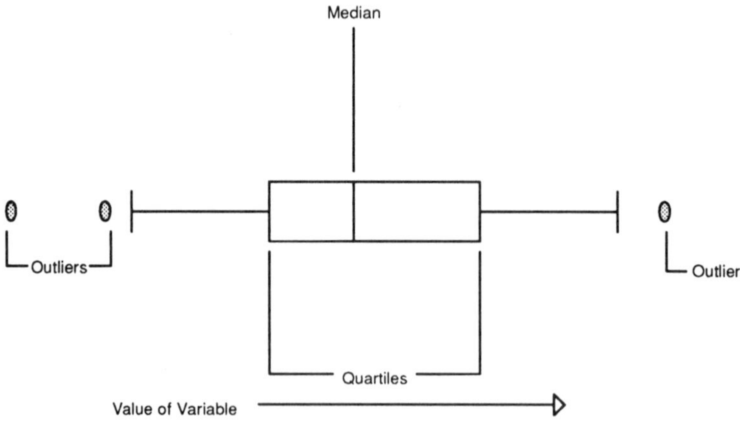

Fig. 7.4 A box and whisker plot.

plot is fairly flat, it is possible to stack several of these in a single diagram. If this is done, it is also often helpful to include a scale of values below the plots, so that exact values of medians, quartiles and so on can be read off. An example of this will be given in the next section.

2.7 The use of transformations

A final consideration when working with univariate data is the use of *data transformation.* Many of the above techniques are used to measure and explore the asymmetries of distribution of the census variables. There are times, however, when symmetrical, bell-shaped distributions of data may be more easily analysed by some statistical techniques. Typically, these will be more formal hypothesis test-based methods than those covered in this chapter, or will be of value when combining one census variable with others (see Chapter 9 later). It is possible to alter the shape of the distribution of a variable by transforming it. This involves applying some mathematical function to the 'raw' values of the census variable with the intention of altering the shape of the histogram for that variable. The choice of function depends on the shape of the original histogram. For example, the square root function tends to increase the values of lower valued arguments but to decrease the values of higher input values. The shape of the transformed histogram will therefore be more 'stretched' in the lower tail, so that this transformation is a useful way of creating a symmetrically distributed variable from one with a positive skew. Similarly, the power function $f(x) = x^a$ (with an a value of greater than unity) provides a means of 'balancing' a negatively skewed distribution.

Choice of the transformation function depends on the initial shape of the distribution of the raw data. Typically, power transforms provide a wide range of possibilities, and the exponent of the power expression may be varied to account for different degrees of skewness of the distribution. A more comprehensive discussion of these ideas, in terms of Tukey's 'ladder of transformations' is given in Tukey (1977) and is also outlined in Thompson and Tapia (1990).

3 Spatial effects in census data

3.1 Census data is geographical data

All of the techniques presented above allow a single census variable to be examined. In fact, these methods would be of use when examining *any* form of univariate data. However, census data are essentially geographical, and this gives rise to some problems that are not generally encountered in the field of data analysis. Most of these stem from the fact that census data were originally collected from individuals, so that each record in the database applied to a single person (or household), but for reasons of confidentiality each record in the census *users'* database applies to a geographical region. Clearly, in each of these regions there are several people, so that each record contains only *aggregate* information about the regional population. This can have particularly far-reaching consequences in multivariate analysis, some of which will be discussed in Chapter 9, but there are also notable effects on univariate studies.

When examining a single variable, much of the emphasis is placed on spotting patterns in the data. In a geographical sense, patterns can occur at many different scales. There are national trends in prosperity between different parts of the country, relative differences in economic growth between towns in a county, more and less exclusive neighbourhoods within a town, and sometimes good and bad ends of a street within a neighbourhood. If all of the individual data were available, they would contain information about patterns at all scales down to individual households. As this is not the case, some detail is lost. When looking at data for a particular set of areal units, all pattern occurring below these units' level of geographical precision is 'averaged out'. Even phenomena at the same scale as the geographical units can get distorted if the boundary positions of the areal units do not coincide well with the 'boundaries' of the phenomena. For a more thorough discussion of the problem see Openshaw (1984).

The outcome of all this is that the values observed in the univariate dataset under study are in part a consequence of the geographical units chosen, as well as any underlying social or demographic process. The shape of the distribution can vary because of this, as can any mapped patterns that may be apparent. As an example, consider again the variable used in the previous section's example. In Fig. 7.5, box and whisker plots are constructed for distributions of the variable (percentage of heads of households in professional occupations) taken for several different sets of zonal units.

It is fairly clear from this diagram that the shape of the distribution alters quite drastically as the choice of units is varied. This occurs for two main reasons. First,

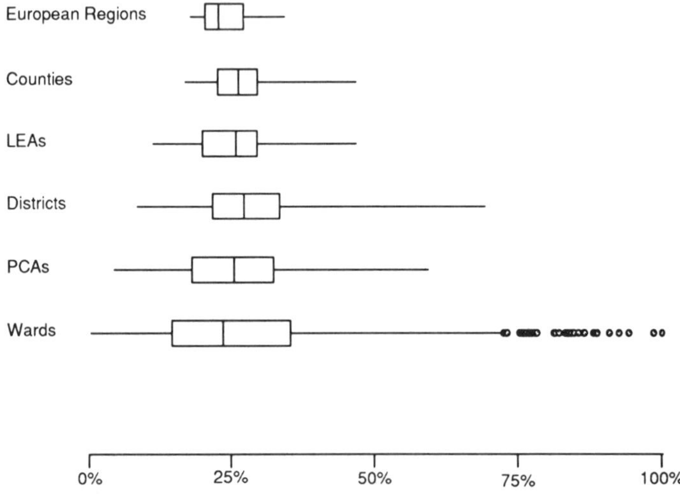

Fig. 7.5 Distribution of professional occupations with changing areal units.

owing to the 'averaging out' effects discussed above the larger zones tend to dilute the effect of extreme local cases. In rough terms, the larger the area is, the greater is the dilution effect. The second cause is particularly notable in the ward-based data, where there are many outlying values in the upper tail. Many of these occur for relatively unusual wards, e.g. those around the City of London which have extremely small populations, sometimes all of whom are classed as 'professionals'. It is quite natural that these extreme values occur in cases where the underlying population is small. Going down to individual or household level, if that were possible, would allow each observation only two possible values, 0% or 100%!

Therefore, the combination of dilution and small sample effects can change the apparent distribution of the same rate variable to a notable degree, if the choice of areal units is altered. This clearly leads to problems when interpreting the data. One way of overcoming this is to consider *all* of the information in Fig. 7.5, rather than any particular areal unit in isolation. For example, here the upper tail retracts fairly quickly once the aggregation level becomes more coarse than ward based. Similarly the lower tail retracts as the size of areal unit increases beyond wards. The particularly marked effect in the upper tail suggests that reasonably well-off people tend to group together geographically at ward level, with some wards having very high percentages of households in professional occupations. However, at larger scales, e.g. parliamentary constituencies, there are fewer extreme cases. Thus there are no constituencies having the extremely high proportion of well-off households seen at ward level. This suggests that there is less evidence of geographical grouping of well-off people over areas of this size. Considering the data in this way gives some idea of 'granularity' of patterns. Here the exploration suggests that there are some ward-sized pockets of high prosperity, but that one is unlikely to find this phenomenon occurring for a whole district.

In some extreme cases, even this approach may not be helpful. It is possible that this granularity may be at a smaller geographical scale than the most detailed areal units allow to be observed. As an example, some urban streets are experiencing a process of gentrification. Newly resident relatively wealthy households are situated side by side with the original residents. The difference in prosperity can sometimes manifest itself in terms of different household size, although the houses themselves may be identical. Thus, a single street could present a checker board of high and low rates of persons per room when mapped at individual household level. The distribution of these rates may well be bimodal. However, even at the level of an enumeration district (which may contain several streets), this pattern would be lost. Incorporating all of the houses in their local areal unit and calculating an average rate would yield some central value of rate, perhaps representing *none* of the houses in the zone well. Worse still, an effect of this sort would be far harder to identify than an atypical value even in a graphical exploratory analysis such as a box and whisker plot, since errors of this sort actually make observations become closer to the central region of the distribution and so appear *more* typical!

The principal argument in this section is that although univariate statistical methods may give the impression of being free from spatial considerations, this is not the case. The fact that the data are spatial in nature runs through the analysis like lettering in seaside rock. A picture of the distribution of some variable may be obtained, but this in itself is meaningless without some consideration of the underlying spatial aggregation process contributing to the creation of the distribution. In many cases, looking at more than one scale of aggregation, together with consideration of the nature of the variable being studied, will give a much clearer view. The previous paragraph perhaps gives an unreasonably pessimistic viewpoint, showing counter-examples where even this will be of no help. Although this problem can arise, many social and demographic phenomena occur at much larger scales than that of gentrification, and these may quite profitably be analysed using appropriate census variables. As stated before, the only guidance as to whether difficulties may occur is to consider the phenomena likely to give rise to the data.

3.2 Examining univariate data as a spatial process

The above example shows that the type of spatial patterns exhibited by the underlying phenomena can have a notable effect on both graphical and tabular summaries. Although these summaries can be useful when considered in conjunction with the spatial effects, it may often be helpful to consider the spatial process on its own. For example, do adjacent wards tend to have similar values for some particular variable? The above methods show information about the values of the variables but convey nothing about their geographical location. In the next sections, graphical and numerical techniques intended to highlight this kind of information will be discussed. Of course, mapping the information is a fundamental tool for carrying out this task, but this subject is covered in Chapters 4 and 6. The techniques considered here will be more in the form of methods of assessing the general degree of spatial clustering exhibited by some variables.

3.3 The semivariogram cloud plot

An important aspect of geographical phenomena is the association of events and features which are near to each other. For examples from the census, do people over the age of 65 tend to live near to each other? Do people owning two or more cars group together? One must first ask what is meant by 'near'. Are there streets with predominantly old populations, or, at a much larger scale, counties? If similar events happen near to each other, or similar demographic features occur close together, what is the relationship between the geographical closeness and the level similarity. A simple way of examining this is to consider the relationship between difference in value and distance for each pair of observations in the data. This is best done using a scatterplot. Since the interest is only in the amount of difference in the variable, not the direction, the squared difference between the variables is plotted on one axis against the distance on the other. Sometimes, however, this can present practical difficulties. Since each *pair* of areas must be plotted, even for large-scale areal units the number of points on the plot increases dramatically.

For 64 counties, for example, there will be 2016 points. The corresponding number for wards is in excess of 54 million. This can be overcome in two ways. First, it is generally accepted that interest is in regions that are reasonably near to each other, so there is little point in considering pairs of areas that are hundreds of miles apart. Thus a 'cut-off distance' could be used to select which points go into the plot. Second, when very large numbers of points are being considered, the distances and variable differences could be split into classes, and counts could be made of the number of points falling in each class. This has been done in the following example, and the information is conveyed in a diagram where circles are drawn at the centroid of each class whose radius is proportional to the count in that class. When using individual points, a graph of this sort is referred to as a semivariogram cloud plot, since the large number of points often resembles a cloud on the diagram. The term semivariogram is borrowed from the work of Matheron (1967) on surface interpolation.

An example of a class-interval-based plot is given in Fig. 7.6. Here the areal units are census wards and the variable of interest is the proportion of households owning three or more cars in Greater London. Wards having very low populations (typically those near the centre of the City of London) are excluded from the diagram. It can be seen that there is a larger spread of possible values at longer distances, but that this is less the case for nearby regions. This suggests that there is some tendency for nearby wards to have similar characteristics in terms of car ownership. It is important to note that, although there are few close wards that differ extremely, at larger distances there are still a reasonable number of wards that have similar rates. This is quite reasonable. One only expects that nearby wards are similar, not that extremely distant wards are dissimilar. For example, there may be a relatively wealthy cluster of wards outside one town, and a similar set outside a neighbouring town.

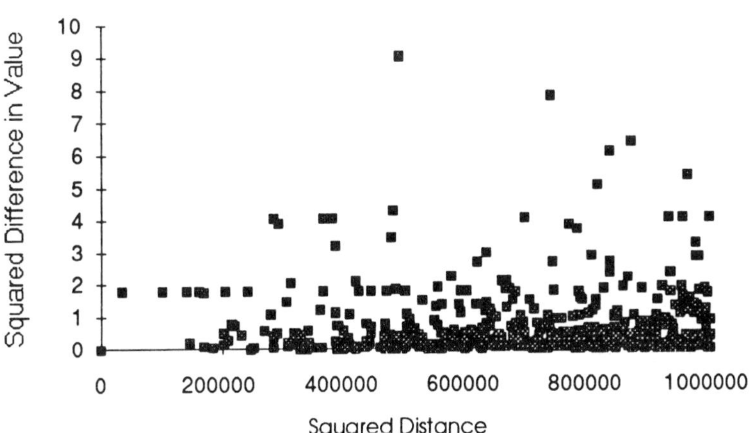

Fig. 7.6 Semivariogram cloud plot.

3.4 Nearest neighbour plots

If it is of interest whether nearby regions have similar characteristics, it could be argued that the previous method not only gives this information but also information about zones that are a long way away from each other. It is also important to note that attention is paid only to the differences in variable values, not the absolute amounts. It may be possible, for example, that there are large clusters of less well-off areas but relatively small clusters of affluent areas. These patterns can be investigated using a nearest neighbour plot. In these plots, only the relationships between very close zones are investigated. For each zone the value of the variable of interest is plotted against that of its nearest neighbour.

The shape of these scatterplots can highlight several characteristics of the spatial patterns exhibited by the variable. For example, if the points lie close to a straight line with a positive slope, this suggests a relatively smooth trend in the data, with high valued zones tending to be close to other high valued zones. In fact, this would be true if the points lay close to any permanently increasing curve. Conversely, a downward-sloping trend in these points would suggest the opposite, that nearby zones had differing characteristics. An example is given in Fig. 7.7, where a nearest neighbour plot is constructed for percentages of households having three or more cars, for all census wards in Greater London.

Another useful feature of a graph of this type is that it may also be used to identify outlying examples. Even if there is generally a smooth spatial pattern on the map, it is possible that there may be a small number of exceptions to this rule, where nearby areas have strikingly different characteristics. These would show up here as outliers, so long as the spatial changes were not excessively smoothed out by an unfortunate choice of ward boundaries as a result of the aggregation effects considered previously. In the example here a number of such outliers can be identified. In some cases they are due to the City of London wards, which have

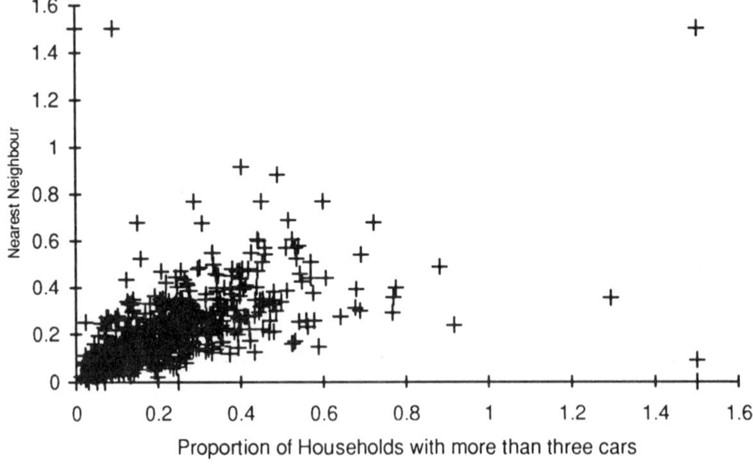

Fig. 7.7 Nearest neighbour plot.

extremely low numbers of residents, although in other cases they may highlight interesting demographic and social patterns in the variable being considered.

There are a number of ways in which this method could be improved upon. One is to plot not just *nearest* neighbour pairs, but also second and third closest pairs. This improves the chances of discovering outliers and unusual spatial variations in the data. An alternative approach may be to consider pairs specified by adjacency of regions rather than nearest neighbours. Thus, for each region, the relationship between itself and all of its boundary-sharing neighbours would be included in the diagram. At times, this approach may be more helpful, since distances between regions are usually based on some form of regional centroid or label point, and these may not represent the centre of population for the region particularly well.

3.5 Autocorrelation

In addition to the above graphical techniques for exploring spatial association, there are also some quantitative techniques. In the same way that the mean, variance and skewness can be used as summary statistics for the shape of a distribution, a *coefficient of autocorrelation* can describe the degree of spatial clustering in a geographical dataset. There are two popular formulae for these coefficients, Moran's I and Geary's C. Both of these measure the difference in value of a variable between nearby zones and use this as a basis for measuring the degree to which nearby regions tend to have similar values. The formulae for both coefficients may be found in Upton and Fingleton (1985). As well as being used as summary statistics, they may also be used in hypothesis testing. For example, in many cases the testing of a null hypothesis of 'no spatial association' against 'some spatial association' is considered.

An important property of these coefficients is that they set out to measure a *global* attribute of the dataset. In both of the above formulae, the coefficient is based on an average measure of discrepancy between nearby regions, taken over the entire study area. It can be thought of as measuring the general tendency of the variable values to cluster. This may not always be helpful. It is possible, for example, that tightly packed urban wards may tend to have a greater amount of agreement in some variable than rural wards where population settlement is sparse. As with statistics summarizing distributions, it is important to consider the variation or spread of the degree of clustering in addition to its aggregated value. It may be constructive for some future research to devise a methodology for investigating this type of phenomenon, partly in terms of graphical and cartographic techniques and also in terms of summary statistics and modelling. At least for the moment it is necessary to make use of some of the graphical techniques described above before considering autocorrelation indices.

This problem also has implications for hypothesis testing. Since the statistic is global, so is any hypothesis associated with it. Thus, tests based on the autocorrelation coefficients can only address questions of the form 'does the process as a whole cluster?' The census analyst will more often require questions such as 'where does the process cluster?' or 'does the process cluster around some specific localities?' to be answered. At the time of writing, techniques aimed at solving this kind of problem are still the subject of much research. One exception to this is the *G* statistic of Getis and Ord (1992).

A further problem which needs to be addressed is the ubiquitous modifiable areal unit problem. As always, the patterns observed in space will depend, to some extent, on the geographical units chosen for data aggregation. A change in these patterns will, in turn, bring about a change in the values of Moran's *I* or Geary's *C* coefficients. Thus, whether a pattern appears to be clustered or not can depend not just on the process underlying the data but also on the method of data collation. As before, it is recommended that if coefficients of this sort are to be used, they should perhaps be evaluated at several different scales of aggregation to understand not only *whether* the data clusters but at what spatial scale any clustering may occur.

3.6 Surface interpolation

With the advent of GIS and three-dimensional computer graphics, it has been suggested that geographical variables may be represented as warped two-dimensional surfaces in three-dimensional space. The census variable is represented as a continuous mathematical function giving the appearance of a terrain over the geographical study area. The high values of the variable correspond to peaks in the terrain, and the low values to valleys. There are many ways that such surfaces can be computed (see for example Tobler 1979; Martin and Bracken 1991), but generally they will take the density of the census variable for each zone as a z value (or a weight in the case of Martin and Bracken's algorithm) and couple this with the x and y coordinates of the zone centroid to give a set of control points in three-dimensional space. These points are used to generate the surface. Since the surface is continuous, this gives a basis for estimating densities at any (x,y) location in the study area, and by numerical integration also allows estimation of values for other zonal systems than those used for the original data.

A surface model can therefore give an *estimate* of the value of some census variable to any degree of spatial resolution required. It is essential to note, however, that this value is no more than an estimate. It can be an interesting exercise to fit surfaces to some census variable tabulated for a set of different areal units. Most methods of interpolation tend to fit smooth surfaces between the control points, and for very coarse levels of spatial resolution (e.g. at county level) this would tend to give smooth trends from the centroid of one region to that of each of its neighbours. For many variables, an examination of ward level data will suggest that this is not the case. Clearly, as an estimation technique, the surface model has not performed well here.

This can perhaps be explained in terms of the ideas of 'graininess' of spatial data suggested earlier. The smoothing approach of the interpolation techniques is equivalent to an assumption that, for levels of geographical accuracy exceeding that of the input data, nearby items are strongly correlated. If the tendency of the underlying process is to show spatial variance at much more local scales than this then the assumption is misleading. The smoothing approach assumes no 'graininess' at smaller scales than the areal units of the data.

This suggests that surfaces should only be generated from data based on the smaller areal units, such as wards or enumeration districts. Even at this scale, however, setbacks can occur. Considering the gentrification example as a worst case, surfaces used for interpolating persons per household would at best be based on the distorted patterns obtained from enumeration districts, giving correspondingly distorted surface models. The variation within enumeration districts would be smoothed out. It can be argued that this is a shortcoming of the initial data rather than of the technique applied. An important point here is that, despite the impression of continuity given, fitted surfaces can be as sensitive to choice of initial areal unit as any other technique. Given that they are often visually striking, they can in the worst case be an effective tool for communicating mistaken impressions. On the other hand, if they do represent the underlying data well, they are a useful and flexible tool for estimating data aggregations to unusual zoning systems. However, it is advised that very careful consideration be given to the variable in hand, and the interpolation process applied, before using a surface-based representation of data.

3.7 Software packages

The final part of this chapter considers some practical aspects of univariate analysis. With the spread of microcomputing in the last decade, most census users will have access to some form of computing facility. This gives the user access to several software packages which may be used to carry out many of the forms of analysis discussed in this chapter. A major change that has occurred in the last few years is in the availability of graphics hardware. Once considered a very specialized and heavily rationed computing resource, most basic PCs now offer reasonably good graphics facilities. At the time of writing, nearly all currently available IBM compatible PCs can display 16-colour graphics at a resolution of 640 × 480 pixels, and many can better this. To many census users, this allows much more frequent use of the graphics-based techniques suggested here and in the previous *Census User's Handbook* (Evans 1983) than has been possible before. It certainly implies that pictorial results can be produced extremely quickly compared with older means of obtaining computer graphics; typically this involved queuing for a limited number of graphics terminals or sending batch jobs to a centralized plotter and then waiting for the results to return. This is particularly relevant for univariate analysis, where much of the emphasis is on data exploration. For example, the user may now experiment with many different class widths when drawing histograms simply by altering a single parameter on a charting package. In addition to this, some micro-based packages offer facilities to query the diagrams interactively. Clicking on an outlying data value in a scatterplot, for example, could display the record in the database or spreadsheet giving this value, perhaps showing which region it corresponded to or some other information. In this way the user may very quickly gain a 'feel' for the data.

Thus, when considering suitable software for carrying out the univariate methods suggested here, as much emphasis should be put on graphical facilities as on quantitative algorithms offered. For many PC users, many of these may be offered in spreadsheet packages. Recently developed spreadsheets often offer facilities to produce histograms or scatterplots such as those used in this chapter. Although many sophisticated formats of graphs are offered, such as histograms in which three-dimensional 'pillars' are drawn instead of bars, it is advisable to forsake these in favour of the more basic styles. Generally the more complex diagrams tend to provide ornamentation that bears little relationship to the data and so draw emphasis away from the fundamental information in the chart. For a more rigorous discussion of this, see for example Tufte (1983).

In addition to the graphical facilities, spreadsheets also allow easy access to some of the statistical methods discussed here. Means and standard deviations (or variances) are usually offered as intrinsic functions, and sorting of data columns provides a good basis for estimating medians and quartiles.

In addition to spreadsheets as PC-based data analysis tools, most of the well-established mainframe-based statistical packages have now been ported onto PCs. There are PC versions of SAS, SPSSx and MINITAB for example. In their PC versions, many of these take advantage of the graphics available, also offering scatterplot and histogram drawing options. In addition to this many also provide direct options for computing summary statistics, such as mean and variance but also skewness and order-based measures. MINITAB also provides commands to produce stem and leaf diagrams and box plots. The XLISP-STAT package (Tierney 1990) provides a public domain tool which has a particularly powerful collection of exploratory data analysis features.

If no PC-based facilities are available, or the dataset being processed is too large to be stored by a PC package, then there are the mainframe versions of these statistical packages also. These are generally more difficult to use (some PC-based versions offer menu-based access to commands, and so on) and are often accessed through text-only terminals and so cannot offer high resolution graphics, but they still provide many of the fundamental tools. For the graphical techniques, for example, line printer graphs are often created, where characters of text are positioned on the printed output to produce low resolution scatterplots and histograms. Whilst not being ideal, this does provide a work-around if more modern equipment is not accessible.

Until this point, most of the discussion has been concerned with software tools for summarizing the distribution shape of variables. Using standard software, it is possible to implement all of the ideas suggested in this text. When considering the spatial aspects of the data, however, direct implementations of the suggested methods are not so readily found. Most statistical packages do not include explicitly spatial techniques, nor suitable data structures for handling spatial data (Goodchild *et al.* 1992). For example, none of the packages mentioned in the text above include an option to compute spatial autocorrelation. It should also be noted that such facilities are not generally offered by GIS either.

Unfortunately, at the time of writing the only way to implement most of the

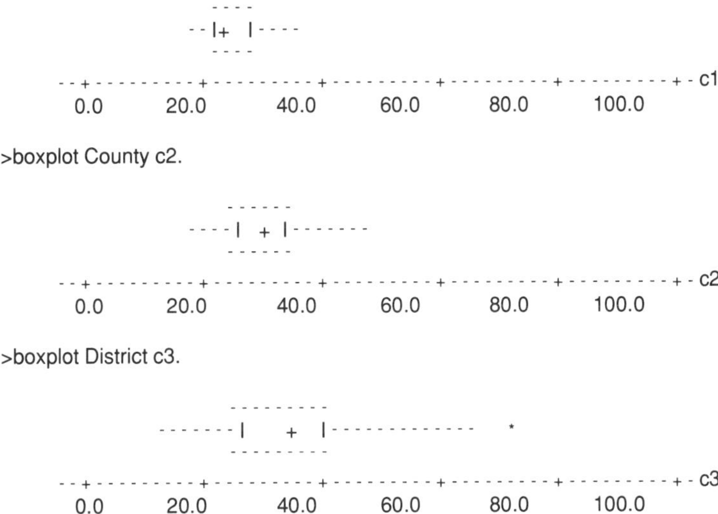

Fig. 7.8 Analysis of spatial data using existing package facilities.

suggestions for exploration of spatial data will involve some amount of programming, even if part of the task can be carried out by some package. For example, the points to be plotted in a nearest neighbour analysis may have to be computed by a stand-alone program, but may then be fed into a spreadsheet or charting program to obtain the final scatterplot. There are some methods, however, which may be applied using existing package facilities. A good example is the type of analysis carried out in Fig. 7.8. Here data tables for one variable are extracted at different levels of spatial aggregation and then box plots for each table are compared. The first stage, data extraction, can be achieved using software to access the census data (e.g. SASPAC), and the second using the box plot facility in MINITAB. However, it should be generally noted that, apart from informal approaches of this sort, spatial techniques are not well supported in statistical packages.

4 Conclusions

4.1 Getting a feel for the variable

In brief, an exploratory approach to univariate data is suggested here. Modern microcomputing environments allow this to be largely graphical, and also interactive. This type of data analysis is essential at an early stage, since it gives a good subjective understanding of any patterns or features in the data. Such understanding is a valuable asset, particularly if the data are to be subsequently passed on to some form of modelling or hypothesis testing. Either of these more formal procedures will make certain assumptions about the data (or the process giving rise to the data), and the justification for their use rests on the validity of these assumptions. After informal data exploration the census analyst should be in a stronger position to view any such assumptions critically, and so hopefully choose an appropriate methodology. In order to achieve this, use can be made of the techniques proposed by Tukey (1977) together with exploitation of some graphical methods. Many of these graphical methods are supported on widely available software packages for microcomputers.

Emphasis has also been placed on viewing univariate census data in a geographical context. This involves mapping of the data, together with some further exploratory techniques suggested in the text. Unlike the earlier univariate methods, these techniques are not readily implemented in established software packages. This perhaps reflects the fact that exploratory spatial analysis is in its infancy and there are few widely adopted methodologies or techniques. It is hoped that future developments in this field may lead to changes in this situation. Indeed, given the statements of the previous paragraph, it is essential that spatial exploration techniques are developed to complement any advances in spatial modelling and hypothesis testing that may well occur in the coming years. For the time being, users are encouraged to experiment either by writing their own software or, if this is impractical, by varying spatial units for extracting census data and carrying out standard techniques.

4.2 Recommendations

Univariate data exploration of each variable should always take place before any modelling or hypothesis testing. A suggested set of techniques to apply are

1. stem and leaf diagrams if the dataset is small, or histograms if large
2. boxplots
3. mean, standard deviation and skewness tables, or order-based equivalents

Note that part of the purpose of 1 and 2 is to identify outlying observations. These should be tagged and examined carefully, particularly if they are to be included in further analysis. In addition to this, some consideration should be given to the areal units chosen for data aggregation. It may be worthwhile checking the effect of altering the aggregation scheme on the previous results. If further exploration of the spatial features of the data is required, draw maps (possibly cartograms may be most helpful – see Chapter 6) and if possible apply some other spatial exploratory techniques. Carrying out these tasks, preferably in an interactive framework, should give a strong feel for the data, with an awareness of any trends that may exist together with any outstanding resistance to these trends. This may be of value on its own, or provide prior knowledge when incorporating a variable into multivariate techniques.

References

Evans, I S 1983 Bivariate and multivariate analysis: relationships between variables. In D W Rhind (ed) *A Census User's Handbook*. London: Methuen.

Getis, A and J K Ord 1992 The analysis of spatial association by use of distance statistics *Geographical Analysis* 24.

Goodchild, M, R Haining and S Wise 1992 Integrating GIS and spatial data analysis; problems and possibilities. *International Journal of Geographical Information Systems* 6.

Martin, D and I Bracken 1991 Techniques for modelling population-related raster databases. *Environment and Planning A* 23.

Matheron, G 1967 Kriging, or polynomial interpolation procedures. *Canadian Mining and Metallurgical Bulletin* 60, 1041–5.

Openshaw, S 1984 *The Modifiable Areal Unit Problem*, Catmog 38. Norwich: Geo-Abstracts.

Thompson, J R and Tapia, R A 1990 *Nonparametric Function Estimation, Modeling and Simulation*. Philadelphia: Society for Industrial and Applied Mathematics.

Tierney, L 1990 *LISP-STAT: An Object Oriented Environment for Statistical Computing and Dynamic Graphics*. Chichester: Wiley.

Tobler, W R 1979 Smooth pycnophylactic interpolations for geographical regions. *Journal of the American Statistical Association*, 74, 519–30.

Tufte E 1983 *The Display of Quantitative Information*. Cheshire, CT: Graphics Press.

Tukey, J W 1977 *Exploratory Data Analysis*. Reading, MA: Addison-Wesley.

Upton, G and B Fingleton 1985 *Spatial Data Analysis by Example*. New York: Wiley.

Velleman, P F and D C Hoaglin 1981 *Applications, Basics and Computing of Exploratory Data Analysis*. Boston, MA: Duxbury Press.

8

Classifying and regionalizing census data

S Openshaw and C Wymer

Editor's note

Many derived census datasets generated by users are characterized by massive multivariate complexity and high levels of data redundancy. Classification is an extremely useful technology for both research and applied purposes as it provides a means of simplifying census datasets. However, the standard methods provided in statistical packages do not adequately handle the geographical nature of census data. The methods described here are regarded as the finest available today and should produce better results than those conventional methods which are still widely used.

1 Data reduction

The 1991 Census provides the user with more data than any previous census. This should today cause relatively little hardship from a census data handling point of view in the light of the major hardware and software progress since 1981; in particular, most users can now store, access and analyse 1991 Census data in a personal computing environment. However, what has not changed at anything like the same speed is the available census analysis technology. Statistical packages abound but offer few really relevant and census-data-safe techniques, particularly in the area of exploratory census data analysis. It would seem that the OPCS is content to drench their data users in numbers without providing either data reduction tools to assist them or any of the new forms of processed census outputs that could be offered to help them, e.g. OPCS census classifications of small area data and classifications at the household level (see Chapter 13). Ten years ago the only national small area census data classifications were expensive commercial systems such as ACORN, MOSAIC Super Profiles and Pins. If users wanted to classify their part of Britain then they had to do it themselves. The same situation applies today. The only real difference is the ease and speed with which census classifications can now be produced and the new opportunities to exploit the descriptive usefulness of classification and regionalization methods as both general purpose and special purpose customization techniques able to provide useful data reduction functions.

There are a number of responses to a data overload situation. First, the user becomes extremely selective and subjective, thereby effectively ignoring most of the data on the grounds that it is probably largely redundant anyway. Indeed, how on earth can so few basic census questions generate orders of magnitude as many census output variables! This selectivity approach may well be valid but it does not look good, can easily be criticized and is difficult to defend. Second, the user can rely only on theory to specify the variables that are important. This scientific ideal is seldom possible with census data because most of the theory-relevant variables are missing and the user has to try and make do with proxies and surrogates based on what is available; for example, there are no income or wealth data. Exceptions to this rule mainly concern certain types of demographic and flow modelling where the relevant information is more or less available or can be estimated reasonably well. The third situation views the census as providing a multivariate data matrix of M variables for N cases and the analyst merely wishes to uncover patterns or empirical census data regularities of some kind. The most unfocused of this form of enquiry is that of classification as a data reduction tool, offering a means of providing a simplified description of the massively complex census database.

It is useful, then, to outline in general terms a number of different practical and potentially useful approaches to census data reduction relevant to a classification and regionalization theme. Indeed it is possible to recognize several different types of census data reduction methodologies.

1. Simplify by reducing the M variables to K new ones that represent most of the 'useful' information contained by the original M ($K < M$). Factor analysis is widely employed to perform this function. Typically, a set of 50 census variables can be reduced to 10 or 20 factors or newly constructed hybrid variables that contain much of the original information. In the 1970s, a large number of census-based factorial ecological studies were performed. Now anyone can do it but it is not always very useful. In particular, the factors reflect the choice of the original variables, the method is, geographically speaking, dumb, and the factor labelling process is often subjective and difficult.
2. Reduce the number of observations by grouping together those cases which have similar profiles in terms of either the original M variables or the K new factor-based ones. This is a classification process. The N original data cases can be reduced to P clusters or groups or types, where P is usually fairly small irrespective of the size of N. For example, the ACORN classification of the 130,000 1981 Census enumeration districts (EDs) contained 38 groups of EDs; i.e. each census ED was allocated to one of 38 'different' types of residential neighbourhood. In the Super Profile system the classification

contained 150, 38, 22 and 10 groups of EDs (Charlton *et al.* 1985). Clearly there is a dramatic amount of data reduction going on here and classification provides a useful means of simplifying the multivariate and geographical complexity of the census data matrix. Methods for performing this function are the concern of this chapter and are discussed in detail later.

3. A radically different approach to classification is termed dynamic regionalization (Openshaw 1970). This is essentially an agglomerative classification procedure with a stepwise classification process being subject to a contiguity restriction. In each step, the two most similar contiguous census areas are grouped together. Their data profile is changed (by aggregation of the data) and the factor scores used in the classification are recomputed. This method is unique in that it seeks to handle the geographical effects of spatial data aggregation explicitly and also to scale the changes on the resulting patterns of factor scores as the regionalization process proceeds. This is relevant because in a census application the classification process is simultaneously also a spatial data aggregation process which progressively modifies the patterns of the spatial associations between the census variables. A dynamic regionalization approach seems to make sense from a geographical point of view. Needless to say, in 1970 computers were about a million times too slow to operationalize a regionalization procedure that would require about 130,000 repeat factor analyses if applied to national data. Today this is less of a problem. The basic concept is simple enough and appealing enough to deserve further investigation.
4. Another form of data reduction involves the regionalization of flow or interaction data. The ability to simplify the patterns of spatial linkage contained in flow data (i.e. journey-to-work and migration origin and destination flows) is extremely useful. A number of simple grouping procedures have been devised to perform this function, e.g. INTRAMAX (Masser and Brown 1975), graph theoretic methods and variants of the SMLA and TTWA algorithms (Coombes *et al.* 1982, 1986). Indeed, it is worth noting that the only explicitly designed statistical reporting areas in use in Britain are the 1981 TTWA definitions (Coombes *et al.* 1986). In many ways these journey-to-work based regionalizations are useful as a descriptive visualization of the functional organization of urban systems. The labour market concept is extremely valuable, defining functional entities that are comparable geographical objects. They also make sense as areal units by which to study urban processes, e.g. London can be compared with Newcastle. The principal difficulty concerns the imposition of a functional structure, based on physical movement, on some regions where this may not be appropriate.
5. A largely under-investigated flow regionalization variant is a combined formal and functional regionalization procedure. Classifications of small areas focus on the characteristics of these places. Flow regionalization concentrates mainly on the between-area flows, with the origin and destination area characteristics being used mainly in the form of size constraints. A combined formal–functional classification would seek to identify regions which were linked by strong within-region flows *and* were composed of either

similar subareas *or* had distinctive profiles compared with the neighbouring regions. Traditionally this objective was regarded as computationally difficult but it may no longer be so hard to achieve and, indeed, it is likely that zone design methods could be employed to identify such areas (see, for example, Openshaw 1978) now that the computing needs can be met. One complication is the prospect that not all parts of Britain may be so conveniently structured as to be susceptible to this type of pattern recognition.

6. A further form of data reduction is to represent flow data or small area data by a mathematical model needing much less information than the original data matrix. A spatial interaction model of 1991 journey-to-work flows, or a neural net equivalent (see Openshaw 1993a), might well constitute the ultimate so far in data reduction. Some users might well find this useful, but there is a major difference between purposeful data reduction and data compression. A major benefit of data reduction is the enhanced descriptive clarity that it provides. It is almost as if we are trying to map out a forest whilst buried by a mass of vegetation which might not even be trees!
7. A final possibility in terms of data reduction is that of pattern recognition. Census analysis is largely aspatial; geography enters via the scale- and aggregation-dependent nature of the areas used to report census statistics. Geography is implicit during the analysis, and only becomes explicit again when the results are mapped. As a result, towns or cities are either reduced to a single set of non-spatial multivariate measurements that provide an aggregate representation of their overall characteristics (although this is not an explicitly spatial representation) or they are analysed in terms of a set of N small areas each of which does not explicitly know where it is or that it belongs to the same town as its neighbours. A pattern recognition approach to census data reduction would involve trying to identify abstract and generalized rotational- and scale-invariant patterns of urban census structure that are recurrent throughout Britain as exemplars. It is easy to spot, when visiting towns, strongly recurrent patterns, but it has so far proved virtually impossible to find any of these striking patterns in census analysis because we have never thought about looking for them as two- or three-dimensional pattern features or, indeed, have had access to the technology that can meet this need. It is argued that developments in artificial intelligence, computer vision and massively parallel processing suggest that this may no longer be true (Openshaw 1994a).

This chapter concentrates on option 2, which might be regarded as the conventional route. The later options are left as a suggested research agenda for others to develop, perhaps in time for the 2001 Census!

2 How to classify census data: a step-by-step approach

Openshaw (1983) provides the basis of what might still be considered best practice. The following 'rule of thumb' recipe based on many years of experience of classifying census data is offered as a checklist for those who need such a device.

Step 1: What is the purpose of the classification?

This is always a difficult question to answer in sufficient detail to guide the subsequent classification process. If the purpose is that of data description, then this will determine the choice of variables in Step 2. If the purpose is more specific, for example to identify poor housing areas, then again this will determine the variables that would be required. However, in both cases there is obviously no unique and 'correct' single set of variables to use. Different people will use different variables for the same purpose, based upon their experience of local conditions and intuition. It is also important to realize that it is frankly doubtful whether satisfactory general purpose classifications can ever be devised. Whilst it is possible that a classification exercise concerned with general census data description will identify areas of poor housing, the precision and the clarity of the definitions would almost certainly be far poorer than if a specific 'poor housing' classification had been carried out. As computing costs become insignificant and the ease by which census classifications can be performed increases, so the virtue of general purpose, widely used, classifications must diminish. In a market research context, it is amazing that throughout the 1980s most large commercial concerns were seemingly content to apply the same general purpose (or no real purpose) classifications as their competitors (Openshaw 1993b).

Classification is a data descriptive and data exploratory tool. Its value to the end-user is not independent of the purpose it was designed to meet. If, as is often the case, there is no clear recollection of what the purpose was that led to the selection of variables, then the results can only be viewed as dangerous. On the other hand, like geographic information systems (GIS), census classifications often have a form of implicit validity. The results are often instantly recognizable as 'self-evident' and plausible. The enhanced ability to show politicians and members of the public a single map, suitably coloured, that summarizes the general 'state' of a county or district or town or ward at the time of the last census is itself a remarkable achievement. It amounts to no more than pure description but, for a while at least, could provide a basis for policy formulation and resource allocation in the broadest sense.

Step 2: Carefully choose variables and census areas

Obviously the choice of variables and of census areas reflects the purpose of the classification. In deciding which areas to classify, you should also bear in mind problems associated with data heterogeneity. Careful consideration is needed in the choice both of spatial scale and of the domain of the study. The 10% census sample data can be unreliable at census ED level. On the other hand 'wards' are not particularly homogeneous areas. Like EDs, they vary in size and census data homogeneity. If there is concern about ecological inference errors (see Openshaw 1984) then the smallest possible geographical areas will be 'best' provided there is some mechanism for handling varying data reliability due to different sizes of census area. Strictly speaking, even the smallest census areas are too large and are possessed of unpredictable levels of social heterogeneity. The best that can be done at present is to hope that these data artefacts are not too damaging and to bear this deficiency in mind when interpreting or using the results.

It is particularly important to remember that a classification of census areas is a classification of places and not of people. The people who live there need not share the area profiles nor need the area profiles represent dominant or majority features, or even any of the features characterizing the people who live there (Openshaw 1984). They could be minority features that are distinctive only because of their relative rareness in the data being studied; an example would be ethnic areas in northeast England. They could also be unreal artefacts created by the aggregation of individual census data. Also the 'places' being classified are often not 'places' with any natural meaning but arbitrary chunks of geographic space that are compatible only in the sense that they are small enough for one census enumerator to cover in one day. This spatial quantity varies with population density and sparsity and is not an obvious natural principle for designing geographical areas for analysis. Not much can be done about this problem, other than performing some aggregation of the census EDs to define a set of areas of approximately equal size and perhaps social homogeneity before analysis begins. Ideally these should have been attended to by the census agency itself and not left to users.

The variables used will normally be formulated as indicators of various socioeconomic conditions and be expressed as rates, ratios or percentages. It is best not to mix measurement scales and to be careful about possible closed number set problems with ratio data. If in doubt about how to define useful indicator variables, then look at those used in previous studies and select an appropriate subset. Generally, the fewer the variables the better; try to avoid large numbers of highly interrelated variables and try to obtain a representative selection that satisfy a given specific purpose. A factor analysis is no substitute for careful thought. If you define 50 variables that reflect housing conditions and five that relate to demographic aspects, then do not be surprised if the classification is dominated by housing condition variables. Factor analysis produces results that reflect the choice of input variables and will not redeem unbalanced or silly choices of variable. There is no statistical technique that is a good substitute for thinking about choice of variable, yet! Appendix 8A lists some of the variables used to create the 1981 Super Profile residential area classification as an illustration of the type of census indicators that some people have found useful. Note that the value of some of these indicators decays with time – in particular car ownership and household amenities.

The results depend on the decisions made here. It is not at all satisfactory to 'bung in any old set of data' that happens to 'pop out of' SASPAC91. You should also be prepared to revise the initial choice of variables once a preliminary classification has been interpreted. It is good practice to check the data before proceeding any further: a simple scan for 'bad' or 'extreme' or 'suspicious' data values is required. It may lead to the exclusion of areas with small populations. Cases with missing values (arising perhaps from data suppression) should certainly be deleted or assigned after the analysis is completed.

Some thought may sometimes be given to the possibilities of applying a data transformation. After all, this sounds like the 'correct' statistical thing to do. Well, think carefully about it and then, perhaps, do not do it! It can be argued that there is little to be gained by data transformations, bearing in mind the exploratory nature of classification and the difficulties it may cause during interpretation; for example, this cluster has high values of the arcsin square root of council housing. Nevertheless, variables which have very peculiar statistical distributions or are very kurtose should be examined. Some peculiarities will indicate poor data, perhaps from mis-specification of variables derived from arithmetic performed on the data or from adjustment effects. They may also indicate outliers in the data which require removal. However, transformations are no substitute for checking the data and thinking about it. If the concern is purely statistical, then remember that transformations not only may change the shape of the frequency distribution but may alter the relationships between the variables. What grounds have you for thinking that log inverse percentage car ownership and arctangent percentage aged is a sensible relationship purely because there happens to be the best transformation for each variable separately?

Step 3: Normalizing and orthogonalizing the data

Since many of the variables will be inter-correlated, it is usually considered good practice to transform the original data from scores on an initial set of variables to scores on a new set of 'derived' variables which have the property that each new 'variable' is uncorrelated with any other and represents as much as possible of the common variance found in the original data. That is, the raw data are orthogonalized and replaced by principal component scores. The M original variables can be replaced by M new variables or principal components without any loss of 'information'. However, normally, you would want rather fewer components than there were original variables. The traditional rule of thumb is that you would seek to retain at least 90% of the total variance found in the original variables. In practice, the number of principal components required might be between one-half and three-quarters the number of original variables.

The principal component stage is used as a data transformation and no attempt is made to interpret the components. It is also desirable that the component scores are weighted by the size of the associated eigenvalues; for this reason it would be unwise to use factor scores where the variance of each set of factor scores is the same, since this will distort the multidimensional space in which the classification is performed. This orthonormalizing data transformation is purely to allow the use of a cluster similarity measure that is a simple distance-based one. It makes some sense, in that otherwise the classification may be unduly influenced by the selection of many different variants of the same variable.

However, it can be argued that this is precisely what is needed, and far from being a problem it is in fact a useful feature.

A contrary view, therefore, is that maybe the data should be normalized but not orthogonalized. Principal component analysis, in common with factor analysis, uses an M by M correlation matrix. Correlation coefficients measure linear relationships and are sensitive to non-normality. Census data, especially for small areas, are often highly skewed, there can be closed number set problems with ratio data, and there is no reason to assume that all the important relationships are linear. As a result, orthonormalization might well be viewed as doing unacceptable damage to the data purely to satisfy an orthogonality assumption that need not be relevant. By forcing noisy, non-normal census data through an orthonormalizing filter, useful information might well be lost. Perhaps the answer is merely to ensure that each variable is represented in the same metric. Z scores are often used but, in a geographical context, positive spatial autocorrelation in the census data combined with weird frequency distributions may also cause unacceptable data damage. Perhaps the answer is to use percentages as the metric for the classification and keep every variable in the same units of measurement. Alternatively, maybe it does not matter. It all depends on purpose!

Step 4: Classify the data using cluster analysis

Cluster analysis technology is now widely diffused and various methods are available via statistical packages. It should be noted that different methods do produce different results and that the differences can be large. Also, as Openshaw and Gillard (1978) demonstrated, the results can be affected by slight changes to the application of a particular method. Various subjective decisions made for operational purposes can have an effect. Choice of clustering method is just another in a long series of highly arbitrary operational decisions.

The choice of the 'best' method is hard. First, the standard texts provide little or no help here. Second, there may be no single best method. Third, there is no universally accepted definition of how to measure 'best' – it depends on purpose. The ultimate criterion of acceptability and plausibility of the results is a very weak evaluation measure. Moreover, a classification can only really be evaluated against the specific purpose for which it is required. There is no magic universal statistical test that can decide this for the user, nor is it likely that classifications exist that are suitable for all purposes. The fact that the results appear to be plausible is not itself sufficient to validate a classification. It helps but is not sufficient.

The choice of the 'best' number of clusters is another extremely important but largely subjective decision. Various magic numbers are always attractive; i.e. 10 or 42. Again this is a highly subjective decision but it is one that matters. The pragmatic answer is to generate and evaluate a range of classifications, perhaps in fine increments – units of two or five. If it now costs very little, then why not?

It has to be accepted, therefore, that classification is a subjective process. Its apparent numerical objectivity is limited in that, if exactly the same method is applied to exactly the same data in exactly the same manner, then the numerical results should be exactly the same. Whether the interpreted results are also the same on replication is in much greater doubt. Classification is an objective numerical task embedded in a highly subjective analysis process.

The onus rests with the user to demonstrate that a classification is reasonable and to identify any weaknesses. It should not and cannot be assumed that the results are automatically of a high quality simply because of the method being employed. Furthermore, purely because a method has certain optimal properties when viewed from a particular perspective does not mean that it is any good at classifying census data. A good example here is the single linkage method. Despite having some optimal mathematical properties, it usually yields fairly poor quality classifications due to chaining.

Step 5: Cluster labelling, interpretation and evaluation

Once a classification has been obtained, it is necessary to try to name the clusters or groups of areas for purposes of communication and description. This is inevitably a highly subjective process that may or may not be coloured by preconceived ideas about which types of area should be present. Once the groups have been 'named', it is necessary to decide whether they make sense – perhaps too few or too many clusters have been specified. Perhaps some suspicious data values have resulted in strange results; outliers will often form highly distinctive clusters.

The task of naming or labelling the groups involves finding key variables that can be used to create either thumbnail images of what the areas are like or a potted description of their distinguishing characteristics. This task can be greatly helped by the provision of diagnostic aids. Statistics such as the mean and standard deviation of each variable for each cluster give some guide. For example, in trying to name a cluster you would look for variables with local cluster means which are substantially higher or lower than the global means and, perhaps also, with smaller standard deviations. Another way is to identify as key diagnostic variables those with cluster means that differ by one, two and three global standard deviations from the global means. All these diagnostics should be calculated from the raw data. The use of these statistics is rarely problem-free; the effects of both small cluster sizes and non-normal distributions can complicate the use of means and standard deviations. An alternative approach is to follow Tukey (1977) and utilize more robust measures. Tukey defines a set of median-based measures – 'far out', 'outer fence', 'inner fence' – which can be used as classification diagnostics. Thus, a key diagnostic variable may be one which has a high proportion of the members of a cluster in either the far out, outer fence or inner fence categories. A distinction also needs to be made as to whether these categories are above or below the global medians of the variables concerned. In practice, it does not appear to make much difference.

Another useful measure is to calculate for each variable the 'within-group' sum of squares as a guide to the 'statistical efficiency' of the classification. It is noted that the total sum of squares for a variable can be partitioned into 'between-cluster' and 'within-cluster' components. In practical terms, if every area being classified is placed in a separate cluster, then the within-group sum of squares would be zero since each cluster is completely homogeneous. Alternatively, if all the areas are assigned to the same cluster then the 'between-group' sum of squares would be zero. A real classification will lie between these two extremes. The percentage 'within-cluster' sum of squares for each variable or aggregated over all the variables measures the amount of information (i.e. variation) 'lost' by a classification of *N* areas into *M* groups.

This within-cluster sum of squares measure provides a guide to whether more or fewer clusters are required. However, it is only a crude guide since there is no way of knowing at what point the loss of information becomes critical to a given purpose. Furthermore, no one really knows what changes in the within-cluster sum of squares mean in terms of the classification in a substantive sense. Moreover, the results vary from one variable to another and they depend on the nature of the areas being classified. For example, ED level classifications have been created with total within-cluster sums of squares that varied from 20% to 36%; and in all cases the classifications were considered useful. Of course, the sum of squares lost by a classification is area- and variable-specific. However, it is useful in helping to determine a suitable number of clusters; but the final decision nearly always depends on the user.

Openshaw (1983) suggests that other numerical measures can also be used to help summarize the properties of different classifications. For instance, the proportion of cases with their nearest neighbours in different groups will provide some indication of 'edge' effects. Other statistics can be computed to summarize the distribution of distances to cluster centroids. Such measures can be calculated separately for each cluster or for all the clusters together.

From an applied perspective, perhaps an even more useful approach is to identify poorly classified cases. The simplest way of doing this is to list those cases which are further away from their cluster centroid than is 'normal' either for the members of the cluster concerned or based on an analysis of all the clusters in the classification. The critical distances again can only be determined by a 'rule of thumb', e.g. if the distance to the cluster centroid exceeds the average distances plus three standard deviations. Median-based measures can also be used to identify 'outer fence' and 'far out' cases. It can be assumed that such cases are poorly classified and that the user needs to know this when interpreting a classification, there may even be grounds for removing them from the data. If more clusters are used, of course, then the proportion of poorly classified cases may well decrease.

Another useful device is to rank the members of each cluster in terms of their distance from the cluster centroid. An examination of the label assigned to the cluster and the data values for cases which are the 'closest' and 'furthest' away may well help with both the interpretation and evaluation processes by allowing the user to label clusters without being hindered by poorly classified cases.

Finally, numerical diagnostics are only an aid to naming and evaluating the clusters. The principal aim of the evaluation stage is to develop by empirical means an understanding of the strengths and weaknesses of a classification. This process is neither easy nor quick, but it is nevertheless essential if an overly naive approach to census data classification is to be avoided. It is noteworthy that this process is very often missing from many classification exercises; indeed it seems that taxonomists have not bothered to spend much time discovering how best to use the results of the classification methods they have invented! As a result, the users of the standard classification package programs are simply left to their own devices once their classifications are produced.

A final health warning. The result of classifying census areas is a classification of areas. It is all very well labelling the clusters as if people of a particular type were likely to be found there, i.e. aged or metro singles; however, this could cause Data Protection Act 1984 problems. Remember that because of ecological inference errors a classification of areas need not provide a good or accurate description of the people actually living there. Accordingly, when labelling clusters, care is needed to avoid attributing to the areal clusters the characteristics of individuals or vice versa.

Step 6: Map the results

The availability of digital representations of census areas and of GIS software makes the graphical presentation of results extremely easy. There is no longer any excuse for not mapping the results. There is no real need, however, to install classification procedures in GIS; instead the classification array only need be input. The within-area type boundaries can be readily dissolved and the resulting classification displayed. Mapping the results in full technicolour greatly extends the power of the classification process as a visual data reduction technique. More needs to be made of these aspects, if only as another means of validating the results. In this respect, it is slightly worrying that so few of the 1981 Census small area classifications could be mapped during their evaluation phase. Today, there is no longer any good excuse.

Step 7: Regionalize

The classification has so far ignored geographical space completely. However, the cluster can be given a contiguous area representation, either via a GIS or by applying a fairly simple region builder to the classification array. An algorithm is given in Appendix 8B.

At one time, long ago, the classification process would have been subjected to an explicit contiguity constraint. That is, either a contiguity restriction was applied to a stepwise or agglomerative classification process or an iterative relocation procedure would be used to swap boundary areas from one cluster to another. The resulting classification would consist of a set of clusters, each of which was composed of contiguous census areas. Openshaw (1973) provided a very efficient algorithm for regionalizing large datasets in this way. The contiguous clusters were termed regional types. A higher order or reclassification of the regional types yielded regional classes. The problem with an explicitly contiguity-constrained regionalization process is that it is very inefficient from a taxonometric point of view. It is true that nearby places are similar but there may well be clumps of similar places which are separated by other places which are highly dissimilar. Openshaw (1973) showed that it is far better to classify without a contiguity restriction and then subsequently contiguise each of the area types into regional types. However, it is worth bearing in mind some of the problems with contiguity lists; i.e. point contiguities and river discontinuities can distort continuous space in unexpected ways.

3 Some difficulties in classifying census data

3.1 Are conventional cluster analysis methods still good enough?

The classification process outlined in Section 2 might well be regarded as a conventional state-of-the-art approach that could be operationalized via a standard statistical package. However, it should also be recognized that a general purpose taxonometric process assumes that there is nothing special about census data and, in particular, that census data can be regarded for analysis purposes as being similar to sample survey data of the general type produced by a household survey. This simplifying assumption might well be good enough for many applications but not for all. If the results of a classification exercise matter because they have financial implications or are to be used as inputs to important decisions, or for commercial purposes, or for serious academic research in which rigour is important, then this conventional classification strategy via a statistical package may no longer be good enough.

It should be appreciated that the classification algorithms often date back to the 1960s and early 1970s when computers were much slower and computing time was very expensive. Shortcuts and algorithms designed to minimize computer costs were necessary. However, these factors are no longer important. If it is possible now, in the 1990s, to obtain better classifications of census data by exploiting much faster computers, or indeed by throwing virtually unlimited amounts of almost zero real-cost computing power at the problem, then we should at least be considering this computer-intensive strategy for those classification exercises that really matter. Classifying the 1991 Census data should not necessarily be regarded as a repeat of the same 1960s classification procedures as were used with the 1981 data. It should now be possible in the 1990s to obtain significantly better results.

3.2 Some major problems with census data

Another important consideration concerns the need to handle rather than ignore some of the problems that exist in census data analysis. These problems are now much better understood than previously. Of course, some of the special problems of classifying spatial census data have been known for a long time; for instance, the likely presence of quite high degrees of positive spatial autocorrelation, the presence of spatial heterogeneities (i.e. non-stationarity or relationships between variables that vary from one part of a study region to another), and the non-sample nature (in a classical simple random sampling sense) of zonal census data. Typically, these problems are ignored. Yet the first biases simple Z score transformations because positive spatial autocorrelation reduces variances. The second is extremely serious since the usual orthonormalization is based on linear correlation coefficients which focus on global or whole map relationships, and this may well filter out as noise relationships which are geographically localized. Moreover it can be argued that the relationships and patterns that are most interesting in census classification are, indeed, geographically localized; e.g. inner city problems or unique Scottish area types rather than British ones. The use of orthonormalization methods (or indeed any statistical method) that emphasize whole-map relationships and which de-emphasize (or even remove) those which are not is problematic and potentially dangerous. The results will be strongly study region dependent and could well miss major patterns that are recurrent but on a more localized scale than others.

Of course it can be argued that a focus on patterns that are highly recurrent is, indeed, a most desirable characteristic. However, this function cannot be reliably entrusted to a multivariate, linear and normal distribution dependent classification process that may or may not succeed, and which contains no obvious mechanism for detecting failure. At least with a regression model, localized heterogeneities may be identified subsequently.

In addition there are a number of specific technical problems with census data that may affect the classification process. These include:

1. non-normality;
2. non-linear relationships;
3. the data being known to contain measurement errors due to non-response imputation;
4. noise being added deliberately to preserve confidentiality;
5. a mix of almost 100% and about 10% sample coded data;
6. the size and homogeneity of the census geographical entities vary even within a class of areas of the same scale or type;
7. under-enumeration (probably spatially biased).

The classification of census data violates the assumptions of classical statistical methods in that the data are analysed while they are known to be wrong in various ways making the strict adherence of those methods difficult to sustain. Conventional classifiers assume that the data are 'correct' apart from the implicit presence of sampling variability. However, the combination of non-random errors due to data imputation (there is no reason to assume that the OPCS can accurately estimate missing responses that contain no bias), the –1, 0, +1 randomization which has a non-random effect on multi-cell count indices, and doubts about both sample size and the randomness of the 10% sample coded variables suggests that from a statistical point of view the census is by no means error free nor subject to only random errors.

Worse follows. The size and internal homogeneity of census reporting areas varies tremendously. For instance, the size of census EDs varies from a few households to a few hundred households. As a result the precision and meaningfulness of the census data values also vary. A small census ED can easily score 100% unemployment, but a large urban ED will probably never exceed 30%. This size-related variation in data precision affects both 100% and 10% data but particularly the latter. An ED with 200 households will have, on average, 10% data based on only 20. The internal homogeneity of social conditions within an ED also varies. It is not purely a function of size but also depends on the interaction between ED boundaries and the underlying patterns of socioeconomic and demographic characteristics. Sadly, this has never been explicitly controlled in census geography. Census areas vary greatly in terms of their ability to represent these patterns, and as a result the representativeness of the multivariate profiles for the small area census data vary. A further major complication is that the size, data precision and spatial representation problems are spatially structured. They can vary with population density and their magnitude depends on location within the urban mosaic. Some areas are very poorly represented, e.g. areas of transition characterized by a mix of households. Small changes in ED boundary location here can make major differences to data values. Elsewhere, the small area data are far more accurate.

The presence of major rural–urban differences in data precision and geographical representation cannot really be ignored but needs to be handled by the development of classification (and also other census analysis methods) that can take it into account. Otherwise, census analysis will amount to trying to compare 'chalk with cheese'.

3.3 Problems of application

In addition to the census-data-related problems, others reflect various aspects of the classification process. In particular, there is no clear *a priori* idea of what results to expect. This is serious because it reduces the ability of the user to make useful performance evaluations. Additionally, there is no good theoretical basis for distinguishing between different results produced by different methods, or different sets of results produced by the same method. With census classifications, it is not even easy to compare the results. The user also has little or no prior theoretical basis on which to choose, or interpret, or judge the results. This is not that uncommon in an exploratory data analysis situation. It forces reliance on a mix of skills, experience and luck and insists that above all else census classification is a subjective art rather than a science. This suggests that audit trails of operational decision making relating to the application of census classification technology are important, particularly in applications where the outcome may well be questioned later.

3.4 Problems of classification

Another class of problems relates to the nature of the classification methods themselves. It has already been remarked that in general many of these methods date from the 1960s. Some of the consequences are quite important. If new classifiers were just being invented, then there are a number of desirable features they should possess. The wish-list includes the following.

1. They should not impose a particular fixed cluster structure or pattern morphology on the data but be responsive to what is found to exist.
2. It is important that fuzziness can survive; some areas may be in between different cluster types and this should be identifiable.
3. They should be able to handle noisy data or at least cope with the known features of census data.
4. They should require a minimum amount of data preprocessing; it is quite unreasonable to expect data 'to speak for themselves' in an exploratory sense if they are massively damaged or otherwise handicapped by data transformations applied purely to meet the theoretical requirements of a particular method.
5. They should have sufficient flexibility, in that the method should be powerful enough to uncover whatever 'natural' structure exists in the data without having to know in advance what to expect.
6. They should have an innate capability to determine how many clusters or groups are most appropriate; and an ability to identify globally optimal results by having some means of avoiding localized suboptima.

There is no suggestion that the conventional methods do not work. They do, but the question is whether they work as well as they should. Are they still the best possible available technology? All too often it seems that it is the users who are having to compensate for the failure and weaknesses of the technology by applying their intelligence to make the best of a mess. Maybe success is more apparent than real. The first step towards improving the situation is to identify the problems that matter, determine what properties are ideal, and then discuss these factors as a means of improving awareness of the problems whilst simultaneously seeking to develop a better census classification technology.

4 Improved methods of classifying census data

4.1 A recommended standard algorithm

It would seem that the best widely available standard clustering method is the *K* means approach. This is what is used in the author's CCP software (see Appendix 8C) and appears in most of the statistical packages. The basic algorithm is as follows:

Step 1

Generate an initial classification by randomly assigning the N original areas to one of M groups, the value for M being a guess at how many groups are needed (if in doubt, try 42).

Step 2

Apply an iterative relocation process.

(i) For any census area i, try moving it from the cluster p it is currently in to another cluster q.
(ii) Calculate the error sum of squares (within-cluster sum of squares) for cluster q with area i assigned to it.
(iii) Consider all possible clusters to which area i could be assigned.
(iv) Move area i into whichever cluster produces the smallest overall error sum of squares.
(v) Process all n cases in a similar fashion.
(vi) If one or more moves occur then return to (i) and start again.

At this point a preliminary classification has been obtained.

Step 3

Examine the classification and compute statistical diagnostics and the within-cluster sum of squares. If more clusters might be needed then return to Step 1 and increase M; if there are too many clusters, then return to Step 1 and reduce M. If uncertain, then try a range of classifications and evaluate them all in parallel.

Step 4

Map and otherwise evaluate the results. A plot of total within-cluster sum of squares might be helpful but do not expect there to be major jumps or discontinuities. Census data classifications are rarely that obliging.

This strategy is by no means a 'one-shot' process. The classification part in Step 2 is fully automatic, but the other steps all involve a degree of thought and human action. Indeed the 'to-and-fro' nature of the classification process is a deliberate attempt to combine a computer approach with human intelligence. It is also necessary because the number of clusters specified in Step 1 cannot be determined with any precision prior to the analysis.

Step 5

Identify poorly classified cases. Decide whether they should be removed and the analysis repeated, or whether the cluster labelling process should be repeated without them.

Step 6

Assess the sensitivity of the classification to various operational decisions, e.g. the number of component scores (try increasing the number used) and the use of different random starting classifications. There is always a possibility, of course, that either no reasonably stable classification exists with the desired number of clusters or that the results are nonsensical or otherwise unsatisfactory. It may be that experience will suggest a different set of variables, or that more clusters are required, or that the original data are suspect – in which case, start again from the beginning, though this is hardly practicable in the case of census data. Remember that classification is inevitably an exploratory process: you will never make best use of the technique unless you are willing to use it in an appropriately exploratory fashion. As Openshaw (1983) puts it: 'In essence, you are groping your way almost blind through an unimaginable complex hyper-dimensional space towards (you hope) a set of usable results' (p. 257).

The question now is how to improve the Step 2 part of the algorithm, bearing in mind that there are possibly major and more easily gained improvements that can be made to most other parts of the process. The main problem with Step 2 is the single-move nature of the heuristic. The process might get stuck at some suboptimal classification. One solution is try several different random starting classifications and simply pick the best. Another involves changing the heuristic.

4.2 A simulated annealing variant

A simple modification can be made to the Step 2 heuristic. In the standard clustering algorithms it is in effect 'all or nothing'. A case is only moved from its parent cluster to another cluster if there is an improvement in the total within-cluster sum of squares. This is clearly computationally efficient but it can result in the classification getting stuck. Equivalent difficulties characterize other types of combinatorial optimization problem. Simulated annealing is viewed as a means of softening, by an annealing process, the heuristic. This is regarded as useful because it avoids local suboptima by allowing the heuristic more time to settle on possibly better solutions. Annealing is the physical process of heating up a solid until it melts and then cooling it slowly until it crystallizes into a state with a perfect lattice. The cooling has to be done carefully to avoid imperfections. Metropolis *et al.* (1953), Kirkpatrick *et al.* (1983) and Cerny (1985) show how the physical annealing process can be modelled successfully by using computer simulation. The same basic algorithm can be applied to census classification.

The basic procedure is as follows.

Step 1

Set an initial temperature t which may be defined as the average change in the within-cluster sum of squares due to a random move in a random starting classification. This can be determined by experimentation.

Step 2

Select an area and try moving it from parent cluster p into each of the available clusters, noting the effect on the classification in F.

Step 3

If any cluster j exists which is an improvement (i.e. $F_j < F_p$) then make the move.

Step 4

Else find the best cluster k ($F_k > F_p$) but make the move if

$$\exp\left(\frac{F_p - F_k}{t}\right) > \text{random}(0, 1)$$

where random(0,1) is a uniform random variate with values between 0.0 and 1.0.

Step 5

Repeat Steps 2 to 4 a reasonable number of times to ensure that the classification has 'melted'; this might be defined as involving $10 * N$ moves with a fixed maximum number of complete scans through the data (e.g. 200).

Step 6

Lower the temperature a little ($t = t * 0.9$) and repeat Steps 2 to 5; if no moves were made then stop the process.

As the temperature is reduced, so the number of uphill moves decreases until eventually the algorithm reduces to the original non-simulated annealing version. Determining an optimal annealing schedule is problematical but seemingly not too critical. Aarts and Korst (1989) provide some advice about this. Another problem is the increase in computing time by a factor of 30 to 50. An application involving 8500 cases and 74 variables took six hours of run-time on a Sun SuperSparc Workstation; so it is not that time intensive. A few weeks should be enough to handle even the biggest problems.

4.3 Neural net classifiers

A seemingly different approach to census classification is to employ what is known as an unsupervised neural net. Cluster analysis, pattern recognition and neurocomputing have some features in common. It is also clear that neural nets offer a very useful basis for pattern recognition in a variety of areas. The question here is whether or not the same technology is able to recognize patterns in multidimensional data originating from a census source rather than a raster representation of an image or a spectral frequency of sounds etc. Most of the published empirical work tends to relate to either small datasets or artificial data; maybe this reflects the commercial relevance of the technologies and the reluctance of the researchers to give away their secrets by publishing them. Whatever the reason, it is quite clear that neural nets would seem to provide a means of applying a new and more flexible approach to census data classification which may be far less dependent on uncertain and unrealistic assumptions than is commonplace with other methods. It would also seem to offer census data a greater opportunity to speak for itself and thus provide a more flexible route to identifying the nature of the patterns that may exist within it. Indeed, some neural nets have already been used for cluster formation; for example, Pao (1989) presents an adaptation of the adaptive resonance theory (ART) of Carpenter and Grossberg (1987) to detect clusters in data. Unfortunately, once the jargon is dispensed with, there is little to distinguish this particular net from a K means approach.

It is worth emphasizing that in the classification applications of interest here it is not possible to utilize a supervised net of the multilayer feedforward form and train it by back propagation, because there are no known results which the net can be trained to reproduce. In census analysis the form and nature of any patterns or structure can only be guessed at, and it is not inconceivable that even the best available prior knowledge may be wrong. Unsupervised neural nets are often advocated as being useful for pattern classification purposes where the target classification is not known, although it is still necessary to make the assumption that the data do contain some natural structure. The purpose is to uncover whatever structure or patterning may be present by some kind of competitive learning process during which a network of neurons fight to represent parts of the training data. The net may well eventually reach a stable state by a process of self-organization which will classify the input data in terms of that output neuron that best represents it. A key design criterion here is the ability to handle at least a few hundred thousand cases and up to 100 input variables, in order that there should be nothing in the proposed technology that will subsequently hinder its application to the largest available census datasets.

The strong theoretical attractions of a neural net approach include the following:

1. its flexibility in representing census data structure;
2. its bottom-up approach with no notion of a global objective function;
3. it is based on a locally adaptive process of self-organization that offers great scope for the data to speak for themselves as to which patterns are most important;
4. it can be modified to handle census data that contain sampling error and varying levels of data precision that conventional classifiers cannot handle; and
5. it provides a useful means of exploiting the rapid speed-up of computers to obtain better classifications of census data.

The novelty and importance of neural net classification is sufficient to insist that the next section focuses on providing further details of what the authors would strongly commend as the class of census classification methods that are today most likely to provide the best practicable results with 1991 Census data.

5 Three unsupervised net architectures

5.1 Choice of architecture?

An immediate concern is the choice of an appropriate architecture for an unsupervised neural net. The general structure is fixed by the nature of the problem and clearly some kind of competitive learning approach will have to be used. The question is which one? The various books on the subject provide no real assistance. Competitive learning is a means whereby a neural net is used to discover structural features in the data; it is essentially a regularity detector. The basic general structure is well described by Rumelhart and Zipster (1986). The problem is deciding upon which of the large and growing number of variations on this theme are worth investigating. Neural nets are a very empirical area where seemingly the only way to proceed is via a trial and error process. Three different architectures are investigated here: two variations of a simple competitive learning net and a variant of a self-organizing map.

5.2 A single-layer competitive net

Possibly the simplest competitive net is that which consists of a layer of fan-out units fully connected to a single layer of processing units (neurons). Each of the N processing units has weights attached to its input lines and combines these with an input vector to produce an output. Thus the output, O_j for neuron j is

$$O_j = \sum_k (w_{jk} - x_{kl})^2$$

where w_{jk} is the weight for input (i.e. variable) k for neuron j and x_{kl} is the kth variable for training case l.

A competition based on these outputs then takes place among the neurons. The winner is the neuron 'nearest' to the input vector for data case l. The winner alone is allowed to adjust its weights so as to strengthen its output when presented with that particular input vector. The following training or weights adjustment procedure is normally used:

$$w_{jk}(\text{new}) = w_{jk}(\text{old}) + \text{alpha}*(x_{kl} - w_{jk}(\text{old}))$$

where $0 < \text{alpha} < 1$ is the training weight.

As different input vectors are presented at random from the training set, each neuron gradually comes to represent a group of input vectors on which it wins against all other neurons, thereby effectively classifying the training set into clusters. In general, the output of a neuron is some form of distance measurement between its weights and the input vector, e.g. the Euclidean distance or Manhattan street block distance. For a given input vector, the competition between neurons simply determines the one closest to the input vector. The adjustment of the winning neuron's weight vector consists of moving it a proportion of the way along the line connecting it to the input vector, thus reducing its distance from the input vector. This method of competition and weight adjustment is usually referred to as Kohonen learning, after Kohonen who brought together much of the earlier work in the area of self-organizing nets (Kohonen 1988). The intention is that, after training, the distribution of weight vectors should represent the distribution of training vectors (i.e. the data to be classified). It is really extremely simple and has been demonstrated to be a very good regularity detector in a variety of application areas.

The simplest method of training this Kohonen layer net is to initialize the weights to small randomly chosen values and repeatedly present the training set vectors (in random sequence), adjusting winning weight vectors by progressively smaller amounts over the training period. This will only work satisfactorily if the initial weight vectors approximate the distribution of the training set vectors, for otherwise there is a tendency in the first iteration for a single weight vector to move to a position where it will subsequently win on a very large number of input vectors, thereby preventing other weight vectors from being trained. The failure of this simple strategy is especially marked when the training set vectors are highly clustered!

Various modifications of the basic training strategy have been developed to try to overcome this problem. Two such were incorporated into the network used to classify census data. The first modification, called the 'radial sprouting' or 'convex combinatorial' method, starts with all input and weight vectors equal (to zero in the case of radial sprouting). As training progresses, the input vectors are gradually relaxed back to their true positions – pulling weight vectors with them. By itself, this method works quite well but it can leave a few weight vectors 'stranded' in no-man's land. The second method, due to Desieno (1988), gives each neuron a 'conscience' bias which it raises if it wins too often and lowers if it wins too little. During the competition the bias is added to the distance between weight vector and input vector. This biasing allows some neurons, which would otherwise become stranded, to win.

A third method is more applicable to census data. A major problem is the use of rates that have variable precision. Areas with small populations can more readily take on extreme rates than large areas. This is a particular characteristic of census data. The neural net solution is to sample the training data in proportion to population size, so that large areas are more important in training the net than small areas with probably misleading extreme values. A variation on this theme would also allow for the mix of 100% and 10% coded census data, with the 10% variables being randomly perturbed to reflect sampling error. Training takes place using these artificially created data. The ability to handle these problems gives neural net classifiers a major advantage over more traditional procedures (Openshaw 1994b).

5.3 A multilayer competitive net

The single-layer Kohonen net can be generalized to a multilayer and multigroup within each layer net. Rumelhart and Zipster (1986) describe such a net for feature detection and pattern recognition of binary data and clearly it can be generalized as a possible tool for census analysis. The neurons in each layer of the network are partitioned into groups of non-overlapping sets. Each neuron in a layer receives identical inputs from all the units in the previous layer. The units in each non-overlapping set 'compete' with each other. The competitions take place within each group with the winner producing an output of one while the losers produce an output of zero. The concatenated output from all groups in the same layer is passed on as input to the next layer. The training process is conducted layer by layer for a given input training vector, in much the same way as for the single-layer version. When real-valued training vectors are applied to this type of network, each group of neurons in the first layer behaves like a Kohonen net. Subsequent layers receive binary inputs and act as higher-order classifiers. Each group forms a 1 in M coding of the input stimuli. This should allow successive levels of abstraction to be identified by the pattern classifier.

As with the single-layer Kohonen net, a conscience mechanism is employed to reduce the number of weight vectors which become stranded. The final layer of this net has a single cluster of neurons and it is the response of this layer that is used to classify the training set. In general, each neuron in this final layer will come to respond to at least one input vector, but occasionally one or more neurons fails to respond to any input vector and the resulting classification has fewer clusters than would be expected. This may be due to the inherent structure of the training data. If so, then this would be an extremely useful property in a classification context, since it would limit the number of clusters that the data can support to a value less than the analyst might expect to find. This can only be a major benefit.

5.4 A self-organizing map

This is a different approach, being based on the self-organizing map developed by Kohonen (1982, 1988). This is an unsupervised net that seeks to learn a continuous topological mapping of a set of inputs onto a set of outputs in such a way that the outputs acquire the same topological order as the inputs, by means of self-organization based on data examples. Kohonen (1982) writes: 'There are no restrictions on the automatic formation of maps of completely abstract or conceptual items provided their signal representations or feature values are expressible in a metric or topological space that allows their ordering' (p. 59). At first sight this type of function mapping net may not seem very well suited to handling classification problems, except that its architecture is not dissimilar from a simpler competitive learning net albeit based on a different kind of lateral inhibition effect. However, it is possible that the maintenance of the topological structure present in the multivariate space that characterizes the training data in the output classification is an advantage that may well assist in uncovering useful data patterns. In essence it means that the Kohonen map will classify input data by the neurons they activate in the output layer but with the restriction that similar cases will activate either the same or nearby neurons in the self-organizing map. The question is whether this offers any real benefits to census classifications.

The Kohonen self-organizing map is used here as both a one- and two-dimensional layered network. It could be extended to higher-dimensional spaces; however, it is thought that there might be some benefit in remaining in one or two dimensions, so that the neurons that represent a particular data case can be visualized. Also the additional dimensions may not be needed because many patterns appear to have limited real dimensional freedom due to a high degree of inter-correlation between the elements of the pattern. A self-organizing map consists of a MAXe by MAXn matrix of processing elements (or neurons). The MAXe or MAXn variables can take a number of values depending on how many clusters are thought likely to exist. The first layer is the input to the network and is fully connected to each processing unit. The processing units are of the familiar form

$$z_{ij} = \sum_{k} abs(w_{ijk} - x_{kl})$$

where z_{ij} is the value of the processing unit in the ith row and jth column, w_{ijk} is the weight for the kth input variable associated with the processing unit in the ith row and jth column, and x_{kl} is the value for the lth input case on the kth variable. The results are thought to be relatively insensitive to the choice of norm.

The processing unit with the smallest z_{ij} value wins the competition. Its weights are updated and so are those surrounding processing units that are within a certain critical distance $d(t)$ of this unit. This is a critical part of the self-organization process. The usual Kohonen updating is used so that

$$w_{ijk}(\text{new}) = w_{ijk}(\text{old}) + \text{alpha}(t) * (w_{ijk} - x_{kl})$$

In the simple training algorithm used here the weight alpha reduces with the number of iterations t as does the critical distance d. They reduce from typical starting values of alpha = 0.5 and d = max(MAXe, MAXn)/2 towards 0.0 in a linear fashion as training proceeds. The process can of course either be forced to converge on a single neuron for each case (if d goes towards zero) or be stopped at the first-order neighbours. In the latter case the trained net retains some fuzziness. Different parts of the map will be attuned to different case profiles. Since there is a one- or two-dimensional spatial structure implicit in the array of neurons, so those neurons excited by the same data case will provide potential alternative classifications for it. If a single allocation is required then a localized tuning process is necessary (Kohonen 1990).

The process of self-organization going on here is very similar to simulated annealing. As the training proceeds so the opportunity for change and restructuring gradually diminishes until the pattern is fixed. Typically a large number of training iterations will be needed, perhaps several million. Fortunately, the processing is extremely simple and it is capable of parallel implementation and vectorization so it is still possible to contemplate the analysis of very large data sets. The problem with this approach is the large amount of computing time needed, especially when the training samples are adjusted to reflect data reliability and sampling uncertainty.

5.5 An example

The data used here are a census dataset for England and Wales consisting of a set of 44 variables (see Appendix 8A) for census wards. This builds on earlier work by Openshaw and Wymer (1991).

A benchmark set of results is obtained by classifying the same data using the CCP program (Openshaw 1982). This might be regarded as one of the best conventional classification procedures. It starts with an orthonormalization of the data by the size of the associated eigenvalues. The classifier is a single-move iterative relocation K means procedure that starts with a random classification of the data and attempts to find a local minimum of the within-cluster sum of squares. Experience suggests that it works very well and tends to produce results that are in accordance with local knowledge of the area. It provides a good benchmark against which to test the neural nets. However, in comparing the

Table 8.1 Cluster sizes for 10 group classifications

Ranked size	*K*: 3*3	*K*: 10*1	CNET (a)	CNET (b)	*K*	CCP
1	2150	2113	2342	2860	2147	1884
2	1935	1887	2255	1535	1956	1437
3	1581	1428	1220	1125	1230	1409
4	1384	1313	1182	897	1228	1183
5	907	943	898	844	1032	1032
6	702	885	733	843	889	850
7	275	265	454	408	253	761
8	254	247	137	377	240	335
9	90	113	56	344	226	304
10	na	84	na	44	76	83

Note: Details of CNET architectures (a) 2: 1= <20>, 1= <10>; (b) 2: 1= <2,4,6,8>, 1= <10>.

results it is important to remember that the benchmark results may not be the best outcome.

It was decided to evaluate the performance of the various methods using a high level of data abstraction. To be of any practical benefit, the wards need to be classified into less than 40 or 50 groups. This is a severe test for any classifier because the data may require considerably more clusters to provide an adequate representation but most users would have difficulties in dealing with more than a few basic area types.

Table 8.1 gives the sizes of each of the groups for a selection of methods. In this and subsequent tables, *K*: $n*m$ refers to a self-organizing map with n rows and m columns described in Section 5.4; CNET is the multilayer and multicluster net described in Section 5.3, with the notation l: n_l = <*a,b,..*>, etc. where l is the number of layers (other than input layer); n_l specifies the number of clusters in the first layer, the first of which has <*a*> units and the second <*b*> units and so on; *K* is the Section 5.2 single-layer net; and CCP is the standard benchmark method. The results would suggest that all the methods provide a range of cluster sizes and most are not too dissimilar from the benchmark. Table 8.2 repeats this analysis for 20 cluster classifications. A similar conclusion applies except that the multilayered methods start to produce less than the target number of groups. This may be a feature of the data but it could also be due to inappropriate architecture or insufficient training.

Table 8.3 offers a comparison in terms of the within-cluster sum of squares that can be computed using the original 44 variables. This is a standard measure of classification performance although it is difficult to know what it means. Nor need there be a direct relationship with classification performance as judged by the user against subjective criteria relating to purpose that is application dependent. Nevertheless, some of the net results seem at least as good in terms of within-cluster sum of squares as the CCP benchmark.

Table 8.2 Cluster sizes for 20 group classifications

Ranked size	*K:* 20*1	*K:* 5*4	CNET (a)	CNET (b)	*K*	CCP
1	1392	1362	2009	1241	1380	973
2	903	1027	979	1240	1005	836
3	893	911	948	1196	932	820
4	884	778	909	963	848	775
5	679	691	866	885	698	745
6	614	635	862	547	606	680
7	604	520	792	511	558	657
8	529	507	553	478	482	616
9	464	472	547	398	476	484
10	421	444	391	364	438	425
11	338	396	231	340	339	401
12	326	342	190	278	319	365
13	304	317	na	224	300	312
14	256	218	na	186	228	292
15	157	157	na	173	153	285
16	142	142	na	144	141	231
17	138	131	na	109	141	147
18	117	114	na	na	121	122
19	59	57	na	na	58	80
20	58	57	na	na	54	32

Note: Details of CNET architectures: (a) 2: 1= <30>, 1= <20>;
(b) 1: 9= <2,4,6,8,10,12,14,16,18>, 2= <20>.

The final question is whether the results are similar. This raises a number of major difficulties because cluster labelling is a subjective process. The other problem is how to match clusters from different classifications. This is essentially insoluble in any rigorous scientific fashion.

Table 8.4 focuses on two particular types of area, those of deprivation and high status. With the exception of CNET (b), there seems to be broad conformity although the precise composition of the groups varies, as does their geographical extent. To some extent this merely demonstrates the immense subjectivity of the classification process. There seem to be multiple different or slightly different sets of plausible results and the distinction between them is mainly a matter of personal preference. Alternatively, the classifications might be tuned for particular subjective definition clarity under certain application-specific circumstances. This is clearly the best way to apply classification methods.

In general the nets do very well given that there is no orthonormalization of the data and the methods contain no concept of within-cluster variances. Indeed all the net results come from a process of self-organization that is performed at the local rather than a global scale. There is therefore no notion of a global function that the classification optimizes. They are also exceedingly easy to

Table 8.3 Within-cluster sum of squares

Description of method	**Number of clusters**	**Percentage within-cluster sum of squares**
CCP	10	40.15
CCP	20	34.21
CCP	30	31.16
CCP	40	27.84
CCP	50	26.53
K: 3*3	9	32.03
K: 10*1	10	30.29
K: 15*1	15	27.48
K: 4*4	16	27.22
K: 20*1	20	25.14
K: 5*4	20	24.93
K: 5*5	25	23.24
K: 25*1	25	22.94
K: 30*1	30	22.00
K: 10*3	30	21.76
K: 6*5	30	21.97
K: 6*6	36	20.91
K: 40*1	40	20.08
K: 8*5	40	20.23
K: 7*7	49	19.05
K: 50*1	50	18.82
K: 10*5	50	18.78
K	10	32.66
K	20	26.82
K	30	23.12
K	40	21.35
K	50	20.20
CNET 2: 1= <20>, 1= <10>	10	58.40
CNET 2: 4=<2,4,6,8>, 1= <10>	10	35.37
CNET 2: 1= <30>, 1= <20>	20	63.86
CNET 2: 9=<2,4,6,8,10,12,14,16,18>, 1= <20>	20	29.80
CNET 2: 1=<40>, 1=<30>	30	42.27
CNET 2: 1= <50>, 1= <40>	40	67.39

program. By comparison with the statistical alternatives, the amount of code is at least an order of magnitude less (Openshaw 1994c). The author's preference would be for the single-layer competitive net. The results are exceedingly clear and seem very plausible. The self-organizing maps may well require larger data sets before their full potential can be realized. A similar conclusion applies to the multilayer nets. The greater subjectivity involved in these two types of architecture is both an advantage (maybe they can be tuned to particular applications)

Table 8.4 Cluster labels for the 30 group classification (number of wards (clusters))

Area label	CCP	*K*	*K*: 20*1	*K*: 5*5	CNET (a)	CNET (b)
High status	893 (1)	848 (1)	893 (1)	569 (1)	0 (0)	1241 (1)
Deprivation	979 (6)	922 (6)	921 (6)	1066 (6)	622 (2)	837 (4)

Note: Details of CNET architectures: (a) 2: 1= <30>, 1= <20> (12 clusters); (b) 2: 9= <2,4,6,8,10,12,14,16,18>, 1= <20> (17 clusters).

and a problem (how to decide how many of each etc.). Moreover, the use of data for smaller census areas (such as enumeration districts) may well require the additional degrees of sophistication that they can offer. In general, the overall impression is that the competitive nets perform extremely well. The problem now is to match net architecture to application type and it may well be a long time before we have enough practical experience to answer that particular question.

6 Conclusions

The chapter provides a wide range of advice about how to go about classifying 1991 Census data. It builds on an earlier attempt on the same topic (Openshaw 1982) by updating the advice on application and method to reflect a decade of progress. Census classification methods have been used to clarify census data ever since the first computer algorithms were developed. The utility of being able to collapse the size of census datasets by grouping together cases which have a similar multivariable profile should not be underestimated and census classifications have been found to be extremely useful as a data description tool in a number of application areas. The ability to simplify the multivariate complexity of census data thereby enabling the key differences between areas to be summarized in a largely non-technical and readily understood form provides a new perspective on the usefulness of census data. Indeed, census data for entire countries have been reduced by classification into a relatively small number of groups or clusters. Hopefully, the advice contained here will allow 1991 classifications to be produced more easily, more efficiently and more usefully than ever before.

Appendix 8A List of the 44 variables used

V1 Males seeking work as a proportion of males economically active
V2 Proportion of married females in private households economically active
V3 Students 16 or over as a proportion of persons in private households
V4 Cars per total private households
V5 Households with two or more cars per total private households
V6 Children aged 0–4 per married female in private households aged 16–44

V7 Proportion residents born in the new commonwealth or Pakistan
V8 Proportion of persons in private households aged 0–4
V9 Proportion of persons in private households aged 5–15
V10 Proportion of persons in private households aged 16–24
V11 Proportion of persons in private households aged 25–44
V12 Proportion of persons in private households aged 45–64
V13 Proportion of persons in private households aged 65+
V14 Proportion of persons in private households over 16 and married
V15 Proportion of single non-pensioner households
V16 Persons per total private households
V17 Rooms per total private households
V18 Proportion of private households owner occupied
V19 Proportion of private households renting from a council or new town
V20 Proportion of private households renting from a housing association
V21 Proportion of private households renting private unfurnished
V22 Proportion of private households renting private furnished
V23 Proportion of private households living at over 1.5 persons per room
V24 Proportion of private households living at 1–1.5 person per room
V25 Rooms per persons in private households
V26 Proportion of private households in shared dwellings
V27 Proportion of private households with no inside WC
V28 Proportion of private households lacking a bath
V29 Proportion of private households occupying seven or more rooms
V30 Proportion of private households occupying one or two rooms
V31 Proportion of workers travelling to work by foot
V32 Proportion of workers travelling to work by bus or train
V33 Proportion of workers in manufacturing
V34 Proportion of workers in agriculture
V35 Proportion of workers in distribution, catering, transport and other services
V36 Proportion of private households with economically active head in Social Class I
V37 Proportion of private households with economically active head in Social Class II
V38 Proportion of private households with economically active head in Social Class IIIN
V39 Proportion of private households with economically active head in Social Class IIIM
V40 Proportion of private households with economically active head in Social Class IV
V41 Proportion of private households with economically active head in Social Class V
V42 Proportion of private households with lone pensioner resident
V43 Proportion of private households with single parent family
V44 Proportion of residents aged 16+ classified as permanently sick or disabled

All variables are expressed as rates per 10,000.

Appendix 8B An algorithm for contiguising a classification

Step 1 Assemble first-order contiguities for each of the *N* areas
Step 2 Take any unprocessed area and make a list of all areas contiguous to it of the same classification type
Step 3 Repeat this process for each of the areas in this list, deleting duplicates, and extend the list as necessary
Step 4 When processing is finished then the areas included in the list are contiguous and members of the same cluster; flag these areas as processed
Step 5 Return to Step 2 or end if no unprocessed areas remain

Appendix 8C Computer software for the classification of census data

Separate programs cover:

- the calculation of principal component scores;
- classification by iterative relocation, including various heuristics for improving a classification;
- the calculation of various diagnostics to help name the clusters;
- the calculation of the classification's sum of squares and other statistical measures;
- the conversion of a classification into a regionalization;
- the generation of random starting classifications.

These programs have been run on a wide range of computers that support a FORTRAN IV compiler with either no, or very little, modification. Full user manuals and program source and test data are available. These programs have also been converted into FORTRAN 77 for UNIX systems. These can be obtained for a small charge by writing to Professor Stan Openshaw, School of Geography, Leeds University, Leeds LS2 9JT.

References

Aarts, E and J Korst 1989 *Simulated Annealing and Boltzmann Machines*. New York: Wiley.

Carpenter, G A and S Grossberg 1987 ART2: self-organisation of stable category recognition codes for analogue input patterns. *Applied Optics* 26, 4919–30.

Cerny, V 1985 Themodynamical approach to the travelling salesman problem; an efficient simulation algorithm. *Journal of Optimisation Theory and Applications* 45, 41–51.

Charlton, M E, S Openshaw and C Wymer 1985 Some new classifications of census enumeration districts in Britain: a poor man's ACORN. *Journal of Economic and Social Measurement* 13, 69–98.

Coombes, M G, A E Green and S Openshaw 1986 An efficient algorithm to generate official statistical reporting areas: the case of the 1984 Travel-to-Work Areas revision in Britain. *Journal of Operations Research Society* 10 943–53.

Coombes, M G, J S Dixon, J B Goddard, S Openshaw and P J Taylor 1982 Functional regions for the Population Census of Great Britain In D T Herbert and R J Johnston (eds) *Geography and the Urban Environment S.* London: Wiley.

Desieno, D 1988 Adding a conscience to competitive learning. *Proceedings of the International Conference on Neural Networks*, vol. I. New York: IEEE Press, 117–24.

Kirkpatrick, S, J Gelatt and M P Vecchi M P 1983 Optimisation by simulated annealing. *Science* 220, 671–80.

Kohonen, T 1982 Self-organised formation of topologically correct feature maps. *Biological Cybernetics* 43, 59–69.

Kohonen, T 1988 *Self-organisation and Associative Memory*. Berlin: Springer.

Kohonen, T 1990 Speech recognition based on topology-preserving neural maps. In I Aleksander (ed) *Neural Computing Architectures*. London: North Oxford Academic, 26–40.

Masser, I and P J B Brown 1975 Hierarchical aggregation procedures for spatial interaction data. *Environment and Planning* A 7, 509–23.

Metropolis, N, A Rosenbluth, M Rosenbluth, A Teller and E Teller 1953 Equation of state calculations by fast computing machines. *J. of Chemical Physics* 21, 1087–92.

Openshaw, S 1970 A dynamic regionalisation algorithm Working Paper, Department of Geography, Newcastle University.

Openshaw, S 1973 A regionalisation algorithm for large datasets *Computer Applications* 3–4, 39–80.

Openshaw, S 1978 An empirical study of some zone design criteria. *Environment and Planning A* 10, 781–94.

Openshaw, S 1982 *Census Classification Program: User Manual.* Department of Town and Country Planning, Newcastle University.

Openshaw, S 1983 Multivariate analysis of census data: the classification of areas. In D Rhind (ed) *A Census User's Handbook*, London: Methuen, 243–64.

Openshaw, S 1984 Ecological fallacies and the analysis of areal census data *Environment and Planning A* 16, 17-31.

Openshaw, S 1993a Modelling spatial interaction using a neural net. In M M Fischer and P Nijtamp (eds) *GIS, Spatial Modelling and Policy*. Berlin: Springer-Verlag, 147–64.

Openshaw, S 1993b Special classification. In B Leventhal, C Moy and J Griffin (eds) *An Introductory Guide to the 1991 Census*. Henley: NTC Publications, 69–82.

Openshaw, S 1994a A concepts rich approach to spatial analysis, theory generation and scientific discovery in GIS using massively parallel computing. In M Worboys (ed) *Innovations in GIS*. London: Taylor and Frances, 123–38.

Openshaw, S 1994b Developing smart and intelligent target marketing systems. *Journal of Targeting, Measurement and Analysis for Marketing* 2, 289-301.

Openshaw, S 1994c Neuroclassification of spatial data. In B Hewitson and R Crane (eds), *Neural Nets: Applications in Geography*. Dordrecht: Kluwer Academic, 53–70.

Openshaw, S and A A Gillard 1978 On the stability of a spatial classification of census enumeration district data. In P W J Batey (ed) *Theory and Method in Urban and Regional Analysis*. London: Pion, 101–19.

Openshaw, S and C Wymer 1991 A neural net classifier system for handling census data. In F Murtagh (ed) *Proceedings of the Neural Networks for Statistical and Economic Data Conference*. Dublin: Munotec Systems.

Pao, Y H 1989 *Adaptive Pattern Recognition and Neural Networks. Reading,* MA: Addison-Wesley.

Rumelhart, D E and J L McClelland 1986 *Parallel Distributed Processing: Explorations in the Microstructure of Cognition*, vol.1. Cambridge, MA: MIT Press.

Rumelhart, D E and D Zipster 1986 Feature discovery by competitive learning. In D E Rumelhart and J L McCelland (eds) *Parallel Distributed Processing*, vol.1. Cambridge, MA: MIT Press, 151–93.
Sokal, R R and P H A Sneath 1963 *Principles of Numerical Taxonomy*. San Francisco: Freeman.
Tukey, J W 1977 *Exploratory Data Analysis*. Reading, MA: Addison-Wesley.

9

Further analysis of multivariate census data

C Brunsdon

Editor's note

The presumption is made that mostly census users will be interested in exploring 1991 Census data for evidence of patterns and relationships that might be of interest. Classification, mapping, GIS-based manipulation and visualization procedures provide alternative ways of tackling the census analysis problem. Another more direct route is to use multivariate statistical methods in either a classical or an exploratory style. This chapter outlines some of the methods that appear most useful. Once again, the spatial nature of census complicates multivariate analysis in many different ways and this chapter provides suggestions about how best to cope.

1 The interaction between census variables

1.1 Introduction

Although the dispersion and overall levels associated with a single variable will be of interest to many census users, the relationships between variables will often be of greater importance. This importance generally hinges on the substantive issues in a given study. For example, how might the age profile of an area relate to levels of population change? In a more general sense, is a high value of one particular variable often accompanied by a high value of another variable, or is the relationship the inverse of this? Perhaps there is little relationship at all. Furthermore, if there does appear to be some relationship between a pair of variables, it may then be necessary to investigate its form in greater detail. Are there any cases that go against the general trends? Does a given change in the level of one of the variables always produce a constant level of change in the other? Issues of this sort are the concern of this chapter.

As in the chapter on univariate analysis, special emphasis will be placed on exploratory techniques and the use of graphics. Whereas summary statistics and mathematical modelling tend to convey impressions of trends in the census *as a whole,* several of the techniques suggested here will either portray the data in their entirety or attempt to highlight outstanding cases as well as provide the summary information for the entire dataset. A great deal of emphasis may be placed on graphical techniques, since computing facilities available to typical census users of today offer extremely high quality and easy to use graphical software packages compared with those available at the time of the last population census. The opportunity for reasonably fast and interactive graphical exploration of census data has increased greatly since that time.

In addition to the graphical techniques, however, attention will also be given to analytical quantitative techniques. There may be various occasions when such techniques become necessary. The techniques considered will address the task of data description and also of modelling relationships between variables. The former becomes particularly important when more than two variables are dealt with in a single study. Although some attempts can be made to visualize data in three dimensions, there are severe problems in graphically representing data when the number of variables is extremely large. To all practical intentions we live in a three-dimensional world; we have some difficulty in perceiving more complex spatial relations even in this world and generally experience problems in envisioning information in more than three dimensions. The latter issue of modelling takes on importance if policy makers wish to consider 'what-if' analysis and forecasting utilizing census variables. If it is possible to encapsulate, to some degree of accuracy, the relationship between a set of census variables, then the outcome of changing some of the values of the variables could be estimated, e.g. when considering possible changes in demographic characteristics of areas in the near future. It will be argued later in the chapter that data modelling and data exploration are complementary techniques. In order to gain some understanding of the relationships between variables, as well as summarizing a *general* pattern in the census variables, exceptions to this trend should also be identified. This is particularly important in a geographical sense, where the identification of unusual cases is essentially the identification of exceptional places.

The question of place and the analysis of multivariate census data raises its own questions. Census information is always geographical in that each variable relates to a specific place. With the exception of the Samples of Anonymized Records (SAR), information is not released at the individual level but is aggregated to spatial zones. Thus, rather than stating whether individuals are unemployed or not, a percentage level is given for some area. The choice of this area can be of fundamental importance. As stated in the chapter on univariate analysis, the patterns observed in the data at one level of spatial aggregation could differ greatly from those at another (see also Chapter 6). This takes on new relevance in multivariate techniques. For example, if 30% of households in one district own two cars, and also 30% of households have one or more pensioners resident, there is no way of ascertaining how many households fall into both categories. On the one hand, it is quite possible that all households in the first category also fall in the second, but if no household fell into both categories it would still be possible to obtain the same percentages. For this reason, interpretation of the observed relationships between some census variables may require more careful consideration than the initial results may suggest. Before any investigation of relationships between variables takes place, it is important to give thought to the geographical relevance of the areal units of aggregation. For all the variables, the spatial scale and 'shape' of the social and economic phenomena in question should be considered.

Readers with some past experience of statistical analysis may note that the emphasis in this chapter is on exploratory analysis techniques rather than 'classical' multivariate analysis methods such as factor analysis, multivariate analysis of variance and so on. This is deliberate, with the following reasons offered as justification. First, much of this material is covered well in other publications, e.g. in Evans (1983). Second, a major aim of this chapter is to outline recent developments in multivariate statistical analysis, many of which have been exploratory, and graphical in nature. Perhaps this reflects upon the increased availability of computer hardware capable of high quality graphical display during the period between the 1981 and 1991 Censuses. The author feels that particular attention should be given to these methods, as they are just now becoming readily available to most census users and will become increasingly commonplace between now and the advent of the next census.

1.2 Bivariate methods

A common problem in the analysis of census data is the investigation of the interaction between a pair of census variables. Typical questions relate to the *strength* of the relationship, and also to its *nature.* When working in only two dimensions the use of graphics is strongly recommended. Plotting scatterplots of the two variables can give some very strong hints towards answering this type of question. For an initial inspection of the data, univariate exploratory analysis of each variable in turn is also advised. The use of such techniques is enhanced even further when considered in terms of maps linking the regions in the scatterplot with their position in the country, and in their own locality. Another way in which graphics could be put to use in the analysis of bivariate data is the investigation of the effect of scale on the relationships observed between the variables. This may give some suggestion of appropriate spatial units when considering the relationship between variables.

Moving towards more analytical techniques, the *correlation coefficient* is also an important tool in summarizing the relationship between a pair of variables. Its use and characteristics will be discussed in greater detail later in this chapter. There are several other techniques that will also be covered, most of these relating to *modelling* the relationship between the variables and also to more formal tests of hypothesis. Graphical techniques are also important at this stage, since they allow easy detection of outlying cases and provide helpful diagnostics when attempting to fit models to the data.

1.3 Three or more variables

Extending a study beyond two dimensions can lead to extra complications. The concept of interaction becomes more complicated when considering the interplay between more than two variables. This leads to greater complexity in any modelling applied to the relationship between the variables, and also when providing a set of summary statistics. This is further compounded by the problems of graphical representation discussed above. As a result, somewhat different techniques may be called for. Generally the problems in interpreting datasets consisting three or more variables can be split into two parts:

1. techniques for a small number of census variables (up to about five or six)
2. techniques for large numbers of census variables

For the former category, exploratory graphical techniques may still be used to some extent. For the latter, it is likely that some purely computational techniques may be unavoidable. However, as with the bivariate case, it is generally profitable to carry out exploratory univariate analysis on each of the individual variables under investigation. In this way, extreme cases and general trends in single variables can be identified. Certainly, for extreme cases, an exceptional value of an individual variable could be linked with unusual behaviour when the data are considered in a multivariate sense.

1.4 The importance of outliers

As suggested in the above sections, the importance of *diagnostic* techniques in modelling cannot be overemphasized. Most methods will attempt to estimate a set of coefficients used in some mathematical model regardless of the suitability of that model. It is then the problem of the census analysts to assess the success of the model-fitting exercise and determine whether it is appropriate. There are two main sources of difficulty here. First the model may be entirely inappropriate, so that the 'optimal' set of coefficients is really no more than the best of a very poor choice. If the number of dimensions is sufficiently low, then graphical diagnostics are generally valuable. Examples of this will be covered in Sections 3 and 4 of this chapter. The second category of problems occur when models may be appropriate to one subsection of the data, but not to another. If the deviant subsection is relatively small compared with the data, the problem is usually approached from the viewpoint of outlier detection. For example, the behaviour of census wards such as the City of London, having a very low population count, may be very different from that of other wards in the country. When examining the relationships between pairs of variables, it is not unusual to find that the value pair for this ward stands out on a graphical representation, and perhaps has a harmful effect on the calibration of regression models or the calculation of correlation coefficients.

A very different problem occurs when the deviant subsection of the data is actually much larger than a handful of exceptions. In this case it is often difficult to determine whether the deviation is attributable to a set of areas each of which is unusual for distinct reasons, or whether there is a coherent 'breakaway group'. For example, might the population age structure of areas experiencing gentrification exhibit a different relationship with employment structure than would other regions? Such areas might form a significant minority in the dataset and might appear as a distinct cluster on a scatterplot. It could be argued in this case that such special subgroups should be partitioned from the main dataset, and that separate models should be applied to them.

1.5 Spatial aspects

A final consideration in the analysis and assessment of multivariate data sets is that of space, and of geography. The concepts of outliers and deviant groups are, as previously suggested, often associated with geography. For instance, patterns associated with census variables related to housing in Scotland often differ from those observed in England, partly as a result of the different proportions of the public rented sector in the two countries (see Champion *et al.* 1987, pp. 90–100). In this case, not only is there a distinct breakaway group in terms of the characteristics of the variables themselves, but there is also a distinct geographical division. This difference may manifest itself in the poor performance of models predicting, say, home ownership in parts of Scotland. Thus, the geographical mapping of areas whose actual values deviate from those predicted in modelling is an important aspect of the identification of outliers and of model diagnostics.

More generally, it is reasonable to assume that the processes that the census variables reflect will often have some geographical qualities. It is almost always useful to investigate the link between the multivariate patterns observed on a scatterplot and the locations of the case areas on a map. Although this borders on the subject matter of the chapters relating to geographical information systems and visualization, there are some specific aspects of these that are particularly helpful when considered in connection with multivariate analysis and modelling. For this reason, such examples will be included in this chapter, serving to give practical examples of the connection between the disciplines.

2 Exploratory techniques and graphics

2.1 Univariate techniques

No investigation of the relationship between several census variables is complete without some consideration of each of the variables in isolation. Before more complicated summaries of linkages between variables are produced, it is essential to describe the typical levels and degree of dispersion associated with each variable in turn. In addition to this, early warnings of troublesome (or indeed interesting!) cases can be obtained if those cases are identified as having outlying

Table 9.1 Five-number summary

	% 16-19	**% Over 65**
Min	3.73	7.32
3rd quartile	6.16	12.63
Median	6.50	14.20
1st quartile	6.80	16.33
Max	9.04	30.67

values in particular variables. This subject matter is covered in much greater detail in Chapter 7, but to demonstrate the connection between univariate and multivariate analyses an example is now given.

For each census district (based on the 1991 Census), the percentage of population between the ages of 16 and 19 was calculated, as was the percentage of the population aged 65 and over. Considering these two variables gives a crude sketch of the age structure of the districts. Before considering the relationship between the two proportions, however, a univariate analysis of each variable in turn is given.

In this case, for each variable, the minimum, third quartile, median, first quartile and maximum are given (Table 9.1). This is sometimes referred to as a *five-number summary* (Tukey 1977). Some basic observations may now be made. First, the proportion of people aged 65 or more is generally greater than those aged between 16 and 19. This is perhaps unsurprising, as the latter category is more tightly defined than the former. The range between proportions is also much greater. The distribution of the 65 and over variable has a distinct positive skew, as can be seen by looking at the value of the maximum compared with the

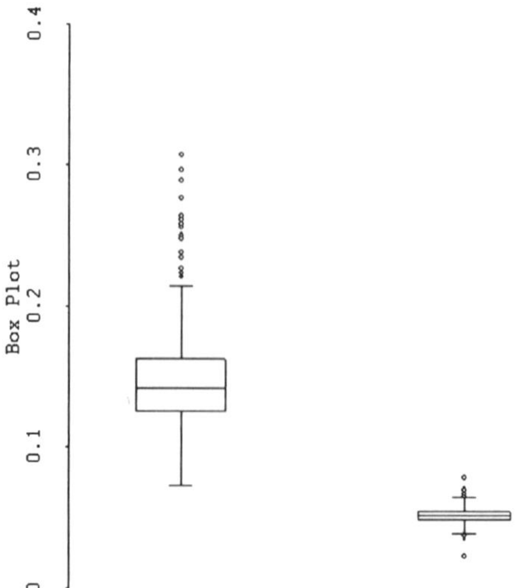

Fig. 9.1 Boxplot of demographic variables.

first quartile. Producing boxplots (Fig. 9.1) of both variables shows that, while the distribution of the proportion of people over 65 has a skewed distribution, there are no outstanding cases. This contrasts with the distribution of 16–19 year olds, which is seen to have outlying values in both the upper and lower ends of the distribution.

As is usual when considering outliers in census data, the next step is to identify the regions associated with them. In this case the low outlier is the proportion for the City of London, and the higher one is Knowsley. Having found outlying regions in the univariate case, valuable clues as to possible 'rogue' observations in multivariate analysis have now been obtained. At this stage, it is often helpful to consider such outlying regions in a more qualitative sense, in order to explain *why* these outstanding values have occurred. Understandings of this sort, and awareness of exceptions to general rules, are of as much importance to policy making as the consideration of general patterns in the data as a whole.

It is important to notice here that these two outlying regions are also clearly visible on a scatterplot of the two variables (Fig. 9.2) and are likely to have some influence on any attempts to summarize the relationship between the variables as a whole. The object of this exercise is to demonstrate that, in many cases where the relationship between variables is under examination, unusual or exceptional regions can initially be identified using univariate techniques and that this in itself is a valuable contribution to multivariate analysis. This is particularly relevant when considering large numbers of variables, when outliers are hard to identify in several dimensions.

2.2 The scatterplot

Having moved on from univariate exploration, the scatterplot provides a powerful tool for examining relationships between pairs of variables. Although

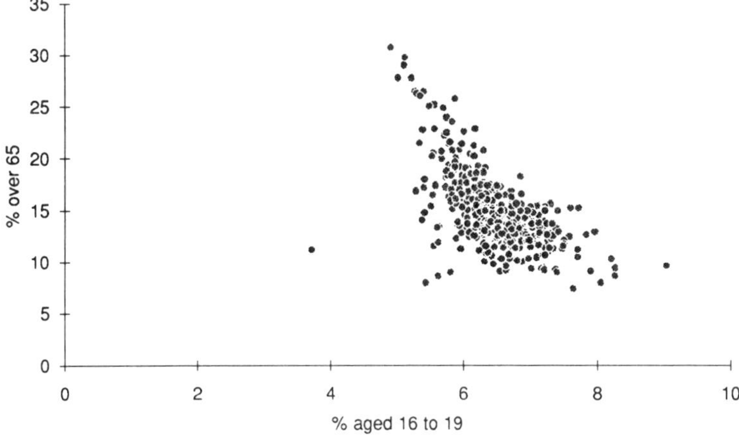

Fig. 9.2 Simple age structure comparison.

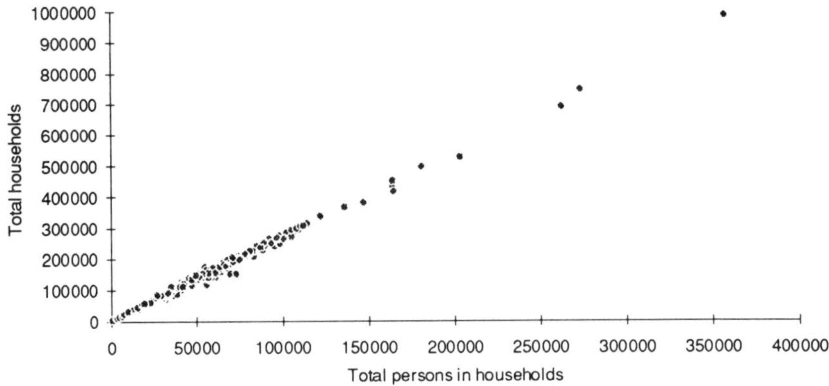

Fig. 9.3 Number of households versus total persons in households.

univariate analysis may identify some useful trends, and interesting cases within the data, it can give no information of how the variables relate *to each other*. This can be thought of as the *interaction* between the variables. When one variable changes in value, how might we expect the other to behave? Consider, for example, the relationship between the total number of households in a district and the total number of persons in households, also by district. Both of these figures were obtained from the 1991 Census. A scatterplot of this is shown in Fig. 9.3. Immediately, various features become apparent. First, there is a very clear linear relationship between the two variables, passing through the origin of the graph. This suggests that the ratio between the two counts, which measures (at a district level) the number of persons per household, is fairly constant throughout the UK. Of course, this is a fairly superficial analysis as it gives no consideration to the *quality* of housing, but it serves to illustrate that producing a scatterplot can give a striking first impression of the relationship between two variables.

Although there are many interesting and relevant features of the data that may be discovered using univariate techniques, there are others which may only become apparent when using techniques in higher dimensions. Figure 9.3 illustrates this point. A univariate analysis of both the total persons in households and the total households would identify outlying areas. In both cases, the districts of Leeds, Glasgow City and Birmingham have exceptionally large counts of both households and occupants. The reason for this is clear: both districts are unusually large in terms of population. What should be noted, however, is that although these places would be identified as unusual in some way, their presence in the dataset does not affect the validity of the assumption of reasonably constant persons to household ratios. An attempt to estimate a mean value of this ratio (e.g. based on the slope of a line drawn through the observations) would not be notably changed by the inclusion of figures for the three cities. This becomes immediately apparent when a scatterplot is drawn.

Although it could be argued that various aspects of univariate analysis could also identify this, it is unlikely that the existence of a strong trend, the exceptional cases, and the fact that the exceptional cases do not actually go against the trend could be as immediately identifiable without the use of a scatterplot.

There are also many other cases where scatterplots can identify relationships and patterns that are mainly linked to the interaction between two variables, rather than the properties of each variable in turn. For example, a pair of variables may have no outlying points, or other unusual features, but it is possible that an unusual combination occurs at a particular place. For instance, generally one would expect the proportion of households owning two or more cars to be related to the proportion of persons occupied in professional and managerial occupations. While this may generally be the case, there may be exceptions. If this were the case, neither of the values of the two variables for these unusual places may be particularly exceptional; what is of note is that they *infrequently occur together*. In Fig. 9.1, Stewartry is such an example. Although the proportions of 16–19 year olds and 65 year olds and over are not unusual in their own right, the point on the scatterplot corresponding to this district stands clear of the main cluster. Again, by plotting scatterplots, such cases may be easily identified by eye, and once again features in the data become immediately apparent.

2.3 Spin plots

The general idea of the scatterplot may be extended into three dimensions. Here the notion of interaction becomes more complex. The way one variable relates to another may in turn affect the value of a third. In the same way that two-dimensional space is used to represent bivariate observations, an attempt is made to represent trivariate datasets in three dimensions. To achieve this, a third axis is added to the scatterplot, extending orthogonally from the plane of the existing two. For each case (again, these would be geographical zones), a symbol is plotted at the position in three-dimensional space corresponding to the values of its three variables. This poses new problems, since although a three-dimensional space can be perceived in a solid world, it cannot be unambiguously represented on a flat piece of paper or a VDU screen. Usually, some form of perspective or projective geometry needs to be employed to represent a set of solid objects as a flat image. However, as in the real world, the choice of viewpoint, the distance away from the objects and the angle of viewing will all affect what may actually be visible. For instance, a small 'breakaway' cluster may not be visible to the viewer of a three-dimensional scatterplot if the main cluster in the data is positioned between it and the viewer's position. In this instance, the particular choice of viewpoint was unhelpful in identifying pattern in the data.

The census user may feel at this point that the idea of a three-dimensional scatterplot is not a particularly helpful avenue to follow. If the advantage of the two-dimensional version is its ability to make patterns become clear, surely the problem of obscurity in three dimensions will greatly reduce this benefit. However, it is possible that some three-way interactions between variables may take place, and that no purely 'flat' approach to graphic data representation would be able to identify these. Fortunately, current advances in computer technology are able to help in this situation. Although no individual viewpoint may be optimal in terms of identifying all the features in the data, the ability to change the position of viewing interactively or to rotate the scatterplot in solid space would allow exploration from several viewpoints. A plot of the data having this property is known as a *spin plot*, since it may be spun in any direction in a similar manner to a ball-bearing resting in a universal joint. In order to implement this on a computer, one would require reasonably fast graphical abilities and a strong degree of user interaction, using a mouse or trackerball. Fortunately, most machines currently being manufactured are able to use software and hardware meeting these requirements. In this application, and others that will be seen later in the chapter, the ability to interact with the data in this manner provides a powerful means of exploration. Examples of packages providing these facilities are SPIDER (see Haslett *et al.* 1990) and XLISP-STAT (Tierney 1990).

As an example, the age structure data will be used again, but this time considering proportions of people aged 65 and over, 16–24 and 25–39. Once again, these figures are computed from counts from the 1991 Census at the district level. Here the age structure data is trivariate. Since a spin plot is interactive, it is hard to demonstrate its full capabilities within a book chapter. However, in Figs 9.4 and 9.5 two different views of the data are given. Note that these interactive displays currently use cruder graphical techniques than those in charting or presentation packages, but this is in order to allow better animation capabilities. The diagrams shown in this chapter are direct screen-dumps, to allow the user to gain an impression of the appearance of tools of this sort when used *in situ.* These figures were obtained using the XLISP-STAT package mentioned above. Clearly, in practice many more views could be obtained.

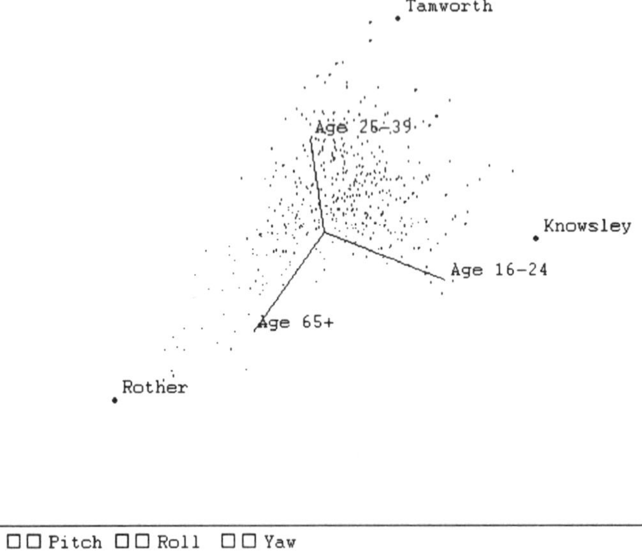

Fig. 9.4 Spin plot of demographic variables.

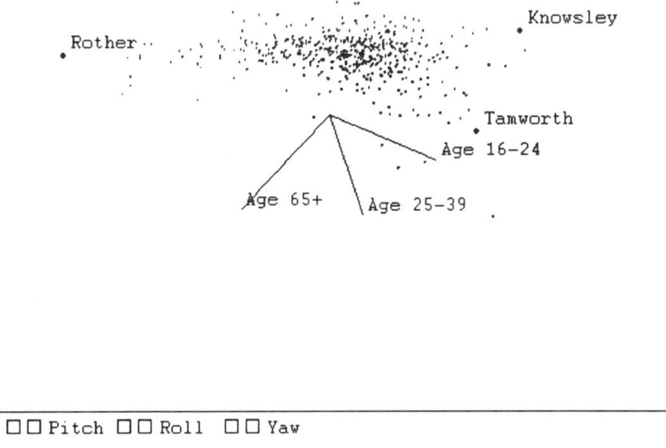

Fig. 9.5 Spin plot after interactive rotation.

The first noticeable feature of the 'clouds' of points in the two figures is that they lie in a fairly narrow band, close to a plane. This is only to be expected, since as all three variables are percentages of the same population they are constrained so that the sum of the three cannot exceed 100. However, looking at various angles it is possible to see outlying points in various directions. These correspond to the districts of Rother, Knowsley and Tamworth. In each case, the composition of the district could then be examined, and possibly further consideration given to the interpretation of this information.

This technique can be extended further by animation, with a prescribed set of rotations applied to the dataset without interaction from the viewer. This can be helpful in giving the viewer clues as to the 'depth' of the data points (in the direction perpendicular to the VDU) or highlighting certain features of the data. Computing suitable sequences of rotation to identify particular assets of the data (such as the 'breakaway' clusters mentioned earlier) is one area where statistical analysis and visualization techniques are profitably combined.

2.4 A small number of variables

As the number of variables in the data increases, the possibility of graphically exploring the interaction between all of these variables reduces. To investigate relationships in three dimensions requires fairly advanced computing techniques by some standards, and in four or more dimensions there is the added disadvantage of difficulties of conceptualization for any given graphical representation. How, then, should an exploratory analysis be carried out when there are more than three variables of interest? Certainly it is difficult to discover any four-way interactions between variables, but it is still possible to investigate less complex schemes of interaction. As a general observation, however, there is a 'law of diminishing returns' on increasing the dimension of analysis. The jump from one to two dimensions gives a notable increase in the utility of graphical techniques used. Although univariate analysis provides some invaluable methods, only by moving up to two dimensions can any examination of interaction take place at all. It is unlikely, however, that addition of an extra dimension to much higher dimensions will bring about such an important change.

In Section 1.2, the utility of scatterplots was discussed, as tools for investigating the relationship between a pair of variables. Providing the number of variables is not large, scatterplots can still be produced for each combination of variables in the dataset. If there are n variables in all, then excluding pairs of scattergrams that have the x and y axes exchanged, $n(n-1)/2$ possible graphs may be produced. Thus, if four variables were considered, there would be six possible charts to draw. Looking at six graphs to investigate unusual patterns or trends is a reasonable task, but if, say, 30 variables were used, then 435 graphs would be necessary to investigate all two-way relationships. This is clearly not a reasonable proposition! This observation effectively identifies two distinct situations when examining datasets having more than three variables; those with an intermediate number of variables that graphical techniques may still be applied to, and those with a large number of variables for which 'raw' exploratory analysis is not viable, except perhaps at the univariate level.

A useful technique which may be applied to this intermediate level of complexity, building on the scatterplot and again making use of an interactive approach, is the *scatterplot matrix*. In this method, all pairs of variables are illustrated using a scatterplot as suggested above. The plots are arranged in a square grid, with the position of each plot corresponding to the pair of row and column variables implicitly labelling the outside of the grid. Providing that there are not too many plots visible at once, an arrangement of plots like this can help to identify any significant patterns in two-way interactions of any of the variables in the dataset.

This alone is little more than bivariate analysis applied to each pairing of variables possible. It is important to bear in mind, though, that the scatterplots can be thought of as being linked, in that any point corresponding to a district on one of the plots matches another on each of the other plots in the matrix. This can be exploited if the software used to produce these diagrams runs in an interactive environment; the scatterplot matrix can become more useful by having its functionality extended to allow interactive query. Making use of a mouse or trackerball based graphical user interface, a user could select a point or set of points from a scatterplot matrix shown on the VDU, from one of the component scatterplots in the matrix. These points would be highlighted, but points on each of the other scatterplots corresponding to the chosen regions would also be highlighted. In this way the groupings of cases for one variable pair could be investigated in relation to other variables, or unusual cases in one plot could be linked to other plots to see if corresponding atypicality occurs with respect to other variables for these cases. In order to carry out several of these 'cross-linking' exercises at once, it is also possible on some software to change

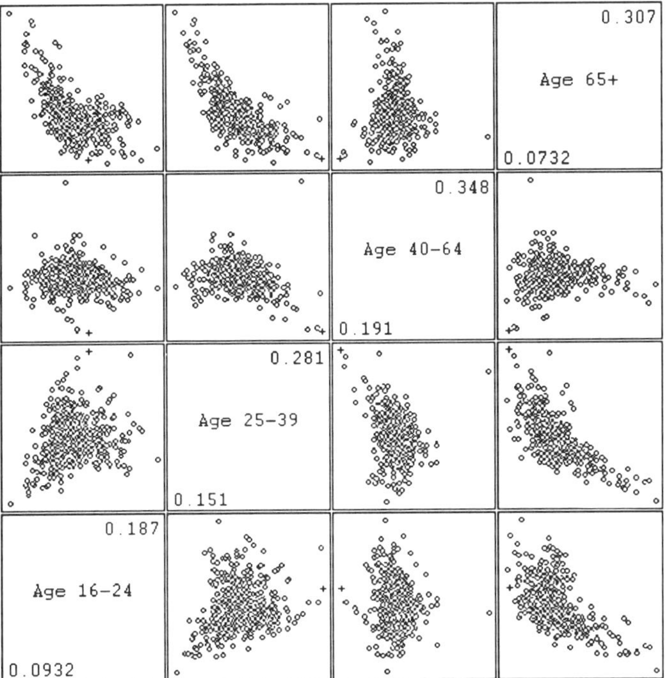

Fig. 9.6 Demographic scatterplot matrix.

either the colour or the symbol of the selected subgroups. By using several colours, or several symbols, it is possible to display linkages between more than one set of cases within the dataset.

As an example, consider once more the age structure information. A scatterplot matrix can be used to examine the relationship between proportions for *four* different sections of the population. Added to the previous age groups, the proportion of the population aged from 40 to 64 (in 1991) will now also be considered. The scatterplot matrix for these data is shown in Fig. 9.6. The unusual point in the plot between the 25–39 and 40–65 age groups corresponds to the City of London. Having been selected interactively, it was then specified that on all plots this point would be represented by an x. On the plots, it can be seen that although the relationship is unusual on some of the plots, the observation is not particularly untypical for the relationship between the 16–24 and over 65 age groups. On the other hand, Tamworth, another observation noted to be outlying and shown in Fig. 9.6 with a + sign, does not appear in the main cluster in any of the plots. This suggests that there is something unusual about the entire age distribution for this district. Again, at this stage it becomes important to look for explanations of these observations. Could the unusual observations be mainly due to small sample size, for example? In the case of the City of London this is certainly possible, as this district has the smallest population of all districts in the

1991 Census. However, for Tamworth this is not the case, and further consideration may be necessary. The power of these exploratory techniques lies in their ability to *generate new hypotheses* rather than test prescribed ones.

2.5 Large numbers of variables

The utility of techniques such as the scatterplot matrix reduces when there are very large numbers of variables to be considered, as indeed does any other attempt to represent graphically the entire information in the dataset. Exploration and the identification of outliers becomes an altogether more difficult problem. One possible way around this, which may also apply to some of the datasets in the previous category, is to make use of *dimensional reduction* techniques. These are best left to the section on analytical techniques but are of some relevance here. In short, a dimensional reduction technique attempts to represent the information in a dataset having a large number of variables using a much smaller dimensional space. Multidimensional scaling, factor analysis and projection pursuit are all examples of these techniques. Often the approach is to search for a projection from a high dimensional space to a lower one which still preserves many of the patterns of the set of data points in the higher dimensional space. If this can be successfully achieved, then some of the techniques discussed above may be applied.

Despite the suggestions above, it must be said that when inspecting a projection of the dataset into a smaller dimensional space the interpretation cannot be as clear as when simple variables are used. First, it is still possible that the projection has obscured some important feature of the data. When specifying some mathematical prescription for a projection it is difficult to guarantee that it will do justice to all aspects of a large multivariate dataset. The problem is intrinsic to all datasets having a large number of variables. Because the data cannot be 'seen' in all their dimensionality, the projection must be chosen 'in the dark'. Perhaps the problem is in attempting to work with too much information at once.

Another problem lies in the interpretation of the dataset once it has been projected. Although it may be possible to discover outliers, trends and clusters in the projected data, it is hard to attribute meaning to these at times, since the values of the variables are not straightforward quantities such as 'percentage unemployed in a district' or 'percentage of households owning three or more cars', but mathematical combinations of these. Although at times an obvious interpretation may be precipitated from the analysis, this is by no means always the case.

There are various methods that one could apply to combat this problem. One simple approach may be to categorize the variables into broad groups, such as 'demographic', 'housing' and 'economic status', and attempt to apply dimensional reduction to each of these groups in turn, perhaps attempting to obtain a projection down to a single dimension in each group. Having done this, the information for each case will be reduced to a single economic indicator, a single demographic indicator and so on. The problem of understanding the meaning of each projection is then reduced to understanding a set of more specialized relationships as opposed to the interaction of all things together. The interaction between the broader categories may then be explored using the techniques for lower dimensional datasets.

The broadness of grouping that is adopted is also of importance here. For more specialized demographic studies, for example, a single 'demographic' grouping would not suffice. This could be addressed by further subdividing the category into more detailed classes, or by projecting variables in the general category onto two- or three-dimensional space. Clearly the choice is fairly subjective, but it may be helpful at the exploratory data analysis stage to obtain a lower dimensional dataset to which at least some understanding can be attached.

2.6 Relating census variables to geography

The final part of this section on exploratory methods addresses the geographical aspects of multivariate census data. As stated in the chapter on univariate analysis, it must be remembered that census data are essentially geographical. Associated with each ward, enumeration district or county, there is a location in space as well as the various census counts. Questions as to whether regions having similar characteristics cluster together or when extremely dissimilar areas are in

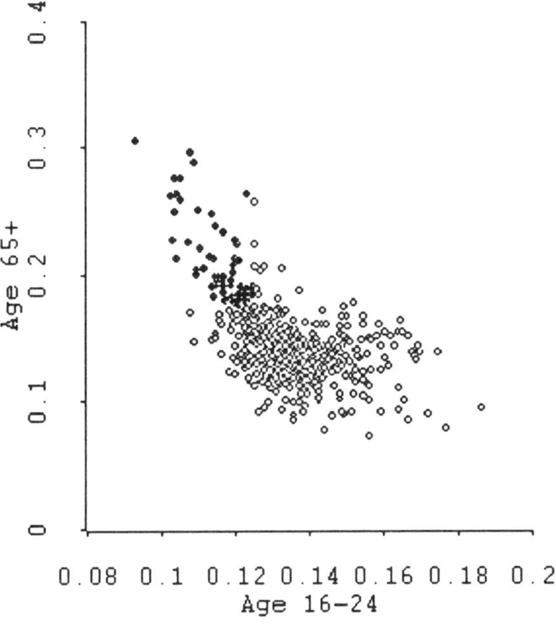

Fig. 9.7 Scatterplot of the proportion of persons in the 16–24 age group against those over 65.

close geographical proximity are often of importance to the census user. In addition to this, the ubiquitous outliers may need to be related to their location in space, or even simply identified as a place. In this area, the use of linked plots and interaction with the computer environment once again proves to be valuable.

The idea of linking several plots by selecting points on one of them was first introduced with the scatterplot matrix. In that case corresponding points on several scatterplots were highlighted in response to the initial selection. To introduce a linkage with geography, it is suggested here that scatterplots are connected with points on maps using this interactive linking technique. In this way, by selecting points on a graph the software would automatically highlight the corresponding set of points on the map. The relevant geographical regions and any patterns in these regions corresponding to the selection on the scatterplot should then become immediately clear. As an example, consider the age structure example once again. In Fig. 9.7, a scatterplot is drawn (using the XLISP-STAT package) of the proportion of persons in the 16–24 age group against those over 65. This is carried out at the district level as before. Selecting the upper part of the scattered points (seen in black) the corresponding points are seen on the linked map (Fig. 9.8). The region of the scatterplot corresponds to areas having a large proportion of residents aged 65 and over. Clearly, from the map, these districts are virtually all coastal, lying on either the southern or western coasts of Great Britain. Selecting the leftmost portion of the cloud on the scatterplot (Fig. 9.9), corresponding to districts with the largest proportion of younger people (aged 16–24), these nearly all correspond to inner city districts in London, Birmingham or Glasgow (Fig. 9.10). It therefore becomes apparent that there are

Fig. 9.8 Linked map corresponding to Fig. 9.7.

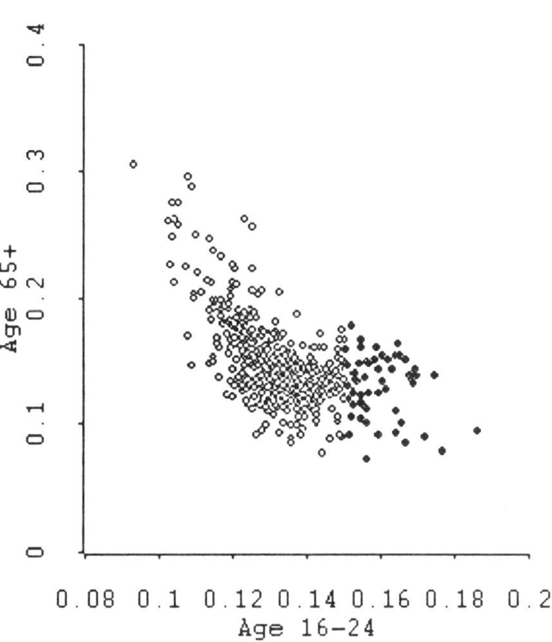

Fig. 9.9 Scatterplot of Fig. 9.7 with points shaded black for the largest proportion of younger people.

Fig. 9.10 Linked map corresponding to Fig. 9.9.

very strong *geographical* patterns in the data in addition to the patterns in the census counts themselves.

Another useful geographical feature, which again could be implemented interactively, is the identification of place names for the selected zones. In this case, selecting a point or group of points using the mouse would cause their names to appear on the chart, or the linked map, or in a separate window. This may, at first glance, appear to be a trivial feature, but it may be important in the identification of outliers or any other regions of interest when the basic map display does not show place labelling as a default.

This last operation is perhaps more akin to a geographical information system (GIS) approach than to statistical analysis, but one great change in the functionality of computers since the time of the last census is the tendency towards overlap in the functionality of several types of software packages. Another reason why there is this overlap is perhaps that both GIS (in some incarnations) and the techniques proposed here encourage adoption of an exploratory approach.

A final geographically related issue that should be mentioned is the effect that changing areal units may have on results. This problem was initially identified by Openshaw (1984), and arises from the fact that altering the zonal system into which counts are aggregated may bring about changes in the data patterns that can be observed. This has been discussed at length in the univariate case elsewhere in this volume, but there are some distinct problems associated with multivariate analysis. A major difficulty is the fact that, when working with several proportions or counts aggregated over a zone, one has no idea whether any apparent interactions between these occur at the individual level or not. Interactions at the district level cannot be unquestioningly attributed to the individual level. A paradox of this kind is a case of the *ecological fallacy.* Since, with the exception of the SAR, no census data are available at the individual level, how may one proceed?

One possibility is to consider the scale at which interaction is thought to be important. Without attributing associations down to the individual level, would a high level of unemployment generally have implications on a community with a high proportion of 16–24 year olds? Could these implications be viewed on a wider scale than immediate community; and if so, then how much wider? Considerations of this sort may perhaps suggest an appropriate areal unit to work with, for a particular study. Alternatively, if such questions prove too difficult to answer with any confidence, a more pragmatic approach could be adopted. If one is unsure which zonal system is most appropriate, it may be helpful to examine the variables of interest over several systems and investigate the effects that changes of scale have on the dataset. To illustrate this, the age structure data from Fig. 9.2 are shown once again, at the county level (Fig. 9.11). Whereas the point corresponding to the City of London was very noticeable as an outlier before, this is no longer the case. However, the general shape of the scatterplot has not altered dramatically. Now moving to a smaller geographical scale, the same data for wards in Greater London are shown in Fig. 9.12. This time many

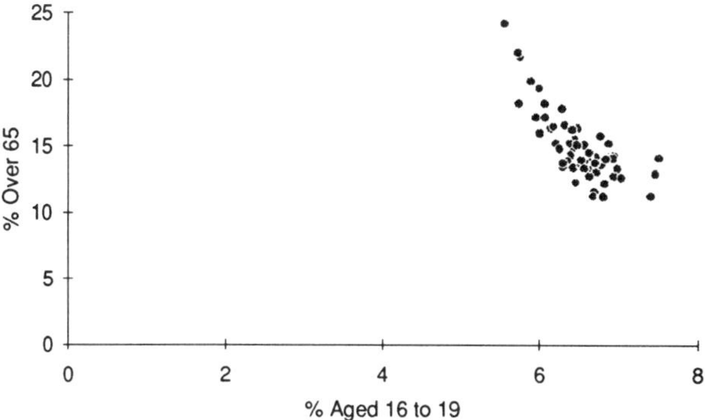

Fig. 9.11 Figure 9.2 redrawn at county level.

more outliers are apparent, with some cases of no people at all in one or other of the age categories. It is interesting to note, however, that although the geographical study area has reduced this time, the general shape of the main part of the scatterplot is similar. There are fewer points in the region corresponding to those areas with a very high proportion of over 65 year olds, but this is perhaps not surprising as the coastal districts identified with these areas previously are not included in this study region. It would seem that, at least in general trends, Greater London is a microcosm of the rest of the country. Looking at all three of these plots certain points can be made. First, outliers here tend to be more prominent the smaller the areal unit used, but the shape of the general trend does not alter with the changes in scale. This may suggest a suitable set of zones to the census user, taking into account the purpose for which the data are used.

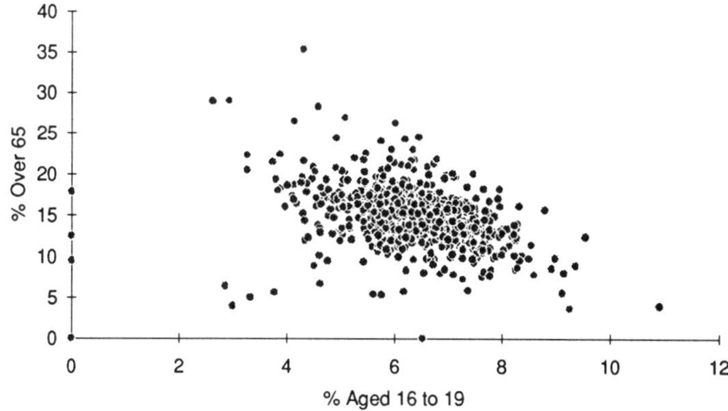

Fig. 9.12 Age structure at ward level (Greater London).

3 Bivariate analytical techniques

3.1 Correlation

In this section, emphasis will be placed on analytical rather than graphical methods. One of the most basic numerical measures of the association between a pair of variables is the *correlation coefficient.* Various forms of correlation coefficient exist, but here attention will be given first to the *product–moment* correlation coefficient of Karl Pearson, usually denoted by r. This coefficient can take values between –1 and +1. A value close to +1 would suggest a strong positive linear association between the two variables, whereas a value close to –1 suggests a strong negative linear observation. A correlation of zero suggests that there is no association between the two variables whatsoever. The use of the term 'linear' in these statements is of importance; this coefficient must be thought of as a measure of *linear* association only. In the case of a perfect non-linear relationship between two variables, the value of the coefficient is unlikely to be equal to +1 or –1.

r is derived for a pair of variables x and y by considering the deviation of each observation from the mean values of each variable, $\bar{x}$ and $\bar{y}$. If there is a strong positive association between the two variables, one would expect that when x was larger than $\bar{x}$ then y would also be larger than $\bar{y}$. That is, cases having above average x values would also have above average y values. Similarly cases where x was below average would be more likely to have below average y values. Consider, then, the quantity $(x-\bar{x})(y-\bar{y})$, calculated for each observation. When x and y are both above average then this quantity is positive, but this is also the case when x and y are both below average, since the two factors in the product are both negative. On the other hand, when there is a negative association between x and y then above average x values are more likely to be accompanied by below average y values, and vice versa. In this case the two factors will be of different signs, so that the product will be negative. Thus the sign of this expression suggests, for each observation, the nature of the association between x and y. Taking the average value of the expression for the entire dataset gives the *covariance*:

$$\text{cov}(x, y) = \frac{\sum (x - \bar{x})(y - \bar{y})}{N}$$

This quantity provides a general measure of the association between the x value and the y value in the data. If very little association exists, then both negative and positive values of $(x - \bar{x})(y - \bar{y})$ are likely to occur, so that the average value will be close to zero. In cases of stronger association, either positive or negative cases will dominate the dataset and so larger magnitudes of covariance will be observed. At this stage, then, a measure of association has been derived, but its value will depend on the units of measure. Taking the age structure example, deciding to work in proportions running from zero to one, rather than percentages, would change the covariance by a factor of 10,000. In order to eliminate this effect, the covariance may be standardized by dividing by the product of the standard deviations of x and y. This then gives a fixed indicator of association regardless of the units of measurement for the variables. This is the correlation coefficient:

$$r(x, y) = \frac{\text{cov}(x, y)}{(\text{var}(x)\ \text{var}(y))^{1/2}}$$

An example of a high value of this coefficient is the correlation between the variables in Fig. 9.3. The scatterplot suggests that there is a strong linear relationship between these variables (total population and total households), and in fact $r = 0.997$. This is an unusually high value of r for much census data, and it may be noted from viewing the examples of several scatterplots in this chapter that the relationships between variables rarely adhere so strongly to a deterministic model of this sort. An important task carried out by the correlation coefficient is to measure the degree of adherence. The greater the magnitude of r, the more closely the scatterplot of the two variables resembles a straight line. In many cases, a linear relationship between the variables is only a general trend, and much more variability about the line should be expected. Consider Fig. 9.12. Although a relationship definitely exists between the variables, this is nothing like the straight line seen in Fig. 9.5. Here, $r = -0.384$. This figure is distinctly different from zero, but not particularly close to -1. In social science data generally, and specifically in census data, r values of this type are commonplace.

A problem when computing correlation coefficients with data expressed as proportions is the fact that in each census aggregation zone there is a different base population. Thus, when working with districts, the City of London as a single observation is given as much importance as any of the other districts, despite having a much smaller base population. One approach to combat this is to work with *weighted* mean values when computing the standard deviations and the covariance. This will reduce the influence of smaller areas of this sort. Usually, weighting should be computed in terms of base populations for each zone. This approach can also be applied to several of the other analytical techniques described in this chapter.

A shortcoming of the product–moment correlation coefficient is the fact that it measures only linear association between the variable pairs. A pair of variables may show some degree of correspondence, but this may not be linear. Therefore values of r may give lower values than might otherwise be expected. To overcome this, one approach is to consider the *ranks* of each variable in the dataset, instead of their actual values. As long as the trend in the relationship between the two variables is *monotone* (i.e. an increase in one variable always leads to an increase in the other, or always leads to a decrease in the other), then the relationship between the ranks of one variable and the other will always appear linear. As an example, consider Fig. 9.11, showing the age structure relationship for counties. This plot suggests that a relationship exists between the two age proportions but that it is not linear. However, in Fig. 9.13, the ranks for each county are plotted;

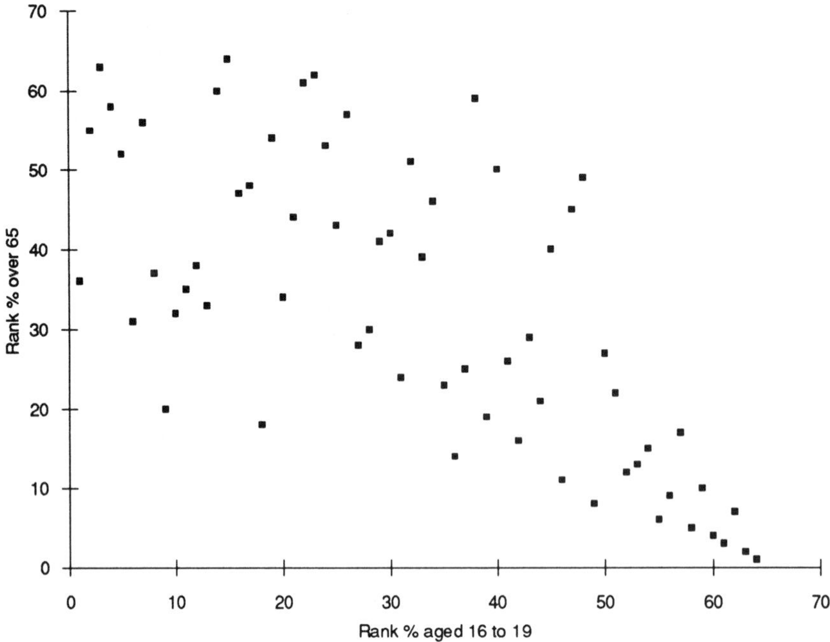

Fig. 9.13 Ranked age structure for each county.

although the pattern of scattering has altered, the trend takes on a more linear shape. This can be used as the basis for another type of correlation coefficient, *Spearman rank correlation coefficient*. Values for each variable are replaced by their rank before the correlation is computed. This coefficient, r_S, can be computed as

$$r_S = 1 - 6\frac{\sum d^2}{N(N-1)}$$

where d is the difference in ranks between the two variables for each zone. It is important to note that r and r_s are not commensurate, so that an r value of 0.4 does not mean the same thing as an r_s value of 0.4. Although both coefficients range from −1 to 1, and values of zero have similar implications, they are measures of different properties of the data. The Spearman rank correlation coefficient allows one to measure a much more general degree of association than a product–moment coefficient, but choice of which coefficient to use will depend on individual studies.

3.2 Regression lines

Regression lines are a commonly used technique for modelling a relationship between two variables x and y. If the relationship appears to be linear, then the relationship between the variables is modelled by $y = ax + b + e$ where a and b are coefficients to be determined and e is an error term. The presence of e is essential in any model that does not assume a perfect mathematical association between x and y. Usually e is modelled as a random variable having a symmetrical distribution (typically Gaussian). This is used as a basis for calibrating a and b; the values of the coefficients giving the most likely set of e values are used as estimates. This technique is often referred to as either 'least squares' or 'maximum likelihood' regression. Regression is strongly related to correlation. The amount of scatter about a fitted line can be thought of as a measure of 'success' of the regression model. Clearly, a large degree of scattering around the fitted line suggests that the model is a poor descriptor of the relationship between x and y. This will also correspond to a low value for r. In fact, the value of $1 - r^2$ is the proportion of the variance in y that is due to the e term in the above model. If r is large, then $1 - r^2$ will be close to zero, suggesting that there is not much deviation from the fitted line. Conversely, if r were zero, then *all* of the variation in y would be due to the error term. x would be considered as having no utility whatsoever as a predictor of y.

There are certain issues in regression modelling which should be raised here. First, the observation should be made that the model described above considers the effect of x as a predictor of y, and that this is not the same as considering y as a predictor of x. The regression model is not symmetric, unlike the correlation coefficient. Coefficients estimated in either case may lead to very different fitted lines on the graph, particularly when r takes on a very low value. Regression models are generally thought of as having a *predictor* variable and a *response*, or sometimes as having an *independent* variable and a *dependent* variable. In this case, the predictor is the x variable and the response is y. This implies a notion of causality in the model, and perhaps this should be reflected in the choice of variables when setting up a regression model. For example, when considering the relationship between proportions of persons employed in professional and managerial employment and of households having three or more cars, it is reasonable to assume that good employment status is a stimulus, and purchasing several cars is a possible response to this. Of course, in view of the ecological fallacy, care should be taken when assumptions of this sort are made. Unfortunately, the distinction between causes and effects is not always clear cut, and this can lead to problems when interpreting the results of regression modelling.

Another important point, linked to the asymmetry of the model, is the fact that only errors in estimating one of the variables are considered in the calibration process. Many statisticians would consider regression to be a univariate rather than a multivariate technique, since it only considers randomness in one of the variables. The technique originates from more controlled environments than that available to the census user. For example, under laboratory conditions, exact amounts of some additive could be dissolved into a compound and the resulting change in the compound's electrical conductivity could be measured. In this case, the x variable could be measured as accurately as possible, and assumed to contain very little error, and the only random effect would be in y, the response to this action. This is not the case with census data. The census user has no ability to control either the x variable or the y variable, effectively making both variables random quantities. In this case, if the purpose of modelling is not to predict one variable from another but to describe the relationship between the two more symmetrically, then different techniques will need to be used. In particular Evans (1983) suggests a line passing through the mean values of x and y whose gradient is equal to the ratio of the standard deviation of x to the standard deviation of y. The sign of the gradient is taken to be that of r. This line has the property of minimizing the perpendicular distances of the points in the scatterplot to the fitted line, rather than the horizontal distances between the fitted line and the points. In this way a symmetrical approach is achieved, and consideration of the linkage between causality and the interpretation of the model is not necessary.

3.3 Non-linearity

In the previous section we discussed various methods for summarizing the relationship between variables using a linear model. However, as noted in the section relating to correlation, the linear assumption is not always valid. In this case no form of linear regression will be of help. Generally, the validity of a linear assumption can be checked by making use of scatterplots. In some cases (Fig. 9.12, for example) there is a clear non-linear relationship between the two variables. One possible approach in cases of this sort is to apply transformations to one or both of the variables. As seen in Chapter 7 a transformation can alter the shape of the distribution of each of the variables, but in two dimensions another important effect is that the shape of the relationship between the variables can also be altered. In this case, the aim is to apply transformations to the data in order to obtain a linear relationship. For example, applying logarithmic transformations to both variables in Fig. 9.12 leads to the scatterplot in Fig. 9.14. In the new scatterplot, a near-linear relationship exists between the two transformed variables.

In this case, then, fitting a line to these data would give a relationship of the form $\log(y) = a+b \log(x)$ which may also be expressed as $y = Ax^B$. Thus an

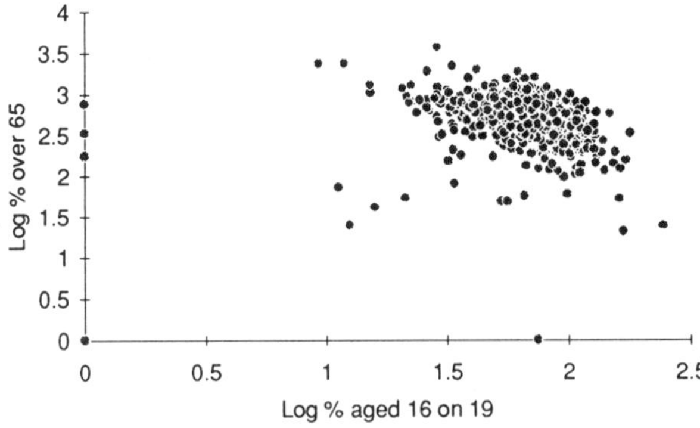

Fig. 9.14 Scatterplot for Fig. 9.12 after logarithmic transformation of both variables.

exponential relationship may be a more suitable model than a linear relationship for these variables. In this example, the correlation coefficient may now be used as a measure of association between the transformed variables, since the relationship between them appears to be linear.

Another issue related to transformations is the phenomenon of uneven scatter or *heteroskedasticity*. When attempting to fit a line to the data, the degree of scatter at one end of the x axis differs from that at the other. This leads to problems when fitting curves. Sometimes, however, this can also be eliminated by the application of transformations. For example, if the degree of scatter increases roughly in proportion to the size of the y value, then taking logs should give a new variable whose variability is fairly constant as the size of the variable increases, since for the unlogged variable the ratio between variability and magnitude of the observation is fairly constant. As ever, the process of finding the right transformation is greatly aided by the use of scatterplots, perhaps also showing the fitted line or curve.

Although transformations are a useful tool, there are cases where the non-linearity of the relationship between variables cannot be resolved by transformation. Some of these can be solved by non-linear regression however. In this case, instead of fitting a straight line to the data, a more complex curve is fitted, such as $y = a + bx + cx^2$. A problem with this approach is that it is not generally a simple matter to calibrate the coefficient values according to the symmetric criteria of the last section, so it is difficult to escape the 'cause and effect' characteristic of least squares linear regression. Generally, the approach in these cases is to 'make do and mend' with the asymmetric techniques, but to bear in mind that the estimates were obtained in this way, particularly when carrying out diagnostics on the results obtained. It is also worth mentioning that although it is generally easy to add complexity to the curve being fitted, for example by increasing the degree of a polynomial being fitted, this is often unhelpful. Having calibrated an algebraically complex curve of this form, it would be extremely difficult (perhaps impossible) to attach meaning to the coefficients, and therefore very little understanding would have been gained from the exercise. Another common problem of interpretation of non-linear curve fitting concerns extrapolation. A particular choice of curve may fit the data well, but *there is no evidence that the same model applies outside the range of observed data.* There are dangers in attempting to predict relationships outside the range of observed figures, or computing asymptotic properties of models from this standpoint. The choice of curve is often a matter of qualitative judgement by the analyst who has inspected the data, and there is no theoretical foundation for any particular functional form. It is therefore unwise to assume that the curve represents some universal law that will apply even at values that have not been observed in the calibration dataset.

Before leaving non-linearity, it is also important to consider the effects that this may have on correlation coefficients. The product–moment coefficient has already been considered, but there are some warnings that must be given relating to Spearman's coefficient also. Although this is capable of measuring some forms of non-linear association, there are cases where even this coefficient can be misleading. If the relationship between a pair of variables is represented by a curve such as $y = a + bx + cx^2$, then it is possible that the non-linear relationship might reach a peak in terms of the y value but then fall off. If this were to happen, the relationship between variables would no longer be monotone, and the ranks given to y variables for low x's would be interlaced with those for high x's. This would give a low value of the statistic, perhaps obscuring a strong, but not monotonic, relationship between the variables. In all cases, then, interpretation of this coefficient should take into account any strong evidence of non-monotonicity suggested by scatterplots or curve fitting.

3.4 Diagnostics, influence and 'robustness'

No discussion on regression and correlation would be complete without some discussion of diagnostic techniques, i.e. techniques which attempt to assess the success of fitting some form of regression model or measurement of correlation. This is a stage in the consideration of two-dimensional modelling where the exploratory techniques in the previous section meet the analytical techniques here. The effect of outliers on regression techniques and correlations is of significance. One might wonder how many district level models of bivariate relationship have had their parameter estimates distorted by the observation for the City of London (Fig. 9.1). The effect of this outlying point can be to 'pull' coefficient estimates away from the values they would attain on the basis of the rest of the data, and so distort the calibration or estimation process. When such unusual observations occur, they should be treated as special cases. If a curve fitting analysis takes place in order to describe a general trend in the data, then clearly these observations are not part of the trend and should not be treated as such.

In bivariate analysis, the easiest way to identify such observations is simply to plot the data. As suggested in the earlier section, extreme cases should then become apparent. When modelling, or curve fitting, another useful approach is the *residual plot*. This is simply a plot of the error in the fitted model for each zone. Usually this is measured in terms of discrepancy of the fitted y value and the true value, but there is no reason why this could not also be applied to the perpendicular differences of the symmetric line relations discussed in an earlier section. Plots of this sort offer an alternative means of identifying outlying cases. Sometimes this approach may be more helpful than plotting the raw values, particularly if the relationship between the two variables is not linear.

Thus, if one is comparing a fitted curve to observed data points, outliers may be discovered. However, the discovery of an outlier then suggests that the fitted curve may have been distorted in some way, since that outlier was actually part of the calibration dataset. An important measure of the validity of the model as it stands might be attained by considering how it would alter if the outlier were not in the dataset. Put another way, a helpful approach to diagnostics would be to take each case in turn and leave them out of the analysis, checking the effect of doing this. This is the basis for the method of *leave-one-out analysis*. Consider, for example, the data in Fig. 9.1. If the correlation coefficient for this dataset were computed, a misleadingly low figure might be obtained owing to the influence of the City of London. A leave-one-out analysis could be carried out here by computing, for each district, the change in the correlation coefficient when it is excluded from the calculation. This produces a new variable for each district, which is, in effect, a measure of its exceptionality. When this is done for the data in Fig. 9.1, the largest value is associated with the City of London. However, looking at the distribution of values for each district, it can be seen that this is the only single observation having such a notable effect on the coefficient. The amount of distorting influence this case appears to have on the entire calculation would suggest that it should indeed be treated as an exception, and that the correlation coefficient computed without this value gives a 'truer' picture for the rest of these data.

The ideas of leave-one-out analysis can be applied to other types of analysis in addition to the correlation coefficient. For example, the difference between an observed y value and its fitted value *when the observation is excluded from the regression* can be a useful detector of rogue cases having an unnecessarily large influence on regression models. There is widespread interest in this kind of technique, taking the ideas beyond the rather simplistic approach advocated here. See Efron (1982) for an example. An important extension of the technique is to consider the effects of leaving more than one point out of the analysis. If there is more than one outlier in the data, then there is a danger that even removing one point at a time will not give distorted analyses. An analytical approach can be taken with leave-two-out or leave-three-out investigations, where all possible two-way or three-way combinations of places would be left out, but it is important to remember that the number of n-way combinations of cases increases factorially with n, and that for very large datasets such as a ward level dataset for the entire country the computational overheads may prove prohibitive. An alternative strategy, perhaps in a more exploratory vein, is to make use of interactive scatterplots again. A scatterplot could be drawn, with a fitted curve superimposed. As points were selected, the curve could be recalibrated without using the selected points. In this way, the user could visually identify potentially troublesome n-way combinations of cases and investigate the effect of their exclusion from the model.

A final point to mention in this section is the concept of *robust regression*. In a similar manner to measures of central tendency such as the median, or measures of spread such as the inter-quartile range, robust regression is designed to be reasonably resistant to exceptional observations. An example of such a technique is given in Mosteller and Tukey (1977). In these techniques, it is expected that although outliers may exist in the data the values of the leave-one-out statistics will not be particularly extreme, as the calibration techniques should be resistant to such phenomena. Although this approach tends to be more computationally intensive than straightforward regression, one can perhaps feel more confident in the relationships that it identifies.

4 Multivariate analytical techniques

4.1 Introduction

In this section, analytical techniques which may be applied to datasets having more than two variables will be considered. In some cases, these may be multidimensional extensions of the techniques considered in the last section, but in other cases they are methods that are unique to datasets having a large number of variables. The concepts of diagnostics and the assessment of the success of analyses are equally important in the multidimensional case. However, as discussed in the section on exploratory techniques, examination and diagnosis in multidimensional space is considerably harder than in the two-dimensional case. Numerical rather than visual approaches are sometimes necessary.

Perhaps owing to the complexity of multidimensional spaces, many of the techniques here aim to express the patterns and structure within several variables in a smaller dimensional space, or to summarize the structure as a set of clusters. The problems of extremely complex datasets are addressed by Openshaw elsewhere in this book, but for completeness, and to serve as a guide to the reader wishing to see these methods in the framework of the other techniques suggested in this chapter, a 'lightning tour' of some of them will be incorporated in this section.

4.2 Correlation and partial correlation

The correlation coefficient was seen to be a useful measure of association between a pair of variables. However, a useful starting point for examining a dataset having more than two variables would be to consider the association between all possible pairs of variables in the dataset. When there are a large number of variables, this could be thought of as a numerical proxy for a scatterplot matrix if the values for all the correlation coefficients are arranged in a square array, with the rows and columns corresponding to each variable in the study. Although this gives no indication of outliers, it may be used to identify pairs of variables having strong association against those which do not. A great deal of insight into the structure of a multivariate dataset can be gained by the highlighting (using a marker pen) of those cells in the correlation matrix having reasonably large values.

The concept of correlation can also be considered in a multivariate sense. Suppose two variables are measuring very similar quantities (say household density and population density per square hectare) and both of these are used to predict a third (unemployment levels, for example). If there is a strong relationship between one of the first two variables and the last one, then one would expect there also to be a relationship between the other of the first two variables and the last, due to the strength of the linkage between the first two variables. This three-way relationship could be summarized using a correlation matrix but another alternative is to make use of *partial correlation*. The partial correlation between a pair of variables, given a third, can be thought of as the linkage between the initial pair of variables *once the effect of the third has been accounted for*. In this case, although the correlation between population density and unemployment may be high, the correlation between these quantities given housing density could be much lower, since there is very little *extra* predictive ability that population density can offer once housing density has already been used as a predictor. It should be noted, however, that this type of analysis takes on board the asymmetric cause and effect nature of a regression model, and that unless distinct causes and effects can be attributed to each of the variables there will be some question as to the validity of the analysis.

4.3 Regression

The concept of regression, introduced as a bivariate technique, can be extended to situations where there are several variables. The problem can be viewed once more as a line fitting exercise, but in this case the model takes the form

$$y = a + b_1x_1 + b_2x_2 + b_3x_3 + \ldots + b_nx_n + e$$

where the linear coefficients for several x values are to be computed. Note that, as in the bivariate case, there is an asymmetrical relationship between the x values and the y value. In this case, the assumption is that all the x values are linked to a cause and that the y variable measures an effect. Also in common with the bivariate case, the only variable in this model that is assumed to be random is the y measure. All the others are considered to be fixed quantities. These assumptions sit uneasily in the context of census data where, as before, *all* of the variables should be thought of as random observations from a multivariate probability distribution. In this context, it seems unreasonable only to include a term for the y error in the model. This also relates to the coefficient estimation procedure. Here the error term measures the discrepancy of the estimation of the y value but does not consider discrepancies relating to any other variables.

If a set of possible 'causal' variables and an 'effect' variable can be identified, then the next problem to be addressed is to determine which of the candidates for causal variables really does seem to have any predictive power. This can be considered in terms of *significance tests*. The introduction of a new variable into the regression model cannot *reduce* the levels of error observed. Clearly, introducing the new variable with a coefficient of zero would have the same quality of fit as the model without that variable, and one expects that some non-zero coefficient would improve on this. The question to be asked is more 'does the introduction of the new variable give a better improvement in the model than one would expect to occur if there were no association?' The typical test of this would be a significance test such as is introduced in many texts on introductory statistical analysis, based on the null hypothesis of no association between the newly introduced variable and the y variable. If a great deal of improvement in the model is observed, then under the null hypothesis it is unlikely that this could have occurred at random, and it would seem reasonable to include the variable in the regression model. It is important to note, however, that the assumption made here is that the error term in the model follows a Gaussian distribution, and if this is not the case then the calculations for the likelihood of obtaining the observed improvement in fit will be inaccurate.

There are also many schemes for *automatic regression*, which attempt to select a subset of variables from a given set to be included in the final model. In such schemes, the criteria for inclusion can take into account the R^2 value, which is a measure of the degree of variation in the y variate attributable the linear predictor part of the model (as opposed to the random error part), the number of variables in the model and the number of cases (these will be census areal units here). Some methods will attempt to fit regression models for all possible combinations of variables (2^p if there are p variables), but clearly this would become impossible for large numbers of variables. In these cases, techniques such as *stepwise regression* are sometimes applied. In these techniques, at a given stage each variable is experimentally added to the model in turn, and the 'best' one according to some criterion is kept. This leads to a new model, and the rest of the variables are once more experimentally added and a 'winner' selected, until a point is reached where the 'best' variable does not offer significant improvement, again by some prescribed criterion. Variations on this theme in which variables are selectively removed from the model are also in existence. There are problems with these sorts of methods, however, since they can be sensitive to changes in the criteria for including a new variable in the model. This can lead to difficulties in interpreting the results of analyses.

In many cases, the relationship between the cases will not be linear. As with the bivariate case, the application of transformations may often be helpful here, although if the number of dimensions is very large there will not be any visual clues available as to how successful the transformations have been. Another possible approach, again extending the bivariate case, is to fit non-linear models in more than two dimensions. As with the use of transformations, however, it is difficult to assess the fit of such models visually, perhaps with the exception of the three-dimensional case where curved surfaces could also be superimposed on spin plots. However, it should be stated that unless there is some strong theoretical justification for a particular mathematical relationship to exist between the variables in the model (which is unlikely with census data), then such modelling and its interpretation is unlikely to provide many fruitful results.

4.4 Principal component analysis

The introductory part of the last section highlights the difficulties associated with the asymmetry between the y variable and the x variables in many multiple regression techniques. With much census data this is likely to be problematic, and as with the bivariate case symmetrical approaches which treat each variable identically are of more value. One such technique, which will be described briefly here, is that of principal components analysis. In this technique, a linear combination of the variables is sought, but it is chosen not for its ability to predict one variable in terms of all of the others (the source of the asymmetry in regression modelling) but to maximize variance. That is, it is an attempt to find an index, which is a linear combination of all the variables, that best highlights the differences between the different census areal units. This linear combination will contain *all* of the variables in the dataset, and does not require the identification and separation of 'cause' and 'effect' variables. The variable obtained from this linear combination is referred to as the *first principal component*. Once this linear combination has been found, a second linear combination is sought which maximizes the variance but is constrained to be independent of the first, so that the correlation between the first and second principal components is zero. A third is then computed, this time subject to the constraint of being independent of both the first and second components. This process may be repeated until the pth component has been found, where p is the number of variables under study.

Given that these components were selected to maximize the level of variance, it is hoped that a small number of these will account for a large proportion of the variance in the data as a whole. In an ideal situation, if the first component accounted for, say, 95% of all variance, then a one-dimensional indicator would suffice to show much of the variety in the dataset. This is not always the case, however, and two or three components may be required to account for most of the variance. However, in two- or three-dimensional space, these components may be plotted and examined using some of the exploratory methods mentioned earlier in the chapter, so that the identification of structures and groupings within the data may then be possible.

Another issue which should be raised here is that of choice of units of measurement for each of the variables in the analysis. Clearly, changing the unit of measurement for one particular variable will also change the variance in that variable. This could lead to difficulties with the interpretation of the principal components, as the coefficients for the linear combination would tend to favour those variables measured in the largest units. One way of overcoming this is to base principal components analysis on the *standardized* variables, i.e. variables that have had their mean value subtracted and have been divided by their standard deviation. In this way, all variables will have a mean of zero and a standard deviation of unity, so that the effects of scale have been removed from the analysis.

A final topic, but a vital one, in the analysis of principal components is that of interpretation. The analysis will provide indices, but what are they indices of? Having found a small set of indices that highlight the variability of the different census areas in the study, the most important question to ask is 'what does vary most notably between places?' An essential aspect of principal components analysis, for the census user, is to interpret the coefficients of the components that have been computed. This process, which attempts to assign meaning to each of the principal component indices, is known as *reification*. For example, a component having large positive coefficients for population density and housing density but a large negative one for number of rooms per household could be thought of as an index of 'crowding', since large positive values of the index would suggest low rooms per household in a densely populated region. In this way, attempts are made to interpret all notable principal components in a particular study. In these studies, it is generally hoped that a clear interpretation is possible, although on occasions it can be a difficult task to attribute meaning to the components.

4.5 Projection pursuit

In a similar vein to principal components is the technique of *projection pursuit.* In the case of principal components, a projection from a high dimensional space to a low one is derived, having the property of maximizing the variance in the low dimensional space. This concept can be extended by finding projections satisfying different conditions. For example, instead of maximizing the variance, projections could be specified having the property of maximizing the effect of outliers. This would help in visualizing the data in two or three dimensions. Another possibility might be to project the variables onto a one-dimensional space but with the aim of minimizing spatial autocorrelation. The value of this would be to highlight the difference between areas and identify geographical regions having very distinct properties from their neighbours.

The general problem of finding projections to meet a given requirement is referred to as projection pursuit (see, for example, the final chapter of Silverman 1986). The technique has become popular since the last census, mainly as a result of the increased graphical and computational abilities of currently available computing equipment, and it is expected that in the coming decade more use will be made of techniques of this kind to explore large collections of census variables.

4.6 Diagnostics

As with bivariate analysis, diagnostics applied to multivariate methods are extremely valuable. When working with very large numbers of variables, it is much harder to make use of visual techniques, but the identification of outliers and of anomalous areas that distort the results of analysis is essential if the output of the analysis is to be of any value. For example, when a principal components analysis takes place, care should be taken that an unusually large contribution to the total variance in the data is not due to a single observation (for example Tamworth in Fig. 9.7), which could lead to a somewhat distorted choice of coefficients. If a very large number of variables were fed into the analysis, then graphical diagnostics may present problems, but use could be made of the 'leave-one-out' approach in Section 3.4. Here, the effect of omitting cases could be measured by changes in the coefficients for the first principal component or for the value of the component itself for each case. In this way, cases having a strong distorting influence on the computation could be singled out.

Another useful kind of diagnostic in multiple regression is the examination of residuals. Residuals are the differences between fitted and actual values for the y variable. Again, if there are a large number of x variables, then identifying areas which do not adhere to the general trend may be difficult graphically, but it is reasonable to expect such areas to have outstandingly large negative or positive residuals. The analysis of residuals is also helpful in identifying when extra variables should be included in a model. If there is a systematic problem with a particular model, then a possible reason for this is that a particular factor has been ignored. If this is the case, there will be a strong correspondence between the residuals and some census-based indicator relating to this factor. If this is suspected to be the case, then scatterplots of these two quantities should be drawn, and if a relationship is apparent then the new indicator should be incorporated into the model.

Finally, the effects of spatial autocorrelation can also be checked by mapping the residuals. If the values of the residual seem to show geographical clustering (for example a large number of negative residuals in neighbouring areas), then there is probably a strong effect of spatial autocorrelation. In this case, care should be taken in the interpretation of any confidence limits placed around parameter estimates, and of any significance tests based around the regression model. In such a case, the analysis may be better executed using a regression technique that takes autocorrelation into account (see Ripley 1981), rather than a standard least squares technique.

5 Conclusion

5.1 Recommended methods

Whenever possible, it is important that the analyst remains aware of the 'raw' data. Understanding of the structure in a dataset cannot be complete if it is based solely on a set of summary statistics. Wherever possible, use should be made of graphical techniques, particularly scatterplots, with the occasional use of spin plots and scatterplot matrices when these are necessary. Linked plots such as those offered by SPIDER and XLISP-STAT are often of use here, as are linked maps. An important task performed by this kind of approach is the detection of outlying values and general trends in the data and for diagnostics applied to other techniques. In all cases, it is valuable to consider the results of univariate analysis of all variables under study before attempting to interpret the outcome of multivariate analysis.

The use of regression techniques should be treated with caution when working with census data. As identified many times in this chapter, regression techniques require the user to identify an 'effect' variable and several cause variables, whereas often in census data the task is to identify structure in the variables, treating each one impartially. For this reason, methods that are 'symmetric', in the sense that the role played by each of the variables in the analysis is interchangeable, are preferred here, unless there are strong substantive reasons for identifying one variable that is dependent on all of the others. Such symmetrical methods include the graphical techniques discussed above, the use of principal components analysis and the computation of correlation coefficients. In the case of principal components analysis, the interpretation may be harder than for the other methods, but a possible benefit of this technique is that it may be possible to 'project' a dataset having a large number of variables into a one-, two- or three-dimensional space, allowing examination using some of the exploratory techniques to take place.

A final consideration when discussing methods for the analysis of census results is that all of these data are geographical. One would expect many of the processes that the census variables reflect to be taking place in a spatial concept. This has many implications for multivariate analysis. First, the assumption in basic regression techniques is that each observation is independent of all others. In a geographical context this is highly unlikely to be the case, since neighbouring regions are likely to be connected in some way by the underlying geographical processes. This is perhaps further argument against the use of such techniques. A second consideration is that of the choice of areal units. As has been demonstrated in this chapter, patterns in the data can alter when different levels of areal aggregation occur. The interpretation of these patterns can also vary if the spatial scale at which the underlying processes take place is considered, alongside the notion of the ecological fallacy. Clearly care has to be taken in deciding which set of areal units is appropriate for any particular study.

5.2 Recommended software

The task of recommending any particular software is a difficult one. Since the time of the 1991 Census, several advances have occurred in computer technology, which has in turn increased the choices available to the user. In the age of the ZX81, high resolution graphics and the ability to compute correlation coefficients for several thousand census wards were the domain of the computer specialist. In the 10 years between then and the current census, high resolution graphics and reasonably powerful 'number crunching' facilities have become available on a desktop PC, and there has been a vast increase in the choice of software packages able to take advantage of these facilities. In particular, the last 10 years has seen the rise of the spreadsheet as a statistical analysis tool. Although lacking some of the more advanced statistical methods, most are able to compute correlation coefficients, fit regression lines (if you must) and produce scatterplots. As an example, Microsoft's Excel package has all of these abilities, but there will be many other systems currently on sale also able to supply this functionality.

Although offering a reasonable number of graphical methods, it is unlikely that spreadsheets will offer many of the techniques suggested in the exploratory data analysis section of this chapter, such as scatterplots linked with maps or spin plots. For this, more specialized data visualization or exploratory software is required, such as the XLISP-STAT, SPIDER or MacSPIN packages. The author has had some experience with XLISP-STAT (which is in the public domain), and since this package also contains a complete programming language (XLISP) it is possible to use it to perform other statistical computations such as the leave-one-out analyses mentioned in this chapter.

Some of the more advanced quantitative methods, such as principal components analysis, are best performed by 'traditional' statistical packages such as SAS and SPSS. Again, there is some overlapping of functionality between these and the packages of the last paragraph, since SAS also offer a data visualization module, allowing spin plots to be produced. Although such packages offer regression techniques, these are not techniques which can take spatial autocorrelation into account, and so should be approached with some caution. Finally, it should be mentioned that although this kind of package will offer many sophisticated techniques, there are dangers in applying such methods blindly to the data. Taking as an example the regression techniques that are available, any analysis will be based on a number of assumptions. These may or may not be appropriate to the data being used, but the user should take a cautious view of any new technique and consider carefully the validity of its assumptions in the context of the current study. For example, the assumption of spatial independence in the regression model is not likely to be reasonable when working with census data. As a 'rule of thumb' any methods on offer that attempt to model a causal relationship between sets of variables are less likely to be of use than those that search for general structures in the data, but as a final word of warning no technique should be applied unless the census analyst is fully aware of the principles involved, the assumptions made and their meaning in the context of the study being undertaken.

References

Champion, A G, A E Green, D W Owen, D J Ellin and M G Coombes 1987 *Changing Places: Britain's Demographic, Economic and Social Complexion*. London: Edward Arnold.

Efron B 1982 *The Jackknife, the Bootstrap, and other Resampling Plans*. Philadelphia: Society for Industrial and Applied Mathematics.

Evans I S 1983 Bivariate and multivariate analysis: relationships between variables. In D W Rhind (ed) *A Census User's Handbook*. London: Methuen.

Haslett, J, G Wills and A Unwin 1990 SPIDER – An interactive statistical tool for the analysis of spatially distributed data. *International Journal of Geographical Information Systems* 4 (3), 285–96.

Mosteller, F and J W Tukey 1977 *Data Analysis and Regression: A Second Course in Statistics*. Reading, MA: Addison-Wesley.

Openshaw, S 1984 *The Modifiable Areal Unit Problem*, Catmog 38. Norwich: Geo-Abstracts.

Ripley, B D 1981 *Spatial Statistics*. New York: Wiley.

Silverman, B W 1986 *Density Estimation For Statistics and Data Analysis*. New York: Chapman and Hall.

Tierney, L 1990 *LISP-STAT: An Object Oriented Environment For Statistical Computing and Dynamic Graphics*. New York: Wiley.

Tukey, J W 1977 *Exploratory Data Analysis*. Reading, MA: Addison-Wesley.

10

Analysis of change through time

A G Champion

Editor's note

The last few decades of the twentieth century are a time of unprecedented socio-economic change. The entire post-war nature of the UK's economy is changing (some might say has changed) in a most fundamental manner. The census provides the only data source able to document the impact of these changes. The ability of the 1991 Census to continue the small area time series started in 1971 and continued by the 1981 Census is very important. This chapter discusses the comparability of census variables over a 20-year period. However, it leaves untouched the even more difficult problem of establishing a small area geography that is also consistent over the 20 years. In general terms this geographical base areas problem probably cannot be solved in a completely accurate and consistent manner, except by changes in the way the Census is managed; although individual users might be able to handle it in their regions and at their scales of interest. Readers might also wish to link this chapter with the census geography sections of Chapters 2 and 5.

1 Introduction

> Regardless of discipline, academic and social scientists believe that the census should enable statements to be made about social change. They are concerned to be able to distinguish real trends from artefactual change brought about by altering census definitions.
>
> (Marsh *et al.* 1988, p. 854)

This statement neatly encapsulates the justification for, and central argument of, this chapter. The identification and analysis of change is essential for several reasons, not least to provide a more informed basis for forward projection and

This chapter contains the latest information available at the time of writing (April 1993).

to obtain a clearer understanding of the way in which society is evolving in its composition, behaviour and relationship to space. Yet the task of studying change through the comparison of data from successive censuses is fraught with difficulty, because of operational changes made between censuses designed to improve their relevance and reliability and because of differences in the degree to which they achieved their aims.

This chapter begins by outlining why it is so important to attempt to study change over time. It then describes some of the principal difficulties in doing this, concentrating on aspects of statistical comparability. These include changes in the range of questions included on the census form, differences in the definitions of individual concepts such as 'household', alterations in the way in which questions are asked or the answers were coded, differences between censuses in the level of coverage achieved in what is theoretically a full (i.e. 100%) enumeration, and differences in the definition of the population base for which tabulations are produced. Greatest attention is given to 1981–91 comparisons, with some reference back to 1971 (the first 100% census for which machine-readable small area statistics were produced systematically). A longer-term perspective on studying intercensal changes since 1801 can be found in Norris and Mounsey (1983), while McKee (1989a, b, c) provides a detailed account of the problems of using the 1971 and 1981 Censuses for studying change.

At the outset, it is important to stress that this account does not aim to be fully comprehensive, but should be used in conjunction with the more detailed documentation provided by the census authorities. The aspects covered should be considered as examples of the types of problems faced. This is one reason, along with limitations of space, why no attention is given to the Census of Northern Ireland which, though somewhat different in design, poses a similar range of problems for the analysis of change over time. Issues relating to comparability of small area geography are also given only the barest mention, these being given separate treatment (see Chapters 2, 4 and 5). Perhaps most importantly for most census users, no attention is given to changes in the way in which variables are cross-tabulated against each other in the standard output datasets. This is a huge topic, given the substantial variations even at a single census between the various outputs (Small Area Statistics (SAS), Local Base Statistics/County Reports (LBS) and Topic Volumes), let alone variations between censuses; and, moreover, it is an issue which takes on a rather different significance now that, in addition to being able to order specially commissioned tables, users can specify their own cross-tabulations by using the Samples of Anonymized Records (SAR) and the OPCS Longitudinal Study and thereby, where desirable and appropriate, regenerate the 1991 data to conform with the specifications of a variable or whole table found in an earlier census.

2 Why study change between censuses?

Before getting into detail about the possibilities and pitfalls of studying change over time from census data, it is important to provide a justification for such analyses. In the present context, there are two elements to the answer. One relates to the general need for a dynamic picture, while the other concerns the particular importance of analysing change in the period up to 1991.

2.1 The general need for a dynamic picture

In the first place, for many purposes it is not sufficient merely to treat the Population Census as a stocktaking exercise relating to a single point in time. This is particularly the case for operations requiring up-to-date intelligence on local populations, such as for government targeting of spatial programmes to address specific policy issues and for private sector planning for mailshots, store location and the like. Problems arise even early on in an intercensal period because the detailed census results may be two years or more out of date before they are available to users, and they become increasingly severe as time elapses after one decennial census before the results of the next one appear, eventually involving a gap of around 12 years.

Because of this, it is vital to know which types of characteristics tend to change most over time and which are relatively static. Where these are not continuously or frequently (say annually) monitored by other data sources – not many can be monitored at the local scale (i.e. within individual local authority districts) and quite a large number cannot be followed in more spatial detail than the standard regions – comparisons between censuses can help to identify the type, direction and scale of trends. Such information can then be used for estimating developments since the most recent census point, adopting some method of onward projection.

Second, this type of information is extremely valuable for forecasting the future, as is required in many applications in both private and public sectors (Champion 1993; Dugmore 1993). The most common approach, using forward projection techniques, needs data on past trends as a basis for extrapolation. Arguably, the results should be more accurate if they are based on a model which has been developed to explain, or at least simulate, past patterns of change and which has been tested out and calibrated by reference to historical experience.

Lastly, empirical analysis of past trends is vital for extending knowledge of the processes producing change. This can provide a more satisfactory basis for the type of forecasting work just described, but it is also of immense importance in its own right both as an intellectual challenge and for the insights which it can reveal about evolving patterns of human behaviour and societal organization. As mentioned at the outset of the book, only the Population Census can provide a sufficiently wide range of information at a local scale to enable the spatial aspects and correlates of these patterns to be explored in any great detail.

2.2 The specific importance of the 1991 Census

The Population Census of 1991 is an especially important source for this type of work. There are primarily two reasons for this. One is that the 1980s is widely deemed to have seen more dramatic economic and social change in Britain than other recent decades, embracing not only a period of major restructuring stemming from wider changes in the world economy but also the timespan of the main impacts of the 'Thatcher experiment'. The other reason is the ability to analyse small area data for more than one period of intercensal change, now possible for the first time because the 1971 Census is the first for which comprehensive machine-readable data are available for small areas.

The possibility of comparing three census points at small area scale has several advantages. One is that it permits the developments of the 'Thatcher decade' to be studied in a longer-term context, allowing an assessment of how different this period was from previous experience. A second benefit is that, for relatively slowly changing aspects of British geography, the 20-year period of change 1971–91 may provide a more sensitive and accurate measure than a single intercensal decade, bearing in mind the sorts of errors and distortions which occur at any single census owing to the quality of the data (particularly for those items coded only for a 10% sample) and to any special features of the timing of the census in relation to short-term fluctuations. A third benefit, as we shall see later, is the fact that the 1991 Census form requested information on several topics which were included in 1971 but omitted in 1981.

2.3 A cautionary note

All these comments on the importance of studying intercensal change and on the benefits of being able to compare data derived from the last three censuses at small area scale need to be borne in mind throughout the rest of this chapter. Such are the problems and pitfalls of comparing the results of separate censuses that only extremely good reasons can justify all the effort and care required. Indeed, the difficulties are sufficient to deter most of the usual purchasers of census data, evidenced by the fact that, owing to the very limited use made of the 1971–81 Change File, no similar dataset on 1981–91 has been produced by the census authorities. As a result, individuals wanting to analyse 1981–91 and 1971–91 change need to construct the datasets for themselves by identifying comparable variables and common geographies. To do this successfully, some vital questions need to be addressed, as outlined in the introduction (Section 1).

3 Variation in the range of topics covered

This section deals with the most obvious and straightforward problem faced when undertaking comparisons between censuses – the addition or deletion of questions. These involve topics for which the analysis of change between censuses is, by definition, impossible – though some exceptions are noted below.

The 1991 Census form contained four completely new questions compared with the 1981 form; these were on ethnic group, limiting long-term illness, term-time address of students and weekly hours worked. In addition, the amenities question included a new section on central heating. Furthermore, thanks to a method based on identifying and classifying household spaces in multi-occupied buildings with a separate or shared entrance, a count of dwellings has been made in 1991 that was not available in 1981. Also, the housing information entered on the form by enumerators in England and Wales in 1991 provided some extra detail on dwelling type that had previously been recorded only in Scotland. Finally, there was no separate question on employment status in 1991.

Though calculation of change over time is generally not feasible for these topics, there are a number of exceptions. In relation to employment status, comparison between 1981 and 1991 is still possible because the categories for the self-employed were included in the question on economic position. There are also several topics for which a 1971-91 comparison is possible because they were covered in 1971 but not in 1981. The 'new' question on weekly hours worked had been included in 1971, so a 20-year change analysis can be made. Similarly, in 1971 an attempt was made to count dwellings, so here too a 1971–91 comparison is possible. There is also some speculation that a relatively accurate calculation can be made of 20-year change in the size of ethnic minority populations, given that the majority of their members in 1971 can be identified by reference to data on parents' birthplaces (a question which was not asked in 1981) – though note that such 1971 estimates will be affected by the fair number of people born of British parents during periods of 'colonial service' in countries which are now part of the New Commonwealth.

In sum, the main effect of changes betweeen 1981 and 1991 in the range of data collected is that extra questions have been asked rather than any main topics dropped. Both of the two latest censuses contained counts of people and households, and information on housing, the availability of cars, the age, sex and marital status of each person, change of address since 12 months before, country of birth, household composition, Welsh and Gaelic language (in Wales and Scotland respectively) and economic activity – all at the 100% level of coding. The common 10% topics comprise household and family composition, occupation, social class, socioeconomic group, industry, workplace and transport to work, and qualifications.

4 Definitional comparability between censuses

Communality of topic coverage in the 1981 and 1991 censuses does not, however, guarantee the practicality or reliability of change calculations because of two other two sources of non-comparability; first, amendment of the form of the question (most commonly, through a change in the categories listed on the census form as alternative answers to a question) and second, alteration of the categories used for presenting the census data in the output data provided for public use (most notably, in the way that the finest set of categories are grouped for publication in the tables in the LBS and SAS). These two provide many pitfalls for the unwary, not least because they are not always apparent from the output tables themselves.

As these two sources of non-comparability overlap to a certain extent in their effects, in the following paragraphs they are treated side by side on a topic-by-topic basis, indicating what is directly comparable and highlighting the cases where problems arise. On the other hand, it is important to recognize a distinction between the two in terms of the potential ability to get round the difficulty. Whereas it is impossible to do anything about the first problem because this arises from the way in which the data have been collected, there is the possibility of using the SAR or of ordering specially commissioned tables to regenerate 1991 variables and tables on a basis comparable to those in earlier censuses.

The account below does not get involved in a high level of detail because space here is limited and because technical guidance is available from the Census Offices, most notably through the Definitions volumes and the User Guides on statistical comparability. It is also the case that the output categories on any particular variable will vary between tables and between the different datasets, normally being at their most disaggregated in the Topic Volumes and progressively more coarse in the LBS and SAS (see Chapter 2). The comments below refer largely to the most disaggregated versions, so anyone wishing to run category-based comparisons at ward or enumeration district level needs to check the groupings used in the relevant datasets.

4.1 Population

The definition of a 'person' for enumeration purposes was virtually the same in 1991 as in 1981. The only differences concerned coverage in relation to shipping. Foreign-registered ships in British ports on census night were enumerated in 1991, whereas they had not been in 1981, while the opposite was the case for people on vessels on coastal trips, fishing voyages and voyages between Great Britain and Northern Ireland, the Isle of Man and the Channel Isles, who had been enumerated in 1981 but were not in 1991.

The only change between 1971 and 1981 in relation to the population count and derived tables was the classification of visitors used in the SAS. In 1971 visitors were differentiated according to whether they came from somewhere else in Great Britain or from outside it. In 1981 the relevant area was the UK, as was also the case in 1991.

Much more important numerically are changes in the population base used in the output tables. In conceptual terms, the change between 1971 and 1981 is the more dramatic, since it involved a shift from 'population present' (i.e. the enumerated population, treated at their place of enumeration) to the 'usually resident' principle in 1981. The 'usually resident (present/absent)' base used in most of the 1981 SAS tables, however, is quite different from the 'usually resident (topped-up present/absent)' base used in most of the 1991 Census LBS and SAS tables, in that whereas the former excludes all households wholly absent from their usual residence on census night, the latter includes both wholly-absent households who sent in their census forms voluntarily on their return and imputed households for occupied household spaces for which no form was available for processing. The significance of this change in base between 1981 and 1991 is examined in more detail below in the section on census coverage (see pages 325-9).

In analyses of change for both 1971–81 and 1981–91, it should also be remembered that a processing error affected the 1981 counts. The result was that the figure given for the population present in private households on census night in 1981 was higher than it was in reality, and the figure for the population usually resident in private households was lower. Nationally, the error was estimated at around 0.2% of the total population present (i.e. around 100,000 people), but the effect was considered to be more pronounced for some districts and counties than for others. For instance, in the southeast region the 'present population' in the 1981 SAS was understated in 100 of the 131 districts, according to McKee (1989c). The effects were considered significant enough for the OPCS to decide that the 1981 'population present' data in the 1991 County Monitors and Reports for England and Wales should be represented by the counts from the 1981 Preliminary Report rather than the 'final' figures from the 1981 SAS and County Reports.

4.2 Households

The definition of a 'household' used in the 1991 Census is identical to that in the 1981 Census, but the latter represented a change from the practice in 1971. In 1971 the sole criterion for identifying a household was that the persons should have a regular arrangement to share at least one meal a day, which could be breakfast, but the 1981 definition allowed an alternative criterion that occupants sharing a common living or sitting room should be regarded as a single household. The effect of this change was that in some cases persons who would have been treated as separate households in 1971 were regarded as just one household in 1981. Comparisons of 1991 households with 1971 will be affected by this change in definition, but not analyses of change between 1981 and 1991.

Lastly, in the same way that the population base changed between 1971 and 1981, so also did the household base used in the bulk of the statistical output. Whereas in 1981 the base comprised households with residents, in 1971 it was defined in terms of households with persons present. The only exception is in the topic volume on household composition in 1971, which used a 'usual residents' definition, though even this varied in detail from the 1981 approach because of its different treatment of absent households. The approach in 1991 was identical to that in 1981, so change analyses for the latest decade can be undertaken as confidently as is permitted by the change in coverage (see below).

4.3 Communal establishments

'Communal establishments' refers principally to establishments in which some form of communal catering is provided. In practice, however, the heading covers everyone who is not enumerated in a private household and who was referred to as 'population not in private households' in 1981 and all previous censuses. The term therefore includes campers and also persons sleeping rough (previously known as 'vagrants').

Data collection for this part of the population was undertaken in a very similar way in 1991 as for the two previous censuses, but the statistical output has changed between each census. Between 1981 and 1991 the number of major categories in the classification of communal establishments identifiable in tables has been expanded from 12 to 18. In some cases this causes no problem of comparability, because a single 1981 category has merely been subdivided. Thus, in 1991 NHS hospitals/homes are split off from non-NHS hospitals/homes, and persons sleeping rough are split off from campers. But the 1981 categories 'homes for the old and the disabled' and 'hospital and homes – other' have been merged and then divided up into four new categories (local authority homes, housing association homes and hostels, other non-NHS nursing homes and other non-NHS residential homes).

There was a similar reclassification of categories and items between the 1971 and 1981 censuses. In particular, 'hostels and common lodging houses' was hived off from 'miscellaneous' in 1971 to form a separate category in 1981, while the category 'prison department establishments' was more narrowly defined in 1981 when community homes, remand homes and police lockups were included in 'miscellaneous'.

The treatment of people enumerated in communal establishments has also altered slightly over time. In 1971 the relatives of staff were entered in the tables as 'other residents', whereas in both 1981 and 1991 the practice has been to include them under 'resident staff'.

4.4 Dwellings and household space type

Mention has already been made of two major changes in 'dwellings and household space type' in the 1991 Census: the count of dwellings and the expansion of the information on type of accommodation. The latter includes a change in the definition of 'self-contained accommodation' which itself was a new question in 1981. The combined result of these changes is that comparisons between censuses must be treated with caution. The full breakdown of the 'household space types' identified at the last two censuses is presented in Table 10.1. Guidance of what aspects are not comparable is given in the 1991 Census Definitions volume, paragraphs 5.24–5.26, but User Guide 28 should be consulted for more detailed advice on exactly which 1981 and 1991 types are comparable.

4.5 Number of rooms and density of occupation

The room count is the only measure of size of dwelling or household space in the

Table 10.1 Full output classification of household space types in permanent dwellings, 1981 and 1991

1981 Census (7 categories)	**1991 Census (15 categories)**
Purpose-built flats and maisonettes	Unshared dwelling – purpose-built
	Detached
Separate entrance from outside building	Semi-detached
	Terraced
Shared access from outside building,	Flat in residential building
self-contained accommodation comprising	Flat in commercial building
(a) 2+ rooms with exclusive use of bath	Unshared dwelling – converted
and inside WC	Flat – separate entrance into building
(b) 1 room and exclusive use of bath	Flat – shared entrance into building
and inside WC ('flatlet')	Flatlet – separate entrance into building
(c) 2+ rooms but without exclusive use	Flatlet – shared entrance into building
of bath and/or inside WC	
	Unshared dwelling – not self-contained
Accommodation not self-contained but	Not self-contained flat
comprising	Not self-contained 'rooms'
(a) 1 room without exclusive use of	Bedsit
Not self-contained unoccupied	
bath and/or inside WC ('bedsit')	Other – not self-contained
(b) 2+ rooms	Not self-contained flats
	Not self-contained 'rooms'
	Bedsit
	Not self-contained unoccupied

Note: The table excludes non-permanent accommodation, which is a separate category in both classifications.
Source: Definitions volumes: 1981 Census, p. 13; 1991 Census, p. 18.

census and is used along with data on the people in the household space for deriving measures of the density of occupation, these being the number of persons per room in England and Wales and what is termed the occupancy norm in Scotland. There have been some changes in the exact definition of 'room' since 1971, so analyses of change in size of dwelling and density of occupation must be made with caution.

The main problem over number of rooms is the way in which they were counted in Scotland in 1981. Then the question was phrased so that the main count referred only to dining rooms, living rooms and bedrooms, followed by two supplementary questions which asked whether cooking was done in one of these rooms or in any other room. In England and Wales, by contrast, kitchens were included in the room count if they were at least 2 m wide. The latter approach was used throughout Great Britain in 1991, so that data for England and Wales in 1991 are (broadly) comparable for 1981 whereas those for Scotland are definitely not. There is one other general difference between 1981 and 1991, however: in 1991 rooms used solely for business, professional or trade purposes were included in the count, but this was not the case previously.

4.6 Tenure of (occupied) accommodation

The categories listed in the question on tenure for households have increased and altered somewhat since 1971. The owner-occupier category was subdivided into freehold and leasehold property in 1981 in England and Wales but kept as a single category in Scotland. This classification was replaced in 1991 by a distinction made in all three countries between those owning outright and those buying the property through a mortgage or loan. Similarly, in 1981 the categories 'renting with a job, shop, farm or other business' and 'renting from a housing association or charitable trust' were identified separately from the two main parts of the private rented sector (furnished and unfurnished). In terms of renting, a further split was made in 1991, with renting from a New Town or Housing Action Trust and renting from Scottish Homes (known formerly as the Scottish Special Housing Association (SSHA)) being hived off from renting from the Council.

The implications for census change analysis are as follows. Owner occupation has to be treated as a single category in all comparisons between the last three censuses. Similarly, those renting from local authorities, New Towns and Scottish Homes/SSHA need to be grouped together at all three censuses. The extra categories of private renting adopted in 1981 – basically tied accommodation and housing associations – can be traced through to 1991. But 1971–81 comparisons are safest if they combine all tenures of private renting, though it would probably be correct to assume that these two new categories had largely been recorded as part of the unfurnished private rented sector in 1971.

4.7 Amenities

The basic household amenities included in 1981 were also covered in 1991, but the form of the question and output altered slightly between censuses. In 1981 the question covered three amenities: a fixed bath or shower permanently connected to a water supply and a waste pipe, a flush toilet (WC) with entrance inside the building and a flush toilet with entrance outside the building, each of these being subdivided into whether the household had exclusive use, shared with another household or had none. In 1991 the first amenity was referred to merely as 'a bath or shower', while the other two were merged in a single question which provides only three categories of output: exclusive use of inside WC, shared use of inside WC, and no inside WC.

The 1981 question represented a significant reduction in information compared with 1971, when the amenities also included cookers or cooking stoves with an oven, kitchen sinks and hot water supply. Lack of these last three had already become rare by 1971 (indeed, most of the 1971 output ignores the first two and refers only to the 'three amenities' of hot water, bath and inside WC), so it is no real problem that they cannot be traced through to 1981 and 1991. The information collected in 1971 on households sharing or lacking bath or inside WC can be compared directly with the two later censuses. The only cautionary note here is that in Scotland in 1971 and 1981 the 'outside' element of the WC question refers to 'outside the dwelling' as opposed to 'outside the building' – which is not necessarily the same thing, involving at least a technical discontinuity in Scotland between 1981 and 1991, though in practice the numbers are likely to be small.

Lastly, as mentioned earlier, the 1991 Census contained a new question on availability of central heating (full, part, none). Obviously, this cannot be used in change analysis. It also has an effect on the form of the output in 1991 compared with previous censuses, because the continuing categories are broken down according to availability of central heating and need to be reaggregated to compare the overall availability of bath and inside WC with 1981 and 1971.

4.8 Cars and vans

This question has stayed the same across the last three censuses. It refers to the number of cars and vans normally available for use by members of the household (and not visitors), including vehicles provided by employers as long as these are normally available for private use and are not used solely for the carriage of goods.

4.9 Age, sex and marital status

The information requested on the 1991 Census forms on these topics was virtually the same as in 1981 and 1971. The only difference is that, for Great Britain in 1991 but only for England and Wales in 1981, 're-married' was distinguished from 'first marriage'. In the LBS/SAS output, however, these two are taken together as a single category and are therefore comparable for change analyses. Moreover, though some of the 1991 LBS tables give data separately for the three other categories of single, widowed and divorced, no tables did so in the 1981 or 1971 Small Area Statistics, so all change analyses using these datasets must use the combined grouping 'SWD'. Also, note that the question on marital status is precisely and only this; it should not be confused with the question on relationship in household which in 1991 includes 'living together as a couple' as a possible response (see below, Section 4.13).

The treatment of age has become somewhat more elaborate since 1971, particularly in the SAS. The normal method of presenting data has been the five-year age group, together with a basic count of younger people by single year of age. The highest age group presented in the 1971 SAS was '75 and over', this being extended to '85 and over' in 1981 and '90 and over' in 1991, so change analysis of the very elderly is somewhat restricted. Moreover, from 1981 15 year olds have been recognized as a separate category by virtue of the raising of school-leaving age to 16.

4.10 Migration

The 'change of address' question in 1991 asked about usual address one year ago, as it had done in 1981, while in 1971 information was collected on usual address both one year ago and five years ago. The form of the question has not changed, so the one-year change of address data for all three censuses can be compared directly. Some care, however, should be exercised in interpreting the data. First, the question does not provide data on all migrations over the 12-month period, treating those who moved twice or more during the year as merely a single change of address and excluding those who have moved and died, those who have been born and moved, those who have moved away and have subsequently returned to the same address, and those who have emigrated. Second, given that migration rates and patterns are highly volatile, they can be affected by short-term circumstances peculiar to the one-year periods concerned, with 1990–1 being a rather different type of economic recession from that in 1980–1 and with both these contrasting with the relatively buoyant state of the economy in 1970–1.

4.11 Country of birth

In contrast to the new question on ethnic group, the 'country of birth' question is of long standing and is self-explanatory. Any problems over changes in the name or geographical extent of countries since birth are dealt with at the coding stage. In terms of comparisons between recent censuses, such problems are also relevant; for instance, what was known as Ceylon in 1971 had become Sri Lanka by the 1981 Census, and 1991 Census output refers to the unified Germany rather than keeping the German Democratic Republic as a separate territory outside the European Union. Similarly, care needs to be exercised in dealing with the groupings of countries used in the more aggregate output, particularly in the SAS.

Close to home, those born in the Channel Isles or Isle of Man and those coded as 'UK (part not stated)' were grouped with Northern Ireland in 1971 and 1981 and, though distinguished from Northern Ireland in 1991, must be treated as a single group for comparative purposes. In terms of higher-order groupings, the headings 'European Community' and 'Remainder of Europe' changed in their constituents between 1981 and 1991 owing to the accession of Spain and Portugal to the European Community. The New Commonwealth included Pakistan in 1971 and 1991 but not in 1981.

4.12 Household composition derived from age, sex and marital status

This classification is produced from the 100% data, in contrast to that produced from the answers to the 'relationship in household' question (see next section). The full breakdown in 1991 comprised 22 categories compared with 19 in 1981, with the effect that it is not possible to produce a change analysis of the male/female breakdown of the adult in one-adult under-pensionable-age households with no, 1 or 2+ dependent children – at least, not without recourse to the SAR or commissioned tables.

Beyond this, however, there are several changes in the specification of the categories which affect 1981–91 comparisons. One is the definition of 'dependent child'. In 1981 it was defined as either a person under 16 years of age or a person under 25 years of age, never married and classified as a student from the economic activity question. The 1991 Census kept the first criterion, but modified the second to refer to persons aged 16–18, never married, in full-time education and economically inactive. The other important change is that the 1991 Census dropped the 'married' criterion in the classification of households with two or more adults. Third, in the 1991 classification more attention is given to the sex of the adult members of households with two or more people.

Two types of related output – household dependant type and lifestage – were introduced in 1991 for the first time and therefore have no equivalents in the output from earlier censuses.

4.13 Household and family composition

This classification differs from the one above in that it distinguishes households according to the number of families in the household (none, one, or two or more) and the type of family. It is derived from the 'relationship in household' question answered by all households but processed only for a 10% sample because of the complexity of allocating members of households to a relationship category (16 alternatives in 1991). In 1991 a total of 60 detailed family unit types were then used to arrange households into 21 'household and family composition' types.

Unfortunately, though many of the types recognized in 1991 appear to be identical to those in the 1981 classification, the extent of sensible 1981–91 change analysis on this topic is extremely limited. This is a clear example of the census authorities having to alter their practices in order to keep pace with the times. The 1991 Census saw the introduction of the answer 'living together as a couple' as an alternative to 'husband or wife' and the alteration of the classification to include six categories of cohabiting couple family. The basic reason for non-comparability is that, though '*de facto* spouse' was used in the 1981 coding of individuals, it was ignored in the eventual classification, with the result that cohabiting couple families were not separately identified in 1981 but would have appeared as households with no family, or as lone-parent families with others or as two-family households, depending on the presence of any children of the cohabitants. On this basis the only categories which would seem to be strictly comparable are those relating to married couples (six categories in 1991 as opposed to eight in 1981, owing to the grouping together of 'with all dependent children' and 'with both dependent and non-dependent children' in 1991), but only the user can decide whether it is useful to consider these types independently of cohabiting couples. This is therefore another case where further processing of the original 1991 data is needed in order to obtain fuller comparison with previous censuses.

4.14 Languages

Questions on Welsh and Scottish Gaelic languages have been included in each of the last three censuses, for completion by all persons aged 3 years and over in Wales and Scotland respectively. Their form has remained virtually unchanged, except for the dropping after 1971 of the question about whether Gaelic speakers could speak English and the dropping of the equivalent question to Welsh speakers after 1981. Thus the information available on this item in 1991 is also available for 1981 and 1971.

A rather different aspect is included in the 1991 Census output under the heading 'language indicator'. Given that no question was asked about 'mother tongue' or language other than English spoken in the home, this measure is based entirely on birthplace data and specifies two groups, those born in the New Commonwealth and all born outside the British Isles, the Old Commonwealth and the USA. This obviously provides only a very crude indication of the possible extent of a language other than English being the first language spoken. Reference to birthplace data in 1981 and 1971 could produce similar, albeit crude, measures.

4.15 Economic activity

Though the form of the question(s) on economic activity has changed with each recent census, essentially the same type of information has been collected on each occasion. Nevertheless, some of the comparisons over time need to be undertaken with care.

The 1991 Census form contained one question on economic activity which attempted to obtain the same information that the 1981 Census elicited through two separate questions on 'persons in employment' and 'employment status'. The results for the two censuses in terms of the output categories are shown in Table 10.2. The main casualty was the dropping of the distinction made in 1981 between employees supervising others and other employees. Also, people who in 1981 would have fallen into the category 'temporarily sick' (i.e. prevented by temporary sickness from seeking work) were instructed to tick the 'unemployed' box in 1991.

The category 'apprentices and trainees' was also dropped for 1991, with any such people presumably viewing themselves as employed. Meanwhile, the category 'on a government employment or training scheme' appeared for the first time in 1991, whereas in 1981 a distinction had been drawn between those on a Job Creation Scheme (treated as full-time employees) and those on a Government Training Course (treated as students). Students cause particular problems in comparing economic activity between 1991 and 1981, because in 1991 for the first time economically active students are included as employees, self-employed or unemployed, as appropriate. Only in certain of the 1991 output tables is enough information given about these students to enable direct comparability between the two censuses.

Table 10.2 Full output classification of persons' economic position and employment status (100% tables), 1981 and 1991

1981 Census	1991 Census
Economic position	*Economic position/employment status*
Economically active	Economically active
Working	Persons in employment
Seeking work	Employees
Temporarily sick	Full-time
	Part-time
Economically inactive	Self-employed
Permanently sick	With employees
Retired	Without employees
Student	On a government scheme
Other	Unemployed
	Waiting to start a job
Employees	Seeking work
Working full-time	Students (included above)
Working part-time	
	Economically inactive
Employment status	Students
	Permanently sick
Apprentices and trainees	Retired
Employees supervising others	Other inactive
Other employees	
Self-employed without employees	
Self-employed with employees	

Note: More elaborate breakdowns are provided in the 10% tables.
Source: Definitions volumes: 1981 Census, pp. 24–5; 1991 Census, p. 34.

Considerably less information was collected on economic activity in 1971, to the extent that only four basic categories can be compared with the two subsequent censuses, namely working, seeking work and sick, retired and other economically inactive (including permanently sick). Also, note that because of the earlier minimum school-leaving age at that time the 1971 data refer to those aged 15 years and over, as opposed to those aged 16 years and over in 1981 and 1991.

4.16 Hours worked per week

This question was asked in 1991 and the results were processed for the 10% sample. It had previously been asked in 1971 but was dropped from the 1981 Census form in favour of additional full-time/part-time boxes in the 100% question on economic activity. A degree of comparability across the last three censuses is afforded by the fact that the full-time/part-time distinction is whether the work involved 31 hours or more a week or not, which is a division used in the 'hours worked per week' output from the 1971 Census. Otherwise, comparisons over time are restricted to 1971–91 and to the categories which are recognized in both years in the datasets being compared, the latter differing somewhat between the two censuses and also between the various types of output from each.

4.17 Occupation etc.

The study of change between censuses in occupational structure, and in the measures of social class and socioeconomic group which are largely derived from information on occupation, is definitely not for the faint-hearted! The classification of occupations has been revised between each census. Although the 1981 Census Definitions volume states that the OPCS Classification of Occupations 1980 (CO80) maintains a high degree of comparability with its 1970 equivalent, users are advised to refer to a tabulation showing the relationship between the two classifications. The output from the 1991 Census uses a new Standard Occupational Classification (SOC) which replaces both CO80 and the Classification of Occupations and Directory of Occupational Titles (CODOT) which has until recently been used widely in the employment service field (see OPCS and Employment Department Group 1990–1).

The structure of the new classification is compared with CO80 and CODOT in Fig. 10.1. The OPCS provides the following general indication of the degree of comparability between the two latest censuses:

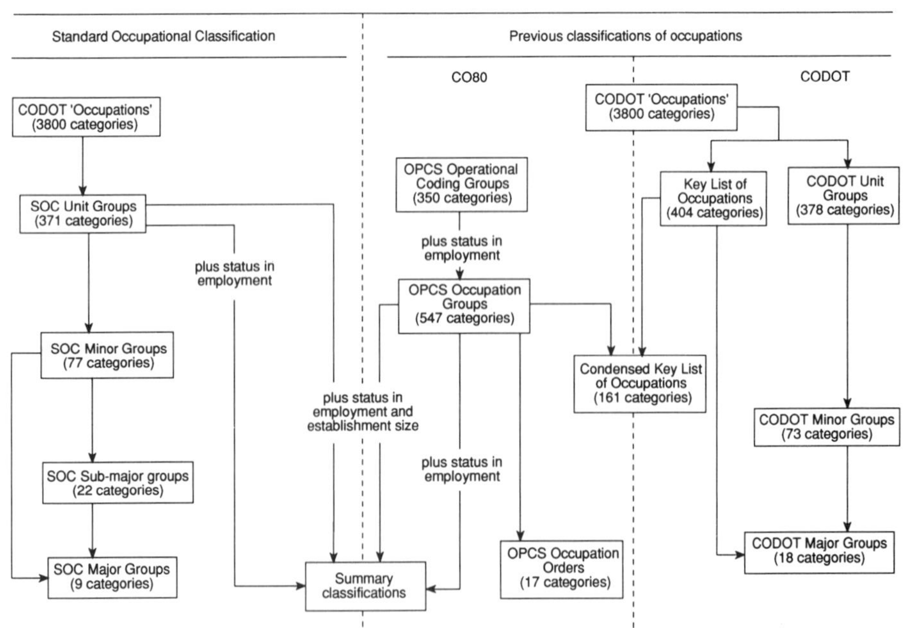

Fig. 10.1 The Standard Occupational Classification used in the 1991 Census compared with the previous classifications of occupations. Source: 1991 Census Definitions, p. 38. Reproduced with the permission of the Controller of Her Majesty's Stationery Office © Copyright.

> Over half (56.3 per cent) of the OCGs [the 350 Operational Coding Groups in CO80] match with the SOC Unit Groups on a one-to-one basis, and a further 4.9 per cent can be exactly reconstructed by aggregating two or more of the SOC Unit Groups. Of the others which cannot be exactly matched, a significant number differ only slightly from the SOC Unit Groups thus providing a reasonably good overall fit. Much of the remaining discontinuity affects the residual 'nec' [not elsewhere classified] groups in CO80.
> (*1991 Census Definitions*, para. 7.36, page 39)

For further information, see the three volumes entitled *Standard Occupational Classification,* published by HMSO for OPCS and the Employment Department Group, and also Table 4 of the *Economic Activity* topic volume and Table 98 of the *County/Region Reports*, which provide extra insights into the degree of comparability between 1981 and 1991 output.

The identification of social class is derived almost exclusively from the classification of occupations, to the extent that its name 'social class', used since the 1911 Census, has been altered to 'social class based on occupation' for the purposes of the 1991 Census. Another change in nomenclature is the switch in the name of Social Class II from 'Intermediate Occupations' to 'Managerial and Technical Occupations'. Despite the changes in the classification of occupations, there is a relatively high level of continuity between 1981 and 1991 Censuses at the aggregate level of the six social classes. OPCS estimate that the biggest effects are a decrease from 18.0% to 16.8% in the proportion of cases assigned to Social Class IV and an increase from 6.2% to 7.6% in Social Class V, with none of the other classes (I, II, IIIN, IIIM) being affected by a difference of greater than +0.3%.

Classification by socioeconomic group (SEG), introduced in the 1951 Census, uses information on both occupation and employment status and thus involves an additional degree of complexity in achieving comparability between censuses. The basis of SEG was extensively amended in 1961, and only a relatively broad grouping of SEGs can be compared with any confidence between 1971 and 1981. The 17 SEG headings used in 1981 are retained for 1991, but the 1991 Census Definitions volume volunteers no information on the likely effects of the changes since 1981 in the occupational classification and the employment status question. Interested researchers should go direct to Volume 3 of the *Standard Occupational Classification.*

4.18 Industry

Data on industry are coded for the 10% sample from replies to the question on the name and business of the employer (or self-employed person). The question did not change in a substantive way between 1981 and 1991, and the same classification was used at both dates, being the *Standard Industrial Classification Revised 1980*. But note that the number of separate headings identified in the 1981 SAS is fewer than in the 1991 LBS/SAS and therefore constrains the fine detail available in change analysis. The industrial classification used in the 1971 output was different, so comparisons with 1971 need much more care.

4.19 Workplace and transport to work

These two 1991 Census questions are similar to those asked in 1981, but there are some detailed differences in questions and/or output. One is that, whereas in 1981 persons resident outside Great Britain were counted as resident in the area of enumeration, in 1991 they are treated as resident outside the workplace area. Second, in 1991 members of the Armed Forces were instructed not to enter their place of work and are treated in the output as working in their area of residence, not at their real workplace as in 1981. Third, in Scotland the workplace question included a note to state 'offshore installation' if appropriate. Lastly, the 1991 question on transport to work excluded the 1981 category 'car or van – pool, sharing driving', so that for direct comparison between 1981 and 1991 only a single group 'car or van' can be used, because the two continuing categories of 'car or van – driver' and 'car or van – passenger' will in 1991 both contain some of the people who would have been caught by the omitted category.

4.20 Qualifications

The same question was put in 1981 and 1991, asking all persons aged 18 and over for details of degrees and professional and vocational qualifications obtained. The only difference was a minor alteration in the population base, in that persons resident outside Great Britain but with a workplace in Great Britain were included in 1981 but omitted in 1991 – a group which numbered only 1240 persons in the 10% sample in 1981.

The procedure in 1971 was rather different. Then the base was restricted to 18–69 year olds. In addition, the question covered a wider range of educational qualifications including A Level or equivalents such as the Ordinary National Certificate. Caution is therefore needed in comparing 1971 with the later censuses.

4.21 Conclusion

This section has dealt with similarities and differences between the last three censuses in the range of topics covered, in the definitions of concepts used in the questions, in the wording of the individual questions on the census forms and in the grouping of answers for the output tables. It has not strived to be totally comprehensive or to go into the fullest details, because the official publications from the Census Office are available for further reference. In particular, more attention has been given here to the comparability between 1991 and 1981, with rather less attention given to 1971. Nevertheless, enough has been said to make clear the extent of comparability and to illustrate the types of problems which will be encountered.

It is clear that only a certain proportion of the statistics collected in the 1991 Census are directly comparable with those collected in 1981. At the same time, however, there are a number of other items which are broadly comparable, where the key question must concern the scale of difference needed between the two census points before the existence of a real change can be stated confidently. The tracing of specific variables across the last two intercensal periods back to 1971 is that much more problematic, both because of changes in definitions and categories and because of the crude level of detail in the 1971 SAS. Nevertheless, the good news is that a number of variables can be followed through all three of the latest censuses, and in addition some extra 1971–91 comparisons can be made even though no equivalent data were collected for 1981.

5 Variation in census coverage

Unfortunately, the ability to make reliable analyses of change between censuses depends not only on the comparability of census questions and output variables. It is also affected by variation in census coverage and quality. These issues form the subject of the next two sections of this chapter.

The issue here relates to the task of achieving an accurate count of the number of people in Britain for the date on which the census enumeration is officially made. This task is not one merely of identifying people at their location on census night but – in relation to the needs of most census users – of being able to provide a reliable measure of the number of people *usually resident* in each area. It requires a means for coping with people who were not at their normal address on census night because of visiting somewhere else including places outside Britain (see Chapter 2). The key point here is that made in Marsh *et al.*'s (1988) observation quoted at the beginning of this chapter, namely that any calculation of change between censuses will include artificial as well as real changes if the level or type of coverage varies between censuses. Given that it is impossible to achieve either a perfect population count or the same enumeration errors at two or more censuses, it is important to assess the scale of the problems so that estimates can be made of the true populations at each census and of the real changes between censuses. This task relates not only to counting overall numbers but also to identifying the extent of any bias in the errors, i.e. the extent to which coverage problems are concentrated on certain subgroups of people rather than being spread evenly across the whole population in any area.

The scale of the coverage problem in 1991 has already been described (see Chapter 2) but is summarized in a somewhat different way in Table 10.3 in order to draw comparisons with the 1981 situation. A total of 54.02 million residents were enumerated on census forms in 1991, the majority of these being in households where at least one member was present on census night but with 680,000 belonging to households which were wholly absent on census night but which completed and mailed back their form voluntarily on their return. This figure of

Table 10.3 Elements of the estimated total population of Great Britain at the 1981 and 1991 Censuses

Element	1981		1991		Difference
	'000s	%	'000s	%	
Residents in population base	53 557	97.7	54 889	98.1	+1 332
Resident population 1981 base – enumerated	53 557	97.7	53 340	95.3	–217
In wholly absent households – enumerated	na	0.0	680	1.2	+680
In wholly absent households – imputed	na	0.0	869	1.6	+869
Coverage adjustments	1 246	2.3	1 053	1.9	–193
In wholly absent households – enumerated	1 005	1.8	na	0.0	–1 005
Net under-enumeration accounted for by CVS	215	0.4	299	0.5	+84
Under-enumeration not accounted for by CVS	26	0.0	754	1.3	+728
Estimated total population on census night	54 803	100.0	55 942	100.0	+1 139
Summary					
Enumerated by census	54 562	99.5	54 020	96.6	–542
Resident population 1981 base	53 557	97.7	53 340	95.3	–217
Resident population 1991 base	na	–	54 889	98.1	–

Note: na, not applicable; CVS, Census Validation Survey. Percentages relate to estimated total population on census night.
Source: Calculated from *1991 Census, National Monitor, Great Britain* (CEN 91 CM 56), Annex A.

54.02 million is 1.92 million people lower than the official estimate of Britain's total number of residents at the census, which is put at 55.94 million – a shortfall of 3.43%. This difference comprises three elements: people in wholly absent households which did not return a form voluntarily (put at 869,000 on the basis of information supplied by enumerators as a result of contacts in the neighbourhood or their own estimates), net under-enumeration identified by the Census Validation Survey (299,000) and other under-enumeration calculated from demographic checks and other means (754,000). The first of these three groups was included in census processing as the 'imputed residents', bringing the total numbers covered by the 1991 Census tabulations to 54.89 million or 98.1% of the estimated total number of residents. The other two groups make up the so-called 'missing million' of the 1991 Census, because not enough was known about them even to estimate their characteristics.

The omission of 1.9% of residents from the census is not unusual by international standards and should not detract substantially from the reliability of most of the findings of that stock-taking exercise, considered as a 98% sample survey of the British population. The implications are potentially much more serious, however, for studying change over time, particularly change in absolute numbers of residents as opposed to change in percentage composition or other types of ratio measure. For instance, in relation to calculating 1981–91 change in the total number of residents in Great Britain, the omission of 1.9% in 1991 is potentially very serious, given that the actual change – according to the best estimates currently available – is an increase of 2.0%, i.e. virtually the same as the estimated error in the 1991 Census. In practice, however, its significance depends on the scale and nature of this type of problem at previous censuses and the geographical incidence of the errors.

Table 10.3 gives details of the coverage of the 1981 Census alongside the 1991 situation. It can be seen that the number of residents not included in the census tables for 1981 is put at 1.25 million, representing 2.27% of the estimated total number of residents at that time. This is a somewhat higher level of effective omission than for 1991, suggesting that any direct comparisons of the number of residents in the full population bases of the two censuses will, if anything, tend to overestimate the rate of population growth between 1981 and 1991 by a small margin, not underestimate it.

At the same time, however, it is also clear from Table 10.3 that the causes of the difference between the estimated total number of residents and the number included in the population base of the census tables for 1981 are not at all the same as those for 1991. The only comparable element is the estimated net under-enumeration discovered by the follow-up survey, termed the Post Enumeration Survey for the 1981 Census (the equivalent of the Census Validation Survey of 1991). Beyond this, there is a major contrast between the two latest Censuses in their treatment of people in households which were wholly absent on census night, a group which accounted for just over 1 million people in 1981 and an estimated 1.55 million in 1991. Whereas in 1991 these were included in the population base of the census tables through the combination of the voluntary returning of census forms and the imputation process, in 1981 the equivalent group – many of whom had completed census forms but elsewhere in Britain or on return from overseas – was entirely excluded from the main census analysis. A second major contrast is that in 1981 there were believed to be very few non-enumerated people beyond those accounted for by the follow-up survey, i.e. people for whom no information at all can be gleaned from the census process itself: only some 26,000 people in Britain in 1981, compared with the three-quarters of a million in this category in 1991.

The fact that the 'missing million' components of the analyses provided by the two latest censuses arise from substantially different sources suggests that they involve different types of people. Certainly, this would appear to be the case in terms of their age structure and household situation. As explained in Chapter 2, demographic checks on the 1991 Census counts indicate that the under-enumeration at that census was particularly large for men aged 20–29 years old, a large proportion of whom are believed to belong to households which were actually enumerated. This is a significant contrast to the 1981 situation where the major component omitted from the census analysis comprised entire households. There is also a strong likelihood that these two groups will differ significantly in their other personal characteristics and in the geographical location of their usual residence.

A pointer to the differences in the geographical location of the 'missing' people is provided by comparing the results of the 1991 Census Validation Survey with those of the 1981 Census Post Enumeration Survey (Table 10.4). It can be seen that in 1981 the estimated net under-enumeration was highest for Inner London

Table 10.4 Geographical variation in net under-enumeration as measured by the 1981 Post Enumeration Survey and the 1991 Census Validation Survey, England and Wales only

Geographical area	**1981 Post Enumeration Survey**		**1991 Census Validation Survey**	
	Thousands	**%**	**Thousands**	**%**
Inner London	58	2.46	3	0.12
Outer London	42	1.01	14	0.33
Other metropolitan counties	17	0.24	106	0.98
Shire counties	87	0.29	170	0.53
England and Wales	215	0.45	292	0.60

Sources: *Census 1981 Monitor* (CEN 82/3, p. 3, Table 1); *Census Newsletter 24* (p. 8, Table 4).

and lowest in the other metropolitan counties – the opposite of the situation in 1991, when the imputation process had compensated for the relatively high level of non-contact in London. Then again, however, it must be realized that the 1991 Census Validation Survey data here exclude the people who were missed by both the census and the Census Validation Survey, amounting to 672,000 for England and Wales. It will need a major research effort to assign geographical locations to the latter group with any reasonable level of confidence, because the demographic checks building forward from the 1981 mid-year estimates depend on the reliability of the monitoring sources, of which the most important at regional and local scale – those on migration (the International Passenger Survey and National Health Service Central Register) – are much less accurate than the registration of births and deaths.

Not surprisingly, therefore, caution should be exercised in studying 1981–91 changes from the census and in interpreting the results of any such analyses. Anyone planning this type of work should first of all heed the following official guidance on the use of 1991 Census data:

> There are two circumstances ... in which the user might find it beneficial to take special action. The first is where the user requires population numbers by age, by sex, or by administrative area, rather than any relationship with other census topics. In this case the mid-year population estimates should be used in preference to the Census resident counts. The second circumstance is where the user is studying census characteristics which are correlated strongly with sex and age and where comparisons might be affected by the known sex/age bias in the under-enumerated population. ... If necessary, approximate correction factors can be supplied for any quinary age group for both males and females. It should be realised, however, that such adjustments would necessarily assume that the relevant characteristics of those missed by the Census are the same as for those counted.
>
> (OPCS 1992, pp. 25–6)

This form of advice will no doubt be extended when the full results of the Census Validation Survey and other checks are available and, hopefully, similar guidance will also be produced for those interested in the analysis of 1981-91 change.

For the moment, probably the best advice is to avoid using the census for studying absolute numbers and change measures based on them. In particular, any such calculations based on 'Resident population – 1981 base' (as used in the 1991 Census County Monitor Table C and as presented in the 1991 LBS/SAS Table 1 as a basis for comparisons with 1981) should be treated with the greatest suspicion. This is because, in omitting people in households wholly absent on census night, they exclude many more people in 1991 than in 1981, indicating a national population decline of 217,000 rather than the 1.14 million increase which is the latest official estimate (see Table 10.3). Instead, where possible, the mid-year estimates for 1981 and 1991 (adjusted for any changes in area boundaries over the decade) should be used, either directly for the district level and above or indirectly as a control for subdistrict level analysis.

6 Other aspects of census quality

The coverage issue may seem alarming at first sight, but it may be no more significant in its effect than other discontinuities between previous censuses that have normally been ignored, either through ignorance or because there is no practical way round them. Most notable among these in relation to the last three censuses is the change in population base between 1971 and 1981, but problems are also raised by the precise timing of the census and by the quality of the answers to individual questions – problems which are more serious for comparisons over time than for the analysis of the data collected by one particular census.

6.1 The change in population base between 1971 and 1981

As mentioned earlier in the chapter (Section 4.1), there was a switch from the 'population present' base (as adopted in 1801 and used through to 1971) to the 'resident' principle in 1981. However, given that the latter involved the 'usually resident (present/absent)' base, comparisons between 1971 and 1981 are affected by two types of major discontinuity. One is that the output from the 1971 Census is more comprehensive in its coverage than that for 1981, since the latter (apart from the 'Usual Residence' topic volume) excluded wholly absent households. The other – very important for geographical analysis and local studies – is that in 1971 analysis took place according to place of enumeration rather than place of usual residence. Table 10.5 shows the composition of the population base for the County Reports and SAS for the latest three censuses in order to emphasize this point.

The scale of these effects at the local level can be assessed from tables in the SAS that compare the population base of one census with that of the previous

Table 10.5 Constituents of the population base for Small Area Statistics, 1971–91

Population group	1971	1981	1991
Present residents	Y	Y	Y
Absent residents (part of household present)	N	Y	Y
Absent residents (wholly absent household – enumerated)	N	Y	Y
Absent residents (wholly absent household – imputed)	N	N	Y
Visitors (resident within or outside UK)	Y	N	N

Note: Y, included in population base; N, excluded from population base.
Source: *1991 Census User Guide 24: Local Base Statistics, Cell Numbering Layouts*, Table 1.

one. Thus in the 1981 SAS, Table 1 shows the 1981 population count on the 1971 base (cell 36), alongside the count on the 1981 base (cell 43), while Table 17 gives 1981 details of household numbers by size on both 1971 and 1981 bases. Similarly, Table 1 in the 1991 LBS/SAS gives the 1991 counts not only for the 1991 population base but also for the definitions used in 1981 and 1971, and the 1991 LBS Tables 18 and 19 give some basic characteristics of the 'imputed' element of residents and households which represents the main definitional change from the 1981 base.

The availability of this information means that it is possible to calculate overall population change between censuses as long as one is happy to use the population base of an earlier census. Thus, in theory, 1981–91 change can be calculated for the 1981 base definition, and 1971–81–91 change can be calculated for the 1971 base definition. Moreover, some other tables in the 1981 SAS and 1991 LBS/SAS use 'population present' as their base, enabling a direct comparison across the three censuses. These relate to disaggregations by age/sex, whether living in a private household or not, and type of communal establishment if not living in a private household (see 1971 SAS Tables 2, 6 and 7; 1981 SAS Tables 1, 3 and 6; 1991 LBS/SAS Tables 1, 3 and 11). The degree of real comparability, however, also depends on the level of census coverage (as outlined in the previous section).

6.2 Comparability problems raised by census timing

The official date of enumeration varies between censuses. This is partly because it always takes place at the weekend, traditionally on the Saturday night but from the 1981 Census on the Sunday night. But the main changes of date arise because it is scheduled in the early spring not nearer than two weeks before or after Easter Day (which itself shifts dates according to the phases of the moon). The dates of the latest three censuses and their relationship to Easter Day are as follows: Saturday night 24–25 April 1971 (two weeks after Easter), Sunday night 5–6 April 1981 (two weeks before Easter) and Sunday night 21–22 April 1991 (three weeks after Easter). This variation in census timing has two sets of implications for change analyses, one relating primarily to the census coverage and the population base, the other more technical concerning the different length of each intercensal period.

The first is particularly significant for any analyses of change based on the 'population present' definition, which as we have seen provides the population base for 1971 and forms the only basis for directly comparing population numbers 1971–81–91. Such comparisons will be affected by differences in the levels of holiday-making resulting from the fact that the Easter weekend is traditionally viewed as the opening of the holiday season as far as UK-based trips are concerned. The weekender factor is probably adequately coped with through the shift of the census to Sunday night in 1981, but particular care is needed in interpreting 1971–81 changes in population present, where the comparison is between a Saturday night two weeks after Easter and a Sunday night two weeks before Easter, with the former finding significantly more people away in popular holiday-making and weekending areas.

The student factor also complicates the comparison of 'population present' data over the past three censuses. Children at boarding school and students in higher education who live away from home in term-time will have their whereabouts on census night recorded at their term-time address if the census falls in term-time, even though the 1981 and 1991 Censuses instructed that the home address should be entered under the 'usual address' question. For most, if not all, higher education establishments the 1981 Census occurred during a vacation period, but in 1971 and 1991 most students would either have started their term already or have just returned to their term-time address in preparation for the start of term. This factor has obvious implications for the population size and composition of places which are important educational centres, particularly those smaller cities where universities and colleges account for a relatively large element of the term-time population.

The significance of such timing problems for the 'population present' measure can be gauged in overall numerical terms by comparing data on enumerated and resident population for each census. Some indication can be obtained from Table 1 in the 1981 and 1991 SAS, but the most comprehensive information can be found in the 'Usual Residence' topic volume of each Census. But it is not possible to assess the compositional effect of those analysed in 1971 at place of enumeration rather than place of usual residence.

These timing problems are much less significant in relation to comparisons just between the latest two censuses because of the 'usual residence' approach used for the population base in both 1981 and 1991. But the difference in census timing in relation to Easter (two weeks beforehand in 1981, as opposed to three weeks afterwards in 1991) may be partly responsible for differences between these censuses in the number of households wholly absent on census night for various places. This would have both numerical and composition effects on 1981–91 comparisons, even if using 1991 data adjusted to the 1981 'present/absent' definition. It also remains to be seen how systematically students living away from home have been entered as usually resident at their parents' home, a check which is theoretically possible in 1991 owing to the instruction to give both term-time and parental address for students.

Lastly, there is a much more technical point concerning the analysis of change between censuses that are not held on exactly the same day of the year, namely that intercensal periods are not precisely 10 years long. The 1971–81 intercensal period was nearly three weeks short of the full 10-year period, while that for 1981–91 was just over two weeks longer than the 10 years. For most purposes these variations will matter little, nor even the fact that the latter intercensal 'decade' is some five weeks longer than the earlier one. There is one potentially important implication, however, relating to cohort studies, in that not every survivor will be in the 10-years-older age group at the next census; for instance, between the 1971 and 1981 Censuses, 1 in 20 people will have had only nine birthdays and will appear in the 'wrong' single-year age group.

6.3 Data quality

This issue needs only a brief mention here, despite its fundamental importance. Mention has already been made (in Chapter 2) of the reliability of individual data items in the 1991 Census, with its dependence on census coverage, accuracy in census form completion and subsequent processing, and (in relation to data deriving from the 10% sample) sampling error. Moreover, earlier sections in this chapter have reinforced the point by commenting on variations between censuses in the quality of coverage.

Census users are strongly advised to study the full results of the Census Validation Survey and see how the quality of the answers to 1991 Census questions compares with that for the earlier censuses. As a basis for comparison, it should be noted that, according to the quality check in the 1981 Census Post Enumeration Survey, there were substantial errors on some questions; a gross error rate of 29% for number of rooms, 16% for socioeconomic group, 13% for social class, 10% for employment status, 9% for means of travel to work and 8% for economic position. Such gross errors usually tend to cancel out in the net distributions for an item, though it is believed that 'Particular categories may have been substantially under- or over-recorded by the Census' (OPCS 1984b, p. 2).

The degree to which such errors can affect comparison between censuses is a thoroughly neglected, and admittedly an extremely intractable, research area. It may be that, with data aggregated to standard output areas and with the possibility of similar patterns of error between successive censuses, the accuracy of change analyses will not be seriously affected. One application of census data, however, is likely to be particularly prone to distortion by these errors, namely the use of the Longitudinal Study to examine changes in the characteristics and circumstances of individuals across the latest three censuses. In this case, the problem of 'artefactual' changes will arise if an analysis includes individuals who have made errors in the completion of at least one of their census records that is being compared, e.g. indicating a change in their circumstances which has not taken place. Clearly, a range of possibilities exists in terms of errors and the extent to which errors cancel themselves out in the process of producing the aggregations which the Longitudinal Study's bar on releasing results for individuals requires, but these are likely to be rather different in nature from those associated with handling results from a single census.

Similar comments can be made about the two other forms of 'error' which are encountered in the census. One is the intentional 'blurring' of data in the LBS and SAS, also known as 'Barnardization' and designed to preserve confidentiality. The other is sampling error in the data items coded only for the 10% sample and thereby affecting the quality of the '10% data'. These have been described in relation to the quality of the 1991 Census data in Chapter 2. The key point here is that similar errors arise in the data for previous censuses and will affect the quality of the results of change analyses.

7 Concluding comments

This is a long chapter, yet it could easily have been made longer. The last two sections have raised important issues over census coverage and other aspects of data quality, which pose more serious difficulties for analysing change than for studying patterns from one single census. The major part of the chapter, however, has concentrated on issues relating to statistical comparability between the latest three censuses, particularly in relation to the degree of similarity of questions asked, definitions used and categories recognized both on the census form and in the output. Even here the above account is not comprehensive, but hopefully it provides enough information to show census users when it is advisable to seek further guidance from official publications or directly from the census authorities themselves. The chapter has not looked at the degree to which 1991 Census data can be assembled for geographical areas that are exactly comparable with the 1981 and/or 1971 Censuses (see Chapter 4 for treatment of this thorny issue and also Chapters 2 and 5), nor has it attempted to address basic statistical questions concerning the most appropriate types of measures, ratios and bases for analysing change over time.

It is clear that, despite the best attempts of the authorities to maintain comparability between censuses, the analysis of change can be a very hazardous operation in many respects. At least three types of reaction can be expected from potential users. One is that it is all too difficult to contemplate, while another is to plough on regardless and assume that there are no comparability problems. Both these seem to have been fairly common after the 1981 Census, for the amount of 1971–81 analysis was relatively limited and most of what was undertaken did not give much attention to the degree of confidence which could be attached to the results. The third type of reaction is to focus attention on the biggest changes in the hope that these could scarcely comprise merely Marsh *et al.*'s 'artefactual change' and be much more cautious in interpreting relatively minor shifts between censuses. Ultimately, it must be hoped that the reliability of censuses for analysing social change will be exposed to much fuller examination, so as to provide better guidance to users in interpreting their results and to assist in the planning for the next census. The Census Offices themselves have already shown the way by starting an investigation into the nature and effects of the 1991 Census's 'missing million', and it is important that this lead should be taken further.

Acknowledgements

I am extremely grateful to Mike Coombes, Daniel Dorling and Chris Denham for their helpful comments on an early draft of this chapter, but I alone am responsible for any remaining errors and omissions; please check your census documentation!

References

Champion, A G 1993 Introduction: key population developments and their local impacts. In A G Champion (ed) *Population Matters: The Local Dimension*. London: Paul Chapman, 1–21.

CSO 1979 *Standard Industrial Classification Revised 1980*. London: HMSO.

Department of Employment 1972 *Classification of Occupations and Directory of Occupational Titles*. London: HMSO.

Dugmore, K 1993 Population pyramids and shifting sands: targeting future investments to give the changing British public their just deserts. In A G Champion (ed) *Population Matters: The Local Dimension*. London: Paul Chapman, 22–32.

Marsh, C, S Arber, N Wrigley, D Rhind and M Bulmer 1988 Research Policy and Review 23. The view of academic social scientists on the 1991 UK Census of Population: a report of the Economic and Social Research Council Working Group. *Environment and Planning A* 20, 851–89.

McKee, C H 1989a Analysis of census data available for measuring local level demographic and socio-economic change in the South East of England between 1971 and 1981. Working Report 10, South East Regional Research Laboratory, Birkbeck College, University of London.

McKee, C H 1989b Local scale socio-economic and demographic change in the South East of England, 1971 to 1981. PhD thesis, Department of Geography, Birkbeck College, University of London.

McKee, C H 1989c The 1971/1981 Census Change Files: a user's view and projection to 1991. Working Paper 13, South East Regional Research Laboratory, Birkbeck College, University of London.

Norris, P and H M Mounsey 1983 Analysing change through time. In D Rhind (ed) *A Census User's Handbook*. London: Methuen, 265–86.

OPCS 1979 *Census 1971, England and Wales: General Report Part 1. Definitions*. London: HMSO.

OPCS 1980 *Classification of Occupations 1980*. London: HMSO.

OPCS 1981 *Census 1981, Definitions, Great Britain*. London: HMSO.

OPCS 1984a *Census 1981, User Guide 84: Guide to Statistical Comparability 1971–81*. Titchfield, Hants: Office of Population Censuses and Surveys.

OPCS 1984b *OPCS Monitor, Census 1981, CEN 84/3: Evaluation of the 1981 Census: Post Enumeration Survey (Quality Check)*. London: Office of Population Censuses and Surveys.

OPCS 1992 *1991 Census, National Monitor, Great Britain (CEN 91 CM 56)*. London: Office of Population Censuses and Surveys.

OPCS and Employment Department Group 1990–1 *Standard Occupational Classification*. vol. 1: *Structure and Definition of Major, Minor and Unit Groups*; vol. 2: *Coding Index;* vol. 3: *Social Classification and Coding Methodology*. London: HMSO.

OPCS/GRO(S) 1992 *1991 Census, Definitions, Great Britain*. London: HMSO.

OPCS/GRO(S) *1991 Census User Guide 28: Guide to Statistical Comparability 1981–91*. Titchfield and Edinburgh: Office of Population Censuses and Surveys and General Register Office Scotland (to be published).

11

Samples of Anonymized Records

E Middleton

Editor's note

The SAR is the single most innovative feature of the 1991 Census. For the first time 1% and 2% samples of census data for anonymous households and people are available. In principle this should extend the usefulness of the census (users can design their own special tables) and create a non-spatial survey data form of census data that standard statistical packages can readily handle in a form that more social scientists might find useful. A particularly interesting aspect of this chapter is the provision of the SAR in a portable form suitable for UNIX and MS-DOS systems.

1 Background

For the first time in a British census the output includes the Samples of Anonymized Records, known as the SAR. These are samples of individual census records anonymized in various ways to ensure that there is no breach of the confidentiality of the census and that no individual can be identified from the data. This is a major new source of census information about people in Britain (see also Marsh 1993).

The SAR can be analysed in the same way as any other randomly sampled household and person survey data using familiar statistical, survey analysis or database software packages. The availability of this census microdata opens up new and exciting areas of research free of many of the technical and methodological problems associated with the spatial census datasets.

2 The demand for microdata

In the past researchers have been restricted to working with tables of aggregated census data but in recent years there has been a growing demand in most industrialized countries for individual level data. As a result of the widespread availability of computing power and statistical software packages, researchers nowadays are very well able to carry out statistical analyses of microdata and to produce their own tables rather than have to rely upon a slow, expensive, census tabulation service.

However, the release of microdata does involve some risks of disclosure of personal information. The public are rightly concerned about the confidentiality of the data and fears have grown about privacy of the individual, possibly in response to the growth of computerized databases in the market research sector and the capacity to link these. Different countries have responded in various ways to the conflict between the needs for access to data and the demands for confidentiality.

One response of countries has been to place strict controls on both the people given access to the data and the setting in which they are allowed to operate. In the UK, the OPCS Longitudinal Study based on a small sample of individual census data from two censuses (1971, 1981) operates in this fashion, with access only via the OPCS themselves after detailed manual scrutiny of the proposed tabulations. Academic researchers in Denmark and Sweden may only receive microdata for specified and delimited purposes. Some countries allow local state authorities access to microdata but deny similar access to academics. Regional governments in Spain and some government departments in Luxembourg have access to microdata as do local government researchers at all levels in Italy. In Italy, academics may be allowed access by special request. In the Netherlands a distinction is made between Public Use Files, which can be obtained without any limitations, and Microdata Under Contract Files, intended for the research community on the basis of a contract (Keller and Willenborg 1992). The alternative approach is to make use of various ways of anonymizing the data: releasing only a sample of records, suppressing obvious identifying variables, grouping detailed classifications, constraining the data structure and perturbing the data.

The USA first released their Public Use Sample Tapes in the 1960s and the Public Use Microdata Samples (PUMS) have been extremely popular with users ever since. Increasingly, the data are also supplied on CD-ROM. There are no restrictions on access to the microdata. The 1990 PUMS are hierarchical files consisting of anonymized records for a sample of housing units, with information on the characteristics of each housing unit and the people in it. Geographical identifiers are for cities, counties and larger areas with a minimum population of 100,000. Currently, the standard PUMS products are the 5% and 1% samples for the USA and Puerto Rico and a special 3% sample dealing specifically with the elderly population. The 5% sample is a county/county equivalent file whereas the 1% sample is basically a metropolitan area file.

A combination of the two approaches to protection of confidentiality is frequently used with users of anonymized microdata signing a licence agreement or undertaking to ensure proper use of the data. This is done in Canada where census microdata was first released in the 1970s. Three files are being released from their 1991 Census: an individual file, a household and housing file and a family file. Australia has also released census microdata since the 1980s. However, Canada and Australia have not released as much information, either in terms of sample size, detail of file structure or fine-grain detail of coding schemes, as the USA. The Australian census microdata in particular contains only the state as a geographic identifier.

In general, the English-speaking countries have tended to make census microdata available in various anonymized forms, whereas other European countries have placed more limitations on uses and users. In France only a restricted subset of census variables is released publicly as microdata in sampling fractions varying from 0.1% to 25%. In Germany, microdata can be released for scientific purposes under certain conditions, provided they are 'factually anonymous'. Recommendations have recently been made for release of data from the German Microcensus, a survey conducted annually with 1% of the population. The recommendations involve both suitable anonymization of records and contractual commitments of recipients of the data (Knoche 1992).

3 The release of the Samples of Anonymized Records

Demand in Britain for microdata increased during the 1980s, mainly from academics (Norris 1983, Marsh *et al.* 1988) but also supported by the British Computer Society team who reviewed security provisions for the 1981 Census. The requests coincided with interest from the Census Office in exploring ways of making census data more directly available to users. Indeed, a census White Paper in 1983 opened up the possibility of there being a Public Use Sample if the demand could be demonstrated and confidentiality fears addressed. The Economic and Social Research Council (ESRC) initiated a series of meetings throughout the 1980s, the first chaired by Professor S. Openshaw leading to an abortive request for a 1981 SAR in 1986, and a later meeting leading to a successful request with a group chaired by the late Professor Marsh. As a result, in good time for the 1991 Census, the ESRC set up a working party to negotiate with the Census Offices in Great Britain in order to present a formal request for microdata. The working party undertook some systematic work in quantifying the risks of disclosure from releasing the microdata and proposed that the Census Offices release two different files of microdata, one to meet the needs of those who wanted the maximum geographical detail and one to meet the needs of those interested in detailed household structure. The statistical risks of anyone in the population being identifiable from the SAR were considered to be extremely small, of the order of 1 in 4 million (Marsh *et al.* 1991), although the risk of incorrectly believing confidentiality had been breached was much greater. These estimates were made from the analysis of 100% microcensus data from the Italian 1981 Census, as a result of a research project between the University of Newcastle, the Regional Government of Tuscany and the Italian Census Agency (ISTAT).

The request for microdata was presented in a report in 1989 (published as Marsh *et al.* 1991) which was favourably received by the Census Offices. Legal advice was sought and it was agreed that the SAR could be released under Section 4(2) of the 1920 Census Act which permits the production of statistical abstracts from the census. Following consultations with the Office of the Data Protection Registrar, with the civil rights campaigning organization Liberty and with the British Computer Society, agreement in principle of the Registrars General to the ESRC request was announced in July 1990. The specification for the SAR was developed by Professor Marsh and submitted to the OPCS technical adviser, Professor Holt of the University of Southampton, who advised on the confidentiality aspects. Finally, parliamentary approval was granted in March 1992 and the SAR became available during 1993.

The ESRC has made a similar request for microdata to the Northern Ireland Census Office. Agreement in principle for release of Northern Ireland SAR has been obtained and the Census Microdata Unit at Manchester University is undertaking to harmonize the Northern Ireland SAR with Great Britain SAR to produce a new SAR dataset for the whole of the UK.

4 Description of the Samples of Anonymized Records datasets

Two different samples of data are being released from the 1991 Census.

4.1 A 2% sample of individuals

This first file is a sample of individuals in private addresses and residents of communal establishments. It has full housing information and some limited information about household structure.

The geography is based on large local authority districts. All non-metropolitan counties in England and Wales, most Scottish regions, all London boroughs (except the City of London) and all metropolitan districts are separately identifiable. Smaller districts are amalgamated with a neighbouring district if their population falls under 120,000 residents. Figure 2.3 in Chapter 2 gives a map of the geographical areas used for the 2% SAR.

4.2 A 1% hierarchical sample of households

This second file is a 1% sample of households and all people who live in them. It has a housing record containing housing and dwelling information, and then a series of subrecords, one for each household member, giving the individual's answers to census questions.

Because of the greater confidentiality risk with more detailed household information, this file will classify data only to standard regions: North, North West, Yorkshire and Humberside, East Midlands, East Anglia, West Midlands,

South West, Inner London, Outer London, Rest of South East, Wales and Scotland.

Table 11.1 gives a list of the variables contained in each SAR file.

4.3 Sampling

The samples are drawn from the 10% of census households which are fully coded. These fully coded census records are ordered by county, enumeration district, then street and grouped together in batches of 10 households. The household sample is drawn first and 1 in 10 households are selected at random. Then the individual sample is drawn from the remainder so that there is no overlapping of the two SAR files. Individuals in communal establishments are stratified into groups of five and one individual is selected at random from each group. Finally, it is noted that the SAR exclude imputed households since these would not be found in the 10% fully coded census records.

5 Reducing the disclosure risk

Great effort has been put into ensuring that the data are safe from individual identification and disclosure (see Skinner *et al.* 1984). Some variables available on the full census database are suppressed and some broad-banding of categories has been applied. Names and addresses are not entered onto the census computer and so do not have to be considered but the precise date of birth is suppressed. Age is available only in yearly bands and is grouped and top coded above 90. A household with a large number of persons may be more easily identifiable and so, where a household containing 12 or more persons is selected for the household file, only housing variables are included and no variables for individuals in that household are included.

The geographical information is also restricted. The usual address of visitors to the household and the former address of migrants are both specified only to the level of standard region. Term-time addresses of students and schoolchildren are specified as being inside or outside the region of usual residence, as is workplace address on the household file. On the individual file, workplace address is stated as being inside or outside the SAR area of usual residence. Distance to work is banded into eight categories, starting with 0-2 km and top coded above 40 km. Further, the distances of move of migrants is banded into 13 categories, starting with the band 0-4 km and top-coded above 200 km.

To reduce the number of rare and possibly unique cases, categories of some variables are grouped together using the rule: *Each category of each variable to be identified on the SAR must have an expected sample count of at least 1 in the smallest geographical area permitted on either file.*

In the individual file, any category of any variable which has less than 25,000 people in the whole of Great Britain is grouped in with another category in the SAR. In the household file, the cut-off falls at 2700 people (Marsh and Teague 1992).

Table 11.1 Details of the information to be supplied in the two Samples of Anonymized Records from the 1991 Census of Great Britain

Item	Household (1%) sample		Individual (2%) sample	
	No. of categories (maximum[a])	Other details	No. of categories (maximum[a])	Other details
Geographical area of enumeration	12	Standard regions of England (with split of South East into Inner London, Outer London, and Rest), Wales and Scotland	278	Local authority districts over 120,000 population. Others amalgamated to form areas over 120,000
Housing/household information				
Accommodation type	14 (14)	Detached, semi-detached or terraced house; purpose-built flat in a commercial or residential building; converted or not self-contained accommodation in a shared house or flat	As household sample	
Availability of amenities				
–bath/shower	3 (3)	Exclusive, shared, or no use	} As household sample (bath/shower, inside WC, central heating)	
–inside WC	3 (3)	Exclusive, shared, or no use		
–central heating	3 (3)	Full, part or none		
Cars (number of)	4 (4)	Top coded: 3 or more	As household sample	
Floor level (lowest) of accommodation (Scotland only)	7 (101)	Basement, ground, 1st/2nd,3rd/4th, 5th/6th, 7th to 9th, 10th or higher	As household sample	
Number of household (accommodation) spaces in dwelling	4 (35)	Top coded: 4 or more	Not included	
Number of persons (enumerated) in household	12 (99)	Top coded: 12 or more	Not included	

Table 11.1 *cont.*

Item	**Household (1%) sample**		**Individual (2%) sample**	
	No. of categories (maximum[a])	**Other details**	**No. of categories (maximum[a])**	**Other details**
Housing/household information—cont.				
Number of residents in household		Derivable	4 (99)	0, 1, 2 to 5, 6 or more
Number of dependent children in household		Derivable	2 (99)	0, 1 or more
Number of pensioners in household		Derivable	2 (99)	0, 1 or more
Number of persons with long-term illness in household		Derivable	2 (99)	0, 1 or more
Number of persons in employment in household		Derivable	3 (99)	Top-coded: 2 or more
Number of rooms	15 (19)	Top-coded: 15 or more	Not included	
Number of persons per room		Derivable	5	Ranging from less than 0.5 to greater than 1.5
Tenure	10 (10)	Owner-occupier or rented (public sector or private)	As household sample	
Wholly moving household indicator	2 (2)	Yes (all resident household members are migrants from the same address) or No	Not included	
Individual information				
Age	94 (111)	Single years 0 to 90, 91–2, 93–4, 95 and over	As household sample	

Table 11.1 *cont.*

Item	Household (1%) sample		Individual (2%) sample	
	No. of categories (maximum[a])	**Other details**	**No. of categories (maximum[a])**	**Other details**
Individual information—cont.				
Status in communal establishment	Not applicable		3 (7)	Visitor, resident staff or resident non-staff
Type of communal establishment	Not applicable		15 (35)	Hotel, hospital, nursing home etc.
Country of birth	42 (102)		As household sample	
Migrants – distance of move (km)	13	5, 10, 20 and 50 km bands; top-coded above 200 km	As household sample	
Distance to work (km)	8	10 km bands; top-coded above 40 km; 0–9 km band split 0–2, 3–4 and 5–9	As household sample	
Economic position				
–primary	10 (12)	Employee, self-employed, unemployed, student, retired etc.	As household sample	
–secondary	7 (10)		As household sample	
Economic position of family head		Derivable	3 (12)	Employed, unemployed or inactive
Ethnic group	10 (10)		As household sample	
Family head indicator	2 (2)	Yes or No	Not included	
Family number	5 (5)	Used to identify individual's family	Not included	
Family type	8 (8)	Married or cohabiting couple family with or without children or lone-parent family	As household sample	

Table 11.1 cont.

Item	Household (1%) sample		Individual (2%) sample	
	No. of categories (maximum[a])	**Other details**	**No. of categories (maximum[a])**	**Other details**
Individual information—cont.				
Gaelic language (Scotland only)	5 (8)	Ability to speak, read or write Gaelic	As household sample	
Hours worked weekly	72 (99)	Single hours 0–70, 71 to 80, 81 and over	As household sample	
Industry of employees and self-employed	185 (334)	Mainly third digit (groups) of 1980 SIC	60 (334)	Mainly second digit (classes) of 1980 SIC
Limiting long-term illness	2 (2)	Yes (individual has illness) or No	As household sample	
Marital status	5 (5)		As household sample	
Migrant – geographical area of former residence	13	Standard regions of England (with split of South East), Wales, Scotland outside Great Britain	As household sample	
Occupation	358 (371)	Mainly unit groups of 1990 SOC	73 (371)	Mainly minor groups of 1990 SOC
Number of higher educational qualifications	3 (7)	0, 1, 2 or more	As household sample	
Level of highest qualification	3 (3)	Higher degree, First degree, Above GCE A-level	As household sample	
Subject of highest qualification	88 (108)	Mainly third digit of Standard Subject Classification	35 (108)	Mainly second digit of Standard Subject Classification
Relationship to household head	17 (17)		8 (17)	

Table 11.1 *cont.*

Item	**Household (1%) sample**		**Individual (2%) sample**	
	No. of categories (maximum[a])	**Other details**	**No. of categories (maximum[a])**	**Other details**
Individual information—cont.				
Resident status	3 (3)	Present resident, absent resident, visitor	As household sample	
Sex	2 (2)		As household sample	
Sex of family head		Derivable	2 (2)	
Social class (as defined by occupation)	8 (8)		As household sample	
Social class of family head		Derivable	8 (8)	
Socioeconomic group	19 (20)		As household sample	
Term-time address of students and schoolchildren	4	Inside or outside region of usual residence	As household sample	
Transport to work (mode)	10 (10)		As household sample	
Visitor – geographical area of residence	13	Standard regions of England (with split of South East), Wales, Scotland, outside Great Britain	As household sample	
Welsh language (Wales only)	5 (8)	Active use of (speak, read or write)	As household sample	
Workplace	5	Inside or outside region of usual residence	5	Inside or outside SAR area of usual residence

Note:[a]The maximum number of categories as available on the full census database.
Source: Reproduced from OPCS *Population Trends* 69, Autumn 1992, with the permission of the Controller of HMSO.

Table 11.2 Some of the variables most affected by grouping

Variable	Number of categories		
	Full census database	**Household 1%**	**Individual 2%**
Occupation	371	358	73
Industry	334	185	60
Degree subject	108	88	35
Country of birth	102	42	42

Some of the variables most affected by grouping are shown in Table 11.2.

Finally, as a further precaution, the SAR files are scrambled to prevent any possible geographical tracing within a SAR area. However, unlike the Small Area Statistics, no perturbation techniques are applied to the SAR data.

6 Access to the Samples of Anonymized Records datasets

6.1 Census microdata unit

The ESRC jointly with the Information Services Committee of the Universities Funding Council, have purchased the data on behalf of the academic community. The SAR are housed at the Census Microdata Unit (CMU) at Manchester University which has been established to undertake research using the SAR and to make the SAR available to others.

The CMU will provide a range of services designed to give census users easy and flexible access to the SAR and to encourage wide and appropriate use of the data. Three major support and dissemination services will be provided.

6.1.1 National on-line access

The SAR will be mounted on-line at Manchester Computing Centre (MCC) and will be accessible over the Joint Academic Network (JANET) using various software packages.

6.1.2 Commissioned tables and analysis service

In the past, commissioned tables from the census were expensive for academic researchers. As an alternative, the CMU will be able to provide a commissioned tables service. In addition to tables, a non-tabular analysis service will be available.

6.1.3 Customized subset service

The CMU will also supply subsets of cases and/or variables from the SAR. For example, some researchers may require data relating to a particular ethnic group or all residents in a particular SAR area. In order to enable users to analyse the data in their own local computing environments, subsets of data will be supplied either as raw data or in a variety of different software formats, such as SPSS, SAS or SIR export format files, QUANTUM/QUANVERT or QUICKTAB system files.

The CMU is undertaking all the necessary subsidiary work connected with running a national support and dissemination service, such as producing documentation on all aspects of the service, calculating the sampling errors and creating derived variables to enhance the datasets. An evaluation of the software packages available for accessing the SAR has been carried out and so advice can be given on using the CMU-supported packages for accessing the SAR (Roberts *et al.* 1992).

6.2 A portable UNIX Samples of Anonymized Records data access system

In addition to supporting a centralized distribution of the SAR at CMU, the ESRC has also sponsored a small project to develop a portable UNIX-based system for accessing the SAR. This USAR product is available and is designed to work on a range of UNIX platforms. A full description is included in Appendix 11A.

6.3 Data availability

The SAR are made available at no cost for academic research, defined as 'research the cost of which is met wholly from within the Higher Education sector in Great Britain or from the Department of Education, Northern Ireland, in Northern Ireland and the results of which may appear in publications made available to the public, and the academic publication of the results of such research'. Since the sponsors of the data have met the full development costs of producing the SAR, they are seeking to recoup these costs by sales of the data to the commercial sector and also to the public sector, for use by central and local government. However, it is possible that the relatively course level of geographical resolution will restrict the usefulness of the SAR in some application areas: e.g. measuring ecological inference errors in geodemographic systems.

The CMU monitors the use of the SAR and has set conditions on their purchase in an End User Licence agreed with OPCS/GRO(S). All organizations using the SAR, including academic institutions, have to sign an End User Licence agreement and give strict undertakings not to attempt to identify individuals on the files, nor to claim to have done so. In addition, SAR data are not to be passed outside the organization without permission from the CMU. Any release of results using the SAR must acknowledge that the data are Crown Copyright and a six monthly report of use of the SAR is to be sent to the CMU. Commercial use of results using the SAR data will be liable to a fee, payable to the CMU, which must be agreed beforehand. The sanctions available in the case of a breach of the regulations are to recall all copies of the data from the offender's institution.

The pricing structure for access to the data has been designed to encourage maximum dissemination of the data and to be simple both to understand and to implement. Detailed information regarding both pricing and the licence agreement is available from the CMU.

7 New forms of census analysis

Many kinds of analysis are possible with the SAR data that are not possible from the published census tables. The SAR provide researchers with a large flexible database which can be installed on the user's own hardware and analysed using a wide range of database, statistical and tabulation software.

7.1 Redefining variables

Variables can easily be recoded to meet the needs of the user. For example, age grouping can be varied as required. Alternative forms of social classification are also possible. The principal form of occupational classification on most predefined census output will be the major groups of the 1990 Standard Occupational Classification. There is a large amount of occupational information available on the SAR and various derived variables can be computed. Some examples are:

- detailed 1990 Standard Occupational Classification;
- 1980 occupational groups; social class Socioeconomic Group;
- 1970 occupational unit groups and social class; and
- various metric scales of the social prestige of the occupation.

These classifications are available for the respondent and for any other household member. Composite scales of social standing can be constructed, perhaps combining information about cars, occupation and tenure in whatever index is considered relevant.

In the 1991 Census the 'householder' was instructed to complete the census form and the Census Offices treat the first person named on the form as the head of household. This person becomes the key person in identifying other household relationships. This definition of 'head of household' can be altered. Using the SAR it would be possible to identify the person who was likely to be the 'chief economic provider' for the household by using the information provided about age, sex, employment status and occupation. Families can also be identifiable from the information given in the relationship box on the census form; there is a strict census definition of a family but, using information provided in the household file, other definitions are possible. For instance, for some purposes we might wish to identify the social class of the head of the family instead of that of the head of household.

Census respondents were allowed to multicode the economic activity box on the census form but no predefined census output makes direct use of this information. New categories of economic activity can now be considered: student-workers, retired and non-retired housewives, those who are both employee and self-employed, and those both in employment and retired.

The SAR may also be useful in supplementing information gained from the Special Migration Statistics which give only limited information about migrants. From the SAR it is possible to get detailed information about migrants and the distance of their move. Households where all resident household members are migrants from the same address are identifiable on the 1% file. Detailed information is also available in the SAR to allow studies of methods of travel to work used by different members of a household. These could take into account each individual's distance to work, the mode of transport to work and the number of cars in the household. These examples illustrate some of the benefits of having access to a SAR.

7.2 Customized tables

The Census Offices now publish a vast array of tables but they cannot predict every user's need. The 1981 Census provided some 5000 cross-tabulated counts and the 1991 Census some 15,000. These were designed by 'committee' as a response to expressed user needs. However, this is a cumbersome process and onerous task. Some 'obvious' tables do not appear in predefined census output, e.g. the new health question cross-tabulated by housing characteristics for detailed areas. A tremendously large number of tables are possible using the SAR. It may still be necessary to commission a table from OPCS to get data to a level of geographical detail or because small numbers demand a 100% run, but by using the SAR first it should be possible to be more confident before commissioning expensive tables from the OPCS.

As a base for tables, the SAR can give both the number of people present on census night and the number of people who usually live in the area. Analysis can be done at different levels. For example, it would be possible to look at children under 5, how many households have children under 5 or how many people live in a household where there is a child under 5. The size of the SAR means that reliable information can be obtained for small subgroups of the population: people over 90, foreign-born doctors, those with pharmaceutical degrees, those working in the computer industry, people not at their usual residence. For example, a table of current occupation by degree subject for graduates under the age of 30 could be produced.

Finally, predefined census output does not provide much information about long-term residents of institutions, those who are sleeping rough or those in temporary accommodation. Tables could be produced to aid research into these disadvantaged groups in society.

7.3 Non-tabular analysis

Non-tabular analysis of the SAR is also possible using techniques such as analysis of variance, regression and cluster analysis. There are already some interval measures on the census: number of children, number of persons in the household, distance of journey to work, age, number of cars. It would also be possible to construct other measures, such as for occupational prestige or material disadvantage, and use these in statistical analysis. For instance, the variation in unemployment between race groups at different ages could be examined, looking at the factors associated with that variation.

7.4 Avoiding ecological fallacies

The SAR will give census users the opportunity of checking for gross ecological fallacies. Most users of the census Small Area Statistics are aware of the problems of drawing conclusions regarding individuals from tables of aggregated data. For example, areas with a high percentage of lone parents may also be areas with low car ownership. It would be wrong to conclude that lone parents do not have cars. The SAR would enable further investigation at an individual level. Openshaw (1984) provides a set of pre-SAR examples that could now be greatly improved upon. One problem though is that methods for multilevel spatial census analysis (combining individual SAR detail with spatial information from the SAS at different levels of geography) need further development.

8 Applications

Census microdata provide a valuable new resource for many fields of research and should prove useful, not only for academics, but for central and local government and in the commercial sector. The SAR could also be useful in meeting the growing demand for data for educational purposes as universities, schools and colleges are increasingly looking for realistic educational aids to explore the structure of contemporary British society.

8.1 Academic research

In North America Public Use Samples have been heavily used by demographers, economists and sociologists studying such topics as migration, patterns of labour force participation, language transfers, household living arrangements and the changing structure of families. Canadian microdata have been used to consider the extent to which different ethnic subgroups have managed to translate their educational qualifications into an occupational advantage (Li 1988). In the USA, estimates of the size and composition of the marriage market have been constructed by sophisticated analysis of age of husband and age of wife, using educational qualifications as predictors of remarriage (Goldman *et al.* 1984). The SAR is likely to stimulate similar activity in the UK and probably throughout the European Union. The data will be used primarily in a substantive census analysis sense and also as a stimulus for further methodological research. Its importance cannot be overestimated.

8.2 Central and local government

The SAR will be useful to researchers involved in analysis of the labour market. The number and characteristics of people working in particular occupations can be examined, as well as the characteristics of those working from home. Detailed studies of ethnic minorities can also be carried out. Occupational and industrial segregation indices can be derived. Status attainment studies would allow new research to be performed, while discrimination and regression analysis could be used to examine the effects of returning to education for different ethnic minorities.

Local authorities often use census data to identify areas with multiple deprivation. These are usually considered to be areas with high unemployment, many single-parent families, relatively low car ownership and many dependants. The SAR give researchers the opportunity of looking directly at households affected by combinations of different aspects of poverty. It is a potentially useful aid to community care planning, as the characteristics of those with a limiting long-term illness can be investigated, distinguishing between children, working age adults and the elderly. The health and employment status of other people in the same household can also be considered. Finally, various cross-authority analyses can be used to research different formulae for distributing government grants.

8.3 The commercial sector

Commercial users of SAR could produce tailor-made tables and statistics relevant to their organization's needs. For example, a SAR would enable the size of any target market group that can be defined in demographic terms to be calculated accurately. In the USA such target group information has been used to convert sales volumes in particular areas into productivity indices of the sales personnel in that area.

A SAR would provide a flexible source of population proportions which could be used by all organizations which regularly conduct survey research, to check the adequacy of a random or quota sample, to yield sensible quotas for a purposive sample, or to provide post-stratification weights for adjusting for non-response or for grossing-up estimates derived from a sample. Again the great advantage of the SAR is its flexibility for deriving appropriate proportions or weights for the precise target populations in surveys.

The pension and insurance industries might be interested in having access to the detailed age composition of different groups of the population. Detailed information is available in the SAR on both occupations and higher qualifications. Obtaining a precise age breakdown of particular subgroups could allow refined estimates to be made of the likely longevity of groups defined in this way, thus permitting life insurance premiums to be determined with greater accuracy.

A possible deficiency is the lack of any plans for labelling the SAR data with geodemographic codes and with lifestyle information. Also the generalized geographic resolution is considerably less than needed. On the other hand, data fusion methods, data estimation procedures and microanalytical modelling techniques might well be sufficiently powerful to generate a whole new range of useful marketing products derived in part from the SAR.

9 Conclusions

The great advantage of the SAR is that they open up so many possibilities for innovative approaches to census analysis and will enable much greater value to be extracted from the 1991 Census than from any previous census. The availability of the SAR datasets might well be viewed later as one of the major milestones in the development of household survey analysis methodology. Probably for the first time, the social statistician has access to a large national, representative, sample of individual data about people in Britain. It will be extremely surprising if this does not stimulate large numbers of applied research papers. The SAR it seems should be good for both the OPCS, the ESRC and British social science generally.

Further information about the SAR can be obtained from The Census Microdata Unit, Faculty of Economics and Social Studies, University of Manchester, Manchester M13 9PL. There is also a user guide (CMU 1993).

Appendix 11A A functional specification for a UNIX-based system for accessing the 1991 Census Samples of Anonymized Records

Ian Turton and Stan Openshaw

11A.1 Introduction

The remit of this ESRC-supported UNIX-based project is to develop portable data access software and SAR data that could be distributed via FTP over JANET to any UNIX workstation with sufficient disk space to receive it. The software and associated databases are distributed by the Census Microdata Unit (CMU) at Manchester University as an alternative means of accessing the SAR and as a complementary supplement to the SAR services provided at Manchester.

It is thought likely that experienced SAR users will want to have the SAR available on their local UNIX systems. It is even possible that as the academic sector's enthusiasm for UNIX continues to increase through the 1990s this may even become the principal future means of accessing the SAR. This Appendix outlines the basic design objectives that this UNIX based SAR diffusion package (USAR) should have; see also Turton and Openshaw (1994a, 1994b) for a fuller description, a user manual, examples, and how to obtain UNIX and MS-DOS versions of USAR.

11A.2 Design objectives – some general principles

It is regarded as essential that the system should be easy to use, requiring virtually zero prior training or at least having a very short learning curve, and should cater for the naive user as well as the more advanced and experienced computer expert. The system needs to have the simplest of possible, intuitively obvious interfaces, to allow rapid ease of use by first-time users who may well have little or no computing experience or knowledge of UNIX. At the same time, it is essential that the system should also cater for the experienced census analyst who, by comparison with the first-time user, may have need for much more complex operations.

It is also important that the documentation provided by the CMU in support of their SAR service should remain relevant to the USAR system. The same data must be available. The same variable names must be used and a similar level of data access and functionality must be provided. In addition there should be a number of 'added-goodies' to make the use of USAR attractive. The added functionality relates mainly to:

1. the ability to provide a greater degree of interactive table design in a workstation environment;
2. easy creation of pseudo SAS/LBS formatted tables;
3. basic table design and visualization tools;
4. a range of UNIX-relevant output formats;
5. a matrix output option (case by selected variables);
6. a degree of intelligent data interpretation, for instance a means of detecting potentially misleading results;
7. advanced data query in that apart from tables a user may wish to formulate fuzzy data queries and obtain counts;
8. data security; and
9. portability.

11A.2.1 Easy, fast and responsive table generation

It is axiomatic that the system should provide a fast response to table requests. In designing tables, particularly complex ones, it is essential to obtain a 'feel' about the sparseness or range of values of the likely results, as quickly as possible if not immediately. A size-adaptive sampling approach has been developed to meet this objective, with the sampling fraction being automatically modified to yield real-time results on platforms of different speeds.

There should also be a comprehensive table design capability able to handle up to 10-way tables (i.e. 10 variables cross-tabulated simultaneously) with the variables being grouped or recoded in any arbitrary manner. Standard recode lists will be provided to make it as easy as possible for the user to create standard tables. A library of recodes to emulate a majority of the SAS or LBS tables with the SAR will be stored. This is important because it is expected that many users will use the SAR to disaggregate standard tables in various ways to obtain the benefits of having access to microcensus data.

11A.2.2 Handling data uncertainty

In a research context table design is often not predetermined but can be an important part of data exploration. The provision of log-linear functionality is beyond the remit of USAR. However, it is not possible to escape from all responsibility in this area. Accordingly, some basic tabled data visualization tools are needed to assist the table design process, mainly by drawing the user's attention to those parts of the table where the reported counts are likely to be so unreliable as to be useless. To this end, a median polishing method linked to simple table colouring displays will be provided as aids to the user in designing 'useful' tables that contain 'meaningful' information. The flexibility of the SAR emphasizes the need for a basic table design tool-kit that goes beyond the table generation task. Previously this seems to have been a greatly neglected topic in statistical packages.

Sparsity is another problem. With the SAR it is expected that even seemingly mild levels of data disaggregation will produce massively empty (i.e. sparse) tables or tables populated by large quantities of small numbers. This may well be intended but the resulting unreliable nature of the tables needs to be detected and the user at least warned about it. The resulting feedback is in our view an important part of the table design process. Indeed, a balance needs to be struck between the degree of cross-tabulation requested and the level of grouping of individual variables needed to produce meaningful results. In this context 'meaningful results' is interpreted as values that can be shown to be different from zero when sampling uncertainty is taken into account, at a reasonably modest level of significance (i.e. a type I error level of 0.05). It is imagined that such values should populate most of the cells in a table, if the user wishes to use the results to demonstrate something of substance.

11A.2.3 Automated table design

Achieving table design in practice might well be difficult if only manual methods are used. It is therefore proposed to offer a semi-automated table design process. The user would specify the cross-tabulating variables and the proportion of non-zero results required; and an auto-table designer would attempt to meet the stated requirements. This is not analysis *per se* but an attempt to allow the user to interact with the SAR data via a semi-automatic table design process that at least attempts to handle rather than completely ignore the sampling nature of the SAR. This process could be left to the user with USAR merely offering a facility to flag possible meaningless cell values in a table (i.e. colour coding them). However, it is also possible to attempt to define optimal recodings of variables that contain large numbers of values, e.g. occupation or age. There are various measures of performance that can be defined for a local optimization. Experiments indicate that an automated table designer can be readily built and would be most useful in the context of the SAR. Either way some means of identifying and reporting data uncertainty is needed and cannot be avoided in the SAR context in particular.

11A.2.4 Query facilities and fuzzy searches

Database query is another need. The user may wish to know how many people or households possess a certain combination of characteristics. This can be regarded as a special case of cross-tabulation with recoded presence or absence values, or as a series of SELECT IF statements linked by Boolean operators such as AND, OR and NOT and shrouded in parenthesis. Nevertheless, it is a valid SAR query and these needs also have to be addressed by USAR.

Extensions to handle 'fuzzy' queries also need to be considered even if they might initially be thought somewhat fanciful. A fuzzy query on the SAR could be considered as a probability that a particular record met the stated SELECT IF criteria even when it would fail the criteria if applied deterministically. The fuzziness could be a reflection of measurement error (of some census kind) in the SAR or in the specification of the SELECT IF statement itself. In the latter case the user might be a little confused about precisely what is needed or would wish to count cases that nearly met the stated criteria. This would not be uncommon as census analysis is an art, not a science.

One way of implementing a SAR-relevant fuzzy query would be for the user to specify a template or ideal set of values and then request the identification of cases that have a certain fraction of the variables in common (i.e. four out of eight) but not necessarily all of them. This idea is also a feature of a data exploration package known as PATFIND. Further facilities should be provided to allow a user to 'explore' the database by specifying a variable value of interest. The program will then produce a list of variables which match records of this type most often. The user can repeat this process until either something of interest is discovered or no further records match.

11A.2.5 Data security in an open systems environment

The USAR is intended to be run in an open systems environment. It is designed to be copied and transferred between sites; at the same time it is recognized that the SAR data are a valuable commodity, that they have a commercial value and that they are covered by a legalistic and mandatory user undertaking and may well be illicitly copied. There is no basic design requirement to ensure that the raw SAR data cannot be easily reconstituted and that the system even when stolen will not readily work. The aim is not to provide 100% guarantees of system security. This is unnecessary because the CMU at the University of Manchester distributes the raw database only to registered users. From a census confidentiality viewpoint, the SAR contains no confidential data; it is an open database. Instead the objective is to preserve the IPR of USAR and offer users an incentive to acquire access rights via official channels.

Data security is ensured by three devices. First, the licensed user will be required to use the standard UNIX file permission modes to prevent unauthorized access to the data. Second, each copy of the system will be uniquely numbered allowing track-back and the user will know that this has been done. Third, the files are compressed using a non-standard algorithm, so that mere access will be insufficient to allow an unlicensed user to read the data.

11A.2.6 Portability

The system is designed to be portable. The software is written in C using standard libraries. The code is self-contained with the exception of the windowing libraries which are freely available by FTP from many locations. It is expected that the system will be portable between commonly available UNIX systems, possibly also to PC systems.

11A.3 User interface

In order to provide a simple interface to users a graphical user interface (GUI) is provided. This is based on the X-windows libraries which are freely available on most UNIX. The interface will also be implemented using the curses screen library to allow the program to be used on intelligent terminals and over JANET. In the future Super-JANET will allow the use of X-based programs on remote machines; however, it will be some time before this is available to all universities.

11A.3.1 X-windows interface

The X-windows system provides a smooth and flexible user interface in an age of open systems. The libraries used in USAR are freely available on a machine with X provided, thus allowing the program to run on the maximum number of machines. The use of a graphical interface allows the user to select actions from a menu of choices or by 'pressing' buttons with the mouse. This means that the application can guide the user through a series of complex activities without them being aware of the complexity.

11A.3.2 Curses interface

The curses screen library is a standard part of the UNIX system distribution that provides screen control on a variety of intelligent terminals (i.e. an IBM PC). This system allows USAR to be used from any terminals commonly found in universities, since it must be remembered that not all researchers have access to an X-terminal. The user interface will be as similar as possible between the two versions; however, the curses interface will inevitably be less intelligent. The user will be required to respond to screen prompts and make use of the arrow keys rather than the mouse to navigate around the screen. Therefore it is expected that users with X-terminals will use the X-windows version of the program and that other users will use the curses-based version. A batch file facility will also be provided to allow the creation of input files to complete a series of jobs while the user is busy (or at home asleep). The functionality of the program will be the same in all versions and it is hoped that the layout and command sequences will be similar wherever possible.

11A.4 Example of use

Figure 11.1 shows the main screen for USAR. The user can move a cursor around the screen, to select the dataset, variables or set other options.

Figure 11.2 shows the screen that is reached after selecting the individual data and the selecting variables on the main screen. The user can now scroll up and down the left-hand column of variables pressing either 'r' or 'c' to select row or

```
USAR 1.0 - (c) Ian Turton, School of Geography, University of Leeds
UniversitLeedsESRC/JICS/DENI          Bugs to: ian@geog.leeds.ac.uk

Data None
Variables              Filters
Tabulate
                       Search
                       Explore

                       Logfile: None
                       Print
Quit

Use arrow keys to choose command - return to select or type first
letter.
```

Fig. 11.1 USAR screen display.

```
USAR 1.0 - (c) Ian Turton, School of Geography, University of Leeds
ESRC/JICS/DENI                                              Bugs  to:
ian@geog.leeds.ac.uk


AREA                  Finished           Row
REGION
AGE
CESTSTAT
CESTTYPE
COBIRTH
DISTMOVE
DISTWORK
ECONPRIM
ECONSEC                                  Columns
ETHGROUP
FAMTYPE
GAELLANG
HOURS
INDUST
LTILL

Use arrow keys to choose variable - press rows or columns
```

Fig. 11.2 Example of variable selection screen.

```
USAR 1.0 - (c) Ian Turton, School of Geography, University of Leeds
ESRC/JICS/DENI                          Bugs to: ian@geog.leeds.ac.uk

  0-  4                                                  finish
  5-  9                                                  Next group
 10- 14                                                  Special
 15- 19
 20- 29
 30- 39
 40- 49
 50- 59
 60- 79
 80- 99
100-149
150-199
200+
Outside UK
Not stated

DISTMOVE
Select class(es) for group 1
Clear
```

Fig. 11.3 Example of variable regrouping screen.

column variables. When a variable is selected the user is presented with a screen like Fig. 11.3 which shows the classes available for the chosen variable which they can then group. The special option allows groups to be constructed by specifying a start and finish class and either the size of the groups or the number of groups required.

Once the user has completed specification of the table, it can be created and viewed on the screen. Again the cursor keys are used to scroll the table if it is larger than the screen.

At this point, it is possible to save the table to a file to be processed in a text editor or spreadsheet. USAR offers a range of print formats. Table 11.3 gives the results produced by USAR directly as a LaTeX file which was then printed without modification. It shows *car* availability *against tenure* by *ethnic* group.

Table 11.3 Results produced by USAR directly as a LaTeX file

		CARS	**0**	**1-3+**
ETHGROUP	**TENURE**			
White	Owning		12.40	87.60
	Rent priv		33.59	66.41
	HA rent		60.90	39.10
	rent LA		58.72	41.28
	rent NT Scot		58.49	41.51
Black	Owning		26.55	73.45
	Rent priv		57.11	42.89
	Ha rent		68.75	31.25
	rent LA		72.07	27.93
	rent NT Scot		0.00	100.00
Indian	Owning		13.89	86.11
	Rent priv		38.89	61.11
	Ha rent		53.09	46.91
	rent LA		52.99	47.01
	rent NT Scot		0.00	0.00
Pakistani	Owning		28.33	71.67
	Rent priv		51.35	48.65
	HA rent		52.47	47.53
	rent LA		54.18	45.82
	rent NT Scot		33.33	66.67
Bangladeshi	Owning		45.77	54.23
	Rent priv		71.51	28.49
	HA rent		67.17	32.83
	rent LA		78.31	21.69
	rent NT Scot		0.00	0.00
Other	Owning		14.93	85.07
	Rent priv		40.20	59.80
	Ha rent		59.31	40.69
	rent LA		57.01	42.99
	rent NT Scot		28.57	71.43

Figure 11.1 also shows the other USAR options: filters, search and explore. *Filters* allows the user to impose restrictions on the persons and households selected for analysis. An example would be to limit the table to just one region or only select persons who are older than 16. *Search* allows the user to limit the data one variable at a time, to see how other variables relate to this restriction and then to add more restrictions. *Explore* provides the fuzzy search facilities described in Section 11A.2.4, where a series of relationships are selected and a specified fraction is matched.

11A.5 Conclusions

The USAR system reflects the view that in 1993 a SAR data access package has to offer more than rudimentary data tabulation functions. It should also seek to exploit the power of modern workstations, open systems, the flexibility of windowing systems and be able to deal effectively with a user base with a wide range of computing skills. The outline functional specification described above has outlined how we plan to meet these objectives. The system is operational and freely available to registered SAR users. Further details can be obtained by writing to either the CMU at Manchester or the authors at Leeds.

References

CMU 1993 *A User Guide to the SARS*. Manchester University: Census Microdata Unit.

Goldman, N, C F Westoff and C Hammerslough 1984 Indicators of the marriage market in the United States. *Population Index* 50 (1), 5–25.

Her Majesty's Government 1991 1991 Census of Population: Confidentiality and Computing. Presented to Parliament by the Secretary of State for Health and the Secretary of State for Scotland, February, Cm 1447. London: HMSO.

Keller, W and L Willenborg 1992 Microdata release policy at the Netherlands CBS. *Proceedings of the International Seminar on Statistical Confidentiality, Dublin,* organized by EUROSTAT and ISI.

Knoche, P 1992 Factual anonymity of microdata from household and person related surveys. The release of microdata files for scientific purposes. *Proceedings of the International Seminar on Statistical Confidentiality, Dublin*, organized by EUROSTAT and ISI.

Li, P S 1988 Ethnic inequality in a class society. Toronto: Wall & Thompson.

Marsh, C 1993 The sample of anonymised records. In A Dale and C Marsh (eds) *The 1991 Census User's Guide*. London: HMSO, 295–311.

Marsh, C and A Teague 1992 Samples of anonymised records from the 1991 Census. *Population Trends* 69, 17–26.

Marsh, C, S Arber, N Wrigley, D Rhind and M Bulmer 1988. The view of academic social scientists on the 1991 UK Census of Population; a report of the Economic and Social Research Council Working Group. *Environment and Planning A* 20, 851–89.

Marsh, C, C Skinner, S Arber, B Penhale, S Openshaw, J Hobcraft, D Lievesley and N Walford 1991 The case for samples of anonymised records from the 1991 census. *Journal of the Royal Statistical Society A* 154, 2.

Norris, P 1983 Microdata from the British Census. In D W Rhind (ed) *A Census User's Handbook*. London: Methuen.

Openshaw, S 1984 Ecological fallacies and the analysis of areal census data. *Environment and Planning A* 16, 17–31.

Roberts, J, E Middleton, K Cole, M Campbell and C Marsh 1992 Software solutions for Samples of Anonymised Records. In A Westlake *et al.* (eds) *Survey and Statistical Computing*. Amsterdam: North-Holland.

Skinner, C,C Marsh, S Openshaw and C Wymer 1994 Disclosure control for census microdata. *Journal of Official Statistics* 10, 31-51.

Turton, I and S Openshaw 1994a A step-by-step guide to accessing the 1991 SAR via USAR. Working paper–94/6, School of Geography, Leeds University.

Turton, I and S Openshaw 1994b USAR – putting the 1991 sample of anonymised records on your workstation. *Environment and Planning A* (to be published).

12

Using microsimulation methods to synthesize census data

M Birkin and G Clarke

Editor's note

Census data will never meet all user needs for data. For some applications microsimulation methods will allow linkage between tables from the census and other data sources, thereby allowing the user to enrich the census resource and extend its usefulness. As computer hardware speeds increase by two or three orders of magnitude during the 1990s, so the ability of users to synthesize their own extra-census data consistent with known real census data will increase and become a potentially extremely useful tool for many research and applied purposes.

1 Introduction

It is widely acknowledged that of all the official government publications the census provides the most comprehensive survey of the national population. It continues to provide the building block for many studies in the social sciences, particularly in areas such as deprivation, population redistribution, allocation of government funds, migration and labour market analysis. In addition, it is the starting point for future population forecasts and provides the inputs into most *applied* urban and regional modelling.

Although it is undeniably a rich resource base for social scientists there are limitations to the information available. In theory, the 24 questions asked in the census should provide a rich cross-classification of the relationships between a wide variety of household and individual characteristics. In practice, the need to protect confidentiality and the necessity to provide aggregated published information means that there is a limit to the number of census tables available and researchers are faced with a rather inflexible information system. In addition, there are simply some issues which are not addressed by the census. The most striking of these omissions are income and expenditure data and a whole range of issues relating to trip patterns (or interaction flows).

The aim of this chapter is first to highlight some of the deficiencies of raw census information for many aspects of urban and social geography (Section 2). Whilst recognizing the importance of the census we stress the need for better microdata and offer a methodology for recreating the detail of the census through synthetically generated samples of individuals and households. This process of microsimulation is explained in Section 3, which also addresses the key advantages of this approach over census tables alone. Some new examples are offered in Section 4.

2 Deficiencies of the published census

2.1 The lack of microdata

The most fundamental drawback with the published census material is the lack of information pertaining to individuals or individual households. For confidentiality reasons, information is only made available at aggregated spatial scales (enumeration districts (EDs) being the smallest). Whilst this is adequate for many social studies there is a feeling of frustration that the rich microdata underpinning the aggregate published information is not available. Indeed, in the survey by Marsh *et al.* (1988) many academics and planners expressed a desire to access results directly and thus felt they could not maximize the use of the census at present. The calls for direct access to microdata go back to the preceding census handbook (Norris 1983) but perhaps the most persuasive arguments appear in Marsh *et al.* (1991). We shall explore and expand on some of these arguments below.

The plea for microdata has been partly met by the agreement to publish samples of anonymized records (SAR data). As Rees (1992) points out, the improved availability of flexible tables based on such samples will widen the appeal of the census (especially in disciplines such as sociology and social policy). However, the SAR data will be based on only a 2% sample of the population, and 1% of households. Perhaps more crucially, they will only be available for very broad geographical regions in order to preserve strict confidentiality conditions. This leads to two problems. First, the relatively broad geographical units will obviously limit the usefulness of SAR data for the study of geographical patterns, and second, the 'sensitive nature' of these datasets will force researchers to abide by very stringent conditions of use (Rees 1992). All in all, the SAR dataset is a useful starting point but for many researchers even this level of data availablity may not be enough.

It is also possible for researchers to order special tabulations on an *ad hoc* basis from OPCS. However, this is likely to be costly, in terms of both money and time. The alternative is the creation of the synthetic dataset outlined in Section 3. The demand for microdata in general emerges as a result of the following problems.

2.2 Missing linkages

Whenever published tables are produced there is clearly a limit to the number of variables that can be shown and hence the interdependences between variables are correspondingly limited. Even though some tables may have a threefold or fourfold classification the majority of tables are two dimensional. An illustration is useful at this point. From the published census material it is possible to obtain unemployment rates by any of the following variables: sex, age, ethnic status and occupation. However, if we wished to calculate the number of 16–19 year old, non-British, unskilled male workers that were currently unemployed we would usually have to undertake some kind of survey. The alternative is to generate a joint probability distribution for this attribute vector and then synthetically create or extract individuals from this distribution (see Birkin *et al.* 1990). The modelling skill is to build up one attribute at a time so that the probability of certain attributes is conditionally dependent on existing attributes (see Section 3).

The best illustration of this work is Birkin and Clarke (1988). They generated a microdata-base for the Leeds Metropolitan District based on five household attributes and seven individual attributes. These are shown in Table 12.1. The beauty of this database is the flexibility to create arrays based on the combination of any of these disaggregate variables, e.g. the number of Pakistani married

Table 12.1 Household and individual attributes in the SYNTHESIS database

Attribute	Number	Details
Household attributes		
Location	1565	1 DAAA01
		2 DAAA02
		⋮
		1565 DABK47
Household structure and composition	5	1 Single person, retired
		2 Single person, not retired
		3 Married couple, no children
		4 Lone-parent family
		5 Married couple with children
Tenure	3	1 Owner-occupied
		2 Council rented
		3 Other
Country of birth of household head	7	1 Great Britain
		2 Eire
		3 New Commonwealth – India
		4 New Commonwealth – Caribbean
		5 Rest of New Commonwealth
		6 Pakistan
		7 Rest of the world
Primary retail location	52	1 Hemsworth
		2 Normanton
		⋮
		52 Bradford

Table 12.1 *cont.*

Attribute	Number	Details
Individual attributes		
Status within household	5	1 Head 2 Spouse of head 3 Child of head 4 Other, dependent 5 Other, not dependent
Exact age	86	0 1 : 85+
Sex	2	1 Male 2 Female
Marital status	3	1 Married 2 Single 3 Widowed or divorced
Economic activity	4	0 Inactive 1 In work 2 Retired 3 Seeking work
Socioeconomic group	7	1 Employers and managers 2 Professional 3 Intermediate or junior non-manual 4 Skilled manual 5 Semiskilled manual 6 Unskilled manual 7 Other or not stated
Industry	7	1 Agriculture 2 Energy and water 3 Manufacturing 4 Construction 5 Distribution and catering 6 Transport 7 Other services

couples with children who live in council-rented property and work in skilled manual occupations within manufacturing industries. The number of potential combinations clearly makes the information system extremely powerful.

2.3 Missing data

In addition to the problem of the limited joint distributions in the published census we have the problem that some information is not available for the simple reason that no question was asked on the topic. Perhaps the most important of the missing variables are household incomes and expenditures (the survey of

Marsh *et al.* (1988) identified an urgent need for indicators of income and receipts of benefits). However, these are available for a sample of households through the New Earnings Survey and the Family Expenditure Survey respectively. The problem is simply how to *link* such survey data with the small area census statistics effectively. Clarke (1986) showed that it was possible to construct an income-generation module based on the industrial sector and occupation of the individual from the New Earnings Survey. The next step is to examine the small area breakdown of occupation groups by industry type and build up probability distributions of household incomes (see Birkin and Clarke 1989). Figure 12.1 plots the income distributions for households in Leeds (based on 1981 Census information).

The census is also deficient in terms of the amount of flow information that it contains. Once again, the study of Marsh *et al.* (1988) is useful for highlighting the problems many researchers feel over the unavailability of interaction data. The Special Migration Statistics and the Special Workplace Statistics offer some information on individual movements across cities and regions although again the coverage does not include all possible interaction groups. However, micro-simulation techniques offer considerable potential here. Let us proceed with an example based on the journey to work.

For many areas of social and economic geography the array *Tij*(*bags*) is a crucial one. *Tij* is the journey to work from residential location *i* to workplace *j*, disaggregated by occupation (*b*), age (*a*), sex (*s*) and industry (*g*). From the census it is possible to get information on the array *Tij*(*m,a,s*), where *m* is additionally mode of travel. What is required now is the link to origin and destination end

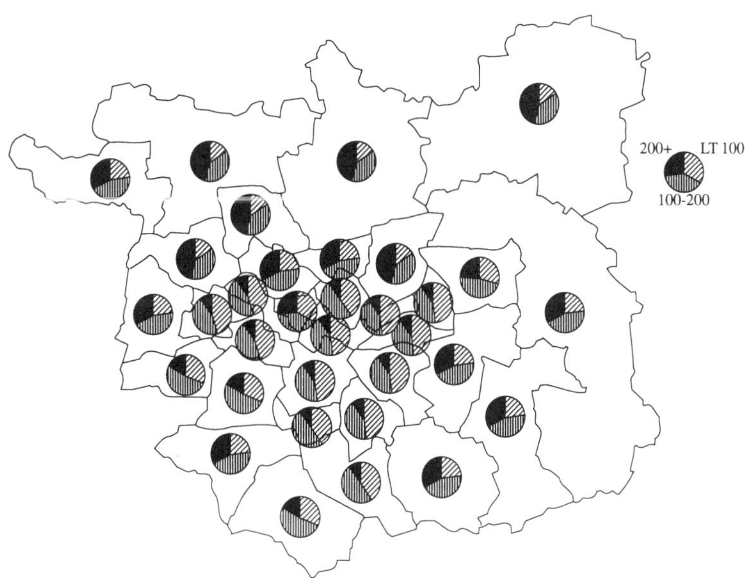

Fig. 12.1 Small area income distributions generated from SYNTHESIS.

totals. We can see from the simulated data described in Section 2.2 that it is possible to estimate the origin array *Pi(bags)* where *Pi* is the residential population in zone *i*. From a combination of the census Special Workplace Statistics and the Census of Employment it is possible to estimate the workplace array *Ej(bags)* where *Ej* defines the workforce in zone *j*. The modelling task therefore is to estimate *Tij(wbags)* from the combination of these three arrays. This example is worked out in detail in Birkin and Clarke (1987) and Birkin *et al.* (1994).

Birkin and Clarke (1988) also included shopping centre locations among their household attribute lists. This was simply based on the LUPIN dataset provided by Pinpoint Ltd which gives known interaction flows for non-food goods by origin postal districts. Although the assigning of individual locations to a 'parent' postal district is fairly crude (and ignores the considerable overlap of real catchment areas) it does provide a useful summary of major shopping flows in the region.

Clarke and Spowage (1985) also showed the power of microsimulation to look at flows related to hospitalization rates. By building a set of morbidity models (again morbidity data are not available in the census but are widely deemed to be important in the survey by Marsh *et al.* (1988)) based on the age, sex, social class and ethnicity of the population they were able to simulate likely hospitalization rates (by small geographical area and by morbidity condition). The model then becomes valuable for policy changes: the closing/opening of a new unit or the rationalization of services in existing units.

The linking of microdata sets to more meso-scale interaction models remains an important and ongoing research programme.

2.4 The aggregation problem

One of the most enduring and least tractable problems in geography and spatial economics is to find methods of problem solving which are mutually consistent at micro, meso and macro levels of resolution. This is known as the 'aggregation problem'. An associated problem is the 'ecological fallacy':

> It is not safe to infer from the evidence of association at one level of aggregation that this association exists at the lower level.
>
> (Marsh *et al.* 1991)

This problem is bound to arise when variables are aggregated into larger spatial units. For many purposes characteristics of households expressed in census EDs or wards are fine for showing the degree of variation across geographical regions. However, as often as not, there are more variations within a zone (of a particular variable) than there are between zones. This is especially worrying when single descriptors are attached to spatial zones to portray the 'typical' population set. This applies in particular to the discriminators used in geodemographic systems. For example, the Superprofiles system has a lifestyle type 'Metro Singles' in which less than 25% actually comprise single individuals. Or again, in the same system, the lifestyle type 'Older Suburbia' has a population in which over 53% of individuals are aged under 45 (see Brown 1989, Tables 1 and 2).

The application of microsimulation methods may be thought of as a direct attack on this problem. The basis of the method is an explicit representation of the attributes of individual actors within the economic system. Because there is no prior aggregation, model outputs can be tailored to the requirements of the user and not constrained by the aggregation process (Clarke and Holm 1987). That said, it may still be useful and appropriate to aggregate individual household results to broader geographical regions. In this way the microsimulation approach offers greatest *flexibility* for aggregation purposes.

2.5 Static database

By the time the 1991 Census was made available to academic and business users it was already some two years out of date. This is inevitable with 10-year snapshots and again for many geographical areas the changes since 1991 will have been minimal. The problem of course gets worse over time, culminating in the period towards the end of the decade when everyone is circumspect about using the data. The problem is compounded in the UK with the uncertainty of the future of the census itself. It will be a harrowing thought to many planners and business people that the 1991 Census might be the last (think of the difficulties on the supply side of the economy since the demise of the Census of Production).

Microsimulation models offer considerable potential in the modelling of both household dynamics and the effects of changes in the supply side of the economy. On the demand side, the main principle is to update individual and household attributes by means of list processing. This involves deriving conditional probabilities for events such as deaths, births, migrations etc. and to invoke Monte Carlo sampling methods to determine whether eligible individuals undergo appropriate transitions (see Section 3 and Clarke 1986, Rees *et al.* 1987, Duley 1989). On the supply side forecasting is more difficult. Datasets such as the Census of Employment help to update changes in the supply side of the economy. However, it is also possible to update and attempt to forecast major supply side changes (loss of major companies in the economy, the building of a new shopping centre or school etc.) through the addition of interaction flows in the manner described in Section 2.3. We shall return to the issues of updating and forecasting in Section 3.

2.6 Summary

In the above sections we have summarized the drawbacks in the information set contained in the 1991 Census and outlined the case for a more detailed microdata set to supplement the census itself (and ultimately replace it if it proves to be the final one!). We have also argued that the SAR dataset provided by OPCS, whilst

Table 12.2 Isle of Wight population profile: 1991 Census

Age	Total persons	Males					Females				
		Total	Single	Married	Widowed	Divorced	Total	Single	Married	Widowed	Divorced
a	b	c	d	e	f	g	h	i	j	k	l
					ISLE OF WIGHT						
ALL AGES	124 577	59 281	23 478	30 568	2 267	2 968	65 296	21 196	30 711	9 511	3 878
0–4	6 806	3 532	3 532				3 274	3 274			
5–9	6 950	3 563	3 563				3 387	3 387			
10–14	7 081	3 665	3 665				3 416	3 416			
15	1 435	727	727				708	708			
16–17	3 067	1 599	1 598	–	–	1	1 468	1 461	5	–	2
18–19	3 032	1 542	1 530	10	–	2	1 490	1 442	45	1	2
20–24	7 262	3 660	3 210	426	1	23	3 602	2 639	902	4	54
25–29	7 405	3 759	2 025	1 594	3	137	3 646	1 251	2 105	8	282
30–34	7 016	3 477	973	2 174	3	327	3 539	542	2 587	18	392
35–39	7 447	3 615	609	2 663	6	337	3 832	304	3 010	32	486
40–44	9 045	4 490	449	3 488	19	534	4 555	251	3 645	69	590
45–49	8 171	4 059	330	3 265	26	438	4 112	194	3 262	124	532
50–54	6 772	3 345	220	2 770	53	302	3 427	177	2 732	153	365
55–59	6 757	3 216	204	2 633	60	319	3 541	208	2 674	356	303
60–64	7 430	3 394	208	2 801	182	203	4 036	283	2 757	725	271
65–69	8 198	3 694	235	3 043	270	146	4 504	326	2 790	1 176	212
70–74	7 137	3 048	161	2 463	330	94	4 089	322	2 030	1 535	202
75–79	6 141	2 430	111	1 842	422	55	3 711	346	1 292	1 972	101
80–84	4 308	1 594	83	991	480	40	2 714	323	631	1 707	53
85–89	2 279	698	38	342	308	10	1 581	234	195	1 127	25
90 and over	838	174	7	63	104	–	664	108	46	504	6

Table 12.2 *cont.*

Age	Total persons	Males					Females				
		Total	Single	Married	Widowed	Divorced	Total	Single	Married	Widowed	Divorced
a	b	c	d	e	f	g	h	i	j	k	l
					Medina						
ALL AGES	71 104	34 210	14 188	17 008	1 218	1 796	36 894	12 476	17 022	5 137	2 259
0–4	4 198	2 195	2 195				2 003	2 003			
5–9	4 086	2 074	2 074				2 012	2 012			
10–14	4 097	2 136	2 136				1 961	1 961			
15	867	433	433				434	434			
16–17	1 809	943	943	–	–	–	866	861	4	–	1
18–19	1 787	936	924	10	–	2	851	814	35	1	1
20–24	4 573	2 303	2 001	282	1	19	2 270	1 627	608	4	31
25–29	4 851	2 514	1 330	1 101	2	81	2 337	789	1 383	5	160
30–34	4 381	2 228	644	1 370	3	211	2 153	332	1 559	13	249
35–39	4 374	2 154	380	1 572	2	200	2 220	176	1 738	17	289
40–44	5 176	2 593	248	1 991	14	340	2 583	145	2 055	42	341
45–49	4 691	2 340	183	1 880	15	262	2 351	119	1 836	71	325
50–54	3 773	1 874	125	1 544	32	173	1 899	98	1 507	90	204
55–59	3 653	1 741	114	1 409	34	184	1 912	105	1 419	207	181
60–64	3 796	1 784	112	1 440	109	123	2 012	133	1 333	401	145
65–69	4 227	1 889	122	1 542	138	87	2 338	165	1 436	619	118
70–74	3 802	1 573	93	1 243	184	53	2 229	181	1 045	888	115
75–79	3 219	1 256	68	931	227	30	1 963	172	647	1 090	54
80–84	2 211	815	40	499	250	26	1 396	178	307	883	28
85–89	1 128	345	18	168	154	5	783	115	85	568	15
90 and over	405	84	5	26	53	–	321	56	25	238	2

useful for helping to calibrate microsimulation models (see Section 3), may not provide the necessary spatial detail required by many geographers.

In the next section we outline the principles of microsimulation in more detail and show how the above issues can be addressed from the technical standpoint.

3 Enhancing the census through microsimulation

3.1 Introduction

It is important to begin this section by emphasizing the distinction between the conventional, array-based representations of spatial data and the alternative representation of individual characteristics on which microsimulation is based. Consider the data in Table 12.2, which is drawn from Table 2 of the County Report for the Isle of Wight (OPCS 1992). The table divides individuals into categories according to their age, sex and marital status in a familiar way. Thus in the Isle of Wight there were 973 single men aged between 30 and 34 in residence on census night in 1991.

An alternative way of representing the same data is as a string of individual characteristics, as illustrated in Table 12.3. Here we have a list of individuals, of which there will be a total of 124,577 in the Isle of Wight. Each individual has four characteristics: a sequence number in the database; an exact age; a sex (1 = male; 2 = female) and a marital status (1 = single; 2 = married; 3 = widowed; 4 = divorced). Thus the first individual is a single man aged 32, and so on.

The power of representing data at the individual level becomes immediately apparent if we extend the list of characteristics. Suppose that we consider the full list of 24 characteristics generated from the 1991 Census forms themselves. It is now clearly impossible to represent counts of all categories of individual within a tabular structure. Even if there were only two possible categories for each characteristic (as in the case of sex, for instance) then there are 2 to the power of 27, or 16 million, possible states in the array! (Note that in practice there will be more than two states for most characteristics, so there are probably of the order of a billion different states, in fact. However, a certain number of cases will

Table 12.3 Typical individuals from an imaginary Isle of Wight database

1	32	1	1
2	65	2	2
3	44	1	3
4	10	2	1
5	51	2	2
6	56	1	2
7	5	1	1
8	34	1	3
9	32	2	1
10	61	1	2
124 577	26	1	1

be mutually exclusive, e.g. ages under 16 and marital states other than single.) What happens in the census is that the individual records are aggregated into about 90 different tables for each of over 100,000 small areas (EDs), each with about 9000 counts of different combinations of characteristics. Nevertheless, since there are of the order of a billion different types of individual for each ED quite a lot of information is lost in this aggregation process, as we argued in Section 2 above. The SAR is to be provided in order to meet the potential need for data which are cross-classified into categories not met in the standard tabulations.

The situation in relation to the census which has been outlined above is quite typical in social science research. What researchers would like to know are detailed sets of cross-classified characteristics for individuals (for the kinds of reasons which were outlined in Section 2). In practice, what is available are either partial tabulations of particular sets of characteristics, or data relating to individuals but only for a sample of cases. Since the first objective of microsimulation is to try and recreate a baseline population, we need to consider two separate methodologies, namely synthetic reconstruction and reweighting.

3.1.1 Synthetic reconstruction of census populations

Where partial cross-tabulations are known then we can use maximum likelihood estimation to try and reconstruct the original population in such a way that all known constraints (the counts represented in the tables) are reproduced. In practice, this is achieved using the technique of iterative proportional fitting (IPF) (Fienberg 1970, 1977; see also Birkin and Clarke 1988). The population reconstruction is a step-by-step exercise. We might begin by estimating the age, sex and marital status of individuals from Table 12.3 (or its small area equivalent). This would be done by Monte Carlo sampling, i.e. generate a list of 124,577 individuals and assign characteristics probabilistically using random number sequences in such a way that the probability that a person is a single man aged between 30 and 34 is 973/124,577 or about 0.8%. Suppose that we then wish to generate a fourth characteristic, say economic position. In this case, we might know economic position by age and sex (from Table 8 of the County Reports) and economic position by sex and marital status (from Table 34). We can use IPF to calculate economic position by age, sex and marital status. Monte Carlo sampling can then be used again to assign economic position given age, sex and marital status of an individual.

This process can then be repeated to generate further new characteristics based on the combinations of those previously generated. As more characteristics are generated, so the process becomes more complex. One of the beauties of IPF is that any number of sets of constraints can be embedded within the procedure.

Notice that no errors are introduced by the IPF process (i.e. we can estimate a complete set of joint probabilities which is completely consistent with all known constraints). However, a certain amount of error is introduced in the Monte Carlo sampling stage, and this level of error increases as we go further along the chain of generation of characteristics. Part of the modeller's art here is to generate new characteristics in an appropriate order so that potential errors are minimized. While the issues are not well understood, they are nevertheless well outside the bounds of the present chapter.

3.1.2 Reweighting

The problems are slightly different when the information at our disposal includes a real sample of individuals. If we assume that the sample is reliable in terms of both size and quality then we can try to reconstruct the original population by reweighting the sample population, i.e. by reproducing individuals in the sample a certain number of times to replicate the parent database in terms of size and composition. An assumption here is that we are again in possession of some known information about the parent population, perhaps in the form of aggregate cross-tabulations. If this is the case, then the techniques necessary to achieve the reweighting are unlikely to be very different from IPF as it becomes necessary to reweight the sample data iteratively to a series of known partial constraints. The procedure has been referred to as multi-raking by Merz (1986). Again, some errors are likely to be introduced through the reweighting procedure as the full variety of the parent population will not usually be present in the sample database, i.e. certain types of individual are not represented.

3.2 Applications of microsimulation

We have seen in the previous section that the technique of microsimulation is relatively complex, data intensive and also computationally expensive. Furthermore the process of population reconstruction is an exact rather than an approximate exercise. We now need to examine some of the benefits which may counterbalance these drawbacks.

3.2.1 Flexible aggregation

This idea has already been introduced in Section 2.1. If we can recreate aggregate tables in terms of sets of individual records then it is possible to reaggregate the data into any set of cross-tabulations which may be desired. Another advantage is that it is often possible to represent attributes at the micro-level as exact values. The obvious example here is age, which means that any categorization involving age can be generated using a single-year classification if desired.

3.2.2 Linkage

We have seen in Sections 2.2 and 2.3 that populations can be recreated synthetically using a step-by-step procedure. There is no reason why this approach needs to be confined to recreating the attributes in a single parent database. So if we can identify constraints which relate census to non-census characteristics then a whole new range of characteristics can be built in.

Notice that we can also use these procedures to add to a micro-level database which has been created through reweighting. For instance we could reweight the SAR to the parent census database and then link in new variables like expenditure and income. This is explored further in Section 4 below. Linkage between micro-level databases may also involve concepts of statistical matching of databases (e.g. Paass 1986).

3.2.3 Updating and forecasting

It is important to distinguish between updating and forecasting. In order to bring a dataset up to date we are likely to feed in new data. Duley (1989) used OPCS Vital Statistics for births and deaths by ward, together with NHSCR migration data and local authority housebuilding statistics to update 1981 Census data. Household forecasting, on the other hand, involves the extrapolation of trends into the future as in any other form of forecasting (see again Section 2.5).

We can also mention that the list processing approach implies an attempt to age a population *dynamically*. So we take an initial population and try to simulate what might happen to individual members of that population over time. An alternative strategy is *static ageing*. In this case, no attempt is made to consider individual transitions, but an initial population is adjusted to reflect macro-level trends. This is therefore another application of reweighting.

3.2.4 Modelling

We have already seen that micro-level databases, whether synthetic or real, provide an efficient way of representing data where the dimensionality is too high to be coped with using array-based representations. This situation can also apply when modelling spatial interactions between small areas, where large and sparse interaction matrices may frequently be generated. The coverage of interactions is also very partial within the census: although there is some consideration of journey-to-work and migration patterns, activities such as shopping, education, health care and recreational pursuits are not considered at all. In this situation, it may be possible to create linked 'micro–macro' models where a microdata-base is used to provide information into some kind of aggregate spatial interaction model. Monte Carlo sampling can then be used again to assign particular patterns of activities to the individuals within the microscale database. See, for example, Birkin and Clarke (1985), where an attempt was made to determine retail activity patterns of a group of individuals, and also Birkin and Clarke (1988).

Microscale representation is also perfect for the representation of large-scale interaction matrices.

3.3 Summary

Microsimulation represents an attempt to recreate a population of individuals in contrast to the more usual focus on counts by category. There are two distinct approaches to the reconstruction phase: reweighting or synthetic approaches. The notion of list processing is also an important one.

Having gone to the (considerable) trouble of generating a micro-level population there are many advantages in terms of flexible aggregation, data linkage, updating, forecasting and modelling activities. We now move on to demonstrate some of these benefits in relation to two distinct areas of application.

4 Some new examples

4.1 Lifestyle data

4.1.1 General discussion

Many companies are now collecting data on the demographic profiles, consumption patterns and interests of the population. NDL International is one such company which has already accumulated data on the characteristics of some 10 million households. The geographical location of these households can be identified right down to the unit postcode level. For each household, some 60 characteristics are recorded, including demographic, social, economic and lifestyle attributes. The data are collected incrementally, and have been built up over a four- or five-year period. The motivation for the development of such a database has been as a direct marketing tool.

In this application we wish to consider the potential benefits of using these data as the basis for an *area profiling system* for small areas. Such a system is currently under development as a collaborative venture between NDL and GMAP Limited, a University of Leeds company. When compared with the census, the main advantage of the NDL database is that it contains information on incomes and on lifestyle types (as well as on other potentially interesting characteristics such as credit card ownership); and new responses are being collected at a rate of about 4 million per year. The main disadvantages are that the coverage of demographic and socioeconomic characteristics is much more sparse than in the census; and that the data are beset by sampling bias.

4.1.2 Objectives

We will not consider the question of partial coverage of characteristics in any more detail. This would need to be addressed through some form of matching of the lifestyles data to other, more extensive, microdata-bases, e.g. to the census SAR, although this in itself would raise all sorts of confidentiality issues. Rather, we will focus on the problem of bias. There are again two possible sources of such bias: misrepresentation of individual responses and systematic biases in the sampling frame. Misrepresentation may arise through misunderstanding of the questions asked, or through a deliberate desire to conceal information. Systematic biases may arise because the data have been generated through questionnaires filled in by people purchasing durable goods; and we would therefore expect the types of people who buy a lot of durable goods to be over-represented in the sample.

The problem to be addressed here is to reweight the sample in such a way that it becomes as representative as possible of the population from which it is drawn (i.e. the population of the UK). This will be done by duplicating individual household records in the database. Duplication will be permitted from zero up to an appropriate maximum number of times. We will end up with a database of some 22 million households 'cloned' from the original 10 million.

4.1.3 Strategy

Clearly in order to reweight the data we need some accurate target information about the parent population. The obvious source is the 1991 Census, which will be a prime source of social, economic and demographic information. Nevertheless there are a number of other sources of potentially useful data, including the New Earnings Survey and Family Expenditure Survey, the General Household Survey and the Registrar General's Population Estimates.

There are two general sets of issues which need to be addressed in relation to the census. The first set relate to defining an appropriate spatial scale for the reweighting. Whilst it might be possible to reweight the data at a very fine spatial scale, such as a postal sector, we would argue that we should not use census data at postal sector level as the major component in the process for a number of reasons. The first is that this is the most computationally burdensome approach, and probably the least robust. Second, there are serious questions regarding the accuracy of the census data themselves. It is known that the census is under-enumerated by around 1.8 million. It is unclear that the damage can be repaired adequately through the OPCS Validation Survey and, in effect, their own re-weighting procedure. There are also difficulties regarding the artificial aggregation of ED-coded census data to postal sector level (e.g. Martin 1992). Third, the census is a one-off, cross-sectional survey. In due course (and probably very soon) we will want to create updated versions of the lifestyle system for which census data will not be available. Finally, the NDL consumer database is a very large one and there is every reason to believe that once the data are reweighted at a spatially aggregate level to represent the major compositional biases in the data, then accurate small area predictions will result automatically (i.e. if we reweight the population so that West Yorkshire is adequately represented, and so that one-parent familes (for example) are properly represented, then we should get right the small area populations within Leeds automatically).

So the ideal strategy is to *constrain* the reweighting process at a relatively coarse spatial level, such as the county; and then *validate* the outcomes at the small area level. We would want to set relatively strict validation criteria for something like small area household counts (e.g. to ensure that totals are within ± 5% of the census figures).

4.1.4 Solution method

There are two elements which are to some extent distinct. We need a heuristic procedure to derive appropriate weights; and we need a procedure to evaluate the quality, or 'representativeness', of the reweighted database.

As an approach to the first problem, we need to begin by defining a set of constraints. This might comprise a number of different types of information: county level household estimates by age and sex from the Registrar-General's population estimates; estimates of the distribution of household types from the census; regional estimates of household income from the Family Expenditure Survey and/or New Earnings Survey; and national lifestyle estimates from the General Household Survey.

The reweighting could then be achieved iteratively. First set the weights arbitrarily. Now adjust them linearly to represent county level population estimates. Now take these weights and move on to household types. Perform further linear adjustments to match up the household types. Obviously this will result in a deterioration in the reweighted county level population estimates but this cannot be helped. Repeat the procedure for incomes and lifestyles. Then go back to the county level population estimates again and keep working through until no further improvements are possible. This procedure is referred to in the literature as 'multi-raking' (Ireland and Kullback 1968; Bungers and Quinke 1986, p. 178; Merz 1986, p. 444).

The second problem is how to identify a good solution when we have found it! The simplest approach here is some kind of quadratic (least squares) minimization between a matrix of characteristics derived from the reweighted sample database and the constraining survey database (census, General Household Survey, etc.). However, there are many other possibilities (e.g. Knudsen and Fotheringham 1986). In this application we have looked at a relatively simple statistic: the mean absolute percentage deviation between the distribution of characteristics in the reweighted database and the constraining distribution from the census (or other source).

4.1.5 Implementation and model testing

A version of the reweighting procedure has been developed using a relatively simple sequential reweighting procedure illustrated in Fig. 12.2. For each county, a database is prepared showing the distribution of household types by composition, income, tenure, car ownership, age, sex and marital status of head; and the occupations of economically active individuals. All of this information, with the exception of income, can be gleaned from the census County Reports (OPCS

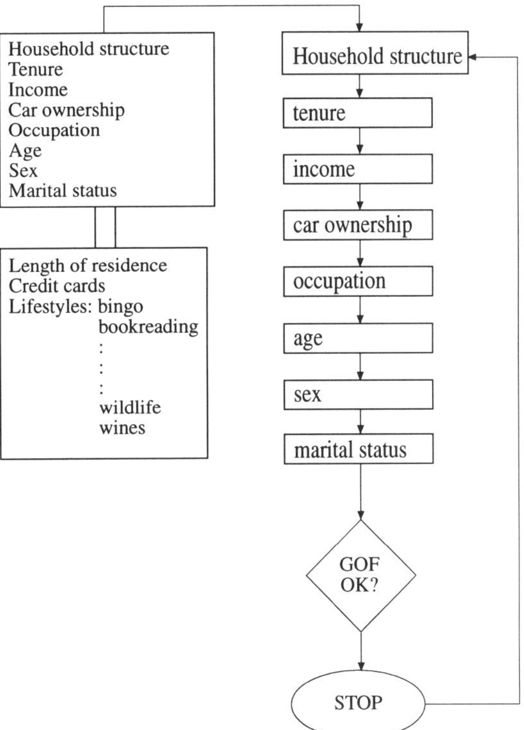

Fig. 12.2 Structure of the NDL reweighting procedure.

1992). At present, income distributions are estimated at the standard region level using Family Expenditure Survey data (Central Statistical Office 1992). We have not yet explored the possibility of linking to the Registrar-General's population estimates, but this may also be necessary once results from the 1991 Census Validation Survey become known.

NDL's database has over 25,000 respondents in total from the Isle of Wight (after deduplication to ensure that each response is from a unique household). However, we have eliminated all households with a partial demographic response (i.e. all those who failed to provide information on income, occupation or any other characteristic). This results in just over 18,000 complete individual records in the sample, so the overall scale of the reweighting is slightly less than 1 in 3 (51,239 households are recorded in the Isle of Wight in the 1991 Census). Under the sequential model, we initially apply weights to each individual so that the pattern of household composition is 'corrected'. The weights are then updated to give the right pattern of household income. Then we repeat the exercise for tenure, car ownership, occupation, age, sex and marital status of head. This comprises one set of inner loop iterations of the model; but of course by the time we get to the end, we no longer have the right pattern of household sizes any

Table 12.4 Sample characteristics of lifestyles data for the Isle of Wight

HOUSEHOLD SIZE AND COMPOSITION	
Number of children	
0	0.786
1	1.669
2	1.524
3+	1.476

HOUSEHOLD INCOME			
< £5,000	0.756	£17,500 – £19,999	0.851
£5,000 – £7,499	1.354	£20,000 – £22,499	0.883
£7,700 – £9,999	1.203	£22,500 – £24,999	0.732
£10,000 – £12,499	1.274	£25,000 – £29,999	0.586
£12,500 – £14,999	1.139	£30,000 – £34,999	0.504
£15,000 – £17,499	0.965	£35,000+	0.443

TENURE					
Owner-occupied	1.086	Council	1.938	Private rented	0.379

CAR OWNERSHIP	
Yes	0.986
No	1.018

OCCUPATION			
Professional		Housewife	1.576
Management	0.756	Retired	0.939
Administrative		Student	0.201
Manual		Other	1.951

AGE OF HEAD					
18-24	3.402	25-34	1.197	35–44	1.268
45-54	1.130	55-64	0.987	65+	0.706

SEX OF HEAD			
Male	1.203	Female	0.543

MARITAL STATUS					
Married	1.235	Single	0.574	WD	0.307

Note: Values greater than one indicate that a population subgroup is oversampled, and vice versa.

more. So we need to iterate through this procedure, hoping for convergence in the distributions.

Our initial tests indicate that the procedure does indeed converge quite quickly for the Isle of Wight case. Table 12.4 shows the values of the weights which we arrive at for each individual characteristic. Note in particular the high level of under-representation in the database of childless families, households in private

Table 12.5 A comparison of small area population distributions against the 1991 census

Postdist	Wted	Unwtd	GDC	Wted%	Unwted%
PO30	10 738	11 064	9 936	8.072	11.359
PO31	5 316	5 378	5 492	3.206	2.078
PO32	2 885	2 829	2 777	3.858	1.862
PO33	11 556	11 673	11 702	1.244	0.251
PO34	1 401	1 419	1 084	29.225	30.846
PO35	1 559	1 632	1 559	0.011	4.674
PO36	5 618	5 642	5 874	4.359	3.959
PO37	2 951	3 062	3 335	11.495	8.181
PO38	4 966	4 618	5 264	5.662	12.270
PO39	788	796	786	0.175	1.253
PO40	2 398	2 145	2 423	1.035	11.479
PO41	1 063	981	1 006	5.613	2.453

Notes: Wted, the number of households in the reweighted NDL sample; Unwted, the number of households in the unweighted NDL sample; GDC, the number of households according to the 1991 Census when EDs are allocated to postal sectors using third-party data provided by the company Graphical Data Capture; Wted%, the absolute percentage difference between the weighted NDL estimates and the census figures; Unwted%, the absolute percentage difference between the unweighted NDL estimates and the census figures.

Mean absolute percentage deviation, NDL versus GDC:

	Districts	Sectors
Weighted	6.163	9.032
Unweighted	7.555	9.927

rented accommodation, households with older than average heads and households without married couples. The obvious interpretation is that these groups purchase fewer durable goods than others. Note also the relatively even weighting by income and car ownership which suggests that social class biases in the sample may not be particularly severe.

Table 12.5 presents a comparison between the census data, the unweighted lifestyle data and the reweighted lifestyle data. At both the postal sector and postal district level, the results are a little better (10%–15%) for the weighted than the unweighted data. If the 5% criterion introduced above is an appropriate one, then this is not quite reached, even in the postal district case. There are couple of particularly large discrepancies, e.g. district PO34 which appears to have 30% too many people in the reweighted (than in the unweighted) database. While these cases might deserve further investigation there are many potential explanations for such variations beyond sampling error, such as the difficulty in matching census and postal geographies and the unknown levels of variation between small areas which arise from the under-enumeration of the census.

One of the potential uses of the system is as a tool for targeting populations of a specific type. The obvious advantage over traditional geodemographic

Table 12.6 Lifestyle types in reweighted Isle of Wight database

Postal sector	Affluent single skiers	Professional households with first child	Pubs and TV sport
1 PO30 1	17	50	7
2 PO30 2	3	39	5
3 PO30 3	5	7	1
4 PO30 4	8	15	11
5 PO30 5	16	74	54
6 PO31 7	15	61	12
7 PO31 8	11	42	13
8 PO32 6	18	44	9
9 PO33 1	15	59	2
10 PO33 2	22	47	8
11 PO33 3	18	55	15
12 PO33 4	10	13	0
13 PO34 5	10	13	5
14 PO35 5	14	20	3
15 PO36 8	9	19	1
16 PO36 9	0	49	26
17 PO36 0	15	24	13
18 PO37 6	10	8	8
19 PO37 7	2	48	42
20 PO38 1	9	40	10
21 PO38 2	3	8	2
22 PO38 3	5	25	1
23 PO39 0	2	13	0
24 PO40 9	1	54	0
25 PO41 0	14	6	1

packages is that we are to identify particular types of household and then produce exact counts of the number of households of that type within a small area. Some examples are shown in Table 12.6, where column 1 is a reweighted count of people who live alone on an income of over £20,000 and enjoy skiing. These people might obviously be targeted for certain types of winter holiday. Column 2 shows the number of households with a single child and a head aged under 35 who has a professional or managerial occupation (this category might be seen as a prime target for a retailer like Mothercare). The third column shows people who have indicated an interest in both pubs and TV sport: perhaps this could be used to indicate where pubs might run live coverage of sports by satellite to boost sales.

4.2 Water consumption

In this section we outline the usefulness of microsimulation methods for the estimation of household water demand and consumption, the subject of a major new research programme sponsored by Yorkshire Water. There are a number of reasons why this is an important time for undertaking such research. First, with the relative absence of domestic metering in the UK, a detailed database on household water consumption is lacking for cities and regions. Although there are estimations of the supply of water at various junction points within a city there is no knowledge of the real spatial variations. Following privatization, the water industry has been forced to examine the costs and benefits of future investment decisions in a far more accountable fashion. It desperately needs better information on current and future consumption patterns.

Second, there is increasing interest in what the implications of small area variations of consumption might mean for future pricing policies. Where meters have been installed it is clear that overall household consumptions do decline (i.e. the Isle of Wight) but there is not much clear evidence of who gains and who loses. In addition, if household consumption patterns are estimated for a city then it may be possible to judge the necessity for metering and the effectiveness of that metering. This could be done by targeting metering to those areas where the water authorities would gain most benefit. In addition to metering, the simulation exercise could look at the effectiveness of alternative household-based pricing policies. The pricing mechanism for water has traditionally been based on the rateable value of a property, ignoring quantity used or the actual income of present occupiers. Any move to change pricing policies would be politically sensitive (we have seen this clearly in changes to the domestic rate system). However, the simulation exercise would allow a variety of future scenarios concerning pricing policies based on actual consumption or income to be tested and evaluated in terms of likely gainers/losers (although it would be interesting to work towards pricing scenarios which might benefit all water users by adopting flexible policies which might then vary across a city).

Although the water industry rarely publishes its methods for estimating domestic consumption it is clear that geodemographic systems are in operation. For example, the Severn Trent Authority has a large metered sample of households which it aggregates into ACORN groups and sells to other regional authorities. By purchasing ACORN data for their regions different authorities can then apply the typical water consumption patterns of these various Severn Trent ACORN groups in order to estimate small area demands in their localities. As in all geodemographics this will work well in some areas, poorly in others. In the case of water consumption the type of house is not as important as the number of residents within it and the number of water appliances they might actually have. Russac *et al.* (1991) looked at ACORN profiles for a sample of metered houses in Brookmans Park, North London. They concluded:

> There are significantly different consumption figures for the same ACORN classifications and also that similar consumptions occur with different ACORN groups.
>
> (Russac *et al.* 1991, p. 350)

The alternative to geodemographics is to build up detailed household profiles

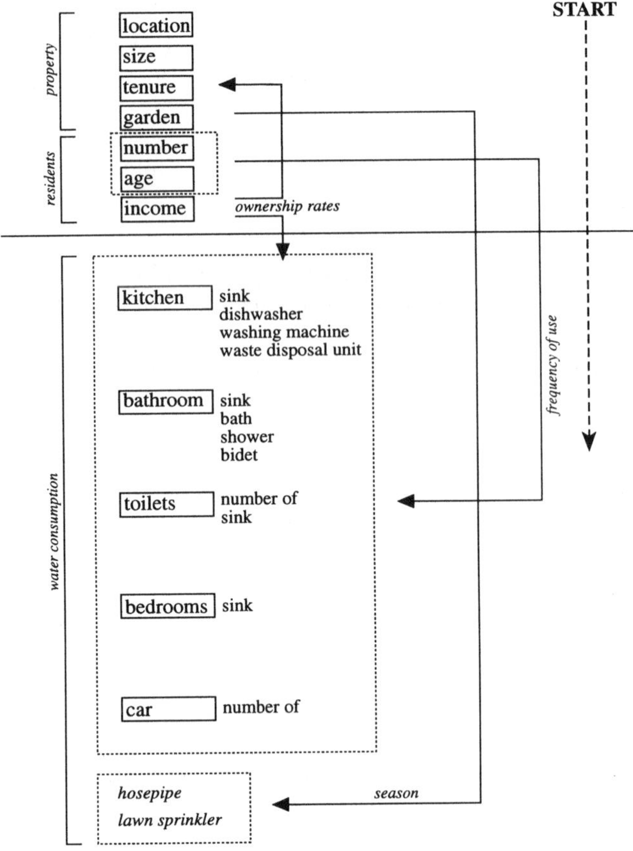

Fig. 12.3 A model structure to estimate domestic water consumption.

containing information related to incomes, family size and likely ownership of water-using appliances. There is a detailed literature on the characteristics which influence the levels of consumption (see Batchelor 1975; Danielson 1979; Gardiner and Herrington 1986). In Fig. 12.3 we show the types of individual and household variables which are most likely to influence both the ownership rates of water-using appliances (normally income related) and the frequency of use of such appliances (household size variables). The diagram also sets out the likely steps in the simulation exercise.

The first step in the procedure is to ascertain the location of the property to be used in the sample (which may be all households in a small area or a selection of households across the entire city). Given the location of the household we can estimate the likely household size and tenure and the characteristics of the tenants (see Birkin and Clarke (1988) for such a procedure within Leeds). This in effect then gives us the top half of Fig. 12.3. From here we can estimate the likely ownership rates of water-using appliances within different households (washing machine, dishwasher etc.) by combining the simulated sample with information contained within the General Household Survey. The household size variables then allow us to calculate the frequency of use. Since the water industry holds detailed information concerning the amount of water used by different appliances, frequency of use can be translated into actual consumption patterns. Combining income and household size variables in this way thus gives us detailed small area estimates of water demand for the first time in the UK. In order to calibrate the models there are a number of factors which additionally help:

1. the known household characteristics of EDs allow us to reproduce the household size and income-related characteristics of our sample confidently (as in Birkin and Clarke 1988, 1989);
2. the information we have from those properties which have been metered allows us to look in more detail at the relationships between household characteristics and water consumption;
3. the known supply totals we have at various supply junctions across a city (though we have to bear in mind leakage here).

Fuller details of the issues raised above appear in Clarke *et al.* (1993).

5 Conclusions

Over the next decade increasing use will be made of microdata-bases in preference to aggregate representations. This trend will be driven by the increasing availability of data about individual people and households, and also by the availability of extra computer power to process the data.

The decision to produce SAR from the 1991 Census goes some way to recognizing the need for microdata. We have argued that for many types of applications we may need to go further than this in at least three respects: we need to move from a sample to a complete representation of the population; we need to include extra characteristics not available within the census; and we need to develop a modelling capability for the manipulation of microdata. The notion of microsimulation provides a convenient umbrella under which these types of application can be considered. For all of these reasons we would expect microsimulation techniques to be explored much more fully in the future than in the past.

References

Batchelor, R A 1975 Household technology and the domestic demand for water. *Land Economics* 3, 208–23.

Birkin, M and G P Clarke (1987) Synthetic data generation and the evaluation of urban performance: a labour market example. Working Paper 502, School of Geography, University of Leeds.

Birkin, M, G P Clarke, M Clarke and A G Wilson 1990 Elements of a model-based GIS for the evaluation of urban policy. In L Worrall (ed) *Geographic Information Systems: Developments and Applications*. London: Belhaven, 133–62.

Birkin, M, G P Clarke, M Clarke and A G Wilson 1994 The application of performance indicator modelling: case studies(1). In C Bertuglia, G P Clarke and A G Wilson (eds) *Modelling the City*, London: Routledge.

Birkin, M and M Clarke 1985 Comprehensive models and efficient accounting frameworks for urban and regional systems. In D Griffith and R Haining (eds) *Transformations Through Space and Time*. The Hague: Martinus Nijhoff, 169–95.

Birkin, M and M Clarke 1988 SYNTHESIS – a synthetic spatial information system for urban and regional analysis: methods and examples. *Environment and Planning A* 20, 1645–71.

Birkin, M and M Clarke 1989 The generation of individual and household incomes at the small area level. *Regional Studies* 23, 535–48.

Brown, P J B 1989 Geodemographics: a review of recent developments and emerging issues. Working Paper 1, Urban Research and Policy Evaluation Regional Research Laboratory, Department of Civic Design, University of Liverpool.

Bungers, D and H Quinke 1986 A microsimulation model for the German Federal Training Assistance Act – principles, problems and experiences. In G H Orcutt, J Merz and H Quinke (eds) *Microanalytic Simulation Models to Support Social and Financial Policy*. Amsterdam: North-Holland, 171–86.

Central Statistical Office 1992 *Family Expenditure Survey 1991*. London: HMSO.

Clarke, G P, A Kashti and A McDonald 1993 Estimating small-area household demand for water. Working Paper, School of Geography, University of Leeds.

Clarke, M 1986 Demographic forecasting and household dynamics: a micro-simulation approach. In R Woods and P H Rees (eds) *Population Structures and Models*. Hemel Hempstead: Allen and Unwin.

Clarke, M and E Holm 1987 Micro-simulation methods in human geography and planning: a review and further extensions. *Geografiska Annaler* 69B, 145–64.

Clarke, M and M Spowage 1985 Integrated models for public policy analysis: an example of the practical use of simulation models in health care planning. *Papers and Proceedings of the Regional Science Association* 55, 25–48.

Danielson, L E 1979 An analysis of residential demand for water using micro time series. *Water Resources Research* 15 (4), 763–7.

Duley, C J 1989 A model for updating census-based population and household information for inter-censal years. PhD thesis, School of Geography, University of Leeds.

Fienberg, S E 1970 An iterative procedure for estimation in contingency tables. *Annals of Mathematical Statistics* 41, 907–17.

Fienberg, S E 1977 *The Analysis of Cross-classified Categorical Data*. Cambridge, MA: MIT Press.

Gardiner, V and P Herrington 1986 *Water Demand Forecasting*. Norwich: GeoBooks.

Ireland, C T and S Kullback 1968 Contingency tables with given marginals. *Biometrika,* 55, 179–88.

Knudsen, D and S Fotheringham 1986 Matrix comparison, goodness of fit, and model performance. *International Regional Science Review* 10, 127–47.

Marsh, C, S Arber, N Wrigley, D Rhind and M Bulmer 1988 The view of academic social scientists on the 1991 UK Census of Population: a report of the Economic and Social Research Council Working Group. *Environment and Planning A* 20, 851–5.

Marsh, C, C Skinner, S Arber, B Penhale, S Openshaw, J Hobcraft, D Lievesley and N Walford 1991 The case for samples of anonymised records from the 1991 Census. *Journal of the Royal Statistical Society A* 154 (2), 305–40.

Martin, D 1992 Postcodes and the 1991 Census of Population: issues, problems and prospects. *Transactions of the Institute of British Geographers, New Series* 17, 350–57.

Merz, J 1986 Structural adjustment in static and dynamic microsimulation models. In G H Orcutt, J Merz and H Quinke (eds) *Microanalytic Simulation Models to Support Social and Financial Policy*. Amsterdam: North-Holland, 423–49.

Norris, P 1983 Microdata from the British Census. In D Rhind (ed) *A Census User's Handbook*. London: Methuen.

OPCS 1992 *1991 Census. County Report: Isle of Wight (Part I)*. London: HMSO.

Paass, G 1986 Statistical match: evaluation of existing procedures and improvements by using additional information. In G H Orcutt, J Merz and H Quinke (eds) *Microanalytic Simulation Models to Support Social and Financial Policy*. Amsterdam: North-Holland, 401–22.

Rees, P 1992 Resources for research: the 1991 Census of Population. *Environment and Planning A* 24, 1371–7.

Rees, P, M Clarke and C Duley 1987 A model for updating individual and household populations. Working Paper 486, School of Geography, University of Leeds.

Russac, D A V, K R Rushton and R J Simpson 1991 Insights into domestic demand from a metering trial. *Journal of International Water Engineering* 5.

13

The future of the census

S Openshaw

Editor's note

Now that the 1991 Census is complete, serious planning and discussions can start for 2001. The OPCS might say simply 'trust in us – we do our best under difficult circumstances'. In this respect the 1991 Census is no different from 1981 or 1971. The question now is whether this process of slow evolutionary development is in the user's best interests. Maybe a more formal but constructively proactive critical response might assist in emphasizing the importance of a more rapid further evolution of the census concept, to bring it more into line with contemporary information technology and user needs. There are of course dangers in being too critical but there are, it is argued, even greater dangers in not being sufficiently critical. The UK census is an extremely important and unique data resource and it is timely and appropriate to consider both the problems and the opportunities for improvement.

1 Introduction

The census is currently the only official source of high quality, accurate and consistent information on population and housing variables available for small (subdistrict) geographical areas in Britain. The value of having this information reported at the sub-local authority and sub-ward levels of geographical scale cannot be overestimated. Census data for small geographical areas is extremely important because it is flexible in use, it can be geographically linked to other small area data from non-census sources (e.g. environmental data, medical information and remotely sensed data), it provides for flexible aggregation, it

---

This chapter was written in summer 1993 based on information available at that time.

reduces the subjectivity and data biases inherent at the ward and district scales, and it offers a detailed geographical picture of the localized variations in Britain's socioeconomic, housing and demographic characteristics that is so useful in planning, marketing, health needs assessment and epidemiology, among many other uses. Moreover, there are probably in excess of 10,000 users, in one form or another, of the 1991 Census data.

Indeed, the vast growth in the usage and perceived value of small area census data (since 1981) has probably rendered the historic demographic purposes of the census of less significance than the new uses in other areas. This trend will undoubtedly continue. Moreover, some of the new uses of census data within government and by industry now have an importance far beyond the purely head-counting statistical traditions of the OPCS and the 1920 Census Act. Examples include (i) its use in allocating billions of pounds of public funds, (ii) its use as a major source of data for a target marketing industry, (iii) its importance as a source of both denominators and covariates in spatial epidemiology and health monitoring, and (iv) its use as a means of describing and explaining within-area differences for a whole multitude of research and applied purposes.

Rhind (1985) and OPCS (1993) neatly summarize the basic strengths of the traditional UK census concept. These are extended and reported in Table 13.1. Indeed it is quite clear that the census is a unique and historically unrivalled source of small area socioeconomic, demographic and housing data about the people of Britain. On the other hand, the very importance of the census as an information source places a heavy burden on the Census Office to 'get it right'. It also increases the pressure on the OPCS to be responsive to the wider needs and concerns of the census user community which now stretches far beyond the traditional remit of demography. The census matters, and as its importance as a data source has increased – so too has the significance of its traditional weaknesses.

Table 13.2 summarizes the principal criticisms of the traditional UK census concept, partly based on Rhind (1985) and OPCS (1993). Many of the key points are elaborated upon in the next two sections. If anything the criticisms have strengthened since the mid-1980s. At the same time the advantages of census geography as a 'safe' spatial reporting system for confidential personal data with geographic file linkage, bringing together the widest possible spectrum

Table 13.1 Strengths of the 1971–81–91 style of census

1 Synchronicity in time
2 Identical questions
3 Exhaustiveness, completeness and high response
4 Fine areal detail
5 Accuracy and reliability
6 Predictability of a decennial census
7 Anonymity and data confidentiality
8 Low cost compared with some countries
9 Apparent responsiveness to user needs
10 Well established, publicly and politically acceptable

Table 13.2 Weaknesses of the 1971–81–91 style of census

1	The need for the highest levels of data accuracy has not been quantified
2	Geographic base reflects standardization of the enumerators workload rather than other factors related to application
3	Use of predetermined, fixed, cross-tabulations of statistics creates vast amounts of data; it is cumbersome, and does not adequately cater for user needs in the 1990s
4	Delays in data availability and long planning lead times
5	Lack of census standardization in Scotland, England and Wales, and Northern Ireland
6	A 10-year census misses or poorly represents localized events and is too infrequent
7	The census is a deficient space–time series data source because each is free standing with incompatible small area geographies
8	The execution of the census is extremely expensive in relative terms
9	Data coverage is too restricted
10	No linkage to other governmental data or use of census to report other governmental data
11	No updating mechanisms and results may soon become out of data
12	The 'Barnardization concept' is unnecessary
13	Quality assurance is problematical
14	Distribution arrangements are not ideal
15	Commercialization aspects poorly handled in both 1981 and 1991
16	GIS aspects ignored
17	Vulnerable to hostile public attitudes

of governmental and public data resources, have never been greater or more obvious.

It would be a very bold step indeed to discontinue a statistical data series that has been a decennial event since 1801 (with the exception of 1941). On the other hand, it is also becoming abundantly clear that the Census of Population probably has no great future in its present form and format, especially when the dust finally settles and the full extent of the 1991 mess may become apparent. The 1991 Census will probably be characterized as being yet another expensive fiasco based on outmoded thinking, obsolete information technology, commercial ineptness and a failure to provide what at least some, maybe most, of the users now seem to want. Of course, being realistic, it is only fair to comment that similar 'criticisms' might well have been written about the previous three censuses, albeit for different reasons. Those familiar with the census usually take a wearily resigned seen-it-all-before view. They tend to voice (in private) rather than write down their criticisms and then get on with making the most from an non-ideal situation. This is by far the 'safest' route, and indeed, this is precisely what we all do. Yet, as a result, most of the criticisms of the census are never published or discussed in public. It seems that this 'not rocking the census boat' approach has really helped no-one other than perhaps OPCS, so it is considered useful, and maybe even essential, to start this chapter with a fairly detailed critique of the 1991 Census and those related aspects of its planning and organization known to the author. If certain unnamed individuals feel aggrieved about this, then maybe this is no more than they deserve. If some of what follows is incorrect then I apologize but it might also be seen as unavoidable in any attempt to provide a critique of the political ecology of this most important of all public data sources about Britain's population. The reader's attention is drawn to the following points.

2 Census criticisms

2.1 Lateness

The Small Area Statistics were two years late in appearing. This delay for data processing was undoubtedly unavoidable in 1971 (and even in 1981) when computers were two or three hundred times slower and smaller than today. However, the continuation of the traditional census delays on into the 1990s is ridiculous! Some aspects of the consequences of this delay are developed further in a later section.

2.2 Obsolete data processing

The census data processing task is apparently so monolithically cumbersome that modern computing and data capture technology has had a minimal impact, if indeed any can be recognized at all over the last two decades. Additionally, users cannot be assured that the census is a really high quality product. In the 1991 case, there has been poor enumeration district (ED) management (how many non-responders do you know, who still have their completed census questionnaire that was never collected?), a failure to allay public fears about census confidentiality in relation to the poll tax, lack of confidence in data coding (the extensive correction that delayed the 1991 Census results might have only been the tip of a bigger iceberg), the imputation magic used to 'fill in' missing responses and even missing returns (really this should have been kept separate from the 'real' data) and on-going confusion about where to locate students.

2.3 Poor management

The census planning management style has seemingly evolved little during the last two decades. The public participation and consultations that accompanied the 1991 Census planning was scarcely any better than a decade previously. It is extremely worrying when it appears that even the civil servants responsible for the public participation exercise do not themselves know how or who makes the final design decisions. Part of the problem seems to be the uneven priorities that the OPCS attribute to the different census-using communities.

The OPCS was created in 1970 with the declared aim of bringing together complementary approaches to information collection which, within the resources

Table 13.3 Rhind's prioritization of the reasons why certain census statistics are collected

Priority rank	Information because of
1	Statutory purposes and needs of central government
2	Central government departments say they need it and will pay for it
3	Local government say they require it and will pay for it
4	Need for definitional comparability with preceding census
5	Academics (perhaps commercial organizations) say they need it and will pay for it

Source: Based on Rhind (1985).

available, will 'best meet the needs of social statistics users in Government, local and health authorities, research and industry and among the public in general' (Denham 1976, p. 3). It is interesting that this is precisely the same order of prioritization that Rhind (1985) later attributes to why certain census statistics are collected. This is summarized in Table 13.3. The question now is whether or not this is still relevant. Seemingly far too much importance has been given to the unclear needs of key central government departments, who generally dither about their requirement for small area data and in any case usually lack any in-house analysis capability to do much with the data they request.

2.4 A reluctance to innovate

An extreme reluctance to innovate is another British census characteristic. The author has endured over two decades of what he now calls 'innovation wither'. It seems to be a distinctive and generic feature of UK Census planning.

Census officials have often stated that the census is firmly based on the main needs of users and on conditions likely to operate when the census is taken and processed (Denham 1976, p. 1). The two points of emphasis here are the main needs of users and the conditions likely to operate when the census is taken. Denham (1976) states that 'any statement to census users which invites discussion can contribute to change *when the views of users are taken into account*' (p. 1, my emphasis). The problem is that of balancing innovation with the presumption 'that in certain quarters there will continue to be active hostility to the census. It is therefore essential that the census should be designed to minimise opposition and to take account of legitimate criticism' (Denham 1976, p. 3). It would seem that public acceptance and other forms of non-specific census hostility are to be 'bought' by a process of innate conservatism, even if this means that important new variables and census modernization needs are overlooked.

The process of 'innovation wither' seems to run as follows. A response is made to an OPCS request for fresh ideas about census outputs. In the case of the 1991 Census this was contained in OPCS Census Newsletter (1987), No. 4. Failing to learn anything from previous experiences, three novel and seemingly sensible suggestions were made and sent to the OPCS (Openshaw and Coombes 1988).

Suggestion 1: A household classification

Census EDs vary greatly in size and social heterogeneity. It is essential to know something about the distribution of different household types (as produced by a multivariate classification of microcensus data) within an ED. This would summarize the thousands of cross-tabulated counts in an efficient multivariate manner, it generates no confidentiality risks and it has been used with the 1981 Italian census data (Openshaw *et al.* 1985).

Suggestion 2: A standard census small area classification

The OPCS were partly responsible for developing the first ACORN (from the 1971 Census). It is quite clear that many users of census data would have found 'official' OPCS census classifications a very useful output from the 1991 Census. There is no reason why this classification product cannot also be developed at the unit postcode level as well. In both cases the classifications could best be performed within the OPCS using the most accurate possible census data, since it is the results and not the data that are reported to third parties. It is argued that attaching a classification code, numbered in the range 1 to say 50, to all postcodes and census EDs in the UK creates no confidentiality problems and threatens no-one. It merely allows the user to identify EDs that are similar in terms of their census characteristics.

Suggestion 3: A standard set of multivariate indicator data

Many census users are only interested in computing indicator variables. The OPCS could create a standard set of variables, expressed as percentages, using non-randomized data and sell these as a census product. This was seen as simplifying access to basic census data, for which there are historical precedents, ensuring a common consistent set of census indicator variables and generally making it easy for users to get value from the 1991 Census.

So what happened to these suggestions? Well the OPCS never wrote to say. The census it seems is an instrument designed to help central government, although it sometimes appears that few government departments will admit to wanting it until it is forced upon them; perhaps in case they have to pay for it out of their budgets. Now obviously, if new ideas are not enthusiastically supported by one (ideally more) government department, perhaps backed with promises of money to pay for it years in advance of the census, then maybe nothing much is likely to happen. Rumour and informal comments suggested that suggestions 1 and 3 simply withered away. Suggestion 2 was considered too risky and that it might discredit the census, although it scarcely makes much difference whether the OPCS or the commercial sector produce the classifications. Maybe the OPCS thought it to be less image tarnishing just to sell the raw census data and let others do their best to classify it. Fair enough; my comments on the sale of census data are made later. However, the quality and geographical resolution of the 1991 Census classifications made by third parties outwith the OPCS are probably significantly poorer than the OPCS should have been able to produce themselves, since only published or publicly available census data could be used and these are deficient compared with the best data available within the OPCS. This assumes that the OPCS can recognize that there is actually an important difference between the raw data used to develop a census classification and the cluster codes that are its outputs. The former might well be highly confidential whilst the highly abstract and generalized nature of the latter renders them safe.

Some attempts were apparently made to consider the development of a joint OPCS and commercial sector census classification as an industry standard but again it withered; and it was not a question of market demand for such products. Seemingly the OPCS prefer that others do their classificatory dirty-work. So instead of having genuine unit postcode level resolution classifications, we will have to rely on various alleged 'fabrications' based on possibly inaccurate representations of what real unit postcode census data might look like. This will presumably discredit the census much more than if the classifications had been done properly with full OPCS support. One should question, however, whether this style of 'pension preserving strategy' is really appropriate in the 1990s. Surely, it is best to extract full value from what always turns out to be an extremely expensive data collection exercise. If the census data are subsequently abused then it will matter little that the OPCS fingers are clean. Indeed by deliberately distancing themselves, the dangers of abuse and misuse by third parties may have actually been increased, perhaps significantly, as they struggle to recoup their initial commercial investment in the data. On the other hand it should also be appreciated that really there is very little 'hard' abuse that can be caused by census data misuse and, as ever, the real danger is incorrect and misinformed speculation, rumour and comment. It often appears that in worrying about these concerns and developing legal restraints on the census users, the OPCS actually make matters worse. For instance, if there really is no confidentiality risk, why the need for user licensing agreements that contain such phrases as, for instance, 'the information shall not be used in any way to attempt to obtain or derive information relating specifically to an identified person or household, nor shall the user claim to have done this'? This immediately creates the impression that such a restriction is needed because it is a real possibility. In reality it cannot be done from the available data; it is impossible!

New output suggestion 1 concerned a household level classification reported at census ED level as frequency counts. The methodology had been tried and tested on Italian census data and the 1991 Census provided an opportunity for it to be applied here. The advantages of a household level classification include the following: it provides a neat and compact multivariate summary of household characteristics, it provides a handle on the levels of ecological inference errors present in all aggregated census data and in conventional classifications of census areas, and it adds a new dimension to census outputs without in any way threatening confidentiality. There was seemingly even some support for it, so what happened to the idea? Of course, it is so easy and trite to argue simply (in private) that the 20,000 or so cross-tabulated cells provide a far better substitute than a household classification with less than 20 categories in it!

A similar fate seems to await most other seemingly 'good ideas'. It also appears that at least two different innovation withering mechanisms exist: ideas can die due to lack of internal OPCS support (never mind what the users want) or they can be made to wither with the blame landing on third parties. The latter is easily engineered or will occur naturally given the right conditions. Consider an example. The England and Wales Census in 1991 was not based on postcode aligned census EDs because of Treasury opposition to the predicted cost in 1985! A subsequent funded request for EDs aligned along unit postcode boundaries was refused because of the perceived dangers of little understood and as yet totally unresearched purely theoretical confidentiality risks caused by differencing data for different sets of areas. New census outputs, it seems, have to be psychologically 'safe' as well as financially self-supporting (i.e. someone has to promise to pay for it well in advance of the census occurring and before the actual cost details can be predicted). Fair enough, you think, but is it a 'fair' test? The same rule if applied to the census as a whole would probably have precluded the 1991 Census from ever happening. Few users are likely to commit themselves years in advance for a census purchase that cannot even be costed at the time the purchase commitment is required. Even fewer users are going to do this for new census outputs.

A final example concerns the one outstanding case of a new idea not withering away despite repeated attempts to wither it. The only really new 1991 Census output is the Sample of Anonymized Records (SAR). The concept of a public use sample is not new and is a feature of some other national censuses. After the 1981 Census, two census White Papers raised the possibility of there being a UK microcensus dataset. The justification for any such data involves a balancing of the perceived risks of confidentiality that the release to the public of individual census data was thought to entail against the benefits obtainable from access to the SAR. Like all other proposed census innovations the potential winners and losers were different. The potential losers were the census agency itself, whilst those who might benefit were a diffuse research community and maybe one or two government departments. The legal case for a SAR depended on the interpretation of a critical part of the 1920 Census Act which stated in para. 4(2): 'The Registrar-General may, if he so thinks fit, at the request and cost of any local authority or person, cause abstracts to be prepared containing any such statistical information, being information which is not contained in the reports made by him under this section and which in his opinion it is reasonable for that authority or person to require, as can be derived from the census returns' taken in conjunction with the usual census confidentiality promise. To the non-legal mind, it seems extremely straightforward.

In 1982 the OPCS noted that there was no UK public use sample because no-one had ever asked for one. When the Economic and Social Research Council (ESRC) subsequently asked in 1985, it was refused on the basis of legal advice.

The fact that individual census data were already available for the 1971 and 1981 censuses in Northern Ireland, ostensibly due to a different interpretation of the same 1920 Census Act, was considered to be irrelevant. The ESRC subsequently tried again and after OPCS received legal advice from a different source and with a new Registrar-General in place, the SAR was born. Two critical factors here were the existence of an identifiable research community shouting for a SAR and the ability of the negotiating team to quantify the confidentiality risks (something the OPCS were seemingly unable to do themselves) by reference to work with microcensus data from Italy. A combination of sustained pressure and demand for a SAR initially from academics but latterly (and perhaps the deciding factor) from within government itself eventually produced the SAR. However, it may now seem churlish to enquire whether it should have required a struggle extending over a decade, especially as the OPCS Longitudinal Study (LS) had been so readily accepted by a different internal route. The LS is of course different in that it never leaves the OPCS computer, eliminating confidentiality fears. On the other hand, it is inherently considerably more 'naughty' from a civil liberties and personal confidentiality perspective, involving the linkage of 1971, 1981 and 1991 Census returns at the individual level, and also tied to other vital events (births, deaths, marriage and morbidity records). From an OPCS perspective all this is acceptable without debate (or indeed without having to ask or inform the persons involved) but a SAR which is inherently safe and anonymous needed almost a decade of what was, at times, extremely acrimonious discussion.

2.5 Commercialization fiasco

The costing of census statistics is highly problematical and is seemingly based on unsound economic and accounting principles. There is a Treasury requirement to recoup the cost of the census from the users. A reasonable principle in theory but its operationalization is a nightmare. The cost of the Small Area Statistics depends on the final number of purchases available to share the cost. This is an interesting but insoluble simultaneous equation problem, because the final number of purchasers can only be guessed at in advance of the data becoming available and whilst its cost is unknown; potential income is further reduced by generous discounts available to government departments. It is noted that with the 1981 Census the ESRC contributed more to the census revenues than any government departments or the private sector.

An even trickier problem is that of separating the 'real' costs of the Small Area Statistics from the cost of a census of population based on small area data but without needing to generate any outputs of the small area type. The latter cost is attributable to central government for deciding to hold a census, since it is government and not the user community who actually invoked the 1920 Census Act; although a user could do so it does not seem to have ever happened. Seemingly, then, the real cost of Small Area Statistics is far less than has historically been charged since it can only be a marginal cost. The cost of the Small Area Statistics should be the cost of copying data created for other purposes.

Census finance is, clearly, an immensely 'grey area'. The price attributed to the 1991 SAR is another example of what can only be described as arbitrary pricing behaviour. The price subsequently charged to the JISC/ESRC was £200 thousand. Why? On what grounds? Surely a single run through a database of census returns cannot really cost that much.

The commercialization of the census outputs has never been handled well. The 1981 Census generated very little by way of commercial sector royalties. Most of the 1981 geodemographic systems were developed from census data originally purchased for about the same price as one licence of the finished system (about £11,000–£16,000). Subsequent licence sales would have generated only a few hundred pounds of royalties. A very nice arrangement for all but the OPCS given a total market for geodemographic products that is informally estimated at about £10 million per year. However, it should be noted that it was the 'geodemographic houses' that provided the value added and that the services they provided (names and addresses indexed by postcode and ACORN or Super Profile or Mosaic or Pin Code) used census data in an extremely tangential manner; geodemographic code was often only one of several discriminators and perhaps seldom the most important one. So it is probably not unreasonable that OPCS received only a fraction of the royalties that the business of profiling client lists probably generated. By itself census data are almost worthless and, indeed, in the case of the 1981 Census they only became a valuable commodity when approximate postcode-to-ED directories were created externally. Without these postcode directories there could have been no geodemographic industry in the UK.

The 1991 commercial details are classed as 'commercial in confidence'. To be a 1991 Census agent, you first apparently have to be 'approved' by the OPCS. It is far from clear what authority the OPCS have to deny access to data paid for by the public purse, or what criteria they apply in judging fitness to receive census data. It seems that not all applicants have been approved. A prospective census agency has to satisfy the Census Office as to its abilities to disseminate census results beyond the boundaries of its own organization and to show that its activities will not damage the good name of the census operation and in particular 'no activity that could threaten the confidentiality of census information or result in risks to confidentiality being perceived'. How? But also are there really such confidentiality risks involved with census agencies? Is someone merely being extremely paranoid and silly, or is it that the OPCS are starting to take census management seriously for the first time? The OPCS will offer an annually renewable (subject to a satisfactory review) licence for only three years. In the case of an ACORN-like geodemographic system, the initially proposed 1991 Census data costs would be £6500 to become an agency and £0.55 per record profiled or £71,500 royalties to OPCS per licence sold. In addition, it would probably be expected that the census agency 'bought' the data used to derive the geodemographic classification at a cost of about £162,500 (assumes up to 200 output counts for 130,000 census EDs). This charging reflects OPCS copyrighting that extends to both the raw census counts but also any material or 'measure obtained from the input counts in any way'. The OPCS also get free use of any products!

Clearly at these prices there would be very little commercial usage of the 1991 Census at the small area scale. They reflect a degree of commercial ineptness that must be hard to match. It appears that for a period of over three years, the OPCS had no consistent and sensible commercial pricing strategy. The potential census agencies could not predict what prices they would be charging for 1991 Census data services and products. These royalty arrangements have now it seems been revised. There is still an agency licence fee of £6000, an annual licence fee of £2000, an annual royalty of £60,000 for geodemographic vendors and a reduced royalty of about £0.30 per record profiled for the sale of census data or processing based on it. The revised royalty charge relates to the number of counts used to create a product and the number of counts actually output. For example, assuming that between 51 and 200 counts are used to create an ED-based geodemographic system, there will be about 130,000 areas with at least one output count. The royalty would be about £26,000. If there were between two and ten outputs per area (i.e. cluster code plus population count) then this would increase to £39,000 per licence. It is estimated that it will cost about £100,000 in data costs just to be in a position to create a 1991 geodemographic system. Even then there is the threat of an annual licence review and uncertainty as to whether there can still be access to 1991 Census data in 1996. At a time of recession, questions might well be asked about the damage this might do to the British economy, if the planned economic revival is thought to be domestic consumer led. Equally it is not clear what value census data have, especially as they are at least two years old before they can be used and at best are available only for what are really fairly large geographic units (i.e. EDs compared with unit postcodes).

Let us return to the key question about what commercial value the 1991 Census data do have. The answer it seems is probably not as much as the OPCS believed, and they may even have no value at all! By overpricing the data, the OPCS have stimulated the need to create small area marketing data from non-census sources. For example, NDL has information on over 9 million individuals which when aggregated to census EDs may yield equivalent or far more powerful geodemographic systems because the variables are much more marketing relevant (many of the census variables are of interest only as income and lifestyle surrogates). It remains to be seen whether this pessimistic state actually materializes but it is not inconceivable that the most valuable census output from the 1991 Census may in fact be the ED-to-postcode directory and not the census data.

2.6 Neglect of GIS

The mid-1980s saw the beginnings of a major revolution in the handling of all kinds of geographical information (Chorley 1987). Yet it is quite clear that as far as the 1991 Census is concerned GIS does not yet exist. This is a major oversight. The 1990 US Census provides a much better example of how to handle a census in the GIS age. Instead the spatial referencing provided by the 1991 Census is no better than 10 years ago and is arguably significantly worse than 20 years previously. This is surprising given the initial innovative use of locational referencing in the 1971 Census. Indeed, some aspects of the advanced nature of the 1971 Census are staggering and even 20 years later have still not been replicated.

The 1971 Census was the first (and so far only) British census in which a National Grid coordinate reference was added to every address enumerated. Denham (1976, p. 6) writes:

> The purpose was to obtain statistics for populations in National Grid squares of 100 m or 1 km, the positioning of which is freely available through Ordnance Survey maps and which can be used as a common spatial base for various sets of data. Moreover the squares have the very considerable advantage of remaining unchanged through time. The regular grid base facilitates the statistical analysis of spatial patterns and also the display of patterns though automated cartography.

Sadly the production of similar statistics for the 1981 Census was cancelled (due to a perceived lack of advanced demand) and was not even seriously considered for 1991. It is interesting that, 25 years after the OPCS first did it, the Ordnance Surveys Address Point product will be replicating the feat of attaching a 1 m grid reference to each postal address in the UK.

2.7 Neglect of census geography

The census ED is an extremely important geographical entity. Its significance extends beyond its OPCS operational utility as it becomes an extremely useful 'safe' geographical area for linking and reporting confidential personal data from non-census sources. Indeed, it is notable that the purchase cost of digital 1991 ED boundaries for Britain probably exceeds that of the associated census data, and it is possible that this will generate more turnover than the census which created it! How ironic.

2.8 Outmoded confidentiality thinking

Questions of census confidentiality dominated many aspects of the 1991 Census. This is understandable. The Census (Confidentiality) Act 1991 makes the disclosure of census information a criminal offence. It is good and very reassuring that the census confidentiality promise is treated so seriously. However, the application of confidentiality constraints is based on a now outmoded technology: that of seeking to render the data 'safe' and of legally restricting what users can do. There is seemingly no concept of census analysis or derived census products that can be performed or manufactured within the OPCS institutional confidentiality barrier. Why, for example, cannot a government department rank full unrandomized census data for unit postcodes to identify deprivation areas within the OPCS, transferring final output results across the census confidentiality barrier that are suitably safe? There is presumably no legal reason why this could not be done, and even a convincing public good argument that it should be done. So why is it not done, or why are such services not routinely provided to the user community for those applications that can sustain and justify the expense? The critical part of the analysis from a confidentiality point of view is when the results cross the OPCS office barrier.

This line of argument can be developed further. Why cannot critical cancer analysis be performed from within the OPCS confidentiality shield so that all the census data are available for analysis? There would be no disclosure of census data. The results would be quite safe. The security services and police have always (presumably) been able to do this and (presumably) identify individuals. The analysis proposed here involves no harm to any personal data subject and is in the public good. It would seem that confidentiality constraints whilst absolute are not being handled creatively or with imagination.

3 Some outstanding generic flaws in the 1991 Census

In addition to these criticisms, the 1991 Census has a number of fairly long-standing generic flaws that hinder users and reduce its usefulness. The same problems can be recognized at least in the 1981 Census and probably others as well.

3.1 Unstable boundaries of census enumeration districts

Boundary changes between the censuses make the creation of small area space–time series almost impossible. For reasons that are difficult to understand, the OPCS seems unable to appreciate the user's need for some ability to measure intercensal change at the small area scale. The Registrar-General for Scotland is an exception here. The trilogy of censuses for 1971, 1981 and 1991 should have provided a good description of changes in Britain's population for small areas. If it is possible at all at sub-local authority scales, then this is chiefly due to the ingenuity of the census user, but it may not be correct. Sadly, it will be least accurate in those areas of greatest change, and thus of greatest interest. Of course, it is hard keeping census ED boundaries intact from one census to the next. However, this mainly reflects the stupidity of continuing to use EDs as both the basic data collection unit and the smallest census output unit. It is possible with modern computers to handle this problem but seemingly there has never been any strong imperative to do so, perhaps reflecting apathy in central government. The solution is also obvious. The census data relate to households who have locations in space. If spatial referencing is used it becomes a fairly trivial task to aggregate the data to any set of areas for which the boundaries are accurately known. The question as to whether the results are safe from a confidentiality point of view is a separate and subsequent issue.

3.2 Changes in census definitions

Changes in definitions are much less of a problem than previously, although again the need for comparability between censuses is still not fully appreciated. In principle it really should not be that difficult to ensure upward and backward comparability of definitions. This is not optional but absolutely fundamental; see also Chapter 10.

3.3 Ten-year data gaps

Much more problematic is the 10-year gap between censuses. At a time of unparalleled historic changes in many aspects of modern life, a 10-year gap is far, far too long. The concept of an updatable annual census really needs more careful consideration. It seems that the Data Protection Registrar considers that personal data more than five years old should not be kept, yet we have to make do with census data that have a mean age of five years, and which can still be used in resource allocation formulae when they are as much as 12 years out of date.

Also, there is an argument that the 1991 Census reflects the height of the longest recession of the post-war years, and a massively depressed static housing market. How long will this state continue? A period of economic boom could see a burst of unparalleled change that would render the census results rapidly inadequate.

It is interesting that the 1920 Census Act does actually place some responsibility on the Registrar-General to provide intercensal data. Section 5 states:

> It shall be the duty of the Registrar-General from time to time to collect and publish any available statistical information with respect to the number and condition of the population in the interval between one census and another, and otherwise to further the supply and provide for the better co-ordination of such information, and the Registrar-General may make arrangements with any Government Department or local authority for the purpose of acquiring any materials or information necessary for the purpose aforesaid.

It is a pity this particular duty was not taken more seriously. One response is that large-scale surveys, such as the Labour Force Survey, do in fact provide intercensal information but not for small areas where the information is most useful. It should be remembered that many users find the census useful as a small area data source.

3.4 Non-linkage

Linkage between the census and other high quality governmental data sources is also a necessity. The inefficiency of having separate unemployment and employment series (i.e. the NOMIS system) that do not link with the census even in census years really needs to be questioned. If the census is regarded as a cross-sectional snapshot of Britain, then it needs to include the full wealth of data available to government reported by census geography. Key statistical abstracts from social security, tax, crime, morbidity and mortality databases need to be added in. This issue is examined in more detail later.

3.5 Incomplete coding of data

The continued use of 10% sample coding of socioeconomic and other key variables (such as journey to work) really needs to be reassessed. This is designed to save coding costs on variables that are difficult to code but these processes should now be capable of being full automated. Other countries such as Italy can manage this task, so why not in the UK? The use of samples reduces the value and reliability of the small area data considerably. Additionally, the analysis of mixtures of 100% and 10% coded variables complicates census analysis and may mislead census users; see also Chapters 7 and 9. It might also be a false economy; for example, the TTWA, used as building blocks for regional aid, are based on 10% coded journey-to-work data. The resulting misallocation of public funds consequent on TTWA definitional errors caused by poor quality census data might far exceed the cost of 100% census coding.

3.6 Randomizing data to preserve confidentiality serves no useful purpose

The continued use of Barnardization or data blurring techniques to adjust the last digit of small area counts randomly needs to be discontinued or at least its utility reassessed. This is a historical sop to mischievous and unwarranted political scaremongering in the late 1960s. It serves no useful purpose other than to degrade the value of Small Area Statistics; it complicates analysis and fosters further the sterile census confidentiality debate. It is unnecessary because there are now legally enforceable confidentiality promises that every census user has to make prior to gaining access to the data. The user promises not to use the information 'in any way to attempt to obtain or derive information relating specifically to an identified person or household, nor shall the user claim to have obtained or derived any such information'. This is more than adequate given the nature of the aggregate census data, as it deals with both the actual (if there are indeed any) and perceived risks of confidentiality. There are also draconian penalties on the user, the host institution and, for a commercial bureau, the clients (past and present). This is a more than adequate safeguard.

3.7 Confidentiality as an excuse for non-analysis

It is right that the census confidentiality promise should be absolute. The issue of whether this is ever breached (or is traditionally regularly breached) by MI5 in the interest of national security is of no relevance here. Of much concern is the traditionally negative application of the basic confidentiality constraint. It is noted that this does not preclude access to individual census data by OPCS staff. It follows then that in principle at least there is no real reason why OPCS staff cannot perform any analysis of the census database provided it is done within the OPCS confidentiality envelope and that the results (if published) are available in a confidentiality safe form. Merely because the individual census data are protected by confidentiality restrictions regarding their release to third parties is no real constraint on the types and nature of analyses that might be performed within the OPCS. When there is good cause for census analysis using all the available data, then it can be done and mechanisms need to be created that will allow this to happen easily, routinely and cheaply. This already happens regularly with the OPCS Longitudinal Study so why not with the full census database itself? Surely in certain policy studies there is a strong and overriding national interest imperative to ensure that the best possible results are obtained, e.g. identifying deprivation areas or computing numbers of deprived individuals etc. Currently, the census database as a national resource is essentially wasted once the planned census outputs have been completed. Users should be allowed (even encouraged) to submit their software to the OPCS to be run on the census database and, provided the results do not breach basic confidentiality constraints, they should be made available.

The message is that the OPCS have to assume the role of more than a data depository and, as 'spare' computer time becomes available, they should adopt a more flexible and proactive function in stimulating the analysis of census data that is perceived to be in the public good. For example, the same census computers that were used to process the census in 1991–3 could well be dedicated to 'national interest' data analysis projects for 1994–2000 rather than presumably standing idle because there is no other census work to keep them fully utilized. In short the OPCS should be more than a data collection agency and should utilize their 'spare' intercensal resources in encouraging the innovative analysis of census data, especially in areas where there are public goods to be gained.

3.8 Census enumeration district geography needs updating

Poor census ED (and, in Scotland, output area) planning and design is another problem. The Victorian concept of an ED is seemingly still alive and well a century after its invention. These areal units need to be most carefully designed since they are the smallest available standard statistical reporting units. Ideally, the units used for census data collection and data reporting should not be the same, but they are in England and Wales. Inconsistencies in ED and output area size, social heterogeneity, density, shape and composition act as a noise-inducing filter that affects and distorts the small area data. It is true that the importance of small area level statistics is a relatively recent innovation (introduced as an experiment with the 1961 Census), but for many census users the small area scale is now the principal and most useful level of geography. Greater recognition is needed of this situation with a corresponding desire to improve matters. Geography-related basic data management confusion was tolerable in 1971, disappointing in 1981 and totally unacceptable in 1991.

The Ordnance Survey's Address Point system is particularly relevant here. The census is about people and people live at discrete postal addresses. The OS/Post Office Address Point system aims to cover 100% of postal addresses. When complete, this will provide a unique data resource that it is wholly inconceivable the 2001 Census would not use. This would provide accurate 1 m references for all addresses in the UK and separate (at last) the dependence of the OPCS on the same areal units for both data collection and reporting. Properly handled, the OS Address Point system would provide an immensely flexible geographical framework for the 2001 Census. Indeed, it is hard to imagine a 2001 Census without something similar. In addition, the census should allow flexible user-defined output reporting areas (differencing areas is yet another confidentiality myth) *and* give users the ability to define their own output areas in an interactive environment. The only 'real' constraint is that the user-defined output areas should match user-defined objectives.

3.9 Lateness of data availability

The continued historic failure to produce the census results either quickly or on time is unacceptable. As Robson (1992) notes: 'It is unforgivable that the results of the census take so long to appear and that the initial publication schedule seems invariably to be hopelessly overtaken by events which should have been anticipated .... Resigned acceptance of the delay seems an inadequate response to what is a national scandal' (p.1). Robson points out that the whole country is affected by the use of out-of-date census data. If the costs of using 'wrong' census information (wrong because it is out of date) could be calculated, it might well be massive. On the other hand, the two-year time lapse with the 1991 Census compares very favourably with the five-year delay associated with the release of the 1971 grid square statistics, except that the tardiness of the latter inconvenienced no-one because it was purely a research product.

3.10 Data quality

The OPCS takes no responsibility for the accuracy or comprehensiveness of the census data and have no obligation to either update or maintain the information. Is this really acceptable as good statistical practice in the 1990s?

4 Rhind's radical solutions

4.1 Can we live without the census?

The combined impact of an increasingly high cost census product that is inflexible, monolithic, out of touch with user needs, and no longer a monopoly data source will be to destroy the census concept as we know it. Certainly, the commercialization problems associated with the 1991 Census have stimulated the need for alternative non-census data sources. At least one planned set of 1991 geodemographic systems contains no census data and yet is based on a 1 in 2 or 3 sample of households. Additionally, there are now several potential sources of census-like data in government computer systems that could be used as census substitutes. Whether any of this happens in time for 2001 and whether European Union legislation will permit it are matters for subsequent debate. It is useful, nevertheless, at least to consider some of the practical possibilities against the results of a recent survey of census users (OPCS 1993). The latter demonstrated that many users need census information particularly in planning, needs assessment, resource allocation and targeting. According to the OPCS interpretation, most are satisfied with the traditional form of compulsory census collected centrally (OPCS 1993, p.1). However, this does not necessarily indicate a desire for more of the same. Indeed, the growing importance of intercensal, annual updates to the census needs to be recognized as an emerging key requirement. These needs are not just at the district scale but extend to small areas.

4.2 Rhind's radical solution

In an important paper Rhind (1985) points out that the need for future censuses is weaker than at any previous time because nearly all the census details (and much more) can in principle be acquired from existing governmental computer systems. Indeed the computerization of the bureaucracy covering all aspects of modern life and more significantly all of a person's interactions with governmental agencies and commerce are now 'captured' by third or fourth generation mature computer systems. This trend is set to continue throughout the 1990s with a progressive improvement in the quality of the available information. The GIS revolution is another contributing factor that is helping make much of this information usable.

Rhind (1985) puts it like this:

> Given all these 'individual' data, it is theoretically possible to link various data sets together and provide both 'stock' and 'change' information by 'piggybacking' existing sources of information. Under these circumstances, the census would then become what it already is in some parts of Europe with a population register; i.e. a calibration exercise, and need not even be carried out on a whole-country synchronous basis. In theory at least substantial savings should be possible and the service to users should be

Table 13.4 Difficulties with Rhind's radical approach

1 Is it legal?
2 Is it acceptable?
3 Is it technically feasible?
4 Is it accurate enough?
5 Is it institutionally possible?
6 Is it affordable?
7 Is it needed?

Source: After Rhind (1985).

> greatly improved. In such a 'cradle to grave' longitudinal scheme, cross-sectional information would never be more than a few months out of data and enormous flexibility would exist in the possible summary statistics.
>
> (p. 34)

A bold vision, although not today particularly novel in that large commercial organizations are seeking to operationalize similar concepts on the lines of what they call behavioural information systems for much less laudable reasons, i.e. to predict credit unworthiness, monitor financial performance and model retail purchase decision making.

Rhind (1985) identifies a number of questions concerning his radical solution (see Table 13.4). The answer to them all is probably now 'yes' but something approaching a complete reorganization of governmental statistics would also be needed. As Rhind (1985) put it:

> Successful 'piggybacking' of existing data sources, therefore, requires some clearly defined central responsibility for all social, demographic, man-power, and housing statistics. Also, it may require legislatively defined access to records of nationalised statutory undertakers ... structural change in government agencies is hence a pre-requisite for the success of the radical approach.
>
> (p. 35)

It is not clear how such a reorganization of the entire government statistical service might be achieved, although there can be little doubt that such a far reaching reform is now needed. Likewise, there is little doubt that the current highly negative application of the 1984 Data Protection Act might well be used or interpreted as a blanket prohibition. The contrary view, that it is a crime against society not to make full and good use of personal data for the public good, is not yet appreciated. Certainly, data protection is important but privacy can be preserved by many different means other than crudely applied abstract data protection principles.

Table 13.5 What users seem to want from the census

1	Very rapid data availability
2	Frequent and reliable updating providing consistent space–time series
3	Broadening of the range of available statistics beyond the scope of traditional census questions
4	Flexible reporting and table design
5	Flexible geographical aggregation and non-census geographical file linkage
6	Digital boundaries for the census areas

Source: Based on Rhind (1985).

4.3 Rhind's strategy for 1991

Other problems relate to the need to rethink what users want from the census. Rhind (1985) makes a number of suggestions which are represented and extended (see Table 13.5). His proposed radical solution would deliver objectives 1, 2 and 3, whilst objective 4 was considered to be of greatest short-term user importance. It was clear that there is a universal need here for flexible user access whilst the confidentiality of the data was not threatened. To this end, Rhind (1985) describes the construction of a secure computer system for interactive table design. A user would be able to define data needs via an interactive table designing system run over a network. Indeed, it is interesting that the USAR system described in Appendix 11A (Chapter 11) illustrates some of the benefits, albeit with respect to SAR data. It would use a rule-based confidentiality machine to check for violation of confidentiality before passing the data request onto a data extraction engine. This was presented as a means of accessing the 1991 Census but really its main use would be as a flexible but safe means of accessing the totality of personal data held in central government's secure corporate British population database, although nothing along these lines yet exists. Nevertheless, a pilot census access system was subsequently built and tested (Rhind *et al.* 1990). So why was it not used with the 1991 Census? Why are users still lumbered with a fixed set of census tables that have now been expanded up to 20,000 cells?

One major problem with the rules machine is that of defining, let alone implementing, current *ad hoc* census confidentiality rules of thumb. Also, the data differencing problem is probably insolvable. However, there is a view that this does not matter in practice because of other 'legal' confidentiality barriers and that it is merely the ultimate technical excuse for ensuring innovation wither in this area too. Nevertheless this broad strategy of flexible, user- controlled, confidentiality safe access is undoubtedly a useful blueprint for accessing personal data held by government. It is imagined that the principal hurdle is really now the institutional one, not the technology.

4.4 Towards a single, corporate, integrated, governmental statistics system

The GIS revolution of the mid-1980s is over. The challenge now is to exploit the software, the associated digital map and the various databases to design and build an integrated, single, governmental statistics system of which the decennial census is really little more than one (small) part.

GIS emphasizes the following aspects of information management:

1. the need for a common corporate view encompassing all relevant governmental departments who have databases;
2. the need for integrated databases based on common standards and with similar levels of geography coding and standard linkages; and
3. an integrated view of governmental information holdings with explicit linkages between the digital map databases and those who hold related attribute data.

Belatedly, all is now revealed. The Governmental Statistical Service and the Ordnance Survey operate what might be regarded as a distributed heterogeneous GIS; the Ordnance Survey own the digital map data and various governmental departments the related attribute data. The main problem is the lack of integration of the pieces at virtually all levels, ranging from copyright issues relating to ED planning maps to ownership of copyright of census geography boundaries. There are also major organization difficulties when different, vast, well entrenched 'empires' collide. The losers as ever are the end-users who are deprived of the information they would like, who will end up being overcharged for all the data they need, and who in consequence will have to tolerate substandard information services. The public also lose because government managers are less efficient than they should be.

How on earth can the OPCS seriously start planning discussions on the geography base for 2001 (Puckey 1993) apparently oblivious to (i) the wider importance and impact of their decisions about census building blocks for reporting non-census governmental data; (ii) the broader need to think in terms of all other governmental data sources; (iii) the need to create a UK-wide postal address file with geography on it (to at least 1 m resolution); (iv) the need to provide the basic digital map data backcloths, boundaries and features without which the 2001 Census data will be of greatly diminished worth; and (v) the fundamental long overdue need to integrate and rationalize, on the one hand, the operations of the government statistical services and various departmental databases, with, on the other, the national digital mapping agency, who owns all the digital map databases that matter, and possibly the Post Office (in view of the importance of postal address data as a linkage device). The census is no longer an end in itself. It can neither safely nor sensibly be divorced from the wider context of the government statistical service and also the national mapping agency.

The obvious answer that only a naive academic could dare suggest is simply to seek to integrate all aspects of the government's corporate GIS under the control of a single department, responsible for both the government's digital map and non-mappable data holdings. It should be charged with the task of producing the 2001 Census (ideally the last) whilst being mandated to create a Rhind style of radical UK corporate information system. This should eventually yield an annually updatable census but it may well take until the middle of the next decade before the task is completed. No new legislation seems to be required since this might be regarded as a legal duty already placed upon the Registrar-General by the 1920 Census Act; i.e. to gather and report data between censuses from government departments and local authorities. It may well be that the principal problem is the pitiful state of the key governmental databases (i.e. tax, social security, health, employment) and an understandable but lamentable desire to cover up decades of ineptness, inefficiency and inadequateness by non-analysis and non-linkage on spurious grounds (i.e. civil liberties, and righteous but false confidentiality concerns).

Certainly the census is still an important information source but during the 1990s its pre-eminence might be expected to decrease. It is now only one of several valuable census-like information sources held by government, and is similar to those being created by the commercial sector. Indeed, the census comes with the unique disadvantage that it is essentially a survey and has to be explicitly and expensively collected, whereas many other census-like data sources are self-collecting, self-updating, self-correcting and real-time. In essence the census is a nineteenth-century concept that will probably be lucky to survive in anything like its present form much beyond 2001. Its day has passed and its death will only be regretted if there is no better substitute. It has done extremely well; a 200-year-long data series will one day be seen as a unique record of persistency and consistency.

5 What might users have expected from the 1991 Census?

It is useful to recall that it was 1994 before all the 1991 Census results were completed. It is trite but necessary to comment that 1991–4 is not the same as 1971–5. Census users are today much better educated, computers are much faster, and the whole information technology scene has radically changed. It is not unreasonable to have expected that the 1991 Census results would have been available in 1992 in appropriate 1990s formats. In particular, the OPCS should have been distributing census information systems not raw data. These systems should have provided easy access to census data without any need for SASPAC, GIS and separate mapping packages. Given that 1994 is GIS revolution plus eight years, they should have contained integrated digital boundaries and other relevant digital map information in an integrated, seamless 1990-style information product. They should also have been a range of non-census data from government sources, able to complement and remedy the coverage deficiencies inherent in the 1991 Census, with some built-in updating mechanisms. In addition, safe and easy to use table design software installed on secure OPCS workstations should have allowed users to specify and buy exactly the information they need. All of this is possible today and yet none of it exists. I wonder why? Meanwhile, we must get on with making the most of what is still a most valuable and precious asset: the 1991 Census.

References

Chorley, R 1987 *Handling Geographic Information*. London: HMSO.
Dale, A and C Marsh (eds) 1993 *The 1991 Census User's Guide*. London: HMSO.
Denham, C J 1976 The future of the Census of Population. Paper presented at IBG Conference, Sheffield, September. London: OPCS.
OPCS 1993 Report on review of statistical information on population and housing (1996–2016). Occasional Paper 40, OPCS, London.
Openshaw, S and M Coombes 1988 1991 Census geography and the case for some new census outputs. NE.RRL Research Report 8814, CURDS, Newcastle University.
Openshaw, S, F Sforzi and C Wymer 1985 National classifications of individual and areal census data. *Systemi Urbani*, 3, 283–312.
Puckey, J 1993 An information paper on the geography base in England and Wales for the 2001 census. IDLG Sub Group, OPCS, London.
Rhind, D W 1985 Successors to the Census of Population. *Journal of Economic and Social Measurement*, 13, 29–38.
Rhind, D W, K J Cole, M Armstrong, L Chow and S Openshaw 1990 An online, secure, and infinitely flexible database system for the national population census. SERRL Working Report 14, SERRL, Birkbeck, London.
Robson, B 1992 Counting the cost. *IBG Newsletter No. 15*, September.

Appendix

Small area statistics: cell numbering layouts

This compact version of the small area statistics cell numbering layouts has been produced by the Office of Population Censuses & Surveys and is reproduced with their permission. No responsibility is accepted for their accuracy.

Notes

1. Each cell in the small area statistics (SAS) has a unique reference number comprising the table number and the cell within the table. Where appropriate, the table number includes an area level indicator, which appears as a prefix in the table layouts but will appear as a suffix on machine readable data.

2. These identification numbers are used in the magnetic media versions of the SAS, although reference should be made to the file specification (*User Guide 21*) as the constituent parts of the identifier are split over several fields. Identifiers may also be included in the documentation for the SAS and in explaining the use of the SAS; for example, to specify how a particular indicator has been calculated from data in various cells. The tables on the following pages provide layouts and cell numbers for the SAS tables. Each cell in the local base statistics (LBS) has a separate unique reference number in the same format. Details of the layouts and the cell numbers for LBS are given in *User Guide 24.*

3. Cells which do not contain counts are marked xxxx (the number of an xxxx cell can be deduced from the surrounding cells). These cells are either impossible counts (e.g. Table 2), repetitive counts (e.g. Table 8) or cells suppressed in the SAS tables (e.g. Table 16). In a table which has no counts in any cell (nil population for that counting base), blank cells may be shown as zeroes, and so are indistinguishable from other cells with no member of population without reference to these tables for SAS and to *User Guide 24* for LBS.

4. Requests for *User Guides* and general enquiries should be directed to:

for England and Wales:	for Scotland:
Census Customer Services	Census Customer Services
OPCS	GRO (Scotland)
Titchfield	Ladywell House
Fareham	Ladywell Road
Hants. PO15 5RR	Edinburgh EH12 7TF
(tel. 0132 981 3800)	(tel. 0131 314 4254)

SAS TOPIC & KEYWORD INDEX

Households Contd/

Women in couples	80 90 91
Workplace outside district of usual residence	76 78 82
Young adults	37
1971/1981 population base	1 27

1991 Census Small Area Statistics - 100% **Area Identifier - <zoneid>** Grid reference - **<Easting/Northing>**
<.Ward / Postcode Sector name..> <........**DistrictName**.........> <.....**County / Region Name**.....>
Table Prefix: S01

Table 1 Population bases: Persons present plus absent residents, in households

	TOTAL PERSONS	In households			Not in households		
		TOTAL	Males	Females	TOTAL	Males	Females
1. Present residents	1	2	3	4	5	6	7
2. Absent residents (part of household present)	8	9	10	11	xxxx	xxxx	xxxx
3. Absent residents (wholly absent household - enumerated)	15	16	17	18	xxxx	xxxx	xxxx
4. Absent residents (wholly absent household - imputed)	22	23	24	25	xxxx	xxxx	xxxx
5. Visitors	29	30	31	32	33	34	35
Resident in UK	36	37	38	39	40	41	42
Resident outside UK	43	44	45	46	47	48	49
PERSONS PRESENT 1991: 1971 BASE (1+5)	50	51	52	53	54	55	56
RESIDENTS 1991: 1981 BASE (1+2)	57	58	59	60	61	62	63
RESIDENTS 1991: 1991 BASE (1+2+3+4)*	64	65	66	67	68	69	70

*All tables for residents on 100% topics are on this population base.

1991 Census Small Area Statistics - 100% **Area Identifier - <zoneid>** Grid reference - **<Easting/Northing>**
<.Ward / Postcode Sector name..> <........**DistrictName**.........> <.....**County / Region Name**.....>
Table Prefix: S02

Table 2 Age and marital status: Residents

Age	TOTAL PERSONS	Males			Females		
		Total	Single widowed or div'ced	Married	Total	Single widowed or div'ced	Married
ALL AGES	1	2	3	4	5	6	7
0 - 4	8	9	10	xxxx	12	13	xxxx
5 - 9	15	16	17	xxxx	19	20	xxxx
10 - 14	22	23	24	xxxx	26	27	xxxx
15	29	30	31	xxxx	33	34	xxxx
16 - 17	36	37	38	39	40	41	42
18 - 19	43	44	45	46	47	48	49
20 - 24	50	51	52	53	54	55	56
25 - 29	57	58	59	60	61	62	63
30 - 34	64	65	66	67	68	69	70
35 - 39	71	72	73	74	75	76	77
40 - 44	78	79	80	81	82	83	84
45 - 49	85	86	87	88	89	90	91
50 - 54	92	93	94	95	96	97	98
55 - 59	99	100	101	102	103	104	105
60 - 64	106	107	108	109	110	111	112
65 - 69	113	114	115	116	117	118	119
70 - 74	120	121	122	123	124	125	126
75 - 79	127	128	129	130	131	132	133
80 - 84	134	135	136	137	138	139	140
85 - 89	141	142	143	144	145	146	147
90 and over	148	149	150	151	152	153	154

1991 Census Small Area Statistics - 100% **Area Identifier - <zoneid>** Grid reference - **<Easting/Northing>**
<.Ward / Postcode Sector name..> <........**DistrictName**.........> <.....**County / Region Name**.....>
Table Prefix: S03

Table 3 Communal establishments: Establishments: persons present not in households

Type of establishment	Number of estab.*	TOTAL PERSONS	Total males	Total females	Not resident		Residents			
							Staff		Other	
					Males	Females	Males	Females	Males	Females
All establishments	1	2	3	4	5	6	7	8	9	10
Medical and care sector	11	12	13	14	15	16	17	18	19	20
NHS hosp./homes - psych.	21	22	23	24	25	26	27	28	29	30
NHS hosp./homes - other	31	32	33	34	35	36	37	38	39	40
Non-NHS hospital - psych.	41	42	43	44	45	46	47	48	49	50
Non-NHS hospital - other	51	52	53	54	55	56	57	58	59	60
Local authority homes	61	62	63	64	65	66	67	68	69	70
Housing association homes and hostels	71	72	73	74	75	76	77	78	79	80
Nursing homes (non-NHS/LA/HA)	81	82	83	84	85	86	87	88	89	90
Residential homes (non-NHS/LA/HA)	91	92	93	94	95	96	97	98	99	100
Children's homes	101	102	103	104	105	106	107	108	109	110
Detention, defence, and education	111	112	113	114	115	116	117	118	119	120
Prison service estab.	121	122	123	124	125	126	127	128	129	130
Defence estab.	131	132	133	134	135	136	xxxx	xxxx	139	140
Educational estab.	141	142	143	144	145	146	147	148	149	150
Other groups	151	152	153	154	155	156	157	158	159	160
Hotels, b'ding houses etc	161	162	163	164	165	166	167	168	169	170
Hostels & common lodging houses (non-HA)	171	172	173	174	175	176	177	178	179	180
Other establishments	181	182	183	184	185	186	187	188	189	190

*The counts in this column are unmodified

1991 Census Small Area Statistics - 100% Area Identifier - <zoneid> Grid reference - <Easting/Northing>
<.Ward / Postcode Sector name..> <........DistrictName.........> <.....County / Region Name.....>
Table Prefix: S04

Table 4 Medical and care establishments: Residents (non-staff) present not in households

Type of establishment	TOTAL PERSONS	Below pensionable age		Pensionable age and over		Migrants
		Males	Females	Males	Females	
ALL MEDICAL AND CARE ESTABLISHMENTS	1	2	3	4	5	6
NHS hospitals/homes - psych.	7	8	9	10	11	12
NHS hospitals/homes - other	13	14	15	16	17	18
Non-NHS hospitals - psych.	19	20	21	22	23	24
Non-NHS hospitals - other	25	26	27	28	29	30
Local authority homes	31	32	33	34	35	36
Housing association homes and hostels	37	38	39	40	41	42
Nursing homes (non-NHS/LA/HA)	43	44	45	46	47	48
Res. homes (non-NHS/LA/HA)	49	50	51	52	53	54

1991 Census Small Area Statistics - 100% Area Identifier - <zoneid> Grid reference - <Easting/Northing>
<.Ward / Postcode Sector name..> <........DistrictName.........> <.....County / Region Name.....>
Table Prefix: S05

Table 5 Hotels and other establishments: Residents (non-staff) present not in households

Type of establishment	TOTAL PERSONS	Below pensionable age		Pensionable age and over		Migrants
		Males	Females	Males	Females	
ALL HOTELS AND OTHER ESTABLISHMENTS	1	2	3	4	5	6
Children's homes	7	8	9	10	11	12
Prison service establishments	13	14	15	16	17	18
Defence establishments	19	20	21	22	23	24
Educational establishments	25	26	27	28	29	30
Hotels, boarding houses etc	31	32	33	34	35	36
Hostels & common lodging houses (non-HA)	37	38	39	40	41	42
Other establishments	43	44	45	46	47	48

1991 Census Small Area Statistics - 100% Area Identifier - <zoneid> Grid reference - <Easting/Northing>
<.Ward / Postcode Sector name..> <........DistrictName.........> <.....County / Region Name.....>
Table Prefix: S06

Table 6 Ethnic group: Residents

Sex and age	TOTAL PERSONS	Ethnic group										Persons born in Ireland
		White	Black C'bean	Black African	Black other	Indian	P'stani	B'deshi	Chinese	Other groups: Asian	Other groups: Other	
TOTAL PERSONS	1	2	3	4	5	6	7	8	9	10	11	12
Males	13	14	15	16	17	18	19	20	21	22	23	24
Females	25	26	27	28	29	30	31	32	33	34	35	36
Age												
0 - 4	37	38	39	40	41	42	43	44	45	46	47	48
5 - 15	49	50	51	52	53	54	55	56	57	58	59	60
16 - 29	61	62	63	64	65	66	67	68	69	70	71	72
30 up to pensionable age	73	74	75	76	77	78	79	80	81	82	83	84
Pensionable age and over	85	86	87	88	89	90	91	92	93	94	95	96
With limiting long-term illness	97	98	99	100	101	102	103	104	105	106	107	108

1991 Census Small Area Statistics - 100% Area Identifier - <zoneid> Grid reference - <Easting/Northing>
<.Ward / Postcode Sector name..> <........DistrictName.........> <.....County / Region Name.....>
Table Prefix: S07

Table 7 Country of birth: Residents

Country of birth	Males	Females
ALL COUNTRIES OF BIRTH	1	2
United Kingdom*	3	4
England	5	6
Scotland	7	8
Wales	9	10
Northern Ireland	11	12
Irish Republic**	13	14
Old Commonwealth	15	16
New Commonwealth	17	18
Eastern Africa	19	20
Other Africa	21	22
Caribbean	23	24
Bangladesh	25	26
India	27	28
Pakistan	29	30
South East Asia	31	32
Cyprus	33	34
Other New Commonwealth	35	36
Other European Community	37	38
Other Europe	39	40
China	41	42
Rest of the World	43	44

* Includes Channel Islands, Isle of Man and United Kingdom (part not stated)

** Includes Ireland (part not stated)

1991 Census Small Area Statistics - 100% **Area Identifier - <zoneid>** **Grid reference - <Easting/Northing>**
<.Ward / Postcode Sector name..> **<........DistrictName.........>** **<.....County / Region Name.....>**
Table Prefix: S08

Table 8 Economic position: Residents aged 16 and over

Sex by economic position	TOTAL AGED 16 AND OVER	Age									Stu-dents (econ. act. or inact.)
		16 - 19	20-24	25-29	30-34	35-44	45 - 54	55 - 59	60 - 64	65 and over	
Males	1	2	3	4	5	6	7	8	9	10	11
Economically active	12	13	14	15	16	17	18	19	20	21	22
Employees - full time	23	24	25	26	27	28	29	30	31	32	33
- part time	34	35	36	37	38	39	40	41	42	43	44
Self-employed - with employees	45	46	47	48	49	50	51	52	53	54	55
- without employees	56	57	58	59	60	61	62	63	64	65	66
On a Government scheme	67	68	69	70	71	72	73	74	75	76	xxxx
Unemployed	78	79	80	81	82	83	84	85	86	87	88
Economically active students (inc. above)	89	90	91	92	93	94	95	96	97	98	xxxx
Economically inactive	100	101	102	103	104	105	106	107	108	109	110
Students	111	112	113	114	115	116	117	118	119	120	121
Permanently sick	122	123	124	125	126	127	128	129	130	131	xxxx
Retired	133	134	135	136	137	138	139	140	141	142	xxxx
Other inactive	144	145	146	147	148	149	150	151	152	153	xxxx
Females	155	156	157	158	159	160	161	162	163	164	165
Economically active	166	167	168	169	170	171	172	173	174	175	176
Employees - full time	177	178	179	180	181	182	183	184	185	186	187
- part time	188	189	190	191	192	193	194	195	196	197	198
Self-employed - with employees	199	200	201	202	203	204	205	206	207	208	209
- without employees	210	211	212	213	214	215	216	217	218	219	220
On a Government scheme	221	222	223	224	225	226	227	228	229	230	xxxx
Unemployed	232	233	234	235	236	237	238	239	240	241	242
Economically active students (inc. above)	243	244	245	246	247	248	249	250	251	252	xxxx
Economically inactive	254	255	256	257	258	259	260	261	262	263	264
Students	265	266	267	268	269	270	271	272	273	274	275
Permanently sick	276	277	278	279	280	281	282	283	284	285	xxxx
Retired	287	288	289	290	291	292	293	294	295	296	xxxx
Other inactive	298	299	300	301	302	303	304	305	306	307	xxxx

1991 Census Small Area Statistics - 100% **Area Identifier - <zoneid>** **Grid reference - <Easting/Northing>**
<.Ward / Postcode Sector name..> **<........DistrictName.........>** **<.....County / Region Name.....>**
Table Prefix: S09

Table 9 Economic position and ethnic group: Residents aged 16 and over

Economic position	TOTAL PERSONS	Ethnic group				Persons born in Ireland
		White	Black groups	Indian, P'stani and B'deshi	Chinese and other groups	
TOTAL PERSONS	1	2	3	4	5	6
Males 16 and over	7	8	9	10	11	12
Economically active	13	14	15	16	17	18
Unemployed	19	20	21	22	23	24
Economically inactive	25	26	27	28	29	30
Females 16 and over	31	32	33	34	35	36
Economically active	37	38	39	40	41	42
Unemployed	43	44	45	46	47	48
Economically inactive	49	50	51	52	53	54

1991 Census Small Area Statistics - 100% **Area Identifier - <zoneid>** **Grid reference - <Easting/Northing>**
<.Ward / Postcode Sector name..> **<........DistrictName.........>** **<.....County / Region Name.....>**
Table Prefix: S10

Table 10 Term-time address: Students (16 and over) present plus absent resident students (16 and over)

	TOTAL STU-DENTS	Age	
		16 - 17	18 and over
TOTAL STUDENTS	1	2	3
Present residents	4	5	6
Term-time address - this address	7	8	9
- elsewhere	10	11	12
Absent residents	13	14	15
Term-time address - this address	16	17	18
- elsewhere	19	20	21
Non-residents	22	23	24
Term-time address - this address	25	26	27
- elsewhere	28	29	30
Students not in h'holds	31	32	33

1991 Census Small Area Statistics - 100% **Area Identifier - <zoneid>** **Grid reference - <Easting/Northing>**
<.Ward / Postcode Sector name..> <........**DistrictName**.........> <.....County / **Region Name**.....>
Table Prefix: S11

Table 11 Persons present: Persons present

Age	TOTAL PERSONS	In households			Not in households						
					Persons present			Residents			
								Staff		Other	
		Total	Males	Females	Total	Males	Females	Males	Females	Males	Females
ALL AGES	1	2	3	4	5	6	7	8	9	10	11
0 - 4	12	13	14	15	16	17	18	19	20	21	22
5 - 9	23	24	25	26	27	28	29	30	31	32	33
10 - 14	34	35	36	37	38	39	40	41	42	43	44
15	45	46	47	48	49	50	51	52	53	54	55
16 - 17	56	57	58	59	60	61	62	63	64	65	66
18 - 19	67	68	69	70	71	72	73	74	75	76	77
20 - 24	78	79	80	81	82	83	84	85	86	87	88
25 - 29	89	90	91	92	93	94	95	96	97	98	99
30 - 34	100	101	102	103	104	105	106	107	108	109	110
35 - 39	111	112	113	114	115	116	117	118	119	120	121
40 - 44	122	123	124	125	126	127	128	129	130	131	132
45 - 49	133	134	135	136	137	138	139	140	141	142	143
50 - 54	144	145	146	147	148	149	150	151	152	153	154
55 - 59	155	156	157	158	159	160	161	162	163	164	165
60 - 64	166	167	168	169	170	171	172	173	174	175	176
65 - 69	177	178	179	180	181	182	183	184	185	186	187
70 - 74	188	189	190	191	192	193	194	195	196	197	198
75 - 79	199	200	201	202	203	204	205	206	207	208	209
80 - 84	210	211	212	213	214	215	216	217	218	219	220
85 - 89	221	222	223	224	225	226	227	228	229	230	231
90 and over	232	233	234	235	236	237	238	239	240	241	242

1991 Census Small Area Statistics - 100% **Area Identifier - <zoneid>** **Grid reference - <Easting/Northing>**
<.Ward / Postcode Sector name..> <........**DistrictName**.........> <.....County / **Region Name**.....>
Table Prefix: S12

Table 12 Long-term illness in households: Residents in households with limiting long-term illness

Age	TOTAL PERSONS	Males	Females
ALL AGES	1	2	3
0 - 15	4	5	6
16 - 29	7	8	9
30 - 44	10	11	12
45 - 59	13	14	15
60 - 64	16	17	18
65 - 74	19	20	21
75 and over	22	23	24

1991 Census Small Area Statistics - 100% **Area Identifier - <zoneid>** **Grid reference - <Easting/Northing>**
<.Ward / Postcode Sector name..> <........**DistrictName**.........> <.....County / **Region Name**.....>
Table Prefix: S13

Table 13 Long-term illness in communal establishments: Residents not in households with limiting long-term illness

Age	TOTAL PERSONS	Males	Females
ALL AGES	1	2	3
0 - 15	4	5	6
16 - 29	7	8	9
30 - 44	10	11	12
45 - 59	13	14	15
60 - 64	16	17	18
65 - 74	19	20	21
75 and over	22	23	24

1991 Census Small Area Statistics - 100% **Area Identifier - <zoneid>** **Grid reference - <Easting/Northing>**
<.Ward / Postcode Sector name..> <........**DistrictName**.........> <.....County / **Region Name**.....>
Table Prefix: S14

Table 14 Long-term illness and economic position: Residents aged 16 and over with limiting long-term illness

Economic position	TOTAL AGED 16 AND OVER	Age				Students (econ. active or inact.)
		16 - 29	30 - 44	45 up to PA	PA and over	
TOTAL PERSONS	1	2	3	4	5	6
Economically active	7	8	9	10	11	12
Employees - full time	13	14	15	16	17	18
- part time	19	20	21	22	23	24
Self-employed	25	26	27	28	29	30
On a Government scheme	31	32	33	34	35	xxxx
Unemployed	37	38	39	40	41	42
Economically active students (included above)	43	44	45	46	47	xxxx
Economically inactive	49	50	51	52	53	54
Students	55	56	57	58	59	60
Permanently sick	61	62	63	64	65	xxxx
Retired	67	68	69	70	71	xxxx
Other inactive	73	74	75	76	77	xxxx

PA = Pensionable age

1991 Census Small Area Statistics - 100% **Area Identifier - <zoneid>** **Grid reference - <Easting/Northing>**
<.Ward / Postcode Sector name..> **<........DistrictName.........>** **<.....County / Region Name.....>**
Table Prefix: S15 **CROWN COPYRIGHT RESERVED**

Table 15 Migrants: Residents with different address one year before census

Age	TOTAL PERSONS	Moved within wards	Between wards but within dist.	A*	B**	C***	From outside Great Britain	Between neigh-bouring dists.	Between neigh. count's /Scot. Regions
ALL MIGRANTS: ALL AGES 1 AND OVER	1	2	3	4	5	6	7	8	9
1 - 15	10	11	12	13	14	15	16	17	18
16 - 29	19	20	21	22	23	24	25	26	27
30 - 44	28	29	30	31	32	33	34	35	36
45 up to pensionable age	37	38	39	40	41	42	43	44	45
Pensionable age and over	46	47	48	49	50	51	52	53	54
Migrants in households	55	56	57	58	59	60	61	62	63

* Between districts but within county
** Between counties but within region
*** Between regions or from Scotland

1991 Census Small Area Statistics - 100% **Area Identifier - <zoneid>** **Grid reference - <Easting/Northing>**
<.Ward / Postcode Sector name..> **<........DistrictName.........>** **<.....County / Region Name.....>**
Table Prefix: S16 **CROWN COPYRIGHT RESERVED**

Table 16 Wholly moving households: Wholly moving households; residents in such households

Household composition and number of residents	ALL TYPES OF MOVE	Moved within wards	Between wards but within dist.	A**	B***	C****	From outside Great Britain	Between neigh-bouring dists.	Between neigh. count's /Soot. Regions
TOTAL WHOLLY MOVING HOUSEHOLDS	1	2	3	4	5	6	7	8	9
TOTAL PERSONS IN WHOLLY MOVING HOUSEHOLDS	10	11	12	13	14	15	16	17	18
*Wholly moving households with dependent children**									
Persons	19	xxxx	xxxx	xxxx	xxxx	xxxx	xxxx	xxxx	xxxx
All households	28	xxxx	xxxx	xxxx	xxxx	xxxx	xxxx	xxxx	xxxx
Wholly moving households, no dependent children, no person aged 60 or over									
Persons	37	xxxx	xxxx	xxxx	xxxx	xxxx	xxxx	xxxx	xxxx
All households	46	xxxx	xxxx	xxxx	xxxx	xxxx	xxxx	xxxx	xxxx
Single person households	55	xxxx	xxxx	xxxx	xxxx	xxxx	xxxx	xxxx	xxxx
Wholly moving households, no dependent children, no person aged under 60									
Persons	64	xxxx	xxxx	xxxx	xxxx	xxxx	xxxx	xxxx	xxxx
All households	73	xxxx	xxxx	xxxx	xxxx	xxxx	xxxx	xxxx	xxxx
Single person households	82	xxxx	xxxx	xxxx	xxxx	xxxx	xxxx	xxxx	xxxx
Other wholly moving households									
Persons	91	xxxx	xxxx	xxxx	xxxx	xxxx	xxxx	xxxx	xxxx
All households	100	xxxx	xxxx	xxxx	xxxx	xxxx	xxxx	xxxx	xxxx

* May include a small number of households with no adults
** Between districts but within county
*** Between counties but within region
**** Between regions or from Scotland

1991 Census Small Area Statistics - 100% **Area Identifier - <zoneid>** **Grid reference - <Easting/Northing>**
<.Ward / Postcode Sector name..> **<........DistrictName.........>** **<.....County / Region Name.....>**
Table Prefix: S17 **CROWN COPYRIGHT RESERVED**

Table 17 Ethnic group of migrants: Residents aged 1 and over

		Ethnic group				
	TOTAL PERSONS	White	Black groups	Indian, P'stani and B'deshi	Chinese and other groups	Persons born in Ireland
TOTAL PERSONS	1	2	3	4	5	6
With different address one year before census (migrants)	7	8	9	10	11	12

1991 Census Small Area Statistics - 100% **Area Identifier - <zoneid>** **Grid reference - <Easting/Northing>**
<.Ward / Postcode Sector name..> **<........DistrictName.........>** **<.....County / Region Name.....>**
Table Prefix: S19 **CROWN COPYRIGHT RESERVED**

Table 19 Imputed households: Wholly absent households with imputed residents

	Households with the following persons		
TOTAL HOUSE-HOLDS	1	2	3 or more
1	2	3	4

1991 Census Small Area Statistics - 100% **Area Identifier - <zoneid>** **Grid reference - <Easting/Northing>**
<.Ward / Postcode Sector name..> <........**DistrictName**.........> <.....**County / Region Name**.....>
Table Prefix: S20 **CROWN COPYRIGHT RESERVED**

Table 20 Tenure and amenities: Households with residents; residents in households

Amenities	All perm -anent	Owner occupied: Owned outr't	Owner occupied: Buying	Rented p'vately: Furn -ished	Rented p'vately: Unfurn -ished	Rented with a job or b'ness	Rented from a housing assoc.	Rented from a LA or new town	Non-perm -anent accomm.	No car
	Tenure of households in permanent buildings									
TOTAL HOUSEHOLDS	1	2	3	4	5	6	7	8	9	10
Exclusive use of bath/shower and inside WC	11	12	13	14	15	16	17	18	19	20
With central heating in all or some rooms	21	22	23	24	25	26	27	28	29	30
No central heating	31	32	33	34	35	36	37	38	39	40
Lacking or sharing use of bath/ shower and/or inside WC	41	42	43	44	45	46	47	48	49	50
With central heating in all or some rooms	51	52	53	54	55	56	57	58	59	60
No central heating	61	62	63	64	65	66	67	68	69	70
Exclusive use of bath/shower	71	72	73	74	75	76	77	78	79	80
Shared use of bath/shower	81	82	83	84	85	86	87	88	89	90
No bath/shower	91	92	93	94	95	96	97	98	99	100
Exclusive use of inside WC	101	102	103	104	105	106	107	108	109	110
Shared use of inside WC	111	112	113	114	115	116	117	118	119	120
No inside WC	121	122	123	124	125	126	127	128	129	130
No car	131	132	133	134	135	136	137	138	139	xxxx
TOTAL PERSONS IN HOUSEHOLDS	141	142	143	144	145	146	147	148	149	150
Exclusive use of bath/shower and inside WC	151	152	153	154	155	156	157	158	159	160
With central heating in all or some rooms	161	162	163	164	165	166	167	168	169	170
No central heating	171	172	173	174	175	176	177	178	179	180
Lacking or sharing use of bath/ shower and/or inside WC	181	182	183	184	185	186	187	188	189	190
With central heating in all or some rooms	191	192	193	194	195	196	197	198	199	200
No central heating	201	202	203	204	205	206	207	208	209	210
No car	211	212	213	214	215	216	217	218	219	xxxx

1991 Census Small Area Statistics - 100% **Area Identifier - <zoneid>** **Grid reference - <Easting/Northing>**
<.Ward / Postcode Sector name..> <........**DistrictName**.........> <.....**County / Region Name**.....>
Table Prefix: S21 **CROWN COPYRIGHT RESERVED**

Table 21 Car availability: Households with residents; residents in households; cars in households

Number of persons aged 17 and over (with or without others)	TOTAL PERSONS (ALL AGES)	TOTAL HOUSE -HOLDS	Households with: No car	Households with: 1 car	Households with: 2 cars	Households with: 3 or more cars	TOTAL CARS*
ALL HOUSEHOLDS**	1	2	3	4	5	6	7
1 male aged 17 and over	8	9	10	11	12	13	14
1 female aged 17 and over	15	16	17	18	19	20	21
2 (1 male and 1 female) aged 17 and over	22	23	24	25	26	27	28
2 (same sex) aged 17 and over	29	30	31	32	33	34	35
3 or more aged 17 and over	36	37	38	39	40	41	42
TOTAL PERSONS (ALL AGES)	xxxx	44	45	46	47	48	xxxx
Persons aged 17 and over	xxxx	51	52	53	54	55	xxxx

* Households with three or more cars are counted as having three cars
** May include a small number of households with no persons aged 17 and over

1991 Census Small Area Statistics - 100% **Area Identifier - <zoneid>** **Grid reference - <Easting/Northing>**
<.Ward / Postcode Sector name..> <........**DistrictName**.........> <.....**County / Region Name**.....>
Table Prefix: S22 **CROWN COPYRIGHT RESERVED**

Table 22 Rooms and household size: Households with residents; residents in households; rooms in household spaces

Households with the following tenure and persons	TOTAL HOUSE -HOLDS	Households with the following rooms: 1	2	3	4	5	6	7 or more	TOTAL ROOMS
ALL TENURES	1	2	3	4	5	6	7	8	9
1	10	11	12	13	14	15	16	17	18
2	19	20	21	22	23	24	25	26	27
3	28	29	30	31	32	33	34	35	36
4	37	38	39	40	41	42	43	44	45
5	46	47	48	49	50	51	52	53	54
6	55	56	57	58	59	60	61	62	63
7 or more	64	65	66	67	68	69	70	71	72
TOTAL PERSONS	73	74	75	76	77	78	79	80	xxxx
Owner occupied	82	83	84	85	86	87	88	89	90
1	91	92	93	94	95	96	97	98	99
2	100	101	102	103	104	105	106	107	108
3	109	110	111	112	113	114	115	116	117
4	118	119	120	121	122	123	124	125	126
5	127	128	129	130	131	132	133	134	135
6	136	137	138	139	140	141	142	143	144
7 or more	145	146	147	148	149	150	151	152	153
Total persons	154	155	156	157	158	159	160	161	xxxx
Rented privately or rented with a job or business	163	164	165	166	167	168	169	170	171
1	172	173	174	175	176	177	178	179	180
2	181	182	183	184	185	186	187	188	189
3	190	191	192	193	194	195	196	197	198
4	199	200	201	202	203	204	205	206	207
5	208	209	210	211	212	213	214	215	216
6	217	218	219	220	221	222	223	224	225
7 or more	226	227	228	229	230	231	232	233	234
Total persons	235	236	237	238	239	240	241	242	xxxx

1991 Census Small Area Statistics - 100% **Area Identifier - <zoneid>** **Grid reference - <Easting/Northing>**
<.Ward / Postcode Sector name..> **<........DistrictName.........>** **<.....County / Region Name.....>**
Table Prefix: S22 **CROWN COPYRIGHT RESERVED**

Table 22 Rooms and household size: Households with residents; residents in households; rooms in household spaces **(Continued)**

Households with the following tenure and persons	TOTAL HOUSE -HOLDS	Households with the following rooms							TOTAL ROOMS
		1	2	3	4	5	6	7 or more	
Rented from a housing association	244	245	246	247	248	249	250	251	252
1	253	254	255	256	257	258	259	260	261
2	262	263	264	265	266	267	268	269	270
3	271	272	273	274	275	276	277	278	279
4	280	281	282	283	284	285	286	287	288
5	289	290	291	292	293	294	295	296	297
6	298	299	300	301	302	303	304	305	306
7 or more	307	308	309	310	311	312	313	314	315
Total persons	316	317	318	319	320	321	322	323	xxxx
Rented from a Local Authority or new town	325	326	327	328	329	330	331	332	333
1	334	335	336	337	338	339	340	341	342
2	343	344	345	346	347	348	349	350	351
3	352	353	354	355	356	357	358	359	360
4	361	362	363	364	365	366	367	368	369
5	370	371	372	373	374	375	376	377	378
6	379	380	381	382	383	384	385	386	387
7 or more	388	389	390	391	392	393	394	395	396
Total persons	397	398	399	400	401	402	403	404	xxxx

1991 Census Small Area Statistics - 100% **Area Identifier - <zoneid>** **Grid reference - <Easting/Northing>**
<.Ward / Postcode Sector name..> **<........DistrictName.........>** **<.....County / Region Name.....>**
Table Prefix: SS22 **CROWN COPYRIGHT RESERVED**

Table 22 Rooms and household size: Households with residents; residents in households; rooms in household spaces

Households with the following tenure and persons	TOTAL HOUSE -HOLDS	Households with the following rooms							TOTAL ROOMS
		1	2	3	4	5	6	7 or more	
ALL TENURES	1	2	3	4	5	6	7	8	9
1	10	11	12	13	14	15	16	17	18
2	19	20	21	22	23	24	25	26	27
3	28	29	30	31	32	33	34	35	36
4	37	38	39	40	41	42	43	44	45
5	46	47	48	49	50	51	52	53	54
6	55	56	57	58	59	60	61	62	63
7 or more	64	65	66	67	68	69	70	71	72
TOTAL PERSONS	73	74	75	76	77	78	79	80	xxxx
Owner occupied	82	83	84	85	86	87	88	89	90
1	91	92	93	94	95	96	97	98	99
2	100	101	102	103	104	105	106	107	108
3	109	110	111	112	113	114	115	116	117
4	118	119	120	121	122	123	124	125	126
5	127	128	129	130	131	132	133	134	135
6	136	137	138	139	140	141	142	143	144
7 or more	145	146	147	148	149	150	151	152	153
Total persons	154	155	156	157	158	159	160	161	xxxx
Rented privately or rented with a job or business	163	164	165	166	167	168	169	170	171
1	172	173	174	175	176	177	178	179	180
2	181	182	183	184	185	186	187	188	189
3	190	191	192	193	194	195	196	197	198
4	199	200	201	202	203	204	205	206	207
5	208	209	210	211	212	213	214	215	216
6	217	218	219	220	221	222	223	224	225
7 or more	226	227	228	229	230	231	232	233	234
Total persons	235	236	237	238	239	240	241	242	xxxx

1991 Census Small Area Statistics - 100% **Area Identifier - <zoneid>** **Grid reference - <Easting/Northing>**
<.Ward / Postcode Sector name..> **<........DistrictName.........>** **<.....County / Region Name.....>**
Table Prefix: SS22 **CROWN COPYRIGHT RESERVED**

Table 22 Rooms and household size: Households with residents; residents in households; rooms in household spaces **(Continued)**

Households with the following tenure and persons	TOTAL HOUSE -HOLDS	Households with the following rooms							TOTAL ROOMS
		1	2	3	4	5	6	7 or more	
Rented from a housing association	244	245	246	247	248	249	250	251	252
1	253	254	255	256	257	258	259	260	261
2	262	263	264	265	266	267	268	269	270
3	271	272	273	274	275	276	277	278	279
4	280	281	282	283	284	285	286	287	288
5	289	290	291	292	293	294	295	296	297
6	298	299	300	301	302	303	304	305	306
7 or more	307	308	309	310	311	312	313	314	315
Total persons	316	317	318	319	320	321	322	323	xxxx
Rented from a local authority	325	326	327	328	329	330	331	332	333
1	334	335	336	337	338	339	340	341	342
2	343	344	345	346	347	348	349	350	351
3	352	353	354	355	356	357	358	359	360
4	361	362	363	364	365	366	367	368	369
5	370	371	372	373	374	375	376	377	378
6	379	380	381	382	383	384	385	386	387
7 or more	388	389	390	391	392	393	394	395	396
Total persons	397	398	399	400	401	402	403	404	xxxx
Rented from a new town or Scottish Homes	406	407	408	409	410	411	412	413	414
1	415	416	417	418	419	420	421	422	423
2	424	425	426	427	428	429	430	431	432
3	433	434	435	436	437	438	439	440	441
4	442	443	444	445	446	447	448	449	450
5	451	452	453	454	455	456	457	458	459
6	460	461	462	463	464	465	466	467	468
7 or more	469	470	471	472	473	474	475	476	477
Total persons	478	479	480	481	482	483	484	485	xxxx

1991 Census Small Area Statistics - 100% **Area Identifier - <zoneid>** **Grid reference - <Easting/Northing>**
<.Ward / Postcode Sector name..> <........**DistrictName**.........> <.....County / **Region Name**.....>
Table Prefix: S23 CROWN COPYRIGHT RESERVED

Table 23 Persons per room: Households with residents; residents in households

Tenure	TOTAL HOUSE -HOLDS	Up to 0.5 ppr	Over 1 and up to 1.5 ppr	Over 1.5 ppr
TOTAL HOUSEHOLDS	1	2	3	4
All permanent buildings	5	6	7	8
Owner occupied - owned outright	9	10	11	12
- buying	13	14	15	16
Rented privately - furnished	17	18	19	20
- unfurnished	21	22	23	24
Rented with a job or business	25	26	27	28
Rented from a housing association	29	30	31	32
Rented from a local authority or new town	33	34	35	36
Non-permanent accommodation	37	38	39	40
TOTAL PERSONS IN HOUSEHOLDS	41	42	43	44
All permanent buildings	45	46	47	48
Owner occupied - owned outright	49	50	51	52
- buying	53	54	55	56
Rented privately - furnished	57	58	59	60
- unfurnished	61	62	63	64
Rented with a job or business	65	66	67	68
Rented from a housing association	69	70	71	72
Rented from a local authority or new town	73	74	75	76
Non-permanent accommodation	77	78	79	80

ppr = persons per room

1991 Census Small Area Statistics - 100% **Area Identifier - <zoneid>** **Grid reference - <Easting/Northing>**
<.Ward / Postcode Sector name..> <........**DistrictName**.........> <.....County / **Region Name**.....>
Table Prefix: S24 CROWN COPYRIGHT RESERVED

Table 24 Residents 18 and over: Households with residents; residents in households

Households with the following persons	TOTAL HOUSE -HOLDS	Households with the following persons aged 18 and over:				TOTAL PERSONS AGED 18 AND OVER
		1	2	3	4 or more	
TOTAL HOUSEHOLDS	1	2	3	4	5	6
1	7	8	xxxx	xxxx	xxxx	12
2	13	14	15	xxxx	xxxx	18
3	19	20	21	22	xxxx	24
4 or more	25	26	27	28	29	30
TOTAL PERSONS	31	32	33	34	35	xxxx

* May include a small number of households with no persons aged 18 and over

1991 Census Small Area Statistics - 100% **Area Identifier - <zoneid>** **Grid reference - <Easting/Northing>**
<.Ward / Postcode Sector name..> <........**DistrictName**.........> <.....County / **Region Name**.....>
Table Prefix: S25 CROWN COPYRIGHT RESERVED

Table 25 Visitor households: Households with persons present but no residents; persons present in such households; cars and rooms in such households

Households with no residents	TOTAL HOUSE -HOLDS	Amen -ities*	No cent. heating	Not self-cont. accomm.	Tenure				TOTAL ROOMS	TOTAL CARS**	Total stu-dents ***
					Owner occ.	Rented priv'ly	Rented from a housing assoc.	Rented from a LA or new town			
TOTAL HOUSEHOLDS	1	2	3	4	5	6	7	8	9	10	11
Households with 1 or more students*** aged 18 and over plus others	12	13	14	15	16	17	18	19	20	21	22
Households with student(s)*** only	23	24	25	26	27	28	29	30	31	32	33
TOTAL PERSONS PRESENT	34	35	36	37	38	39	40	41	xxxx	xxxx	xxxx
Students*** present	45	46	47	48	49	50	51	52	xxxx	xxxx	xxxx

* Lacking or sharing use of bath/shower and/or inside WC
** Households with 3 or more cars are counted as having 3 cars
*** Includes all students aged 18 and over, whether economically active or inactive

1991 Census Small Area Statistics - 100% **Area Identifier - <zoneid>** **Grid reference - <Easting/Northing>**
<.Ward / Postcode Sector name..> **<......,.DistrictName.........>** **<.....County / Region Name.....>**
Table Prefix: S26

Table 26 Students in households: Households with residents; residents in households; persons present in households; rooms in household spaces; cars in households

Households with residents enumerated with resident or visitor students aged 18 and over***	TOTAL HOUSE -HOLDS	Amen -ities*	No central heating	Not self-cont. accomm.	Tenure: Owner occ.	Tenure: Rented priv'ly	Tenure: Rented from a housing assoc.	Tenure: Rented from a LA or new town
TOTAL HOUSEHOLDS	1	2	3	4	5	6	7	8
Households with students*** (resident or visitor only)	18	19	20	21	22	23	24	25
Households with students*** (resident or visitor) and non-students	35	36	37	38	39	40	41	42
*Number of students*** in household (included above)*								
1	52	53	54	55	56	57	58	59
2	69	70	71	72	73	74	75	76
3 or more	86	87	88	89	90	91	92	93
TOTAL PERSONS RESIDENT OR PRESENT	103	104	105	106	107	108	109	110
Students*** resident or present	120	121	122	123	124	125	126	127

TOTAL ROOMS	TOTAL CARS**	Total stu-dent*** v'tors	Total stu-dent*** r'dents	Households with the following persons present or resident: 1	2	3	4	5 or more	Households with residents enumerated with resident or visitor students aged 18 and over***
9	10	11	12	13	14	15	16	17	**TOTAL HOUSEHOLDS**
26	27	28	29	30	31	32	33	34	Households with students*** (resident or visitor only)
43	44	45	46	47	48	49	50	51	Households with students*** (resident or visitor) and non-students
									*Number of students*** in household (included above)*
60	61	62	63	64	65	66	67	68	1
77	78	79	80	81	82	83	84	85	2
94	95	96	97	98	99	100	101	102	3 or more
xxxx	xxxx	xxxx	xxxx	xxxx	xxxx	xxxx	xxxx	xxxx	**TOTAL PERSONS RESIDENT OR PRESENT**
xxxx	xxxx	xxxx	xxxx	132	133	134	135	136	Students*** resident or present

* Lacking or sharing use of bath/shower and/or inside WC
** Households with 3 or more cars are counted as having 3 cars
*** Includes all students aged 18 and over, whether economically active or inactive

1991 Census Small Area Statistics - 100% **Area Identifier - <zoneid>** **Grid reference - <Easting/Northing>**
<.Ward / Postcode Sector name..> **<........DistrictName.........>** **<.....County / Region Name.....>**
Table Prefix: S27

Table 27 Households: 1971/81/91 bases:
Line 1: 1991 households with persons present (1971 population base):present residents and visitors; rooms
Line 2: 1991 households (1981 population base); present and absent residents; rooms
Line 3: 1991 households enumerated or absent (1991 population base); present and absent residents and imputed members of wholly absent households; rooms

	Households with the following persons: 0*	1	2	3	4	5	6	7 or more	TOTAL HOUSE-HOLDS	TOTAL PERSONS (1991)	TOTAL ROOMS (1991)
1. 1971 population base	xxxx	2	3	4	5	6	7	8	9	10	11
2. 1981 population base	12	13	14	15	16	17	18	19	20	21	22
3. 1991 population base	23	24	25	26	27	28	29	30	31	32	33

* Private households with a visitor or visitors present but no usual residents i.e a household with '0 persons'

1991 Census Small Area Statistics - 100% **Area Identifier - <zoneid>** **Grid reference - <Easting/Northing>**
<.Ward / Postcode Sector name..> <........**DistrictName**.........> <.....**County / Region Name**.....>
Table Prefix: S28 **CROWN COPYRIGHT RESERVED**

Table 28 Dependants in households: Households with residents; residents in households

Household composition	TOTAL HOUSE -HOLDS	No non-depen-dants	1 male non-dependant: Not in emp.	1 male non-dependant: In emp.	1 female non-dependant: Not in emp.	1 female non-dependant: In emp.	1 male and 1 female non-dependants: Neither in emp.	1 male and 1 female non-dependants: One in emp.	1 male and 1 female non-dependants: Both in emp.
TOTAL HOUSEHOLDS	1	2	3	4	5	6	7	8	9
Households with no dependants	16	xxxx	18	19	20	21	22	23	24
Households with 1 dependant									
Age of dependant									
0 - 15	31	32	33	34	35	36	37	38	39
16 up to pensionable age	46	47	48	49	50	51	52	53	54
Pensionable age and over	61	62	63	64	65	66	67	68	69
Households with at least 2 dependants									
Age of youngest dependant 0 - 15 and age of oldest									
0 - 15	76	77	78	79	80	81	82	83	84
16 up to pensionable age	91	92	93	94	95	96	97	98	99
Pensionable age and over	106	107	108	109	110	111	112	113	114
Age of youngest dependant 16 up to pensionable age and age of oldest									
16 up to pensionable age	121	122	123	124	125	126	127	128	129
Pensionable age and over	136	137	138	139	140	141	142	143	144
Age of youngest dependant pensionable age and over	151	152	153	154	155	156	157	158	159
TOTAL PERSONS	166	167	168	169	170	171	172	173	174
Persons in households with dependants									
Non-dependants	181	xxxx	183	184	185	186	187	188	189
Dependants	196	197	198	199	200	201	202	203	204

emp. = employment

1991 Census Small Area Statistics - 100% **Area Identifier - <zoneid>** **Grid reference - <Easting/Northing>**
<.Ward / Postcode Sector name..> <........**DistrictName**.........> <.....**County / Region Name**.....>
Table Prefix: S28 **CROWN COPYRIGHT RESERVED**

Table 28 Dependants in households: Households with residents; residents in households **(Continued)**

2 same sex non-dependants: Neither in emp.	2 same sex non-dependants: One in emp.	2 same sex non-dependants: Both in emp.	3 or more non-dependants: None in emp.	3 or more non-dependants: One in emp.	3 or more non-dependants: 2+ in emp.	Household composition
10	11	12	13	14	15	**TOTAL HOUSEHOLDS**
25	26	27	28	29	30	Households with no dependants
						Households with 1 dependant
						Age of dependant
40	41	42	43	44	45	0 - 15
55	56	57	58	59	60	16 up to pensionable age
70	71	72	73	74	75	Pensionable age and over
						Households with at least 2 dependants
						Age of youngest dependant 0 - 15 and age of oldest
85	86	87	88	89	90	0 - 15
100	101	102	103	104	105	16 up to pensionable age
115	116	117	118	119	120	Pensionable age and over
						Age of youngest dependant 16 up to pensionable age and age of oldest
130	131	132	133	134	135	16 up to pensionable age
145	146	147	148	149	150	Pensionable age and over
160	161	162	163	164	165	Age of youngest dependant pensionable age and over
175	176	177	178	179	180	**TOTAL PERSONS**
						Persons in households with dependants
190	191	192	193	194	195	Non-dependants
205	206	207	208	209	210	Dependants

emp. = employment

1991 Census Small Area Statistics - 100% **Area Identifier - <zoneid>** **Grid reference - <Easting/Northing>**
<.Ward / Postcode Sector name..> <........**DistrictName**.........> <.....**County / Region Name**.....>
Table Prefix: S29 **CROWN COPYRIGHT RESERVED**

Table 29 Dependants and long-term illness: Households with residents; dependants in households

Household composition	TOTAL HOUSE -HOLDS	Dependants: TOTAL DEPEND -ANTS	Dependants: Aged 0 - 15: With long-term illness	Dependants: Aged 0 - 15: With no long-term illness	Dependants: Aged 16 - 18: A*	Dependants: Aged 16 - 18: B**	Dependants: C***	Dependants: D****
TOTAL HOUSEHOLDS	1	2	3	4	5	6	7	8
1 or more non-dependants, no dependants	9	xxxx	xxxx	xxxx	xxxx	xxxx	xxxx	xxxx
1 dependant, living alone	17	18	19	20	21	22	23	24
2 dependants, no non-dependants	25	26	27	28	29	30	31	32
3 or more dependants, no non-dependants	33	34	35	36	37	38	39	40
1 non-dependant with 1 or more dependant	41	42	43	44	45	46	47	48
2 non-dependants with 1 or more dependant	49	50	51	52	53	54	55	56
3 or more non-dependants with 1 or more dependant	57	58	59	60	61	62	63	64

* A Single, in full-time education and economically inactive
** B With long-term illness and permanently sick/retired
*** C Aged 19 up to pensionable age with long-term illness and permanently sick/retired
**** D Pensionable age and over with long-term illness and permanently sick/retired

1991 Census Small Area Statistics - 100% **Area Identifier - <zoneid>** **Grid reference - <Easting/Northing>**
<.Ward / Postcode Sector name..> <........**DistrictName**.........> <.....**County / Region Name**.....>
Table Prefix: S30 **CROWN COPYRIGHT RESERVED**

Table 30 'Carers': Households with residents; residents in households with dependants

Number, sex, and age of non-dependants	TOTAL HOUSE -HOLDS	H'holds with no depend -ants	Households with 1 or more dependants: Age of youngest d'dant 0-15 and age of oldest: 0-15	Households with 1 or more dependants: Age of youngest d'dant 0-15 and age of oldest: 16 up to PA	Households with 1 or more dependants: Age of youngest d'dant 0-15 and age of oldest: PA and over	Households with 1 or more dependants: Age of youngest d'dant 16 up to PA and age of oldest: 16 up to PA	Households with 1 or more dependants: Age of youngest d'dant 16 up to PA and age of oldest: PA and over	Households with 1 or more dependants: Age of y'gest d'dant PA and over	Persons in households with dependants: Non-depend -ants	Persons in households with dependants: Depend -ants
TOTAL HOUSEHOLDS	1	2	3	4	5	6	7	8	9	10
No non-dependants	11	xxxx	13	14	15	16	17	18	xxxx	20
1 Male	21	22	23	24	25	26	27	28	29	30
16-44	31	32	33	34	35	36	37	38	39	40
45-64	41	42	43	44	45	46	47	48	49	50
65 and over	51	52	53	54	55	56	57	58	59	60
1 Female	61	62	63	64	65	66	67	68	69	70
16-44	71	72	73	74	75	76	77	78	79	80
45-64	81	82	83	84	85	86	87	88	89	90
65 and over	91	92	93	94	95	96	97	98	99	100
1 Male and 1 Female	101	102	103	104	105	106	107	108	109	110
Both of pensionable age	111	112	113	114	115	116	117	118	119	120
1 under, 1 of pensionable age	121	122	123	124	125	126	127	128	129	130
Both under pensionable age	131	132	133	134	135	136	137	138	139	140
2 of same sex	141	142	143	144	145	146	147	148	149	150
Both of pensionable age	151	152	153	154	155	156	157	158	159	160
1 under, 1 of pensionable age	161	162	163	164	165	166	167	168	169	170
Both under pensionable age	171	172	173	174	175	176	177	178	179	180
3 or more	181	182	183	184	185	186	187	188	189	190
All of pensionable age	191	192	193	194	195	196	197	198	199	200
1 or more under pensionable age	201	202	203	204	205	206	207	208	209	210

1991 Census Small Area Statistics - 100% **Area Identifier - <zoneid>** **Grid reference - <Easting/Northing>**
<.Ward / Postcode Sector name..> <........**DistrictName**.........> <.....**County / Region Name**.....>
Table Prefix: S31 **CROWN COPYRIGHT RESERVED**

Table 31 Dependent children in households: Households with residents; residents in households

Households with the following adults	House -holds with no d'dent ch'dren	All house -holds	Households with dependent children: With one d'dent child: Aged 0 - 4	Households with dependent children: With one d'dent child: Aged 5 and over	Households with dependent children: With two or more dependent children: All aged 0 - 4	Households with dependent children: With two or more dependent children: All aged 5 and over	Households with dependent children: With two or more dependent children: A**	Persons in households: With no d'dent child(ren): All persons	Persons in households: With no d'dent child(ren): Persons econ. active	Persons in households: With dependent child(ren): D'dent ch'dren	Persons in households: With dependent child(ren): Adults	Persons in households: With dependent child(ren): Persons econ. active
ALL HOUSEHOLDS*	1	2	3	4	5	6	7	8	9	10	11	12
1 male	13	14	15	16	17	18	19	20	21	22	23	24
1 female	25	26	27	28	29	30	31	32	33	34	35	36
2 (1 male and 1 female)	37	38	39	40	41	42	43	44	45	46	47	48
2 (same sex)	49	50	51	52	53	54	55	56	57	58	59	60
3 or more (male(s) and female(s))	61	62	63	64	65	66	67	68	69	70	71	72
3 or more (same sex)	73	74	75	76	77	78	79	80	81	82	83	84

* May include a small number of households with no adults
** A. 1 or more aged 0 - 4 and 1 or more aged 5 and over

1991 Census Small Area Statistics - 100% **Area Identifier - <zoneid>** **Grid reference - <Easting/Northing>**
<.Ward / Postcode Sector name..> <........**DistrictName**.........> <.....**County / Region Name**.....>
Table Prefix: S32 **CROWN COPYRIGHT RESERVED**

Table 32 Children 0 - 15 in households: Households with residents; residents in households

Households with the following persons aged 16 and over	House -holds with no persons aged 0 - 15	All house -holds	Households with persons aged 0 - 15: With one person aged 0 - 15: Aged 0 - 4	Households with persons aged 0 - 15: With one person aged 0 - 15: Aged 5 - 15	Households with persons aged 0 - 15: With two or more persons aged 0 - 15: All aged 0 - 4	Households with persons aged 0 - 15: With two or more persons aged 0 - 15: All aged 5 - 15	Households with persons aged 0 - 15: With two or more persons aged 0 - 15: A**	Persons in households: With no person aged 0 - 15: All persons	Persons in households: With no person aged 0 - 15: Persons econ. active	Persons in households: With person(s) aged 0 -15: Persons aged 0 - 15	Persons in households: With person(s) aged 0 -15: Persons aged 16 and over	Persons in households: With person(s) aged 0 -15: Persons econ. active
ALL HOUSEHOLDS*	1	2	3	4	5	6	7	8	9	10	11	12
1 male	13	14	15	16	17	18	19	20	21	22	23	24
1 female	25	26	27	28	29	30	31	32	33	34	35	36
2 (1 male and 1 female)	37	38	39	40	41	42	43	44	45	46	47	48
2 (same sex)	49	50	51	52	53	54	55	56	57	58	59	60
3 or more (male(s) and female(s))	61	62	63	64	65	66	67	68	69	70	71	72
3 or more (same sex)	73	74	75	76	77	78	79	80	81	82	83	84

* May include a small number of households with no persons aged 16 and over
** A. 1 or more aged 0 - 4 and 1 or more aged 5 - 15

1991 Census Small Area Statistics - 100% **Area Identifier - <zoneid>** **Grid reference - <Easting/Northing>**
<.Ward / Postcode Sector name..> <........**DistrictName**.........> <.....**County / Region Name**.....>
Table Prefix: S33 **CROWN COPYRIGHT RESERVED**

Table 33 Women in 'couples; economic position: Females resident in households of one male aged 16 and over and one female aged 16 and over with or without persons aged 0 - 15; number of persons aged 0 - 15 in such households

In households with:	TOTAL FEMALES	Economically active females: Employees: Full-time	Economically active females: Employees: Part-time	Economically active females: Self-emp-loyed	Economically active females: Other	Econ. active stu-dents	Econ. inact. females
No persons aged 0 - 15	1	2	3	4	5	6	7
Person(s) aged 0 - 4 only	8	9	10	11	12	13	14
Person(s) aged 5 - 15 only	15	16	17	18	19	20	21
Persons aged 0 - 4 and 5 - 15	22	23	24	25	26	27	28
TOTAL PERSONS AGED 0 - 15	29	30	31	32	33	34	35
Persons aged 0 - 4	36	37	38	39	40	41	42

1991 Census Small Area Statistics - 100% Area Identifier - <zoneid> Grid reference - <Easting/Northing>
<.Ward / Postcode Sector name..> <........DistrictName.........> <.....County / Region Name.....>
Table Prefix: S34

Table 34 Economic position of household residents: Residents aged 16 and over in households

Economic position	TOTAL PERSONS	Males: Single widowed or div'ced	Males: Married	Females: Single widowed or div'ced	Females: Married	Students (econ. act. or inact.)
TOTAL PERSONS AGED 16 AND OVER	1	2	3	4	5	6
Economically active	7	8	9	10	11	12
Employees - full time	13	14	15	16	17	18
- part time	19	20	21	22	23	24
Self emp. - with employees	25	26	27	28	29	30
- without employees	31	32	33	34	35	36
On a Government scheme	37	38	39	40	41	xxxx
Unemployed	43	44	45	46	47	48
Economically active students (inc. above)	49	50	51	52	53	xxxx
Economically inactive	55	56	57	58	59	60
Students	61	62	63	64	65	66
Permanently sick	67	68	69	70	71	xxxx
Retired	73	74	75	76	77	xxxx
Other inactive	79	80	81	82	83	xxxx

1991 Census Small Area Statistics - 100% Area Identifier - <zoneid> Grid reference - <Easting/Northing>
<.Ward / Postcode Sector name..> <........DistrictName.........> <.....County / Region Name.....>
Table Prefix: S35

Table 35 Age and marital status of household residents: Residents in households

Age	TOTAL PERSONS	Males: Total	Males: Single widowed or div'ced	Males: Married	Females: Total	Females: Single widowed or div'ced	Females: Married
ALL AGES	1	2	3	4	5	6	7
0 - 4	8	9	10	xxxx	12	13	xxxx
5 - 9	15	16	17	xxxx	19	20	xxxx
10 - 14	22	23	24	xxxx	26	27	xxxx
15	29	30	31	xxxx	33	34	xxxx
16 - 17	36	37	38	39	40	41	42
18 - 19	43	44	45	46	47	48	49
20 - 24	50	51	52	53	54	55	56
25 - 29	57	58	59	60	61	62	63
30 - 34	64	65	66	67	68	69	70
35 - 39	71	72	73	74	75	76	77
40 - 44	78	79	80	81	82	83	84
45 - 49	85	86	87	88	89	90	91
50 - 54	92	93	94	95	96	97	98
55 - 59	99	100	101	102	103	104	105
60 - 64	106	107	108	109	110	111	112
65 - 69	113	114	115	116	117	118	119
70 - 74	120	121	122	123	124	125	126
75 - 79	127	128	129	130	131	132	133
80 - 84	134	135	136	137	138	139	140
85 - 89	141	142	143	144	145	146	147
90 and over	148	149	150	151	152	153	154

1991 Census Small Area Statistics - 100% Area Identifier - <zoneid> Grid reference - <Easting/Northing>
<.Ward / Postcode Sector name..> <........DistrictName.........> <.....County / Region Name.....>
Table Prefix: S36

Table 36 'Earners' and dependent children: Households with residents; resident adults; resident dependent children

Households with the following adults: Number	Economically active	In employment	TOTAL HOUSE-HOLDS	Households with the following dependent children: 0	1	2	3 or more	TOTAL DEPEN-DENT CHILD-REN
None	None	None	1	xxxx	3	4	5	6
One	None	None	7	8	9	10	11	12
One	One	None	13	14	15	16	17	18
One	One	One	19	20	21	22	23	24
Two or more	None	None	25	26	27	28	29	30
Two or more	One	None	31	32	33	34	35	36
Two or more	One	One	37	38	39	40	41	42
Two or more	Two or more	None	43	44	45	46	47	48
Two or more	Two or more	One	49	50	51	52	53	54
Two or more	Two or more	Two or more	55	56	57	58	59	60
TOTAL HOUSEHOLDS			61	62	63	64	65	66
TOTAL ADULTS			67	68	69	70	71	xxxx
Economically active			73	74	75	76	77	xxxx
In employment			79	80	81	82	83	xxxx

1991 Census Small Area Statistics - 100% Area Identifier - <zoneid> Grid reference - <Easting/Northing>
<.Ward / Postcode Sector name..> <........DistrictName.........> <.....County / Region Name.....>
Table Prefix: S37

Table 37 Young Adults: Residents aged 16 - 24 in households

Age	TOTAL PERSONS		Married		Lone 'parent' aged 16 - 24 with children aged 0 - 15		Economically active		On a Government scheme		Unemployed		Students (including those econ. active)	
	Males	Females	Males	Females	Males	Females	Males	Females	Males	Females	Males	Females	Males	Females
ALL AGES 16 - 24	1	2	3	4	5	6	7	8	9	10	11	12	13	14
16	15	16	17	18	19	20	21	22	23	24	25	26	27	28
17	29	30	31	32	33	34	35	36	37	38	39	40	41	42
18	43	44	45	46	47	48	49	50	51	52	53	54	55	56
19	57	58	59	60	61	62	63	64	65	66	67	68	69	70
20	71	72	73	74	75	76	77	78	79	80	81	82	83	84
21	85	86	87	88	89	90	91	92	93	94	95	96	97	98
22	99	100	101	102	103	104	105	106	107	108	109	110	111	112
23	113	114	115	116	117	118	119	120	121	122	123	124	125	126
24	127	128	129	130	131	132	133	134	135	136	137	138	139	140

1991 Census Small Area Statistics - 100% **Area Identifier - <zoneid>** **Grid reference - <Easting/Northing>**
<.Ward / Postcode Sector name..> **<........DistrictName.........>** **<.....County / Region Name.....>**
Table Prefix: S38

Table 38 Single years of age: Residents aged 0 - 15 in households

Age	TOTAL PERSONS	Males	Females
ALL AGES 0 - 15	1	2	3
0	4	5	6
1	7	8	9
2	10	11	12
3	13	14	15
4	16	17	18
5	19	20	21
6	22	23	24
7	25	26	27
8	28	29	30
9	31	32	33
10	34	35	36
11	37	38	39
12	40	41	42
13	43	44	45
14	46	47	48
15	49	50	51

1991 Census Small Area Statistics - 100% **Area Identifier - <zoneid>** **Grid reference - <Easting/Northing>**
<.Ward / Postcode Sector name..> **<........DistrictName.........>** **<.....County / Region Name.....>**
Table Prefix: S39

Table 39 Headship: Residents in households

Age	TOTAL PERSONS	Males			Females		
		Total	Single widowed or div'ced	Married	Total	Single widowed or div'ced	Married
Heads of households							
All ages 16 and over*	1	2	3	4	5	6	7
16 - 29*	8	9	10	11	12	13	14
30 - 44	15	16	17	18	19	20	21
45 - 59	22	23	24	25	26	27	28
60 - 64	29	30	31	32	33	34	35
65 - 74	36	37	38	39	40	41	42
75 - 84	43	44	45	46	47	48	49
85 and over	50	51	52	53	54	55	56
All persons in households by head's age, sex and marital staus							
All ages 16 and over**	57	58	59	60	61	62	63
16 - 29**	64	65	66	67	68	69	70
30 - 44	71	72	73	74	75	76	77
45 - 59	78	79	80	81	82	83	84
60 - 64	85	86	87	88	89	90	91
65 - 74	92	93	94	95	96	97	98
75 - 84	99	100	101	102	103	104	105
85 and over	106	107	108	109	110	111	112

* May include a small number of heads aged under 16
** May include a small number of persons in households with heads aged under 16

1991 Census Small Area Statistics - 100% **Area Identifier - <zoneid>** **Grid reference - <Easting/Northing>**
<.Ward / Postcode Sector name..> **<........DistrictName.........>** **<.....County / Region Name.....>**
Table Prefix: S40

Table 40 Lone 'Parents': Lone 'parents' aged 16 and over in households of one person aged 16 and over with person(s) aged 0 - 15; persons aged 0 - 15 in such households.

Age of child(ren)	TOTAL LONE 'PAR-ENTS'	Male lone 'parents'						
		Total male lone 'p'nts'	Economically active					Econ. inact.
			Employees Full -time	Employees Part -time	Self -emp-loyed	Other	Econ. active stu-dents	
Total households	1	2	3	4	5	6	7	8
Child(ren) aged 0 - 4 only	16	17	18	19	20	21	22	23
Child(ren) aged 5 - 15 only	31	32	33	34	35	36	37	38
Child(ren) aged 0 - 4 and 5 - 15	46	47	48	49	50	51	52	53
TOTAL CHILDREN AGED 0 - 15	61	62	63	64	65	66	67	68
Children aged 0 - 4	76	77	78	79	80	81	82	83

Female lone 'parents'							Age of child(ren)
Total female lone 'par-ents'	Economically active					Econ. inact.	
	Employees Full-time	Employees Part-time	Self-emp-loyed	Other	Econ. active stu-dents		
9	10	11	12	13	14	15	**Total households**
24	25	26	27	28	29	30	Child(ren) aged 0 - 4 only
39	40	41	42	43	44	45	Child(ren) aged 5 - 15 only
54	55	56	57	58	59	60	Child(ren) aged 0 - 4 and 5 - 15
69	70	71	72	73	74	75	TOTAL CHILDREN AGED 0 - 15
84	85	86	87	88	89	90	Children aged 0 - 4

1991 Census Small Area Statistics - 100% Area Identifier - <zoneid> Grid reference - <Easting/Northing>
<.Ward / Postcode Sector name..> <........DistrictName.........> <.....County / Region Name.....>
Table Prefix: S41

Table 41 Shared Accommodation: Households with residents not in self-contained accommodation; rooms in such households.

Households with the following persons:	TOTAL HOUSE -HOLDS	Over 1 person per room	A*	B**	C***	Central heating: All or some rooms	Central heating: No rooms	No car	TOTAL ROOMS
TOTAL HOUSEHOLDS	1	2	3	4	5	6	7	8	9
1 person	10	xxxx	12	13	14	15	16	17	18
2 persons	19	20	21	22	23	24	25	26	27
3 or more persons	28	29	30	31	32	33	34	35	36

* A. Exclusive use of bath/shower and inside WC
** B. Bath/shower and inside WC available, one or both shared
*** C. Lacking use of bath/shower and/or inside WC

1991 Census Small Area Statistics - 100% Area Identifier - <zoneid> Grid reference - <Easting/Northing>
<.Ward / Postcode Sector name..> <........DistrictName.........> <.....County / Region Name.....>
Table Prefix: S42

Table 42 Household composition and housing: Households with residents; dependent children in households

Household composition: Adults	Dependent children	TOTAL HOUSE -HOLD	Over 1 and up to 1.5 ppr	Over 1.5 ppr	A*	No central heating	B**	Not self cont. accomm.
ALL HOUSEHOLDS***		1	2	3	4	5	6	7
1 adult of pensionable age	0	17	18	19	20	21	22	23
1 adult under pensionable age	0	33	34	35	36	37	38	39
1 adult any age	1 or more	49	50	51	52	53	54	55
2 adults (1 male and 1 female)	0	65	66	67	68	69	70	71
	1 or more	81	82	83	84	85	86	87
2 adults (same sex)	0	97	98	99	100	101	102	103
	1 or more	113	114	115	116	117	118	119
3 or more adults (male(s) and female(s))	0	129	130	131	132	133	134	135
	1 or more	145	146	147	148	149	150	151
3 or more adults (same sex)	0	161	162	163	164	165	166	167
	1 or more	177	178	179	180	181	182	183
TOTAL DEPENDENT CHILDREN AGED 0 - 18		193	194	195	196	197	198	199
Dependent children aged 0 - 4		209	210	211	212	213	214	215
Dependent children aged 5 - 15		225	226	227	228	229	230	231
Dependent children aged 16 - 17		241	242	243	244	245	246	247

Tenure: Owner occupied: Owned outr't	Owner occupied: Buying	Rented p'vately: Furn -ished	Rented p'vately: Unfurn -ished	Rented with a job or b'ness	Rented from a housing assoc.	Rented from a LA or new town	No car	Two or more cars	Household composition: Adults	Dependent children
8	9	10	11	12	13	14	15	16	ALL HOUSEHOLDS***	
24	25	26	27	28	29	30	31	32	1 adult of pensionable age	0
40	41	42	43	44	45	46	47	48	1 adult under pensionable age	0
56	57	58	59	60	61	62	63	64	1 adult any age	1 or more
72	73	74	75	76	77	78	79	80	2 adults (1 male and 1 female)	0
88	89	90	91	92	93	94	95	96		1 or more
104	105	106	107	108	109	110	111	112	2 adults (same sex)	0
120	121	122	123	124	125	126	127	128		1 or more
136	137	138	139	140	141	142	143	144	3 or more adults (male(s) and female(s))	0
152	153	154	155	156	157	158	159	160		1 or more
168	169	170	171	172	173	174	175	176	3 or more adults (same sex)	0
184	185	186	187	188	189	190	191	192		1 or more
200	201	202	203	204	205	206	207	208	TOTAL DEPENDENT CHILDREN AGED 0 - 18	
216	217	218	219	220	221	222	223	224	Dependent children aged 0 - 4	
232	233	234	235	236	237	238	239	240	Dependent children aged 5 - 15	
248	249	250	251	252	253	254	255	256	Dependent children aged 16 - 17	

* A. Lacking or sharing use of bath/shower and/or inside WC
** B. Lacking or sharing use of bath/shower and/or inside WC and/or no central heating
*** May include a small number of households with no resident adults
ppr = persons per room

1991 Census Small Area Statistics - 100% Area Identifier - <zoneid> Grid reference - <Easting/Northing>
<.Ward / Postcode Sector name..> <........DistrictName.........> <.....County / Region Name.....>
Table Prefix: S43

Table 43 Household composition and ethnic group: Households with residents; residents in households

Household composition	TOTAL HOUSE-HOLDS	Ethnic group of head of h'hold: White	Black groups	Indian, P'stani and B'deshi	Chinese and other groups	House-hold head born in Ireland
ALL HOUSEHOLDS	1	2	3	4	5	6
Households with adults and dependent children	7	8	9	10	'11	12
Single adult households	13	14	15	16	17	18
TOTAL PERSONS	19	20	21	22	23	24

May contain a small number of households with no resident adults or with adults but no dependent children

1991 Census Small Area Statistics - 100% **Area Identifier - <zoneid>** **Grid reference - <Easting/Northing>**
<.Ward / Postcode Sector name..> **<........DistrictName.........>** **<.....County / Region Name.....>**
Table Prefix: S44

Table 44 Household composition and long-term illness: Households containing persons with limiting long-term illness; residents in such households

Household composition		TOTAL HOUSE-HOLDS	ALL PERSONS		Total with limiting long-term illness		Persons with limiting long-term illness aged: 0 - 15		16 - 44	
Adults	**Dependent children**		Males	Females	Males	Females	Males	Females	Males	Females
ALL HOUSEHOLDS*		1	2	3	4	5	6	7	8	9
1 adult	0	16	17	18	19	20	xxxx	xxxx	23	24
	1 or more	31	32	33	34	35	36	37	38	39
2 adults (1 male and 1 female)	0	46	47	48	49	50	xxxx	xxxx	53	54
	1 or more	61	62	63	64	65	66	67	68	69
2 adults (same sex)	0	76	77	78	79	80	xxxx	xxxx	83	84
	1 or more	91	92	93	94	95	96	97	98	99
3 or more adults (male(s) and female(s))	0	106	107	108	109	110	xxxx	xxxx	113	114
	1 or more	121	122	123	124	125	126	127	128	129
3 or more adults (same sex)	0	136	137	138	139	140	xxxx	xxxx	143	144
	1 or more	151	152	153	154	155	156	157	158	159
Households with										
0 persons economically active		166	167	168	169	170	171	172	173	174
1 person economically active		181	182	183	184	185	186	187	188	189
- in employment		196	197	198	199	200	201	202	203	204
- unemployed		211	212	213	214	215	216	217	218	219
2 or more persons economically active		226	227	228	229	230	231	232	233	234
- 1 or more in employment		241	242	243	244	245	246	247	248	249
- all unemployed		256	257	258	259	260	261	262	263	264
Persons economically active		xxxx	272	273	274	275	xxxx	xxxx	278	279
Persons in employment		xxxx	287	288	289	290	xxxx	xxxx	293	294

* May include a small number of households with no resident adults

1991 Census Small Area Statistics - 100% **Area Identifier - <zoneid>** **Grid reference - <Easting/Northing>**
<.Ward / Postcode Sector name..> **<........DistrictName.........>** **<.....County / Region Name.....>**
Table Prefix: S44
CROWN COPYRIGHT RESERVED

Table 44 Household composition and long-term illness: Households containing persons with limiting long-term illness; residents in such households **(Continued)**

Persons with limiting long-term illness aged: 45 up to pensionable age		Pensionable age - 74		75 and over		Household composition	
Males	Females	Males	Females	Males	Females	**Adults**	**Dependent children**
10	11	12	13	14	15	**ALL HOUSEHOLDS***	
25	26	27	28	29	30	1 adult	0
40	41	42	43	44	45		1 or more
55	56	57	58	59	60	2 adults (1 male and 1 female)	0
70	71	72	73	74	75		1 or more
85	86	87	88	89	90	2 adults (same sex)	0
100	101	102	103	104	105		1 or more
115	116	117	118	119	120	3 or more adults (male(s) and female(s))	0
130	131	132	133	134	135		1 or more
145	146	147	148	149	150	3 or more adults (same sex)	0
160	161	162	163	164	165		1 or more
						Households with	
175	176	177	178	179	180	0 persons economically active	
190	191	192	193	194	195	1 person economically active	
205	206	207	208	209	210	- in employment	
220	221	222	223	224	225	- unemployed	
235	236	237	238	239	240	2 or more persons economically active	
250	251	252	253	254	255	- 1 or more in employment	
265	266	267	268	269	270	- all unemployed	
280	281	282	283	284	285	Persons economically active	
295	296	297	298	299	300	Persons in employment	

* May include a small number of households with no resident adults

1991 Census Small Area Statistics - 100% **Area Identifier - <zoneid>** **Grid reference - <Easting/Northing>**
<.Ward / Postcode Sector name..> <........**DistrictName**.........> <.....**County / Region Name**.....>
Table Prefix: S46

Table 46 Households with dependent children; housing: Households with dependent children; residents in such households

Household composition	TOTAL HOUSE-HOLDS	Over 1 and up to 1.5 ppr	Over 1.5 ppr	A*	No central heating	Not self cont. accomm.
ALL HOUSEHOLDS WITH DEPENDENT CHILDREN	1	2	3	4	5	6
Households of 1 adult with 1 or more dependent children	13	14	15	16	17	18
Dependent child(ren) aged 0 - 4 only	25	26	27	28	29	30
Dependent child(ren) aged 5 and over only	37	38	39	40	41	42
Dependent child(ren) aged 0 - 4 and 5 and over	49	50	51	52	53	54
Dependent children in households of 1 adult with 1 or more dependent children						
All dependent children	61	62	63	64	65	66
Dependent children aged 0 - 4	73	74	75	76	77	78
Dependent children aged 5 - 15	85	86	87	88	89	90
Dependent children aged 0 - 17	97	98	99	100	101	102
Other households with dependent children	109	110	111	112	113	114
Dependent child(ren) aged 0 - 4 only	121	122	123	124	125	126
Dependent child(ren) aged 5 and over only	133	134	135	136	137	138
Dependent child(ren) aged 0 - 4 and 5 and over	145	146	147	148	149	150
Persons in other households with dependent children						
All adults	157	158	159	160	161	162
All dependent children	169	170	171	172	173	174
Dependent children aged 0 - 4	181	182	183	184	185	186
Dependent children aged 5 - 15	193	194	195	196	197	198
Dependent children aged 0 - 17	205	206	207	208	209	210
Households with 3 or more dependent children	217	218	219	220	221	222
Households with 3 or more persons aged 0 - 15	229	230	231	232	233	234
Households with 4 or more dependent children	241	242	243	244	245	246
Households with 4 or more persons aged 0 - 15	253	254	255	256	257	258

* A. Lacking or sharing use of bath/shower and/or inside WC
ppr = persons per room

1991 Census Small Area Statistics - 100% **Area Identifier - <zoneid>** **Grid reference - <Easting/Northing>**
<.Ward / Postcode Sector name..> <........**DistrictName**.........> <.....**County / Region Name**.....>
Table Prefix: S46

Table 46 Households with dependent children; housing: Households with dependent children; residents in such households **(Continued)**

Tenure						
Owner occ.	Rented priv'ly	Rented from a housing assoc.	Rented from a LA or new town	No car	TOTAL PERSONS IN HOUSE -HOLDS	**Household composition**
7	8	9	10	11	12	**ALL HOUSEHOLDS WITH DEPENDENT CHILDREN**
19	20	21	22	23	24	**Households of 1 adult with 1 or more dependent children**
31	32	33	34	35	36	Dependent child(ren) aged 0 - 4 only
43	44	45	46	47	48	Dependent child(ren) aged 5 and over only
55	56	57	58	59	60	Dependent child(ren) aged 0 - 4 and 5 and over
						Dependent children in households of 1 adult with 1 or more dependent children
67	68	69	70	71	xxxx	All dependent children
79	80	81	82	83	xxxx	Dependent children aged 0 - 4
91	92	93	94	95	xxxx	Dependent children aged 5 - 15
103	104	105	106	107	xxxx	Dependent children aged 0 - 17
115	116	117	118	119	120	**Other households with dependent children**
127	128	129	130	131	132	Dependent child(ren) aged 0 - 4 only
139	140	141	142	143	144	Dependent child(ren) aged 5 and over only
151	152	153	154	155	156	Dependent child(ren) aged 0 - 4 and 5 and over
						Persons in other households with dependent children
163	164	165	166	167	xxxx	All adults
175	176	177	178	179	xxxx	All dependent children
187	188	189	190	191	xxxx	Dependent children aged 0 - 4
199	200	201	202	203	xxxx	Dependent children aged 5 - 15
211	212	213	214	215	xxxx	Dependent children aged 0 - 17
223	224	225	226	227	228	Households with 3 or more dependent children
235	236	237	238	239	240	Households with 3 or more persons aged 0 - 15
247	248	249	250	251	252	Households with 4 or more dependent children
259	260	261	262	263	264	Households with 4 or more persons aged 0 - 15

1991 Census Small Area Statistics - 100% **Area Identifier - <zoneid>** **Grid reference - <Easting/Northing>**
<.Ward / Postcode Sector name..> **<........DistrictName.........>** **<.....County / Region Name.....>**
Table Prefix: S47

Table 47 Households with pensioners; housing: Households with one or more residents of pensionable age; residents in such households

Household composition	TOTAL HOUSE -HOLDS	Up to 0.5 ppr	A*	No central heating	B**	Not self cont. accomm.
TOTAL HOUSEHOLDS WITH 1 OR MORE PENSIONER(S)	1	2	3	4	5	6
Lone male 65 - 74	15	16	17	18	19	20
Lone male 75 - 84	29	30	31	32	33	34
Lone male 85 and over	43	44	45	46	47	48
Lone female 60 - 74	57	58	59	60	61	62
Lone female 75 - 84	71	72	73	74	75	76
Lone female 85 and over	85	86	87	88	89	90
2 or more, all pensioners, under 75	99	100	101	102	103	104
2 or more, all pensioners, any aged 75 and over	113	114	115	116	117	118
1 or more pensioners with 1 non-pensioner	127	128	129	130	131	132
1 or more pensioners with 2 or more non-pensioners	141	142	143	144	145	146
TOTAL PERSONS IN HOUSEHOLDS WITH PENSIONERS	155	156	157	158	159	160
Total persons of pensionable age	169	170	171	172	173	174
Pensionable age - 74	183	184	185	186	187	188
75 - 84	197	198	199	200	201	202
85 and over	211	212	213	214	215	216
Persons with limiting long-term illness						
Pensionable age - 74	225	226	227	228	229	230
75 - 84	239	240	241	242	243	244
85 and over	253	254	255	256	257	258

* A. Lacking or sharing use of bath/shower and/or inside WC
** B. Lacking or sharing use of bath/shower and/or inside WC and/or no central heating
ppr = persons per room

1991 Census Small Area Statistics - 100% **Area Identifier - <zoneid>** **Grid reference - <Easting/Northing>**
<.Ward / Postcode Sector name..> **<........DistrictName.........>** **<.....County / Region Name.....>**
Table Prefix: S47

Table 47 Households with pensioners; housing: Households with one or more residents of pensionable age; residents in such households **(Continued)**

Tenure								
	Rented privately							
Owner occup'd	Furn -ished	Unfurn -ished	Rented with a job or b'ness	Rented from a housing assoc.	Rented from a LA or new town	No car	Persons with lim'ing long -term illness	Household composition
7	8	9	10	11	12	13	14	**TOTAL HOUSEHOLDS WITH 1 OR MORE PENSIONER(S)**
21	22	23	24	25	26	27	28	Lone male 65 - 74
35	36	37	38	39	40	41	42	Lone male 75 - 84
49	50	51	52	53	54	55	56	Lone male 85 and over
63	64	65	66	67	68	69	70	Lone female 60 - 74
77	78	79	80	81	82	83	84	Lone female 75 - 84
91	92	93	94	95	96	97	98	Lone female 85 and over
105	106	107	108	109	110	111	112	2 or more, all pensioners, under 75
119	120	121	122	123	124	125	126	2 or more, all pensioners, any aged 75 and over
133	134	135	136	137	138	139	140	1 or more pensioners with 1 non-pensioner
147	148	149	150	151	152	153	154	1 or more pensioners with 2 or more non-pensioners
161	162	163	164	165	166	167	168	**TOTAL PERSONS IN HOUSEHOLDS WITH PENSIONERS**
175	176	177	178	179	180	181	182	**Total persons of pensionable age**
189	190	191	192	193	194	195	xxxx	Pensionable age - 74
203	204	205	206	207	208	209	xxxx	75 - 84
217	218	219	220	221	222	223	xxxx	85 and over
								Persons with limiting long-term illness
231	232	233	234	235	236	237	xxxx	Pensionable age - 74
245	246	247	248	249	250	251	xxxx	75 - 84
259	260	261	262	263	264	265	xxxx	85 and over

1991 Census Small Area Statistics - 100% **Area Identifier - <zoneid>** **Grid reference - <Easting/Northing>**
<.Ward / Postcode Sector name..> **<........DistrictName.........>** **<.....County / Region Name.....>**
Table Prefix: S48

Table 48 Households with dependants; housing: Households with residents

Household composition	ALL HOUSE -HOLDS	Over 1 person per room	A*	No central heating	Not self-cont. accomm.	No car
TOTAL HOUSEHOLDS	1	2	3	4	5	6
1 or more non - dependants, no dependants	7	8	9	10	11	12
1 dependant male living alone	13	xxxx	15	16	17	18
1 dependant female living alone	19	xxxx	21	22	23	24
2 or more dependants, no non - dependants	25	26	27	28	29	30
1 male non - dependant with 1 or more dependant(s)	31	32	33	34	35	36
1 female non - dependant with 1 or more dependant(s)	37	38	39	40	41	42
2 or more non - dependants with 1 or more dependant(s)	43	44	45	46	47	48

* A. Lacking or sharing use of bath/shower and/or inside WC

1991 Census Small Area Statistics - 100% Area Identifier - <zoneid> Grid reference - <Easting/Northing>
<.Ward / Postcode Sector name..> <........DistrictName.........> <.....County / Region Name.....>
Table Prefix: S49

Table 49 Ethnic group; housing: Households with residents; residents in households

	TOTAL HOUSE-HOLDS	Ethnic group of household head				Household head born in	
		White	Black groups	Indian, P'stani and B'deshi	Chinese and other groups	New Common -wealth	Ireland
ALL HOUSEHOLDS	1	2	3	4	5	6	7
Over 1 and up to 1.5 persons per room	8	9	10	11	12	13	14
Over 1.5 persons per room	15	16	17	18	19	20	21
Owner occupied	22	23	24	25	26	27	28
Rented privately	29	30	31	32	33	34	35
Rented from a housing association	36	37	38	39	40	41	42
Rented from local authority or new town	43	44	45	46	47	48	49
No central heating	50	51	52	53	54	55	56
No car	57	58	59	60	61	62	63
ALL RESIDENTS IN HOUSEHOLDS	64	65	66	67	68	69	70
Over 1 and up to 1.5 persons per room	71	72	73	74	75	76	77
Over 1.5 persons per room	78	79	80	81	82	83	84

1991 Census Small Area Statistics - 100% Area Identifier - <zoneid> Grid reference - <Easting/Northing>
<.Ward / Postcode Sector name..> <........DistrictName.........> <.....County / Region Name.....>
Table Prefix: S50

Table 50 Country of birth; household heads and residents: Residents in households; household heads

Country of birth of household head	TOTAL PERSONS	All ages Inside UK	All ages Outside UK	0 - 4 Inside UK	0 - 4 Outside UK	5 - 15 Inside UK	5 - 15 Outside UK	16 - 29 Inside UK	16 - 29 Outside UK
ALL COUNTRIES OF BIRTH	1	2	3	4	5	6	7	8	9
United Kingdom*	17	18	19	20	21	22	23	24	25
England	33	34	35	36	37	38	39	40	41
Scotland	49	50	51	52	53	54	55	56	57
Wales	65	66	67	68	69	70	71	72	73
Northern Ireland	81	82	83	84	85	86	87	88	89
Irish Republic**	97	98	99	100	101	102	103	104	105
New Commonwealth	113	114	115	116	117	118	119	120	121
Rest of the World	129	130	131	132	133	134	135	136	137

* Includes Channel Islands, the Isle of Man, and United Kingdom (part not stated)
** Includes Ireland (part not stated)

30 - 44 Inside UK	30 - 44 Outside UK	45 up to PA Inside UK	45 up to PA Outside UK	PA and over Inside UK	PA and over Outside UK	TOTAL HOUSE -HOLD HEADS	Country of birth of household head
10	11	12	13	14	15	16	**ALL COUNTRIES OF BIRTH**
26	27	28	29	30	31	32	**United Kingdom***
42	43	44	45	46	47	48	England
58	59	60	61	62	63	64	Scotland
74	75	76	77	78	79	80	Wales
90	91	92	93	94	95	96	Northern Ireland
106	107	108	109	110	111	112	Irish Republic**
122	123	124	125	126	127	128	New Commonwealth
138	139	140	141	142	143	144	Rest of the World

* Includes Channel Islands, the Isle of Man, and United Kingdom (part not stated)
** Includes Ireland (part not stated)
PA Pensionable age

1991 Census Small Area Statistics - 100% Area Identifier - <zoneid> Grid reference - <Easting/Northing>
<.Ward / Postcode Sector name..> <........DistrictName.........> <.....County / Region Name.....>
Table Prefix: S51

Table 51 Country of birth and ethnic group: Residents in households

Country of birth	TOTAL PERSONS	Ethnic group			
		White	Black groups	Indian, P'stani and B'deshi	Chinese and other groups
TOTAL PERSONS	1	2	3	4	5
United Kingdom*	6	7	8	9	10
New Commonwealth	11	12	13	14	15
Rest of the World	16	17	18	19	20

Includes Channel Islands, the Isle of Man, and United Kingdom (part not stated)

1991 Census Small Area Statistics - 100% Area Identifier - <zoneid> Grid reference - <Easting/Northing>
<.Ward / Postcode Sector name..> <........DistrictName.........> <.....County / Region Name.....>
Table Prefix: S53

Table 53 'Lifestages: Residents aged 16 and over in households

Lifestage category	ALL PERSONS In a couple h'hold	ALL PERSONS Not in a couple h'hold	ALL HOUSE-HOLD HEADS In a couple h'hold	ALL HOUSE-HOLD HEADS Not in a couple h'hold
Aged 16 - 24				
No children aged 0 - 15 in household	1	2	3	4
Child(ren) aged 0 - 15 in household	5	6	7	8
Aged 25 - 34				
No children aged 0 - 15 in household	9	10	11	12
Child(ren) aged 0 - 4 in household	13	14	15	16
Child(ren) in household, youngest aged 5 - 10	17	18	19	20
Child(ren) in household, youngest aged 11 - 15	21	22	23	24
Aged 35 - 54				
No children aged 0 - 15 in household	25	26	27	28
Child(ren) aged 0 - 4 in household	29	30	31	32
Child(ren) in household, youngest aged 5 - 10	33	34	35	36
Child(ren) in household, youngest aged 11 - 15	37	38	39	40
Aged 55 - pensionable age				
Working or retired	41	42	43	44
Unemployed or economically inactive (but not retired)	45	46	47	48
Pensionable age - 74	49	50	51	52
Aged 75 and over	53	54	55	56

1991 Census Small Area Statistics - 100% Area Identifier - <zoneid> Grid reference - <Easting/Northing>
<.Ward / Postcode Sector name..> <........DistrictName.........> <.....County / Region Name.....>
Table Prefix: S54

Table 54 Occupancy (occupied, vacant and other accommodation): Household spaces; rooms in household spaces; rooms in hotels and boarding houses

Occupancy type	TOTAL HOUSE -HOLD SPACES	TOTAL ROOMS
All TYPES OF OCCUPANCY	1	2
Households with residents	3	4
Enumerated with person(s) present	5	6
Absent households (enumerated)	7	8
Absent households (imputed)	9	10
Vacant accommodation	11	12
New, never occupied	13	14
Under improvement	15	16
Other	17	18
Accommodation not used as main residence	19	20
No persons present	21	22
Second residences	23	24
Holiday accommodation	25	26
Student accommodation	27	28
Persons enumerated but no residents	29	30
Owner occupied	31	32
Not owner occupied	33	34
Hotels and boarding houses	xxxx	36

1991 Census Small Area Statistics - 100% Area Identifier - <zoneid> Grid reference - <Easting/Northing>
<.Ward / Postcode Sector name..> <........DistrictName.........> <.....County / Region Name.....>
Table Prefix: S55

Table 55 Household spaces and occupancy: Household spaces in permanent buildings, dwellings

Occupancy type	TOTAL HOUSE -HOLD SPACES	B** 1	B** 2	B** 3 or more	A*
All TYPES OF OCCUPANCY	1	2	3	4	5
Households with residents	6	7	8	9	10
Enumerated with person(s) present	11	12	13	14	15
Absent households (enumerated)	16	17	18	19	20
Absent households (imputed)	21	22	23	24	25
Vacant accommodation	26	27	28	29	30
Accommodation not used as main residence	31	32	33	34	35
No persons present	36	37	38	39	40
Persons enumerated but no residents	41	42	43	44	45
TOTAL DWELLINGS	46	47	48	49	xxxx

*A. Unattached household spaces (not in a dwelling)
**B. Household spaces in dwellings with the following number of household spaces

1991 Census Small Area Statistics - 100% Area Identifier - <zoneid> Grid reference - <Easting/Northing>
<.Ward / Postcode Sector name..> <........DistrictName.........> <.....County / Region Name.....>
Table Prefix: S56

Table 56 Household space type and occupancy: Household spaces

Occupancy type	TOTAL HOUSE-HOLD SPACES	Household space type in permanent buildings: Unshared dwellings - purpose built: Det-ached	Semi-det-ached	Terr-aced	Purpose built flat in: Res. b'ding	Comm. b'ding	Unshared dwellings - converted: Conv. flat	Conv. flatlet	Unshared dwellings - not self-contained: Not self-cont. flat	Not self-cont 'rooms'	Bedsit	Other household spaces - not self-contained: Not self-cont. flat	Not self-cont 'rooms'	Bedsit	Non-perm. accomm.
All TYPES OF OCCUPANCY	1	2	3	4	5	6	7	8	9	10	11	12	13	14	15
Households with residents	16	17	18	19	20	21	22	23	24	25	26	27	28	29	30
Enumerated with person(s) present	31	32	33	34	35	36	37	38	39	40	41	42	43	44	45
Absent households	46	47	48	49	50	51	52	53	54	55	56	57	58	59	60
Vacant accommodation	61	62	63	64	65	66	67	68	69	70	71	72	73	74	xxxx
New, never occupied	76	77	78	79	80	81	82	83	84	85	86	87	88	89	xxxx
Other	91	92	93	94	95	96	97	98	99	100	101	102	103	104	xxxx
Accommodation not used as main residence	106	107	108	109	110	111	112	113	114	115	116	117	118	119	xxxx
No persons present	121	122	123	124	125	126	127	128	129	130	131	132	133	134	xxxx
Persons enumerated but no residents	136	137	138	139	140	141	142	143	144	145	146	147	148	149	150

1991 Census Small Area Statistics - 100% Area Identifier - <zoneid> Grid reference - <Easting/Northing>
<.Ward / Postcode Sector name..> <........DistrictName.........> <.....County / Region Name.....>
Table Prefix: S57

Table 57 Household space type; rooms and household size: Household with residents; residents in households; rooms in household spaces

	TOTAL HOUSE-HOLDS	Household space type in perm. buildings: Unshared dwellings - purpose built: D'ched semi or t'aced	Purpose built flat	Unshared dwellings: Con-verted	Not self-cont.	Other h'hold spaces - not self-cont.	Non-perm. accomm.	With migrant head
Households with the following rooms								
TOTAL	1	2	3	4	5	6	7	8
1	9	10	11	12	13	14	15	16
2	17	18	19	20	21	22	23	24
3	25	26	27	28	29	30	31	32
4	33	34	35	36	37	38	39	40
5	41	42	43	44	45	46	47	48
6	49	50	51	52	53	54	xxxx	56
7 or more	57	58	59	60	61	62	xxxx	64
TOTAL ROOMS	65	66	67	68	69	70	71	72
Households with the following persons								
TOTAL	73	74	75	76	77	78	79	80
1	81	82	83	84	85	86	87	88
2	89	90	91	92	93	94	95	96
3	97	98	99	100	101	102	103	104
4	105	106	107	108	109	110	111	112
5	113	114	115	116	117	118	119	120
6	121	122	123	124	125	126	127	128
7 or more	129	130	131	132	133	134	135	136
TOTAL PERSONS	137	138	139	140	141	142	143	144
Households with the following persons per room								
TOTAL	145	146	147	148	149	150	151	152
Over 1.5	153	154	155	156	157	158	159	160
Over 1 and up to 1.5	161	162	163	164	165	166	167	168
Over 0.5 and up to 1	169	170	171	172	173	174	175	176
Up to 0.5	177	178	179	180	181	182	183	184

Note: Maximum number of rooms in non-permanent accommodation is 5

1991 Census Small Area Statistics - 100% Area Identifier - <zoneid> Grid reference - <Easting/Northing>
<.Ward / Postcode Sector name..> <........DistrictName.........> <.....County / Region Name.....>
Table Prefix: S58

Table 58 Household space type: tenure and amenities: Household with residents

Tenure and amenities		TOTAL HOUSE-HOLDS	Household space type in perm. buildings: Unshared dwellings - purpose built: D'ched semi or t'aced	Purpose built flat	Unshared dwellings: Con-verted	Not self-cont.	Other h'hold spaces - not self-cont.	Non-perm. accomm.
TOTAL HOUSEHOLDS		1	2	3	4	5	6	7
Owner occupied	- owned outright	8	9	10	11	12	13	14
	- buying	15	16	17	18	19	20	21
Rented privately	- furnished	22	23	24	25	26	27	28
	- unfurnished	29	30	31	32	33	34	35
Rented with a job or business		36	37	38	39	40	41	42
Rented from a housing association		43	44	45	46	47	48	49
Rented from a local authority or new town		50	51	52	53	54	55	56
Exclusive use of bath/shower and WC		57	58	59	60	61	62	63
With central heating	- all or some rooms	64	65	66	67	68	69	70
No central heating		71	72	73	74	75	76	77
Lacking or sharing use of bath/shower and/or WC		78	79	80	81	82	83	84
With central heating	- all or some rooms	85	86	87	88	89	90	91
No central heating		92	93	94	95	96	97	98
With central heating	- all rooms	99	100	101	102	103	104	105
	- some rooms	106	107	108	109	110	111	112
No central heating		113	114	115	116	117	118	119

1991 Census Small Area Statistics - 100% Area Identifier - <zoneid> Grid reference - <Easting/Northing>
<.Ward / Postcode Sector name..> <........DistrictName.........> <.....County / Region Name.....>
Table Prefix: S59

Table 59 Household space type; household composition: Households with residents; residents in households

Household composition: Adults	Dependent children	TOTAL HOUSE-HOLDS	Household space type in perm. buildings: Unshared dwellings - purpose built: D'ched semi or t'aced	Purpose built flat	Unshared dwellings: Con-verted	Not self-cont.	Other h'hold spaces - not self-cont.	Non-perm. accomm.
ALL HOUSEHOLDS*		1	2	3	4	5	6	7
1 adult of pensionable age	0	8	9	10	11	12	13	14
1 adult under pensionable age	0	15	16	17	18	19	20	21
1 adult any age	1 or more	22	23	24	25	26	27	28
2 adults (1 male and 1 female)	0	29	30	31	32	33	34	35
	1 or more	36	37	38	39	40	41	42
2 adults (same sex)	0	43	44	45	46	47	48	49
	1 or more	50	51	52	53	54	55	56
3 or more adults (male(s) and female(s))	0	57	58	59	60	61	62	63
	1 or more	64	65	66	67	68	69	70
3 or more adults (same sex)	0	71	72	73	74	75	76	77
	1 or more	78	79	80	81	82	83	84
Households containing persons of pensionable age only (any number)		85	86	87	88	89	90	91
Households containing persons aged 75 and over only (any number)		92	93	94	95	96	97	98
All dependent children		99	100	101	102	103	104	105
Dependent children aged 0 - 4		106	107	108	109	110	111	112
Dependent children aged 5 - 15		113	114	115	116	117	118	119
Persons pensionable age - 74		120	121	122	123	124	125	126
Persons aged 75 - 84		127	128	129	130	131	132	133
Persons aged 85 and over		134	135	136	137	138	139	140

* May include a small number of households with no resident adults

1991 Census Small Area Statistics - 100% Area Identifier - <zoneid> Grid reference - <Easting/Northing>
<.Ward / Postcode Sector name..> <........DistrictName.........> <.....County / Region Name.....>
Table Prefix: S60

Table 60 Dwelling and Household spaces: Converted or shared accommodation; dwellings; household spaces; rooms in such households

Converted or shared accommodation	TOTAL CONVER-TED OR SHARED ACCOMM.	TOTAL DWELL-INGS	Total shared dwell-ings	Shared dwellings with the following h'hold spaces: 2	3 or more	Unatt-ached spaces	Total house-hold spaces	Household space type: Conv-erted flat	Conv erted flatlet	Bedsit	Other not self-cont.	TOTAL ROOMS
TOTAL CONVERTED OR SHARED ACCOMMODATION	1	2	3	4	5	6	7	8	9	10	11	12
Unconverted accommodation	13	14	15	16	17	xxxx	19	xxxx	xxxx	22	23	24
Partly converted accommodation*	25	26	27	28	29	30	31	32	33	34	35	36
Converted accommodation	37	38	xxxx	xxxx	xxxx	xxxx	43	44	45	46	47	48

* Includes unshared dwelling(s) plus an unattached household space (not in a dwelling)

1991 Census Small Area Statistics - 100% **Area Identifier - <zoneid>** **Grid reference - <Easting/Northing>**
<.Ward / Postcode Sector name..> **<........DistrictName.........>** **<.....County / Region Name.....>**
Table Prefix: S61 **CROWN COPYRIGHT RESERVED**

Table 61 Dwelling type and occupancy: Dwellings; non-permanent accommodation

Occupancy type	TOTAL DWELL -INGS	Unshared dwellings: Total unsh'd dwell -ings	Unshared dwellings - purpose built: Det-ached	Semi det-ached	Terr-aced	Purpose built flats in: Res. b'lding	Comm. b'lding	Unshared dwellings - converted: Conv-erted flat	Conv-erted flatlet	Unshared dwellings - not self-contained: Not self-cont. flat	Not self-cont. 'rooms'	Bedsit	Shared dwell -ings	TOTAL NON-PERM. ACCOMM.
All TYPES OF OCCUPANCY	1	2	3	4	5	6	7	8	9	10	11	12	13	14
Dwellings with residents	15	16	17	18	19	20	21	22	23	24	25	26	27	28
Vacant accommodation	29	30	31	32	33	34	35	36	37	38	39	40	41	xxxx
Accommodation not used as main residence	43	44	45	46	47	48	49	50	51	52	53	54	55	56
No persons present	57	58	59	60	61	62	63	64	65	66	67	68	69	xxxx
Persons enumerated but no residents	71	72	73	74	75	76	77	78	79	80	81	82	83	84

1991 Census Small Area Statistics - 100% **Area Identifier - <zoneid>** **Grid reference - <Easting/Northing>**
<.Ward / Postcode Sector name..> **<........DistrictName.........>** **<.....County / Region Name.....>**
Table Prefix: S62 **CROWN COPYRIGHT RESERVED**

Table 62 Occupancy and tenure of dwellings: Dwellings with persons present or resident

Occupancy type	TOTAL DWELL -INGS	Owner occupied: Owned out'ght	Buying	Rented p'vately: Furn -ished	Unfurn -ished	Rented with a job or b'ness	Rented from a housing assoc.	Rented from a LA or new town
All TYPES OF OCCUPANCY	1	2	3	4	5	6	7	8
Dwellings with residents	9	10	11	12	13	14	15	16
Dwellings with person(s) present	17	18	19	20	21	22	23	24
Dwellings with no person(s) present	25	26	27	28	29	30	31	32
Dwellings with persons enumerated but no residents	33	34	35	36	37	38	39	40

1991 Census Small Area Statistics - 100% **Area Identifier - <zoneid>** **Grid reference - <Easting/Northing>**
<.Ward / Postcode Sector name..> **<........DistrictName.........>** **<.....County / Region Name.....>**
Table Prefix: S63 **CROWN COPYRIGHT RESERVED**

Table 63 Dwelling type and tenure: Dwellings with residents; non-permanent accommodation

Tenure	TOTAL DWELL -INGS	Unshared dwellings: Total unsh'd dwell -ings	Unshared dwellings - purpose built: D'ched semi or t'aced	Purpose built flat	In conv. or partly conv. accomm.	Shared dwell -ings	TOTAL NON-PERM. ACCOMM.
All TENURES	1	2	3	4	5	6	7
Owner occupied - owned outright	8	9	10	11	12	13	14
- buying	15	16	17	18	19	20	21
Rented privately - furnished	22	23	24	25	26	27	28
- unfurnished	29	30	31	32	33	34	35
Rented with a job or business	36	37	38	39	40	41	42
Rented from a housing association	43	44	45	46	47	48	49
Rented from a local authority or new town	50	51	52	53	54	55	56

1991 Census Small Area Statistics - 100% **Area Identifier - <zoneid>** **Grid reference - <Easting/Northing>**
<.Ward / Postcode Sector name..> **<........DistrictName.........>** **<.....County / Region Name.....>**
Table Prefix: S66 **CROWN COPYRIGHT RESERVED**

Table 66 Shared dwellings: Shared dwellings; household spaces in shared dwellings

Number of household spaces within dwelling	TOTAL HOUSE -HOLD SPACES	Type of not self-contained housedold space in shared dwellings: Not self-cont. flat	Not self-cont. 'rooms'	Bedsit	Not self-cont. unocc.	TOTAL SHARED DWELL -INGS
TOTAL SHARED DWELLINGS	1	2	3	4	5	6
2	7	8	9	10	11	12
3	13	14	15	16	17	18
4	19	20	21	22	23	24
5	25	26	27	28	29	30
6	31	32	33	34	35	36
7	37	38	39	40	41	42
8 or more	43	44	45	46	47	48

1991 Census Small Area Statistics - 100% **Area Identifier - <zoneid>** **Grid reference - <Easting/Northing>**
<.Ward / Postcode Sector name..> **<........DistrictName.........>** **<.....County / Region Name.....>**
Table Prefix: SS67

Table 67 Gaelic language: Residents

Age	TOTAL PERSONS		Gaelic speakers		Reads Gaelic		Writes Gaelic		Speaks and reads Gaelic		Speaks, reads and writes Gaelic		Either speaks, reads or writes Gaelic	
	Males	Females	Males	Females	Males	Females	Males	Females	Males	Females	Males	Females	Males	Females
ALL AGES	1	2	3	4	5	6	7	8	9	10	11	12	13	14
0 - 2	15	16	xxxx	xxxx	xxxx	xxxx	xxxx	xxxx	xxxx	xxxx	xxxx	xxxx	xxxx	xxxx
3 - 4	29	30	31	32	33	34	35	36	37	38	39	40	41	42
5 - 11	43	44	45	46	47	48	49	50	51	52	53	54	55	56
12 - 15	57	58	59	60	61	62	63	64	65	66	67	68	69	70
16 - 17	71	72	73	74	75	76	77	78	79	80	81	82	83	84
18 - 19	85	86	87	88	89	90	91	92	93	94	95	96	97	98
20 - 24	99	100	101	102	103	104	105	106	107	108	109	110	111	112
25 - 29	113	114	115	116	117	118	119	120	121	122	123	124	125	126
30 - 34	127	128	129	130	131	132	133	134	135	136	137	138	139	140
35 - 39	141	142	143	144	145	146	147	148	149	150	151	152	153	154
40 - 44	155	156	157	158	159	160	161	162	163	164	165	166	167	168
45 - 49	169	170	171	172	173	174	175	176	177	178	179	180	181	182
50 - 54	183	184	185	186	187	188	189	190	191	192	193	194	195	196
55 - 59	197	198	199	200	201	202	203	204	205	206	207	208	209	210
60 - 64	211	212	213	214	215	216	217	218	219	220	221	222	223	224
65 - 69	225	226	227	228	229	230	231	232	233	234	235	236	237	238
70 - 74	239	240	241	242	243	244	245	246	247	248	249	250	251	252
75 - 79	253	254	255	256	257	258	259	260	261	262	263	264	265	266
80 - 84	267	268	269	270	271	272	273	274	275	276	277	278	279	280
85 and over	281	282	283	284	285	286	287	288	289	290	291	292	293	294
Aged 16 and over	295	296	297	298	299	300	301	302	303	304	305	306	307	308
Not in households	309	310	311	312	313	314	315	316	317	318	319	320	321	322
Born in Scotland	323	324	325	326	327	328	329	330	331	332	333	334	335	336

1991 Census Small Area Statistics - 100% **Area Identifier - <zoneid>** **Grid reference - <Easting/Northing>**
<.Ward / Postcode Sector name..> **<........DistrictName.........>** **<.....County / Region Name.....>**
Table Prefix: SS68

Table 68 Floor level of accommodation: Households in permanent buildings; residents in such households

Household type and age of residents	Households in permanent buildings - lowest floor level of accommodation						
	Base -ment	Ground	1 or 2	3 or 4	5 or 6	7 to 9	10 and over
TOTAL HOUSEHOLDS	1	2	3	4	5	6	7
Lone male 65 - 74	8	9	10	11	12	13	14
Lone male 75 - 84	15	16	17	18	19	20	21
Lone male 85 and over	22	23	24	25	26	27	28
Lone female 60 - 74	29	30	31	32	33	34	35
Lone female 75 - 84	36	37	38	39	40	41	42
Lone female 85 and over	43	44	45	46	47	48	49
2 or more persons, all pensioners, under 75	50	51	52	53	54	55	56
2 or more persons, all pensioners, any aged 75 and over	57	58	59	60	61	62	63
1 or more pensioners with 1 non-pensioner adult	64	65	66	67	68	69	70
1 or more pensioners with 2 or more non-pensioner adults	71	72	73	74	75	76	77
Households of 1 adult with 1 or more dependent children	78	79	80	81	82	83	84
Dependent child(ren) aged 0 - 4 only	85	86	87	88	89	90	91
Dependent child(ren) aged 5 and over only	92	93	94	95	96	97	98
Dependent child(ren) aged 0 - 4 and 5 and over	99	100	101	102	103	104	105
Other households with dependent children	106	107	108	109	110	111	112
Dependent child(ren) aged 0 - 4 only	113	114	115	116	117	118	119
Dependent child(ren) aged 5 and over only	120	121	122	123	124	125	126
Dependent child(ren) aged 0 - 4 and 5 and over	127	128	129	130	131	132	133
TOTAL PERSONS	134	135	136	137	138	139	140
0 - 2	141	142	143	144	145	146	147
3 - 4	148	149	150	151	152	153	154
5 - 15	155	156	157	158	159	160	161
16 up to pensionable age	162	163	164	165	166	167	168
65 - 74 male	169	170	171	172	173	174	175
60 - 74 female	176	177	178	179	180	181	182
75 and over male	183	184	185	186	187	188	189
75 and over female	190	191	192	193	194	195	196
All persons with limiting long-term illness	197	198	199	200	201	202	203

1991 Census Small Area Statistics - 100% **Area Identifier - <zoneid>** **Grid reference - <Easting/Northing>**
<.Ward / Postcode Sector name..> <........**DistrictName**.........> <.....**County / Region Name**.....>
Table Prefix: SS69

Table 69 Occupancy norm: households: Households in permanent buildings with residents

Adults	Dependent children	TOTAL HOUSE-HOLDS	Occupancy norm +1 or more	0	-1	-2 or less
ALL HOUSEHOLDS*		1	2	3	4	5
1 adult under pensionable age	0	6	7	8	9	10
1 adult of pensionable age	0	11	12	13	14	15
1 adult any age	1 or more	16	17	18	19	20
2 adults (1 male and 1 female)	0	21	22	23	24	25
	1 or more	26	27	28	29	30
2 adults (same sex)	0	31	32	33	34	35
	1 or more	36	37	38	39	40
3 or more adults	0	41	42	43	44	45
	1 or more	46	47	48	49	50
Tenure						
All permanent buildings		51	52	53	54	55
Owner occupied - owned outright		56	57	58	59	60
- buying		61	62	63	64	65
Rented privately - furnished		66	67	68	69	70
- unfurnished		71	72	73	74	75
Rented with a job or business		76	77	78	79	80
Rented from a housing association		81	82	83	84	85
Rented from a local authority		86	87	88	89	90
Rented from a new town		91	92	93	94	95
Rented from Scottish Homes		96	97	98	99	100
Amenities						
Exclusive use of bath/shower and inside WC		101	102	103	104	105
Shared use of bath/shower and inside WC available - 1 or both shared		106	107	108	109	110
Lacking use of bath/shower and/or inside WC		111	112	113	114	115
With central heating - all rooms		116	117	118	119	120
- some rooms		121	122	123	124	125
No central heating		126	127	128	129	130

* May include a small number of households with no resident adults

1991 Census Small Area Statistics - 100% **Area Identifier - <zoneid>** **Grid reference - <Easting/Northing>**
<.Ward / Postcode Sector name..> <........**DistrictName**.........> <.....**County / Region Name**.....>
Table Prefix: SS70

Table 70 Occupancy norm: residents: Residents in households in permanent buildings

	TOTAL PERSONS	Occupancy norm +1 or more	0	-1	-2 or less
TOTAL PERSONS IN HOUSEHOLDS	1	2	3	4	5
All dependent children aged 0 - 18	6	7	8	9	10
Dependent children aged 0 - 4	11	12	13	14	15
Dependent children aged 5 - 15	16	17	18	19	20
All persons of pensionable age	21	22	23	24	25
Persons pensionable age - 74	26	27	28	29	30
Persons aged 75 - 84	31	32	33	34	35
Persons aged 85 and over	36	37	38	39	40
All persons with limiting long-term illness	41	42	43	44	45
0 - 15	46	47	48	49	50
16 up to pensionable age	51	52	53	54	55
Pensionable age - 74	56	57	58	59	60
75 - 84	61	62	63	64	65
85 and over	66	67	68	69	70

1991 Census Small Area Statistics - 100% & 10% **Area Identifier - <zoneid>** **Grid reference - <Easting/Northing>**
<.Ward / Postcode Sector name..> <........**DistrictName**.........> <.....**County / Region Name**.....>
Table Prefix: S71

Table 71 Comparison of 100% and 10% counts: Residents; households with residents

	Residents				Households	
			In households			
	TOTAL	Not in house-holds	Enum-erated	Imputed	Enum-erated	Imputed
100% counts	1	2	3	4	5	6
10% sample counts	7	8	9	xxxx	11	xxxx

1991 Census Small Area Statistics - 10% Area Identifier - <zoneid> Grid reference - <Easting/Northing>
<.Ward / Postcode Sector name..> <........DistrictName.........> <.....County / Region Name.....>
Table Prefix: S73

Table 73 Industry (10% sample): Residents aged 16 and over; employees and self-employed

Sex and age	TOTAL PERSONS	Industry										
		Agric. f'estry and fishing	Energy and water	Mining	Manufac -turing metal etc.	Other manufac -turing	Const- ruction	Distrib -ution and cat'ing	Trans- port	Banking and finance etc.	Other serv -ices	Not stated, id*, or w'place out. UK
TOTAL PERSONS	1	2	3	4	5	6	7	8	9	10	11	12
Males aged 16 and over	13	14	15	16	17	18	19	20	21	22	23	24
16 - 19	25	26	27	28	29	30	31	32	33	34	35	36
20 - 29	37	38	39	40	41	42	43	44	45	46	47	48
30 - 44	49	50	51	52	53	54	55	56	57	58	59	60
45 - 64	61	62	63	64	65	66	67	68	69	70	71	72
65 and over	73	74	75	76	77	78	79	80	81	82	83	84
Females aged 16 and over	85	86	87	88	89	90	91	92	93	94	95	96
16 - 19	97	98	99	100	101	102	103	104	105	106	107	108
20 - 29	109	110	111	112	113	114	115	116	117	118	119	120
30 - 44	121	122	123	124	125	126	127	128	129	130	131	132
45 - 59	133	134	135	136	137	138	139	140	141	142	143	144
60 and over	145	146	147	148	149	150	151	152	153	154	155	156

* id = Inadequately described

1991 Census Small Area Statistics - 10% Area Identifier - <zoneid> Grid reference - <Easting/Northing>
<.Ward / Postcode Sector name..> <........DistrictName.........> <.....County / Region Name.....>
Table Prefix: S74

Table 74 Occupation (10% sample): Residents aged 16 and over, employees and self-employed

Standard Occupational Classification - Major Groups	Males aged 16 and over					Females aged 16 and over				
	16 - 19	20 - 29	30 - 44	45 - 64	65 and over	16 - 19	20 - 29	30 - 44	45 - 59	60 and over
ALL OCCUPATIONS	1	2	3	4	5	6	7	8	9	10
1 Managers and Administrators	11	12	13	14	15	16	17	18	19	20
2 Professional occupations	21	22	23	24	25	26	27	28	29	30
3 Associate professional and technical occupations	31	32	33	34	35	36	37	38	39	40
4 Clerical and secretarial occupations	41	42	43	44	45	46	47	48	49	50
5 Craft and related occupations	51	52	53	54	55	56	57	58	59	60
6 Personal and protective service occupations	61	62	63	64	65	66	67	68	69	70
7 Sales occupations	71	72	73	74	75	76	77	78	79	80
8 Plant and machine operatives	81	82	83	84	85	86	87	88	89	90
9 Other occupations	91	92	93	94	95	96	97	98	99	100
Occupation not stated or inadequately described	101	102	103	104	105	106	107	108	109	110

1991 Census Small Area Statistics - 10% Area Identifier - <zoneid> Grid reference - <Easting/Northing>
<.Ward / Postcode Sector name..> <........DistrictName.........> <.....County / Region Name.....>
Table Prefix: S75

Table 75 Hours worked (10% sample): Residents aged 16 and over; employees and self-employed

Sex, age, marital status and long-term illness	TOTAL PERSONS	Hours worked weekly						
		15 and under	16 - 21	22 - 23	24 - 30	31 - 40	41 and over	Not stated
TOTAL PERSONS	1	2	3	4	5	6	7	8
Males								
16 - 29	9	10	11	12	13	14	15	16
30 - 44	17	18	19	20	21	22	23	24
45 - 64	25	26	27	28	29	30	31	32
65 and over	33	34	35	36	37	38	39	40
Females								
16 - 29	41	42	43	44	45	46	47	48
30 - 44	49	50	51	52	53	54	55	56
45 -59	57	58	59	60	61	62	63	64
60 and over	65	66	67	68	69	70	71	72
TOTAL MALES	73	74	75	76	77	78	79	80
Single, widowed or divorced	81	82	83	84	85	86	87	88
Married	89	90	91	92	93	94	95	96
TOTAL FEMALES	97	98	99	100	101	102	103	104
Single, widowed or divorced	105	106	107	108	109	110	111	112
Married	113	114	115	116	117	118	119	120
Persons with limiting long-term illness								
Total	121	122	123	124	125	126	127	128
Males	129	130	131	132	133	134	135	136
Females	137	138	139	140	141	142	143	144

1991 Census Small Area Statistics - 10% Area Identifier - <zoneid> Grid reference - <Easting/Northing>
<.Ward / Postcode Sector name..> <........DistrictName.........> <.....County / Region Name.....>
Table Prefix: S76

Table 76 Occupation and Industry (10% sample): Residents aged 16 and over, employees and self-employed

Standard Occupational Classification - Major Groups	TOTAL PERSONS	Industry											Working outside dist. of usual res.
		Agric. f'estry and fishing	Energy and water	Mining	Manufac -turing metal etc.	Other manufac -turing	Const-ruction	Distrib -ution and cat'ing	Trans-port	Banking and finance etc.	Other serv -ices	Not stated, id*, or w'place out. UK	
ALL OCCUPATIONS	1	2	3	4	5	6	7	8	9	10	11	12	13
1 Managers and Administrators	14	15	16	17	18	19	20	21	22	23	24	25	26
2 Professional occupations	27	28	29	30	31	32	33	34	35	36	37	38	39
3 Associate professional and technical occupations	40	41	42	43	44	45	46	47	48	49	50	51	52
4 Clerical and secretarial occupations	53	54	55	56	57	58	59	60	61	62	63	64	65
5 Craft and related occupations	66	67	68	69	70	71	72	73	74	75	76	77	78
6 Personal and protective service occupations	79	80	81	82	83	84	85	86	87	88	89	90	91
7 Sales occupations	92	93	94	95	96	97	98	99	100	101	102	103	104
8 Plant and machine operatives	105	106	107	108	109	110	111	112	113	114	115	116	117
9 Other occupations	118	119	120	121	122	123	124	125	126	127	128	129	130
Occupation not stated or inadequately described	131	132	133	134	135	136	137	138	139	140	141	142	143
Working outside district of usual residence	144	145	146	147	148	149	150	151	152	153	154	155	xxxx

* id = Inadequately described

1991 Census Small Area Statistics - 10% Area Identifier - <zoneid> Grid reference - <Easting/Northing>
<.Ward / Postcode Sector name..> <........DistrictName.........> <.....County / Region Name.....>
Table Prefix: S77

Table 77 Industry and hours worked (10% sample): Residents aged 16 and over, employees and self-employed

Hours worked weekly	TOTAL PERSONS	Industry										
		Agric. f'estry and fishing	Energy and water	Mining	Manufac -turing metal etc.	Other manufac -turing	Const-ruction	Distrib -ution and cater-ing	Trans-port	Banking and finance etc.	Other serv -ices	Not stated, id*, or w'place out. UK
TOTAL PERSONS	1	2	3	4	5	6	7	8	9	10	11	12
15 and under	13	14	15	16	17	18	19	20	21	22	23	24
16 - 21	25	26	27	28	29	30	31	32	33	34	35	36
22 - 23	37	38	39	40	41	42	43	44	45	46	47	48
24 - 30	49	50	51	52	53	54	55	56	57	58	59	60
31 - 40	61	62	63	64	65	66	67	68	69	70	71	72
41 and over	73	74	75	76	77	78	79	80	81	82	83	84
Not stated	85	86	87	88	89	90	91	92	93	94	95	96

* id = Inadequately described

1991 Census Small Area Statistics - 10% Area Identifier - <zoneid> Grid reference - <Easting/Northing>
<.Ward / Postcode Sector name..> <........DistrictName.........> <.....County / Region Name.....>
Table Prefix: S78

Table 78 Occupation and hours worked (10% sample): Residents aged 16 and over, employees and self-employed

Standard Occupational Classification - Major Groups	TOTAL PERSONS	Hours worked weekly						
		15 and under	16 - 21	22 - 23	24 - 30	31 - 40	41 and over	Not stated
ALL OCCUPATIONS	1	2	3	4	5	6	7	8
1 Managers and Administrators	9	10	11	12	13	14	15	16
2 Professional occupations	17	18	19	20	21	22	23	24
3 Associate professional and technical occupations	25	26	27	28	29	30	31	32
4 Clerical and secretarial occupations	33	34	35	36	37	38	39	40
5 Craft and related occupations	41	42	43	44	45	46	47	48
6 Personal and protective service occupations	49	50	51	52	53	54	55	56
7 Sales occupations	57	58	59	60	61	62	63	64
8 Plant and machine operatives	65	66	67	68	69	70	71	72
9 Other occupations	73	74	75	76	77	78	79	80
Occupation not stated or inadequately described	81	82	83	84	85	86	87	88

1991 Census Small Area Statistics - 10%   Area Identifier - <zoneid>   Grid reference - <Easting/Northing>
<.Ward / Postcode Sector name..>   <........DistrictName.........>   <.....County / Region Name.....>
Table Prefix: S79

Table 79 Industry and employment status (10% sample): Residents aged 16 and over, employees and self-employed

Employment status	TOTAL PERSONS	Industry: Agri-culture	For-estry and fishing	Energy and water	Mining	Manufac-turing metal etc.	Other manufac-turing	Const-ruction	Distrib-ution and cater-ering	Trans-port	Banking and finance etc.	Other serv-ices	Not stated, id*, or w'place out. UK
Males	1	2	3	4	5	6	7	8	9	10	11	12	13
Self-employed	14	15	16	17	18	19	20	21	22	23	24	25	26
With employees	27	28	29	30	31	32	33	34	35	36	37	38	39
Without employees	40	41	42	43	44	45	46	47	48	49	50	51	52
Employees	53	54	55	56	57	58	59	60	61	62	63	64	65
Working 31 or more hours per week	66	67	68	69	70	71	72	73	74	75	76	77	78
Working 30 or fewer hours per week	79	80	81	82	83	84	85	86	87	88	89	90	91
Economically active students (included above)	92	93	94	95	96	97	98	99	100	101	102	103	104
Females	105	106	107	108	109	110	111	112	113	114	115	116	117
Self-employed	118	119	120	121	122	123	124	125	126	127	128	129	130
With employees	131	132	133	134	135	136	137	138	139	140	141	142	143
Without employees	144	145	146	147	148	149	150	151	152	153	154	155	156
Employees	157	158	159	160	161	162	163	164	165	166	167	168	169
Working 31 or more hours per week	170	171	172	173	174	175	176	177	178	179	180	181	182
Working 30 or fewer hours per week	183	184	185	186	187	188	189	190	191	192	193	194	195
Economically active students (included above)	196	197	198	199	200	201	202	203	204	205	206	207	208

1991 Census Small Area Statistics - 10%   Area Identifier - <zoneid>   Grid reference - <Easting/Northing>
<.Ward / Postcode Sector name..>   <........DistrictName.........>   <.....County / Region Name.....>
Table Prefix: S80

Table 80 Working parents; hours worked (10% sample): Women in couple families and lone parents in employment

	Age of youngest dependent child in family	TOTAL PERSONS	Hours worked weekly: 15 and under	16 - 21	22 - 23	24 - 30	31 - 40	41 and over	Not stated
Women in couple families in employment		1	2	3	4	5	6	7	8
No dependent child in family	-	9	10	11	12	13	14	15	16
1 or more dependent child(ren)	0 - 4	17	18	19	20	21	22	23	24
	5 - 10	25	26	27	28	29	30	31	32
	11 - 18	33	34	35	36	37	38	39	40
Male lone parents in employment		41	42	43	44	45	46	47	48
No dependent child in family	-	49	50	51	52	53	54	55	56
1 or more dependent child(ren)	0 - 4	57	58	59	60	61	62	63	64
	5 - 10	65	66	67	68	69	70	71	72
	11 - 18	73	74	75	76	77	78	79	80
Female lone parents in employment		81	82	83	84	85	86	87	88
No dependent child in family	-	89	90	91	92	93	94	95	96
1 or more dependent child(ren)	0 - 4	97	98	99	100	101	102	103	104
	5 - 10	105	106	107	108	109	110	111	112
	11 - 18	113	114	115	116	117	118	119	120

1991 Census Small Area Statistics - 10%   Area Identifier - <zoneid>   Grid reference - <Easting/Northing>
<.Ward / Postcode Sector name..>   <........DistrictName.........>   <.....County / Region Name.....>
Table Prefix: S81

Table 81 Occupation and employment status (10% sample): Residents aged 16 and over, employees and self-employed

Employment status	TOTAL PERSONS	Standard Occupational Classification Major Groups: Man-agers and admin.	Profess-ional	Assoc. profess-ional	Cler'al and sec.	Craft and related	P'sonal and pro'ive service	Sales	Plant and machine op'ives	Other occup-ations	Not stated or inad desc.
Males	1	2	3	4	5	6	7	8	9	10	11
Self-employed	12	13	14	15	16	17	18	19	20	21	22
With employees	23	24	25	26	27	28	29	30	31	32	33
Without employees	34	35	36	37	38	39	40	41	42	43	44
Employees	45	46	47	48	49	50	51	52	53	54	55
Working 31 or more hours per week	56	57	58	59	60	61	62	63	64	65	66
Working 30 or fewer hours per week	67	68	69	70	71	72	73	74	75	76	77
Economically active students (included above)	78	79	80	81	82	83	84	85	86	87	88
Females	89	90	91	92	93	94	95	96	97	98	99
Self-employed	100	101	102	103	104	105	106	107	108	109	110
With employees	111	112	113	114	115	116	117	118	119	120	121
Without employees	122	123	124	125	126	127	128	129	130	131	132
Employees	133	134	135	136	137	138	139	140	141	142	143
Working 31 or more hours per week	144	145	146	147	148	149	150	151	152	153	154
Working 30 or fewer hours per week	155	156	157	158	159	160	161	162	163	164	165
Economically active students (included above)	166	167	168	169	170	171	172	173	174	175	176

pro'ive = protective
op'ives = operatives

1991 Census Small Area Statistics - 10% **Area Identifier - <zoneid>** **Grid reference - <Easting/Northing>**
<.Ward / Postcode Sector name..> <........**DistrictName**.........> <.....**County / Region Name**.....>
Table Prefix: S82

Table 82 Travel to work and SEG (10% sample): Residents aged 16 and over, employees and self-employed

Socio-economic group (SEG)		TOTAL PERSONS	Means of transport to work: BR train	Other rail	Bus	Car: Driver	Car: P'enger	Motor cycle	Pedal cycle	On foot	Other	Works at home	Not stated	Working outside dist. of usual res.
TOTAL PERSONS		1	2	3	4	5	6	7	8	9	10	11	12	13
Total males		14	15	16	17	18	19	20	21	22	23	24	25	26
Total females		27	28	29	30	31	32	33	34	35	36	37	38	39
1,2	Employees and managers	40	41	42	43	44	45	46	47	48	49	50	51	52
3,4	professional workers	53	54	55	56	57	58	59	60	61	62	63	64	65
5	Intermediate non-manual workers	66	67	68	69	70	71	72	73	74	75	76	77	78
6	Junior non-manual workers	79	80	81	82	83	84	85	86	87	88	89	90	91
8,9,12	Manual workers (foremen, supervisors, skilled and own account)	92	93	94	95	96	97	98	99	100	101	102	103	104
7,10	Personal service and semi-skilled manual workers	105	106	107	108	109	110	111	112	113	114	115	116	117
11	Unskilled manual workers	118	119	120	121	122	123	124	125	126	127	128	129	130
13,14,15	Farmers and agricultural workers	131	132	133	134	135	136	137	138	139	140	141	142	143
16,17	Members of armed forces, inadequately described and not stated occupations	144	145	146	147	148	149	150	151	152	153	154	155	156
Working outside district of usual residence		157	158	159	160	161	162	163	164	165	166	xxxx	168	xxxx
Employed and self-employed persons resident in households with:														
No car		170	171	172	173	174	175	176	177	178	179	180	181	182
1 car		183	184	185	186	187	188	189	190	191	192	193	194	195
2 cars		196	197	198	199	200	201	202	203	204	205	206	207	208
3 or more cars		209	210	211	212	213	214	215	216	217	218	219	220	221

1991 Census Small Area Statistics - 10% **Area Identifier - <zoneid>** **Grid reference - <Easting/Northing>**
<.Ward / Postcode Sector name..> <........**DistrictName**.........> <.....**County / Region Name**.....>
Table Prefix: S83

Table 83 Travel to work and car availability (10% sample): Residents aged 16 and over, employees and self-employed

Households with the following number of resident employees or self-employed aged 16 and over and means of transport to work

Cars available	1: Car	1: Public trans -port	1: Other	2: Both car	2: Both public trans -port	2: 1 car and 1 public trans -port	2: 1 car and 1 other	2: 1 public t'port and 1 other	2: Others	3 or more: All car	3 or more: All public trans -port	3 or more: A*	3 or more: B**	3 or more: C***	3 or more: Others
TOTAL HOUSEHOLDS	1	2	3	4	5	6	7	8	9	10	11	12	13	14	15
No car	16	17	18	19	20	21	22	23	24	25	26	27	28	29	30
1 car	31	32	33	34	35	36	37	38	39	40	41	42	43	44	45
2 or more cars	46	47	48	49	50	51	52	53	54	55	56	57	58	59	60

* A: Any car and any public transport with or without other(s)
** B: Any car and any other(s) - no public transport
*** C: Any public transport and any other(s) - no car

1991 Census Small Area Statistics - 10% **Area Identifier - <zoneid>** **Grid reference - <Easting/Northing>**
<.Ward / Postcode Sector name..> <........**DistrictName**.........> <.....**County / Region Name**.....>
Table Prefix: S84 **CROWN COPYRIGHT RESERVED**

Table 84 Qualified manpower (10% sample): Residents aged 18 and over

Level of highest qualification, age and economic position	TOTAL PERSONS	Males	Females
ALL PERSONS AGED 18 AND OVER	1	2	3
All persons qualified	4	5	6
Level a (higher degree)	7	8	9
Level b (degree)	10	11	12
Level c (diploma etc.)	13	14	15
All persons qualified at level a, b, or c			
18 - 29	16	17	18
30 - 44	19	20	21
45 up to pensionable age	22	23	24
Pensionable age and over	25	26	27
All persons qualified at level a, b, or c aged 18 up to pensionable age	28	29	30
Employee or self-employed	31	32	33
On a Government scheme	34	35	36
Unemployed	37	38	39

1991 Census Small Area Statistics - 10% **Area Identifier - <zoneid>** **Grid reference - <Easting/Northing>**
<.Ward / Postcode Sector name..> <........**DistrictName**.........> <.....**County / Region Name**.....>
Table Prefix: S86 **CROWN COPYRIGHT RESERVED**

Table 86 SEG of households and families (10% sample): Households with residents; residents in households; families of resident persons

Socio-economic group	Households						
		Tenure of households in permanent buildings					
	TOTAL HOUSE-HOLDS	Owner occ.	Rented priv-ately	Rented from a housing assoc.	Rented from a LA or new town	Migrant head of house-hold	No car
	By SEG of economically active head of household						
TOTAL	1	2	3	4	5	6	7
1 Employers and managers in large establishments	14	15	16	17	18	19	20
2 Employers and managers in small establishments	27	28	29	30	31	32	33
3 Professional workers - self-employed	40	41	42	43	44	45	46
4 Professional workers - employees	53	54	55	56	57	58	59
5.1 Ancillary workers and artists	66	67	68	69	70	71	72
5.2 Foremen and supervisors - non-manual	79	80	81	82	83	84	85
6 Junior non-manual workers	92	93	94	95	96	97	98
7 Personal service workers	105	106	107	108	109	110	111
8 Foremen and supervisors - manual	118	119	120	121	122	123	124
9 Skilled manual workers	131	132	133	134	135	136	137
10 Semi-skilled manual workers	144	145	146	147	148	149	150
11 Unskilled manual workers	157	158	159	160	161	162	163
12 Own account workers (other than professional)	170	171	172	173	174	175	176
13 Farmers - employers and managers	183	184	185	186	187	188	189
14 Farmers - own account	196	197	198	199	200	201	202
15 Agricultural workers	209	210	211	212	213	214	215
16 Members of armed forces	222	223	224	225	226	227	228
17 Inadequately described and not stated occupations	235	236	237	238	239	240	241
Economically inactive	248	249	250	251	252	253	254
TOTAL PERSONS	261	262	263	264	265	266	267
Persons economically active	274	275	276	277	278	279	280
Dependent children	287	288	289	290	291	292	293

1991 Census Small Area Statistics - 10% **Area Identifier - <zoneid>** **Grid reference - <Easting/Northing>**
<.Ward / Postcode Sector name..> <........**DistrictName**.........> <.....**County / Region Name**.....>
Table Prefix: S86 **CROWN COPYRIGHT RESERVED**

Table 86 SEG of households and families (10% sample): Households with residents; residents in households; families of resident persons **(Continued)**

Persons				Families		Socio-economic group
TOTAL PERSONS	Persons econ. active	D'dent child-ren	Adults with lim'ing long-term illness	TOTAL FAM-ILIES	Lone parent with d'dent child-(ren)	
By Socio-economic group of economically active head of household				*By Socio-economic group of economically active head of family*		
8	9	10	11	12	13	**TOTAL**
21	22	23	24	25	26	1 Employers and managers in large establishments
34	35	36	37	38	39	2 Employers and managers in small establishments
47	48	49	50	51	52	3 Professional workers - self-employed
60	61	62	63	64	65	4 Professional workers - employees
73	74	75	76	77	78	5.1 Ancillary workers and artists
86	87	88	39	90	91	5.2 Foremen and supervisors - non-manual
99	100	101	102	103	104	6 Junior non-manual workers
112	113	114	115	116	117	7 Personal service workers
125	126	127	128	129	130	8 Foremen and supervisors - manual
138	139	140	141	142	143	9 Skilled manual workers
151	152	153	154	155	156	10 Semi-skilled manual workers
164	165	166	167	168	169	11 Unskilled manual workers
177	178	179	180	181	182	12 Own account workers (other than professional)
190	191	192	193	194	195	13 Farmers - employers and managers
203	204	205	206	207	208	14 Farmers - own account
216	217	218	219	220	221	15 Agricultural workers
229	230	231	232	233	234	16 Members of armed forces
242	243	244	245	246	247	17 Inadequately described and not stated occupations
255	256	257	258	259	260	Economically inactive
xxxx	xxxx	xxxx	xxxx	272	273	**TOTAL PERSONS**
xxxx	xxxx	xxxx	xxxx	285	286	Persons economically active
xxxx	xxxx	xxxx	xxxx	298	299	Dependent children

1991 Census Small Area Statistics - 10% **Area Identifier - <zoneid>** **Grid reference - <Easting/Northing>**
<.Ward / Postcode Sector name..> **<........DistrictName.........>** **<.....County / Region Name.....>**
Table Prefix: S87

Table 87 Family type and tenure (10% sample): Households with residents; residents in households

Household composition	Households								Persons	
		Tenure of households in permanent buildings								
	TOTAL HOUSE-HOLDS	Owner occ.	Rented priv-ately	Rented from a housing assoc.	Rented from a LA or new town	Migrant head of house-hold	No car	2 or more cars	TOTAL PERSONS	Depen-dent child-ren aged 0 - 18
TOTAL HOUSEHOLDS	1	2	3	4	5	6	7	8	9	10
Households with no families	11	12	13	14	15	16	17	18	19	xxxx
One person	21	22	23	24	25	26	27	28	29	xxxx
Two or more persons	31	32	33	34	35	36	37	38	39	xxxx
Households with one family	41	42	43	44	45	46	47	48	49	50
Married couple family	51	52	53	54	55	56	57	58	59	60
with no children	61	62	63	64	65	66	67	68	69	xxxx
with dependent child(ren)	71	72	73	74	75	76	77	78	79	80
with non-dependent child(ren) only	81	82	83	84	85	86	87	88	89	xxxx
Cohabiting couple family	91	92	93	94	95	96	97	98	99	100
with no children	101	102	103	104	105	106	107	108	109	xxxx
with dependent child(ren)	111	112	113	114	115	116	117	118	119	120
with non-dependent child(ren) only	121	122	123	124	125	126	127	128	129	xxxx
Lone parent family	131	132	133	134	135	136	137	138	139	140
with dependent chil(dren)	141	142	143	144	145	146	147	148	149	150
with non-dependent child(ren) only	151	152	153	154	155	156	157	158	159	xxxx
Households with two or more families	161	162	163	164	165	166	167	168	169	170
All dependent children aged 0-17 in lone parent families	171	172	173	174	175	176	177	178	xxxx	xxxx

1991 Census Small Area Statistics - 10% **Area Identifier - <zoneid>** **Grid reference - <Easting/Northing>**
<.Ward / Postcode Sector name..> **<........DistrictName.........>** **<.....County / Region Name.....>**
Table Prefix: S89

Table 89 Family composition (10% sample): Families of resident persons

Family composition	TOTAL FAM-ILIES	Type of family		
		Married couple	Cohab -iting couple	Lone parent
TOTAL FAMILIES	1	2	3	4
No children	5	6	7	xxxx
With dependent child(ren)	9	10	11	12
With non-dependent child(ren) only	13	14	15	16
In households with two or more families	17	18	19	20

1991 Census Small Area Statistics - 10% **Area Identifier - <zoneid>** **Grid reference - <Easting/Northing>**
<.Ward / Postcode Sector name..> **<........DistrictName.........>** **<.....County / Region Name.....>**
Table Prefix: S90

Table 90 Social class of households (10% sample): Households with residents; residents in households

Social class as defined by occupation of household head	TOTAL HOUSE -HOLDS	TOTAL PERSONS	Persons aged 0 - 15	Persons of pens. age	Females in couples *
Economically active heads					
Total	1	2	3	4	5
I Professional etc. occupations	6	7	8	9	10
II Managerial and technical	11	12	13	14	15
III(N) Skilled occupations - non-manual	16	17	18	19	20
III(M) Skilled occupations - manual	21	22	23	24	25
IV Partly skilled occupations	26	27	28	29	30
V Unskilled occupations	31	32	33	34	35
Armed forces	36	37	38	39	40
On a Government scheme	41	42	43	44	45
Occupation inadequately described or not stated	46	47	48	49	50
Economically inactive heads					
Retired	51	52	53	54	55
Other inactive	56	57	58	59	60

* Females in married or cohabiting couples

1991 Census Small Area Statistics - 10% Area Identifier - <zoneid> Grid reference - <Easting/Northing>
<.Ward / Postcode Sector name..> <........DistrictName.........> <.....County / Region Name.....>
Table Prefix: S91

Table 91 Social class and economic position (10% sample): Residents aged 16 and over in households

Social class based on occupation	TOTAL PERSONS			Economic position					
				In employment			Unemployed		
		Females			Females			Females	
	Males	Total	In a couple*	Males	Total	In a couple*	Males	Total	In a couple*
Economically active									
Total	1	2	3	4	5	6	7	8	9
I Professional etc. occupations	10	11	12	13	14	15	16	17	18
II Managerial and technical	19	20	21	22	23	24	25	26	27
III(N) Skilled occupations - non-manual	28	29	30	31	32	33	34	35	36
III(M) Skilled occupations - manual	37	38	39	40	41	42	43	44	45
IV Partly skilled occupations	46	47	48	49	50	51	52	53	54
V Unskilled occupations	55	56	57	58	59	60	61	62	63
Armed forces	64	65	66	67	68	69	70	71	72
On a Government scheme	73	74	75	76	77	78	xxxx	xxxx	xxxx
Occupation inadequately described or not stated	82	83	84	85	86	87	88	89	90
Economically inactive									
Retired	91	92	93	xxxx	xxxx	xxxx	xxxx	xxxx	xxxx
Other inactive	100	101	102	xxxx	xxxx	xxxx	xxxx	xxxx	xxxx

* Females in married or cohabiting couples

1991 Census Small Area Statistics - 10% Area Identifier - <zoneid> Grid reference - <Easting/Northing>
<.Ward / Postcode Sector name..> <........DistrictName.........> <.....County / Region Name.....>
Table Prefix: S92

Table 92 SEG and economic position (10% sample): Economically active residents

Socio-economic group	TOTAL PERSONS		Economic position				Persons with different address 1 year before census (migrants)	
			In employment		Unemployed			
	Males	Females	Males	Females	Males	Females	Males	Females
TOTAL PERSONS	1	2	3	4	5	6	7	8
1.1 Employers in large establishments	9	10	11	12	13	14	15	16
1.2 Managers in large establishments	17	18	19	20	21	22	23	24
2.1 Employers in small establishments	25	26	27	28	29	30	31	32
2.2 Managers in small establishments	33	34	35	36	37	38	39	40
3 Professional workers - self-employed	41	42	43	44	45	46	47	48
4 Professional workers - employees	49	50	51	52	53	54	55	56
5.1 Ancillary workers and artists	57	58	59	60	61	62	63	64
5.2 Foremen and supervisors - non-manual	65	66	67	68	69	70	71	72
6 Junior non-manual workers	73	74	75	76	77	78	79	80
7 Personal service workers	81	82	83	84	85	86	87	88
8 Foremen and supervisors - manual	89	90	91	92	93	94	95	96
9 Skilled manual workers	97	98	99	100	101	102	103	104
10 Semi-skilled manual workers	105	106	107	108	109	110	111	112
11 Unskilled manual workers	113	114	115	116	117	118	119	120
12 Own account workers (other than professional)	121	122	123	124	125	126	127	128
13 Farmers - employers and managers	129	130	131	132	133	134	135	136
14 Farmers - own account	137	138	139	140	141	142	143	144
15 Agricultural workers	145	146	147	148	149	150	151	152
16 Members of armed forces	153	154	155	156	157	158	159	160
17 Inadequately described and not stated occupations	161	162	163	164	165	166	167	168
On a Government Scheme	169	170	171	172	xxxx	xxxx	175	176

1991 Census Small Area Statistics - 10% Area Identifier - <zoneid> Grid reference - <Easting/Northing>
<.Ward / Postcode Sector name..> <........DistrictName.........> <.....County / Region Name.....>
Table Prefix: S94

Table 94 Former industry of unemployed (10% sample): Residents on a Government scheme or unemployed

	TOTAL PERSONS	Industry of most recent job in last 10 years										
		Agric. f'estry and fishing	Energy and water	Mining	Manufac-turing metal etc.	Other manufac-turing	Const-ruction	Distrib-ution and cater-ing	Trans-port	Banking and finance etc.	Other serv-ices	Not stated id*, or w'place out. UK
TOTAL PERSONS	1	2	3	4	5	6	7	8	9	10	11	12
Males	13	14	15	16	17	18	19	20	21	22	23	24
Females	25	26	27	28	29	30	31	32	33	34	35	36

* id = Inadequately described

1991 Census Small Area Statistics - 10% Area Identifier - <zoneid> Grid reference - <Easting/Northing>
<.Ward / Postcode Sector name..> <........DistrictName.........> <.....County / Region Name.....>
Table Prefix: S95

Table 95 Former occupation of unemployed (10% sample): Residents on a Government scheme or unemployed

	TOTAL PERSONS	Occupation (SOC Major Groups) of most recent job in last 10 years									
		Man-agers and admin.	Profess-ional	Assoc. profess-ional	Cler'al and secret-arial	Craft and related	P'sonal and pro'ive service	Sales	Plant and machine op'ives	Other occup-ations	Not stated or inad desc.
TOTAL PERSONS	1	2	3	4	5	6	7	8	9	10	11
Males	12	13	14	15	16	17	18	19	20	21	22
Females	23	24	25	26	27	28	29	30	31	32	33

Pro'ive = Protective
Op'ives = Operatives

INDEX